The twilight of a military tradition

The twilight of a military tradition
Italian aristocrats and European conflicts, 1560–1800

Gregory Hanlon
Dalhousie University, Halifax, Nova Scotia

PRESS

First published in 1998 by UCL Press

UCL Press Limited
1 Gunpowder Square
London EC4A 3DE
UK

The name of University College London (UCL) is a registered
trade mark used by UCL Press with the consent of the owner.

British Library Cataloguing-in-Publication Data
A catalogue record for this book is available from the British Library.

ISBNs: 1-85728-703-7 HB
       1-85728-704-5 PB

Typeset by Best-set Typesetter Ltd, Hong Kong
Printed by Arrowhead Books Limited, Reading, UK.

Contents

List of figures

Graphs

Preface

The inspiration for this book sprang from my encounter with a single source, the *Compendio Istorico di Sanesi Nobili*, a list of accomplishments of Sienese aristocrats, compiled by the canon Antonio Sestigiani in 1695. I had just begun research on a long-term project, funded by the Social Sciences and Humanities Research Council of Canada, focusing on relations of authority and deference around Siena in the Medicean period, and knew that I had to acquire information on the background of the city's patriciate. From the elegant calligraphy surged hundreds of military careers, complete with service dates, ranks achieved and often the fate of individuals never fortunate enough to achieve the fame they sought. I had only a gentleman's knowledge of the maritime campaigns in the Levant, and only passing familiarity with prominent Italian generals serving Spain, France and the Empire. Here was much of European history witnessed and acted out by a great gallery of heroes and rogues, whose number tapered off substantially after the middle of the seventeenth century.

Without abandoning my 'official' research project, I began to collect Sienese data on the subject. The SSHRC has contributed to this book more than it knows. I gradually expanded the scope of this study in tandem with a gifted MA student, Elmar Henrich, who wanted to explore the Habsburg monarchies' reliance on Italians in the sixteenth and seventeenth centuries in both Madrid and Vienna. It was Elmar who ferreted out the Fascist encyclopedias. Their compilations allow a glimpse of the military activity of nobles from all over the peninsula. There was no way of knowing how reliable they were without looking at the political evolution of the peninsula and the military infrastructure over the long term. This we did by drawing upon the resources, the goodwill and the patience of the people in the Dalhousie University Killam Library inter-library loan department, in particular Gwyn Pace and Kelly Hawley. Libraries on two continents deposited truly wondrous and rare books into the mail for our purposes over the last few years. In addition, Tommaso Astarita allowed me to consult his valuable *tesi di laurea* on the Neapolitan garrison army in the period of Spain's decline, and Martine Lambert-Gorges sent me the typescript of an important article on Spanish military orders which is presently in press.

The text of this book was composed pretty much in isolation. Only an unexpected teaching appointment at the Ecole Nationale des Chartes and the Sorbonne in 1996 allowed me to bounce the results off the eminent French historians Jean Bérenger, Yves-Marie Bercé and Emmanuel Le Roy Ladurie. Michel Fontenay and Jean-François Pernot were helpful too, on specific points, while Jean-Pierre Bost in Bordeaux provided background assistance. In Britain, Jeremy Black's encouragement has accelerated the publication process. I owe thanks to Bruce Bonaney, for his appreciated logistical support in my trips to the Robarts Library in Toronto. Marie-Blandine Duclap in Paris has helped this project and all the others in ways too numerous to account for individually. And finally I would like to thank my wife Anne for tolerating periods when I spent long evenings in front of a word processor.

Introduction

Hilarity erupts – "Short book!" – whenever I reveal that the subject of this book is Italian war heroes: an oxymoron, I am assured, by Italians or foreigners, in Italy and outside, since "Italians are anything but". Virtually everyone has an idea about the subject, inspired by superficial knowledge of battles since the Risorgimento, such as Novara (1848), Adowa (1885), Caporetto (1917) and the débâcle of the Second World War. The consensus is that Italian society, whatever its other characteristics, and for good or ill, is not militarily inclined. Fascist attempts to transform Italians simply dissolved into tragic slapstick. This impression of Italian disinclination for fighting has venerable roots and a long pedigree, dating back at least as far as Guicciardini. His portrayal of bloodless *condottieri* campaigns still holds sway among the literati. In the view of that remarkable historian, Italians were content for many years with the images of war, but not its substance, and at the critical moment they lacked the resolve to confront the "*furore francese*". His portrayal of mercenary pseudo-war and bellicose posturing, "explains" the collapse of Italian armies when confronted with the French invasion of 1494.[1]

   This book will therefore address a historical enigma. After situating the place of Italian military commanders, officers and adventurers at the close of the wars of Italy in 1559, I will chart their progress and decline. It is hard not to discern the progressive estrangement of Italian society from martial pursuits, over more than two centuries between Lepanto (1571) and the invasions by French revolutionary armies in the 1790s. Given the extreme diversity of the material available, and the uneven interest of generations of historians, some parts of this account will be more detailed than others. The treaty of Câteau-Cambrésis in 1559 is probably a good place to begin, for it brought to a complete halt the long series of regional wars devastating most of the peninsula over more than half a century. The treaty imposed a *Pax Hispanica* on the peninsula, followed by the demobilization of the captains and their soldiers. If one can argue that Italian society was militarily amateurish at the end of the fifteenth century, this was certainly untrue after two

---

[1] F. Guicciardini, "Storia d'Italia", in *Opere*, V. de Caprariis (ed.) (Milan: 1961), p. 434.

generations of 'decisive battles' like Fornovo, Ravenna, Marignano and Pavia, and of great sieges like those of Rome, Naples and Siena. If Italy was a battlefield for mercenaries hailing from Andalusia to Switzerland, nevertheless Italian knights, mercenaries, militias and cities were caught up in the fighting more than they cared. By the time of Napoleon, however, the passivity of Italian states to his conquering armies revealed both a lack of spirit, and a lack of means, with which to resist the invader. The peninsula (with the notable exception of Piedmont) had demilitarized to such an extent that the Italian states considered organized resistance to be impractical and hopeless. Bonaparte in turn came to realize the full extent of it as he strove to create a modern, efficient, and disciplined army from scratch. Over a century later, would-be Fascist warlords sought to complete this process.

Italy's case stands in stark contrast to the general European experience of the seventeenth and eighteenth centuries, that of the gradual establishment of permanent armies, and the thronging of aristocracies into them. The increase in effective forces was of an order not dreamt of in the Renaissance. Whether this was a military 'revolution' is a matter of debate, the terms of which have been formulated by Michael Roberts and Geoffrey Parker.[2] André Corvisier supplies some rough figures for this. A first approximation for 1621 gives about 500,000 men under arms, of whom 200,000 were situated in Eastern and Balkan Europe. By 1710, this figure, still excluding militias, reached 1.3 million soldiers, of whom 800,000 at least served in west European armies. In France alone, there were 100,000 men under arms in 1635, 200,000 in 1640, and maybe 500,000 in 1690, when one man in ten of age to carry arms and one gentleman in three was serving in the army.[3] In short, northern Europe armed and regimented itself just as Italian patricians and feudatories consigned their armour and weapons to display cases. This development has many implications for the ulterior evolution of the peninsula's history. What effect did it have on the development of the modern state in Italy? What effect did demilitarization have on the dynamic of Italian society, for military careers carry a baggage of cultural assumptions about social discipline, order and efficiency, technical progress and other 'virtues'? These are important questions, with ramifications far removed from the traditional historiography of 'battle history'. To cite a formula coined by the Italian military historian Piero Pieri, war constitutes *"une certaine façon de voir, de considérer, d'expliquer l'histoire générale*

---

[2] For a succinct formulation of the argument, see the introduction to Geoffrey Parker's pathbreaking book, *The army of Flanders and the Spanish Road (1567–1659): the logistics of Spanish victory and defeat in the Low Countries' wars* (Cambridge: 1972), pp. 3–21.

[3] A. Corvisier, "Introduction", in *Guerre et paix dans l'Europe du XVIIe siècle* (Paris: 1991), vol. 1, pp. 19–31. John Lynn has recalculated these figures for France in a recent article, reducing them by a quarter. The general trend, however, remains clear. See J. Lynn, "Recalculating French army growth during the *Grand siècle*, 1610–1715", *French Historical Studies*, 1994, pp. 881–906.

des hommes".[4] These issues revolving around war are pregnant with significance for social history and the history of behaviour, although it is premature to assign to demilitarization any causal role in the long subjugation of the peninsula to Great Power politics.

Though the work here is the first of its kind in scope and direction, the subject is slowly growing on the consciousness of Italian historians, each in their region. What I plan here is to survey the secondary literature, both Italian and foreign over the last century and a half. Rather than a conventional research monograph based on archival material, this work is what the French sociologist and epistemologist Raymond Boudon would call a '*pré-enquête*', a summary of the question aiming to review some of our preconceptions, and to reveal some trends. These impressions can be confirmed or undermined by further research.[5] Before dealing with the material here, though, the historiography of the topic invites some reflections and hints at useful directions and correctives. The literature available, quantitatively almost inexhaustible, is of mixed quality. Previous generations of historians were keenly sensitive to military and diplomatic history, so we have some excellent works based on proper archives, explored with judicious reflection and analysis.[6] Other authors, oblivious of the need to cite sources, were content to repackage historical writing of previous centuries. In such cases, the origin of the information remains mysterious or suspect. Given the patriotic or celebratory nature of this literature, some individuals, some events, and some campaigns were better treated than others, as more glorious, inspiring, or to employ the terminology of the time, as "worth remembering".

The greatest obstacle in collecting pertinent local studies has been Italian dislike for the period, although this is changing. The Risorgimento cast the terms in which the period is studied. These are called the "forgotten centuries", where the history of the peninsula was overshadowed by events unfolding elsewhere. The French invasion of 1494 inaugurated a period in which foreign armies of more warlike lands subjugated and imposed their will on Italians. Their rapid success was a reflection of Italian military inefficiency that Macchiavelli likened to dilet-

---

[4] P. Pieri, "Sur les dimensions de l'histoire militaire", *Annales: Economies, Sociétés, Civilisations*, 1963, pp. 625–38, at p. 626.

[5] R. Boudon, *Les méthodes en sociologie* (Paris: 1969), p. 33.

[6] The work by Camillo Manfroni on the knights of Santo Stefano, now over a century old, comes to mind as a dispassionate evaluation of their place in maritime history, and how well their actions corresponded to their intentions. See C. Manfroni, *La marina militare del granducato mediceo* (Rome: 1895). Similarly, the substantial work by N. Giorgetti, *Le armi toscane, 1537–1860*, 3 vols (Città di Castello: 1916). Less scholarly books include: L. Conforti, *I Napoletani a Lepanto: ricerche storiche* (Naples: 1886); C. Randaccio, *Storia delle marine militari italiane, dal 1750 al 1860, e della marina militare italiana dal 1860 al 1870* (Rome: 1886); and two books by A. Bernardy at the turn of the century, derived from printed sources, *Venezia e il Turco nella seconda metà del secolo XVII* (Florence: 1902), and *L'ultima guerra turco–veneziana (1714–18)* (Florence: 1902).

tantism, a degeneration of the warlike spirit perverted by the famous *condottieri*. They preferred bloodless manoeuvring in chess-like fashion, to the bloody chaos and risk of a pitched battle.[7] These warlords had waxed fat by prolonging limited wars that made them both rich and indispensable. Historians of this century, from Frederick Taylor and Piero Pieri to Michael Mallett concur, describing the art of war of the *condottiere*, as a "kind of giant kriegspiel". The 'national' armies invading the peninsula came as pupils to improve their knowledge of war as a performance art.[8]

According to the Risorgimento or nationalist interpretation, refined but not revised by Benedetto Croce, the most influential Italian historian of the first half of the twentieth century, Renaissance *condottieri* wielded power in a society that had become civilian, or 'soft'. City militias disarmed, and states maintained public order with small garrisons. Tyrant princes and oligarchic republics had good reason to disarm their subjects and confide their security to mercenary warlords. Only the *condottieri* retained the 'military spirit,' a sense of self-confidence, pride and *prepotenza* with respect to civilians. This would lead, in the Crocean idealist language employed by Piero Pieri, to a generalized 'spiritual insufficiency' of the social élite as citizens and as Italians, once the geographical expression that was Italy was invaded by a large army led by an aggressive prince and a warrior nobility. Risorgimento historians see the collapse of the Italian military spirit as part of a larger crisis of national identity and constitutional wrangling of petty states unable to place their *Italianità* over vested interests and regional hegemony.[9] Military agents remaining in Italy (and they were still plentiful) cravenly placed themselves in the service of foreign princes. Without admitting that this princely rivalry and territorial competition was a kind of Italian civil war, historians felt rather that the main problem was that Italian forces were fighting each other in wars where the only victor could be a foreign monarch: the king of Spain, as it turned out. I am oversimplifying the argument I have just traced. Croce himself noted how the Neapolitan aristocracy perceived the Spanish imperial system that emerged from the wars of Italy as an opportunity. The Neapolitan philosopher–historian lamented that the memories of those actions were obliterated in modern

---

[7] I have used an older volume of collected works, for the Florentine statesman's thought. N. Macchiavelli, *Il principe dell' arte della guerra, ed altri scritti politici* (Milan: 1961), F. Costero (ed.). Macchiavelli's view has been partially vindicated by a recent historian of the *condottieri*, Michael Mallett, who writes that "Defensive and unduly complex tactics were weaknesses of Italian warfare, and the Italian wars would prove over and over again that a new concept of warfare was emerging, with the desire to seek conclusions on the battlefield, to conquer, rather than to manoeuvre for the preservation of the balance of power". Mallett then nuances his judgement, and rehabilitates some of the Italian tactics. See his book, *Mercenaries and their masters: warfare in Renaissance Italy* (London: 1974), pp. 242ff.

[8] The term is Frederick Lewis Taylor's, in *The art of war in Italy, 1494–1529* (Westport, Conn.: 1973; first publ. 1921), p. 9. See also M. Mallett, n. 7 above. The classic book on this theme by Piero Pieri is *Il Rinascimento e la crisi militare italiana* (Turin: 1952).

[9] Pieri, *Il Rinascimento e la crisi militare italiana*, p. 341.

times (1924), because the families were extinct, or their interests had shifted, and that this tradition was belittled when not simply forgotten. Historians, influenced by the resounding lack of recent success of Neapolitan arms, and confusing the political reliability of an army with the military attitudes of a nation, rendered a superficial and derogatory judgement.[10]

Despite its militant nationalism, Fascist historiography usually turned a blind eye to Spanish domination in the sixteenth and seventeenth centuries. The period constitutes a real 'black hole' of Italian military historiography.[11] When Fascist writers did examine the era, they were inclined to prove that the military 'spirit' of Italians survived the long Spanish peace (1560–1700). The Spanish imperial system gave Italians a vast theatre on which to display their martial prowess. Spain's reach created a zone of influence that made the Mediterranean an Italian lake, and stretched tentacles of activity into Flanders, Hungary, Germany, Spain, the Levant and far-off Brazil. Reviving the glory of forgotten military heroes became a propaganda vector for the regime in the 1920s and 1930s. One title, *Condottieri italiani in Germania* (published in 1941!) imparts a good impression of the tone of their work.[12]

The biographical encyclopedia projects gave perfect scope for this revival; the regime needed a catalogue of heroes in every age who could mobilize modern Italians to emulation. Emphasizing the past vigour of the race was a way of masking Italy's social and economic lag compared to reference countries like France, Britain and Germany. The fascist material is best epitomized by three sets of encyclopedias, apparently intended to complement each other.[13] They encapsulated the names, place of origin, dates of activity and career *cursūs* of some 4,000 military nobles active between the reign of Philip II and the end of the seventeenth century. The volumes devoted to military heroes appear curious today, but they were sumptuous projects in their time, lavishly illustrated with reproductions of contemporary works, dramatic nineteenth-century engravings, and some period pieces of upright stern-faced paragons of Fascist strength. These beautifully bound volumes continued to appear in the years immediately after the Second World War, until this kind of militant nationalism evaporated in the 1950s. Unlike their Crocean contemporaries, the compilers were not professional academic histori-

---

[10] B. Croce, *Storia del regno di Napoli* (Bari: 1972; first publ. 1924), pp. 99–101.

[11] P. del Negro, "La storia militare dell' Italia moderna nello specchio della storiografia del Novecento", *Cheiron*, 1995, pp. 11–33.

[12] V. Mariani & V. Varanini, *Condottieri italiani in Germania* (Milan: 1941).

[13] The volume compiled under the direction of C. Argegni, *Enciclopedia biografica italiana, vol. 19: Condottieri, capitani e tribuni* (Rome: 1936), included Italian military figures from many periods, from the middle ages to the eighteenth century. This was augmented considerably by Aldo Valori in his complementary work in the same collection, *Condottieri e generali del Seicento* (Rome: 1940) and reprinted after the war in 1946. The several volumes of Luigi Maggiorotti, *L'opera del genio italiano all' estero*, 3 vols (Rome: 1933–9), while more lavishly illustrated, followed the same general format.

ans, but rather were soldiers, and good Fascists whose work echoed the ideology of the Party.[14] I doubt their university credentials because of the proliferation of errors of dates, reigning monarchs, and the frequent confusion of the Spanish and Austrian branches of the Habsburgs. A multitude of easily detectable printer errors, which derived from typesetters working from manuscripts, compounded the flaws in erudition. The errors of detail are compensated in part by the sheer enthusiasm of the compilers who, in their eagerness to expand the project and prove the eternal military vitality of the Italian race, inserted notices of officers of whom they knew virtually nothing. They also included many conspicuous incompetents, a sprinkling of court soldiers and captains of urban militia, some of whom may never have fired a shot in battle. They included nobles hailing from regions under the sovereignty of Italian states, that is, Savoyards and Dalmatians, and some cosmopolitan aristocrats living outside Italy, of whom Prince Eugene of Savoy is the most brilliant example. Pride of place in these volumes was nevertheless allotted to actors in primarily 'Italian' wars, especially of Venetians fighting Turks in the Aegean. Del Negro's characterization of Fascist historians, that they waxed longingly over the lives and gestures of great figures who possessed "*la forza del carattere*", is apt in this regard.[15]

They were all deemed virtuous, these scions of Italian families serving in European armies. In the inimitable rhetoric of the regime, Aldo Valori praised the world of Italian military nobles active in a land thought dead to arms and evoked how they gloriously carried the name of Italy to other, more fortunate (!) countries where war was present and felt, where there was the will and the possibility to cultivate that art; lands where lively political energies were fermenting, but which lacked brilliant and experienced military leaders that Italy possessed in abundance. Italian generals and captains showed to all the world, through their judicious use of armed might, all the energy and all the capacity of a people and of a state.[16] Fascist rhetoric frequently evoked futurist images of force and energy, and the poet Marinetti might have recognized his influence. They echoed the highly charged Baroque rhetoric of the literary sources they were using, often discernible in their images and their prose. This heroical style was a variant of an

---

[14] A systematic search of bibliographical reviews contained in the *Archivio Storico Italiano*, the *Rivista Storica Italiana*, the *Nuova Rivista Storica*, the *Rivista Storica Lombarda*, and the *Archivi Storici per le Provincie Napoletane* between 1935 and 1948 uncovered not the slightest trace of these writings. A lengthy historiographical essay on early modern Italy by P. F. Palumbo, "Formazione e sviluppo degli studi di storia moderna in Italia", *Archivio Storico Italiano*, 1941, pp. 154–82, does not mention these projects. Aldo Valori thanks in passing the "assiduous and resourceful researchers in the archives", to whom he attributed the precision and the thoroughness of the information provided. The people he mentions, various *dottori*, *avvocati*, and even a count, bear no academic or archival affiliation. See Valori, *Condottieri e generali del Seicento*, p. vii.

[15] Del Negro, "La storia militare dell' Italia moderna", *Cheiron*, 1995, pp. 11–33.

[16] Valori, *Condottieri e generali del Seicento*, pp. vii–xx.

older aesthetic tradition, celebrating military culture and valour, in the way it extolled "a whole flowering of heroism, sacrifices, brilliant initiatives, honourable gestures and deeds; one can still perceive at once the infinite vitality of the Italian temperament, always vigorously present and active wherever the love of great adventure and the sense of military honour calls".[17]

Despite the intellectual and methodological shortcomings of these fascist propagandists, and the naïvely celebratory nature of their labour, they were hardly wrong. In retrospect, they were perfectly correct to point out that hundreds of high-ranking Italians waged war for the Habsburgs from the sixteenth to the eighteenth centuries. These officers, not '*condottieri*' in the purely mercenary sense of that word, played a conspicuous part at the highest levels of the Spanish and Austrian imperial systems. Uncovering traces of their activity and influence is not difficult. Their vocations reveal something about the cosmopolitan nature of the Italian aristocracy, and the way it identified with the Habsburg Catholic cause that the Risorgimento neglected or deprecated. Italian patricians and feudal lords retained their military traditions and refurbished them with every new generation. Moreover, service to the Habsburgs was not the attribute solely of the Neapolitan, Sicilian or Milanese aristocracy, over which the king of Spain was the legitimate sovereign. The appeal of the Flanders and Hungarian theatres lured young men away from their Ligurian, Tuscan, Emilian, Umbrian and even Terraferma *palazzi*. Another important direction of this specifically Catholic activity lay in the appeal of the maritime military orders, of Malta and of Santo Stefano. Their raiding and amphibious campaigning reached paroxysmic levels during the late sixteenth and early seventeenth centuries, and their activity remained notable until the 1720s.

What escaped the fascist authors entirely, and therefore is my purpose here, is that their compilations reveal a startling decline of military activity abruptly around the middle of the seventeenth century. Italian states virtually ceased making war against each other after the curious Castro War (1642–4), an episode of Italian history that has yet to find a modern historian. Most of these states were no longer capable of what the nineteenth century would call 'grand politics' of alliances and armies, and contemporaries like Botero were conscious of it. What is more important, Spanish exhaustion in the aftermath of the Thirty Years War, coupled with Austrian fiscal limitations, deprived the Italian military aristocracy of its traditional outlets. This, and a deep, prolonged crisis of the Mediterranean economy, provoked a demilitarization of the upper reaches of Italian society that continued apace until the time of Napoleon. Except for the Piedmontese, who followed what one might call the north European model, Italian élites lost interest in military affairs.

While the decline of Italian military activity is my primary interest here, the chief difficulty is to demonstrate an *absence*. What follows is therefore a hypothesis in need of verification by proper empirical methods using more systematic

---

[17] *Ibid.*

sources, a stage to which I will allude in the conclusion. I elaborate this hypothesis by narrating events, which I bolster episodically by elementary quantitative evaluation of desultory sources that, like the encyclopedia biographies, allow me to make rough generalizations. Narrative is the most appropriate form of explication, since the process under examination follows a chronological progression, subject to the impact of events unfolding in different European states. There is another compelling reason to adopt the narrative, perhaps even more pressing than the first. Much of what follows will be tied to the political and military history of Europe from the sixteenth to the eighteenth century. Readers will find little there that is new. However, the political and military context of the various Italian states in the period is not generally known, even to Italians. Even when I cover familiar territory, it will sometimes be from an unfamiliar Italian perspective. The narrative serves to provide a loose factual framework upon which every analysis must ultimately hang.[18]

---

[18] Lawrence Stone's argument in favour of historical narrative suits this particular topic well, I think. See, "The revival of narrative. Reflections on a new Old History", *Past and Present* **85**, 1979, pp. 3–24.

Chapter 1
Knights and corsairs in the Mediterranean

Originality of Mediterranean warfare

The galley as a warship was so particularly suited to the geographical features of the Mediterranean region that its essential characteristics changed little in two thousand years. The advantage of the oared vessel was that it could move even in the calm weather that bedevilled sea travel in the Mediterranean. A standard galley possessed two masts retaining lateen (triangular) sails, and was propelled by twenty-five to thirty oars per side. Its narrow hull was just wide enough to fit benches for three or four oarsmen per oar, separated by a central walkway. The vessel, which lay less than a metre above the water-line in the centre, had an upraised stern containing command and steering functions and a raised bow platform for artillery and storage. All these characteristics enhanced its manoeuvrability, enabling it to circle its target and 'bite' it at the right spot (the side of another oared vessel, the bow or stern of a roundship). A common but not universal feature was the bronze spur on the bow that hooked on to an enemy ship and provided simultaneously a walkway for the boarding party.[1] The vessel had such shallow draught that it could operate close to shore, or be beached with no difficulty. Thus, the galley served better a military function than a commercial one. Built in a similar manner in Barcelona, Venice and Constantinople, galleys from all over the Mediterranean were used side-by-side by their captors and sometimes changed hands several times.[2]

The crucial innovation in the sixteenth century was the replacement of the trireme, where oarsmen on three levels each wielded a single oar, by a galley fitted out with a single bank of oars, each powered by several men. Such a system

---

[1] J. F. Guilmartin, *Gunpowder and galleys: changing technology and Mediterranean warfare at sea in the sixteenth century* (New York: 1974), p. 61.

[2] M. Aymard, "Chiourmes et galères dans la seconde moitié du XVIe siècle", in *Il Mediterraneo nella seconda metà del '500 alla luce di Lepanto*, G. Benzoni (ed.) (Florence: 1974), pp. 71–94. See in particular p. 90. John Francis Guilmartin nuances this by examining modifications of galley construction from Turkey, to Venice and Spain. See *Gunpowder and galleys*, p. 212.

enabled the vessel to carry more oarsmen, and increased its speed. By the late sixteenth century, the crowding was truly daunting. Men were crammed into every nook and cranny, from the oarsmen chained to the benches, to the soldiers and seamen gripping the gunwales and the platforms. A normal complement comprised 150 to 250 oarsmen, fifty seamen and a variable number of soldiers and officers. A typical galley forty metres (133 ft) long might contain 300 to 400 men, packed into 200 or 250 square metres (2150–2700 sq ft).[3] The large number of soldiers, seamen and oarsmen, these last sometimes salaried and liable to be armed, made it possible for galleys to approach the more vulnerable parts of an enemy ship and overwhelm the defenders. Only very good gunners could fire accurately from more than a few hundred metres and guns were generally unable to sink ships. Neither the attacking ship nor its target could release more than one salvo before collision. It sufficed for the galley to connect to its victim, hold fast in order to get enough men aboard, and support them with missile fire of swivel guns, arquebuses and arrows.[4] The galley could do this effectively even when the victim was a roundship, because until the seventeenth century these were generally slow-moving, unwieldy and cumbersome, with their only advantage being their higher sides. Most merchant ships surrendered without a struggle, hoping for lenient treatment.[5]

The galley's strength in manpower was also its chief drawback. It consumed provisions at a rate commensurate with the number of people wedged into it, and extreme crowding made disease a likely occurrence. The overwhelming filth and stench of the vessel were breeding grounds for typhus. The danger was offset only by constant exposure to the sun and wind, since the canopies draped over the hull only became common in the seventeenth century. Fresh water was a scarce and precious commodity, requiring frequent halts along the coast to replenish the barrels, a procedure known as the *acquata* or the *aiguade*. Above all, the narrow, low galley was unable to keep to sea in bad weather, and was reduced to operating for a few months in the summer and autumn. The requirements of crews, of equipment (oars, canvas, masts, rope, food) and also the short navigational season made galleys dependent upon their bases. A fleet's range of operations was in inverse proportion to its size, such that a large fleet could not venture very far. Only a few Mediterranean ports were capable of collecting the massive stores required for a major operation, building or repairing galleys and casting ordnance, holding crews available and combing the hinterland for more. Only three great centres

---

[3] M. Aymard, "Chiourmes et galères", in *Il Mediterraneo nella seconda metà del '500*, p. 78.

[4] There are several good sources on galley warfare: Guilmartin, *Gunpowder and galleys*, p. 61. See also J. R. Hale, "Men and weapons: the fighting potential of sixteenth-century Venetian galleys", in *War and society: a yearbook of military history*, B. Bond and I. Roy (eds) (London: 1975), pp. 1–23. More recently, see Franco Gay, "Considerazioni sulle navi dell' ordine di Santo Stefano", in *Le imprese e i simboli: Contributi alla storia del Sacro Militare Ordine di S. Stefano (s. XVI–XIX)* (Pisa: 1989), pp. 99–122.

[5] P. Earle, *The corsairs of Malta and Barbary* (London: 1970), pp. 136ff.

could support whole navies: Barcelona, Venice and Constantinople. Naples, Messina, Genoa, and Malta were staging areas able to store supplies and crews, but few other cities played an important role.[6] Imagine the arrival in port of a hundred galleys, a number frequently cited in the late sixteenth century! That was the equivalent of 30,000 or 40,000 men, more than the largest European armies, and entirely dependent upon local stocks of food as they spent long months in port waiting for developments. Forty thousand men equalled the daily food requirements of a major European city of the time.

To compensate for the logistical fragility of the galley fleet, Christian armadas eventually included roundships containing food, water, ammunition and the myriad implements required to repair ship damage or lay siege to coastal forts. Fleets and flotillas still had to halt every three or four days to replenish water, to take on fresh provisions, and to rest the crews. Dependency upon the resources of the coast and islands was another limitation, but galleys had removable rudders permitting them to be beached in a predicament, with their guns pointing menacingly out to sea, while the precious crews scrambled ashore for safety. The shallow draught allowed raiding parties to land in a twinkling on the beach, to storm a castle or a port. Working close to shore in a way not possible for sailing ships, galleys could perform valuable work in a siege, firing their cannon at vulnerable flanks of a fortress, and drawing away defenders.[7] They could disembark their valuable heavy guns to batter a fortress from the landward side; and their crews could dig entrenchments or participate in assaults. Conversely, a fleet threatened by a larger one could beach itself under the guns of a friendly fortress, and be unapproachable by sea.

Guilmartin ventures that the main purpose of assembling a galley armada, apart from offering combat to any enemy navy, was to capture enemy bases that would support friendly fleets thereafter. Such was the purpose of the Hispano-Italian attack on Djerba in 1560, the invasion of Malta in 1565, the Ottoman invasion of Cyprus in 1570, the Venetian attack on Navarino in 1572, and the Spanish expedition against Tunis the same year. Removal of threatening bases in the heart of their shipping routes motivated the Turkish invasion of Crete (1645), and attempts against Algiers (1545 and 1600) and Peñon (1563) by the Spaniards. These shoreside targets were more worthwhile objectives than the destruction of an enemy fleet arrayed in battle order.[8]

The naval history of the period was nevertheless punctuated by clashes of galley fleets, usually the size of squadrons, but occasionally much larger. A surprised galley fleet in dispersed order without the advantage of wind had no chance of winning. Its only defence was to veer towards the enemy, and deploy in a line-abreast formation, a solid front of prows and cannon. This formation took hours to achieve and much discipline and luck to maintain, since keeping formation

---

[6] Guilmartin, *Gunpowder and galleys*, p. 100.

[7] *Ibid.*, p. 76ff.

[8] *Ibid.*, p. 98ff.

slowed the fleet speed to about two knots. It was virtually impossible to maintain a compact formation of more than sixty galleys abreast. Changing direction required superhuman efforts from the end galleys to keep up. Elsewhere an accordion effect bunched galleys up or spread them apart, opening dangerous gaps to the enemy, who was assured victory if allowed to attack from the side. A second line of reserve galleys made it possible to stop some of the gaps. Moreover, they could attach themselves to the rear of a friendly galley and feed reinforcements into the mêlée combat taking place on its deck.[9]

When galleys fought each other they paired off and accelerated at the last minute to close. Gunnery exchanges were not crucial because only the nimble and accurate Venetian gunners were capable of two salvoes or more, from the great bronze pieces mounted on the bow. In the sixteenth century good bronze guns were expensive and rare, like the great hand-carved stone balls they fired. The single bronze piece was usually flanked by a couple of iron ones of lesser calibre. An assortment of smaller swivel pieces mounted on the forecastle or the stern and loaded with stones or metal pellets and shards, accompanied those. The Spanish and Hispano-Italian galleys in particular bristled with ordnance, like a floating castle, in contrast to the nimbler Venetian equivalents, with their smaller detachment of soldiers.[10] After the brief exchange of salvoes, a mêlée on the deck of the target ship decided the outcome. In this terrible throng, Christian troops had the relative advantage of more body armour: breastplates, helmets, thigh guards of plate. They were variously armed with arquebuses, pikes, longswords, crossbows and longbows. Arquebusiers were easy to train and their weapons were effective at short ranges, though they were so slow to reload that each carried a sword and dagger too. The Turkish recurved bow was still a redoubtable weapon and remained in service throughout the seventeenth century and even after. Bows were accurate, powerful and rapid, but it took years to train an effective archer, and in a long battle they would tire. Numbers being equal, the advantage belonged to those higher up, particularly on the bow superstructure looking down onto the deck of the target ship.[11]

At Lepanto the Venetians introduced a secret weapon that, if it did not spell the demise of galley fleets for more than a century, at least introduced a self-defeating logic. Francesco Duodo fitted out twelve cumbersome merchant galleys, the galeasses, with four times the hull displacement of a normal galley, and packed the sides with cannon and swivel guns.[12] For much of the campaign, they had to be towed by the lighter (sensile) galleys, despite the efforts of up to 500 oarsmen. They provided a stable platform for hundreds of soldiers and gunners. By their size and

[9] Guilmartin, p. 73ff.

[10] Ibid., p. 175ff; p. 212ff.

[11] Ibid., p. 149; See also Hale, "Men and weapons", in War and society, pp. 1–23; and Gay, "Considerazioni sulle navi", Le imprese e i simboli, p. 103ff.

[12] M. Morin, "La battaglia di Lepanto", in Venezia e i Turchi: Scontri e confronti di due civiltà (Milan: 1985), pp. 210–31, at p. 219.

armament, and their ability to spew projectiles from the sides and the bow, the six galeasses present at Lepanto inflicted crippling losses on the Turks.[13] Galeasses figured in every Christian fleet thereafter, and even normal galleys tended to increase in length and armament in the subsequent decades. But the increased operating cost limited their numbers. The price of food more than quintupled in the sixteenth century, reducing the 'cost-effectiveness' of galleys as warships.[14] A Tuscan version, built around 1600, reportedly carried 36 heavy guns and 64 pierriers, and 1,200 men. It must have been ruinous to operate, and unlikely to catch any prey.[15] The increased size also nullified the ship's manoeuvrability, and thus its offensive capacity. Some improvements after Lepanto, such as the introduction of a third mast, made the galeass faster, but it could not operate independently. It functioned instead as a floating gun-platform for use in set-piece battles. The evolution towards the galeass inaugurated a new period defined by the importance of ship-borne artillery.

The next stage was the appearance after 1590 of the improved North Sea roundship, the *bertone*, as the Italians called it. A typical English one displaced 300 to 500 tons, broad and round, a three-master with square sails and a crew of only about sixty men. It could carry 30 or even more cannon all around it, and still leave room to transport soldiers and cargo. Such ships were not invulnerable to galleys, for expert gunners could disable one from afar, before closing in on its vulnerable stern. One Italian galley squadron was able in 1637 to capture an entire Dutch convoy, composed of such vessels.[16] Over time their agility improved, and by 1650 galleys served as adjuncts to fleets of roundships. The teeth of the still unwieldy *bertone* consisted of the many iron cannon it contained. A sixteenth-century revolution in casting techniques in northern Europe made it possible to multiply the number of cheap cannon. They were heavier, bulkier, less accurate and more dangerous than the bronze guns commonly in use as the main gun on warships. Because there were so many of them, the quality of gunnery suffered. However, the sheer number of these guns transformed seaborne warfare.[17]

Logistical requirements for the concentration of numerous galleys could be daunting for sixteenth-century administrators. Since they were not large ships, the

---

[13] *Ibid*, p. 219.

[14] Guilmartin, *Gunpowder and galleys*, p. 273.

[15] See Gay, "Considerazioni sulle navi", in *Le imprese e i simboli*, p. 112, for details on Tuscan galleys and galeasses. The monstrous galeass containing 1,200 men is mentioned by Gino Guarnieri, but I have never encountered its presence in any accounts, if indeed it ever existed. See G. Guarnieri, *I cavalieri di Santo Stefano, nella storia della marina italiana (1562–1859)* (Pisa: 1960), p. 80.

[16] R. C. Anderson, "The Thirty Years' War in the Mediterranean", *Mariner's Mirror*, 1969, pp. 435–51, at p. 440.

[17] On the impact of iron cannon on naval warfare, see Guilmartin, *Gunpowder and galleys*, p. 175ff. For the appearance of the *bertone* and Venice's adaptation to it, see A. Tenenti, *Piracy and the decline of Venice, 1580–1615* (London: 1967, first publ. 1961), p. 53ff.

hulls could be built quickly and fairly cheaply, if seasoned timber was on hand. The Venetians and Turks proved this by constructing large fleets of them in short order. Philip II of Spain (1556–98) created fleets of galleys at Barcelona and at Naples, in both cases using large numbers (153 in 1587) of expensive Genoese craftsmen, caulkers and carpenters, under the expert direction of Genoese over-seers.[18] For quality construction at reasonable cost, it was necessary to have forests situated close to the coast for the transport of timber to the shipyards, like the Dalmatian forests at the disposal of the Arsenal in Venice. By far the most expensive and laborious part of any galley expedition was to find the oarsmen. In medieval Venice, service at the oar was a duty incumbent on able-bodied men, and mobilization stripped the shops and workshops of merchants and artisans. The increase in urban living standards made artisans so recalcitrant that by the mid-sixteenth century, many oarsmen were impressed seamen, captured pirates or convicts, recruited from as far away as Bavaria. By 1580, when Venice was committed to floating more than a hundred galleys, the quality of the workforce declined.[19] By 1592 only the pilot (or lantern) galleys, equivalent to flagships, were using crews of freemen; all the others used convicts and prisoners chained to their benches where they lived permanently. The Venetians sometimes solved their manpower problems by scooping hapless villagers off the Greek coast.[20] Spanish fleets were similarly strapped. The great cost of maintaining galleys at sea tempted many captains to cut corners at the expense of the oarsmen.[21] Food rations that were balanced and copious enough for the seamen and the soldiers, were limited to bread and water for them.[22] The atrocious conditions caused many oarsmen to fall sick and die, making it necessary to renew them continually.[23] Tenenti affirms that serious negligence or indiscipline on the part of the captains or *sopracomite* was rare, but it was common for them to make unofficial trips and unauthorized halts, to smuggle contraband goods or engage in unauthorized trade.

These administrative headaches led the Spanish to suspend efforts to build their own fleet and turn to entrepreneurs, primarily Genoese, with galleys for hire. Indeed, the private agents kept their galleys cleaner, with better conditions for the crew in order to avoid the costly search for oarsmen. The crown leased vessels from owners who built and commanded them as an investment. Studying a

---

[18] D. Goodman, *Power and penury: government, technology and science in Philip II's Spain* (Cambridge: 1988), p. 100.

[19] Tenenti, *Piracy and the decline of Venice, 1580–1615*, p. 108.

[20] A. E. Vacalopoulous, *The Greek nation, 1463–1669* (New Brunswick, New Jersey: 1976), pp. 85–90.

[21] Tenenti, *Piracy and the decline of Venice, 1580–1615*, p. 116ff.

[22] J. J. Hémardinquer, "Vie matérielle et comportements biologiques, bulletin no. 11: A propos de l'alimentation des marins, sur les galères de Toscane au XVIe siècle", *Annales: Economies, Sociétés, Civilisations*, 1963, pp. 1141–9.

[23] All of these problems of manning the galleys are illustrated in the article by Maurice Aymard, "Chiourmes et galères", in *Il Mediterraneo nella seconda metà del '500*, pp. 71–94.

contract between King Philip II of Spain and the Genoese admiral and entrepreneur Gian Andrea Doria in 1566, Guilmartin underscores the fiscal rationale for the monarch to lease a flotilla for 2,000 ducats annually per galley, at an annual interest rate of 14 per cent (with inflation running at around 4 per cent) on the unpaid balance. For the entrepreneur, an *asiento* for a galley was also a means of realizing hidden profits, such as having access to jealously guarded currency export licences, or the right to purchase Sicilian grain free of taxes and duties, for resale elsewhere at a profit. Genoese captains and commanders did not hesitate to transport merchandise or smuggle cash whenever the occasion presented itself, even when this was forbidden in the contract.[24] Including all the hidden costs, Spain paid about 10,000 ducats annually for the operation of a Genoese galley during the Lepanto era, which Guilmartin maintains was ten per cent more expensive than operating a Spanish one.[25] Thompson counters that the Genoese alternative was cheaper, more efficient and clearly preferable when there was not enough money available to finance a larger Spanish fleet, even in the 1630s when a single galley cost 18,000 ducats annually.[26] Considerations of sovereignty still spurred the Spaniards occasionally to build and operate their own ships, despite the greater expense. At Lepanto about ten per cent of the entire Christian navy consisted of rented galleys belonging to Genoese entrepreneurs, who were conspicuous at the division of the spoils. They purveyed galleys to Spain during the entire seventeenth century.[27]

The clash of great fleets

It is easy to forget that when historians speak of the Spanish fleet, they refer mostly to Italian galleys based in Naples and Sicily, with others rented from Genoese and Roman entrepreneurs. Add to those the Tuscan, Papal and Savoyard auxiliary

---

[24] This could also have a negative impact on military operations. During the Djerba campaign of 1560, where private galleys outnumbered state vessels 31 to 16, owners avoided exposing their capital whenever possible, and were more inclined to attack merchant ships than enemy galleys. See C. Monchicourt, *L'expédition espagnole de 1560 contre l'île de Djerba* (Paris: 1913), p. 89.

[25] Guilmartin, *Gunpowder and galleys*, p. 34.

[26] I. A. A. Thompson, *War and government in Habsburg Spain, 1560–1620* (London: 1976), p. 86ff.

[27] For example, the king of Spain attempted twice to create a Sardinian flotilla by recourse to such naval entrepreneurs. In 1639, four galleys were provided by the Genoese Giovan Antonio Saulì, costing 15,000 ducats each for six months service. See F. F. Olesa Muñido, *La organizacion naval de los estados mediterraneos y en especial de España durante los siglos XVI y XVII*, 2 vols (Madrid: 1968), vol. 1, p. 380ff. A similar contract to provide eight galleys was passed soon after with the Genoese-born prince of Melfi, Giovanni Andrea Doria. Only two of his personal galleys ever saw service, and despite provisions in the contract stipulating that the officers ought to be native Sardinians, the Genoese predominated. See G. Sorgia, "Progetti per una flotta sardo-genovese nel Seicento", *Miscellanea di Storia Ligure*, 1966, pp. 177–90.

flotillas in Spanish pay, and the enormous Venetian navy, it becomes apparent that the great majority of the Catholic fleets in the Mediterranean, probably more than 70 per cent, were in reality Italian, with seamen and soldiers of predominantly Italian origin. The peninsula, moreover, was the appropriate base from which to strike at the heart of the Ottoman Empire, the Barbary pirate coast from Tunisia and Tripolitania to present-day Algeria, and the hostile Greek and Albanian coast. Italy, rather than Iberia, was the Spanish bulwark in the Mediterranean, the staging area for the great fleets. Turkish ascendancy at sea, the outcome of the running battle of Prevesa in 1538, limited Spain's chances to reduce these pirate bases. Spanish expeditions against them were nevertheless largely Italian affairs, conceived and directed from Italy, with Messina being the ideal port for assembling men and ships.[28]

The first offensive project was an operation against Tripoli at the end of 1559, organized by the Viceroy of Sicily, Medina Celi, and involving the Spanish flotillas, the Knights of Malta, a Genoese contingent, a few Papal galleys and the new Tuscan navy. Barbary galleys could only operate in conjunction with Turkish ones in summer, and for the rest of the year they were on their own. The fleet leaving Syracuse in December consisted of 47 galleys, four galiots and three galleons, with supply vessels ferrying 12,000 Spanish, German and Italian soldiers. Almost all the galleys were Italian or commanded by Italians, who comprised about half the soldiery too. Bad weather forced them to wait in Malta until February 1560 where 2,000 men were lost to illness. In early March, Medina Celi and Gian Andrea Doria chose to occupy the island of Djerba instead of Tripoli, and the troops that were disembarked there fell to building a fort to serve as a permanent base. In response, the Turkish galley fleet left Constantinople in April, earlier than the Hispano-Italians thought possible. It arrived off Djerba on 11 May, weeks before it was expected. The consequence was so predictable that the scattered Catholic fleet gave no thought to forming a proper battle deployment. Many Christian soldiers were still on the island, and the galley commanders' only instinct was to escape in a 'sauve qui peut'. The Turks took half the galleys and most of the supply ships. Medina Celi readied a relief force of 14,000 troops (again largely Italians) in Sicily to rescue the stranded troops on Djerba, and launched new galleys to replace those lost, but they dared not attack the Turkish fleet. At the end of July the Djerba garrison surrendered for lack of water. After that, the combined Turkish and Barbary navy cruised with impunity off the coasts of Tuscany before raiding the southern coast of Sicily and burning the city of Augusta. They probably captured about 7,000 prisoners in these raids alone.[29]

---

[28] Thompson, *War and government in Habsburg Spain*, p. 17.

[29] The most detailed and scholarly study of the Djerba expedition, based partially on Turkish and Arab sources, is by Monchicourt, *L'expédition espagnole de 1560 contre l'île de Djerba*. For the raids on Sicily, see K. Setton, *The Papacy and the Levant (1204–1571): vol. IV, The sixteenth century from Julius III to Pius V* (Philadelphia: 1984), p. 765. See also Dennis Mack Smith, *A history of Sicily, vol. 1: medieval Sicily, 800–1713* (London: 1968), p. 129ff.

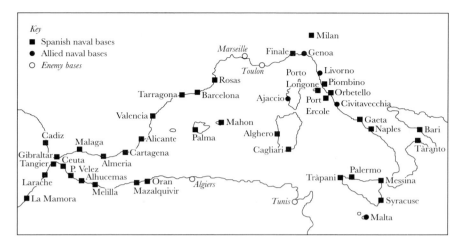

Map 1.1 Naval bases in the western Mediterranean in the seventeenth century *(after J. Alcala-Zamora y Queipo de Llano)*

The disaster befalling the fleet at Djerba was only one of a string of reverses suffered by the Catholic states at the hands of the Moslems since the beginning of Sultan Suleiman's reign in 1521. The 'Spanish' fleet suffered another catastrophe in November 1562 when a savage storm sank 25 of 28 galleys assembled off the Màlaga coast, with the loss of several thousand lives. This required the urgent assembly of most of the available Italian galleys off Spain, ferrying Spanish troops, to effect the relief of the Oran garrison. That force contained only four Spanish galleys out of forty-two. An expedition by the same fleet to capture Peñon de Velez failed for the loss of surprise in July 1563. Another armada of galleys collected in Italy attempted it again in 1564. The fleet formed off the south coast of Andalusia numbered 90 to 100 galleys, plus auxiliary vessels with 16,000 troops on board. Early in September this armada inaugurated the siege of Peñon and captured this pirate base in a few days.[30]

Given the scale of expenditure, this success was meagre. Repeated Spanish galley mobilization in the 1560s shows Philip II's desire to hold the Moslem threat at bay and not to relinquish the initiative in the Mediterranean. An ongoing drain on the treasury was the maintenance of a string of bases in North Africa, like Melilla, Ceuta and Oran, sometimes held only to prevent them from falling into enemy hands. Finding galleys, crews and especially oarsmen was the most difficult part of that task, and resulted in makeshift solutions. Madrid rented ships from Genoa and Tuscany, and subsidized their construction. It also called upon the

---

[30] F. Braudel, *The Mediterranean and the Mediterranean world in the age of Philip II*, 2 vols (New York: 1967, first publ. 1949), vol. 2, p. 1000. Braudel's masterpiece inspires most of the subsequent literature on the great conflict in the Mediterranean, and it has not really been superseded.

Knights of Malta for assistance. Philip succeeded in inducing the Italian states, Florence particularly, to increase the number of their own warships since the Catholic effort was seen as a joint one. Spain furnished part of the 'start-up' capital, either in the form of guaranteed leasing fees, or else in direct subventions.[31] As a result, the Catholic powers reconstituted their losses after each setback. By 1564 the Hispano-Italian effort made it possible to collect about a hundred galleys for one expedition.[32]

The Turkish offensive against Malta in 1565 attempted to reassert Moslem ascendancy in the central Mediterranean. Its capture would remove a crucial base of Catholic raiding activity, and transform it into an advance position against southern Italy. The port of Borgo was a tiny community, despite its ample, deep-water harbour. When the knights settled there in 1530, there were only 12,000 people on the island and 5,000 more on nearby Gozo. By quickly establishing its ascendancy over the inhabitants, the order reorientated the economy around privateering against Moslem vessels. In 1564 they captured a vessel carrying rich possessions to the sultan's harems.[33] The knights had just enough time to prepare for a siege; more than 600 of them and over 7,000 professional soldiers and local militiamen thronged into the fortress. A combined Turkish–Barbary fleet surpassing 150 sail, landed about 25,000 soldiers and workers on the island on 18 May. They quickly overran it save for the old capital of Città Vecchia and the Borgo, which was protected by Fort St Elmo on the tip of a barren peninsula. This fort kept the Turkish fleet away from the town, and it was held at all costs. Reinforcements for it arrived by boats at night to replace the fallen. An assault finally overwhelmed it after four weeks of constant battery. Despite repeated assaults along its ramparts, the Ottoman besiegers made no progress against the Borgo, which held out. Meanwhile, the Spanish Captain-General Don Garcia de Toledo gathered his forces in Italy. By the end of August 1565 he had 100 galleys available, with levies of soldiers hired throughout southern Europe and concentrated at Messina and Syracuse. Hundreds of noble volunteers, for the most part Italians, joined them. When 10,000 Spanish, German and Italian troops landing on the coast opposite the siege checked the Ottoman forces sent against them, the

---

[31] Camillo Manfroni's *La marina militare del granducato mediceo* contains many details concerning Duke Cosimo's role as a Spanish satellite, eager to make some political capital out of Spain's need for Tuscan galleys. See p. 106ff.

[32] Besides Braudel, the events of these campaigns are related with more detail in several more recent works. The most detailed, and least analytical, is R. C. Anderson's compilation, *Naval wars in the Levant, 1559–1853* (Princeton, New Jersey: 1952). Rambling, but useful and fastidiously researched is Kenneth Setton's *The Papacy and the Levant (1204–1571), vol. IV: The sixteenth century from Julius III to Pius V* (Philadelphia: 1984). In the Braudellian vein is the substantial analytical work by Francisco-Felipe Olesa Muñido, *La organizacion naval de los estados mediterraneos y en especial de España durante los siglos XVI y XVII*, 2 vols (Madrid: 1968).

[33] Q. Hughes, *Fortress: architecture and military history in Malta* (London: 1969), p. 40ff.

Turks hurriedly abandoned their siege and re-embarked their army. They also feared that their fleet would be attacked while most of the soldiers necessary to defend them were on land. The Turks sailed away on 11 September. For the Order of Malta it was an expensive victory, costing them 300 knights and 2,500 soldiers killed.[34]

Malta was a 'defensive' victory, won by a few thousand knights and Maltese with the king of Spain and Italian princes speeding to their aid. Their rescue was feasible only because the invaders could not fight on land and sea simultaneously. Only an alliance between Spain and Venice could confront the combined resources of the Ottoman Empire on equal terms. Luckily for them, Constantinople played into their hands after the death of Sultan Suleiman in 1566. The Turkish fleet bared its teeth at Venice that year, perhaps because the new sultan, Selim II, contemplated an easy conquest in that theatre. Selim sent a fleet of 100 galleys to the Adriatic, into waters hitherto under the protection of the Venetian republic. It burned some coastal towns in the Abruzzi, Ortona and Francavilla, abandoned by their populations, and raiding parties foraged into the interior. In anticipation, the Venetians launched 100 galleys of their own, but the Turks withdrew without attacking them. After that both were diverted from the Mediterranean. The nervous Venetians prepared their fortresses for the likelihood of a repeat attack. The Spaniards were distracted in turn by the Dutch revolt and the Moorish uprising in the kingdom of Granada in 1569. The necessity of ferrying troops, including many Neapolitans, to Andalusia and the Sierra Nevada, weakened Spain's hold over the waters around Sicily. In January 1570, friendly Tunis fell to a Calabrian renegade in Turkish service, named Euldj Ali. The Ottomans marked one more success in their quest for control of north Africa and the Mediterranean.[35]

Spanish preoccupation with an Islamic guerrilla war in Iberia left the door open for an Ottoman attack on Venetian Cyprus in 1570. The *Serenissima* traditionally held itself aloof from the great fleet expeditions of Spain and the rest of Italy, anxious to retain access to the Middle East, foundation of its prosperity. Venice was no weakling. Perhaps two million people inhabited its empire, mostly in the prosperous Terraferma and the rest in the Dalmatian and Greek dominions. The latter included Corfù and the Ionian islands, Crete and Cyprus. Venice's thin corridor along the eastern Adriatic shore was tenuously held, however. The Turks began with some diversionary raids into Dalmatia from Bosnia, overwhelming

---

[34] Some contemporary accounts of the siege from the perspective of the knights have been reprinted. The standard narration by an eye-witness is in H. A. Balbi, *The siege of Malta (1565)* (Copenhagen: 1961). See also E. Montalto, *Diario dell' assedio di Malta* (Rome: 1965), which contains a list of the volunteers and adventurers, and a list of the knights engaged in the siege.

[35] For the place of the Morisco revolt in the struggle between Spain and Islam, see A. C. Hess, "The Moriscos: an Ottoman fifth column in sixteenth-century Spain", *American Historical Review*, 1968, pp. 1–25.

smaller outposts on the Montenegrin coast like Dulcigno, Antevari and Budua. They besieged Zara, Spalato and Sebenico vainly. This invasion triggered a complex process of mobilization, ordered by the patrician civilians in the capital, through their system of deputized proveditors to the army and navy. Venetian officials called out the local militias and the feudal levies, who would not exceed the numbers of professional troops until an attack was imminent. John Hale has shown how the Venetian peacetime force of about 9,000 men quadrupled in the space of a few months by drawing upon hired professional soldiers and large territorial militias simultaneously.[36] The republic beefed up its garrisons everywhere. Mercenaries habitually sent to the Greek islands were untrustworthy, because they had established families there and had begun to till the soil. There was little sympathy for the republic among its Cypriot Greek subjects. With the new levies of Italian soldiers, the Venetian governor built a huge rampart 8 km (5 mi) long around Nicosia, and used forced labour and mass evictions to prepare the city for a siege. At sea Venice was able to muster 136 galleys plus 11 of the new galeasses. From the total they managed to assemble a high seas strike fleet of 77 galleys and 20 roundships. The empire also had to contribute to the build-up of the fleet, with Crete producing 29 galleys on its own. Despite these efforts, only the massive fortifications of Nicosia and Famagusta delayed the quick Turkish conquest of the island. Nicosia fell after about a month's siege and six assaults, and most of the surviving Italians were massacred in the main square. By early 1571 it was Famagusta's turn, having only 2,000 Italian soldiers in garrison besides the local Greeks, but it was a seaport and received providential relief from a Venetian squadron under Marco Querini that scurried through the blockade, and then escaped in a heaven-sent fog.[37]

Scores of nobles stepped forward offering to raise troops. Sixty such captains or personalities proposed to raise 75,000 professional soldiers for the republic, and cities offered more. The greater number of professional soldiers was Italian, chiefly from outside the Terraferma, from Corsica to Naples. The largest number

---

[36] J. R. Hale, "From peacetime establishment to fighting machine: the Venetian army and the War of Cyprus and Lepanto", in *Il Mediterraneo nella seconda metà del '500 alla luce di Lepanto*, G. Benzoni (ed.) (Florence: 1974), pp. 163–84. Useful details can be culled from Federico Paleologo Oriundi, *I Corsi nella fanteria italiana della Serenissima repubblica di Venezia* (Venice: 1912), p. 7. See also Luciano Pezzolo, "Aspetti della struttura militare veneziana in Levante fra Cinque e Seicento", in *Venezia e la difesa del Levante, da Lepanto a Candia, 1570–1670* (Venice: 1986), pp. 86–96. In the same collection, see the short but pithy piece by Robert Mantran, "L'Impero Ottomano, Venezia e la guerra (1570–1670)", in *Venezia e la difesa del Levante*, pp. 227–32. Note that, here and elsewhere, the continental convention has been followed, whereby contributions in published colloquia do not as a rule carry the names of the editors, at least for bibliographical purposes.

[37] The best recent narrative of these events can be found in Setton, *The Papacy and the Levant (1204–1571)*, vol. IV, pp. 1004–10.

of non-Italians was Swiss, followed by some French and Germans. If the figures cited by Hale are accurate, this levy of mercenaries was extraordinary for the time. Recruiters provided 12,000 soldiers for the Armada of 1570, then 5,000 reinforcements in 1571, and sent another 15,000 overseas before the battle of Lepanto, for a total of at least 37,000. It proved harder to find oarsmen. Muster-rolls always ignore the continual replenishment of crews: losses from dysentery in the Venetian fleet alone were close to 20,000 men in 1570–71.[38] Venice tradition-ally raised crews in Greek islands like Zante and Cefalonia, or in the Peloponnesis (Morea). They were not above raiding the Greek archipelago to carry off men as slaves; islands like Andros, Paros, and Naxos were favourite targets. The entire navy under Admiral Zane eventually consisted of 145 galleys, 11 galeasses and 20 ships, with 12,000 infantry on board.

Spain mobilized simultaneously, despite its war in Granada, by gathering its galleys at Messina and recruiting troops of Spaniards and Italians for Sicily and for the galleys themselves. The combined squadrons of Sicily, Naples and Genoa comprised about sixty galleys, carrying several thousand troops. Catholic forces combined in Crete were therefore considerable. Venetian, Spanish and Pontifical forces reached a total of 205 galleys and galeasses, with about 17,000 infantry aboard, and 4,000 adventurers.[39] Zane dared not risk a confrontation with the Turkish fleet, however, and the coalition forces withdrew when the weather turned.

Pope Pius V finally sewed together a formal Holy League to confront the Ottoman navy and save Venice. Three commanders were designated: Don Juan, Philip II's bastard son for Spain, and the chief of the triumvirate; MarcAntonio Colonna, a Roman patrician for the Papal States, and admiral Sebastiano Venier for Venice. The Venetian flotillas at Crete united with Spanish and Papal ships (most of which were rented from Florence) at the end of August, 1571. The entire Catholic fleet was not assembled until September. By colossal effort, Venice found soldiers and crews sufficient for its galleys and its garrisons too. This network of fortifications was the real armature of its resistance. Crete alone absorbed 8,500 soldiers in 1571, or 29 per cent of all the overseas garrisons of the republic.[40] The

---

[38] M. Mallett and J. R. Hale, *The military organisation of a Renaissance state* (Cambridge: 1984), p. 237.
[39] Setton, *The Papacy and the Levant, vol. IV*, pp. 970–90. See also Hale, "From peacetime establishment to fighting machine", in *Il Mediterraneo nella seconda metà del '500*, pp. 163–84.
[40] Pezzolo, "Aspetti della struttura militare veneziana in Levante fra Cinque e Seicento", in *Venezia e la difesa del Levante*, pp. 86–96, at p. 86. All the infantry garrisons, excluding Venice and the Terraferma (a few thousand troops, probably) comprised 17,350 men, of whom more than 5,000 were in Zara, 2,197 in Sebenico, 3,780 in Cattaro, 4,576 in Corfù, 8608 in Crete and 3,290 were holding out desperately in Famagusta. Smaller garrisons were scattered throughout the empire.

epic siege of Famagusta, which lasted eighteen months proved the technical superiority of the Venetians over the Turks. Its garrison surrendered only after it had exhausted its gunpowder.[41]

With such a narrow demographic base, and such a huge arc of territories to garrison against the Ottomans, the Venetians were hard pressed to find troops for their galleys. They had to hire Calabrian and Neapolitan captains and their companies at premium prices. The Venetians relied heavily on Croat subjects, and on Greek and Albanian mercenaries. The Corfiote militia was extremely enthusiastic, for the devastation wrought there by the Ottoman siege in 1538 was keenly remembered.[42] Greeks and Croats also provided many of the officers leading the militias and the infantry companies. Only Venetian patricians commanded the galleys. To compensate for the scarcity of soldiers, the Venetians led raids into Bosnia and Hercegovina, and spurred Serbs, Albanians and Greeks to rise up against the Ottomans from Bosnia to the Peloponnesis. At sea they offset their numerical inferiority by adapting their galleys for greater speed, and focused on improving their gunnery. Unlike the Spaniards or Ottomans, the Venetians had an elaborate training régime for their gunners.[43] Artillery was complemented by the musketry of the soldiers, protected by their body armour, and removable wooden shutters on the sides of their galleys protected soldiers and crews from arrows.[44] The most effective ships the Catholics possessed at Lepanto, six lumbering galeasses, were also Venetian.

The 'Spanish' contribution measured up to the Venetian one. To begin with, there were 45 galleys from the Neapolitan and Sicilian squadrons, carrying two élite *tercios*, part of a Sicilian *tercio* and regiments from Lombardy and Naples. Providing soldiers in abundance was not so difficult for Philip II. Even the suspicious Venetians accepted 1,500 Spanish, Italian and German soldiers in the Catholic king's pay on its galleys to compensate for their own lack of troops. In total there were 25,000 soldiers in Spanish pay. Though no Neapolitan commanded any of the 21 galleys of the kingdom's squadron at Lepanto, they were numerous among the soldiers and gentlemen adventurers. The kingdom also provided 4,000 soldiers, purportedly Calabrians.[45] Sicily contributed additional resources. If the island covered ten per cent of the visible expenditures, in reality it paid much more by provisioning the fleet united at Messina.[46] Sicily spent 5.3

[41] For details of the siege, see Kenneth Setton, *The Papacy and the Levant, vol. IV*, p. 1032.

[42] William Miller, *Essays on the Latin Orient* (Cambridge: 1921), p. 221.

[43] Guilmartin, *Gunpowder and galleys*, p. 175.

[44] Guilmartin, *Gunpowder and galleys*, p. 212. See also Hale, "Men and weapons", in *War and society*, p. 17.

[45] G. Parker, "Lepanto (1571): the costs of victory", in *Spain and the Netherlands, 1559–1659* (Short Hills, New Jersey: 1979), p. 129; see also L. Conforti, *I napoletani a Lepanto: ricerche storiche* (Naples: 1886), p. 36; and K. Setton, *The Papacy and the Levant, vol. IV*, pp. 1047–50.

[46] Parker, "Lepanto (1571)", in *Spain and the Netherlands, 1559–1659*, p. 126.

million *scudi* for three successive campaigns between 1571 and 1573, which was more than its total tax revenue.[47]

The third pillar of the Holy League was the Pope, who bankrolled one-sixth of the total cost of the Catholic fleet, and provided his own squadron of 12 galleys, with Tuscan crews, rented from the grand duke. MarcAntonio Colonna had once owned a private corsair flotilla, and knew something about warfare at sea. Aboard were 3,000 troops in Papal pay, and many adventurers. The Tuscan crusading order of Santo Stefano manned five of these galleys themselves, with about a hundred knights aboard.[48] Minor Italian states, like Genoa, Savoy and Malta, provided three galleys each with their own crews and soldiers. Maltese galleys contained the highest proportion of knights and the largest number of gentlemen adventurers and men-at-arms. The Genoese had the best reputation for seafaring skills and as fighting men at sea. The republic's official contribution was dwarfed by the private flotillas of Genoese patrician entrepreneurs in Spanish pay. Gian Andrea Doria, the most famous of them, provided 11 of his own galleys, while other patrician families, like the Grimaldi, the Centurione and the Sauli, furnished 15 more.[49]

The entire Catholic fleet at Lepanto on October 7 1571, comprised 207 galleys, six galeasses, 30 vessels carrying 1,815 cannon, 28,000 soldiers, 13,000 seamen (who were armed), and 43,500 men at the oars, mostly slaves and convicts. There were about two hundred soldiers and armed seamen aboard every light galley. Commanders removed the iron shackles from the feet of Christian convict oarsmen so they might help too in exchange for freedom. They shuffled the different contingents of galleys throughout the line to stimulate competition between 'nations'. Nevertheless, the great majority of the ships and crews were Italian, along with half of the soldiers, and most of the adventurers, like the princes Alessandro Farnese of Parma, and Francesco Maria Della Rovere of Urbino, who were accompanied by the nobility of their respective duchies.[50] They confronted 222

---

[47] P. Castiglione, *Storia di un declineo: il seicento siciliano* (Syracuse, Italy: 1987), p. 27.

[48] Gino Guarnieri, *I cavalieri di Santo Stefano nella storia della marina italiana (1562–1859)* (Pisa: 1960), p. 124. For the Papal expedition in great detail, see A. Guglielmotti, *Storia della marina pontificia, vol. VI* (Rome: 1892).

[49] Various authors provide lists of such galleys and their paymasters, such as Luigi Conforti, *I napoletani a Lepanto*, p. 36. More recently, so does Kenneth Setton, *The Papacy and the Levant, vol. IV*, p. 1047ff. The campaign is covered primarily from the Christian side by André Zysberg and René Burlet, *Gloire et misère des galères* (Paris: 1988), accompanied by rich illustration. A view from the Turkish archives can be found in Michel Lesure, *Lépante: crise de l'empire ottoman* (Paris: 1972). Guilmartin encapsulates the course of the battle, with special consideration for tactical issues arising from the galley mêlée. See his *Gunpowder and galleys*, p. 221ff.

[50] It is difficult to determine the number of these adventurers and their provenance. For the role of Alessandro Farnese, see Giovanni Drei, *I Farnese: Grandezza e decadenza di una dinastia italiana* (Rome: 1954). On the contingent from Urbino see James Dennistoun, *Memoires of the Dukes of Urbino (1440–1630)* (London: 1851), vol. 3, p. 133.

galleys and 60 galiots of the combined Turkish and Barbary fleets, carrying 34,000 soldiers and 13,000 seamen, but only 750 cannon, with 41,000 men tugging at the oars, again mostly captives and convicts. The details of the battle of Lepanto are not well known. The Catholic secret weapon was the Venetian galeass. Six of them carried between 22 and 42 pieces of artillery each, most with shot weighing more than 14 pounds (6.5 kg). They were floating fortresses the like of which had never been seen, with six times the armament of a normal galley.

Placed 700 metres (2,300 ft) in front of the Catholic array, they broke the cohesion of the Ottoman line, and meted out punishment by firing from the flanks. Almost certainly the Turks were unaware of their capability, and had no means of neutralizing them.[51] Then the two fleets collided by the bows. Don Juan made the most of the Catholic fleet's artillery advantage by removing the bow spurs to improve the field of fire. The Turks tried to force the Christian left wing along the shore, but Barbarigo's Venetian galleys prevented this by pinning them there. Then, at close quarters, great boarding parties lunged at each other with swords, scimitars, iron maces, knives, arrows, arquebuses and fireballs. Many of the engagements were duels, one ship versus another, but wherever there was an opening, several galleys combined on a target. Seven Ottoman galleys over-whelmed the Maltese flagship, killing a substantial portion of the knights.[52] An opening developed between the Catholic centre and its right flank commanded by Gian Andrea Doria, such that the Maltese and Tuscan galleys there were badly handled by Euldj Ali. As was the custom, the flagships engaged each other. The soldiers on Don Juan's galley surged onto the deck of the Turkish flagship after the fourth attempt, and killed the admiral Ali Pasha himself. His severed head displayed aloft was the signal to the Catholics that they had won. In that day's carnage, between 8,000 and 9,000 Christians died, despite that fact that only 12 of their galleys remained in Ottoman hands at the end of the day. Catholic arms killed over 30,000 Turks and captured or destroyed 200 of their ships, freeing 20,000 Christian slaves in the process. To preclude their being ransomed, the Venetians slaughtered many prisoners they thought were soldiers.

Lepanto was the largest battle in European history since ancient times. As such it was a major event: but Turkish sea power was not broken.[53] The sultan immediately rebuilt his fleet. By 1573 it boasted 250 galleys, 13 great galleys (mahones)

---

[51] Morin, "La battaglia di Lepanto", in *Venezia e i Turchi*, pp. 210–31.

[52] Fra B. dal Pozzo, *Historia della sacra religione militare di S. Giovanni Gerosolimitano, detta di Malta* (Verona: 1703), pp. 8–30.

[53] A. C. Hess, "The battle of Lepanto and its place in Mediterranean history", *Past and Present*, **57**, 1972, pp. 53–73. Hess sees Lepanto as an important episode in the great war between Christianity and Islam from the time of Charles V, and which finished in stalemate after the destruction of a Portuguese crusading army at Alcazar in Morocco in 1578. For their part, the Ottomans recaptured Tunis and La Goletta in 1574, restoring all of their losses.

and 30 smaller craft, though often built of green wood and carrying green troops, mostly arquebusiers.[54] While they refrained from confronting another Christian navy, they pointedly sailed into the Adriatic and burned the Puglian town of Castro near Òtranto. Another great battle between the fleets was almost joined off Cerigo on 7 August, as Euldj Ali's galleys rowed towards the Catholic fleet. They veered away at the last moment, doubtful of the outcome. The Spanish–Italian fleet of 104 galleys took Tunis that year, but when they dispersed for the winter, the Ottoman fleet sallied forth. A large army landed in Tunisia, captured La Goletta with its 2,000 soldiers, and then reduced the stranded Tunis garrison of 4,000 in 1574.[55] Meanwhile, the Holy League alliance came unstuck as Venetians and Spaniards disagreed on campaign objectives. The Spaniards hoped to make progress against the Barbary states by recapturing Tunis, and aimed their fleet in that direction. Their policy was to secure the western Mediterranean lifeline by capturing all the potential corsair bases along the coast. The Venetians desired for their part to relieve Famagusta and if not recapture Cyprus, then at least occupy Greek coastal territory as compensation, with the help of the Christian uprisings that followed the great battle.

Having different strategic aims from the Spaniards and the Pope, Venice preferred to go its own way. The republic's strength was still considerable, with 130 galleys and 23,000 infantry in the Adriatic and the Aegean garrisons. Peace with Turkey and a resumption of commerce in the Levant was preferable to an exhausting war for the sole advantage of the king of Spain. The peace they made with the sultan in 1574 triggered a gradual demobilization of these forces. There were still 5,000 troops on Crete in 1575 and 3,000 in 1577, though the real figure was probably below this paper strength.[56] The level of garrisons thereafter stabilized at about 9,000, of which 7,000 was infantry, supplemented by 760 noble gens d'armes or heavy cavalry and about 1,000 light horse, mostly Greeks, Albanians and Croats. The empire overseas absorbed about two-thirds of this, about 4,000 men being regularly based on Crete. The naval demobilization was less marked, and more ships existed on paper than had taken part in the Lepanto campaign. In 1581 there were 146 light galleys and 18 galeasses available, costing about a third of the republic's revenue. Many of these were laid up at the great Arsenal. Venice was still at the height of its commercial prosperity and possessed enormous resources. Like the Dutch republic of the next century, its military strength was out of all proportion to its demographic weight.

Both the Spaniards and the Turks were diverted from the Mediterranean after

---

[54] For the rapidity of reconstruction, see Setton, *The Papacy and the Levant, vol. IV*, p. 1076.

[55] *Ibid.*, p. 1076ff.

[56] Luciano Pezzolo, "Aspetti della strutture militare veneziana", *Venezia e la difesa del Levante*, pp. 86–96. Another article by the same author places the considerable Venetian effort into a comparative Italian perspective, "Esercito e stato nella prima età moderna. Alcune considerazioni preliminari per una ricerca sulla Repubblica di Venezia", in *Guerre, stati e città: Mantova e l'Italia padana dal secolo XIII al XIX* (Mantua: 1988), pp. 13–30.

1574, so that henceforth any effort against the adversary was episodic. Guilmartin stresses that it was virtually impossible for a fleet to achieve strategic victory since galleys could be launched easily and the bases were difficult to capture and hold, year-in, year-out.[57] In view of the ensuing stalemate, both empires focused their attention elsewhere. For Spain, reconquest of the Netherlands drained its considerable resources, both Spanish and Italian, until the early seventeenth century. Only by dint of co-operation with Malta, Savoy, Tuscany, Rome and Genoa, was Spain capable of concentrating a fleet for a short period. In 1601 70 galleys and 10,000 troops converged on Algiers, hoping that a slave rising would give them advantage over the city. The attempt failed and the squadrons dispersed.[58] Gian Andrea Doria was finally relieved of his command for irresolute leadership in this fiasco. The strains on the Spanish empire resulted in fewer resources directed to galley patrols. The 33 galleys in the Naples flotilla in 1583 numbered only 26 in 1621 and 17 in 1633, increasingly decrepit and poorly manned. There was no peace, though, since the Jihad and the Crusade justified continuing the war by other means.

Corsairs and maritime raiding

The repeated clash of galley fleets was exceptional for the huge short-term mobilization it entailed. Galleys remained the mainstay of Mediterranean fleets for a century after Lepanto, but they no longer waged war by themselves.[59] Their dispersal did not make the Mediterranean safer, for galleys and lighter vessels were then allotted into small flotillas and made to earn their keep by scouring the seas and coasts in search of plunder. To repeat Tenenti's formula, the Mediterranean "was not exactly sailed by ships exchanging cheerful greetings at every encounter; to use a contemporary simile, it much more resembled a forest teeming with bandits".[60] Their raids were intermittent from the 1540s onwards on the Sicilian coast. In 1558 it was calculated that corsairs enslaved more than 12,000 people in the kingdom of Naples, from Calabria to Torre del Greco in Campania, almost within sight of the capital.[61] The Djerba fiasco then unleashed a wave of Barbary and Ottoman ships on Europe. In Corsica, rebels against Genoese overlordship plotted with renegades and Ottoman admirals to establish Turkish control there. The rebel leader Sampiero Corso con-

---

[57] Guilmartin, *Gunpowder and galleys*, p. 100ff.
[58] Manfroni, *La marina militare*, pt 2, p. 27.
[59] Anderson, *Naval wars in the Levant*, p. 66ff.
[60] Tenenti, *Piracy and the decline of Venice*, p. 61.
[61] Manfroni, *La marina militare*, pt 1, p. 49. For an outline of the great raids in the 1540s and 1550s, see S. Bono, *Corsari nel Mediterraneo: Cristiani e musulmani fra guerra, schiavitù e commercio* (Milan: 1993), pp. 125–43.

ducted negotiations in Constantinople with the Calabrian renegade Euldj Ali, before seeking French support.[62] Effective defence on land and sea was limited, and the galley squadrons available were too small to intercept any large force. In the 1580s and 1590s Moslem attacks on the Italian coast reached alarming proportions, though there was no longer a fear of invasion and conquest. Particularly vulnerable to raids mounted from Algeria, Tunisia and Tripolitania was the south coast of Sicily, Sardinia and Calabria. Sardinia's population declined absolutely as it fled from the coastline, cutting it off ever further from the outside world.[63] Moslem pirates operated occasionally in larger fleets of galleys and small ships; Dragut Pasha sacked Reggio Calabria in 1585; in 1594, Sinan Pasha, a Sicilian renegade, punished the coast of his native land around Syracuse with some 70 oared vessels, before falling upon Reggio Calabria again.

Farther up the coast, in Lazio, Tuscany and Liguria the danger was not so much from large concentrations of warships as from tiny corsair flotillas lurking off the islands in search of easy targets. Even the River Tiber saw Moslem ships penetrate almost as far as Rome.[64] The Tuscan and Ligurian shore was hit from time to time, and even more so the little islands between Corsica and the coast. They were convenient places where corsairs could take on fresh water.[65] Then, around 1615 smaller, oared ships penetrated the Adriatic, attacking grain boats and small fishing towns from Puglia to the Abruzzo, to the Marches, Romagna and close to Venice itself. Operating from Albania, these galiots or *fuste* contained 200 men each, six to an oar, such that they could outrun most of the galleys sent to intercept them. In 1580 (that is, in peacetime), the Venetians claimed they lost 25 vessels in a month just off Cattaro.[66]

Islamic states had no monopoly of corsair activity, even though they probably depended upon it to a greater degree than did the Catholics. Michel Fontenay has tried to establish the true dimensions of this corsair economy in the Mediterranean midway through the seventeenth century. Following Earle, Michel Fontenay calculates that perhaps 8,000 to 10,000 men were employed in the huge Algiers pirate fleet of 100 ships in 1625. This privateering 'industry' may have occupied as much as 25 per cent of the active population in Algiers, not including the other

[62] R. Emmanuelli, *Gênes et l'Espagne dans la guerre de Corse (1559–69)* (Paris: 1963), p. 115.

[63] Maurice Le Lannou, *Pâtres et paysans de la Sardaigne* (Tours: 1941), p. 100ff. See also G. Sorgia, "Progetti per una flotta sardo-genovese nel seicento", *Miscellanea di Storia Ligure*, **IV**, 1966, pp. 177–93, esp. pp. 180–84.

[64] Jean Delumeau, *Vie économique et sociale de Rome dans la séconde moitié du XVIe siècle*, 2 vols (Paris: 1957–9), vol. 1, p. 89ff.

[65] On the incursions against Liguria in the sixteenth century, see Vilma Borghesi, "Il magistrato delle Galee (1559–1607)", in *Guerra e commercio nell' evoluzione della marina genovese tra XV e XVII secolo* (Genoa: n.d. *circa* 1970), pp. 187–223, at p. 209.

[66] Tenenti, *Piracy and the decline of Venice*, pp. 17–23.

activities related directly to the port.[67] The fleet shrank to only about 25 ships in the 1680s, but the vessels were larger than before, and still employed some 7,000 men. To these one must add about 2,500 men in Tripoli, 3,000 in Tunis, and several thousand more in the minor bases such as Bona, Susa, Bizerta, Sale and so on. Some corsairs were Turks and Arabs; there were many Greeks, Albanians, Syrians and Berbers in this trade, but a larger number were renegades, especially Corsicans, Sardinians and Calabrians.

Since the corsairs had uncanny knowledge of the Italian coast, most targets were not selected at random. Renegades guided the flotillas to their native villages. Seizing as much as possible at first, they then lingered to sell back to the coastal communities the livestock, the elderly captives, and any cumbersome objects better left behind on the return journey. Coastal towns subjected periodically to such raids got to know their tormentors, to bargain and to negotiate with them.[68] They could correspond regularly with North Africa and buy the liberty of captives held there, sending merchants or monks as emissaries entrusted with the ransom money. Some of the most successful Barbary pirate captains and admirals were renegade Italians. Two of the most celebrated were Euldj Ali (Lucciali) from Calabria, whose galleys escaped unscathed from the disaster at Lepanto, and Sinan Pasha, alias Scipione Cicala, a Messinese patrician captured at sea during the Djerba expedition with his father, who was a galley entrepreneur for Spain.[69] Some of his brothers and nephews were Jesuits. His brother Carlo was a founder of the military Order of the Star, a company of knights in Messina, ostensibly raised to aid the struggle against the Turks. Carlo then defected to Constantinople, and eventually became governor of the island of Naxos for the Turks.[70] Scipione became a corsair captain and rose to command large fleets for the Sultan. In 1594 he appeared off Syracuse and burned many villages, before moving on to overwhelm Reggio Calabria, which he sacked for two days. In September 1598, in exchange for a truce, he persuaded the Viceroy of Sicily to allow him to visit his aged mother in Messina and other relatives (including some knights) in the port; seventy Moslem galleys fired salutes in the harbour in the honour of the aged Signora Lucrezia and the corsair admiral lavishly entertained

---

[67] See the book by Earle, *Corsairs of Malta and Barbary* (London: 1970), p. 45. This is expanded by Michel Fontenay, "La place de la course dans l'économie portuaire: l'exemple de Malte et des ports barbaresques", *Annales: Économies, Sociétés, Civilisations*, 1988, pp. 1321–47, p. 1427ff.

[68] The most detailed work on these relations is the splendid book by Bartolome and Lucile Bennassar, based on the Inquisition files on escaped slaves and recaptured renegades, *Les Chrétiens d'Allah: l'histoire extraordinaire des rénégats (XVIe–XVIIe siècles)* (Paris: 1989).

[69] Borghesi, "Il magistrato delle Galee", in *Guerra e commercio nell' evoluzione della marina genovese*, p. 201.

[70] C. Trasselli, "Naufragi, pirateria e doppio giuoco", in *Le genti del mare Mediterraneo*, Rosalba Ragosta (ed.) (Naples: 1981), vol. 1, pp. 499–510.

his Italian relatives on board.[71] Leaving Sicily in peace, as he promised, he looted Malta on his way home, but was driven off by the knights and militia.[72]

Italy's defence against such raids usually took the form of active defensive patrolling in the waters around the peninsula and the islands. The galley squadrons of Sicily, of Naples, the Papal States, Genoa and Tuscany operated either in small flotillas under a single flag, or in combination. Spain's galley flotillas, in separate Sicilian and Neapolitan squadrons, were the largest. A good portion of Sicilian tax revenue was spent maintaining the squadron, ordinarily ten or twelve units propelled by 200 oarsmen each, besides seamen and soldiers.[73] In 1561 the pirate captain Dragut captured seven of the Sicilian galleys in a single blow, capturing dignitaries in the event. Naples' squadron oscillated in size, depending upon the availability of cash or the urgency of its mobilization. By 1616, only ten galleys remained, which was smaller than the viceroy's personal corsair flotilla.

The line between defensive patrolling and active raiding against Moslem commerce was so nebulous that they should be considered together. Catholic retaliation against Moslem ships and coastal towns of the Ottoman Empire was also vigorous. The problem of finding oarsmen justified corsair operations too, since galley slaves were too numerous and expensive to leave idle for long. Captives taken at sea, if they were fit, were pressed into service on the benches, and could be bought in groups in the slave markets in Malta, Venice, Palermo, Naples and Livorno.[74] Losses suffered generally corresponded to the vigour of the patrolling

---

[71] The story of Scipione Cicala, *alias* Sinan Pasha, is related in numerous sources. Alberto Guglielmotti provides the most detail, in his *Storia della marina pontificia: vol. VII: la squadra permanente, 1573–1644* (Rome: 1892), p. 136. Monchicourt lists him as a captive in the Djerba expedition itself, and provides some information on his life. Scipione was eventually made grand vizir, and married one of the daughters of the Sultan Ahmed, around 1610. See Monchicourt, *L'expédition espagnole de 1560 contre l'île de Djerba*, p. 139. While exceptional, the career of Scipione Cicala is not untypical of the Ottoman 'system' which promoted renegades to high position. Gino Benzoni affirms that of 48 grand vizirs appointed between 1453 and 1623, at least 33 were renegades. He does not stipulate how many of those were Italians. See Benzoni, "Il 'farsi turco', ossia l'ombra del rinnegato", in *Venezia e i Turchi: scontri e confronti di due civiltà* (Milan: 1985), pp. 91–133, at p. 107.

[72] Dal Pozzo, *Historia della sacra religione militare*, vol. 1, p. 407.

[73] M. Aymard, "Chiourmes et galères", in *Il Mediterraneo nella seconda metà del '500*, pp. 71–94, at p. 77.

[74] Michel Fontenay attempts to determine the importance of this market at Malta in the seventeenth century, where most of the oarsmen were slaves. See "La place de la course dans l'économie portuaire: l'exemple de Malte et des ports barbaresques", *Annales: Economies, Sociétés, Civilisations*, 1988, pp. 1321–47. For the view from Turkey, see his article, "Chiourmes turques au XVIIe siècle", in *Le genti del mare mediterraneo*, vol. 2, pp. 877–903. According to Fontenay, in the mid-seventeenth century, four-fifths of the 20,000 oarsmen in the Turkish navy (excluding the Barbary pirates) were slaves, and about ten per cent of those were Italians. The proportion of Italian slaves in the Barbary ships was probably much higher.

and raiding. In 1606 the Sicilian squadron, supported by the knights of Malta, attacked Hamamet in Tunisia, but almost 600 men perished in the expedition.[75] The number of galleys declined continually from 22 around 1585, to twelve in 1600 and ten in 1610, and even those proved difficult to fit out. In the 1620s, after considerable effort, Spain could collect at Naples some 25 galleons and 24 galleys, and another five roundships and twelve galleys from Sicily, but these forces were scraped together by various expediencies for limited duration.[76] The viceroy planned operations not so much according to the number of galleys afloat or in storage, but rather depending on the number of oarsmen available. Volunteers for the oarsmen's benches (the *buonavoglie*) were ever harder to find, representing only about a quarter of the necessary manpower in 1610.[77] In Sicily, as everywhere in Italy, the judges condemned criminals to the galleys rather than to capital sentences or exile, so that the term galley became a synonym for prison in the Italian language.[78]

The Papacy tried to maintain its own galley fleet to protect the Adriatic coast and the Tyrrhenian waters. After the Turks seized all five Papal galleys at Djerba in 1560, the only ships available for several years were the seven owned by MarcAntonio Colonna. Then, with the establishment of the Holy League in 1570, the pontiff rented a dozen *sensile* or light galleys from Venice, and in 1571 leased a similar number from the grand duke of Tuscany. The permanent squadron and sound financing for it were the fruit of that most wilful of Counter-Reformation popes, Sixtus V Peretti (1585–90). He launched ten in 1587, but they were not well-built, and their crews were inexpert. Within a few years the papal flotilla maintained only five galleys, a number that remained constant over most of the two subsequent centuries. By the mid-seventeenth century, a few roundships rented from Flemish captains complemented these. Galley officers tended mostly to be drawn from the aristocracy of Rome and the Papal States, with a sprinkling of Tuscans and others, depending upon the provenance of the Papal family.[79] Apart from some concerted actions with Hispano-Italian and Tuscan galleys, the Papal navy kept strictly to its task of coastal patrol.

A more effective, continuous riposte to the attacks on the Italian coast came from a surviving medieval institution, the religious order of crusading knights. Sultan Suleiman the Magnificent ejected the Knights Hospitaller of Saint John of Jerusalem from the island of Rhodes in the Greek archipelago in 1522. Charles V

---

[75] Dal Pozzo, *Historia della sacra religione militare*, vol. 1, p. 519.

[76] Anderson, *Naval wars in the Levant, 1559–1853*, pp. 89–105, follows the varying size and effectiveness of the Neapolitan flotillas, both public and private.

[77] Aymard, "Chiourmes et galères", in *Il Mediterraneo nella seconda metà del '500*, p. 79.

[78] *Ibid.*, p. 80.

[79] The creation and operations of the Papal flotilla are recounted with numbing detail in the multi-volume work by P. Alberto Guglielmotti, *Storia della marina pontificia*, vol. VII: *la squadra permanente, 1573–1644*, and vol. VIII: *a Candia ed alla Morea; storia dal 1644 al 1699* (Rome: 1892).

established them on the island of Malta south of Sicily in 1530. It was a military order composed of noblemen who took ecclesiastical vows of celibacy and charity, and consecrated several years of their youth serving on the galleys of the order. After this they became fully fledged 'monks' and were eligible to draw income from the order's landed holdings spread throughout Europe. While assistance in the hospital of the order was important in the training of each member, the focus of the activity of the knights was service in the flotilla. The order held Malta as an independent and sovereign state, under the spiritual jurisdiction of the pope. It was in reality something of a Spanish satellite in the Mediterranean, although a half or more of the knights were French. The population of the island tripled between 1530 and 1700, and, as a result, it was totally dependent upon supply from Sicily. The knights were responsible too for the defence of the Barbary port of Tripoli, which they held until 1551. With the loss of that base, the south coast of Sicily was wide open to devastating Moslem raids. Malta then expanded as a base of operations, an advance post and a bulwark, ideally situated to intercept Turkish communications with the Barbary coast.

The great siege of 1565 was another turning point, for it was followed by a flow of new recruits and a widening of their activities.[80] No sooner had the Turks departed than the knights built a great fortress on the promontory of St Elmo. The new town was laid out on the peninsula inside the port. The scale of its fortification had few equals anywhere in the world. The city and fortress were designed by the engineer Francesco Laparelli from Cortona in Tuscany, with the aid of the veteran general Gabrio Serbelloni of Milan. While their first estimates called for 345,000 man-days to complete the project, the ramparts required 4,000 men working continually for two years, or eight times as much. They completed the great perimeter only in 1569, leaving a vast empty space inside. By 1592 almost all of the public buildings had been transferred across the harbour to this new town, called Valletta, after the grand master of the order during the siege.[81] Its population expanded to about 20,000 inhabitants by the early seventeenth century and the port became one of the most important in the central Mediterranean. To offset the increased power and range of artillery, it was necessary to push the defences farther out and reduce the concentration of an attacker. By 1770, Valletta boasted five lines of fortification.

---

[80] Fra Bartolomeo dal Pozzo, *Ruolo generale de' Cavalieri Gierosolomitani della Veneranda Lingua Italiana* (Messina: 1689). This is a nominative list of all the Italian knights of Malta, the year of their admission to the order, and their place of origin. Roughly speaking, Italian entries increased gradually in the first half of the sixteenth century, and then surged upward after 1560, levelling off in the 1580s, before a long and gradual decline. Angel Antonio Spagnoletti analyzes the fluctuation in the Italian recruitment to the order from the sixteenth to the end of the eighteenth century, primarily with regard to determining how likely peninsular nobles were to serve a supra-national organization. See A. A. Spagnoletti, *Stato, aristocrazie e Ordine di Malta nell' Italia moderna* (Rome: 1988).

[81] Hughes, *Fortress*.

The raiding by the flotilla increased in scale too, with mixed results at first. The order lost three galleys out of five in a single day off the Torre di Montechiaro in 1570, where 80 knights were killed or captured. Three galleys fought at Lepanto the next year, where 70 more knights perished.[82] These were grievous losses for the order that counted 300 or 400 knights on active service. With the end of fleet-sized operations, the knights returned to their traditional occupations of patrolling and raiding. After 1600 most of the operations took place in the eastern Mediter-ranean, and were offensive rather than defensive in nature. To accomplish this task, however, the knights had only five galleys in the 1590s, six in 1628, seven in 1651 and finally eight from 1685 to 1690, and one or two galleons operating in the first decades of the seventeenth century. The patrolling was continual, year after year for over two centuries. They made annual cruises along the coasts of Tunisia and Libya; rowed to an island in the Greek archipelago to wait for the Turkish Alexandria convoy; and then made a quick run to Barcelona to pick up cash.[83] Like the Turkish and Barbary galleys, they hugged the coasts, or sprinted from one island to another, while the warning towers announced their advance. Their battles against the Turkish flotillas and their coastal raids could be murderous. In one clash in the Greek archipelago in 1597, they captured a few ships and reaped 271 slaves and 80,000 *scudi* worth of plunder, but lost 'many dead' and 140 injured. The raid on Hamamet in Tunisia in 1606 finished in disaster: 39 knights and 70 soldiers of Malta died, and 500 Sicilians drowned.[84]

Adventure under a religious banner held great appeal for Catholic noblemen in the late sixteenth and early seventeenth centuries. The recruits came from noble houses exclusively. Admission to the order was considered a genealogical bench-mark, and a certificate of good lineage. Each family prepared a thick application file, complete with genealogical tree and other proof of pedigree, to be considered for admission. In Italy only nobles from cities where they exercised power in local government could apply. The order tightened entry requirements in the 1590s, by excluding those candidates whose families had still practised 'vile', 'mechanical' or commercial activities within recent memory. Only nobles from the four commer-cial cities of Genoa, Lucca, Florence and Siena were exempt.[85] Families desig-nated children to be knights at each generation, for it prevented dispersal of family patrimony. Better to be a 'fighting monk' than a poor cadet. Once admitted, the

---

[82] Dal Pozzo, *Historia della sacra religione militare*, vol. 1, pp. 8–12.

[83] M. Fontenay, "Corsaires de la foi ou rentiers du sol? Les chévaliers de Malte dans le 'corso' méditerranéen au XVIIe siècle", *Revue d'Histoire Moderne et Contemporaine*, 1988, pp. 361–84. Similar details can be found, aside from the work by the Veronese knight Bartolomeo dal Pozzo, in the book by Ettore Rossi, *Storia della marina dell' Ordine di S. Giovanni di Gerusalemme, di Rodi e di Malta* (Rome–Milan: 1926). Rossi glosses over the fact that the French comprised at least half of all the knights, and sees in the activity of the order the demonstration that the Mediterranean was an "Italian sea".

[84] Dal Pozzo, *Historia della sacra religione militare*, vol. 1, pp. 393, 463, 492, 519.

[85] C. Donati, *L'idea di nobiltà in Italia (secoli XIV–XVIII)* (Rome: 1988), p. 249.

youngster had to spend five years on the island, and complete four 'caravans' of six months each on the galleys of the order, either at sea or available in port. Normally there were 20 to 25 knights per galley, and 30 on the flagship, complemented by a few score of soldiers and a comparable number of seamen. These latter hailed generally from Malta, Corsica, Sardinia, Sicily or Calabria.[86] While there was some obligation to learn the nautical arts, most of these youths thought of themselves as soldiers, not seamen, and entrusted the navigation of the ship to professional mariners. On board, the knights spent their time playing cards, and in port caroused in taverns and brothels.

By the early seventeenth century, privateers using the island of Malta as a base outstripped the raiding actions of the galleys of the order. Corsairs were often knights 'retired' from compulsory service in the flotilla and now in business for themselves.[87] The naval crusade against Islam easily blurred into corsair activity for profit, which contemporaries considered a legitimate pursuit. The picture at Malta was not much different from that at Algiers.[88] In addition to the half-dozen galleys of the order, many ships were fitted out privately and given licence to plunder in exchange for ten per cent of the 'official' or declared booty. Between 1600 and 1624, the chancellery gave out 280 licences, involving 350 ships, an average of 14 annually. There was an increase in this activity during the Cretan War (1645–69), and at the peak between 1660 and 1675, 20 to 25 corsair ships flying the Maltese banner plied Ottoman waters. The size of the ship virtually decided the ambition of the privateers. Smaller oared vessels had the shortest range, restricting them to the barren coast of North Africa. Larger ships generally preferred the Levant, and the Greek archipelago in particular. A ship carrying some 30 guns and a complement of over 100 seamen and soldiers, roving the seas for up to a year, might require an outlay of 30,000 *scudi*. The corsair in these operations supplied part of the capital, plus his competence, and various shippers in Malta furnished the rest, at a usurious 30 per cent interest annually. The shippers, too, were mostly former knights. It was obvious that these vessels should avoid battle with enemy warships, and hunt instead the bulky, slow-moving Greek *caiques* carrying sugar, rice, coffee and other products along the major trade routes of the Ottoman Empire. Any crews captured could be sold on the slave market. Most of the corsair captains flying the Maltese ensign were French subjects, but a large fraction of them were Italian, and the bulk of the seamen and 'workers' in the business were Maltese and Sicilian.

Officially, corsairs operating out of Malta brought in 160,000 *scudi* annually,

---

[86] Fontenay, "Corsaires de la foi ou rentiers du sol?", *Revue d'Histoire Moderne et Contemporaine*, 1988, p. 372ff.

[87] Earle, *Corsairs of Malta and Barbary*, p. 112ff. See also two articles by Michel Fontenay, "L'empire ottoman et le risque corsair au XVIIe siècle", *Revue d'Histoire Moderne et Contemporaine*, 1985, pp. 185–208, and "La place de la course dans l'économie portuaire", *Annales: Economies, Sociétés, Civilisations*, 1988, pp. 1321–47.

[88] See John B. Wolf, *The Barbary coast: Algeria under the Turks* (New York: 1979).

but this hides much or most of the true profit. Like their Barbary counterparts, they stole most of the food they consumed on their trip from the ships they seized. By immediately selling back much of the booty and ransoming the common captives, they earned some unreported windfall cash.[89] Nor does this account for substantial fraud. The booty declared in Malta was then split up among the investors, the crew, the order, and a host of institutions, like the quarantine station, or the convents of nuns who prayed for the successful outcome of Catholic arms, and officials hovering around the port. It was not a way to make a fortune quickly. Ironically, individual knights left legacies for the construction and maintenance of galleys of the order, as acts of Christian charity, permitting the gradual increase in the size of the flotilla just as the number of knights was declining. By the 1660s, there were about 30 corsair vessels operating out of Malta, which was not much smaller than the Algerine fleet.[90] Sometimes the official flotilla worked in combination with corsairs. In 1604 a raid on Patras and Lepanto on the west coast of Greece mobilized four galleys of the order, four corsair frigates, three galleons, five other roundships and two hired merchantmen. There were strict guidelines placing Greek Christian merchant ships off-limits, and a court in Malta sometimes gave Greek merchants redress in those frequent occurrences when the guidelines were ignored.[91] Maltese seizures of Greek commerce and plunder of Greek Christian islands were endemic, though occulted in the archives of the order.[92] Venetian ships were off-limits too, but more dissuasive than litigation was the republic's retaliation against Maltese vessels by their own warships.[93]

The place of this raiding in the finances of the order and the economy of Malta is quite impressive. In 1590 the galleys of the order were able to embark ten per cent of the active population of the island. This share grew in subsequent decades. In 1632 the galleys took to sea some 3,080 persons, of whom 1,284 were slaves and 175 were convicts. Half the total complement comprised of knights, soldiers and seamen, for some 1,600 men. Add to the official fleet a fluctuating population of corsairs and privateers numbering between 800 and 1,500 men, and this raiding economy employed some 15 to 20 per cent of the active population, and maybe about 25 per cent in 1665.[94] Of these, the Maltese themselves were a

---

[89] B. Bennassar & L. Bennassar, *Les Chrétiens d'Allah: L'histoire extraordinaire des rénégats, XVIe–XVIIIe siècles* (Paris: 1989), pp. 216–17.

[90] Fontenay, "La place de la course dans l'économie portuaire", *Annales: Economies, Sociétés, Civilisations*, 1988, pp. 1321–47.

[91] Earle, *Corsairs of Malta and Barbary*, pp. 112 and 144.

[92] Fontenay, "L'Empire ottoman et le risque corsair au XVIIe siècle", *Revue d'Histoire Moderne et Contemporaine*, 1985, pp. 185–208.

[93] Tenenti, *Piracy and the decline of Venice*, p. 39.

[94] Fontenay, "La place de la course dans l'économie portuaire", *Annales: Economies, Sociétés, Civilisations*, 1988, pp. 1321–47.

minority alongside the southern Italians, Corsicans, Tuscans, Provençaux, as well as Greeks and Croats. The landing and auction of plunder produced spin-off benefits for related sectors of the economy, such as ship construction in Malta, purchase of food and naval stores, and the administration and servicing of the port. The knights spent 200,000 *scudi* annually on their fleet, which Fontenay claims is more than Richelieu spent on the entire French navy at the time.[95]

The military obligations of the order prevented them from placing all of their energies in corsair expeditions. Maltese participation in Spanish naval defence of southern Italy and aid to the beleaguered Venetians in Crete was significant and expensive. When, after 1677, Louis XIV forbade them to launch raids on Ottoman territory in Anatolia and Greece, they lost some valuable liberty. Turkish and Ottoman merchants then resorted to transporting their merchandise in French vessels, which the Sun King rendered untouchable.[96] Soon the diminishing value of booty no longer covered the upkeep of the squadron. The order gradually relied more on its landed holdings, the *commende* or 'commanderies' which were revenue-bearing properties in Catholic Europe. There were some 500 of them in Italy, Spain and France, and another sixty in the Holy Roman Empire. Their revenue of 750,000 *scudi* in the mid-seventeenth century was equivalent to half the money the king of Spain drew from the bullion mines in the New World. Only a fifth of that sum reached the treasury in Malta to pay for the galleys, the fortifications, and the upkeep of the 400 or 500 'monks' resident on the island.[97] In an emergency, extra funds had to be found to defend the island. In 1645, fearing an Ottoman invasion, 4,000 troops were recruited by agents of the order in the kingdoms of Naples and Sicily, and 1,500 elsewhere in the peninsula. The knights and their servants converged on the island to help in the defence. There were 1,400 of them, 4,000 regular troops, and 10,000 local militia, not including others who came at their own expense.[98]

Both Fontenay and Spagnoletti view the knights of Malta as a flourishing anachronism in the seventeenth century, a feudal organization drawing revenues from land in Europe in exchange for military service to protect Christendom. If most knights did not stand out for their piety, they did give themselves to the ethic of the crusade, a life of adventure fighting a religious enemy. This entailed considerable risk and a chance of some windfall treasure, but allowed the knight to retire to the security of one of the *commende* of the order, or some military or diplomatic employment elsewhere. The seventeenth century represents the last

---

[95] *Ibid.*

[96] R. Mantran, "La navigation vénitienne et ses concurrentes en Méditerranée orientale aux XVIIe et XVIIIe siècles", in *Mediterraneo e Oceano indiano* (Florence: 1970), pp. 375–87.

[97] Fontenay, "Corsaires de la foi ou rentiers du sol?", *Revue d'Histoire Moderne et Contemporaine*, 1988, pp. 361–84, at p. 380.

[98] Dal Pozzo, *Historia della sacra religione militare*, vol. 1, pp. 98–110.

full flowering of this crusading institution before the onset of its slow decline after 1700.[99]

The success of the knights of Malta in the second half of the sixteenth century provoked emulation in other Catholic states. Spain's knights of Santiago boarded the Catholic king's galleys during the Lepanto campaign.[100] The crusading order of knights with quasi-ecclesiastical status was reproduced elsewhere in Italy during the sixteenth century. Insignificant was the Mantuan Order of the Redeemer, created by Duke Vincenzo I Gonzaga in 1608, for it had no galleys and Mantua disposed of no ports. There were never more than 15 knights simultaneously. This order served as an honorific device exalting the duke's person.[101] The Piedmontese Order of the Knights of Santi Maurizio e Lazzaro, inaugurated in an important ceremony in Rome in 1573, played only a marginal role.[102] There were about 70 knights at the outset, most of them subjects of the duke of Savoy, who maintained a tiny flotilla of two or three galleys operating from the port of Villefranche near Nice. Piedmont possessed a minimal coastline to protect, so its galleys helped patrol the wider Tyrrhenian sea and made themselves available for Spanish fleet actions. Spain subsidized its existence, which could be augmented by smaller ships fitted out by corsairs and other naval entrepreneurs using Villefranche as a base, or others flying the Savoyard banner for convenience.

The most important maritime effort in Italy after those of the Spanish crown and Malta was that of Tuscany. This has been the object of some admirable studies over the past century, most notably that of Camillo Manfroni.[103] The

---

[99] Fontenay, "Corsairs de la foi ou rentiers du sol?", *Revue d'Histoire Moderne et Contemporaine*, 1988, p. 384; Spagnoletti, *Stato, aristocrazie e ordine di Malta nell' Italia moderna* (Rome: 1988), pp. 43–9.

[100] M. Lambert-Gorges, "Le roi, les ordres et le péril barbaresque: un exemple d'utilisation des ordres militaires castillans par le pouvoir royal dans l'Espagne du XVIe siècle", in *Potere e ordini militari–cavallereschi nell' Europa mediterranea dell' età moderna* (Brussels–Rome: in press).

[101] C. Mozzarelli, *Mantova e i Gonzaga dal 1382 al 1707* (Turin: 1987), p. 104.

[102] Guglielmotti, *Storia della marina pontificia, vol. VII*, p. 9. The order is also described by Nicola Brancaccio, *L'esercito del vecchio Piemonte: Gli ordinamenti: vol. 1, 1560–1814* (Rome: 1923), p. 59.

[103] Manfroni, *La marina militare del granducato mediceo*. Much of the same material was reworked in Niccolò Giorgetti, *Le armi toscane e le occupazioni straniere in Toscana (1537–1860)*, 3 vols (Città di Castello: 1916), pp. 288–301 and pp. 375–98. Working from the same archives, Gino Guarnieri published a more celebratory work, *I cavalieri di Santo Stefano, nella storia della marina italiana, 1562–1859* (Pisa: 1960); and more substantially, *L'ordine di S. Stefano nei suoi aspetti organizzativi interni sotto il gran magistero Mediceo* (Pisa: 1966), 4 vols; Franco Angiolini is more sensitive to the social signification of admission to the order, in his articles, "Politica, società e organizzazione militare nel principato mediceo; a proposito di una 'Memoria' di Cosimo I", *Società e Storia*, **9**, 1986, pp. 1–51; and "La nobiltà 'imperfetta'; cavalieri e commende di S. Stefano nella Toscana moderna", in *Signori, patrizi, cavalieri nell' età moderna* (Bari: 1992), pp. 146–66. Finally, a collection of scholarly works was published recently under the title, *Le imprese e i simboli: Contributi alla storia del sacro militare ordine di S. Stefano (s.XVI–XIX)* (Pisa: 1989).

Tuscan navy was largely the creation of the remarkable duke of Florence, Cosimo I, who placed his initiatives under the aegis of the Emperor. He built the first galley in 1547 and created a fortified base for it at Portoferraio on the island of Elba. He bought another galley from the viceroy of Naples, complete with 170 slaves. By 1548 there were two more galleys under construction, but this was too ambitious, for there was no corresponding supply of oarsmen. Cosimo chose the easiest solution in 1551 when he leased his four galleys to a naval entrepreneur, Jacopo d'Appiano, prince of Piombino. Appiano selected crews, captains and oarsmen, fed them, and maintained both men and equipment for six months of the year, presumably the active months. There were soon five galleys, manned by 554 convicts, 243 slaves and 144 volunteer oarsmen. Two more galleys were then built in 1559 by shipwrights from Messina and Venice, and high salaries were offered to attract competent seamen. Soldiers and gentlemen adventurers who fought on board drew their pay from the grand duke. Tuscany had no active maritime population of its own from which to draw seamen. The officers and seamen were Genoese, Venetian, Corsican, Greeks, renegades and other riff-raff (*rifiuto*).[104] A series of disasters then beset the fledgling Tuscan navy. The Turks captured two of the four galleys sent to Djerba in 1560. Venetians seized a third galley preying on Turkish shipping off Cyprus in order to prevent complications with the sultan. Of the three remaining galleys sent to Corsica, two were captured by Algerine ships because they were unseaworthy and their crews incompetent.[105]

Between 1557 and 1560 Cosimo decided to establish a proper seaborne militia on the model of the knights of Malta.[106] He recruited cadets of noble houses, and established them with ecclesiastical benefices or *commende*, consisting of property set aside by their family and exempt from most taxes. Candidates had to submit proofs and genealogies for admission, as they did for the knights of Saint John. He granted many a dispensation of some shortcomings in their genealogy in exchange for contributing more property to the order.[107] Unlike the Order of Malta, the new organization, called the Order of Santo Stefano, permitted its knights to marry. The time they spent at 'headquarters' in Pisa was not as long, and their religious obligations were minimal. All of the knights were conferred special status and privileges, such as the right to sport swords in public; they were judged by special tribunals and obeyed little other authority than that of the Order. The Grand Master and effective head of the institution was the grand duke in person. He could grant dispensations of noble titles, admit or legitimize bas-

---

[104] Manfroni, *La marina militare del granducato mediceo*, pt 1, p. 48.

[105] *Ibid.*, p. 78.

[106] Angiolini, "Politica, società e organizzazione militare nel principato mediceo", *Società e Storia*, **9**, 1986, pp. 1–52.

[107] *Ibid.*, p. 83ff. On the noble background of the knights, and their various 'imperfections', see Franco Angiolini, "La nobiltà 'imperfetta'", in *Signori, patrizi, cavalieri nell' età moderna* (Bari: 1992), pp. 146–66.

tards, exempt members from serving on the galleys, or pardon the knights their crimes.

Cosimo required each of the knights to be available during three years of effective navigation. During these years, they resided in the 'convent' of Pisa to learn navigation and the military arts. These barracks served as an academy and as a finishing school for these youngsters while they awaited action. Guarnieri describes these youngsters as knights 'without stain and without fear' who were devoted to every sacrifice, motivated by a sense of altruism, of Christian charity and Italian brotherhood.[108] Manfroni, who has laboured in their archives, paints a more sombre picture, showing that boredom was a serious problem. There were regional rivalries among the young knights, quarrels of precedence, widespread duelling and a tendency to resolve quarrels by force. Once their regulatory time was accomplished, they were not eager to serve again at sea.[109] At the outset in 1562 there were about 60 knights, but that number expanded quickly to several hundred, attracting virtually as many Italians as the Order of Malta. The peak came early in the seventeenth century when there were about 600 knights of all nations, who were supported by a personnel of noble volunteers, soldiers, seamen and oarsmen totalling some 2,000 men. The substantial majority of the 3,756 knights accepted into the order between 1562 and 1737 were subjects of the grand duke (68 per cent), 28 per cent were natives of other Italian territories, mostly the adjacent Papal States, and 4 per cent originated elsewhere, primarily in Spain and the Holy Roman Empire.[110] At the end of the sixteenth century, about six *commende* were established yearly, with average annual revenues of a modest 300 *scudi*.[111]

Their ships depended upon a variety of revenues: ecclesiastical tithes on properties transferred to the order; duties on the *commenda* and entry fees; proceeds from the sale of plunder and subsidies from the king of Spain, who drew upon the services of Tuscan galleys at will. It is not always easy to distinguish the galleys belonging to the order and those comprising the Tuscan 'navy'.[112] Cosimo rented

---

[108] Guarnieri, *L'ordine di S. Stefano nei suoi aspetti organizzativi interni*, vol. 1, p. 66.

[109] Manfroni, *La marina militare del granducato mediceo*, pt 1, p. 89ff.

[110] S. Burgalassi, "La 'Religione' di Santo Stefano P.E.M.; saggio di sociologia religiosa", *Le imprese e i simboli*, pp. 145–77. Burgalassi notes that 40 per cent of the knights came from just four cities: Florence, Pisa, Pistoia and Siena. The entire list of knights admitted to the order, with their city of origin and date of entry, is reprinted by Gino Guarnieri in volume 4 of his work, *L'ordine di S. Stefano*.

[111] Angiolini, "La Nobiltà 'imperfetta'", in *Signori, patrizi, cavalieri*, pp. 146–66, at p. 158.

[112] Manfroni, *La marina militare del granducato mediceo*, p. 138. In 1574, of the eight galleys that Grand Duke Francesco wished to place in Spanish service, only four belonged to the knights. The legal separation of the two forces was a subterfuge allowing Francesco to seek commercial links with Ottoman Turkey, like Venice, while allowing his crusaders to seize Moslem ships. See the synthesis of Tuscan history under the Medici grand dukes by Furio Diaz, *Il granducato di Toscana: I Medici* (Turin: 1987), p. 253ff.

galleys for profit to Philip II in the 1560s, like a private naval entrepreneur. By 1565 the duke had seven galleys of his own, and rented others from MarcAntonio Colonna. The oarsmen were mostly convicts from Tuscan jails. The expeditions were fraught with risk; in 1569 no less than four of the ten galleys were lost, along with many knights, seamen and soldiers of the Tuscan militia. With each setback Cosimo began afresh, setting the arsenals and shipyards at Pisa and Portoferraio to work, with 400 such workers employed in 1570. Twelve galleys were ready to rent to the Pope for the Lepanto campaign in 1571, and 100 knights embarked to take part. In 1572 the Tuscan navy consisted of eleven 'light' galleys, two big galeasses, two galleons, six frigates and some transports, carrying in all 200 guns (which was considerable for the sixteenth century), 900 seamen, 100 knights and 2,500 oarsmen. With the end of the Spanish subsidy, in 1574, the navy shrank to about four galleys.[113] Most of the subsequent patrols hugged the Tuscan and Roman coast, teasing the corsairs out of their island lairs.

Grand Duke Ferdinand I (1587–1609), who was a naval enthusiast, set out to enlarge the scope of operations. He began by enlarging the arsenal and the port at Livorno, which became the new base of operations. The former cardinal with a Midas touch might have had loftier crusading ideals, but the targets he chose reveal a desire to reap a harvest of booty from Moslem shipping and towns. The expeditions frequently degenerated into acts of savage piracy against Moslems and Christians alike, mostly in the Aegean and the Levant.[114] An expedition against the Greek city of Chios in 1599 nearly succeeded, but when the troops forcing entry to the town dispersed to gather plunder, they were cut off and captured by the Turkish garrison. Five Tuscan galleys figured in the allied fleet sent to surprise Algiers, but that failed too. The knights of Santo Stefano maintained a flotilla of four galleys, and the proceeds of their frequent prizes permitted them to launch two more. Under the direction of the Volterran admiral Jacopo Inghirami in 1604, the order counted six galleys, three roundships, two *bastardelli*, a galleon and a galeass along with two transports, supplemented by still other ships financed by corsair entrepreneurs flying the Tuscan banner. Their foray against the Greek port of Prevesa in 1605 with five galleys and 400 infantry drawn from the Tuscan militia was a striking success. As a result, there were more slaves to propel the galleys, and more experienced seamen gravitated to Livorno. There were even some Catholic Englishmen in Tuscan employ, like Sir Robert Dudley, duke of Northumberland (1574–1649), who designed large vessels; Sir Kenelm Digby (1603–65), an Oxford scholar who spent 25 years in Livorno as a corsair plundering Venetian, French and Spanish shipping; and others who served as

---

[113] Giorgetti accompanies the relation of these events with a useful table of the galleys launched, and their fates, in a systematic manner. See *Le armi toscane e le occupazioni straniere in Toscana (1537–1860)*, vol. 1, p. 301, and also p. 378.

[114] Manfroni, *La marina militare del granducato mediceo*, pt 2, pp. 1–59 recounts with some detail the various operations during the reign of Ferdinand I.

captains on roundships, or who rented their own ships for the lucrative Tuscan expeditions.[115]

In 1606 the bastard son of the grand duke, Don Cosimo de'Medici commanded six galleys and some roundships, along with 150 knights and 600 soldiers on an expedition to Turkey, bringing back much booty and many slaves. Their expectations rose with each success. The order's archives contain scores of sketches of the coasts, plans of towns and locations of castles from Tunisia to Syria, all potential targets.[116] They intended to capture Famagusta in Cyprus in 1607, to serve as a logistical base supporting a Syrian uprising. Adventurers from all over Italy volunteered to take part in that mission. It failed utterly when the galley carrying the storming ladders arrived late, and then when these proved too short. Undaunted, another force left to attack the north African port of Bone in 1607, with eight galleys, nine *bertoni* and a galleon, carrying almost 2,000 soldiers, 100 knights and 200 gentlemen volunteers under the Sienese Silvio Piccolomini. Like most of the targets of these raids, Bone was not well defended and the Tuscans carried off 1,500 people as slaves, at a toll of 150 dead and wounded.[117] From 1560 to 1609, the Tuscan fleet captured 76 galiots, seven galleys, two large roundships and 67 minor craft, taking 9,620 slaves and liberating 2,076 Christians. The clear preponderance of smaller vessels among the prizes reveals that most of the trophies were easy victories.

The growing fleet of roundships or *bertoni* after 1600 attests to the changing technology of naval warfare as artillery became cheaper, and exorbitant food costs made the large galley crews less cost-efficient. Tuscans were pioneers with some early constructions. They launched several big ships at Portoferraio after 1601, with an armament of about 40 guns each and a complement of only 60 seamen. Eight of them around 1610, all commanded by Dutch or English captains, floated a total of 200 guns, and were capable of transporting 800 infantry.[118] They began to sail independently of the galleys on long voyages to the Levant. The greater outlay for construction and fitting out had to be recovered as booty. They scored their most resounding success off Cape Celidonio and Rhodes in 1608, when three galleys and four roundships intercepted a Turkish convoy of 42 vessels, of which they seized nine. At a cost of about 400 Tuscan casualties, they netted some 600 slaves and a booty of one million ducats, equivalent to about two years' revenue for the grand duchy. With such rewards, the new Grand Duke Cosimo II (1609–21) continued these operations, sending seven roundships with 1,800 soldiers for a year and a half into the eastern Mediterranean, from 1609 to 1611. This time the loss of 800 men, and four ships disabled, announced the era of less

[115] Guarnieri, *I cavalieri di Santo Stefano, nella storia della marina italiana*, p. 125.

[116] Guarnieri, *L'ordine di S. Stefano nei suoi aspetti organizzativi interni*, vol. 2 contains maps, sketches and plans.

[117] G. Guarnieri "Il 'Registro delle prede' dei cavalieri di Santo Stefano", *Archivio Storico Italiano*, 1973, pp. 257–86, at p. 263.

[118] Manfroni, *La marina del granducato medo*, pt 2, p. 58.

profitable ventures. Alongside the knights of Santo Stefano and the galleys and roundships of the Tuscan navy, the grand dukes enticed corsair captains from around the Mediterranean to use Livorno as a base of operations. Twelve English corsairs set up there in 1610, some of them secretly enticed out of north African ports by a granducal emissary. In exchange for their conversion to Catholicism, they were pardoned all their previous misdeeds. They operated thereafter almost exclusively against Christian ships, especially French and Venetians. Livorno was soon Italy's largest corsair base, generating ample capital reinvested back into new private expeditions.[119]

After 1612 the grand duke progressively laid up his roundships, and narrowed the scope of the galleys to coastal patrol and policing the Tyrrhenian sea between Liguria, Sardinia and Sicily.[120] The quality of the crews declined and the units deteriorated quickly, culminating in the capsizing of a galley off Corsica in 1618.[121] After 1630 only two Tuscan galleys were maintained, and a third held in reserve, to deter the little pirate boats that still infested coastal waters. Only a couple of dozen knights could serve their terms at once. While the number of ships dwindled, the number of knights admitted to the convent in Pisa continued to climb. The *commende* remained in the same families, and the status of knight became virtually hereditary, and not necessarily predicated upon real military service. The admiral Achille Sergardi lived in his Sienese *palazzo* and dispatched orders by letter. Galleys began to transport bales of raw silk from Messina to Livorno to help defray operating costs. Occasionally the ships joined Papal or Neapolitan galleys to confront flotillas of Barbary vessels. The register of prizes of the order lists some 238 vessels they captured from 1563 to 1688; enemy galleys captured from 1568 to 1599 were eleven (for the loss of an identical number); another seventeen were seized between 1602 and 1635; and only one galley was captured after 1635.[122] The last important prizes were two Barbary pirate vessels captured off Sardinia in 1719, and the galley fleet was scrapped with the end of the Medici dynasty in 1737.

The rapid transition from galleys to roundships by the Barbary pirates gradually rendered the Italian galleys all but obsolete, or rather, useful in strictly limited roles such as close shore support, and summer patrol. Venetians, Maltese and Tuscans integrated a few sailing vessels into their flotillas early in the seventeenth century, but they were expensive, and Mediterranean crews were not used to them. By 1609, the Venetians were commissioning *bertoni* with as many as 80 guns. An allied French and Spanish fleet of 16 such ships, carrying 435 guns among them, forced the harbour of Algiers that same year, and destroyed 23 vessels in port before withdrawing. The first important battle between these

---

[119] S. Bono, *Corsari nel Mediterraneo: Cristiani e musulmani fra guerra, schiavitù e commercio* (Milan: 1993), p. 61.

[120] Manfroni, *La marina del granducato mediceo*, pt 2, p. 60.

[121] Giorgetti, *Le armi toscane*, vol. 1, p. 409.

[122] Guarnieri, *I cavalieri di Santo Stefano, nella storia della marina italiana*, p. 457ff.

roundships (six, carrying 191 guns) and galleys (55, carrying about 250 guns), was a protracted affair off Cape Celidonia in 1616. Two of the roundships were damaged, and 25 galleys were disabled.[123] As the Barbary pirates converted to roundships themselves (with Dutch and English captains and crews, occasionally), the Christian galleys learned not to cross their path unless they had to.

Subduing *bertoni* whenever they could be caught was fraught with difficulty. Guglielmotti relates a telling example in October 1624, where the galleys of Naples, Rome, and Tuscany joined forces off Sardinia to track the pirate squadron of Hassan Pasha. Fifteen Catholic galleys found the five pirate vessels in a dead calm near the island of San Pietro off the south-west coast, a favourite mooring place.[124] The plan of attack required seven galleys to overwhelm the pirate flagship, while the remaining eight took the others. At dawn, the galleys raised their banners to the sound of trumpets, and then their combined 30 cannon fired in salvo. The size of the flagship made it difficult for the assailants to attach themselves; but the low profiles of the galleys made it impossible for the cannon of the pirate ship to hit anything. On the seven galleys were 1,000 knights and soldiers, all firing upwards, and then trying to clamber up the sides. A pirate crew 300 strong fought heroically to repair the damage, to repulse the assault, and to pour down projectile fire on the galleys with muskets, arrows, rocks, and anything else on hand. After the third futile assault with their rope ladders, the Neapolitan galleys attached themselves to the prow with their bow-hook. The pirates fought back there with firearms and steel, mortally wounding the general Pimentello. At that point, the galleys decided to detach themselves, and to fire at their leisure with their cannon, until they wore down the resistance. The calm made this easy, without exposing the galleys to a pirate broadside. The Neapolitan galleys, however, were still attached to their target with the bows having penetrated the hull. To get away, they had to saw their own prows off, under the protective fire of arquebusiers on the forecastle to keep the heads of the pirates down.

For several more hours, the galleys raked the flagship from bow to stern from point-blank range, the balls smashing away the sides and hurtling down the decks. Seven galleys converging their fire on the immobile ship soon dismasted it. It responded fruitlessly with its own cannon, for it could not fire other than laterally, nor could it swing around. At one point, Hassan brought up a sheep to the deck to sacrifice it and thus induce providence to create wind. In the heat of combat he splashed the blood and the entrails of the victim over the ship, but with no result. Some pirates jumped overboard to surrender to the galleys. Finally, Hassan went into the powder magazine and attached a long wick to a barrel, before lowering his ensign in sign of surrender. Then with a few followers, he lowered himself into a skiff, and fled in the direction of the only other pirate ship to escape that day. The suspicious galleys did not approach, letting two skiffs of Catalans board first in search of plunder. Then the ship exploded, erupted into flame, and blew apart.

---

[123] Anderson, *Naval wars in the Levant*, p. 87.

[124] Guglielmotti, *Storia della marina pontificia, vol. VII: la squadra permanente*, p. 286ff.

Hassan Pasha escaped in the night and returned to Algiers. The ten-hour battle resulted in three ships taken, one sunk, and three prizes recaptured, 400 pirate dead, 200 prisoners, and 60 Christians liberated. There were 60 Christian soldiers and knights killed in the fight, including the general of the Naples squadron, and 200 wounded.

Although the efforts to combat corsair raids by the Italian flotillas were insufficient, the impact on coastal populations seems to have declined after the 1640s. No longer would hundreds or thousands of captives be swept off to sea in a single raid, until the French Revolution distracted European fleets from their patrolling.[125] Braudel speculates that piracy ebbed and flowed with the Mediterranean economy as a whole. The decline in pirate activity just reflects the economic crisis that gripped the region, and Italy in particular, after 1620.[126] Fontenay has speculated that losses due to seizures by pirates represented about two to three per cent of French commerce in the 1660s, and he extends that figure to the entire region. The Order of Malta and the corsairs took an estimated 330,000 *scudi* annually at their peak in the 1660s. In comparison, the French privateer fleet operating from the North Sea port of Dunkirk against the English and Dutch at the end of the century netted four times that amount.[127]

Its impact on the Greek archipelago seems to have been more crippling. The whole area seethed with pirates in the seventeenth century, primarily French, but operating under the Tuscan and Maltese flags, and this in addition to the depredations of the galleys of Malta and Santo Stefano. Venetians participated as well during their protracted wars against the Ottoman Empire. A few islands, like Ios and Melos actually prospered by encouraging pirates to anchor there and sell their plunder and take on stores.[128] Since the Turks lacked roundships viable in all weather, many Christian pirates wintered for months in relative security in the very heartland of the enemy state.[129] The Greek Orthodox populations encouraged Catholic monks to settle among them, mostly to intercede and negotiate with the corsairs. In most of the region however, the attacks were crippling. Coastal commerce was ravaged by continual attacks, and even the largest islands like Cyprus, Crete, Rhodes and Chios were frequent targets.

Raids against Moslem-controlled coasts everywhere supplied captives to the slave markets of the Italian world. One estimate for the early seventeenth century gives a slave population of around 30,000 individuals, most of whom were held in Sicily and Naples. Unlike Moslems, who captured slaves primarily to sell them back by ransom, Christian states captured slaves to use them on the galleys, and

[125] Bono, *Corsari nel Mediterraneo*, p. 178.
[126] F. Braudel, *The Mediterranean and the Mediterranean world in the age of Philip II* (New York: 1966, first publ. 1949), vol. 2, p. 883.
[127] Fontenay, "La place de la course dans l'économie portuaire", *Annales: Economies, Sociétés, Civilisations*, 1988, p. 1335ff.
[128] Vacalopoulos, *The Greek nation, 1453–1669*, p. 90.
[129] Earle, *Corsairs of Malta and Barbary*, p. 144ff.

ransomed few.[130] Malta contained a few thousand of these slaves; the few women served as domestics and many eventually married there and were freed, while the men served on the galleys as long as they were fit.[131] Livorno and Genoa also had a slave market. There was also much slave-running from the north African coast to Sicily. The viceroy levied 10 per cent of the slaves and 20 per cent of the proceeds of their sales, and there were some impressive fortunes built on this commerce.[132] To keep this in perspective, as many as 60,000 Europeans languished in north Africa, principally in Algiers.

European princes held that corsair activity stimulated the whole maritime economy, aided in coastal defence, and prevented the development of a Moslem merchant marine simultaneously.[133] Yet the undisciplined nature of piracy probably helped cripple the Italian maritime economy, for its principal victim was the Venetian commercial empire. As the European state most deeply inserted into the trading circuits of the Middle East, Venice was considered fair game by Christian and Moslem privateers alike. Its merchant galleys generally travelled without benefit of convoy and had to run the gauntlet of zones infested with pirates. The Serbian Uskoks, among the most ferocious, seized ships just south of Istria.[134] Albania served as a lair for Barbary pirates, and the waters off Crete were also favoured hunting grounds for Barbary and Christian privateers. Venetian war galleys patrolled constantly from their bases in the Adriatic, Corfù and Crete, but they could not be ubiquitous. They also had to avoid creating a *casus belli* with the Ottoman Empire by allowing the crusading orders logistical support for their strikes against Islam. Venetian galleys seized the occasional Maltese or Tuscan war galley operating in its waters to avoid provoking the Porte.

The viceroys of Naples and Sicily sometimes fitted out privateer vessels on their own account after 1585, and these attacked Moslem and Venetian commerce in the Levant. Similarly, the sultan's representatives in Tripoli, Tunis and Algiers profited personally from piracy. Venetian merchants were not so much victims of regular Spanish warships as of privateers and pirates operating out of Sicily, Calabria and Puglia with official complicity, and these pirates then returned to Habsburg territory with their prizes. In 1603 at least 12 large Venetian vessels were pulled into south Italian ports. The maverick Duke Osuna, viceroy of Sicily and Naples (1610–20), was especially ambitious, for he bought or built a whole

---

[130] Bono, *Corsari nel Mediterraneo*, pp. 191–9.

[131] C. Petiet, *Ces messieurs de la religion: l'ordre de Malte au dix-huitième siècle, ou le crépuscule d'une épopée* (Paris: 1992), p. 154. Petiet claims there were 10,000 slaves living on Malta in the first decades of the eighteenth century, which is so considerable for the population of the island that the figure is doubtful.

[132] D. Mack Smith, *A history of Sicily, vol. 1: medieval Sicily 800–1713* (London: 1968), p. 133ff.

[133] Bono, *Corsari nel Mediterraneo*, p. 67.

[134] A good relation of the conflict between Venice and the Uskoks is found in the article by Fulvio R. Babudieri, "Gli Uscocchi: Loro formazione e loro attività a terra ed in mare", in *Le genti del mare Mediterraneo*, R. Ragosta (ed.) (Naples: 1981), vol. 1, pp. 445–98.

fleet of privateer ships operating under his orders, considerably larger than the royal squadron of galleons and galleys. The official pretext of such a build-up was to protect the coast from pirate raids. His preferred vessels, however, were not the faster galleys, but the roundships. He visited England once to study these new ships, and had 12 of them built, and sailed with French seamen.[135] At least on this fleet, the personnel were paid on time, the equipment was of good quality, the captains were competent and the operations were conducted quickly and boldly. In 1616, this 'private' squadron consisted of 17 galleys and five vessels, compared to the Naples galley squadron of 16 units. Five of his vessels once scattered a Turkish fleet of 55 galleys. By 1620 Osuna's navy consisted of 23 sailing ships, assembled against the express orders of King Philip III. The reasons for his eventual downfall that year had much to do with his strong-arm policy against Venice using his private navy in lieu of the official Spanish one. He concentrated a battle fleet consisting of 17 sailing vessels and 33 galleys off Brindisi in 1617 in order to intimidate Venice to conclude its war with Austria. Venice and Spain came within an inch of war, prodded by the initiatives of the viceroy. To pay for this force, Osuna browbeat Neapolitans into paying for it. He ordered on his own authority a levy of 12,000 troops and 20 sailing ships, spent over a million ducats on this, and another 600,000 ducats of secret funds. He overstepped the line by using soldiers of the Naples *tercio* to fight aboard his flotilla and by pretending that some of the galleons and slaves were his, and selling them to the Crown.[136] Coastal fortresses in southern Italy and the islands continued to harbour corsairs thereafter. There were 20 corsair captains based in Trapani alone in 1675–8, although it is difficult to determine who their preferred targets were.[137]

Quite apart from the stakes of high politics, where the republic gambled resolutely, Venetian shipping was continually harassed by the large *bertoni* after 1600. Most of them were sailed by Protestants, primarily the Dutch and English, but sometimes also by the Maltese and Tuscans. The Protestants were intent on taking most of the Levant commerce away from Venice, and they combined piracy with legitimate trading. Unencumbered by ideological baggage, they tended to seize every opportunity that presented itself, and they had some willing accomplices among the Italian princes, like Grand Duke Ferdinando of Tuscany, or Charles Emanuel of Savoy, who offered Livorno and Villefranche to them as bases. When the king of England made peace with Spain in 1604, these English privateers went into Dutch service, using Turkish bases. Venetian ships trading along the Spanish coast were also considered legitimate targets. Venetian traders, who once dominated the economy of Puglia, gradually retreated into the Adriatic. Merchants from the lagoon city began to employ Dutch and English roundships to carry their cargoes to the Levant and to the Atlantic. Venice's shipbuilding industry and the maritime freight business were notable victims of this evolution,

[135] Anderson, *Naval wars in the Levant*, pp. 77–89.
[136] Anderson, *Naval wars in the Levant*, p. 90ff.
[137] Bono, *Corsari nel Mediterraneo*, p. 65.

despite shipbuilding subsidies granted by the republic. The quality of local crews deteriorated. After 1610 the *Serenissima* decided to hire foreign ships and to build its own *bertoni*. In 1619 the Venetians had at their disposal 50 galleys and 50 *bertoni*. They built more galeasses that were powerfully armed. All these measures maintained Venice as an important maritime power until mid-century, but the cost of such power increased dramatically.[138]

The great days of Mediterranean piracy were over after 1680, though it was still endemic in the region until the conquest of Algiers by France in 1830. The prohibition of attacks on the Ottoman Empire by Louis XIV in 1679, which he enforced on the knights of Malta, is probably the decisive date. The galley squadrons gradually disappeared after 1700, and the galley as a warship a century later. Their long twilight attests to their continued usefulness in the Mediterranean, where the long beaches and the irregular wind made navigation by sailing vessels aleatory. Moreover, these were the vessels of small or poor states with few available seamen.[139] Gradually the maritime powers with their large fleets of men-of-war (a development after 1660) supplanted the little squadrons of galleys maintained by the Pope, Tuscany, Genoa, Savoy and the Spanish dominions.

---

[138] Tenenti, *Piracy and the decline of Venice*, pp. 53–84, and p. 138ff.

[139] J. Meyer, "Gens de mer en Mediterranée au XVIIe siècle: la France et l'Espagne, essai de comparaison", in *Le genti dal mare mediterraneo*, vol. 2, pp. 905–36.

Chapter 2
Italy in the age of Habsburg hegemony, 1560–1620

The Spanish system in Italy

The treaty of Câteau-Cambrésis in 1559 between France and the Empire, ending over six decades of intermittent warfare, left Spain in uncontested control of Italy through its hold over Sicily, Naples and Milan. Ultimately, this strength rested on Spanish naval supremacy in the western Mediterranean, and on a network of naval bases and friendly ports stretching from Andalusia to the straits of Òtranto, and encompassing the Balearic islands along with Sardinia, Sicily and Corsica. Only a relatively short stretch of the coast of Provence, with the French bases of Toulon and Marseille, was in potentially hostile hands. The success of Spanish and Imperial arms in the peninsula did the rest. Venice withdrew from the contest in 1530. France's Sienese ally was overwhelmed by Hispano-Imperial troops with Tuscan backing in 1555, and the Papal States fell into line after the death of the Carafa Pope Paul IV in 1559.[1] Both France and Spain placed garrisons in Piedmont, the latter to provide an effective bulwark for Spanish power in Milan. An alliance with Genoa further buttressed Spain's central strategic position in Lombardy. The republic's prosperity depended on the lucrative *asientos*, or supply contracts of the Spanish monarchy.[2] Free passage to Milan through Liguria was an axiom of Spanish policy, and each time that access was threatened, the king held Genoa a little more tightly. Spain helped the republic secure the restless island of Corsica, whose nobles plotted with the French and the Turks to throw off the Genoese yoke.[3] Tuscany and the Papal States were kept respectful by strong

---

[1] Two general political histories of Italy are still very useful. The most detailed is still Romolo Quazza, *Storia politica d'Italia: preponderanza spagnuola (1559–1700)* (Milan: 1950, first publ. 1938). Also, see the abundantly illustrated *L'Italia nell' età della controriforma, 1559–1700; Storia d'Italia*, vol. 2, Nino Valeri & Vittorio de Caprariis (eds) (Turin: 1965).

[2] See Fernand Braudel on the place of Genoa in international commerce and finance, in *Civilisation matérielle, économie et capitalisme, XVe–XVIIIe siècles: vol. 3, Le temps du monde* (Paris: 1979), pp. 130–44.

[3] R. Emmanuelli, *Gênes et l'Espagne dans la guerre de Corse (1559–1569)* (Paris: 1963), p. 13ff. Emmanuelli's book illustrates with meticulous detail the vital support that Spain was prepared to give to Genoa in exchange for the republic's good offices.

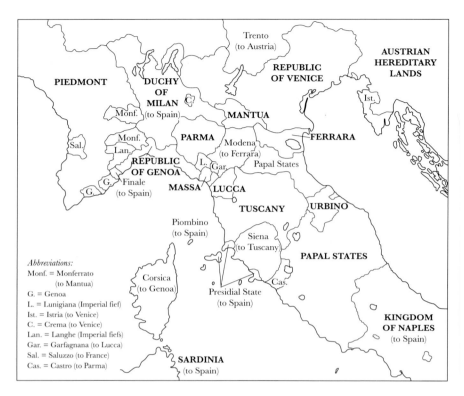

Map 2.1 Political boundaries in Italy, after 1560

Spanish garrisons lodged on the Tuscan coast, at Piombino, Orbetello and the island of Elba. Similar garrisons held strategic points in northern Italy, such as the Farnese capital of Piacenza (until 1585), the crucial Ligurian port of Finale, which linked the Mediterranean with Milan, and La Spezia, the alternative route to Milan through the Lunigiana.

Spanish policy confided strongpoints in Italy to Spanish or German garrisons, and drew upon Italians to serve elsewhere in the empire. The ethnic 'Spanish' *tercios* based in Italy – those of Milan, Naples and Sicily respectively – were administrative rather than tactical units. Their 12,000 to 15,000 men, maintained on a permanent footing, were paid out of the treasury of each territory, and their effective numbers were augmented or rotated by new arrivals. The Spanish crown found it easy to find Spaniards for service in Italy, where the recruits received a modicum of training before moving on to more active duty on the galley fleet or in the Flemish theatre. Geoffrey Parker suggests that the rationale for rotating garrisons was that the military efficiency of a unit improved in direct proportion to the distance from the area where it was raised.[4] The different territories belonging to the House of Austria were so geographically dispersed, and inhabited by so many different peoples, that the garrisons constituted an essential instrument of government for the maintenance of public order.

The kingdom of Naples was the resource base for the Spanish monarchy in Italy. From the time of its conquest in 1503, it was the principal reservoir of men, of horses, of ships and provisions for Spanish imperial defence. Until about 1580 the level of taxation there remained tolerable and constant with inflation.[5] Thereafter, until 1609, tax pressure increased as the war in the Netherlands intensified. Beyond dispatching troops to 'Flanders,' Naples disbursed about a third of the military expenditures accruing to Lombardy, and paid for the garrisons on the Tuscan coast too.[6] This whole military establishment cost about 800,000 ducats annually, or about a third of the kingdom's revenues. Moreover, the public debt also had a military origin, and the interest payments on it devoured 40 per cent of tax income.[7] Despite massive borrowing to meet these expenditures, the kingdom of Naples could redeem the debt and pay an attractive ten per cent interest in full to lenders all across Italy.

Spanish ascendancy in the peninsula also rested upon the active support and participation of Italian aristocracies, first and foremost in those territories where the Catholic king was the legitimate sovereign. It would be inaccurate to see the exclusion of the Neapolitan aristocracy from holding sensitive fortresses or galley commands in the kingdom as an indication of their demilitarization (as Giovanni Muto does), because Italians served in other theatres by virtue of the same policy.[8] Furthermore, while the troops in the kingdom were under the command of the viceroy, Neapolitan nobles enjoyed ascendancy in the key assemblies and committees that financed and administered the army. They monopolized the *Consiglio di Stato*, the military wing of the *Consiglio Collaterale*.[9] Similarly in Milan, only *bona fide*

---

[4] G. Parker, *The army of Flanders and the Spanish Road, 1567–1659: the logistics of Spanish victory and defeat in the Low Countries' wars* (Cambridge: 1972), p. 29. For the general organization of a Spanish *tercio*, see the book by René Quatrefages, *Los tercios españoles (1567–1577)* (Madrid: 1979). The cultural backdrop of military service in the Spanish infantry is treated in the book by Raffaele Puddu, *Il soldato gentiluomo. Autorittrato di una società guerriera; la Spagna del Cinquecento* (Bologna: 1982).

[5] A. Calabria, *The cost of empire: The finances of the kingdom of Naples in the time of Spanish rule* (New York: 1991), p. 5ff.

[6] On Neapolitan and Sicilian contributions to Milan, see Domenico Sella, *Lo stato di Milano in età spagnola* (Turin: 1987), p. 54 and p. 123ff.

[7] Calabria, *The cost of Empire*, p. 10 and p. 78.

[8] G. Muto, "'I segni d'onore'; rappresentazioni delle dinamiche nobiliari a Napoli in età moderna", in *Signori, patrizi, cavalieri in età moderna* (Bari: 1992), pp. 171–92.

[9] R. Villari, "La feudalità e lo stato napoletano nel secolo XVII", in *Potere e società negli stati regionali italiani fra '500 e '600*, pp. 259–77, Elena Fasano-Guarini (ed.) (Bologna: 1978), p. 275.

patricians with deep roots in Lombardy were eligible to sit among the 60 decurions comprising the Senate, the state's legislative body, and they governed in the monarch's name alongside the governor.

Most contemporaries saw the Spanish régime in a positive light. For one, it brought southern Italy two centuries of almost unbroken stability. An invading army descending from the north and moving provisions by sea along the coast could be checked by the garrisons placed in the Tuscan Maremma.[10] The Ottoman fleet and the incessant incursions by Barbary pirates were more pressing dangers. In 1480, an Ottoman landing in Puglia underscored how vulnerable Italy was to the Moslem threat. Emperor Charles V devoted special effort to modernizing the fortifications of the port cities there. These expensive projects were rarely realized in a single spurt. In Sicily most of the emphasis was placed on Palermo where thousands of workers erected bastions and dug the ditches.[11] Italian engineers applied the modern principles of fortification to the ramparts of Bari, Tàranto, Brìndisi, Òtranto, Lecce, Barletta, Naples, Salerno, Messina, Syracuse, Tràpani, Cagliari, Pescara, Gaeta, Catania and a number of smaller ports besides. In addition to the bastioned perimeter of the typical Italian trace design (angular bastions set deep in the earth, serving as a platform for artillery and capable of defending the approaches with crossfire from several points), the viceroys provided the larger cities with one or several forts or citadels where a handful of soldiers could maintain watch over the population, or hold strategic points until reinforcements arrived. Smaller redoubts, forts and watchtowers studded the coast and overlooked each of the little bays and anchorages. Normally, they were all weakly held. After Lepanto there were only about 1,600 Spanish infantry, and some light cavalry, lodged in these little outposts and towers, in small detachments all along the coast. The largest of these garrisons, in Naples, consisted of only several hundred soldiers. Most of the cities contained a mere hundred, or even less, regular soldiers. A skeleton military presence sufficed to hold the kingdom of Naples 'in submission' to Spain, despite its turbulent, unruly population of over three million inhabitants.[12] In 1612 it was calculated that the entire kingdom contained only 27 companies of Spanish infantry (that is, between 3,000 and 4,000 men, on paper), augmented by 16 companies of noble

---

[10] The importance of these fortresses is highlighted in the article by J. Alcalà-Zamora y Queipo de Llano, "Razon de estado y geoestrategia en la politica italiana de Carlos II: Florencia y los presidios, 1677–1681", *Boletin de la Real Academia de la Historia*, **173**, 1976, pp. 297–358. On the construction of fortresses there, see the final chapters of the book by Simon Pepper and Nicholas Adams, *Firearms and fortifications: military architecture and siege warfare in sixteenth-century Siena* (Chicago: 1986).

[11] D. Mack Smith, *A history of Sicily: vol. 1, medieval Sicily, 800–1713*, pp. 140–1.

[12] T. Astarita, "Istituzioni e tradizioni militari", *Storia del Mezzogiorno*, vol. 9, G. Galasso & R. Romeo (eds) (Naples: 1988–1993), pp. 121–56. See also the substantial work by Francisco-Felipe Olesa Muñido, *La organizacion naval de los estados mediterraneos y en especial de España durante los siglos XVI y XVII* (Madrid: 1968), p. 977ff.

gens d'armes and four companies of light horse, perhaps 1,000 horsemen in all. These latter were mostly Neapolitan or Albanian mounted arquebusiers employed in police duties. An undisclosed number of soldiers guarded castles and coastal defences.[13] Finally, the galley squadron employed about a hundred soldiers per vessel, accounting for about 1,000 additional troops. Such light-handed control extended over Sicily too. Expert opinion held that it required 6,000 men to hold the island, but in 1574 there were said to be only 800.[14]

Not only was this number of soldiers insufficient to impose a vice-grip over the Italian kingdoms; these garrisons themselves often constituted a menace to public order. Benedetto Croce depicts a few of these soldiers serving in Naples and the Mediterranean theatre, from their autobiographies. Miguel de Castro ingenuously recounted the disastrous impact that passing troops could have on small communities, especially if the troops were veterans and had a clear idea of what they could get away with. The picaresque lifestyle of these Spaniards resulted in vendettas with families of girls they deflowered and then abandoned. When the viceroy employed Spanish soldiers to repress banditry or levy taxes in the mountainous interior, their marauding was as calamitous for the peasantry as the brigandage itself.[15]

This regular military establishment was barely sufficient to hold the coast against Barbary incursions and the interior against bandit gangs. It could not hope to form a solid line of defence by itself. In 1563, the viceroy duke of Alcalà recast a militia on a more centralized footing, to supplant the motley feudal levies of medieval times. This *battaglione* was similar to peasant militias in Piedmont, Tuscany and Venetia. Its purpose was to support the regular soldiers and urban militias mounting the ramparts whenever danger threatened. Each community was to supply four foot-soldiers and a cavalryman for every 100 hearths. In this way it was possible to raise about 22,000 men. The crown conceded special legal privileges to militiamen in peacetime to encourage them to volunteer. Sicily had a similar force of urban militiamen, created by Charles V in 1548 as a defence against corsairs.[16] Their task was to deter pirates from landing on the beaches, for their frequent *aiguades*, the water-fetching parties necessary for galley fleets. Further study might show whether these militiamen were the reservoir from which Spain recruited regular soldiers for service elsewhere. Besides this infantry, which

---

[13] Alfred von Reumont's history, the English translation of which was published in 1854, is still often cited by historians of Naples. *See The Carafas of Maddaloni: Naples under Spanish dominion* (London: 1854), p. 45. More recently, see Astarita, "Istituzioni e tradizioni militari", *Storia del Mezzogiorno*, vol. 9, pp. 121–56.

[14] Mack Smith, *A history of Sicily: vol. 1, medieval Sicily, 800–1713*, p. 144.

[15] Benedetto Croce, "Scene della vita dei soldati spagnuoli a Napoli", *in Uomini e cose della vecchia Italia* (Bari: 1927), pp. 109–45. For campaigns against bandits, see Alfred von Reumont, *The Carafas of Maddaloni*, p. 163ff., and more extensively, Rosario Villari, *La rivolta antispagnola a Napoli: le origini (1585–1647)* (Bari: 1976), pp. 59–90.

[16] P. Castiglione, *Storia di un declino: il seicento siciliano* (Siracusa, Italy: 1987), p. 26.

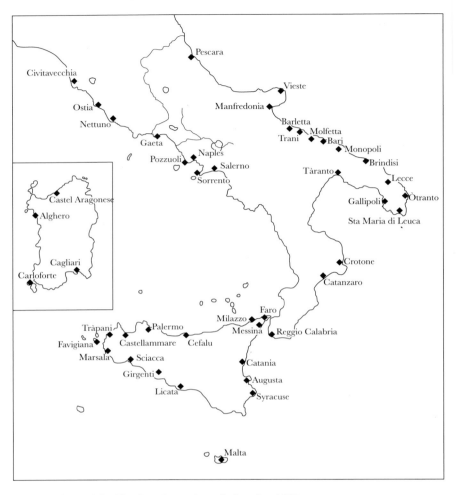

Map 2.2 Coastal fortifications in southern Italy, after 1600

was virtually untrained, there was a cavalry militia called the *sacchetta* whose troopers were wealthy enough to provide their own horses. In the Mezzogiorno they numbered on paper about 2,400 soldiers. In Sicily too, there was a local mounted militia, but by all accounts, it was singularly unwarlike. Astarita is probably right to suggest that the absence of peril hindered the constitution of an effective force.[17]

The government in Naples also used regular soldiers and militiamen to maintain order in the countryside, since the cities were generally free of 'political'

---

[17] Astarita, "Istituzioni e tradizioni militari", *Storia del Mezzogiorno*, vol. 9, pp. 121–56.

unrest, vendettas notwithstanding. Banditry was endemic in more remote districts, but the 1580s and 1590s saw it increase to epidemic proportions almost everywhere. In the 1580s Calabrian bandits formed a troop of some 600 horse and elected a 'king', Marco Berardi of Cosenza. These marauders governed themselves by a regular council and levied 'taxes' from small communities entirely at their mercy. They nearly captured the ancient coastal town of Crotone, before they were scattered by a force of 1,000 Spanish infantry and 400 cavalry under the marchese Cerchiara Pignatelli.[18] In 1586 the whole countryside around Salerno and Eboli fell to the bandit chief Benedetto Mangone, and the famous bandit Marco Sciarra held sway over most of the Abruzzi, dodging soldiers by crossing the border with the Papal States to elude capture. These bands scaled the walls and plundered the houses of significant towns like Vasto in the Abruzzi and Lucera in Puglia. While their numbers fluctuated continually, they commonly collected hundreds and even thousands of adherents for single objectives. In the aftermath of the famine of 1590–91, the scourge reached unprecedented proportions and extra troops had to be levied to combat them. Don Carlo Spinelli, who like Pignatelli was a Neapolitan noble, tracked Sciarra through the Abruzzi with an army of 4,000 men in 1591 and 1592, operating in conjunction with a similar Pontifical army across the border. Together they drove the bandit leader and his stalwarts out of the region and into Venetian service abroad.[19]

While Naples and Sicily served as a shield and a bulwark in the Mediterranean, Milan performed quite a different geostrategic function. It entered the Spanish orbit definitively in 1554 when Charles V split the Habsburg dominions into a Spanish sphere falling to his son Philip II (consisting of Iberia and the overseas empire, Italy, the Low Countries and the Franche-Comté), and an Austrian or German sphere under his brother Ferdinand I, Holy Roman Emperor, who ruled the hereditary lands of Austria and Bohemia, together with the remnants of the kingdom of Hungary not occupied by the Turks. While the north Italian territories still belonged theoretically to the Holy Roman Empire, in practice Madrid ruled them through the governor of Milan. A thick swath of semi-independent feudal territories lay between Piedmont, Liguria and southern Lombardy, against the peaks of the Apennines. Their holders paid scant attention to the distant emperor in Vienna, who was poor and in comparison powerless, and so they became clients of Spain.[20] The feudataries themselves were either patricians in nearby cities or, like the Malaspina, abandoned their rural castles to take up residence in an urban *palazzo* and seek lucrative sinecures in the princely courts.[21]

---

[18] Von Reumont, *The Carafas of Maddaloni*, pp. 163–4.

[19] Villari, *La rivolta antispagnola a Napoli*, pp. 82–94. See also L. von Pastor, *The history of the popes from the close of the middle ages; vol. XXIV: Clement VIII (1592–1605)* (London: 1952), p. 375ff.

[20] S. Pugliese, *Le prime strette dell' Austria in Italia* (Milan–Rome: 1932), p. 46 and p. 70.

[21] *Ibid.*, pp. 46–85.

In the duchy of Milan, the Catholic king took care to leave intact the medieval institutions, by which the landed patriciate administered the state in the king's name.[22] The Spanish presence in Milan virtually eliminated French designs on Naples, discouraged by Spain's entrenched strength in northern Italy. In addition, Milan was the hub of the most developed manufacturing and commercial economy anywhere on the planet, harnessing the powerful north Italian economy in support of Spanish imperial policy.[23] Milan was also an armoury of the utmost strategic importance at the end of the sixteenth century. Its strategic role widened after 1565 with the revolt of the Netherlands against Philip II. The surest way to send, train and equip troops for Flanders was to collect them in Lombardy and to march them over the Alps, through Savoy, Franche-Comté and Lorraine. From 1567 onwards, the Spanish governor of Milan played the role of linchpin in effectively organizing this route, establishing alliances with the Swiss Catholic cantons for easy passage into Germany, or negotiating with Savoy and Genoa for access to passes and ports respectively. Officials improved administrative procedures in order to increase the number of troops awaiting transit without overburdening the numerous rural population.[24] In 1570 Spanish troops occupied the coastal enclave of the marquisate of Finale, and turned it into a transit base. It afforded easy access into landlocked Lombardy. Spain purchased Finale outright in 1602, built a citadel and a large quay to accommodate new arrivals, and based a galley squadron there.[25]

The Spanish hegemony over northern Italy was reinforced by the governor of Milan, Count Fuentes (1596–1610), who tightened Madrid's military grasp in response to the stabilization of France under Henri IV, and the resurgence of French military potential at the close of the wars of religion. When France closed the access of Spanish troops to Franche-Comté across the Rhône, and encouraged Savoy, Venice and Tuscany to shake off Spanish domination, Fuentes responded. First, he extended his control over the Tuscan coastline by building an imposing fortress on the island of Elba at Porto Longone in 1602.[26] Enemy of the house of Farnese, he then threatened the duchy of Parma with a military occupation, and sought to place a new Spanish garrison in Piacenza, evacuated almost twenty years earlier as recognition of Duke Alessandro's service.[27] He had just concluded,

---

[22] G. Vismara, "Il patriziato milanese nel cinque-seicento", in *Potere e società negli stati regionali italiani fra '500 e '600*, E. Fasano-Guarini (ed.) (Bologna: 1978), pp. 153–72. See also D. Sella, *Lo stato di Milano in età spagnola* (Turin: 1987), pp. 21–39.

[23] On this strength, see Sella, *Lo stato di Milano in età Spagnola*, p. 109ff.

[24] M. Rizzo, "Militari e civili nello stato di Milano durante la seconda metà del Cinquecento: in tema di alloggiamenti militari", *Clio*, 1987, pp. 563–96.

[25] Y.-M. Bercé, "Les guerres dans l'Italie du XVIIe siècle", in *L'Italie au XVIIe siècle* (Paris: 1989), pp. 313–31, at p. 314.

[26] Bercé, "Les guerres dans l'Italie du XVIIe siècle", *L'Italie au XVIIe siècle*, p. 315.

[27] G. Drei, *I Farnese: grandezza e decadenza di una dinastia italiana* (Rome: 1954), pp. 175–8. Specifically, Fuentes forced Duke Ranuccio I to dismantle the recent fortification of his western frontier at Borgo San Donnino (today's Fidenza), under the threat of invasion.

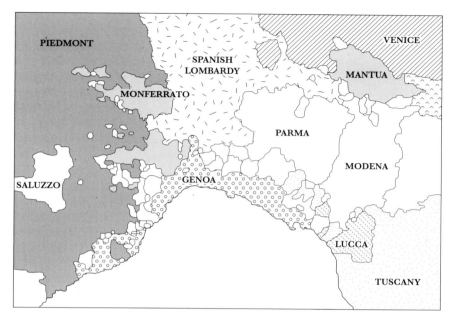

Map 2.3 Principalities and fiefs in northern Italy, *circa* 1600

in 1600, an alliance with the Swiss Grison league, giving Spanish troops free access to the Valtellina and Austrian Tyrol. A citadel at Bormio and a more powerful fortress at the entrance to the valley, called appropriately Fort Fuentes, could strangle commerce traversing Switzerland. Every year, Spanish and Italian troops took this road to the Low Countries. By holding this valley, Spain was also able to prevent Venice from receiving troops she recruited beyond the Alps. The Valtellina became the hub of international relations and a flashpoint of conflicting interests. For the time being, it remained the *voie royale* of Spanish imperial policy in central Europe.[28]

Beyond the brute force of Spanish military occupation, the increasing grasp of its fortified tentacles, and the loyalty of the Sardinian, Neapolitan, Sicilian and Milanese aristocracy toward their king, the strength of the Habsburg monarchy lay in the moral pre-eminence of Philip II. It was in the interest of most of the Italian states, most of the time, to support the *Pax Hispanica*. Genoa's commercial interests dictated its policy. In 1608, for example, as many as 7 per cent of the patrician families resided outside the republic, scattered from Chios in Greece, to Flanders and Mexico. About three-quarters of the 154 expatriate households

---

[28] The best overview of the tensions in the alpine region over the Valtellina–Grison route is the book by Pedro Marrades, *El camino del Imperio: notas para el estudio de la cuestiòn de la valtelina* (Madrid: 1943).

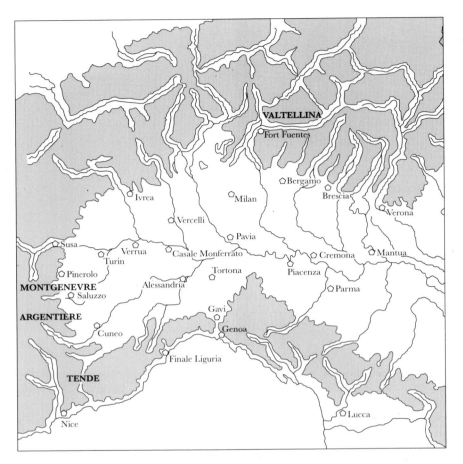

Map 2.4 Mountains, passes and major fortresses in north-west Italy, *circa* 1610

resided in various Spanish dominions.[29] While technically neutral, Genoa opened its ports and the gates of its fortresses to Spanish garrisons on occasion. Philip II intervened in the brief civil war of 1575 between the 'new' and 'old' factions of the patriciate, establishing a *modus vivendi* favourable to his interest.[30] The republic needed Spanish aid to help maintain its own hold over fractious Corsica. Genoese galley entrepreneurs were essential to the constitution and maintenance of the Spanish fleet, and many of the galleys that comprised it could often be found in the Ligurian capital, where they took on soldiers, seamen and oarsmen. In Spain's

---

[29] E. Grendi, *La repubblica aristocratica dei genovesi: politica, carità e commercio fra cinque e seicento* (Bologna: 1987), p. 19.

[30] C. Bitossi, *Il governo dei magnifici: patriziato e politica a Genova fra cinque e seicento* (Genoa: 1990), p. 18.

shadow, the Genoese virtually ceased to think about their own defence, save from the occasional corsair raid. The inventory of the Republic's artillery around 1616 reveals that most of its pieces were old or unserviceable. Virtually all of its guns, apart from 100 held back in the central arsenal, were dispersed in small numbers in the coastal castles and citadels. No cannon armed the forts guarding the passes into Lombardy. Genoa spent about 50,000 *scudi* on defence annually, an insignificant sum in absolute terms, and especially derisory relative to the wealth of the city.[31]

Each Italian prince had his own specific reasons for supporting the *status quo*, although some were common. Spain exploited its hegemony to prevent the territorial ambitions of the different states from upsetting the peace. There was no lack of controversial issues capable of creating discord. Most states had claims against neighbours, or intended to diminish feudal autonomies by swallowing up lesser jurisdictions. Both Piedmont and Genoa claimed sovereignty over parts of the Langhe fiefs in the northern Apennines, and along the western Riviera. Tuscany and Parma contested each other's claims on the Lunigiana, where the Malaspina feudal lords held sway. Close by, Lucca and Modena fought a bitter border war over the Apennine district of the Garfagnana. The Papal States claimed jurisdiction over Parma, and prepared to swallow the states of Ferrara and Urbino when their dynasties became extinguished in the direct line. After the devolution of Ferrara to Rome in 1597, the house of Este based in Modena schemed to recover the territory by any means. Venice maintained ancient claims on the estuary of the Po, and was ready to wreck any Papal attempt to establish a rival port in the Adriatic. Mantua and its subject territory of Monferrato were eyed greedily by most of its neighbours. The *status quo* was fragile because of the fragmentation of the duchy into competing feudal holdings of the different branches of the house of Gonzaga. Parma sought to incorporate the powerful fiefs held by the Pallavicini and Landi dynasties by force, although those houses were faithful clients of the Habsburgs. Northern Italy therefore seethed with potential for renewed outbreaks of open warfare, but Spanish influence always stifled them.

When dealing with the larger Italian states, Spain relied more on *realpolitik* than on moral suasion or threats. A series of bilateral treaties that took the form of defensive alliances between the House of Austria and individual states, cemented the peace of Câteau-Cambrésis. Spain subsidized and otherwise flattered their princes with honours and employment. Madrid bought the complicity of the smallest states, and individual seigneurs living in them. The crown's aim by this policy of cultivating *los Potentados* was to overcome the political fragmentation of Italy with a network of private clients and 'friends'.[32] After 1600 Philip III paid out

---

[31] D. Zanetti, "Le artiglierie genovesi all' inizio del secolo XVII", *Nuova Rivista Storica*, 1966, pp. 643–64.

[32] Manuel Rivero Rodriguez, "Felipe II y los 'Potentados de Italia'", *La dimensione europea dei Farnese; Bulletin de l'Institut Historique Belge de Rome*, **63**, 1993, pp. 337–70, at p. 339.

'subsidies' of some 100,000 ducats to the dukes of Urbino, Modena and Mirandola, which was a considerable sum for those princes.[33] Another practice was to encourage Italian client princes to send one or more of their sons to Madrid to serve at the Spanish Court. In due course the child would grow to appreciate the justice of the Spanish cause, but meanwhile he could be held hostage against the policies of his father. Alessandro Farnese, future duke of Parma (whose mother Margarita was an illegitimate daughter of Charles V), was brought up at the court of Castile, and his haughty Spanish manner offended the sensitivities of his future subjects. The princes of Savoy, the Della Rovere of Urbino and the Medici were similarly sent to Madrid.[34]

More subtle was the crown's conferral of Spanish aristocratic titles, orders and revenues on Italian princes, as upon great aristocrats of Naples and Sicily, sometimes for services rendered, but also preventively. When Ranuccio Farnese, son of Alessandro, went to Madrid as the Pope's emissary in 1601 to be present at a royal baptism, he received the Order of the Golden Fleece for his pains.[35] Philip III bestowed the same distinction upon the Medici prince Don Pietro, son of the Grand Duke Ferdinando I; Don Pietro was a general of Italian infantry living at the court of Madrid. I have not found a complete list of the beneficiaries of the Golden Fleece, which was confined to great dignitaries. The Catholic kings appointed other great princes to the position of viceroy over different Spanish dominions. They liberally distributed the 'habits' of the military orders of Santiago, Alcántara, Calatrava and Montesa to even modest noble families whose service and loyalty made them clients in the peninsula, often at odds with their own sovereigns.[36] Knightly orders such as those of Santiago brought little wealth

---

[33] For Urbino, see J. Dennistoun, *Memoirs of the dukes of Urbino (1440–1630)* vol. 3, p. 104.

[34] Alessandro Farnese, whose mother Margarita was a bastard daughter of Charles V, grew up in Spain during the 1560s. See Drei, *I Farnese: grandezza e decadenza di una dinastia italiana*, p. 106. Prince Francesco Maria della Rovere spent two and a half years there during the same period, passing his time with military games before ascending to the throne in 1574. See Dennistoun, *Memoirs of the dukes of Urbino*, vol. 3, p. 124. Several Medici princes spent time there, beginning with the black sheep of the family, Pietro, brother of Grand Duke Francesco, who was cast off as a child by his relatives. He went to Spain in 1579 and never returned. His bastard half-brother Giovanni went with him, and became a career officer in Imperial, Spanish and Venetian service. See the compendium of Medici biographies by E. Grassellini and A. Fracassini, *Profili Medicei: origine, sviluppo, decadenza della famiglia Medici attraverso i suoi componenti* (Florence: 1982). Ferrante Gonzaga of the Guastalla branch went to Spain in 1599, where he was awarded the Golden Fleece. His son Vincenzo achieved the highest ranks in the Spanish administration in Spain and Italy. Vespasiano Gonzaga of the Sabbioneta branch was created Grandee of Spain in 1558, in a long career in the service of Charles V and Philip II. See Giuseppe Coniglio, *I Gonzaga* (Mantua: 1967), pp. 477–97.

[35] Drei, *I Farnese*, p. 175.

[36] See two catalogues published at the turn of the century by V. Vignau and F. Chagon, *Indice de pruebas de los caballeros que han vestido el habito de Santiago, desde el ano 1501 hasta la fecha*

to the recipients: their value was more symbolic than financial or military. In the sixteenth century, and especially after 1560 when these awards multiplied, Italians were frequent beneficiaries. Over the century, 208 Italians, constituting more than 11 per cent, received the habit of Santiago. Most resided in political capitals or major cities. The Habsburg kings saw, in these awards to beneficiaries who were not their vassals, a way of reinforcing a community of pro-Spanish and pro-Catholic sentiment, as well as a means of applying pressure on the courts of their respective princes.[37] Strategic marriages between Italian princes and the House of Austria also solidified these alliances, and Hispanicized the Italian courts through the introduction of Spanish etiquette.[38] Historians often consider this feature to denote the enhanced dignity of the monarch.

Lastly, the king of Spain allowed nobles and princes living outside his domains to acquire fiefs in his states. The Medici, the Farnese, and the Gonzaga were all important fiefholders in the kingdom of Naples, and drew substantial revenues from them. These fiefs could be confiscated if those princes strayed from Madrid's interests. Carlo Bitossi claims that of 2,700 feudal communities in the kingdom of Naples, 1,200 were held by Genoese families. All the leading houses were extensive landholders either there or in Sicily, or both: the Doria, the Spìnola, the Grimaldi, the Centurioni, Sauli, Ravaschiero, De Mari, Saluzzo and others were real stakeholders in the Spanish system. Branches of those families established in Naples maintained close links with their city of origin, and on at least one occasion the Senate elected one of these Neapolitans doge.[39] Others, like the Doria, Spìnola and Pallavicino, held fiefs in Lombardy, or Spain itself. Similarly, the great feudal families around Rome, the Orsini, Colonna, Caetani, Savelli, Frangipani and Caffarelli, held fiefs across the border in Campania or the Abruzzi.[40] They too

---

(Madrid: 1901), and *Indice de Pruebas de los Caballeros que han vestido el Habito de Calatrava, Alcántara, y Montesa* (Madrid: 1903). The entries identify the year of admission and the place of origin of the candidate.

[37] M. Lambert-Gorges, "Le roi, les ordres, et le péril barbaresque: un exemple d'utilisation des ordres militaires castillans par le pouvoir royal dans l'Espagne du XVIe siècle", forthcoming in *Potere e ordini militari–cavallereschi nell' Europa mediterranea dell' età moderna*, (Brussels–Rome: in press). I wish to thank Mme Lambert-Gorges for graciously sending me the typescript of her contribution.

[38] As an example, at Charles Emanuel's marriage to the Infanta of Spain in 1584, the Duchess's court at Turin comprised over a hundred people, mostly Spaniards. See Pierpaolo Merlin, *Tra guerre e tornei: la corte sabauda nell' eta di Carlo Emanuele I* (Turin: 1991), p. 160.

[39] The logic of conceding fiefs to Italian princes is underscored by Marzio dell' Acqua, "Al servizio della Spagna: la corrispondenza tra Vespasiano Gonzaga e Alessandro Farnese", in *Guerre, stati e città: Mantova e l'Italia padana dal secolo XIII al XIX* (Mantua: 1988), pp. 375–87, at p. 382. The figure for Genoese fiefholders is in Bitossi, *Il governo dei magnifici* p. 44.

[40] L. von Pastor, *The history of the popes from the close of the middle ages, vol. XXIV: Clement VIII (1592–1605)*, p. 430. This phenomenon of courting great families is analyzed more exten-

were frequent recipients of the king of Spain's coveted distinctions and titles. Their task was to maintain a discreet lobby in favour of Spanish policy, and promote Spanish candidates for ecclesiastical preferment, and more generally to tilt curial politics in that direction.

The military potential of Italian states with respect to the Spanish empire was meagre. The Pope was sometimes hostage to the goodwill of the king of Spain and the governor of Milan. In peacetime, Papal forces barely maintained order.[41] They spent much money and energy tracking bandits; there were said to be 15,000 bandits on the lists of wanted criminals in the 1580s and the early 1590s.[42] The 2,600 Roman and Corsican soldiers hunting them in the Marches and Latium pillaged almost more than did the delinquents. When not in the kingdom of Naples, Marco Sciarra could raise hundreds of men or more for spectacular raids on walled towns. Co-operation with Spanish forces operating from Naples and Tuscan troops to the north was therefore crucial. There were only two significant fortresses in the state, Ancona and Civitavecchia, both seaports. The popes never extended Rome's great fortifications to the right bank of the Tiber where most of the population lived. The 30,000 men in the peasant militia were entirely untrained. There was no military force in existence by which the Pope could exercise a continual pressure on his neighbours. Armies could be raised from scratch, however, as they were everywhere else. In 1597 for example, Cardinal Pietro Aldobrandini, the papal nephew, raised one on the occasion of the Ferrara devolution.

Clement VIII Aldobrandini declared the direct Este line in Ferrara to be extinct, and that the duchy of Ferrara with its dependency of Comacchio was to be incorporated into the Papal States. The Este Duke Cesare, cousin and heir of the late sovereign, also fortified his state and levied thousands of local militiamen to contest the Papal decree, which in feudal law was perfectly legitimate.[43] Grand Duke Ferdinando I de'Medici increased his peasant militia to some 10,000 men,

---

sively in an article by Manuel Rivero Rodriguez, "Felipe II y los 'Potentados de Italia', *La dimensione europea dei Farnese; Bulletin de l'Institut Historique Belge de Rome*, **63**, 1993, pp. 337–70.

[41] We can catch a glimpse of the Papal military organization in the article by Andrea da Mosto, "Ordinamenti militari delle soldatesche dello stato romano nel secolo XVI", *Quellen und Forschungen aus Italienischen Archiven und Bibliotheken*, 1904, pp. 72–133.

[42] Von Pastor, *The history of the popes, vol. XXIV*, p. 375ff. This summary has been explored more deeply by Jean Delumeau, *Vie économique et sociale de Rome dans la séconde moitié du XVIe siècle*, 2 vols (Paris: 1957–9), vol. 2, pp. 544–67; and Irene Polverini Fosi, *La società violente: il banditismo dello stato pontificio* (Rome: 1985).

[43] Von Pastor, *The history of the popes, vol. XXIV*, p. 393. The corresponding mobilization on the Ferrarese side is examined in M. Cattini, "Dall' economia della guerra, alla guerra 'in economia'. Prime indagini sull' organizzazione militare estense nei secoli XV e XVI", in *Guerre, stati e città: Mantova e l'Italia padana dal secolo XIII al XIX* (Mantua: 1988), pp. 31–40.

strengthened the westward fortifications against Spain and east in the Tuscan Romagna. The king of France, Henri IV, contemplated coming to the aid of these states too. Confronted with this challenge, the Pontifical effort was considerable. Aldobrandini gave out contracts to great aristocrats to levy troops in Italy, such as Duke Pietro Caetani's *condotta* authorizing him to enrol 3,000 infantry and 300 horse. To everyone's surprise, within a few months there were 20,000 Papal infantry and 3,000 horse camped near Faenza, ready to besiege Ferrara. There was still a significant military aristocracy in the Papal States, the leading houses of which were the Capizucchi, the Conti, the Savelli and the Sforza. The outcome of war was not a certainty, however, given the strength of Ferrara's ramparts, the popularity of the new duke, the resolve of his peasant militia, the still rudimentary siegecraft of the day and the dubious quality of the papal levies. Many junior officers were untrained peasant notables nominated by the communities providing troops, and one expert considered them worthless.[44] Spanish diplomatic intervention in favour of the papal claim convinced the Este to desist and relinquish his capital. Another occasion when Spain lent powerful support to Papal policy arose not long after, in 1606, when Pope Paul V Borghese placed an interdict on the republic of Venice, and both the Papal State and the Venetians prepared for war. Spanish military preparations on Venice's vulnerable border with Lombardy encouraged the republic to seek a diplomatic solution to the crisis, which entailed no territorial dispute.[45] Spanish aid to Rome to resolve these conflicts was therefore critical.

One dispute to flare up into open warfare was the border conflict between the tiny republic of Lucca and the duchy of Modena over some hilltop villages in the Garfagnana. The Modenese raised an army of two or three thousand soldiers to besiege Castiglione Garfagnana in 1602, but it was stoutly defended by its inhabitants, and the Luccan urban and peasant militias led by the republic's patricians went to its rescue. When Spain took Lucca under its protection, the governor of Milan, Count Fuentes, mediated a truce. Border warfare between the two states erupted again in 1613. Lucca mobilized several thousand militiamen for the occasion and launched raids on villages and towns in the mountain district with considerable destruction. The Modenese retaliated by dispatching General Bentivoglio and two Este princes with a professional army of several thousand infantry, a big artillery train and a crowd of noble adventurers. Again, there were

---

[44] Stefano Andretta, "Da Parma a Roma: la fortuna dei Farnese di Latera tra armi, curia e devozione tra XVI e XVII secolo", *La dimensione europea dei Farnese: Bulletin de l'Institut Historique Belge de Rome*, **63**, 1993, pp. 7–32, at p. 17.

[45] A good account of the dispute is contained in von Pastor, *The history of the popes, vol. XXV: Paul V* (London: 1937), p. 126ff. On military advice to the pope not to risk a war with Venice, see Stefano Andretta, "Da Parma a Roma: la fortuna dei Farnese di Latera tra armi, curia e devozione tra XVI e XVII secolo", *La dimensione europea dei Farnese; Bulletin de l'Institut Historique Belge de Rome*, pp. 7–32.

pitched battles around key villages and castles. Lucca mobilized more resources in turn, its patricians heading columns of hundreds of regular soldiers and militia. Spanish envoys in the form of Italian notables dispatched to the scene restored the peace after a few months, this time permanently.[46] The massive fortifications undertaken at Lucca around the same period were not just for show. Militia garrisons were enough to hold it against most other states. A besieging army had to be enormous to blockade it effectively, and Lucca's immediate neighbours were incapable of such efforts. Spanish success in imposing peace in the Garfagnana was easy because even minimal intervention on one side or the other would prove decisive.

Despite Spanish success in keeping localized unrest within bounds, they could never take the compliance of Italian princes for granted. Most of them desired to retain a margin of manoeuvre and enhance the status and territory of their state, and their counsellors were continually hatching schemes to that effect.[47] Duke Cosimo I of Tuscany (1537–74) prepared his principality for any eventuality. He raised about 30,000 men, between regular soldiers and peasant militias, for the war resulting in the conquest of Siena, from 1553 to 1559. Permanent armies were still far in the future, so in subsequent decades Cosimo paid at most a couple of thousand infantry to guard his castles, and a few hundred cavalry to patrol the coast. His originality was to embark on a precocious policy of fortification. Like other princes, Duke Cosimo asserted his sovereign power and curbed the restiveness of his subject towns by building citadels, commanded invariably by outsiders. Florence had three; the other cities, Pistoia, Prato, Pisa, Volterra, Livorno, Siena, Arezzo, Cortona, Montepulciano, Grosseto, Portoferraio and Borgo San Sepolcro each had one.[48] The grand dukes then ringed the duchy with fortresses and castles, as Vauban would do on a larger scale in France a century later, closing off all the avenues into the principality. Some of these strongpoints were substantial, like the mountain-top fortress of Radicòfani towering over the highway to Rome, or Città del Sole, near Forlì, which threatened to pinch off communications in the Papal states between Romagna and the Marches.[49] Cosimo used extensive corvées and heavy local taxes to erect these fortifications, which were maintained and improved under his several successors.

While Cosimo's policies never swerved from the Spanish alliance, his son, Gand Duke Ferdinando I (1587–1609) was more provocative in his dealings with Madrid. He intervened in the French wars of religion on the side of the Protestant Henri IV, capturing and holding the Château d'If guarding the harbour of

---

[46] An account of this lilliputian war is contained in Luigi Amorth, *Modena capitale: storia di Modena e dei suoi duchi dal 1598 al 1860* (Milan: 1967), p. 40ff.

[47] On this point, see *Quazza, La preponderanza spagnuola*, p. 8.

[48] G. Spini, "Introduzione", in *Architettura e politica da Cosimo I a Ferdinando I* (Florence: 1976), pp. 9–77. For the background to much of this construction, see Pepper and Adams, *Firearms and fortifications in sixteenth-century Siena* (Chicago: 1987).

[49] Spini, "Introduzione", in *Architettura e politica da Cosimo I a Ferdinando I*, p. 57.

Marseille, with a Tuscan garrison. Ferdinando was instrumental thereafter in bringing about the conversion of Henri IV to Catholicism, and his intercession with Clement VIII Aldobrandini, a Florentine pope, helped lift the Papal excommunication. He scored his greatest coup by marrying his niece Maria de'Medici to the Bourbon king in 1599. It seemed in 1593 as if Spain would invade Tuscany over this maverick policy, and Spanish troops disembarked at Port' Ercole in the presidial state, but nothing followed. Diplomats assumed that Tuscany harboured various grievances against Madrid, notably over the Spanish fortresses along the Tuscan coast, and that Ferdinando would be willing to fight the House of Austria in order to possess them. An anonymous Venetian intelligence report dating from about 1607 gauged Tuscan military potential in the hope of an anti-Spanish alliance with the republic. The writer judged the grand duchy able to spend up to 800,000 ducats annually on war, which was a significant sum, equal to half the revenue of the kingdom of Naples but drawn from only a quarter of its population.[50] Although the grand duke maintained garrisons of only 2,500 men, in war it was thought he could raise 40,000 infantry or more, and up to 2,000 cavalry, recruited among the Tuscan militiamen, Corsicans, and Romagnoles, all reputed to be good soldiers. The anonymous Venetian observer noted the 'affection' of gentlemen in other states who could be expected to rush to the prince's aid with their retainers, to be an important asset. The feudal count of Santa Fiora (a Sforza) was mentioned in the document by name, but the grand duke had many such 'friends' in Bologna, Perugia and Città di Castello, such as Baglioni, Còppoli, Vitelli and Bourbon del Monte. Behind this moral and professional support of friends, clients and relatives lay a mythical treasure of twenty million ducats in gold, and the inestimable wealth of the palace. There was, too, the military order of Santo Stefano and the granducal fleet of galleys and galleons. This report was wildly optimistic about the real muscle of the grand duke, but it did have some basis in fact. Attachment to the Spanish cause by Tuscany was not exclusively the result of frailty. Before the days of standing armies, small Italian military forces were not a sign of weakness, for money and clientage could produce some sort of decent force in short order.

In case of crisis, the grand duke kept some military speciaists on call, called *lancie spezzati*, like Alfonso Montecùccoli, Silvio Piccolòmini and Virginio Orsini. They were fed at his table, and he gave them pensions in return for military service in time of need. Their task was to raise such an army and render it serviceable in a hurry.[51] Silvio Piccolòmini, a scion of the foremost Sienese house, and father of the future Spanish–Imperial general, Ottavio, seems typical of the *lancie spezzati* on

---

[50] A. Zanelli, "Una relazione inedita dello stato del granducato di Toscana nel 1607", *Bullettino Senese di Storia Patria*, 1926–7, pp. 185–212.

[51] Similarly, the grand duke paid riding and martial arts instructors, called *cavallerizzi*, to teach military skills to noble youths. See Zanelli, "Una relazione inedita", *Bullettino Senese di Storia Patria*, 1926–7, pp. 185–212, at p. 198.

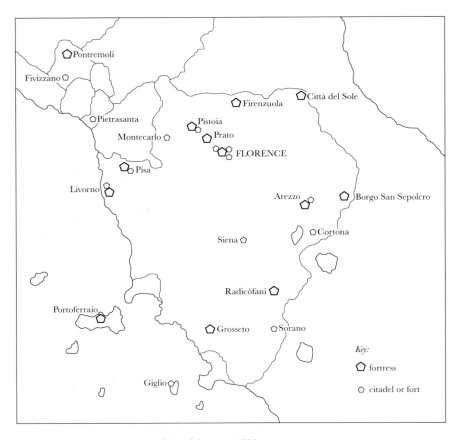

Map 2.5 Tuscan fortresses and citadels, *circa* 1620

the payroll of all the Italian courts. His father raised him to be a soldier, and took him to Flanders for his apprenticeship under Farnese in the Capizzuchi *tercio*. In 1595 the grand duke sent him in the capacity of military adviser and specialist in fortifications and siegecraft to aid the prince of Transylvania against the Turks. In 1599 he joined an expedition of the knights of Santo Stefano against Negroponte in Greece. By 1605, being one of the pre-eminent warriors at the Tuscan court, Ferdinando I appointed him Grand Constable of the Order of Santo Stefano, succeeding his maternal uncle Scipione in that charge, and he was one of the commanders of the Tuscan expedition against Bona in 1607. At Florence, he occupied a variety of military and courtly functions, like Master of Artillery, Grand Chamberlain, cup-bearer, and captain of the granducal body-guard. Of his three sons, two, Enea Silvio and Ottavio were destined to follow in his footsteps, while Celio was ushered into the Church, eventually becoming archbishop of Siena.[52]

Spanish policy tolerated some military potential in Italian states, provided it was employed in the framework of its alliance with them. The treaty bound the grand dukes of Tuscany, for example, to send 5,000 men to the Spanish army if ever Lombardy or Naples were attacked. In 1613, when the duke of Savoy launched an invasion of the Monferrato, Cosimo II sent 2,000 infantry and 300 cavalry to Milan under the command of his brother, Don Francesco de'Medici, and with them rode a cluster of Tuscan and Roman noble adventurers. The concentration of 'Spanish' troops in Lombardy in 1615, and the subsequent battle of Asti in May against Piedmontese troops featured contingents from Tuscany, Parma, Lucca and Urbino, although they were not all employed in the front line.[53]

Tuscany was blessed in the calibre of its princes, who were all conscientious administrators. They compare favourably with many of their contemporaries. In some principalities there was a contrast between the 'Apollonian' regularity and caution of those dukes who remembered the period of the Italian wars, and their young 'Dionysian' successors eager to acquire military glory for themselves. Certainly this is the case with the Gonzaga in Mantua, the Farnese of Parma, and the Savoy of Piedmont. In Mantua, Duke Guglielmo (1550–87) was the antithesis of a charismatic hero. The miserly administrator of a prosperous state reduced the court and pared back noble privileges. He held closely to the Spanish alliance in his foreign policy, marrying Eleonora of Austria in 1561. The tiny, but wealthy Mantuan state – wedged between Spanish Lombardy and Venice – seemed unlikely to have much scope for great and bellicose deeds. Half of it was constituted by the territory of Monferrato, astride the Po between Piedmont and Lombardy. After it had rebelled against Mantuan rule in 1565, Guglielmo held it in subjection by force. Piedmont had definite designs on it. Guglielmo needed Spanish support to reduce the restive territory, and to quell an incipient uprising backed by the duke of Savoy. Spanish cavalry augmented the Mantuan force of 3,000 troops employed to put down the rebellion.[54]

In contrast, Duke Vincenzo I of Mantua (1587–1612) spent much of his life trying to live up to the dimensions of the chivalric heroes galloping out of the pages of Ariosto and Tasso. Vincenzo too submitted himself to Spanish policy

---

[52] T. Barker, "Ottavio Piccolomini (1599–1659): a fair historical judgement?", in his collection, *Army, aristocracy, monarchy: essays on war, society and government in Austria, 1618–1780* (Boulder, Colorado: 1982), pp. 61–111. For much of his material on Silvio, Barker draws upon the compendium of Fra Isidoro Ugurgieri Azzolini, *Le Pompe Sanesi, overo relazione delli huomini e donne illustri di Siena e suo stato*, 2 vols (Pistoia: 1649), vol. 2, p. 201ff.

[53] N. Giorgetti, *Le Armi toscane e le occupazioni straniere in Toscana (1537–1860)*, vol. 1, p. 399.

[54] G. Coniglio, *I Gonzaga* (Mantua: 1967), pp. 319–23.

aims in the hope of promotion to the stature of Alessandro Farnese. Soon after becoming duke, he lent Philip II 300,000 ducats (the equivalent of a year's taxes) in exchange for the Golden Fleece.[55] Vincenzo built one of Europe's strongest fortresses at Casale Monferrato, as a showcase of Mantuan sovereignty and military power. Ironically the reinforcements destined for it had to request permission from the governor of Milan each time they wished to cross Spanish Lombardy. A decade later Vincenzo was vainly petitioning to serve Spain in the capacity of governor in Flanders, or as admiral of the Spanish fleet.[56] In Mantua itself, Vincenzo modernized the fortifications and built an important and well-stocked arsenal. He had occasion to quarrel with two of his neighbours, Duke Alfonso d'Este of Ferrara, and Duke Ranuccio Farnese of Parma, and in both cases launched punitive cavalry raids across the border.[57] He was disappointed not to play a more decisive role in the Imperial campaigns in Hungary and Croatia, and left that army under a cloud. In 1606 he offered aid to Venice against the Pope, in exchange for the rank of Captain-General of the republic. He swore vengeance when the Serenissima turned him down. After 1608 his thoughts turned more towards the idea of crusade, so he founded a military order to fight the Turks. The Pope, however, offered no concessions of ecclesiastical revenue; Genoa would concede him no ports, and he had no galleys. In 1610 some Albanian refugees convinced him that by raising an army of 10,000 men and sending them across the Adriatic, he could lead a successful insurrection and become king of Albania. A scouting mission to the coast was a complete fiasco, however.[58] When he died in 1612, all dreams of Mantuan military destiny vanished.

The evolution of neighbouring Parma was similar, although the recent establishment of the duchy under the upstart house of Farnese rendered its legitimacy more fragile. Originally from the Lake Bolsena district of northern Latium, they usurped the duchy after Alessandro Farnese became Pope Paul III (1534–50). Piacenzan nobles, angry over the erection of a citadel there, assassinated the first duke, Pier Luigi, on the instigation of the duke of Mantua.[59] Duke Ottavio (1547–88) more cautiously attempted to centralize the duchy and reinforce the prestige of his house. His marriage with the natural daughter of Emperor Charles V aided

---

[55] *Ibid.*, p. 370.

[56] *Ibid.*, p. 377.

[57] M. Bellonci, *A prince of Mantua: the life and times of Vincenzo Gonzaga* (New York: 1956), p. 118 and p. 145.

[58] Bellonci, *A prince of Mantua*, p. 264. For an overview of the various Italian schemes to create kingdoms in the Balkans, of which Vincenzo's was but one, see the book by Angelo Tamborra, *Gli stati italiani, l'Europa e il problema turco dopo Lepanto* (Florence: 1961), p. 53. See by the same author, "Dopo Lepanto: lo spostamento della lotta antiturca sul fronte terrestre", in *Il Mediterraneo nella seconda metà del '500 alla luce di Lepanto*, G. Benzoni (ed.) (Florence: 1974), pp. 371–91.

[59] Giovanni Tocci, *Il ducato di Parma e Piacenza* (Turin: 1987), p. 19.

this design. By conferring important fiefs and jurisdictions on the couple in Lombardy (Novara), the Papal States (Camerino) and the kingdom of Naples, Charles V made certain of the duke's docility. His son Alessandro was raised at the court of Spain. These first three dukes were first and foremost warriors, naturally involved in the maintenance of the Spanish 'system'. A Spanish garrison in Piacenza until 1585 ensured this. After they left, the dukes required only a handful of soldiers to maintain order, such as the 400 soldiers in the castle of Parma, of whom 16 were colonels and captains, and a personal ducal guard composed of 13 Germans. To this tiny force, Ottavio added a militia in 1581, which Ranuccio I refounded and reinforced in 1595. The dukes gave this enormous militia of 37,000 eligible men privileges and exemptions in exchange for service.[60] The dukes selected the colonels and the captains, and paid them from public revenues. Finally, Duke Alessandro desired, purely for reasons of dynastic prestige, that Parma have an imposing citadel of its own. He undertook the project in 1589, and followed its progress from Flanders by letter and by plan. Furthermore, he used his personal resources and credit to build it, without increasing taxation.[61]

Secure in their duchy, the Farnese dukes performed valuable service for the kings of Spain. Alessandro was present at the battle of St Quentin as an adolescent in 1557, and further distinguished himself during the war against the Turks, before departing for the Low Countries in 1575. His son Ranuccio I served under him in France and the Low Countries in 1590, and thereafter episodically contributed his person and Parman resources to expeditions against Moslem pirates. In 1600 he accompanied the expedition against Algiers, with 200 knights and gentlemen adventurers from his state. For these efforts, and as a down-payment on his future compliance, Philip III awarded him the Golden Fleece, and designated him godfather to his eldest daughter in 1602.[62] After the death of Count Fuentes, who was hostile to his house, Ranuccio hoped to be appointed governor of Milan, or be given command of Spanish forces in Italy. He tamely sent contingents to join the Spanish army after the Monferrato crisis erupted in 1613, but never obtained the recompense he desired.[63] Tocci feels that among the Parman nobility, there existed a deep anti-Spanish sentiment that expressed itself in the persistent un-

---

[60] G. Tocci, *Le terre traverse: poteri e territori nei ducati di Parma e Piacenza tra sei e settecento* (Bologna: 1985). Some of the privileges are listed in the book by Giovanni Drei, *I Farnese*, p. 193. On the small garrisons of the Parman state, see Marzio Achille Romani, "Finanza pubblica e potere politico: il caso dei Farnese (1545–1593)", in *Le corti farnesiane di Parma e Piacenza (1545–1622)*, 2 vols (Rome: 1978), pp. 3–78.

[61] Giuseppe Papagno & Marzio Romani, "Una cittadella e una città (il Castello Nuovo farnesiano di Parma, 1589–1597): tensioni sociali e strategie politiche attorno alla contruzione di una fortezza urbana", *Annali dell' Istituto Storico Italo–Germanico di Trento*, **8**, 1982, pp. 141–209.

[62] Drei, *I Farnese*, p. 175.

[63] *Ibid.*, p. 178ff.

popularity of the dynasty. Ranuccio I discovered, or perhaps invented, a plot hatched against his life by leading aristocrats, and destroyed them on the scaffold and by confiscation.[64] New emphasis placed on the court transformed it into a theatre of devotion to the prince.

Like Guglielmo Gonzaga and Ottavio Farnese, Emanuel Philibert of Savoy (1553–80) was a prince of simple tastes. This brilliant general led the Spanish army to decisive victory over the French at St Quentin. He remained Spain's lieutenant in northern Italy for a generation after the end of the Italian wars, ever mindful, however, of solidifying his authority over his own principality. Under his guidance, the Piedmontese attempted to recover territories, including Geneva, lost to the Swiss confederation as a result of the Reformation. Thousands of his soldiers, or Spanish troops in his pay, also served to restore Catholicism in the French wars of religion.[65] His principal military legacy was the establishment of a territorial militia in his alpine state, and the creation of a military infrastructure serving himself more than the king of Spain.[66]

Quixotic is how one might describe the next duke of Savoy, Charles Emanuel I (1580–1630), who spent his long reign chasing crowns and seeking vainly to extend the frontiers of Piedmont in every direction. Of the six princely dynasties in north-central Italy, only Piedmont under Charles Emanuel stepped out of line. Until 1600, however, he deployed his efforts against France, and tried as well to recover the lost district of Geneva. In these ventures, the Piedmontese were Spanish allies, often with the benefit of Spanish troops in ducal pay.[67] The sole success was to seize the marquisate of Saluzzo, a French-held fief in Piedmont in 1588.[68] Piedmontese intervention in support of the Catholic League and an invasion of Provence backfired when the French conquered and annexed the territory of Bresse, north of the Rhône, in 1600. Charles Emanuel next looked

---

[64] Giovanni Tocci discusses the anti-Spanish current in aristocratic circles in *Il ducato di Parma e Piacenza*, p. 44. On the details of the supposed plot to kill Ranuccio, see Giovanna Solari, *The house of Farnese* (New York: 1968; first publ. 1964), p. 141ff.

[65] For example, the 6,400 foot and horse serving under Alfonso d'Este in 1567: see E. Faldella, *Storia degli eserciti italiani, da Emanuele Filiberto di Savoia ai nostri giorni* (n.p.: 1976), p. 16.

[66] The literature on the dukes of Savoy is voluminous. For Emanuel Philibert and his military proclivities, see N. Brancaccio, *L'esercito del vecchio Piemonte: gli ordinamenti, vol. 1, 1560–1814* (Rome: 1923), pp. 14–60; Vittorio Mariani & Varo Varanini, *Condottieri italiani in Germania* (Milan: 1941), p. 47ff. Recent works include Martha Pollak, *Turin, 1564–1680: urban design, military culture and the creation of the absolutist capital* (Chicago: 1991), pp. 16–19; R. Devos & B. Grosperrin, *La Savoie de la Réforme à la Révolution* (Rennes: 1985), pp. 38–50, covers the same material from a Savoyard perspective. The military preparations are set into their sixteenth-century context in the thesis of Walter Barberis, *Le armi del principe: la tradizione militare sabauda* (Turin: 1988), pp. 7–35. See also Pierpaolo Merlin, *Tra guerre e tornei* (Turin: 1991), pp. 1–3.

[67] Devos & Grosperrin, *La Savoie de la Réforme à la Révolution*, p. 47ff.

[68] Merlin, *Tra guerre e tornei*, p. 11ff.

towards France for subsidies and troops in order to expand in Italy. That was to bring him into collision with Madrid.

Wars of religion in Flanders and France

Most Italian military nobles were ready to devote their military talents to the crown of Spain. Only a few score seem to have preferred exile in France at the close of the Italian wars. There they offered their swords to royal and Catholic armies as the kingdom sank into protracted civil wars over religion, from 1561 to 1594.[69] A few struck roots there: the Gonzaga-Nevers became part of the great French aristocracy. Some of the families siding with the king of France before the emperor took control of the peninsula were obliged to leave. The Fieschi and Fregoso of Genoa, the Strozzi of Florence, and the Ornano of Corsica figure among these important exiles. Some Sienese departed after the duke of Florence, Cosimo I, annexed their homeland. A handful of Florentines was attached to the clientèle of the queens, Caterina de'Medici, and Maria de'Medici after 1600. Overall, the number of Italian courtiers in France, especially in comparison to Spain, appears to have been modest. These exiles were joined after 1562 by Italian reinforcements to the Catholic cause, when it seemed that France was about to topple into the heretic camp. Both Philip II of Spain and the Pope subsidized soldiers in the French religious wars, primarily German and Italian professionals. In July 1562, Pope Pius IV dispatched his own nephew to France with 2,500 infantry.[70] The Queen Regent entrusted Pietro Strozzi with a separate command. During the second civil war, triggered by the Huguenot rising of 1567, more troops from Piedmont and the Papal states joined Strozzi's army in Poitou. Pius V raised 4,000 foot and 800 horse from central Italy to fight in France in 1569 under the count of Santa Fiore. They were accompanied by a thousand others sent by Duke Cosimo of Florence, who needed Papal consent to acquire the granducal title.[71] These Italians figured prominently in the defence of Poitiers, the siege of Châtellerault and the battle of Moncontour, on 3 October 1569, where they numbered about 700 horse and 2,500 foot, a fifth of the royal army.[72] During the wars of the League after 1588, Charles Emanuel of Savoy intervened actively against the royalists under Henri IV, occupying first the marquisate of Saluzzo in Piedmont, and then scheming to detach all of southern France east of the Rhône. With Spanish subsidies and support, Piedmont waged fruitless war against France

---

[69] The Encyclopedia notes that two important nobles converted to Calvinism and fought for them, for a time at least: the Neapolitan Ferrante San Severino, and Enrico di Savoia. See C. Argegni, *Condottieri, capitani, tribuni*, vol. 3, p. 122; and *ibid.*, vol. 3, p. 177.

[70] J. W. Thompson, *The wars of religion in France* (New York: 1910), p. 157.

[71] F. Rocquain, *La France et Rome pendant les guerres de religion* (Paris: 1924), p. 85.

[72] Thompson, *The wars of religion in France*, p. 383.

continuously from 1588 until 1601.[73] Finally, in the critical years of Henri IV's reign as a Protestant monarch, the papacy made a tremendous effort to topple him. Gregory XIV Sfondrato raised 6,000 Swiss and 3,000 Italians under his Milanese nephew Ercole Sfondrato, to help the Catholic League. By taking the Spanish road over the Alps to Lorraine, they joined Farnese's army campaigning in Normandy and the Ile de France.[74] Soon after, Clement VIII Aldobrandini dispatched shiploads of soldiers, reportedly 8,000 in all, to Avignon in an attempt to stem the Huguenot progress.[75]

Just as crucial to the political scene of sixteenth-century Europe was the spread of Calvinism from France to the Netherlands in the 1560s, culminating in the anti-Spanish revolt there. The rebellion always maintained this double quality, of subjects rising against their legitimate prince, and of a religious war. If the king of Spain's generals sometimes downplayed the religious component, both Spanish and Italian memorialists and historians felt that religion was the principal issue, and that the army furthered the Catholic cause.[76] Italian noble warriors in search of a cause now that the conclusion of the wars of Italy brought peace to their homelands found one here. Most Italian warriors joined Habsburg service, and of the two branches, Madrid's was without doubt the larger, richer and more ambitious. Joining the Spanish banner, they were integrated into the largest and most modern army of the period.

The Spanish infantry *tercios* were named after the place where they were quartered in peacetime, while new ones took the name of their commander, the *maestro di campo* or the colonel. Its full complement varied between 1,200 and 1,600 men, according to the prestige and authority of the recruiting captains. In the late sixteenth century the Spanish and Italian *tercios* consisted of eight or ten companies of 200 men or less. To raise a *tercio*, the royal treasury contracted with the company commander, the captain, to muster the desired number of soldiers. The contracting captain had the right to designate officers, the lieutenants and ensigns, and left room as well for a few gentlemen adventurers and volunteers who received preferred treatment and drew higher pay.[77] Companies in any case were not permanent units, but were recruited to operate in a wartime field army, to supplement the garrisons. Each consisted of a captain, an ensign, a sergeant and ten corporals, two drummers and a fife, and roughly one hundred and fifty ranks. The ratio of officers to men in a full-strength company was quite low, although gentlemen volunteers linked officers and ranks and helped keep morale high. At

---

[73] R. Quazza, *Storia politica d'Italia: preponderanza spagnuola (1559–1700)*, p. 389ff.

[74] Rocquain, *La France et Rome pendant les guerres de religion*, p. 438.

[75] Guglielmotti, *Storia della marina pontificia, vol. VII: La squadra permanente*, p. 92.

[76] L. van der Essen, "Croisade contre les hérétiques ou guerre contre des rebelles? La psychologie des soldats et des officiers espagnols de l'armée de Flandre au XVIe siècle", *Revue d'Histoire Ecclésiastique*, 1956, pp. 42–78.

[77] L. van der Essen, *Alexandre Farnèse, Gouverneur-Général des Pays-Bas (1545–1592)*, 5 vols (Brussels: 1935), vol. 2, pp. 8–15.

a higher level, the regimental staff consisted of the *maestro di campo*; the second-in-command, the *sergente-maggiore*, who was frequently the effective commander in the field; the provisions officer or quartermaster; and a field-officer of justice. Characteristic of the *tercio* (and quite rare in other armies) was the presence of chaplains or almoners, generally friars.

I have never found sources attesting explicitly to the geographical origins of the soldiery. Many seem to have been recruited by officers they knew personally. All carried swords and daggers, but the main combat arms consisted of pikes and arquebuses.[78] It was the older weapon, the pike, which required more training and expertise in battle for, to be effective, pikemen had to learn to wield that weapon in unison. At the end of the wars of Italy, an infantry unit might comprise six pikemen for every arquebusier, but that ratio diminished gradually until, by 1600, half or more of the soldiers bore firearms.[79] What rendered the Spanish units superior to their adversaries in an open battle was their ability to dissolve their great squares into companies and small units where firepower dominated.[80] Cavalry was fairly ineffectual against disciplined bodies of infantry, so mounted troops generally only constituted from five to ten per cent of an army. There was still the occasional company of heavily-armoured gens d'armes, or noble men-at-arms on armoured mounts, employed for charges with lances in close formation. Companies of them were retained for ceremonial purposes after those tactics were abandoned. More common, however, were companies of mounted arquebusiers, a light cavalry for reconnaissance, foraging and skirmishing. This was apparently a Neapolitan strength, although Spain also levied companies of Albanians, who were sometimes Italians by birth or by naturalization. Their task was to serve as scouts, and to find fodder and livestock necessary for the maintenance of the army on campaign, or else to punish recalcitrant villages for non-compliance.[81] Marauding was their real speciality.

The Castilian Duke of Alba's success in wielding such troops effectively in Italy in the war against Pope Paul IV Carafa in 1555–9 led Philip II to entrust him with repressing the rebellion in the Low Countries in 1567. Alba gathered the *tercios* of Naples, Lombardy, Sicily and Sardinia (most of whom were in effect Spaniards), and marched them over the Alps. Alba established supply stations, or *étapes* through Piedmont, Franche-Comté and Lorraine to keep his units fed. Braudel writes of an army of 5,000 Spaniards and 7,000 Italians, the best troops available, making the journey northwards. Maltby counts 8,650 infantry and 1,200 horse,

---

[78] The equipment of the Hispano-Italian forces is described in the work by René Quatrefages, "Un professionnel militaire: l'*Infante* du *Tercio*", in *L'homme de guerre au XVI siècle* (Saint-Etienne: 1992), pp. 191–204. The context and a broader view of the tactical evolution is treated in the book by Geoffrey Parker, *The military revolution: military innovation and the rise of the West, 1500–1800* (Cambridge: 1988).

[79] Parker, *The military revolution*, p. 17ff, on the development of volley tactics.

[80] Quatrefages, "Un professionnel militaire", in *L'homme de guerre au XVIe siècle*, p. 196.

[81] L. van der Essen, *Les Italiens en Flandre au XVIe et au XVIIe siècle* (Brussels: 1926), p. 11.

with Alba in command, seconded by the Tuscan Chiappino Vitelli. Whatever the number of troops, contemporaries were struck by their smart appearance, their gorgeous equipment and their discipline. Once engaged in the ferocious repression of rebels, both Catholic and Calvinist, troop discipline broke down quickly.[82]

Alba's Hispano-Italian army was the first to cross the Alps in the direction of Flanders, along a corridor that became known as the 'Spanish Road'. Italian contingents generally comprised from ten to twenty per cent of the entire Spanish army in Flanders, and this ratio remained roughly constant until after 1640.[83] Alba relied on Spanish and Italian administrators to govern the rebellious provinces, just as he relied on Spanish and Italian troops and commanders to carry out orders with enthusiasm. This further marginalized and antagonized the Flemish, Walloon and German aristocracy.[84] The severity of Alba's repression ultimately resulted in his recall to Spain. Since his ferocity resolved none of the issues behind the revolt, resentment exploded again in 1573. France was only too eager to offer refuge to the rebels, as were German Protestant states, spurring the Netherlanders to widen their rebellion. In the 1570s, Philip II tried to contain the rebellion and shore up his support with the aid of troops raised in the Low Countries themselves, but they turned out to be insufficient to the task.[85] Gradually, Spain relied on foreign troops, most of whom were probably subjects of the House of Austria. About 5,000 Spaniards and 4,000 Italians in four *tercios* arrived there in 1582. The Italian contribution compared well to the Spanish one. One historian lists 18 separate Italian *tercios* dispatched to the theatre between 1565 and 1600.[86] They attracted a large number of noble adventurers or volunteers from the peninsula who placed themselves under the commander-in-chief, Alessandro Farnese, duke of Parma. Croce aptly states that the hearts, thoughts and imaginations of a generation of Italian nobles were turned towards the plains of 'Flanders'. Reading the letters and reports of friends and relatives, they became familiar with the region before setting out for it themselves. This interminable distant war served as a military school for loyal subjects, and simultaneously purged the Italian dominions of bad characters.[87] By the end of 1582 there were 60,000 men in this 'Spanish' army, representing almost every nation in Europe. To offset this force, the Dutch and Walloon rebels forged alliances with French Huguenots, England

---

[82] W. Maltby, *Alba: a biography of Fernando Alvarez de Toledo, third Duke of Alba, 1507–1582* (Berkeley, California: 1983), p. 142.

[83] R. A. Stradling, *Europe and the decline of Spain: a study of the Spanish system, 1580–1720* (London: 1981), p. 60ff.

[84] Maltby, *Alba*, p. 264.

[85] A comprehensive account of the Dutch revolt, based on vast archival erudition, is Geoffrey Parker's *The Dutch revolt* (Harmondsworth, Middlesex: 1977).

[86] Olesa Muñido, *La organizacion naval de los estados mediterraneos*, vol. 2, p. 832.

[87] Croce, "I Caracciolo d'Avellino", in *Uomini e cose della vecchia Italia* (Bari: 1927), p. 150.

and German Protestant states, and hired foreign mercenaries from Scotland to Hungary. 'Flanders' became the rendezvous of those who desired to learn the art of war, and it remained the foremost arena of military competition throughout the seventeenth century.

While Italian units were identical in structure to Spanish ones, they were less highly esteemed. Philip II did not trust them much at first, but there were not enough Castilians to go around; perhaps there were never more than 10,000 of them in the theatre. Spanish troops were frequently veterans, while the Italian levies were more often raw recruits. Different nationalities were held to excel in different kinds of situations. General military opinion held that, while the Italians were as brave as the Spaniards, they lacked resilience. Italians were thus choice troops in an assault, a skirmish or improvised encounters. They were considered excellent as light horsemen, for harassing, skirmishing and ambushing the enemy.[88] These mounted arquebusiers fought generally on foot, as precursors to dragoons. Their commander and commissioner-general was Giorgio Basta, an Italian of Albanian descent, who wrote an instruction manual for that arm.

Italians had no peers in the technical arms of artillery and fortification. Between 1554 and 1600, of the 32 published works on fortification we can account for, 26 are Italian, four French, two Spanish, one is German and one Dutch.[89] French kings imported almost all their engineers from Italy around the mid-sixteenth century, to erect fortifications and to improve artillery.[90] In Flanders, they were propagators of the Italian trace in both the construction of fixed fortresses and in field fortification. Van der Essen names several who were active in the theatre and renowned in their day, like Francesco Paciotto, architect of the massive citadel of Antwerp, Pompeo Targone, Properzio Barocchi and Rafaello Barberini, uncle of the future pope.[91] Even the duke of Parma designed fortifications and employed hydraulic devices in the attack and defence of places. The crucial siege of Antwerp in 1585 was a contest of Italian engineering skill: the defector Federigo Giannibelli built a floating explosive device that destroyed Parma's pontoon blockade, but Farnese ultimately prevailed by constructing water diversions, field fortifications and dykes.[92] Experienced Italians went also to Spain to train gunners and engineers, where they enjoyed great prestige and were commissioned with the greatest

---

[88] Van der Essen, *Les Italiens en Flandre au XVIe et au XVIIe siècle* (Brussels: 1926), p. 20.
[89] H. Vérin, *La gloire des ingénieurs: l'intelligence technique du XVIe au XVIIIe siècle* (Paris: 1993), p. 96.
[90] Vérin, *La gloire des ingénieurs*, p. 112.
[91] Van der Essen, Les Italiens en Flandre, p. 24. On Paciotto, see Dennistoun, *Memoirs of the dukes of Urbino*, vol. 3, p. 249. On fortifications experts, see Pollak, *Turin, 1564–1680*, p. 5. For such engineers in Spanish service generally, see David C. Goodman's book, *Power and penury: government, technology and science in Philip II's Spain* (Cambridge: 1988), pp. 125–9.
[92] On the siege of Antwerp, see Parker, *The Dutch revolt*, pp. 214–15. On Federico Gianibelli's contribution to the rebel cause, see Solari, *The House of Farnese*, p. 73.

projects. Goodman notes how few Spaniards were considered competent in this business, and that all of the 25 foreigners employed there were Italians.[93] Italians also invented many 'machines' of war, most of which proved impractical. They offered, among the more intriguing designs, prototypes for rapid-firing artillery, transportable bridges, and "a multi-barrelled arquebus arranged in rows, on a tripod, four to a wagon".[94]

Alessandro Farnese, heir to the duchy of Parma, commanded the Spanish forces in the theatre from 1578 until shortly before his death in 1593. Alessandro grew up at the court of Spain, and, convinced of the righteousness of Philip II's cause, wanted nothing more than to fight for it. After serving under Don Juan (to whom he was very close), in the Lepanto expedition, he followed him to Flanders in 1577 to serve as understudy, and on the death of the prince the following year, was considered the logical choice to succeed him. Farnese was considered a strict disciplinarian, who sometimes executed officers for insubordination. An expert on the employment of mercenaries, he was deemed most capable of reducing a polyglot assembly of companies and *tercios* to work cohesively. He created a praetorian guard of Italians and Albanians with which he tried to prevent or repress the mutinies for lack of pay.

Farnese oversaw the rapid build-up of Spanish forces in the theatre. The army that numbered only 35,000 in 1570 attained 70,000 troops in the 1590s, and some years even more, making it Europe's largest permanent force since Roman times.[95] Some 20 to 30 per cent of this number arrived every year in new recruits to maintain these numbers, compensating for losses due to battle, disease and desertion. Farnese maintained control partly through the creation of a corps of élite officers, the *entretenidos*, of whom there were several score, entrusted with special missions or dangerous assignments. As Captain-General and Governor-General of the Low Countries, he lived an opulent lifestyle at his 'court' in Brussels, surrounded by a numerous retinue of Spanish, Italian, German and 'Belgian' courtiers, and a turbulent crowd of aides, servants and *bravi* (hired assassins, frequently employed in Italy), some 1,500 people in all. It was all that he could do to prevent the ticklish honour of sixteenth-century nobles from erupting into internecine combat. Intractable problems of protocol and precedence were posed by competing Spanish and Italian *maestri di campo*, and other prepotent aristocrats. Farnese paid his Spanish units more, and more regularly, because

---

[93] D. Goodman, *Power and penury*, pp. 125–9. One illustrious example was Tiburzio Spannocchi of Siena, see Ugurgieri Azzolini, *Le Pompe Sanesi*, vol. 1, p. 668; or G. Hanlon, "The demilitarization of an Italian provincial aristocracy: Siena (1560–1740)", *Past and Present*, **155**, 1997, pp. 64–108.

[94] Goodman, *Power and penury*, p. 129. See the Encyclopedia for Pompeo Targone's prototype of a tank. C. Argegni, *Condottieri, capitani, tribuni*, vol. 3, p. 304.

[95] For fluctuations in the effective numbers in the army of Flanders, see Geoffrey Parker, *The army of Flanders and the Spanish Road, 1567–1659: the logistics of Spanish victory and defeat in the Low Countries' wars* (Cambridge: 1972), p. 29ff.

everyone considered them élite troops.[96] Apart from that precaution, he was held to be partial to the Italians.

By years of sieges, surprises, skirmishes and the occasional battle, Farnese consolidated his hold on the southern Low Countries. To Namur and Arras, he added Brussels, Antwerp, the Flemish coast and most of the northern Netherlands to the lands controlled by Spain. From the capture of Maastricht in 1579 to that of Antwerp in 1585, the prince of Parma and his generals captured thirty major towns. His light cavalry penetrated deep into enemy territory to forage and skirmish, and the Dutch rebels were increasingly inclined to talk of submission. By seeking to reconcile and pardon, Farnese himself was more elastic than his master, Philip II, who could tolerate no Protestants in his states. Massive English intervention on the side of the rebels in 1586 slowed his progress. It still seemed likely in 1587 that the Army of Flanders would constrain the rebels to settle. At precisely that moment, however, Philip II decided to change targets.

The diversion of resources away from Flanders and towards the Armada against England, took the pressure off the Dutch at the critical moment. Farnese was ordered to interrupt his sieges and collect an invasion army of 20,000 men near the English channel. Professional soldiers on board the Armada itself matched this number. He scattered the remaining troops of the Army of Flanders across scores of strongpoints. Spanish strategy shifted to the static defence of a series of forts and earthworks facing the Dutch behind their own similar defences. Complete failure of the Armada in 1588 at least liberated Farnese for operations against Holland. The assassination of Henri III in 1589, however, triggered the most paroxysmic phase of the French wars of religion, when the new Protestant Bourbon king Henri IV lay siege to Paris, which held for the Catholic League. Philip ordered Farnese to intervene in the French civil war on the side of the League and lift the siege of Paris. Farnese's troops were more than a match for Henri IV, but France was not a theatre in which a decisive result could be achieved quickly.[97] Philip II finally dismissed the duke of Parma in 1592 for disobeying instructions to use the Army of Flanders to more effect in northern France. The Dutch under Maurice of Orange-Nassau profited from this respite to mark points and occupy towns along the Flemish coast and the Scheldt estuary.

Thereafter, war in Flanders slowed to a static affair of skirmishes and sieges along the line of earthwork fortifications. Once the Dutch mastered the intricacies of Italian design with makeshift but effective earth works, the contest of attrition continued until the king exhausted his credit. Spain's financial overextension gradually paralyzed its crack army. The entire silver fleet income from Mexico barely covered ten per cent of the huge expenditures. Spanish troops were em-

---

[96] Parker, *The army of Flanders and the Spanish Road*, p. 108.
[97] The details of both the reconquest of the Low Countries and the quagmire of the French religious wars are treated in great detail in the monumental work by Léon van der Essen, *Alexandre Farnèse, prince de Parme, gouverneur-général des Pays-Bas (1545–1592)*, 5 vols (Brussels: 1935–9).

ployed on galleys and the Indies galleons; explored and extended the reach of the Catholic king from Chile to Florida; stood watch along the Iberian coast and in the Pyrenees, in the Balearic islands and the north African coast; sweltered in garrisons along the coasts of Naples, Sicily, Sardinia, and Tuscany; supported Piedmontese forays into Provence and Switzerland; guarded Milan and the alpine passes; stiffened the frontier against the Turks in Hungary; and clung grimly to the Irish coast to divert the queen of England. With so many vital points to garrison, it proved impossible to support the Army of Flanders. The troops themselves went unpaid and ill-fed for years and lacked every kind of equipment. With the accession of Philip III in 1598, the monarchy's military expenditures equalled total tax revenue. The monarchy avoided financial collapse only because foreign financiers, mainly Genoese, found the high rates of interest on Spanish loans irresistible.[98]

Farnese's removal and his death in 1593 lifted the relative protection by which the Italians benefited. Spanish commanders lost no time avenging past slights, humiliating Italian officers and mistreating their *tercios*. After 1590 Italian units practically ceased to be paid, at least under normal circumstances. Discipline again deteriorated. Even under Farnese, whenever troops went unpaid for extended periods, they deserted to scrounge for food and plunder the peasantry.[99] Like other soldiers, the Italians had women and children to maintain (probably themselves not often Italians), since a host of civilians followed the armies. Troops eventually learned to mutiny to demand pay and provisions. There were forty major mutinies in the Army of Flanders in the twenty years after 1590, and complaints were especially vociferous in the Italian garrisons. At Aerschot in 1594 and 1596, six companies of the *tercio* of Don Gastone Spìnola mutinied for not having received any pay for six or seven years. They threatened to go over to the Dutch who, if they were heretics, at least had a better reputation for paying their soldiers. These were merely threats, because a senior Italian officer, Giovanni Giacomo di Belgioioso, was able to placate them, like almost all the mutinous units. More serious was the mutiny of the *tercios* of Vespasiano Carcano, and of Sanminiato: they seized the town of Sichem in Brabant and invited other soldiers to join them. The archduke Ernesto ordered Camillo Caràcciolo to besiege the town and end the mutiny, but the Neapolitan rejected the order, as did all the other Italian commanders in the theatre.[100] These dramas underscore the gradual

---

[98] Valeri indicates that Philip II borrowed money at five to seven per cent interest in good years, but this was often the camouflage for more devious means of mining the resources of the Spanish empire. See Nino Valeri & Vittorio de Caprariis, *L'Italia nell' età della controriforma, 1559–1700* (Turin: 1965), vol. 2, p. 495.

[99] Van der Essen, *Les Italiens en Flandre*, p. 16ff.; see also Parker, *The army of Flanders and the Spanish Road*, p. 195.

[100] Croce, "I Caracciolo d'Avellino", in *Uomini e cose della vecchia Italia*, p. 148; see also Parker, *The Dutch revolt*, pp. 230–2.

paralysis of the Spanish army as the war of Flanders wore on. Moreover, Italian commanders were victims of insubordination by ethnic Spanish officers: Ferrante Gonzaga, a cavalry general, was humiliated in such a manner in 1600, and Francesco Bourbon del Monte Santa Maria resigned his commission because of another incident.[101]

Seemingly endless warfare placed increasing stress on the human resources of Spain too, beginning with Castile. In 1575, the duke of Alba calculated that 43,000 Castilians had left the kingdom since 1567, mostly in a military capacity, and not including emigrants to the Indies. This represented perhaps four per cent of the adult male population of that kingdom. He could find only a handful of Spanish veterans for his army that conquered Portugal in 1580, and relied on Germans and Italians for the rest.[102] New levies were also those that experienced the heaviest losses, whatever their nationality. In 1587 some 9,000 Italian infantry marched to Flanders, but a year later there were only 3,600 left, the others having died or deserted. Soldiers contracted incurable diseases like syphilis, malaria and tuberculosis, and Italians especially found the humid and cold climate of the Netherlands difficult to adapt to. Desertion among Spaniards and Italians tended to be lower than for other nationalities; Parker calculates such losses at 1.5 per cent monthly in the 1580s, compared with two to seven per cent for soldiers of other origins. If soldiers deserted, it might be to enrol in some other unit, or to serve in Catholic armies of the emperor in Hungary, or to fight in the French wars of religion. Recruiters found it ever more difficult to fill out their companies. After deducting all the garrisons, the field forces of the Spanish army of Flanders in 1598 numbered no more than 20,000 infantry, of whom about 6,000 were Spanish and 2,000 Italians.[103] The archduke, Albert, was only able to muster less than half that number to attack a Dutch army isolated in the dunes outside Nieuwport in 1600, where Spain suffered its first significant defeat in a set-piece battle at the hands of Maurice of Nassau. Since the Dutch were not strong enough on land to recapture significant towns in areas held by Spain, the stalemate continued.

Officers gradually withdrew too, or their motives for serving changed. It became apparent than an officer's ostentatious lifestyle was unlikely to be supported by his pay, and the strategic impasse precluded capturing rich booty. Increasingly the crown confided leading posts to contractors who could afford to raise their own companies, or would-be courtiers who needed to make their curriculum vitae look attractive to the king. Military service gradually became a rite of passage

---

[101] On Francesco Bourbon del Monte Santa Maria (1559–1622), see Aldo Valori, *Condottieri e generali del Seicento*, Enciclopedia biografica e bibliografica 'italiana' (Rome: 1946), p. 53.
[102] Maltby, *Alba*, p. 280ff.
[103] C. Martinez de Campos, *España belica: el siglo XVII* (Madrid: 1967), p. 34.

instead of a career commitment.[104] The Spanish nobles are said to have with-drawn from war as a career at this juncture.[105]

Paradoxically, the stalemate was broken when Philip III gave command of his army to a rich Genoese financier with little military experience. Ambrogio Spìnola, born in 1569, excelled at mathematics at school, and seemed destined like other patricians to pursue a mercantile vocation. Deeply embroiled in the finances of the Spanish monarchy, these patricians were all dependent on the outcome of the struggle in Flanders. His enterprising younger brother, Federigo Spìnola, joined Spanish service in 1591 as a gentleman adventurer at sea, and at the age of 20 was already considered an expert in galley warfare. He equipped four galleys at his own expense and leased them to Spanish service. Still in his early twenties, Federigo Spìnola submitted a report in 1593 to the Spanish crown suggesting that a galley squadron be established on the coast of Flanders with the aim of raiding Dutch maritime commerce in the Rhine, Meuse and Scheldt estuaries.[106] In 1597 Philip III called him to Madrid as a consultant advising galley raids against the English coast, and Federigo offered 470,000 ducats of his own money to launch the project. The raids were so successful that the English and Dutch seriously considered building their own galleys to counter the threat to shipping and coastal security. In 1600, Federigo (to whom Stradling refers as a "maritime genius") led a flotilla of nine Italian galleys from the Mediterranean to Dunkirk, with troops on board. Under his direction, the flotilla was remarkably successful at tormenting the Dutch coast and plundering its commerce. After he was killed in 1603 in a naval engagement off Ostend, the fleet was gradually laid up for lack of money.[107]

Meanwhile, Ambrogio was required to marry and continue the dynasty, and dabbled in the treacherous waters of Genoese republican and municipal politics by vying for pre-eminence with the house of Doria. Disgusted with his lack of success, he decided to join Spanish service in 1599 to gain distinctions and honours that would finally ensure the pre-eminence of his house. After the defeat of Archduke Albert at the battle of the Dunes, Ambrogio offered to raise 8,000 men at his own expense, in exchange for sole command over them. The bargain was not entirely altruistic, for Spìnola was to be reimbursed for the outlay, and

---

[104] Quatrefages, "Un professionnel militaire: l'*Infante* du *Tercio*", in *L'homme de guerre au XVIe siècle*, pp. 191–204.

[105] Henry Kamen, *Spain 1469–1714: a society of conflict* (London: 1983), p. 244.

[106] This flotilla has been the object of research by several British scholars: Hubert Reade deals with it in his substantial and often insightful book, *Sidelights on the Thirty Years War* (London: 1924), vol. 1, p. 9ff.; see the article by R. Gray, "Spinola's galleys in the narrow seas", *Mariner's Mirror*, **64**, 1978, pp. 71–83. Most recently, R. A. Stradling devotes a chapter to it in his work on the 'Spanish' naval forces in Flanders, *The armada of Flanders: Spanish maritime policy and European war, 1568–1668* (Cambridge: 1992), p. 13ff.

[107] Stradling, *The armada of Flanders*, p. 13.

be paid interest in the interim, along with several perks, such as a cardinal's hat for one of his sons, grain export licences from Sicily, and the right to provide galleys to transport coin across the Mediterranean. Like other military enterprisers, he also made a middleman's profit by equipping these men, and retaining the pay due to casualties and deserters. Nevertheless, to advance huge sums of money to the desperate Spanish monarchy in 1602 entailed enormous financial risk. The appointment was advantageous for Spain too, for military operations required such massive borrowing. Ambrogio was familiar with the milieu of Genoese finance, and could find credit in hidden places. Much of the money for the operation, a huge treasure of two million ducats, was his family's own. Over time, he may have advanced five million florins to the Spanish treasury, and was not repaid in full until 1619. Spìnola was therefore not simply a military commander, but remained a financier, a politician and an administrator of the Low Countries, all roles in which, providentially for Spain, he displayed enormous talent.[108]

With 8,000 fresh troops mustered in northern Italy, many of whom were veterans, Ambrogio Spìnola broke the strategic deadlock in Flanders. He could be a harsh disciplinarian, and hanged 100 of these men to restore march discipline. When he reached the Low Countries in July 1602, he raised an additional 5,000 Walloons and Germans to constitute a field army capable of important projects. Archduke Albert gave him enough autonomy to have effective command of all the forces in the theatre. Spìnola gave priority to the siege of Ostend, held by the Dutch and continually supplied by sea. His field army of 15,000 men gradually inched towards the massive fortifications by dint of fieldworks and redoubts. Italian engineers played the leading technical role. Drawing their pay more regularly, the troops sapped and mined with more enthusiasm.[109] In the last twenty months of siege, an estimated 18,000 besiegers died (and were replaced), and some 250,000 cannonballs and 50,000 bombs were fired.[110] The successful conclusion of the epic siege in 1604 established Spìnola's reputation as a soldier and a strategist. In subsequent years, he staked his personal credit and reputation to raise new troops for offensive operations against the northern Netherlands itself.[111] To succeed, he needed two field armies, one operating on each side of the

---

[108] On Spinola as a military commander, see Reade, *Sidelights on the Thirty Years War*, vol. 1, pp. 16–56. Parker discusses his role as a military administrator, in *The army of Flanders and the Spanish Road, 1567–1659*, p. 116. His political finesse in the Low Countries, and his relations with Archduke Albert, are discussed in the work by Henri Pirenne, *Histoire de Belgique des origines à nos jours*, vol. 2 (Brussels: n.d., *circa* 1939), p. 390.

[109] E. Belleroche, "The siege of Ostend: or the New Troy, 1601–1604", *Proceedings of the Huguenot Society of London*, vol. 3, 1889, pp. 427–539, at p. 472ff.

[110] Martinez de Campos, *España belica: el siglo XVII*, p. 42.

[111] The campaign of 1606 was launched on a loan in Genoa on Spinola's own security, of 2 million *scudi*. See Reade, *Sidelights on the Thirty Years' War*, vol. 1, p. 42.

Rhine. The capture of the river fortress of Rheinberg in 1606 unlocked new possibilities, and allowed him to occupy much of Friesland. Credit ran out soon after. The sudden loss of territory convinced Maurice of Orange-Nassau that he should strike a truce with the king of Spain, but Spìnola was eager to conclude one too, before the complete financial ruin of the monarchy.[112]

Another part of Spìnola's success lay in his ability, like Farnese, to co-ordinate troops of different nationalities. In 1610 one of his Neapolitan colonels, Lelio Brancaccio, complained of the rigid protocol that resulted in continuous litigation between Spanish and Italian officers, creating confusion in the camps, the order of march and even during battle.[113] Spìnola could co-ordinate the Spanish, Italian, Walloon and German contingents effectively, and as Lieutenant-General of the Low Countries after 1605 dispensed his patronage even-handedly. Like his predecessor Farnese, he maintained an opulent court in Brussels, surrounded by aides and a troop of noble guards. This was a training ground for a whole generation of senior Italian officers and future generals. Besides Giorgio Basta, there was Pompeo Giustiniani, a Corsican-born Genoese patrician who trained German troops for siege warfare at Ostend before receiving autonomous detachments and screening forces to command; and Silvio Piccolòmini, a captain in the *tercio* of Camillo Capizucchi, before becoming a leader of Tuscan forces on land and sea. There were six or seven Italian infantry *tercios* serving in Flanders at any one moment, employing hundreds of regular officers and gentlemen adventurers from all over the peninsula.

The confidence of the archduke, Albert – Philip II's representative in Brussels, who commanded the army there before Spìnola's arrival, but who was unlucky in war – contributed to Spìnola's success. When in 1605 the former Genoese banker was given the title of *Maestro di Campo Generale* with complete control over the army, the archduke was deprived of the better part of his authority and prestige. Far from being jealous, Albert took Spìnola into his confidence and made him a kind of *maire du palais*, the real power behind the throne. The Genoese thus directed the war effort alone, with little interference.[114] Spìnola retained command over Spanish forces in the Low Countries after the truce of 1609, and used his rank to insert his family into the Spanish court. His influence obtained a military command for his son Filippo, whose talents were mediocre. The Genoese banker–general rivalled the houses of Lerma and Guzman (Olivares) for political influence in the reigns of Philip III and Philip IV. Ironically, the general was a moderating influence on Spanish imperialism, mindful of the financial stake he held in royal finances. More charitably, he appreciated the military limits of the Catholic king.[115]

---

[112] Parker, *The Dutch revolt*, pp. 237–40.

[113] Martinez de Campos, *Espana belica: el siglo XVII*, p. 18.

[114] Pirenne, *Histoire de Belgique des origines à nos jours*, p. 390.

[115] Stradling, *The armada of Flanders*, p. 66.

Crusade in Hungary against Islam

Historians have often dismissed the Holy Roman Empire and the Imperial mystique as an outworn relic of medieval times, of which Charles V briefly revived the shadow but not the substance. Early in his reign, however, Charles taxed independent states in Italy on the basis of his Imperial title alone. Most of the minor principalities, such as Massa-Carrara, Mirandola, the Malaspina in the Lunigiana, Lucca, Siena and the host of tiny fiefs in the Langhe freely recognized Imperial suzerainty. This attachment was not reciprocated, however: Italy, apart from Savoy, was for the Empire a conquered land without representation in the Imperial Diet. Pugliese thought that Imperial jurisdiction in Italy was deliberately left ambiguous to allow for future claims. Although north Italian states were clients of the king in Madrid, they never ceased to depend legally on the emperor with his seat in the Danubian hereditary lands. The power of the emperor in Italy was to a large degree a legal fiction in 1560. The only reason Italians needed the emperor at all was to arbitrate their competition for titles and precedence, or confirm investiture when a direct line became extinguished.

After the division of the House of Austria into two branches in 1554, the German side was very much the junior partner. The emperors' poverty forced them to consent to Spanish hegemony in Italy. These sovereigns had only limited means of suasion to raise money and troops, even from territories and cities inside the Habsburg patrimonial lands. Emperor Ferdinand I stooped to selling the granducal title to Cosimo I for 100,000 ducats in 1569, so desperate was he for funds with which to confront the Turks.[116] Pugliese estimates his ordinary revenues at 1.2 million ducats in 1562, half of which was committed to maintaining garrisons in Hungary. This was perhaps only double the income of the duke of Savoy or the grand duke of Tuscany, and fell far short of the 7.5 million ducats available to the king of Spain from Castile alone.[117] Even in the hereditary territories (Austria, Bohemia, Moravia and Silesia) there were jealous and niggling estates and assemblies to contend with, requiring arduous negotiations for every new request for money. Protestant influence was everywhere predominant, and even in Austria, Bohemia and Hungary the greater part of the nobility was Lutheran or Calvinist, although the emperor remained Catholic.[118] After the assertion of Habsburg jurisdiction over the part of Hungary not occupied by the Turks, the emperor acquired a whole new range of commitments and problems. These Hungarian territories in Slovakia and Croatia had to be held against Turkish encroachment, and the Danubian road to Vienna barred.

---

[116] Pugliese, *Le prime strette dell' Austria in Italia*, p. 58.

[117] *Ibid.*

[118] For an overview of the evolution of the Habsburg monarchy between the Reformation and the heady expansion of the end of the seventeenth century, see R. J. W. Evans, *The making of the Habsburg monarchy, 1550–1700: an interpretation* (Oxford: 1979), pp. 5–60.

The emperor was not entirely unsupported by Italian princes, supposedly his vassals, first in the brief war in 1566, and again in the longer conflict known as the Fifteen Years War, fought against the Turks in the Danubian basin. In 1566, rather than offer money, Duke Alfonso II of Ferrara offered troops to serve in Hungary, hopeful that the emperor would allow Modena to remain in the Este domains if the direct line were extinguished, and mindful not to be upstaged by the duke of Florence. Cosimo I lent 200,000 *scudi*, and then sent 3,000 foot, on the understanding that the emperor would consent to grant the granducal title.[119] Italians contributed more in the way of expertise. During the 1560s and 1570s, many Italian engineers erected fortifications along a vast frontier arc from the Dinaric Alps to Transylvania.[120] By the time the Turkish armies were ready to advance again in earnest, in 1593, most of these fortifications were complete. The war was provoked by the destruction of a Turkish raiding force outside Sisak, in Croatia. Turkish armies then attempted to break through the line of forts and castles. Both sides conducted sieges in a zone of marsh and forest rendered sterile by the continual raiding, where large armies lacked the means of subsistence.[121] Emperor Rudolf II persuaded the Turkish satellite princes in Transylvania, Wallachia and Moldavia to revolt against the Sultan and to join him in an alliance, and then appealed to the Pope for aid in money. Tuscany, Ferrara and the Pope all sent money from the onset of hostilities, but Pope Clement VIII sought to expand this commitment into a full-blown crusade.[122] This entailed mobilizing Italian contingents and dispatching them to Hungary.

The first contingents to depart belonged to states having close dynastic ties to Austria, like Tuscany and Mantua. Emperor Rudolf named Giovanni de'Medici general of artillery in Hungary, and grand duke Ferdinando disbursed 100,000 *scudi* to send a corps of 3,000 infantry and 400 horse. Recruiters beat their drums in the Apennine valley of the Mugello, just north of Florence, and youths descended from the entire district to join up.[123] Ferdinando's 19-year-old nephew Don Antonio de'Medici followed as an adventurer with a company of 100 gens-d'armes and 100 mounted arquebusiers, purportedly all Tuscan gentlemen, on his own account. Don Antonio's Tuscans went to garrison the fortress of Györ on the Raab river, soon besieged by the Ottoman army. Of the 2,400 sent into the place,

---

[119] Pugliese, *Le prime strette*, pp. 70–75.

[120] For details on the engineers and their projects, see G. Maggiorotti, *L'opera del Genio italiano all' estero*, 3 vols (Rome: 1933–9).

[121] John Stoye provides the best description of the difficult terrain for armies in the theatre, a good century later, since his subject, Count Marsigli was a military geographer–cartographer. See *Marsigli's Europe, 1680–1730: the life and times of Luigi Ferdinando Marsigli, soldier and virtuoso* (New Haven, Connecticut: 1994).

[122] Von Pastor, *The history of the popes, vol. XXIII: Clement VIII*, p. 266–74; see also A. Tamborra, "Dopo Lepanto: lo spostamento della lotta antiturca sul fronte terrestre", in *Il Mediterraneo nella seconda meta del '500*, pp. 371–91.

[123] M. Niccolai, "Il contributo toscano nelle guerre contro il Turco in Ungheria (1590–1606)", *Corvina*, 1952, pp. 59–71.

only 500 emerged to become prisoners. Tuscans left in smaller groups after that, as experts in fortification and artillery. Silvio Piccolòmini of Siena commanded about a hundred Italian officers and technicians in the service of Sigismund Bathory, prince of Transylvania in 1595. These 'advisers' taught Hungarian and Romanian bands how to site batteries and capture Turkish strongpoints along the lower Danube.[124] The Tuscans encountered many other Italians already serving Bathory in similar roles, while scores of renegade Italian officers chose the Turks instead.[125] Giorgio Basta also served in Transylvania as a commander of Imperial light horse, though he exercised a rough authority over the Hungarians and Romanians there, in the name of the emperor.[126]

Another Italian prince making a significant contribution was the erratic Duke Vincenzo I of Mantua, son of a Habsburg mother and brother-in-law to the Austrian archduke. His first contribution was a contingent of three well-equipped companies of mounted arquebusiers, consisting of the flower of the Mantuan nobility. The units contained some seasoned veterans of Flanders under Carlo Rossi. This first expedition in 1595 left in a pageant atmosphere, following a solemn mass in Mantua celebrated by the bishop, with the troops forming up in the square to receive benediction. The duke followed later with several hundred soldiers more, including his personal guard of 100 German halberdiers. Vincenzo even constrained his court composer, Claudio Monteverdi, to join the expedition, which cost some 100,000 crowns.[127] Vincenzo then liberally sprinkled money through allied contingents, lending 25,000 florins to the archduke, Matthias, and 10,000 crowns to induce Walloon soldiers not to plunder and thereby antagonize the peasantry. He obviously hoped for high command in an army of competing German, Italian and Walloon regiments. Bickering over operations provoked his departure in October 1595. He returned to Croatia in 1597 with a sterner mindset, with better-equipped troops fitted out in Brescia. During the siege of Györ alongside Giorgio Basta, the duke of Mantua became embroiled in a cavalry mêlée with some Turks, in which the Italian force prevailed. This gave him at least the aura of military bravura and competence he craved.[128]

Hopes of attaining high command induced him to join the Imperial army again

---

[124] Pernice notes the presence of other Italian adventurers in the region, such as the Venetian *condottiere*, Gaspare Furloni. They were sponsored by the Papal nuncio, Visconti. See the article by Angelo Pernice, "Un episodio del valore toscano nelle guerre di Valacchia alla fine del secolo XVI", *Archivio Storico Italiano*, 1925, pp. 249–97.

[125] Pernice, "Un episodio del valore toscano", *Archivio Storico Italiano*, 1925, pp. 249–97, at p. 263.

[126] Von Pastor, *The history of the popes, vol. XXIII: Clement VIII*, p. 300ff.

[127] Tamborra, "Dopo Lepanto: lo spostamento della lotta antiturca sul fronte terrestre", *Il Mediterraneo nella seconda metà del '500*, pp. 371–91, at p. 385. More details are provided by Maria Bellonci, *A prince of Mantua*, p. 163. Useful too are some passages in Giuseppe Coniglio, *I Gonzaga*, especially p. 364.

[128] Bellonci, *A prince of Mantua*, p. 167.

in 1601. This time he had to compete with Giovanni de'Medici, bastard son of Grand Duke Cosimo I, who refused to defer to him or place the Tuscan contingent of 2,000 men under his orders.[129] At the siege of the Croatian town of Kanizsa, where Archduke Ferdinand of Austria commanded, Vincenzo Gonzaga served as his lieutenant, surrounded by a luxurious court. Both were incompetent, and the siege foundered. Petty dissensions undermined the Christian army as the operation dragged on. Some of his own Mantuan captains were placed under the orders of de'Medici, and Vincenzo was not privy to the strategy sessions plotted out by one Colonel Orfeo. Officials allotted his Mantuan troops the worst encampments, where many died of dysentery and typhus. Nevertheless he persevered against the well-stocked fortress, and even ordered a play celebrated in Mantua on the fall of the city, prematurely as it turned out. Desperately trying to force a successful conclusion, he instructed his court alchemist to prepare poisons, and invent poison-gas cannonballs that would kill or incapacitate the Turkish defenders. On 30 September he ordered an unprotected and unsupported assault on the Turkish defences, the failure of which resulted in the deaths of hundreds of his troops. In November, with his troops suffering the onset of the winter, he ordered a second fruitless and bloody storming of the fortress. Not long after, the emperor dismissed him and the Mantuan contingent withdrew.

Pope Clement VIII Aldobrandini sent more substantial help. The pontiff urged total war against the Turks from the very beginning of the Turkish offensive in 1592, when the town of Bihac fell. Clement addressed briefs to the various Italian princes, exhorting them to "extinguish the conflagration in blood".[130] He first allowed the emperor to levy taxes from church properties normally exempt, and similarly raised money from Church revenues in Italy, but this was not sufficient. Following the Turkish defeat at Sisak in Croatia, Clement hatched the idea of a great coalition, including the Shah of Persia. The whole of eastern Europe could be reconquered from the Turk by Austria, Poland, Venice and the Italian states. Venice quickly rejected the idea, and was content to build the fortress of Palmanova in Friuli, ostensibly to prevent Turkish raids into the Terraferma.[131]

The Pope's attentions then focused on the emperor as the instrument of this crusade. The pontiff's emissary Giambattista Doria reported, however, that the Imperial army was in a sorry state, owing to bickering among the commanders, and the military incompetence of Archduke Mattias. When Györ fell in September 1594, Clement decided to send an army of his own, placed under the command of his nephew Gianfrancesco Aldobrandini. Aldobrandini raised some

---

[129] Bellonci, A prince of Mantua, p. 182ff.; see also Coniglio, I Gonzaga, pp. 372–7; and Von Pastor, The history of the popes, vol. XXIII, p. 300.

[130] Von Pastor, The history of the popes, vol. XXIII, p. 266. See also Tamborra, "Dopo Lepanto", Il Mediterraneo nella seconda metà del '500, pp. 371–9.

[131] See the section on Venetian fortifications by J. R. Hale in M. Mallett & J. R. Hale, The military organization of a Renaissance state (Cambridge: 1984), pt 2, p. 428.

of the troops by granting pardons to notorious outlaws. The recruiters' drums beat principally in Rome and Perugia, while the weapons were furnished by the great arsenal of Italy, Brescia, in the Venetian Terraferma.[132] Some commanders of this army were veterans of Flanders, like Paolo Sforza, the second-in-command. After the army left Rome, with banners and insignia blessed by the Pope on 4 June 1595, it recruited more troops along the way in the Marches and Romagna. Papal forces sent to the theatre in 1595 numbered some 11,800 infantry and 650 horse. By early July, the bulk of this army was in Vienna, and united soon after with the other Italian contingents at the siege of Gran (Esztergom). They were conspicuous at the capture of that city, and of Visgrad in September, both towns on the Danube above Buda. It was an auspicious beginning. Progress halted with the onset of the rains. The Pontificals complained they were badly treated by the Imperials in matters of quarters and food and there were suspicions that Protestant counsellors were behind this. By October, contagious diseases broke out in camp and the army began to dissipate. The year's campaign cost the Pope 600,000 *scudi.*

Germans felt that Italian troops did not function well in winter, so the experience was not renewed immediately. In 1596 the Imperials, without the Italian contingent, were defeated in a great battle with the Ottomans at Keresztes. Clement VIII decided to send another army under Gianfrancesco Aldobrandini, again with the participation of Vincenzo Gonzaga. The Papal nephew enlisted over 7,000 Pontifical troops for the campaign of 1597, who took part in the capture of the town of Papa, near Lake Balaton. When the rains began in the autumn, most of this force took sick or deserted, and the troops were reduced to only 2,000 when they were disbanded. As the war dragged on, Pope Clement sent another Papal army of 8,000 troops to the theatre to serve in the ill-fated siege of Kanizsa in 1601. The town had fallen to the Turks the previous year, and opened Austria itself to Ottoman cavalry raids. Gianfrancesco Aldobrandini died of fever soon after arriving in summer, but the rest of the army joined the siege in September. As the weather turned, the mortality in the trenches and in the camp was very high. There were only 3,500 Pontificals left when the siege was lifted at the end of November and the armies disbanded for winter. Papal aid to the Imperial cause was sporadic after that, and the war slowed to a stalemate. The Imperial army made no progress, partly because of the poor logistics in the theatre of war, and partly because the officers pocketed the money allocated for the troops. These were practices widespread in all the European armies, and were difficult to check. Finally, the cavalry general Giorgio Basta, applying a zealous policy of Catholicization in the towns of Imperial Hungary (modern Slovakia) and Transylvania, provoked the Protestant towns into open rebellion.

There was a final episode to this Italian activity in the Balkans. Orthodox

---

[132] Von Pastor, *The history of the popes, vol. XXIII,* p. 281.

Christians sought the right moment to revolt against the Ottomans, and Serbian, Greek, Bulgarian and Albanian monks visited European courts looking for assistance. Only the Italian duchies responded. Charles Emanuel I negotiated with Jovan, the Patriarch of Pécs, to send a force to the region in 1607, and liberate the Balkans in exchange for the 'Crown of Macedonia'.[133] Jovan assured the duke that an army of 'only' 20,000 soldiers and 25 guns, and weapons for 25,000 more to be distributed in the Balkans, would easily overwhelm the sultan.[134] After years of scheming, nothing concrete came of it, because such an expedition required Spanish naval and logistical support. In 1610 and again in 1612, Vincenzo Gonzaga was ready to act, for one of his ancestors was a Paleologue of the Byzantine ruling dynasty. Giddy with visions of Imperial splendour, the duke of Mantua sent plenipotentiaries to the Dalmatian coast near Dubrovnik, trying to meet Serb and Montenegrin headmen. With the death of the voivode, Grdan, in 1612, and the subsequent internment of Jovan in Constantinople, this too came to nought.[135] Not discouraged, Charles Gonzaga, the French-born duc de Nevers, took the bait when some Greek emissaries offered him their services in 1614. They assured him that a mere 12,000 Catholic soldiers would ignite such a revolt that, assuredly, at least 160,000 Balkan Christians would converge upon Skopje in Macedonia. Charles ordered warships constructed in Holland for the great project, and founded in 1619 the Order of the Christian Militia to serve on them. He was ready to sail in 1621, when the king of France commandeered his vessels for the wars of religion.[136]

At the end of the sixteenth century, Italian states retained enough of a military infrastructure to support the Habsburg cause in Italy, France, Flanders and Hungary with significant numbers of men. We should keep in mind that the maritime war against the Ottomans and their Barbary allies was simultaneously intense. Nobles also left to serve as adventurers at their own considerable expense, usually in the framework of the Habsburg and Catholic crusade against Turks and Protestants. The Italian military aristocracy placed itself in the Counter-Reformation cause of the militant church, and aided in its triumphs. Those triumphs were mostly defensive, in limiting the conquests of the Turks, stalling the spread of Protestantism, and in reconquering the greater part of the rebellious Low Countries. Their enthusiastic contribution helps explain why the Habsburg dynasty was still immensely powerful in 1620.

---

[133] On this project, see Ruth Kleinman, "Charles-Emanuel I of Savoy and the Bohemian revolt of 1619", *European Studies Review*, 1975, pp. 3–29, at p. 7; A. Tamborra, *Gli stati italiani, l'Europa e il problema turco dopo Lepanto* (Florence: 1961), p. 21; for the duke's craving for prestige, see Pierpaolo Merlin, *Tra guerre e tornei: la corte sabauda nell'eta di Carlo Emanuele I* (Turin: 1991).

[134] Tamborra, *Gli stati italiani*, pp. 21–35.

[135] Tamborra, *Gli stati italiani*, pp. 40–53. See also Bellonci, *A prince of Mantua*, p. 264.

[136] See the book by Emile Baudson, *Charles de Gonzague, duc de Nevers, de Rethel et de Mantoue (1580–1637)* (Paris: 1947), p. 130 and p. 176.

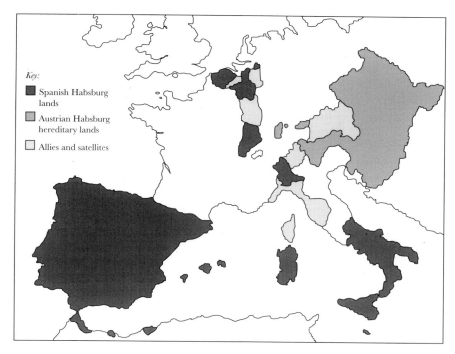

Map 2.6 Habsburg territories and their allies, *circa* 1620

First challenge: Venetian–Piedmontese alliance

One state never fitted conveniently into the framework of the Habsburg imperial system: Venice. The republic was the single most powerful state in the peninsula, and during the Lepanto war displayed its incipient power by arming 140 galleys and raising an army of almost 40,000 men, excluding militias. This was comparable to the potential of the Viennese Habsburgs, and perhaps equivalent to a third of the Spanish forces. Venice was also intensely jealous of its independence. Venetian patricians forfeited their political rights if they served any other state, and were discouraged from joining even the knights of Malta. In order to enhance its independence, the republic chose the chief religious dignitary in the state, the patriarch, and established its own branch of the Inquisition to preclude interference from the Roman equivalent. Finally, the republic's policy of friendly relations with the Ottoman Porte contravened the fundamental thrust of both Spanish and Papal policy.

There were several occasions before the Thirty Years War where Venice had to scramble to raise troops to defend its interests. The first was in 1606 when Pope Paul V Borghese slapped an interdict on the *Serenissima*, and both the king of Spain and the emperor offered to raise armies to overthrow the republic.[137] Not intimidated, partly because of French diplomatic support, Venice raised troops and refurbished its fortresses briskly, while its diplomats defused the crisis. It was in this atmosphere that fra Paolo Sarpi's pen justified the separation of Church and State. The senators and patricians whose views he expressed contemplated the creation of a 'Catholic' church under government control, akin to Henry VIII's Anglican solution in England. Popular solidarity with the excommunicated Senate, and Saint Mark's military preparedness, persuaded Paul V to back down and accept limited Papal jurisdiction in the Venetian state.

The Gradisca war (1614–17) against Austria was further confirmation of the republic's determination to defend its interests. For decades, merchant vessels of the *Serenissima* had suffered from the attacks by Christian pirates, known as Uskoks, in a zone of the northern Adriatic under the suzerainty of the emperor. Tension was compounded by Venice's unilateral claim to a monopoly over shipping in the Adriatic, to the detriment of the Austrian port of Trieste, but also of the Papal States and the kingdom of Naples. In 1613 the Venetians attacked the Uskok stronghold of Senj on the Adriatic coast, ignoring the suzerainty of its Austrian overlord. Archduke Ferdinand reacted by sending raiding parties into Venetian Istria, and devastating border communities. Hostilities escalated into full-blown war where both armies sparred indecisively along the Isonzo river frontier for almost three years, while the Venetians laid siege to Gradisca and Gorizia. There was not one set-piece battle in the entire conflict. A petition to the Venetian Senate from a Corsican captain gives a flavour of the operations. In it, he related the exploits of his recent career, boasting "that he had burned Horci; was among the first to storm and penetrate Moschenizza, and was made governor of the place; that he fought against the Uskoks holed up in the fortress of Serisa, and hatched the stratagem to kill the enemy commander there; he put down a mutiny of the Albanian soldiery; was the first to break into Buccari; and in Friuli helped devastate the villages of S. Martino di Crusca, and of Lucianis".[138]

The élites of the Terraferma seconded the Venetian senate. Bergamo, Verona and Padua each offered to raise hundreds of troops. There were two or three thousand such volunteers with the army on the frontier, and their deportment was not much different from that of the other troops.[139] The best units were Germans and Swiss, but Spanish efforts to block the Swiss passes made them difficult to obtain. Sporadically there were Dutch Protestant troops in Venetian service too.

---

[137] Von Pastor, *The History of the popes: vol. xxv, Paul V Borghese* (London: 1937), p. 126 and p. 162.

[138] F. Paleologo Oriundi, *I Corsi nella fanteria italiana della Serenissima repubblica di Venezia* (Venice: 1912), p. 8.

[139] An overview of the war can be found in R. Quazza, *Storia politica d'Italia: preponderanza spagnuola (1559–1700)*, p. 420ff. On the Venetian mobilization, see Mallett & Hale, *The military organization of a Renaissance state*, p. 241ff.

The republic hired 4,000 of them, commanded by Ernest of Nassau, to serve in Italy in 1612 and in 1616 ferried 3,100 more Dutch soldiers into the Adriatic at great expense. Protestants also figured among the French troops.

This war against the Austrian archduke led to a confrontation with Habsburg Spain, although neither side desired to escalate the dispute into full-scale war. There was considerable brinkmanship in the confrontation of the two fleets off Puglia late in 1616. A year later, on 20 November 1617, war was very close as the 'private' fleet of the viceroy, Osuna, acting in defiance of orders from Madrid, provoked the Venetians to attack. Each fleet numbered about 18 ships and 33 galleys, most of the Venetian ships being hired Dutch and English merchantmen. Since the respective commanders hesitated to come to grips, the day claimed only 50 casualties per side.[140] Osuna, having raised 12,000 soldiers and 2,000 seamen, increased the stakes by mobilizing the kingdom of Naples and sought a pretext committing Madrid to war.[141] After having disarmed a Spanish 'plot' to overthrow the republic in 1618, Venice felt more assertive.[142] A Venetian fleet of more than 30 sail appeared off Brindisi and captured some ships not having paid tribute to Venice. In 1619, a larger fleet of 40 galleys, five galeasses and 38 ships went to the Puglian coast to intimidate Spain into maintaining neutrality. Osuna's fleet commander, Ribera, raided the Dalmatian coast in turn. Finally in 1620, Philip III sacked Osuna and imprisoned him for disobeying instructions not to embroil Spain in war with the republic.

Meanwhile, Venice paid subsidies to Duke Charles Emanuel I of Savoy to occupy the Monferrato and so distract Spain, preventing her from mounting an invasion from Lombardy. The duke needed little encouragement, due to his thirst for military glory and for territorial expansion, anywhere. Already in 1589, the Venetian ambassador to Turin, Francesco Vendramin, noted that the prince showed an extraordinary lust for military glory almost from infancy. He wished to measure up to the deeds of his ancestors, who built up the state by conquest. Each of them had fought at least one great battle, most often victoriously, and they blazed the path to follow.[143] After the disastrous treaty of Lyons in 1601, which amputated much of the French-speaking part of the state, Charles Emanuel sought an opening in Italy, in Genoa, the Monferrato, or even Lombardy. The pretext first presented itself in 1613 when the duke of Mantua died and his widow,

---

[140] G. Coniglio, "Il duca d'Ossuna e Venezia dal 1616 al 1620", *Archivio Veneto*, 1955, pp. 42–70. See also R. C. Anderson, *Naval wars in the Levant, 1559–1853* (Princeton, New Jersey: 1952), p. 89.

[141] Anderson, *Naval wars in the Levant*, p. 100; see also Francesco Benigno, *L'ombra del rey: la lotta politica nella Spagna dei Validos (1598–1643)* (Palermo: 1990), pp. 70–82.

[142] On the doubtful existence of the plot by the Spanish ambassador in Venice, Count Bedmar, to seize control of the city with the aid of French mercenaries in Venetian service, see G. Spini, "La congiura degli Spagnoli contro Venezia del 1618", *Archivio Storico Italiano*, 1949, pp. 17–53.

[143] Merlin, *Tra guerre e tornei*, p. 186.

the childless daughter of Charles Emanuel, was sent home to Turin. The duke claimed the Monferrato as compensation and quickly followed up his claim with an invasion. Spanish military intervention, supported by other Italian states, together with French pressure, forced Charles Emanuel to withdraw. Draped in the rhetoric of defending Italian liberty against the Spanish yoke, in 1615 he invaded the Monferrato again with an army composed largely of French and German troops, with Venice underwriting at least a third of the cost.[144] Spanish and Italian confederate troops checked his advance at Asti.[145] Chastened, but no wiser, he approached England, Venice and the German Protestant states, with the aim of establishing a vast anti-Habsburg alliance. English ships were supposed to transport troops to the Mediterranean and attack Genoa. Then Holland and France would invade the Spanish Netherlands.

These grandiose projects were real, and were instrumental in creating the anti-Habsburg climate that ignited the Thirty Years War.[146] Expecting Venetian and French military assistance (or hoping to force their hands), Charles Emanuel invaded the Monferrato and Spanish Lombardy again, until Spain captured the key town of Vercelli after a protracted and bloody siege in 1617. The two-month Iliad focused all the tensions of the Spanish hegemony in Italy, by illustrating the vigour of the Piedmontese military challenge, but it also underscored the commitment of most of Italy's young warriors to the Spanish cause.[147] Only French diplomatic protection saved the duke from complete humiliation. Charles Emanuel married his son to the sister of Louis XIII soon after, thus lodging Piedmont in the French camp arrayed against Spain.[148] In April 1619, the formal treaty between the duchy and the Venetian republic was made public. The Catholic duke next sought entry into the German Protestant League so that he might be elected king of Bohemia, as the diet in Prague cast about for alternative candidates to the emperor, Ferdinand II.[149] The outbreak of new religious wars in France in 1620 undermined the ability of Piedmont and Venice to profit from the Habsburg problems in Germany and the Low Countries. They remained isolated in a nation enthusiastic for the advancement of the Catholic cause.

Ultimately, the solidity of the Habsburg 'system' in Italy was amply demon-

---

[144] E. Stumpo, "'Vel domi vel belli'. Arte della pace e strategie di guerra fra cinque e seicento: casi del Piemonte sabaudo, e della Toscana medicea", in *Guerre, stati e città: Mantova e l'Italia padana dal secolo XIII al XIX* (Mantua: 1988), pp. 53–68, at p. 60.

[145] The best narrative of these "Monferrato Wars" is contained in Romolo Quazza, *Storia politica d'Italia: la preponderanza spagnola*, pp. 409–20.

[146] This was first articulated by Hubert Reade, *Sidelights on the Thirty Years War*, vol. 1, p. 167. See also the article by Ruth Kleinman, "Charles-Emanuel I of Savoy and the Bohemian election of 1619", *European Studies Review*, 1975, pp. 3–29.

[147] Quazza, *La preponderanza spagnola*, p. 419.

[148] Merlin, *Tra guerre e tornei*, p. 22.

[149] Kleinman, "Charles-Emanuel I of Savoy and the Bohemian Election of 1619", *European Studies Review*, 1975, pp. 3–29.

strated. Italian states had enough interest in the continuation of the *Pax Hispanica* to counterbalance the destabilizing influence of Charles Emanuel, and the egoism of the Venetian senate. One should not forget as well, that Italian nobles generally had allegiances outside the narrow confines of their states, and followed princes other than their 'natural' one. The charisma of the Habsburg dynasty stemmed in part from its Catholic mission at the onset of the Counter-Reformation.

Chapter 3
The Forty Years War, 1618–59

The German civil war

It is not my purpose to relate the events leading up to the Bohemian Diet's revolt against its Habsburg overlord, the Emperor Ferdinand II in 1618, and the subsequent mobilization of Catholic and Protestant armies around these adversaries. The ever-increasing clarity of Ferdinand's intention to restore the Catholic faith in the hereditary lands of the House of Habsburg, in Austria, Bohemia, Moravia, Silesia and Hungary, worried the élites that had rallied to Calvinism or Lutheranism in the sixteenth century.[1] The Jesuit-bred Ferdinand was an Italophile who drew extensively on their talents as advisers. Equating Protestantism with disloyalty, he felt that Italians served him unflinchingly, and shared his own views of confessional absolutism more readily than his native German and Czech subjects. As emperor, he consulted religious advisers in all matters political, tended to reinterpret past agreements and compromises regarding religious toleration in the Empire in a sense favourable to the Catholic Church, and swore a solemn vow at Loreto to uproot Protestantism in his realms.[2] Vienna became the hub of a Catholic reconquest of Central Europe, led by talented and motivated Counter-Reformation clerics of diverse ethnic background. Italians, particularly Jesuits and Capuchins selected by Rome, were the most visible exponents of this offensive. Simultaneously, Vienna became the most Italianate city north of the Alps, a character it retained until the end of the eighteenth century. Italian, more than German, was the language of the educated nobility at court, on par with the more cosmopolitan Latin.

Imperial policy had never been decided in Madrid, for the emperor's poverty precluded an aggressive line against the Protestants outside his states.[3] His rev-

---

[1] The book by R. J. W. Evans is an excellent introduction to this material. See his book, *The making of the Habsburg monarchy, 1550–1700* (Oxford: 1979).

[2] P. Brightwell, "Spain and Bohemia: the decision to intervene, 1619", *European Studies Review*, 1982, pp. 117–41, at p. 120. See also Evans, *The making of the Habsburg monarchy*, p. 59.

[3] P. Brightwell, "The Spanish origins of the Thirty Years' War", *European Studies Review*, 1979, pp. 409–31.

enues of 2.26 million ducats in 1614 were only marginally higher than other German princes, and much of them were committed to garrison Hungary to block the Turks, or to maintain the Imperial court.[4] Ferdinand I, Rudolph II and Matthias had multiple attachments to Lutheran princes and intellectuals, and were disinclined to act against them for confessional reasons alone. But neither did the emperors oppose Spanish policies, and they resigned themselves to Spanish co-option of Imperial sovereignty in Italy and the Rhineland, where Madrid's strategic interests were paramount. In exchange for non-interference, the kings of Spain sympathized with the plight of their poor German cousins, and sent them subsidies in various forms. What was different in the affair of the Imperial succession in 1618 was the depth of the split between the prince and his subjects, and the danger of allowing the Protestant Union to dictate the outcome of Imperial elections.

The rupture between Catholics and Protestants in Central Europe in 1618 made it easy for Italian nobles looking for a war to choose their camp with good conscience. Pope Paul V Borghese immediately aligned Rome with the Habsburg dynasty, and promised it troops and money. The grand duke of Tuscany, Cosimo II, brother-in-law to the emperor Ferdinand, resolved immediately to send some companies of cavalry to Germany under the Walloon Count Dampierre, with some Tuscan captains and volunteers.[5] Small detachments like these were the nucleus to which noble adventurers attached themselves. With the truce holding in the Low Countries between Spain and the Netherlands, and with the duke of Savoy quiescent, the outbreak of a religious war in Germany was a conflict made to order for them. Glory could be earned in a worthwhile cause, in service of God, His Holy Church, and the emperor.

Philip III and his ministers, particularly Zuñiga, decided to help their Austrian cousins in the hour of peril, for dynastic reasons first, and because of Germany's place in the Spanish imperial system as a reservoir of troops, and its corridor to Flanders. Madrid began to dispatch money to Vienna. The king's lieutenants were men of war, who knew the urgency of the situation and sometimes anticipated the king's instructions. The governor of Milan, Oñate, made available to Vienna the 'Spanish' troops in Friuli supervising the application of the treaty of Madrid between Austria and Venice.[6] As the outnumbered Imperial forces sparred indecisively against the Bohemian rebels and their Hungarian and Transylvanian allies, Madrid sent them Walloon and Neapolitan *tercios*. The viceroy, Duke Osuna, who had levied large contingents of soldiers in Naples and Sicily to strike at Barbary corsair bases and to intimidate the Venetians, sent these

---

[4] S. Pugliese, *Le prime strette dell' Austria in Italia* (Milan–Rome: 1932), p. 109.

[5] T. M. Barker, "Ottavio Piccolomini (1599–1659): A fair historical judgement?", in his *Army, aristocracy, monarchy: essays on war, society and government in Austria, 1618–1780* (Boulder, Colorado: 1982), pp. 61–111, at p. 71ff.

[6] Brightwell, "The Spanish origins of the Thirty Years' War", *European Studies Review*, 1979, pp. 409–31.

to Vienna early in 1619.[7] Ambrogio Spìnola collected troops in Flanders for the offensive southward into Germany, while the marchese di Campo Lattaro led 7,000 Neapolitans north to converge on the Moselle region. Another body of 7,000 Neapolitan troops under Carlo Spinelli went to Austria itself in November 1619, where they doubled the size of the field army. By 1620, there were six *tercios* in Bohemia paid out of the Spanish war treasury, totalling about 18,000 infantry, or more than all the 'Germans'.[8] Madrid replenished them with a steady stream of fresh recruits from Naples, Lombardy and Flanders. The overall commander was the Walloon Count Bucquoi, but after his death in 1622 he was succeeded by the Neapolitans Caràcciolo and Girolamo Carafa, count of Montenegro. There was a Papal contingent of 20 companies too, under Pietro Aldobrandini, serving in Hungary and Moravia.

It is difficult to determine how many rank and file were Italian, but nobles from the peninsula commanded units of other nationalities. Pietro de'Medici, for example, led a regiment of arquebusiers, called 'the Florentine' only because it was paid out of the Tuscan treasury, but which comprised Germans and Walloons hired in the Low Countries. The Roman Torquato Conti led Walloons, while the Modenese Ernesto Montecùccoli commanded German arquebusiers. This multi-ethnic army overwhelmed the Czechs and Germans at White Mountain outside Prague in 1620. Almost simultaneously, Spìnola's army occupied the Rhine Palatinate, neutralizing the coalition of Protestant states in a few months. By 1622, the emperor's allies restored his authority. Fighting continued after that in spasms, as the Protestants found hesitant friends like Holland and England, ready to send money and volunteers, but unwilling to commit troops. The king of Denmark next took up the Protestant cause until his shattering defeat in 1625. Spanish forces were by then diverted by the resumption of hostilities with the Netherlands.

In Vienna the war occasioned a change of political personnel as several generals joined the Imperial Privy Council and the War Council, or *Hofskriegsrat*.[9] The battle of White Mountain was followed by a massive expropriation of nobles who had helped the rebels, to the advantage of those who remained faithful to the emperor, or who came from abroad to help. A vigorous Counter-Reformation in all of the Imperial hereditary lands provoked the exile of hundreds of Austrian nobles.[10] One who profited from the upheaval was the Czech *condottiere*, Albert, Count Wallenstein, who converted to Catholicism in his youth, and was one of the few non-Protestants from the empire in Imperial service. Wallenstein employed and worked with so many Italians that jealous Germans accused him of preferring

---

[7] Brightwell, "Spain and Bohemia: the decision to intervene", *European Studies Review*, 1982, pp. 117–41.
[8] J. V. Polisensky, *War and society in Europe, 1618–1648* (Cambridge: 1978), p. 80.
[9] H. F. Schwarz, *The Imperial privy council in the seventeenth century* (Cambridge, Mass.: 1943), p. 114.
[10] Evans, *The making of the Habsburg monarchy*, p. 59ff.

them, a charge that his biographer, Golo Mann, disputes.[11] A surfeit of Protestant colonels made Italian appointments to that rank attractive to the emperor. He held them to be the outstanding strategists, and could count on their 'hawkish' disposition towards Protestant rebels. Indeed, too much flexibility on Wallenstein's part proved to be his undoing. A disproportionate number of senior commanders were Italians, who had fought in Imperial service since the early years of the century, like Rambaldo Collalto, from Treviso in the Venetian Republic. His family had deep-rooted links to the Imperial cause, and one of his ancestors, Giacomo Collalto, commanded two German regiments in Hungary against the Turks.[12] At fifteen, Rambaldo served his apprenticeship in the same war. He was not particularly successful as a general, and even less as a diplomat and negotiator for the emperor. Sent to represent Imperial interests in Transylvania, his high-handedness soon provoked a revolt there. His single major victory was the capture of Mantua in 1630, but he was thought to have been assassinated by his own troops not long after, during a rigorous winter march. While an indifferent general, Collalto was a major power broker in Vienna, and gave valuable support to an entire generation of Italian military enterprisers.

His contemporary Matteo Galasso was a direct subject of the emperor, born at Trento in 1584. Matteo's father, a Neapolitan gentleman, served in the army of Farnese in the Low Countries. Galasso began his military career as an adult, probably in 1615 when he received an ensign's commission in the feudal cavalry of the lord of Trento, Cardinal Madruzzo. Galasso's opportunity came in 1620 when he led the count of Anhalt's unit in the Bohemian invasion, and by 1625 he was colonel of his own regiment. Subsequently, his career took him to the most famous battlefields of the war as commander of an important segment of the Imperial army: at Mantua in 1629, at Lutzen in 1632, and then Nordlingen in 1634 where he led the Imperial contingent of the combined Habsburg army. His later autonomous operations in Burgundy and in Bohemia were not successes, but he blamed those failures on the bungling of his Italian subordinates, the colonel, Salazar and the cavalry general, Pallavicino. Galasso himself sank into obesity and, unusually for an Italian, alcoholism.[13] During his last campaign in 1647, his entire army dissolved in a forced march through Silesia.

Ernesto Montecùccoli, born near Modena in 1584, belongs to the same generation. He fought his first campaigns against the Turks under Giorgio Basta, and he

---

[11] Golo Mann, *Wallenstein: his life narrated* (New York: 1976; first publ. 1971), pp. 214 and 305.

[12] V. Mariani & V. Varanini, *Condottieri italiani in Germania* (Milan: 1941), p. 186.

[13] Considering his importance, it is interesting that he has not been the subject of an extended biography. See Mariani & Varanini, *Condottieri italiani in Germania*, p. 181ff. There are glimpses of him in the books by Golo Mann, *Wallenstein*, p. 479, and dispersed throughout the great work by Fritz Redlich, *The German military enterpriser and his work force: a study in European economic and social history*, 2 vols (Wiesbaden: 1964).

continued to fight against the prince of Transylvania until he was captured in 1609. He must not have had much standing among his relatives, for only the duke of Modena could persuade his family to pay the ransom.[14] In 1620 he was colonel of a regiment of Spanish soldiers, and entered Spanish service in the Low Countries soon after. Montecùccoli passed back into Imperial service and fought under Tilly and Wallenstein, and served in the duke of Lorraine's army against the French in 1633. As a general, he was adept at skirmishes and small-scale guerrilla harassment. He was killed in just such an encounter against the Swedes in Alsace in 1634. Like most of the other officers from this Emilian dynasty, Ernesto was not above reproach: Redlich refers to him as a "real extortionist".[15]

This generation of commanders who cut their teeth before the revolt in Bohemia was gradually superseded by younger men who followed paths blazed by their countrymen. When Wallenstein reorganized the Imperial army in 1631–2, he appointed or confirmed a clutch of Italian generals and colonels, who comprised perhaps as much as a fifth of the Imperial high command. They were not all paragons of discipline, and two of them, Giovanni Luigi Isolani, commander of the Croat light cavalry, and Francesco del Caretto di Grana earned sinister reputations as looters and perpetrators of atrocities.[16] Among the generals were two Germanized Italians, Rodolfo and Girolamo Colloredo, from Friuli. After the crisis of 1631, the grand duke of Tuscany sent three of his brothers along with 6,000 foot and 1,000 horse to aid his Imperial uncle. Two of the princes died during the subsequent campaigns, but Mattias de'Medici became general of artillery and served for a decade before retiring at the ripe age of 28.[17] Highborn but still more mediocre generals were quite indispensable, even for Wallenstein, if their purse was deep. Duke Federico Savelli was a wealthy Roman patrician whose talents proved dismal as he bungled every operation entrusted to him.[18]

The most singular career belonged to Ottavio Piccolòmini, from a Sienese family of Papal origin, but whose more immediate ancestors were soldiers. Ottavio and his elder brother Enea Silvio were destined from childhood to emulate their warlike father, Silvio. Enea was the designated heir of the family, brought up at the court in Florence as a page, and who had sired some heirs by the time the revolt of Bohemia broke out. He figured among the noble adventurers accompanying the Tuscan expedition to Germany, but was killed within months when scaling the walls of Pechin. Ottavio, born in 1600, was destined to

---

[14] There are interesting details on Ernesto Montecùccoli in the book by Tommaso Sandonnini, *Il generale Raimondo Montecùccoli e la sua famiglia* (Modena: 1913), p. 191.

[15] Redlich, *The German military enterpriser and his work force*, vol. 1, p. 367.

[16] On Isolani, see Redlich, *The German military enterpriser and his work force*, vol. 1, p. 456. Golo Mann notes Wallenstein's dislike for the rapacious del Caretto, whom he once rewarded on the battlefield for valour. See his *Wallenstein*, p. 756.

[17] N. Giorgetti, *Le armi toscane*, vol. 1, p. 429.

[18] Redlich, *The German military enterpriser and his work force*, vol. 1, p. 395.

be a knight of Malta, but he joined Spanish service in Lombardy in 1617 and saw his first action at the siege of Vercelli. After the death of his brother, he served in Moravia and Hungary under Girolamo Carafa, where he rose quickly to the rank of lieutenant-colonel under General Pappenheim. He returned to Italy at the head of 1,000 horse in 1625, when the emperor sent aid to Spain to face the French and Piedmontese. Back in Germany, Count Wallenstein appointed him captain of his bodyguard, and approved his command of a regiment in a promotion brokered by Collalto. He owned a second regiment by 1628, which was superbly fitted out at the expense of the townspeople of Stargard in Pomerania. Appreciated by Wallenstein, he showed himself to be a fanatical and pitiless scourge of Protestants and rebels at the sack of Magdeburg in 1630. Piccolòmini was also present in Wallenstein's army at Lutzen in 1632, and was close to the Tuscan infantry that killed the king of Sweden that day, a stroke of luck for which he took credit. More importantly, his repeated cavalry charges against the advancing Swedes turned the bloody battle into something resembling an Imperial success.[19]

Like the other Italians, Piccolòmini was a 'hawk' in favour of prosecuting the war to its utmost. It was easy to convince him that his patron, Count Wallenstein, was engaged in treasonous negotiations. The Sienese was, with Matteo Galasso, and the princes Mattias and Francesco de'Medici, one of the ringleaders of the plot to assassinate the Czech field marshal. Once they accomplished the deed, Emperor Ferdinand lavishly rewarded them from the spoils. With the command of two regiments, he was already one of the foremost commanders of the Empire, and sat on the Imperial War Council. Months after Wallenstein's assassination, Piccolòmini's regiments played a stellar role in the destruction of the Swedish army at Nordlingen, although Silvio, one of his nephews and a colonel, was killed there.[20] Despite his extraordinary talent, the climate towards Latin officers, most of whom were Italians, turned cold. Germans feared that they would monopolize the senior ranks of the Imperial army. This persistent ill-feeling towards Italians led him to request permission to serve the king of Spain in 1635, engaged in earnest now against the French and the Dutch in the Low Countries and northern France.

For the next few years, Ottavio flourished in Spanish service and was tremendously successful in Picardy in 1636, and in Lorraine in 1639. He was hampered only by a short political leash, and by the Spanish monarchy's increasingly

---

[19] The most recent biography is the long article by Thomas Barker, "Ottavio Piccolomini (1599–1659); a fair historical judgement?", in his *Army, aristocracy, monarchy; essays on war, society and government in Austria, 1618–1780* (Boulder, Colorado: 1982), pp. 61–111. Barker was working partly from the biography compiled by the Sienese ecclesiastic, Isidoro Ugurgieri Azzolini, published in the general's lifetime. See *Le Pompe Sanesi, overo relazione delli huomini e donne illustri di Siena e suo stato*, 2 vols (Pistoia: 1649), vol. 2, p. 206 et sq. See also the article by G. B. Mannucci, "Il maresciallo Ottavio Piccolòmini", *Bullettino Senese di Storia Patria*, 1929, pp. 3–27, which publishes some of the general's correspondence.

[20] Ugurgieri Azzolini, *Le Pompe Sanesi*, vol. 2, p. 216ff.

desperate financial situation. The defensive style of warfare to which he was now forced in the Low Countries was not of his choosing. Despite receiving feudal investiture of the duchy of Amalfi and the Order of the Golden Fleece, he was ready to return to Imperial service in 1647. He fought his final campaign in Bavaria with an Imperial army, trying to stem the Swedish tide before the conclusion of negotiations in Westphalia. At this late juncture, Emperor Ferdinand III appointed him supreme commander of all the Imperial forces. At the conclusion of the war (which he was one of the very few to fight from start to finish), he settled in Austria and founded through his surviving nephews a German branch of the family. He maintained a lavish lifestyle on his Bohemian estate at Nachod and in his Vienna palace where he died in 1659.

Similarly successful was another Montecùccoli, Raimondo, born in the Modenese Apennines in 1609. His father too, had been a military noble in Imperial service in Hungary, though he fled there to escape prosecution for murder. After their father was killed in a vendetta, the Montecùccoli children were brought up at the court of Modena. Rambaldo Collalto spotted Raimondo there in 1625, and gave him an ensign's place in his regiment. Montecùccoli always boasted that he began his profession at the bottom, as a non-commissioned gentleman adventurer and a pikeman. Whether or not this is true, his advancement was due to more than diligence. When the emperor appointed Collalto President of the Imperial War Council after 1628, Montecùccoli began his ascent. Between 1628 and 1630 he served as a captain of infantry, then cavalry captain in his cousin Ernesto's regiment. His unit was routed in a skirmish with the Swedes near Magdeburg in 1631 and he spent six months as a captive before paying his own ransom. Freedom brought promotion to the rank of major, and then lieutenant-colonel of infantry, tantalizingly close to one of the colonelships that unlocked riches. The death of his cousin in 1634 left him without a proper patron, so he took active charge of regiments belonging to Italian princes, that of Borso d'Este of Modena, and then of Annibale Gonzaga of Mantua.

Finally, Montecùccoli inherited Ernesto's old regiment and with his brother Galeotto, continued to perform well despite the indiscipline of the troops. He was arrested once after his troops plundered the personal baggage of the Elector of Brandenburg, an ally. He needed the support of all his influential friends, Prince Mattias of Tuscany, Annibale Gonzaga, Matteo Galasso and Luigi Pallavicino, members of the influential 'Italian party', to be exonerated. In 1639, the Swedes captured Raimondo again during a rearguard skirmish, and held him in Stettin for three years. Giving himself to the study of philosophy and military science, it was there that he composed and meditated the most important general treatise on the art of war of the seventeenth century. He was released in 1642 after the duke of Modena obtained his freedom, in exchange for his service against the Papacy in the Castro War. As soon as operations against the Pope were suspended at the end of 1643, Raimondo returned to Vienna. He was immediately welcomed into the charmed circle of successful generals, joining the Imperial War Council, and became Imperial Chamberlain in 1645. Montecùccoli took the field in 1647 and

1648, as something of a specialist in rear-guard actions. Along with Piccolòmini, he was the Empire's leading commander at the close of the great war, and he was to rise to still greater importance.[21]

The resumption of the Netherlands War

Resumption of hostilities between Spain and the Netherlands in 1621 soon extended the war beyond Germany. Neither side wished to renew the twelve-year truce of 1609, which had eliminated the obstacles in the way of Dutch commercial exploitation of the Spanish and Portuguese empires. Philip III feared losing control of his own colonies.[22] The rivals also competed for influence in north-western Germany, the Netherlands' economic hinterland. In 1610 a European war almost erupted over the succession to the duchy of Julich, between Liège and Cologne. Spìnola's army of Flanders seized the territory before the Dutch Republic and its German Protestant allies could react, and the assassination of Henri IV precluded French support for their cause. Spìnola, whose quick campaign to conquer the Palatinate in 1620 confirmed his reputation as one of the most talented commanders of the age, personally opposed resuming the war against the Netherlands. For him it was an unnecessary diversion when the Habsburg dynasty had victory against the German Protestant Union in its grasp.[23] Philip and his advisers decided nevertheless for war. If they did not feel that total reconquest of the rebel republic was possible, they could hope for a better treaty. Even in peacetime, the Flanders army cost the Spanish treasury about 1.75 million ducats annually. The cost of launching a fleet in the Atlantic to confront the Dutch was only a half-million ducats more, and by bringing the Dutch to a favourable peace, Spanish and Portuguese trade profits might compensate for the expenditure.[24]

The Genoese commander displayed a real grasp of economic warfare, intent as he was on subduing the Netherlands by blockading its river lifeline in Germany. It sufficed to occupy the fortresses along the lower Rhine and Meuse to stop the flow of merchandise and food into the Republic, while unleashing simultaneously a fleet of warships and privateers from Ostend and Dunkirk against Dutch

---

[21] T. Barker, *The military intellectual and battle: Raimondo Montecuccoli and the Thirty Years War* (Albany, New York: 1975). The introduction of the book comprises one of the most recent biographies. On his family background, see by Tommaso Sandonnini, *Il generale Raimondo Montecùccoli e la sua famiglia* (Modena: 1913).

[22] J. I. Israel, "A conflict of empires: Spain and the Netherlands, 1618–1648", *Past and Present*, **76**, 1979, pp. 34–74.

[23] P. Brightwell, "The Spanish system and the twelve years' truce", *English Historical Review*, 1974, pp. 270–92.

[24] *Ibid.*

merchant shipping and the fishing fleet.[25] Then his field army gnawed away at the great ring of fortresses protecting the heartland of the northern provinces, in a series of expensive sieges that was Spìnola's speciality. The long siege of Julich in 1621–2, and the unsuccessful attempt to take Bergen-op-Zoom in 1623 consumed vast resources in men and material. This strategy was finally vindicated in 1625 with the capitulation of Breda, a great fortress and seat of his adversary, Prince Maurice of Orange, which opened up the whole territory south of the Meuse to reconquest by Spain.

Spìnola's success fuelled fears that Spain would become too powerful. After surreptitiously financing Holland, both France and England launched attacks on Spanish shipping and planned to strike at the heart of the Spanish imperial system by attacking Genoa by land and sea. The garrison and Andalusian militia routed the Anglo-Dutch descent on Cadiz in 1625, while local forces also undid a Dutch attempt to conquer Brazil. Despite success in keeping its enemies at bay, Spain's mobilization had to meet the scale of the threat. Stradling suggests that by the late 1620s, Spain had 80,000 men fighting in four field armies in Europe, and 150,000 regular soldiers in garrison, all exclusive of militia.[26] Anderson, citing Parker, suggests that the Spanish army may have continued to increase its effective strength to 300,000 men by the early 1630s, although it was increasingly less Spanish as it expanded.[27] Olivares wanted to maintain this level by having each component part of the Empire contribute to the maintenance of a segment of it, in a policy known as the Union of Arms. The financial burden of the war was becoming intolerable, although a Spanish field army had yet to be defeated in battle.[28] Castile's treasury as it was constituted failed to bear the weight of the war. Tax receipts in 1627 amounted to fifteen million ducats, half of which went to service the debt. A bankruptcy that year frightened away foreign investors, who had always been attracted by the high rates of interest on Spanish loans.[29] Spìnola wanted Philip IV to withdraw from the war that year, and went to Madrid to challenge Olivares' policy. His personal fortune was entirely engulfed in the Spanish treasury's debt, as was an enormous sum lent by a Genoese finance consortium of which he was the instrument. In the past, he rarely requested prompt payment of the interest, but now he was demanding full reimbursement. Capture of the Spanish treasure fleet, arriving from the Indies in 1628, compounded his problems.

Some historians maintain that the drain on Spanish manpower began to take its

---

[25] Israel, "A conflict of empires", *Past and Present*, **76**, 1979, p. 55ff; see also R. A. Stradling, *Europe and the decline of Spain: a study of the Spanish system, 1580–1720* (London: 1981), p. 56ff.

[26] Stradling, *Europe and the decline of Spain*, p. 64.

[27] M. S. Anderson, *War and society in Europe of the old regime, 1618–1789*, (London: 1988), p. 17.

[28] R. A. Stradling, *Philip IV and the government of Spain, 1621–1665* (Cambridge: 1988), p. 71.

[29] Stradling, *Europe and the decline of Spain*, p. 65.

toll by the 1620s and that it was harder to find recruits in Spain to replace losses in the *tercios*.[30] I doubt there was a real depletion in available manpower, for while there was continual emigration to the Indies, and while thousands left annually in the *tercios* or the fleets, this was largely compensated by peasant immigration to Iberia from southern France. Only detailed research can quantify the flow of Spanish, Portuguese and Italian troops moving northwards. Stradling notes how the proportion of Italians in the Spanish army of Flanders crept upwards after 1600. I have no firm figures here, but at least one author emphasizes how the ethnic characteristic of the *tercios* gradually broke down once they were in the theatre, with captains replacing men in their companies any way they could.[31] Lonchay establishes the number of Italians in Flanders at around 6,000 during the 1630s, equivalent to the Spaniards.[32] At Rocroi, about a fifth of the 20,000 infantry engaged in the battle were Italian, that is four *tercios* out of 20, compared to five Spanish and two Burgundian, the rest being Walloon or German. As in the late sixteenth century, troops fitted out in Milan marched to Flanders through the Valtellina, and the Swiss cantons to Alsace or the Breisgau. This was the experience of about 10,000 miserably equipped Italian troops in 1633, who had to fight their way to the Low Countries through Swedish-held Alsace.[33] The loss of Breisach to France in 1638 made it difficult to march reinforcements overland. Until the battle of the Dunes in 1639 it was occasionally possible to send sizeable contingents of them by sea. After that, Italians had to travel to Spain by sea, and leave the Basque ports in small groups to avoid attracting the enemy, as we read in a letter written by the Sienese officer Giovanni Nuti, giving an account of his terrifying journey to Ostend in 1642.[34]

Despite comprising a diminishing fraction of the troops in the north, a high proportion of the generals were Italian, even after Spìnola left Flanders in 1628. His successor was the Spanish marquis of Santa Cruz, whose preferment of ethnic Spaniards demoralized the army and provoked a revolt among the local nobility in 1632.[35] After 1634, command in the theatre was entrusted to the heir to the throne, the Infanta Cardinal Philip, who presided over the turbulent council of war. Lonchay attributes the Spanish reverses less to the mediocrity of the generals, and more to their rivalry that was in part ethnic.[36] For example, at the attempt to

---

[30] For recruiting difficulties in Spain, see I. A. A. Thompson, *War and government in Habsburg Spain, 1560–1620* (London: 1976), p. 146ff.

[31] H. Lonchay, *La rivalité de la France et de l'Espagne aux Pays-Bas (1635–1700)* (Brussels: 1896), p. 35.

[32] *Ibid.* The figures for Rocroi come from Aumale, *La journée de Rocroy*, p. 48ff; it is unclear whether the Sardinian *tercio* is counted as Spanish or Italian, p. 63.

[33] *Ibid.*, p. 25.

[34] Biblioteca Comunale Intronati di Siena, Autografi Porri, filze **6**: Letter from Giovanni Nuti to his family from Brussels, 1642.

[35] Lonchay, *La rivalité de la France et de l'Espagne*, p. 24.

[36] *Ibid.*, p. 100.

relieve the French siege of Arras in July 1640, the Neapolitan general Cantelmo gave two Italian regiments the task of leading the assault on the French entrenchments, preceding the Spaniards. To avenge the affront, the Spaniards refused to support the Italian attack, which was repulsed.

Three Italians rose to prominence after the French entered the war in 1635, but none achieved status comparable to Spìnola. Andrea Cantelmo, prince of Pettorano, enlisted in Spanish service at the age of 15, in 1613. Seven years later he was only a company commander in the Valtellina and Palatinate campaigns. He followed his colonel into Austrian employ in Transylvania, before returning to Spanish service in Lombardy in 1625. By the time of the siege of Casale Monferrato in 1628, he led his own *tercio*. Cantelmo commanded next in Flanders, where Maurice of Nassau trounced him in the vicinity of Maastricht. His unit was one of those to advance far into France in the 1636 breakthrough in Picardy. In 1638 Madrid appointed him general of artillery, and then governor of the army of the Low Countries, in command of the field army around Antwerp. Finally, in 1640 the king appointed him field commander-in-chief in Catalonia, where he held his own until his army was defeated utterly by Harcourt at Llorens on 22 June 1645. He died the following November, reportedly of despondency.[37]

Meteoric was the rise of a prince of Piedmont, Tommaso of Savoy, trained in war from infancy by his bellicose father. He fought his first campaigns beside his father against Spain, with the French as allies. Heartily and wisely mistrustful of Richelieu's intentions towards the alpine principality, Tommaso offered his services to Philip IV in 1634. He went to Brussels with no promise of suitable employment, but he had great expectations, since he was prince of a ruling house, and possessed ample talent. When the French invaded the Low Countries in 1635, he was inauspiciously trounced by an army three times more numerous than his 10,000 men. Before the campaign was over, however, he helped expel the French and Dutch armies by forcing them to abandon their sieges, and then recaptured all the territory lost. In 1636, as commander of the main field army, Tommaso administered a stunning lesson in military initiative to the French, whose commanders lacked experience fighting a modern war. He captured several small border fortresses in a couple of weeks, opening a path for his army of 22,000 infantry and 15,000 cavalry, most of the latter under the direction of Ottavio Piccolòmini. After the capture of Corbie, a minor fortress on the Somme near Amiens, the army surged southwards unopposed towards Paris, stopping only at Pontoise, some 30 km short. It was too difficult to supply such a large army moving so quickly, so they receded gradually before the French militias, returning to Flanders in August loaded with an immense amount of booty. Tommaso then

---

[37] Mariani & Varanini, *Condottieri italiani in Germania* (Milan: 1941), p. 147. For a short biography, see the Encyclopedia entry in Argegni, *Condottieri, capitani, tribuni*, vol. 1, pp. 131–2; and the account of the battle of Rocroi by the duc d'Aumale, *La journée de Rocroy (19 mai, 1643)* (Paris: 1890), p. 48.

returned to Piedmont on the death of his brother Victor Amadeus I, a French ally, determined to pull the duchy out of the anti-Spanish alliance.[38]

The other general of the hour was Ottavio Piccolòmini, who needed to be rehabilitated after his involvement in Wallenstein's assassination. Like Prince Tommaso and Cantelmo, the Sienese general was a Francophobe. Initially he led an Imperial contingent working in conjunction with, and as a subordinate to, the prince of Savoy in the Low Countries. According to Lonchay, their co-operation was not seamless, with Piccolòmini refusing to take orders from the prince, and threatening to take his men home. Nevertheless it was a lucrative assignment during the year of Corbie, when villages near Paris sent envoys bearing gifts and provisions to him, hoping to buy exemption from plunder by marauding cavalry patrols, from the Croats in particular.[39] In 1639 he took the offensive in Lorraine with his own autonomous command, and completely destroyed a French army under La Feuillade at Thionville. Italians commanded quite a few of his regiments, like the Marchese Gonzaga, the Marchese del Carretto di Grana, and the colonels Altieri, Gerardini, Petazzo, Galasso, Savelli and Frangipani. Like their leader they were perhaps purging their unpopularity after Wallenstein's demise. After these successes, Philip IV called him to Spain itself, succeeding Cantelmo to the task of extinguishing the Catalan revolt. When he returned to Flanders in 1643, the king made him duke of Amalfi (a fief that had belonged to his ancestors), bestowed on him the Golden Fleece and the rank of Grandee of Spain, and awarded him pay of 24,000 *scudi* with a gift of four horses from the royal stables. In exchange, he received the remnants of the army destroyed at Rocroi, and promised to preserve it. Political and strategic decisions were not his to make, so he fought a defensive war until 1647. By then, he was ready to return to Vienna in a more autonomous capacity.[40]

Besides the three Italian commanders mentioned here, at least seven lesser lights led armies for the king of Spain between 1635 and 1660.[41] The skill of these generals was quite insufficient to surmount the odds against Spain after 1640, especially since talent was not all on their side. Spanish fortunes rose and fell for over a decade after that. A great effort to renew the fleet in the 1620s served Madrid well for over a decade. In 1637, Stradling estimates that there were some

---

[38] Prince Tommaso of Savoy as a Spanish general is the subject of a biography by Romolo Quazza, *Tommaso di Savoia-Carignano, nelle campagne di Fiandre e di Francia, 1635–1638* (Turin: n.d., 1941?)

[39] Lonchay, *La rivalité de la France et de l'Espagne*, p. 76ff.

[40] See the article with attached correspondence by G. B. Mannucci, "Il maresciallo Ottavio Piccolòmini", *Bullettino Senese di Storia Patria*, 1929, pp. 3–27.

[41] De Campos identifies some of them, without entering into details, some of which could be gleaned from the encyclopedias. They were the Neapolitans Francesco Toraldo and Francesco Tuttavilla, the Hispano-Genoese sons of Ambrogio, Filippo and Cardinal Agostino Spìnola, the Milanese Cardinal Trivulzio and Giovanni Serbelloni, and the Parman prince Alessandro Farnese.

150 seaworthy warships in the various armadas, capable of coping with the Dutch, the French and the Turks. A great fleet of 128 sail, including 30 warships and 29 galleys, could be dispatched from Naples to relieve the siege of Tarragona in Catalonia in 1641.[42] This was gradually worn down, without the losses being replaced.[43] In the Low Countries, the Duc d'Enghien (future Duc de Condé) halted an offensive under the Portuguese general Francisco de Melo at Rocroi on 19 May 1643, and smashed the Italian and Spanish *tercios* after the German and Flemish troops bolted.[44] He almost obliterated Spain's élite infantry corps in a single day. During the 1640s, recruiting in Spain itself for armies elsewhere collapsed. Stradling estimates that only about a thousand recruits a year sailed from Spain to Flanders. Officials placed new emphasis on foreign mercenaries, chiefly German and Irish, hired outside the empire. By 1648, when peace was signed with the Netherlands, the monarchy was financially exhausted. Bankruptcies in 1627, 1647 and 1652 undermined future attempts at borrowing. The crown put up taxes on everything, and still this was not enough. These financial hardships are reflected in the amount of money sent to prosecute the war in Flanders. Dominguez Ortiz calculates that, from 1634 to 1641, Madrid sent almost four million *scudi* each year. In 1647 it dispatched only two and a half million, while in 1656–7, it paid only 800,000 *scudi* in eighteen months.[45] With decreasing revenues, the government in Brussels had to fend for itself. French armies improved after the civil war of the Fronde, and the campaign of 1655 marked the definitive turning point. The duke of Lorraine, another former ally, went over to the French. The balance tipped further in 1656 when England sent an expeditionary force to aid Mazarin. In 1658 there were still almost 50 infantry regiments in Spanish employ in the Low Countries, and 16 cavalry regiments, but these were under strength, and nationalities of every sort far outnumbered Castilians and Italians.[46]

Campaigns in the Iberian peninsula, from Catalonia to Portugal, reflected the gradual exhaustion of the monarchy. After the Portuguese routed an invasion force at Elvas in 1658, it took months to find reinforcements to build another. The subsequent armies were composed of Italian recruits, and Irish and German

---

[42] R. C. Anderson, "The Thirty Years' War in the Mediterranean", *Mariner's Mirror*, **15**, 1969, pp. 435–51, at p. 450.
[43] Stradling, *The Armada of Flanders: Spanish maritime policy and European war, 1568–1668* (Cambridge: 1992), p. 127. Unlike the galley flotilla under Federigo Spìnola, whose officers were mostly Italian, the frigate fleet based in Dunkirk after 1621 was overwhelmingly staffed by Flemish captains.
[44] A fairly detailed account of the battle, in which two of three Italian *tercios* were also destroyed, is contained in a book by the duc d'Aumale, *La journée de Rocroy (le 19 mai, 1643)* (Paris: 1890), p. 137.
[45] A. Dominguez Ortiz, "España ante la paz de los Pireneos", in *Crisis y decadencia de la España de los Austrias* (Barcelona: 1969, first publ. 1959), pp. 157–93, at p. 170.
[46] *Ibid.*, p. 177.

mercenaries. The Spanish levies were all green troops, completely worthless in combat. Peace with Holland (1648) and with France and England (1659) was not respite enough for Spain to reconquer Portugal with all the means of its empire.

The war in Italy and its impact

Spanish power was strong enough in Italy that it was not immediately threatened by the outbreak of war in the Empire. Given the unpredictability of the duke of Savoy, Charles Emanuel I, Madrid explored other routes over the Alps. The logical one was the Valtellina, a valley running east–west from Lake Como and north of Venetian Lombardy, and linked by passes to both the Swiss Cantons and the Austrian Tyrol. After France annexed the right bank of the Rhône from Savoy in 1601, this route took on the utmost strategic importance. Held by the Swiss Protestant Grison Leagues, the pass was also the road that German, French and Swiss troops took into Venetian employ. Politically, the Valtellina was a powder keg, because the German-speaking Swiss Calvinists imposed a heavy hand on the Catholic Italians living in the valley. In July 1620 the Italians rose and massacred several hundred of the former in a 'sacred slaughter', with the connivance of the duke of Feria, governor of Milan. Spanish troops (many of whom were Italians) immediately occupied and fortified the towns to deny control of the region to Venice.[47] In the aftermath, France and Venice prodded the Grisons to block the entry to the valley at Chiavenna.[48] Venice raised 11,000 troops and considered joining the German Protestant Union and the Dutch Republic in 1621. But Spain's hold was firm. By 1622 its troops holding the valley allowed easy passage of reinforcements to Germany through Alsace, where there were more Spanish and Italian troops in garrison.[49] To ease the tension, Spain allowed Pontifical troops to hold the valley forts in its stead, but this legitimized control in favour of the Catholic cause.[50]

In the early 1620s Spain never seemed stronger, to the envy of its traditional enemies, the Netherlands, England and France along with Piedmont and Venice in Italy. The 'weak underbelly' of this Spanish imperial system, as Parker calls it, was the weakly defended coast of the republic of Genoa. Apart from the Spanish base at Finale, there were few troops in garrison along the Ligurian coast, and the Genoese tranquilly occupied themselves with the lucrative Spanish *asientos*.[51] The

---

[47] The best study is that of Pedro Marrades, *El camino del imperio: notas para el estudio de la cuestiòn de la Valtelina* (Madrid: 1943).

[48] *Ibid.*, p. 49.

[49] Geoffrey Parker, *The army of Flanders and the Spanish road, (1567–1659): the logistics of Spanish victory and defeat in the Low Countries' wars* (Cambridge: 1972), p. 70ff.

[50] Marrades, *El camino del imperio*, p. 127.

[51] H. Reade, *Sidelights on the Thirty Years' War*, vol. 1, p. 104.

garrison of the busy city of 60,000 inhabitants numbered only about 600 German and 200 Swiss soldiers. None of the other fortresses amounted to much. A couple of thousand Corsicans comprised most of the other troops in the republic, scattered in dozens of tiny garrisons.[52] In 1624, Charles Emanuel of Savoy tempted Louis XIII to back an alliance of Holland, England, Venice and Piedmont, intending to strike Liguria from land and sea. The immediate pretext for war was the sale of the imperial fief of Zuccarello to the Genoese. Its rapid occupation was much resented by Charles Emanuel. He had been plotting a vast anti-Spanish alliance for years, especially since marrying his heir in 1619 to Christine de Bourbon, sister of the French king. Since the Bohemian diet rebuffed his overtures for the royal crown in 1618, he looked across the Alps for support for his expansion in Italy. Only after 1624, however, when Cardinal Richelieu emerged as chief minister was the French king willing to embark on a policy of direct confrontation with Spain. In February 1625, French troops crossed the Alps under the old marshal, Lesdiguières, a former Huguenot. He joined the duke of Savoy's army (also largely composed of French soldiers) at Asti at the beginning of March.[53]

Together, the substantial field army comprised 30,000 infantry and 3,000 horse, with a battery train of 38 guns intended to hammer down the walls of fortresses in his path. The army took Novi, on the north edge of the Apennines, on 23 March, and prepared to move across the mountains to the coast, where they were expecting an English fleet to support them. French and Piedmontese soldiers committed unspeakable outrages passing through the towns of neutral Monferrato, and sacked churches indiscriminately. Genoese forces were completely unprepared. In the capital, Stefano Raggi with 40 other young patricians stepped forward to raise companies of soldiers at their own expense, in order to command them in the field.[54] As none of them had any combat experience, this was expensive bravado. There were capable militiamen in the Riviera valleys, and the peasants of the mountains were skilled in the use of firearms, living as they did with bandits and smugglers, experienced in the ways of the vendetta. Nevertheless, the Genoese garrisons on the Riviera had no will to resist the Piedmontese, and quickly surrendered, despite the presence of 30 Spanish and Genoese galleys patrolling the coast without opposition. The forces of the republic, under the Flanders veteran Gian Girolamo Doria, were dissolving.[55]

Spain saved its beleaguered ally by putting troops at Genoa's disposal. Not wishing to confront France directly while the war in the Low Countries was in

---

[52] See the article by Dante Zanetti, "Le artiglierie genovesi all' inizio del secolo XVII", *Nuova Rivista Storica*, 1966, pp. 643–84.

[53] The ethnic composition of this army is a mystery to me. Charles Dufayard specifies that only a third of Lesdiguières' army comprised of French troops. See C. Dufayard, *Le connetable de Lesdiguières* (Paris: 1892), p. 542.

[54] See the encyclopedia entry, Valori, *Condottieri e generali del seicento*, p. 315.

[55] See the narrative by H. Reade, *Sidelights on the Thirty Years' War*, vol. 2, p. 455ff.

flux, Madrid allowed the Genoese to employ Spanish troops ferried from Naples. Some 6,000 untested Neapolitans under Tommaso Caràcciolo, disembarked and camped outside the walls, were surprised by Lesdiguières at Serravalle and routed. Piedmontese forces put them to flight again at Voltaggio, but only after a bitter struggle. Before long, there were 15,000 troops under Genoese supervision, of which many were Spanish veterans.[56] The strategic evolution nullified Franco-Piedmontese successes, too. Despite their previous assurances, the Venetians were not willing to invade Spanish Lombardy from the east. Moreover, the English and Dutch fleet that was supposed to invade Liguria was attracted by the lure of booty at Cadiz instead, and was upset there. Feria, the governor of Milan, could therefore bolster his field army in Lombardy and wait for the right moment to attack the French and Piedmontese from the rear. As the armies of Charles Emanuel and Lesdiguières advanced, their supply link became more tenuous. The neutral duchy of Mantua reinforced its garrisons in the Monferrato, largely with foreign troops; its neutrality just succeeded in alienating both France and Spain.[57] One observer complained that for a small state like Mantua to have two royal enemies contesting its soil, and not having the means to defend itself, was to be treated as an enemy by both sides.

The Spanish system of alliances then came into its own, to good effect. Both Parma and Modena dispatched a couple of thousand troops to Lombardy to reinforce Feria's field army. Tuscany's five galleys transported Spanish troops from Naples to Genoa, though the admiral Montauto had strict orders not to help the Spaniards in a fleet action or shore operations against France directly.[58] Genoese and Spanish galleys for their part prevented ferrying any French reinforcements by sea. The balance of forces gradually swung in the direction of Spain and her north Italian allies. Meanwhile, the Franco-Piedmontese army proceeded into the mountain passes leading to Genoa. On its route were two mediocre strongholds: Ovada and Gavi. The army stopped and laid siege, but once it was immobile, and no booty was to be had, troops began to desert. Gavi surrendered on 17 April, but the strategic situation was too perilous for the allies to continue their advance. The captured towns had to be relinquished and the army retreated into Piedmont as Feria's army now attacked from behind, through the Monferrato. The Polish and Albanian light horse in Spanish pay marauded and plundered worse than the French. Initiative now lay entirely with Spain, since the siege of Breda in the Netherlands ended with a Habsburg triumph. Feria felt confident enough to confront French forces directly. His army bottled up much of

---

[56] Dufayard, *Le connetable de Lesdiguières*, p. 550.

[57] R. Quazza, *Mantova e Monferrato nella politica europea alla vigilia della guerra per la successione (1624–1627)* (Mantua: 1922), p. 86: "Lo star neutrale ad un Principe picciolo fra due eserciti Reali, che non ha il modo da se di difendersi, non e altro che haverli tutti e due per nemici".

[58] C. Manfroni, *La marina militare del granducato mediceo* (Rome: 1895); pt 2, p. 81ff; see also N. Giorgetti, *Le armi toscane*, vol. 1, p. 423.

the French and Piedmontese in the Po stronghold of Verrua, and there commenced a proper siege. The emperor, fresh from victory against Denmark and its
German Protestant allies, dispatched 5,000 German and Italian troops to speed
up the operation. Before long, Richelieu and Charles Emanuel I were happy to
negotiate a return to the *status quo ante*.[59]

Papal diplomacy defused the crisis. Urban VIII Barberini favoured a muscular
neutrality of Italian states. As the war raged, he mobilized his own field army of
12,000 infantry around Ferrara, and collected 6,000 more around Rome, and
deployed much activity improving fortifications.[60] Now that the adversaries were
ready to negotiate, they called upon the Papal army to keep them apart. Some
5,000 Papal troops were given the task of replacing the Spanish in the Valtelline
garrisons again, after having abandoned them under French pressure without a
fight in 1624. This prevented a return of the Protestant Grisons and let Spain to
feed reinforcements again to the Low Countries. Cardinal Richelieu had to quell
the incipient revolt of French Protestants in Languedoc, and France disappeared
from the scene again. This left Charles Emanuel waiting for a new opportunity to
act.

The new pretext was not long in coming, with the impending extinction of the
direct line of the Gonzaga in Mantua. The reigning duke, Vincenzo II, insisted on
establishing the French branch of the family, the Gonzaga-Nevers, rather than
one of the minor branches, in particular that of Francesco Gonzaga of Guastalla,
allied with Spain. It was a thorny problem, for any heir to the duchy would have
to receive formal investiture from the emperor in Vienna. Carlo Gonzaga-Nevers
was one of the great nobles of France, who could be expected to uphold French
strategy in northern Italy. Moreover, he was an experienced and charismatic
soldier. After serving the emperor in Hungary in 1600, he later prepared an
expedition to liberate the Balkan Christians from the Turks. Worse still for Spain,
both Mantua and the fortress watching over the Monferrato, Casale, were among
the most powerful strongpoints in northern Italy, and both were situated at vital
crossroads on each side of Spanish Lombardy. The Spanish chief minister, or
valido, Olivares and Duke Charles Emanuel I of Piedmont saw the succession crisis
as the opportune moment to divide the Monferrato between them, and to install
the more pliant Guastalla branch on the ducal throne. In the face of this opposition, Charles de Nevers and his son, the duke of Rethel stole into Mantua, where
they had long cultivated ties, just before the death of Vincenzo II.[61] They mortgaged or sold their French possessions to raise troops, and placed French
mercenaries alongside volunteers and peasant militias in fortresses across their
domains.

War began with some raiding from Guastalla against towns in the Mantuan

---

[59] Quazza, *Mantova e Monferrato nella politica europea*, p. 96.
[60] *Ibid.*, p. 104.
[61] See the biography by Emile Baudson, *Charles de Gonzague, duc de Nevers, de Rethel et de Mantoue (1580–1637)* (Paris: 1947), p. 248.

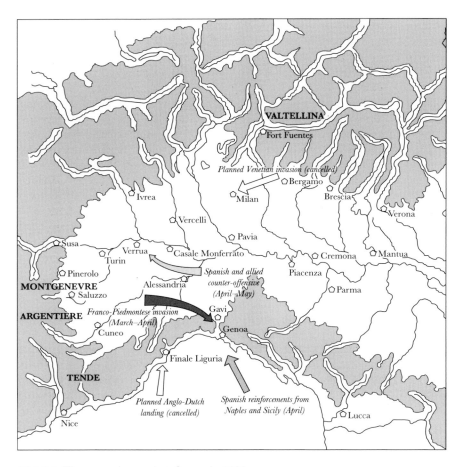

Map 3.1 The campaign against Genoa in 1625

district. By December 1627, the duke of Feria and Charles Emanuel were collecting troops to occupy the Monferrato. Again, the opportune context north of the Alps spurred Spain to action. Count Wallenstein's army was completely victorious in Germany, but it was premature to disband it. Part of the Imperial army of 120,000 men could be dispatched to Italy to further the Habsburg cause there. Emperor Ferdinand II decided that Mantua and Monferrato should surrender to his arbitration as the ultimate feudal lord. Despite Spìnola's advice to Philip IV warning him against a new war in Italy, the more optimistic Olivares and the new governor of Milan, Gonzalo de Cordoba, prevailed.[62] They prepared a field army of 9,000 infantry and 3,000 cavalry in Milan for operations in the Monferrato. It

---

[62] On the role of Olivares, see Stradling, *Europe and the decline of Spain*, p. 84.

was to be joined by the 6,000 Piedmontese infantry and 2,000 cavalry being assembled at Vercelli. The governor of Milan activated the system of alliances again, mobilizing Neapolitan troops by placing them in Genoese pay, under the command of Niccolò Doria. A good part of the Spanish forces comprised of four *tercios*, two of Neapolitans, one of Germans and one of Corsicans. They joined the 10,000 infantry and 1,000 horse already assembled at Alessandria under the Milanese general, Trotti. Another force of 4,000 troops under Girolamo Carafa, prince of Montenegro, screened the Mantuan border from Cremona, and 2,000 troops under another Milanese general, Count Giovanni Serbelloni, guarded the lake district and the exit from the alpine passes.[63]

While the new Duke Charles and his son Charles, duke of Rethel, prepared to defend their duchy, they tried to persuade the emperor to grant them investiture. Many at the court of Vienna, including Wallenstein, favoured this solution.[64] Louis XIII allowed the duke of Mantua to raise troops in France, and provided him with some money to pay them. Some of his best officers were dispatched to Mantua as military advisers.[65] Duke Charles also enlisted two regiments in Mantua and two more in the Monferrato, together with a paltry number of horse. He scattered most of them in garrisons in both sections of his states, separated by 150 km (95 ml) of hostile territory. The size of the army, 12,000 infantry and 2,000 horse, was considerable considering the tiny dimensions of the state whose entire population probably did not exceed 300,000 people, but it is uncertain how much of this was militia.[66]

Charles Emanuel invaded the Monferrato on 29 March 1628, and besieged the town of Trino (north of the Po) with another force. The Spanish army laid out its lines of contravallation before Casale, hoping for a quick conclusion. Its troops were recent levies, since the veterans were in Flanders. When the siege began to stretch into months, desertion depleted the army. Neapolitan and German reinforcements took their place, but finding money to keep the work going was increasingly problematic. Genoese financiers had to be prevailed upon to commit 500,000 *scudi* in July 1628, and in January 1629 for 1,300,000 ducats. The Piedmontese, on the other hand, were reaping most of the advantages. Trino fell to them on 12 May. Their plunder included 5,000 bags of provisions, 40 cartloads of forage and all of the local livestock.[67] In June the Piedmontese army, reinforced with mercenaries formerly in the service of their Mantuan enemy, occupied many towns of the Monferrato. The town of Nizza Monferrato surrendered after a

---

[63] The most detailed, and learned, account of the Mantuan Succession crisis is still the work by Romolo Quazza, *La guerra per la successione di Mantova e del Monferrato (1628–1631)* (Mantua: 1926). On the mobilization, see vol. 1, p. 90.

[64] Mann, *Wallenstein*, p. 479.

[65] Quazza, *La guerra per la successione di Mantova e del Monferrato*, vol. 1, p. 66.

[66] *Ibid.*, vol. 1, p. 125. For the large number of militia in 1619, see Coniglio, *I Gonzaga*, p. 418.

[67] Quazza, *La guerra per la successione di Mantova e di Monferrato*, vol. 1, p. 145.

three-week siege, despite Duke Charles' spending over a million *scudi* in its defence. The bitter fighting there depleted the Piedmontese and Spanish forces, though, and Casale still held out. In September, Charles Emanuel lent part of his army to Gonzalo de Cordoba to speed up the operations. New levies in all of its Italian territories, as well as in Genoa and Burgundy, increased Spain's forces. Important towns had been lost in Flanders due to the requirements of the siege of the great fortress on the Po.[68]

Olivares' new fear was that King Louis XIII, fresh from his triumph over Protestant La Rochelle and England, would come to rescue his ally over the Alps. The siege of Casale was then slowed by the necessity of diverting troops to block passes leading out of France. Duke Charles raised an additional army of almost 10,000 men in France by selling his estates there. A large body of it under the Marquis d'Uxelles tried to force its way across the mountains at Casteldelfino, but it was caught, battered and then dispersed by the Piedmontese.[69] Casale was still holding out when Louis XIII resolved to come to its aid with a large army of his own, on 1 March 1629. Leading his army in person, the king of France broke a mediocre Spanish and Piedmontese force trying to bar the way at Susa. Many of the Spanish forces were composed of green levies drawn from Lombardy. Like most of the Piedmontese militia, they bolted without firing a shot when charged by French and Swiss veterans.[70] The French army's appearance changed the strategic picture entirely, for the besiegers around Casale had to lift the siege hurriedly and throw detachments into fortresses in the path of the Bourbon king. Once it was clear that Louis was ready to act, Venice promised to help Duke Charles of Mantua with its own army, which its French commander, the Duc de Candale assembled in the Terraferma.[71] Flush with confidence, Duke Charles went on the offensive, attacking Casalmaggiore in Spanish Lombardy. Venice was supposed to join him in a siege of Cremona with an army of 12,000 men, but the Senate refused to commit itself to an open breach with the Habsburgs.

After placing a French garrison in Casale, Louis abandoned his Italian allies again and took his army back to France to deal with another Protestant rebellion in Languedoc. This was the beginning of disaster for Mantua. Venice feared doing irreparable damage to its own security, and remained on the defensive. The Habsburgs took the initiative again. Philip IV appointed Ambrogio Spìnola as governor of Milan and commander in Italy, with the task of capturing Casale, as he had captured Ostend, Julich and Breda. He brought with him as his chief engineer Ferdinando Giovanni La Capra, the foremost military engineer in Spain. Spìnola then set about creating a massive field army in Lombardy. Besides the 16,000 soldiers still mobilized, he would add 12,000 German troops, 6,000

---

[68] Stradling, *Philip IV and the government of Spain*, p. 98.
[69] Quazza, *La guerra per la successione di Mantova e di Monferrato*, vol. 1, p. 235.
[70] *Ibid.*, vol. 1, p. 323.
[71] *Ibid.*, vol. 1, p. 323.

fresh Neapolitans, 4,000 Tuscans and 2,000 Parmans. He meant this army to overwhelm Casale and the isolated Mantuan garrisons in the Monferrato, but also to intimidate his untrustworthy ally, Charles Emanuel of Piedmont, whom he suspected was negotiating secretly with France. Spìnola ordered Grand Duke Ferdinando II of Tuscany to comply with the alliance treaty provisions with Spain, and furnish 4,000 men. Not daring to refuse, the latter readied 1,600 men in Livorno, but neglected to transport them.[72]

More troops assembled in Catalonia and Naples, where Olivares prevailed upon the aristocracy to open its purse and to arm itself. In line with a century-old tradition, many of them complied. Tuscany eventually complied too. A *tercio* under Camillo Bourbon del Monte finally disembarked in Liguria to join Spìnola's army, and 500 horse followed under the Florentine Cosimo Ricciardi. Tuscany also agreed to pay for 4,000 Swiss infantry and to improve its coastal fortifications. Grand Duke Ferdinando II promised to send 6,000 men to Lombardy for two years, and to place his galleys under Spanish command, but avoided complying. Despite all of this energy and organizing, bullying and exhorting, Spìnola's array was not as fearsome as it looked on paper. Few of the troops were very good. There were many *tercios* and companies, but the lack of food and pay incited the soldiers in them to desert. The siege of Casale began again in the summer of 1629, this time against a predominantly French garrison under Marshal Thoiras. In December, although the garrison was dwindling, Casale was still holding out.

The Bourbon king's hesitations created a pall of incertitude everywhere. In December 1629, Louis XIII marched back into Piedmont, to Susa, and this time Charles Emanuel declared himself a French ally. He promised the French king he would lead 10,000 men on Milan and expel the Spaniards from northern Italy. It was a short dalliance. Louis returned to France again to settle the fundamental direction of his policy, torn between the pro-Spanish and Catholic policies of his mother and her advisers, and the expansionist and secular *realpolitik* of Cardinal Richelieu. Without French protection, Charles Emanuel changed sides again and promised 6,500 troops for Spìnola's army shivering around Casale.[73] The besieging army gradually swelled again with the spring of 1630.

Having decided to back Cardinal Richelieu, who was now unchallenged chief minister of France, and having settled the Huguenot rebellions definitively, Louis XIII decided to force his way back into Italy. A Piedmontese army of 10,000 infantry and 2,500 horse blocked the way. Spìnola dispatched 7,000 Spanish infantry and 2,000 Germans, mostly good troops, and almost 5,000 horse, to bar the route to the French. Reinforcements arrived from Naples, Tuscany, Parma and now even Modena and Lucca, in the form of soldiers and money. Two thousand more Tuscans arrived in May. Unable to break this force in the confined space of an alpine valley, Louis conquered Savoy instead, held by only 6,000

---

[72] *Ibid.*, vol. 1, p. 323. See also N. Giorgetti, *Le armi toscane*, vol. 1, p. 427.
[73] Quazza, *La guerra per la successione di Mantova e del Monferrato*, vol. 2, p. 36.

Piedmontese and an unenthusiastic peasant militia. Casale was slowly being reduced, with only 2,000 French and 1,000 Monferrini and Italians left in the garrison. Spìnola wàs making preparations for the final assault on the city with his army of 20,000 infantry and 4,000 horse, the bulk of the troops being Spanish and Italian.[74]

As Spìnola built up his forces in Lombardy in the spring of 1629, Emperor Ferdinand II decided to settle the Mantuan crisis by besieging Mantua itself with an Imperial army. At the end of May the first contingents marched through Switzerland under Merode and Galasso, wreaking havoc *en route*. By August there were 30,000 infantry and 6,000 Imperial horse in northern Italy. While most of the soldiers were Germans, with Walloons and Croats making up the difference, at least ten colonels were Italians in Imperial service.[75] They seemed ready to overwhelm the vastly outnumbered French and Mantuan troops and their timid Venetian friends too, if they got in the way. In Mantua, Duke Charles employed 3,000 Venetian soldiers to dig trenches around the city. There were 4,000 more Venetians dispersed in the Mantuan strongholds of Castelgoffredo, Gazzuolo, Canneto and Goito, and a corps of 3,000 Mantuan infantry under Cosimo del Monte available for offensive operations. A Venetian field army sat behind the Oglio river in its entrenchments, waiting for developments.[76]

In October 1629 the German army under Galasso and Collalto advanced into the duchy, capturing Viadana and Canneto almost without a siege. The Serenissima's field army poised to prevent this was large and well supplied, but its troops lacked the experience, training, leadership and sinister reputation of the Germans. Venetian troops broke and ran almost everywhere, allowing the Imperials to advance beyond the Chiesa river border. The mere reputation of Wallenstein's army demoralized the recent Italian levies. The strongest of the outlying fortresses, Gazzuolo, had a garrison of 2,500 men and plenty of provisions. It surrendered after an initial bombardment of two days, and 500 of the garrison enlisted in the enemy army. To ease his conscience, the fortress commander, Angelo Corner, discussed with Ottavio Piccolòmini whether a good Italian could deliver his post to the emperor.[77] On 22 November, Goito surrendered, again mostly owing to the poor quality of the soldiers recruited, especially in the Venetian army that disbanded under the slightest pressure. To stiffen their

---

[74] *Ibid.*, vol. 2, p. 76.

[75] On the composition of the Imperial army, see Quazza, *La guerra per la successione di Mantova e del Monferrato*, vol. 1, p. 457. See also Golo Mann, *Wallenstein*, p. 479ff. Selwyn Brinton provides a list of 17 regiments besieging Mantua in 1630, of which nine were commanded by Italians; see S. Brinton, *The Gonzaga, lords of Mantua* (New York: 1927), p. 226.

[76] Quazza, *La guerra per la successione di Mantova e del Monferrato*, vol. 1, p. 464ff.

[77] On this point of honour, see the encyclopedia entry by A. Valori, *Condottieri e generali del seicento*, p. 97. On the surrender of Mantuan fortresses to the Imperials, see Quazza, *La guerra per la successione di Mantova e del Monferrato*, vol. 1, p. 464ff.

resistance it was necessary to find veterans. Duke Charles relied increasingly on a couple of thousand *oltremontani*, generally French and Swiss, to stiffen the garrison of his capital.

Having ravaged the duchy of Mantua in late autumn, Collalto tried to profit from the momentum to storm the defences of Mantua itself. The garrison repulsed this easily, forcing the Imperials to disperse their army into winter quarters and subject the city to a blockade. The soldiery settled in the swath of Imperial fiefs around the duchy, where the emperor demanded that their holders pay taxes for their upkeep. The autonomous minor branches of the Gonzaga envied ducal power, and eagerly collaborated with Spain and the emperor. Parma and Modena paid contributions too.[78] Ottavio Piccolòmini had the task of persuading the grand duke to contribute money as an Imperial vassal. In this he failed, but only because Tuscany contributed large sums to the Spanish campaign in Liguria in 1625, and assisted Spìnola around Casale. Grand Duke Ferdinando II promised moreover to lend money and to send troops and material to Germany, under the command of his brothers.[79] For the emperor, the episode served to revive Imperial pretensions in northern Italy despite the Spanish hegemony. These pretensions rested entirely upon the presence of the army, which became restive when supplies were lacking. Around Mantua, formerly one of the richest districts in all of Europe, the destruction wrought by the invading army was colossal. At Volta Mantovana, marauding soldiers killed about 150 peasants, an atrocity akin to those committed in Germany, and by which the Thirty Years War is so tragically famous.[80] As the Venetian army would not defend it, much of the rural population fled the district. Then a new scourge appeared to ravage the invader and the invaded alike, in the bubonic plague. This was part of a lethal pandemic that devastated much of Europe, but nowhere more than northern Italy. Seeking safety in flight, Venetian troops deserted in bands. The epidemic then seeped into Mantua and took a heavy toll on both the civilians and the garrison. By early May, before the contagion's peak, there were only about 3,000 regular troops left, divided equally between French and Italians, and 400 militiamen, barely enough to guard the ramparts. Between April and July, some 25,000 soldiers and civilians inside the city died of the plague. In mid-July there were only 700 soldiers left fit for service.[81]

The Imperial army just waited for resistance to collapse from disease. On 29 May, Galasso's army stormed the Venetian camp at Villabuona near Goito. The Venetian leaders panicked completely: an army of 15,000 infantry and 2,500

---

[78] Pugliese, *Le prime strette dell' Austria in Italia*, p. 122 et sq. On Modena see L. Amorth, *Modena capitale: storia di Modena e dei suoi duchi dal 1598 al 1860* (Milan: 1967), p. 59. For Parma, see Giovanni Drei, *I Farnese: grandezza e decadenza di una dinastia italiana* (Rome: 1954), p. 201.

[79] Pugliese, *Le prime strette dell' Austria in Italia*, p. 127.

[80] Quazza, *La guerra per la successione di Mantova e del Monferrato*, vol. 2, p. 36.

[81] *Ibid.*, vol. 2, p. 119.

horse behind good earthworks was put to rout with over 2,000 casualties by an inferior force. It might have been feasible for Galasso to occupy the cities of the Venetian Terraferma, but such was not his mandate. Rather, on 18 July 1630, the Imperials launched their assault on Mantua, by crossing the lake in boats. Since the garrison was too small to cover the entire perimeter, the troops scaling the wall irrupted into the city almost unopposed. By military convention, a city taken by storm could be looted. The scale of booty to be drawn from a rich and noble capital city like Mantua led the commanders of the day, Rambaldo Collalto, Mattia Galasso, Ottavio Piccolòmini and the Lorrainer, Aldringhen, to carry out the sack in a methodical fashion. For three days, 14,000 soldiers combed the city in search of booty. Collalto and Aldringhen were well placed to take the choicest spoils, including the ducal palace with its art collection, reputedly the most important in Europe. The booty from the palace alone was said to be eighteen million ducats, several times the value of silver the king of Spain received from Mexico and equivalent to three times the tax revenue of the kingdom of Naples! Moreover, the soldiery emptied all of the noble palaces, bourgeois houses and every pauper's garret. Mantua never recovered its former importance. From 30,000 inhabitants before the siege, there left only 6,000 or 7,000 plague-dazed survivors living in complete destitution.[82]

The successful conclusion to the Imperial siege of Mantua contrasted with Spìnola's inability to crack Casale. Mantua's capture ended the pretext for hostilities. The emperor concluded *his* war from a position of strength. Duke Charles relinquished his claim on Guastalla to his cousin Don Cesare Gonzaga, a Spanish client, and ceded Trino, Alba and some other towns in the Monferrato to the duke of Savoy, all in exchange for Imperial investiture. Mantua, however, retained Casale, and the duke remained part of the French clientèle in northern Italy. After the duke's death in 1638, Venice guaranteed the city's integrity by placing its own troops in garrison there, maintained by Mantuan taxes. It was vastly weaker in wealth and power, never recovering its former population.[83] Papal diplomacy conducted by the young Giulio Mazzarini brought a suspension of arms around Casale, on the eve of a decisive battle between the Spanish army and a French relief force. Ambrogio Spìnola died of exhaustion – some say disappointment – because of his failure to capture it.[84] Hubert Reade sees the siege of Mantua as the beginning of a resurgence of Imperial power in Italy, a prelude to Austria's intention of restoring the Holy Roman Empire to its former grandeur south of the Alps. After it, Italian princes would look more towards

---

[82] *Ibid.*, vol. 2, p. 150. On the orderly sacking, see Redlich, *The German military enterpriser and his work force*, vol. 1, p. 359ff.

[83] C. Mozzarelli, *Mantova e i Gonzaga dal 1382 al 1707* (Turin: 1987), p. 116.

[84] This whole episode is placed in the context of the incipient struggle between France and Spain, by Michel Devèze, *L'Espagne de Philippe IV (1621–1665)* (Paris: 1970), vol. 1, p. 124.

Vienna than to Madrid.[85] That is premature, for Spain still had plenty of fight left in it, and the subsequent campaigns would prove just how resilient Spanish power remained.

For Spain and Austria, the Mantuan succession crisis appeared in a window of opportunity when both could divert the greater part of their resources to Italy. Stradling views Olivares' intervention as an all-or-nothing gamble to reassert Spanish hegemony in Italy, and to impose a 'Spanish peace' there. Since it demanded a huge commitment of resources, it compromised the Spanish position in Flanders, which had been promising before the removal of Spìnola in 1628. By 1630, the military conjuncture had worsened for Spain, having failed to strengthen its position in Italy, having neglected to make a compromise peace in Flanders, and having failed to drive Richelieu from the entourage of Louis XIII. At that juncture, the invasion of Germany by the Swedish Protestant armies of Gustavus Adolphus presented new dangers to the House of Austria. Spain would have to tax its resources still further. Italy was thereafter relegated to the periphery. This meant that Naples, Sicily, Sardinia and Lombardy resumed their role of bankrolling and reinforcing Spanish imperial aims elsewhere.

At Madrid, the *valido* Olivares put in place a plan to institutionalize this military contribution from the Spanish realms outside Castile. The Union of Arms, as he called it, set military quotas for each dominion to fill and maintain. The goal was the maintenance of an army of 130,000 men. Olivares assigned the largest contingent, 44,000 men, to Castile and the Indies. Catalonia, Portugal, Aragon and Valencia, with the Balearics and the Canaries would support another 54,000. The Netherlands could pay for 12,000 on their own. Finally, the Italian states could provide 30,000: 6,000 for Sicily, 8,000 for Milan and 16,000 for Naples.[86] Philip IV called upon Spanish aristocrats to reverse their declining participation in royal armies, and to prove their loyalty by setting an example. They paid no heed, however. Titled feudal lords in Castile who were to recruit and maintain a body of horsemen, or else pay an equivalent sum to the treasury, claimed immunity from such taxation.[87] Twenty-eight grandees were assigned the rank of colonel, and requested to levy a regiment as their private property, in which they could dispose of the officers' commissions as they wished. Only four of them raised the obligatory 1,500 men, and only two decided to follow these troops into the field. Olivares then tried to purchase their co-operation, by granting them immu-

---

[85] Reade, *Sidelights on the Thirty Years War*, vol. 3, p. 488. Pugliese notes that while the Thirty Years War persisted, Vienna was more solicitous of its Italian vassals than they were of it. See Pugliese, *Le prime strette dell' Austria in Italia*, p. 128.

[86] Devèze, *L'Espagne de Philippe IV*, vol. 1, p. 183. I have seen no figures for the thinly-populated Sardinia, or the intensely loyal Franche-Comté.

[87] F. Benigno, *L'ombra del rey: la lotta politica nella Spagna dei Validos (1598–1643)*, (Palermo: 1990), pp. 183–4.

nity from debt litigation in exchange for their contribution to the war. An important lever was the conferral of military orders on families that petitioned for them. Few of these brought meaningful wealth to their holders in the form of a *commenda*. Rather, bestowing the 'habit' exclusively on noble families served to legitimize the aspirations of upwardly mobile houses. They remained therefore a much sought-after commodity, which Philip IV and Olivares exploited to the hilt. Obtaining one for a son became crucial to the thousands of Spanish families in the hidalgo class, but they were also very appreciated in Italy. Olivares in fact 'sold' these titles to families that contributed to the war effort. Wright notes that the gradual upward curve of grants suddenly steepened after 1621, until the rate had tripled, and conferrals remained very high until 1655.[88]

Surprisingly, the Italian states provided the bulk of the money expected from them, despite the devastation wrought by the plague of 1630. The active participation of the peninsula's nobility was crucial for the continuation of war, and this participation may have retained some vitality for another generation in Italy, particularly in Naples. Von Reumont, although he is miserly with dates, provides some examples.[89] The most eminent families were the greatest of warriors. The prince of Belmonte Pignatelli raised and conducted a regiment of 14 companies to Lombardy. Outdoing that, the prince of Satriano Ravaschiero raised 22 companies that served in Liguria and the Monferrato in 1625. Marzio Carafa di Maddaloni enlisted in the same campaign, commanding four regiments of cavalry and 16 companies of gens d'armes he had helped raise. The duke of Maddaloni summoned 500 of his own vassals, and raised two regiments of horse for the sum of 25,000 ducats, and took them to the siege of Vercelli in 1617. Diomede Carafa, a relative, raised his company of horse when he was only 15 years old, but his parents refused to let him go to Lombardy. In 1640 he reached into his purse to furnish 24 companies of troops drawn from his vassals, and helped to defray the cost of the war. Comparato, however, is probably right to see in this generosity an indirect form of taxation of their rural vassals, especially inasmuch as von Reumont maintains that the opulent lifestyle of the baronage was hardly curtailed during the war.[90]

By 1637 the viceroy of Naples warned Olivares that only a few nobles were still inclined to raise companies of troops on their own account, and that the greatest families were losing their taste for war. Naples purportedly raised about 50,000 new recruits between 1630 and 1635, which was more than Castile, from a

---

[88] L. P. Wright, "The military orders in sixteenth and seventeenth century Spanish society: the institutional embodiment of a historical tradition", *Past and Present*, **43**, 1969, pp. 34–70.
[89] Alfred von Reumont, *The Carafas of Maddaloni: Naples under Spanish dominion* (London: 1854), p. 155ff.
[90] See the article by Vittorio Ivo Comparato, "Toward the Revolt of 1647", in *Good government in Spanish Naples*, A. Calabria & J.A. Marino (eds) (New York: 1990, first publ. 1974), pp. 275–316, at p. 278.

population only half the size.[91] It is difficult to confirm contemporary impressions that the scale was so considerable. On the basis of the accounts of the Sommaria in Naples, Antonio Calabria confirms that Naples provided, or at least paid for, 10,000 soldiers and 1,000 horses annually, from 1631 to 1643. This was in addition to a subsidy of one million ducats to the war effort, over and above the cost of soldiers and ships for the kingdom's defence. Naples also equipped these recruits and bought cannon, muskets and pikes for them, and then transported them by sea to Genoa or Finale, and later to Spain itself. The kingdom also paid about a third of government expenditures in Lombardy, which had to bear the brunt of the war. It is not easy to identify the recruits, and where they came from. By 1640, recruits were not easy to find. A common practice was to pardon bandits and criminals in exchange for their enlistment, or even recruit whole troops of bandits to fight as a unit under their leader, who became a commissioned officer into the bargain. Spain also pressured its client states in Italy to provide troops for the Catholic cause. In 1634 Ottavio Villani, a regent of the Council of Italy, tried to persuade the princes of Tuscany, Modena and Parma to send 15,000 soldiers to Milan and Germany, in exchange for titles and offices in the Empire. None complied.[92]

Sardinia raised its first *tercios* for the Spanish empire too. In the sixteenth century, the islanders were considered too brutal, bloodthirsty and undisciplined to make good soldiers. In 1628, aristocrats from the kingdom's leading houses, the Castelvì and Cervellon, raised the island's first *tercio* for service in Lombardy. This marked the very beginning of a military vocation among Sardinian aristocrats. Another Castelvì raised a *tercio* for service in Flanders in 1637, which was destroyed at Rocroi. A third was raised with difficulty in 1641 for service in Catalonia, but sickness destroyed most of it very quickly. Two years later an infantry *tercio* and a cavalry regiment were drawn from the island for the war in Spain. Between 1628 and 1650, from 8,000 to 10,000 soldiers were recruited from the island, which Antonello Mattone sees as being in line with Spanish recruitment in Italian dominions, running at four to five per cent of the total population.[93] Behind the recruits was money. Sicily contributed little to the *tercios* of the empire, but it did provide half a million *scudi* annually for military operations

---

[91] A. Calabria, *The cost of empire: the finances of the kingdom of Naples in the time of Spanish rule*, (New York: 1991), p. 90. The figures cited by Antonio Calabria have been advanced previously by other authors, notably Rosario Villari, but there is little direct evidence offered that these numbers were effectively levied. James B. Collins emphasizes the difference between sums demanded, and sums received in contemporary France, in his *Fiscal limits of absolutism: direct taxation in early seventeenth-century France* (Berkeley, California: 1988). Still in France, the true effective numbers never represented more than 60 per cent of those called for in the levies; see A. Corvisier, *Louvois* (Paris: 1983), p. 82.

[92] R. Canosa, *Milano nel seicento: grandezza e miseria nell' Italia spagnola* (Milan: 1993), p. 138.

[93] A. Mattone, B. Anatra, R. Turtas, *Storia dei Sardi e della Sardegna, vol. 3: l'età moderna: dagli Aragonesi alla fine del dominio spagnolo* (Milan: 1989), pp. 95–8.

elsewhere after 1620.[94] Giuseppe Giarrizzo estimates that Sicily raised no less than ten million *scudi* for the war effort between 1620 and 1650, of which more than half was made up by alienating crown property.[95] Pressure on Sicily to raise troops intensified over time. In 1642 the island's parliament approved a *donativo* to enrol over 4,000 troops to send to war theatres, but the troops levied may not have been islanders.[96] Similarly in Lombardy, the tax pressure was applied forcefully. In Como, studied by Domenico Sella, taxes tripled between 1618 and 1688, with the level of taxes per capita increasing until about 1660, or the end of the war with France.[97] Because of its greater size, the kingdom of Naples was the most important contributor. There as well, taxes tripled after 1620, in the absence of any real inflation, and despite a serious economic decline. This played havoc with the fundamental rules of state finance. The king of Spain was truly concerned to avoid measures prejudicial to the lower classes by providing tax exemptions for the elderly and the poor. There were privileged classes or groups too, like the clergy, and the inhabitants of the city of Naples. To meet its obligations, the viceroy (on Philip's and Olivares' urgings) resorted to two instruments; indirect or sales taxes on the one hand; and borrowing on the other. Taxes were applied on most items, but especially those consumed by the wealthy.[98]

By borrowing massively to pay for the war, money was no longer available to replant vines and orchards, buy seed grain or press olives. Naples imposed a tax on the number of sheep, so that it was in the short-term interest of the crown to encourage an extension of grazing at the expense of the secure provisioning of Naples, Palermo and Messina. Landlords took more and more land out of cultivation and converted it to pasture.[99] The whole economy began to stagnate and then falter as the crown imposed taxes on exports of raw materials like silk and oil. Borrowed money also had to be repaid eventually, and interest had to be paid immediately. Until 1620 the kingdom of Naples had always been able to redeem its debt, at attractive interest rates. The renewal of the Dutch war in 1621 and the Genoese war of 1625 upset this balance. By 1626 officials employed over half the revenues to pay the interest. After 1638 the crown began to renege on some of its debts, or bargained interest payments against new loans, which struck at investor confidence and drove interest rates upwards. After 1640, the viceroy could only continue financing the war by desperate financial measures, such as alienating revenues to creditors. In simple figures, the Neapolitan debt rose from ten million ducats in 1612, to forty million in 1636, and the interest to service this was roughly

---

[94] D. Mack Smith, *A history of Sicily: medieval Sicily, 800–1713* (London: 1968), p. 208.

[95] G. Giarrizzo & V. d'Alessandro, *La Sicilia dal Vespro all' unità d'Italia* (Turin: 1989), p. 287.

[96] P. Castiglione, *Storia di un declino: il seicento siciliano* (Syracuse, Italy: 1987), p. 109.

[97] D. Sella, *Lo stato di Milano in età spagnola* (Turin: 1987), p. 123ff.

[98] Calabria, *The cost of empire*, p. 65ff.

[99] John Marino, *Pastoral economics in the kingdom of Naples* (Baltimore: 1988), p. 22 and p. 158.

57 per cent of ordinary revenues. In 1646, the public debt reached over fifty million ducats, for an economy that had contracted owing to the economic crisis in the Mediterranean.

To continue borrowing, the viceroy had to alienate the new taxes, that is, place their collection in the hands of state creditors. About 50 per cent of the tax money was thereby alienated in 1637, and about 90 per cent by 1644. This meant that the state paid an effective interest rate of 70 per cent annually on the money it borrowed to fight the war.[100] Speculative fever created colossal fortunes overnight; although for the crown to refuse to reimburse particular creditors meant that they might lose fortunes too. One of the few avenues left was to swell the categories of 'extraordinary revenue'. Philip IV began to sell the crown assets to anyone with the money to buy them, and this was usually the barons or Genoese bankers. Like his ancestors, he sold titles, so that a dizzying spiral of princes and marcheses followed year after year, inflated like the coinage. He allowed lateral branches of noble families to consolidate their grasp over the fiefs of their kin, despite laws to the contrary. The viceroys leased royal buildings, forests, prisons and even fortresses to private individuals. Judicial prerogatives were sold to the barons. Pardons were sold for every crime but treason.[101]

These redoubled efforts seemed to pay off strategically, despite the worsening financial situation of the Habsburg monarchy. A new Hispano-Italian field army assembled in Milan in 1634 under the command of the son and heir of Philip IV, Ferdinando, the Cardinal–Infante. Marching into Germany, this force combined with the Imperials under Galasso and Piccolòmini, and laid siege to the city of Nordlingen, hoping to entice the Swedish army to attack them in their entrenchments. The Swedes, despite their numerical inferiority, decided to attack, unaware that Piccolòmini was circling behind them with his cavalry. The battle of 6 September 1634 almost ended the war in Germany.[102] After Habsburg forces destroyed Sweden's army utterly, the Spanish continued triumphantly to the Low Countries to confront the Dutch. Sweden was abandoned by most of its German Protestant allies, who made their peace with the emperor.

After Nordlingen, only France could save the German Protestant cause and thwart the triumph of the Habsburg dynasty. Richelieu had been subsidizing both the Dutch and Swedish war effort, preferring to fight Spain and Austria by proxy rather than risk an all-out war. Nordlingen convinced Richelieu and Louis XIII they should escalate their policy into one of full-blown war with the House of Austria at the beginning of 1635, by waging war simultaneously on all its borders. We have seen how, in the Low Countries, the first campaigns

---

[100] L. De Rosa, "L'ultima fase della guerra dei trent' anni e il regno di Napoli: inflazione, tassazione, speculazioni e drenaggio di capitali", *Nuova Rivista Storica*, 1983, pp. 367–86.

[101] Rosario Villari, *La rivolta antispagnola a Napoli: le origini (1585–1647)*, p. 230.

[102] On the importance of the battle of Nordlingen, see Geoffrey Parker *et al.*, *The Thirty Years' War* (London: 1984), pp. 140–2.

were successes for Spain. Richelieu had prepared French operations in the Italian theatre by beckoning to the Italian princes to enter an anti-Habsburg alliance. The new duke of Savoy, Victor Amadeus I, was the linchpin of this construction, with his consort, Marie-Christine, daughter of Henri IV. However, as an insurance policy, his brother Tommaso of Savoy was commander of the Spanish forces in the Low Countries; this ambivalence was typical of Piedmontese policy, and may have been replicated by the behaviour of local military families too, who had family members in each camp. Duke Charles of Mantua, now dependent upon French support, entered the alliance too, promising to provide a little field army of 3,000 men, alongside the glory-seeking Odoardo Farnese, duke of Parma, who levied 4,000 foot and 500 horse to serve in the coalition.[103] Olivares upset French designs by launching a seaborne attack on Provence. A fleet of 35 galleys and ten other vessels transported 7,500 Spanish and Italian troops to the islands off the east coast of Provence where they cut coastal links between France and its Italian allies Piedmont and Parma.[104]

Richelieu had no intention of making Italy the foremost theatre of operations, and sent only 8,000 men under Marshal Créqui, who directed operations under the nominal authority of Duke Victor Amadeus. The allied army moved first on the Lombard town of Valenza, situated on the Po between Genoa and Milan. Another French and Swiss army under the duc de Rohan invaded Lombardy from the north, winning a battle against a small Italo-Spanish army under Serbelloni at Morbegno.[105] Success would have cut Lombardy off from outside aid. Multiple commanders in the alliance played havoc with the direction of siege operations in 1635. The Spanish defenders and Italian defenders proved to be more spirited and experienced than anticipated and so the allied troops began to desert. Odoardo Farnese was the first to flinch, pulling his troops back into his duchy to protect it from cavalry raids, but he lost contact with his allies by doing so.[106] The duke was punished first by the seizure of his fiefs in the Abruzzo, and next by the systematic looting of his duchy by cavalry. Habsburg troops then routed Odoardo with his little army at Rottofreno, near Piacenza in June 1636.[107] When the Mantuans pulled back too, and sat on the defensive, the initiative passed to the 'Spaniards'.

The allied armies made no progress in subsequent years. Rohan did not advance south of the Alps in 1636, and in 1637 the Grisons pulled out of the

---

[103] G. Solari, *The House of Farnese* (New York: 1968, first publ. 1964), p. 222ff.

[104] R. C. Anderson, "The Thirty Years' War in the Mediterranean" (pt 1), *Mariner's Mirror*, **15**, 1969, pp. 435–51.

[105] J. A. Clarke, *Huguenot warrior: the life and times of Henri de Rohan, 1579–1638* (The Hague: 1966), p. 183ff.

[106] Solari, *The House of Farnese*, p. 229. See also Drei, *I Farnese*, pp. 204–6; and Giovanni Tocci, *Il ducato di Parma e Piacenza* (Turin: 1987), p. 56.

[107] Tocci, *Il ducato di Parma e Piacenza*, p. 56.

French alliance altogether. In the Piedmontese campaigns of 1636 and 1637, Victor Amadeus emerged victorious from two minor battles, at Tornavento and Mombaldone. It was a harbinger of successes to come when, in quick succession, the principal figures of the coalition died. Duke Charles Gonzaga died in Mantua in September 1637, followed by the sudden demise (from poison?) of Victor Amadeus in October, and then the marshal, Créqui, in March 1638. The anti-Habsburg alliance, never strong, began to fall apart. Mantua, after the death of Duke Carlo, reverted quickly to the Spanish orbit under the regent Maria. The French occupied the Monferrato and were ensconced in Casale with a sizeable garrison. Only Monferrato's being held hostage stood in their way of joining Spain actively.[108]

Olivares and the governor of Milan, Liganes, then pressured their allies into taking firmer positions. Genoa had too much stake in the Spanish system to defect, but it gave more thought to its own defence. Spanish bankruptcy in 1627, and the death of Spìnola in 1630, created new fears. After the events of 1625, the republic constructed an enormous new rampart around and above the capital city. Philip IV sought to entice Tuscany into taking a more active role by promising to appoint one prince or the other, Mattias or GianCarlo de'Medici, as Spanish General of the Sea. Ferdinand II could not refuse to send the Tuscan galleys to join the Spanish fleet, but he did order his admiral, Verrazzano, to desist from attacking French ships. Tuscany began to play a double game of paying lip-service to its traditional alliance with Spain, but without participating in aggressive actions against the French. The Tuscan galleys therefore limited themselves to transporting troops between Barcelona and La Spezia, convoying supply ships, or patrolling the coast.[109] Tuscany also diminished its financial support. The Monte di Pietà in Florence had served as a state bank from which Grand Duke Ferdinando II lent money to Spain at low rates of interest. This was discontinued too. Tuscany spent much of its revenue on preparation for war, however: improving the fortresses, augmenting the garrisons, and maintaining, like the Pope, a muscular neutrality benevolent to Spain. In contrast, Modena was less ambiguous. Duke Francesco I d'Este had martial yearnings like Odoardo Farnese in Parma. Both built citadels and fortified the principal towns of their duchies. Without committing himself to the Spanish alliance actively, Duke Francesco did what he could to further the success of its armies. His brother Rinaldo served in Lombardy as colonel, and an important clientèle from the duchy followed him. Duke Francesco alternately acted as mediator and menace to induce Odoardo Farnese to quit the French alliance in 1637.[110]

The chaos in Piedmont underlines just how attractive the Spanish party was. The death of Victor Amadeus I in 1637 precipitated a political crisis, since the

---

[108] For Mantua in the years after the siege, see Selwyn Brinton, *The Gonzaga: lords of Mantua*, p. 230ff.

[109] Manfroni, *La marina militare del granducato mediceo*, part 2, pp. 96–9.

[110] Amorth, *Modena capitale*, pp. 59.

French duchess-regent Marie-Christine differed with her pro-Spanish brothers-in-law Prince Tommaso and Cardinal Maurizio. Prince Tommaso was the most gifted soldier the family had ever produced. Of all his military and political education, the lesson learned best was to be wary of French promises. Richelieu had left Piedmont in the lurch in 1635, expecting his Italian allies to do the fighting and to suffer the consequences. Tommaso also rightly suspected that France had designs on annexing Savoy, and over the strongholds guarding the entry into the Po valley, beginning with the hilltop fortress of Pinerolo ceded to the kingdom by Victor Amadeus as part of the pact of Rivoli.[111]

Immediately upon the death of Victor Amadeus, Richelieu wanted to place French troops in all the key strongpoints of the duchy. Many Piedmontese officials were also 'gratified' with French money. The meagre French forces in the theatre were put on the defensive by Leganès, who besieged the important city of Vercelli in 1638. The two princes then raised their own armies from among their followers in Piedmont, and many military commanders joined Tommaso out of tradition, or from clientèle interest. For Piedmont, the onset of the civil war in 1638 was the most sombre period in its history. By 1639, the princes backed by a few thousand Spanish troops were well on their way to capturing all the towns in the territory adjoining Spanish Lombardy, often with little resistance. Even Turin refused to lodge the French troops sent to help it. Tommaso seized most of the territory north and east of the capital. Cardinal Maurizio at the head of his own army occupied much of the south, with some towns welcoming his forces.[112]

In July 1639, Prince Tommaso's army of 8,000 infantry and 2,500 horse entered Turin by surprise, and the regent Marie-Christine barely had time to remove herself and her infant son Charles Emanuel II to the citadel with the French garrison. For Richelieu and Louis XIII, the contest looked bleak: Habsburg armies had bested them recently in the Basque Country and in Luxembourg, and Spanish troops had laid siege to Casale too, far to the east of French forces in Piedmont. By the end of autumn the tide began to shift, after the French dispatched one of their abler generals, the Comte d'Harcourt. French soldiers frequently committed atrocities when they took towns held by the princes, as a dispiriting example to others. The Piedmontese themselves were so polarized that they feared endless vendettas. Control of Turin was the ultimate prize. Prince Tommaso in the city blockaded the citadel with his army. Harcourt invested Prince Tommaso's troops with the French army. Then Leganès invested the French army with the Spanish one, making four concentric circles of troops besieging each other. Spanish attempts to break and carry the French entrenchments in July were repulsed, and experiments to pack provisions into bombs and fire them into the city proved impractical. On 24 September, Prince Tommaso

---

[111] M. Pollak, *Turin, 1564–1680*, p. 88.

[112] The most detailed analysis of the civil war is contained in a short book by Guido Quazza, *Guerra civile in Piemonte, 1637–1642 (nuove ricerche)* (Turin: 1960).

turned Turin over to Harcourt and withdrew with what was left of his army. He was vacillating now, believing that Leganès was jealous of his talents, and had no intention of helping him win. Despite the fact that his wife and children were held hostage in Spain, Prince Tommaso began to negotiate with Richelieu. In 1641 the Habsburg field commander, the Milanese Cardinal Trivulzio, offered Tommaso as much support as possible, but after the outbreak of rebellion in Portugal and Catalonia the previous year, Spain was desperate for troops and money. Spanish forces would not risk a field battle with French and Piedmontese loyalist troops, so Tommaso reluctantly decided to change sides, along with his brother. In May 1642 they reached an accord with the princess regent Marie-Christine, and offered their forces to France.[113] This was a serious defeat for Spain, but as Guido Quazza argues, it was a serious defeat for Piedmont too. Piedmontese forces would play but a subordinate role from now on, while the French continued to garrison the critical fortresses, beginning with Turin. In the years following, neither side was ready to exploit the strategic advantage. Prince Tommaso was appointed commander-in-chief of French armies in the theatre, but the lack of troops and resources kept him on a short leash.

The year 1640 marked the onset of an era when the Spanish strategic conjuncture passed from bad to catastrophic. Revolts in Iberia stretched resources ever thinner, while denying the crown important sources of taxation. Madrid created new armies only by scavenging military resources in the less threatened districts, like southern Italy. It reduced the galley squadron to a skeleton, ceased buying horses for the cavalry and suspended casting of cannon in the kingdom. Sardinian defences were not worthy of the term. In 1638 there were 81 coastal towers guarding the beaches, most of them built between 1591 and 1610, to deter pirate attacks. In addition, the island contained only three fortified towns, Alghero, Castel Aragonese and Cagliari, none of which had significant garrisons, and where the few guns were lying on the earth, without powder or ammunition. A French landing in 1637 was not so much repulsed as monitored by the local militia.[114] The viceroy of Sicily was told to recruit soldiers in the island in 1638, but he reported that this was impossible, due to the lack of inclination for soldiery by Sicilians. They would not even enlist in units to defend the island, held now by only a few hundred Spanish troops. Barbary pirates made important raids on cities in Calabria, like Catanzaro in 1644, secure in the knowledge there were no forces to oppose them. Confident in the loyalty of the population of southern Italy and the islands, Olivares and Philip IV continued to feed the armies in Lombardy, Flanders, Catalonia and Portugal by starving the garrisons in the peninsula. These undermanned fortresses eventually proved irresistible for Cardinal Mazarin, the Italian chief minister of France, successor to Richelieu after 1643.

France's Roman-born chief minister was well placed to pry apart the *status quo* supporting Spanish hegemony in the peninsula. For one, he was formerly a client

---

[113] *Ibid.*, p. 73ff.

[114] Mattone, Anatra, Turtas, *Storia dei Sardi e della Sardegna, vol. 3: l'età moderna*, p. 73.

of the Barberini nephews, Taddeo and Cardinal Antonio, who were the centre of a pro-French faction in the Papal curia. They had plans to upset Spanish rule in southern Italy, and were thought powerful enough to bring Rome into the war on the side of France in 1641, before the crisis of Castro.[115] Mazarin then wanted to entice Tuscany and Modena into his anti-Spanish alliance by giving the Italian theatre new prominence. In 1646 Prince Tommaso of Savoy embarked an army on the French fleet with the aim of occupying the Spanish fortresses on the Tuscan coast and on Elba. Mazarin signalled to Tuscany to join him in the spoliation of the coastal fortresses, the vital link between Naples and Milan. The Tuscan pretence of alliance with Spain had worn very thin. In 1642 GianCarlo de'Medici took the galley squadron to Spain, but the grandees snubbed and publicly humiliated him.[116] Mazarin offered incentives to Prince Mattias to commit the grand duchy to war on the French side. Grand Duke Ferdinando II would not budge, however. Instead, he improved fortifications along the coast, and called out a militia force of 10,000 men to observe the fighting across the border at Orbetello between the besieging French and Spanish forces. Ferdinando's circumspection was understandable. Spain still plied the sea lanes in the Mediterranean with its galleys, reinforced by warships sent from Flanders. Neapolitan and Sicilian galleys, towing warships behind them, pounced on the French fleet off Port' Ercole and killed the French admiral. When Spanish troops occupied the high ground around Port' Ercole, the siege of Orbetello had to be scuttled, after much of Prince Tommaso's army had perished from typhus and malaria in the coastal plain. Prince Tommaso ferried a new army along the Tuscan coast the following year, looking for opportune targets that might be turned into French bases. Porto Longone, built on Elba in 1602 with barracks for 2,000 men, contained a mere 80 soldiers when assailed in September.[117] Nevertheless, it held out for two weeks. Piombino on the mainland also surrendered to the French after a short siege. An important Spanish fleet of 28 ships and 11 galleys, operating out of Naples, drove off the French flotilla at the year's end, and restored control of the western Mediterranean to Spain.[118]

The stalemate focused new attention on Duke Francesco of Modena, who desired to serve the Spanish alliance with a glorious role similar to that of Alessandro Farnese, Ambrogio Spìnola or Prince Tommaso of Savoy. He was not interested in expanding his little duchy in the direction of Lombardy, but wished to recover Ferrara in the Papal States for the Este dynasty.[119] France promised aid

---

[115] A. Musi, *La rivolta di Masaniello nella scena politica barocca* (Naples: 1989), p. 52.

[116] Manfroni, *La marina militare del granducato mediceo*, pt 2, p. 96.

[117] J. Alcalà-Zamora y Queipo de Llano, "Razon de estado y geoestrategia en la politica italiana de Carlos II: Florencia y los Presidios, 1677–1681", *Boletìn de la Real Academia de la Historia*, 1976, pp. 297–358, at p. 312.

[118] R. C. Anderson, "The Thirty Years' War in the Mediterranean" (pt 2), *Mariner's Mirror*, **16**, 1970, pp. 41–57.

[119] L. Simeoni, *Francesco I d'Este e la politica italiana del Mazarino* (Bologna: 1922), p. 25.

and territory easily, but rarely followed through in the form of troops and supplies. After ten years of war in Piedmont and Lombardy, Spanish power there was intact. What finally pushed Francesco into the French camp was a political discourtesy in Rome, where the Spanish Admiral of Castile refused to stop his coach to salute the duke's brother, the Cardinal d'Este. Thinking that the time had come to punish Spain, and confident that Parma and Tuscany would join him, he began to mobilize an army. Duke Francesco announced in 1646 his intention to raise an army of 6,000 infantry and 1,000 horse. This was not an easy task in the 1640s, partly because the reserve of willing recruits was much depleted, and partly because would-be soldiers were already serving in other armies. The troops available in states like Modena or Tuscany were citizen militias in the towns and peasant militia in the countryside, none of whom had much experience in war, apart from the recent operations against the Papal States in the Castro War (1643–4). These were complemented by some noble cavalry troops and the ducal bodyguards, some of whom might have served in other armies. To wage war against a country like Spain, even enfeebled, required hiring mercenaries on the international market; Germans, Swiss (frequently Germans, in fact), Corsicans, Albanians or Frenchmen. Duke Francesco needed French money to fortify Brescello (his advance base on the Po), to garrison his fortresses, and to expel the Spanish garrison from Correggio. Then he could think about offensive operations.[120]

By June 1647, when he was ready to act, Duke Francesco had put 4,000 infantry in the field, most of them French, and expected 4,000 more to arrive by sea. Prince Tommaso was supposed to invade Lombardy from the west as a diversion. The Modenese army, led by the French marshal Serion, finally crossed the Po late in the campaigning season, at the end of September. It occupied the unfortified town of Casalmaggiore as a bridgehead, but the troops lacking supplies soon disbanded to plunder the countryside. Before long they were skirmishing with the peasants and the Lombard militia. This last was a recent creation in both the cities and the countryside of the principality, set up to meet the French invasion after 1636, and entrusted to leading Milanese patricians. Normally their activities were limited to stiffening garrisons, guarding prisoners or escorting supply convoys.[121] They had time to help the Spaniards shore up the fortifications of Cremona, and added to the meagre professional garrison troops of perhaps 2,000 men. They proved too strong for the little Modenese army that, after some sparring, started to disband from the bad weather and lack of food. Cremonese nobles led peasant militia raids at their heels. Despite receiving reinforcements, Francesco decided that the army would fall back on Casalmaggiore on 6 October. Much of it then deserted into Mantuan and Parman territory.[122]

---

[120] *Ibid.*, p. 99.

[121] E. Dalla Rosa, *Le milizie del seicento nello stato di Milano* (Milan: 1991), pp. 21, 81, 155 and 210.

[122] Simeoni, *Francesco I d'Este e la politica italiana del Mazarino*, pp. 120–3.

Unchastened, Duke Francesco decided to correct his mistakes in a new campaign. A more skilled French general, Plessis-Praslin, took over the command role completely. At the end of June 1648, the army composed mostly of French troops advanced on Cremona again, and laid siege after 22 July. The army was still too small to capture such a large city, it being impossible to encircle the place and conduct active approaches simultaneously. Cremona therefore received support from Lombardy almost without obstacle, and by October, the besieging army had barely advanced. The onset of the Fronde in France then deprived the Modenese of vital support, and Plessis-Praslin was reduced to spending his own considerable fortune.[123] The Spanish were able to strike back and attack Reggio. In February 1649, Duke Francesco admitted defeat, sent his soldiers back to France, and promised to support Spanish forces in Lombardy, in exchange for an honourable command in another theatre.

Stradling's argument that the battle of Rocroi in 1643 was not the death-knell of Spanish power is borne out in the Italian theatre, at least on first sight.[124] When France descended into civil war in 1648, its gains in Italy had been negligible. Casale in Monferrato and Pinerolo in Piedmont were the main acquisitions, taken from its allies. Its conquests along the Tuscan coast were vulnerable to a superior Spanish–Italian navy. Richelieu and Mazarin were never able to deliver any of what they promised to Italian princes, who were understandably cautious. Simultaneously, Spain concluded a separate peace with the Low Countries, Sweden and the German Protestant states, ending its participation in the Thirty Years War.

By 1648, however, the Spanish imperial system was beyond fatigue; it began to break down under the strain of uninterrupted war since 1617. The fiscal pressure first came to a head at Palermo in May 1647, sparked by a grain riot. Notables loyal to the king quickly commandeered the revolt against the viceroy and it hardly spread beyond the city. By September it was over, having entailed only some episodes of bloody rioting.[125] More dire was the revolt that broke out on 7 July 1647, in Naples, shortly after the viceroy duke of Arcos imposed a tax on fruit. Faced with the threat of a French invasion in 1640, the viceroy had created a 'popular' militia in the city, under its own leaders, in effect dispossessing the aristocracy of its monopoly of military command.[126] When the city rebelled against the Spanish regime seven years later, Arcos was bereft of all military support, except for a few hundred men in two of the forts in Naples, one overlook-

---

[123] J. Chagniot, "Ethique et pratique de la 'profession des armes' chez les officiers français au XVIIe siècle", in *Guerre et pouvoir en Europe au XVIIe siècle*, (Paris: 1991), pp. 79–93, at p. 84.

[124] Stradling, *Europe and the decline of Spain*, p. 125ff.

[125] H. G. Koenigsberger, "The revolt of Palermo in 1647", *Cambridge Historical Journal*, **8**, 1944, pp. 129–44.

[126] Musi, *La rivolta di Masaniello nella scena politica barocca*, p. 89.

ing the city (Castelnuovo) and another on the waterfront (Castel dell' Uovo). The crowd assembled around a charismatic fishmonger, Tommaso Aniello (called Masaniello), who reconstituted the militia of tens of thousands within a few days, many bearing firearms. While the viceroy and his handful of soldiers and nobles barricaded themselves into the Castelnuovo overlooking the city, the crowd killed some nobles, their henchmen, and other notables notorious for their lucrative dealings in the tax farms. Rebellion also spread quickly through the countryside, where a widespread anti-feudal sentiment held sway.[127] Large districts of the Abruzzi, Puglia and Calabria were taken over by rebels, sometimes led by rich and influential personalities. Masaniello himself did not survive. Some extravagances resulted in his assassination, but the incident only intensified feelings against the viceroy, and the crowds began to lay siege to the fortresses, though without much artillery.[128]

Military operations intensified after early October when a Spanish fleet bearing Don Juan (bastard son of Philip IV) arrived in the region. It carried very few soldiers, since there were none to spare, and the Spanish crown hoped that the charisma of House of Austria would return people to obedience.[129] Instead, the prince's presence tended to polarize the process. Most of the important nobles decided to support Spain, and fled Naples first to their estates (if they were safe) or to Capua, a strong fortress near the Papal border. They combed their lands and called upon their clientèles to raise an army. Diomede Carafa, whose estates were not far from Capua, raised 350 horsemen and 342 foot. The Avalos of Vasto in the Abruzzi found 190 horsemen and 220 'infantry', while the prince of Montesarchio raised 130 horse and 70 foot. The majority of these levies were horsemen: 146 from the Caracciolo; 70 from the Piccolòmini of Naples, and many small contingents made up of individual noblemen, their immediate relatives and some farm hands. It was hardly an army, especially since the nobles serving in it were more used to giving, than following, orders. So many troopers were peasants mounted on cart horses, or domestics, or bandits and *bravi* out for the adventure legitimized by the congregation of great families, that it is amazing they accomplished anything at all. One professional soldier, General Vincenzo Tuttavilla, who mustered less than two hundred veteran soldiers, that is 50 Germans and 120 Spaniards and Flemings, soon asserted his pre-eminence. He concentrated his men at Aversa in the plain north of Naples, blocking the road by which the great city was fed. From there the royalist bands skirmished ruthlessly with the rebel militia companies, neither side giving any quarter. The noble army of 4,000 horse

---

[127] On this sentiment, see Villari, *La rivolta antispagnola a Napoli*, p. 61.

[128] The long account of the revolt of Naples and the military operations around the capital by Alfred von Reumont is frequently cited in recent literature and is still very useful; see his *The Carafas of Maddaloni: Naples under Spanish dominion*, p. 313ff. See also the most recent analysis by Aurelio Musi, *La rivolta di Masaniello nella scena politica barocca*, p. 129ff.

[129] Musi, *La rivolta di Masaniello nella scena politica barocca*, p. 129ff.

and 500 infantry was able to harass the rebels and threaten the city with starvation, but it was powerless to do more.[130]

In Naples the revolt quickly radicalized, calling into question the legitimacy of the Spanish connection. The rebels killed their leader Francesco Toraldo, a high-ranking veteran of many Habsburg campaigns abroad, for his loyalty to Philip IV, and a non-noble lawyer, Gennaro Annese took his place as *generalissimo*. The revolt reached another stage in November when the quixotic French Duc de Guise arrived in Naples with an escort of French gentlemen, with the understanding that he would become the king of the Neapolitan republic. Despite his difficulty in imposing discipline among his many followers, he led the militia to break the ring of encirclement, by capturing Salerno to the south, then Avellino to the east, and after a dogged siege, Aversa too. Only Capua and the coastal fortress of Gaeta, each held by a paltry force of regulars, remained in Habsburg hands. Had Mazarin wanted to play the Naples card for all it was worth – that is, by sending a French army and fleet under an able commander – the barons might have been overwhelmed. Mazarin, however, had little confidence in the Duc de Guise's ability to rally the Neapolitans behind him. Influential personalities began to desert the cause. Many barons abandoned Capua to wage a war of vendetta on the peasant uprisings in the Abruzzi, in Puglia, in Calabria and other zones of resistance.[131]

Guise was also unable to break the Spanish resistance in their city strongholds. Worse, he acted like the seventeenth-century monarch he longed to become, claiming absolute power for himself, notwithstanding the fragile base of his authority. His attempt to win over a substantial part of the great nobility was rebutted pointedly by their spokesmen.[132] As his popularity declined, the strain of

---

[130] Von Reumont, *The Carafas of Maddaloni*, p. 357.

[131] R. Villari, "La feudalità e lo stato napoletano nel secolo XVII", in *Potere e società negli stati regionali italiani fra '500 e '600*, E. Fasano-Guarini (ed.) (Bologna: 1978), pp. 259–77, at p. 261.

[132] Musi, *La rivolta di Masaniello nella scena politica barocca*, p. 233. The author reproduces a speech attributed to Carlo Carafa, duca d'Andria, which is worth reproducing, for it gives the reasons why Neapolitan nobles adhered so closely to the King of Spain:

> . . . il mio sentimento e quello di tutta la Nobiltà, e che la Republica [*sic*] non essendoci propria, non potiamo né vogliamo giammai udirne a parlare, noi non sopportaremo giammai che il popolo dividi l'autorità con noi, e noi siamo d'un genio così attivo, e naturalmente si glorioso, che non ci è possiblie, senza mangiarsi un l'altro, dividerci molti in egualità di potere: ne arriverebbe infallibilmente divisioni, odii e gelosie, che sarebbero assolutamente ruinare e perdere il paese. Noi siamo nati per il stato Monarchico, non ci sapressimo passar d'un Re. E d' huopo che una autorità suprema ci tenga in pace, ed in reposo col acquietar le nostre dissensioni ed inimicitie a che ci porta il naturale; e l'educazione havuta. E supposto questo, bisogno di necessità che noi ci resolviamo a perdere gli beni e la vita per conservarci sotto il dominio del nostro Re, abbenché rude noi ci siamo assuefatti, e noi crediamo che quello di Francia non ci sarebbe più dolce, noi non guadagneremmo niente a questo cambio, e forse vi

the war on the civilian population in the metropolis was felt more keenly. Then on 5 April 1648, the new viceroy Don Luis de Haro with 500 soldiers, mostly Spanish, surged out of the waterfront citadel in Naples and stormed the barricades. Before the end of the day they reoccupied the great city, joined by much of the citizenry as they pushed their way through the streets. The insurrection collapsed. Mazarin sent Prince Tommaso with a fleet and an army to the coast to incite a new revolt, but nobody moved. Don Luis de Haro then reined in the baronage. He waged war on the bandit gangs that infested the country in the aftermath of rebellion, and punished those barons who gave refuge to such outlaws in their estates, by depriving them of their lands and jurisdictions.[133]

The siege of Cremona and the revolt of Naples marked a pause in the fighting between France and Spain. When the Thirty Years War ended formally that spring, Spain granted full independence to the Netherlands. The 1640s may have witnessed the apex of fighting in Europe, and it might be worthwhile to take stock of the process. It was never possible to know the size of the armies in the period exactly, given the illness and desertion that plagued each army. There were field armies in Flanders, the Basque Country and Catalonia, in the Franche-Comté and northern Italy. In addition, there were soldiers assigned to the several galley squadrons and to the Indies fleet. There were garrisons from Acapulco and Cuba to the Canaries and Iberia. The coastal defences in the Mediterranean had to be manned, the passes through the Alps to Austrian Tyrol kept safe. Garrisons in Italy and Flanders probably exceeded by far the number of troops available in the field.[134] A great many of those troops must have been Italian, but curiously, we have absolutely no information about who the rank and file were, and where they came from.

Despite the absence of real information as to the origin of the troops, Yves-Marie Bercé has tried to estimate the number of soldiers Italy might have paid for in the given year of 1643.[135] That year saw the mobilization of virtually the entire peninsula, both in the Castro War and in the Thirty Years War. He estimates that the Pope normally employed six or seven thousand good troops, of which

---

perderemmo, noi vederessimo allo stesso modo la nostra nazione sommessa a stranieri, le nostre cariche, gli nostri impieghi, gli governi delle nostre Piazze, e delle nostre Provincie nelle loro mani, gli nostri beni e le nostre ricchezze passarebbero all' ordinario in un altro paese, che arricchiressimo col poverirci, e saressimo sempre sforzati di far la corte e piegar il ginocchio davanti il Viceré che non sarebbe nato di più che noi altri. Per quello voi vedde bene che cio non sarebbe un ammendare la nostra condizione, e di più, l'humor spagnuolo è più confacente al nostro, il Francese sendo e troppo allegro e troppo galante per gente seriosa e gelosa come noi siamo naturalmente.

[133] Von Reumont, *The Carafas of Maddaloni*, p. 385ff.

[134] G. Parker, *The military revolution: military innovation and the rise of the West, 1500–1800* (Cambridge: 1988), p. 40. Parker notes that half the Spanish army was placed in garrison in the Low Countries, and that there were no fewer than 208 garrisons.

[135] Y.-M. Bercé, "Les guerres dans l'Italie du XVII siècle", in *L'Italie au XVIIe siècle* (Paris: 1989), pp. 324–6.

perhaps a fifth were Swiss, and an equal proportion Corsicans. The mobilization of 1643 raised the number to at least 12,000 infantry and 3,000 cavalry, besides the urban and rural militias that played a role in the fighting. Of their adversaries, Venetian forces in the theatre numbered about 15,000 infantry, including several thousand in garrison in the Terraferma. He considers that most of the infantry would have been French, Dutch, Germans and Swiss, supplemented by Italians of various origin. The best cavalry units consisted of Croats, Dalmatians, Albanians and Greeks who traditionally fought for the Republic. The armies of Parma, Modena and Tuscany would have numbered 4,000 to 5,000 good troops each, again presumably mostly Swiss and French mercenaries. In Lombardy, French and Spanish effective forces numbered about 10,000 for each, onto which one must aggregate the Lombard militia. Bercé gives no figure for the Ligurians or the Piedmontese. Finally there were about 10,000 to 15,000 troops of various origins in the Spanish garrisons in the presidial territories, Naples, Sicily and Sardinia. In all, the forces paid for by Italy amounted to about 100,000 men, for a population of some twelve million, representing approximately one per cent of the total population, which Bercé sees as falling within a European norm. My own sense is that some armies he cited were larger, and Italians comprised a larger proportion of them: say 20,000 for the Papal States and 10,000 for Tuscany, 5,000 for the Republic of Genoa and maybe 20,000 in Piedmont just emerging from its civil war. When war raged in Italy, many local militiamen fought too, so that the distinction between soldiers and civilians became blurred in some regions. While many troops were undoubtedly foreign mercenaries, this was counterbalanced by thousands of Italians serving in the armies of the emperor and the duke of Bavaria in Germany. Venetian garrisons in Dalmatia and the Aegean, a couple of regiments of Italians in French service, and the Italian *tercios* of the king of Spain employed in other theatres. Nor should we forget the knights of Malta and Santo Stefano, with their galleys and garrisons. Nevertheless, these would not total much more than the one per cent that Bercé suggested. As for their specific origin, who knows? We know that many Piedmontese served in France, and the Corsican mercenary tradition is well known. Beyond that, we know very little.

Whoever they were, they seem less numerous after the end of the Thirty Years War in Germany, the onset of the Fronde, and the end of the rebellion in Naples. To begin with, the mobilization of nobles in the defence of the king of Spain spurred few new vocations; most of them returned to their urban palaces or their estates and put away their banners. The army collected in Naples for the reconquest of the presidial states was quite small, probably no more than 7,000 men, transported by a substantial fleet. The great rebellion forced Spain to lighten the kingdom's tax burden, and the revenues derived from it collapsed.[136] Noble

---

[136] On the lightening of the fiscal burden, see Villari, "La feudalita e lo stato napoletano nel secolo XVII", in *Potere e societa negli stati regionali italiani*, Fasano-Guarini (ed.), pp. 259–77, p. 261. Calabria notes that in 1648 private receivers were granted most of the royal gabelles for only 300,000 ducats; *The cost of empire*, p. 2.

ardour for the cause of Spain was not extinct: GianGirolamo Acquaviva raised 300 infantry and 70 horse for this expedition, and recaptured Piombino with them. The siege of Porto Longone in Elba took longer: its 1,500-man garrison held out for ten weeks and inflicted grievous losses on the Neapolitans before it too capitulated. During the Fronde, the marquis of Caracena, governor of Milan, finally brought Mantua back into the Spanish camp, and captured Casale Monferrato in 1652 with only modest effective forces. Its Mantuan garrison was paid from the Spanish and Imperial treasury, while the unwarlike Duke Carlo was gratified with the title of Imperial *generalissimo*. By rallying Lombards into effective militia companies, Caracena was able to hold the French at bay.

The French cardinal–minister was able to break the strategic stalemate only by separating the smaller states that constituted the passive alliance in Spain's favour. Genoa's relations with Madrid cooled when it appeared that the alliance's protective value had lost most of its credibility. When Spain questioned Genoa's right to levy taxes on its military base of Finale in Liguria, those two states moved close to a rupture, with Mazarin proffering promises of support to the republic.[137] Individual patricians, however, continued to lease warships to Spain for a profit, and the Spanish party never lost control. Duke Francesco of Modena let Mazarin talk him into a new alliance in 1654, for he still hankered after military glory, and Spain had turned him down.[138] Before he was even organized, the governor of Milan, Caracena, marched on Reggio Emilia and disrupted everything, though he soon withdrew. The following year the Modenese co-ordinated their invasion with Prince Tommaso, invading Lombardy from the west with French and Piedmontese troops. Their siege of Pavia was a complete failure, owing to the small size of their armies and the combativeness of the local militia.[139] The duke was wounded in the operation, while Prince Tommaso contracted malaria and died. In 1656 the combined armies besieged and captured the small town of Valenza, without accomplishing much more.

In 1657, after they had failed to capture Alessandria, Mantua tightened its alliance with Spain. Despite his personal military ineptitude and the ridicule in which his allies held him, the emperor appointed Duke Carlo as commander of Imperial troops coming to Spain's aid.[140] He fielded 3,000 infantry and 2,000

---

[137] Quazza, *La preponderanza spagnola*, p. 515. See also the long article by Gian Carlo Calcagno, "La navigazione convogliata a Genova nella seconda metà del seicento", in *Guerra e commercio nell' evoluzione della marina genovese tra XV e XVII secolo* (Genoa: n.d., 1970?), pp. 265–392, at p. 279.

[138] For the general context, see Stradling, *Philip IV and the government of Spain*, p. 288. For more details on Modena, see Simeoni, *Francesco I d'Este e la politica italiana del Mazarino*, p. 181.

[139] On the city's militia and its organization, see M. Rizzo, "Istituzioni militari e strutture socio-economiche in un città di antico regime: la milizia urbana di Pavìa nell' età moderna", *Cheiron*, 1995, pp. 157–85.

[140] Coniglio, *I Gonzaga*, p. 448.

cavalry from his own state against the French and Piedmontese, in the hope of maintaining control of the Monferrato and keeping Habsburg armies operational. Duke Francesco d'Este was out on a limb for, as an enemy of the Habsburg dynasty, the emperor considered him a rebel and contemplated sending Imperial troops against Modena. In 1657 it looked as if Vienna and Mantua would join Spain to crush the little duchy from the north. Finally, during a last campaign at the head of combined French, Piedmontese and Modenese armies, Francesco penetrated the heart of Lombardy, taking Mortara and pushing his cavalry patrols to the outskirts of Milan. He lacked the infantry and artillery necessary to capture a large town, however, especially since its garrison was greatly augmented by urban militiamen well stocked with arms and ammunition.[141] After capturing a couple of small border towns, he too contracted malaria and died in October 1658.[142] With his death, the belligerents agreed to halt operations until the Peace of the Pyrenees put a formal end to the war between France and Spain, and their respective allies. Ironically, as his biographer Luigi Simeoni points out, Francesco d'Este never ceased to be a Hispanophile. He spoke Spanish, and offered his support to Spain sincerely, although Simeoni thinks the Spaniards were correct to mistrust such enthusiasm, and to confide their troops to commanders of proven ability. Culturally and intellectually, most of the Italian princes were inclined towards Spain. Spanish cultural ascendancy, however, had run its course by 1660. Despite the successful defence of its Italian territories, the Spanish monarchy was being supplanted as the pole of attraction by the emerging Louis XIV.

The Castro War, 1642–9

Along with Piedmont, only one other Italian state continued to expand and assert its authority over more territory with enhanced effect: the Papal States. Rather than reconduct feudal states to lateral branches when the ruling branch was extinguished in the direct line, the popes asserted their sovereignty over these territories and ruled them through a cardinal legate. Thus, the Este dynasty was displaced to Modena in 1598, as Ferrara reverted to Papal rule. Urbino was similarly absorbed with its state on the confines of the Marches, Umbria and Tuscany when the direct line of the Della Rovere family disappeared in 1631. The enlargement of the Papal possessions did not occur without envy or worry among the other Italian states, and they added these to the tally of grievances they held against Rome and the Pope as a secular ruler.

What appeared to be the final straw was the high-handed manner by which Pope Urban VIII Barberini seized the duchy of Castro and the nearby town of Ronciglione from the reigning duke, Odoardo Farnese of Parma, as collateral for

---

[141] Dalla Rosa, *Le milizie del seicento nello stato di Milano*, p. 109.

[142] Simeoni, *Francesco I d'Este e la politica italiana del Mazarino*, p. 186.

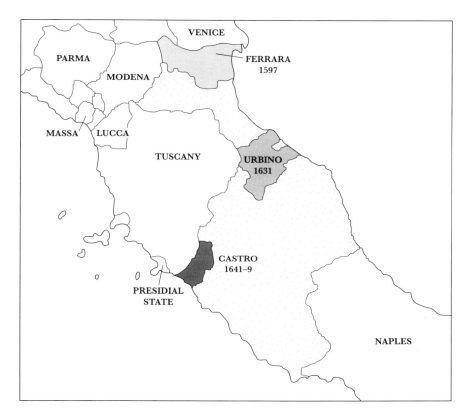

Map 3.2 Papal annexations, 1597–1649

debts he owed to the Papal treasury, in 1640. The duchy was a feudal enclave in northern Latium, and the ancestral seat of the house of Farnese. Castro itself was a modest-sized fief of grain-producing hills and plains north of Rome. Because of the pervasive malaria, the walls of its minuscule capital enclosed but three streets and 500 inhabitants, not including the garrison in the little citadel. The Farnese floated loans in Rome in the 1580s and again in the 1630s to finance military operations of the dukes, using the revenues of the duchy as collateral. In the 1630s, the revenues of these territories were so deeply mortgaged that interest was no longer being paid out. The duke also refused to pay for grain export licences that Rome considered part of its domain. When the Barberini pope insisted on payment, Duke Odoardo responded by fortifying Castro and hired a couple of hundred soldiers barely tolerated by the population. In October 1641 the Papal army under Taddeo Barberini invested the town and laid siege. The 6,000 infantry and 900 horse that the Pope had mobilized for the expedition was a significant effort for the Papal states, for it was in addition to the garrisons and the galley squadron. Few defenders wished to die for such a cause, so Castro capitulated after a week.[143]

Duke Odoardo then cultivated the other Italian states to oppose in unison an arbitrary measure. Venice was worried about Papal attempts to develop Ancona and Comacchio near the Po delta into trading centres on the Adriatic, to the detriment of the Serenissima. Moreover, new Papal fortifications near the mouth of the Po held an implicit threat to the vital navigation of the river, one of the republic's lifelines. The Este of Modena had never really assimilated the loss of Ferrara and its dependencies in Romagna. Duke Francesco pretended that Comacchio had never belonged to Ferrara (and by extension, had never been a Papal fief), and ought to revert to his house. The Tuscans had two bones of contention: Ferdinando II had married Vittoria Della Rovere and expected Urbino to pass to the Medici family in 1631; and the Papal States had undertaken a drainage project in the Val di Chiana and the upper basin of the Paglia river near the Tuscan border without co-operation, with the result that a Papal dyke ruined an important tract of Tuscany's most fertile soil near Chiusi.[144] Beyond these conflicts over territory, they all desired to limit the Pope's jurisdiction in their state. The tax exemptions on Church property, the fiscal privileges of ecclesiastics used brazenly as tax havens for the wealthy, the extensive rights of sanctuary, the invasive curiosity and rigidity of the Roman Inquisition, the jealously guarded ecclesiastical jurisdiction that transformed every minor bishop of central Italy into a bulldog with regard to his prince: all these issues were implicit in the grievances between the Pope and the states of northern Italy. Bercé believes the latter all desired a French-style *concordat* which would have conferred on the prince extensive rights of patronage and control over ecclesiastical benefices.

The personality of Urban VIII Barberini was not amenable to conceding Papal prerogatives to minor potentates. He was the last of the warrior–popes, who invested much energy and treasure into military preparedness.[145] During the Genoa war of 1625, and then again in 1629–30, Urban amassed troops around Ferrara, and constructed and improved fortifications. He built a fortress of major proportions (called Forte Urbano) on the Modenese border near Castelfranco Emilia, as well as a huge arsenal at Tivoli, outside Rome. Urban VIII's advice to other Italian princes was that peace and respect could only come

[143] For the background leading up to war, see G. Demaria, "La guerra di Castro, e la spedizione de' Presidi (1639–1649)", *Miscellanea di Storia Italiana*, 3 ser., vol. IV (Turin: 1898), pp. 191–256.

[144] Y.-M. Bercé, "Rome et l'Italie au XVIIe siècle: les dernières chances temporelles de l'état ecclésiastique, 1641–1649", in *Etudes réunies en l'honneur du doyen G. Livet* (Strasbourg: 1986), pp. 229–37. See also by the same author, "Urbain VIII s'en va t-en guerre", *Historama*, November 1988, pp. 34–42.

[145] See L. von Pastor, *Storia dei papi*, vol. 13 (Rome: 1943), pp. 865–9.

from strength, and that preparation for war had deterrent value. It may have been this level of preparedness that enboldened the Pope to be firm with Odoardo Farnese.

Tuscany, Modena and Venice signed a formal alliance with Parma on 31 August 1642, but none of them had made any warlike preparations. Undaunted, Odoardo Farnese assembled a force of 3,000 cavalry, a similar number of infantry, his palace guard and a crowd of noble adventurers, most of whom were horsemen and utterly incapable of besieging a modern town. The French exile Annibal de Coeuvres, the septuagenarian duc d'Estrées, handled them in the field. This army was faced with a larger force of Pontificals based in Forte Urbano under the direction of the Pope's nephew, Taddeo Barberini. As the Parmans advanced, the Pontificals clung to their fortresses. The Parmans therefore skirted the cities and continued their march by foraging, for such a small force could live off the country as long as it kept moving. Odoardo's army chased away the Pontificals not far from Bologna, in what resembled a race more than a skirmish. Imola opened its gates to the host, which passed through the town as if on parade. Similar processions took place at Faenza and Forlì, the Parman forces proving to be well disciplined and high-spirited. The cavalcade then crossed the Apennines into allied Tuscany, and emerged into Latium at Aquapendente, near the duchy of Castro, early in October. Rome was only a few days distant, and no Papal army ventured to block their path. Urban VIII assembled a new army, 15,000 strong around Rome, under the French sieur de Valençay, a knight of Malta, and Cardinal Antonio Barberini, another nephew. They mustered garrison troops, Corsican mercenaries, peasant militias and any other force on hand in a climate of impending doom, since Romans remembered the sack of 1527. In Rome both patricians and artisans fitted themselves out in military apparel and underwent a bit of weapons drill. The new city militia soon counted 6,000 'soldiers' under five colonels and 40 noble captains, although everyone doubted its effectiveness.[146] Odoardo and the duc d'Estrées halted not far from the Papal camp at Città Castellana to take stock of their situation and, with the army immobilized and vulnerable to raids against their supplies, the troops began to slip away and desert. On 22 October, having made his point, and unable to recover Castro by means of a siege, Odoardo withdrew and returned to Parma a conquering hero.

These easy successes stimulated war preparations in Florence, Modena and Venice. None of these states could mount by itself a force large enough to conquer important fortified towns in the Papal states, like Ferrara. They lacked money, first, and experienced troops, second. The troops were bought in Germany and France, along with some of the officers. It was necessary to obtain permission from these foreign princes to recruit in their lands. Both Ferdinando II of Tuscany and Francesco I of Modena entertained visions of conquest as they called upon their

---

[146] L. Nussdorfer, *Civic politics in the Rome of Urban VIII* (Princeton, New Jersey: 1992), p. 211.

expatriate military nobles serving Spain or Austria. Francesco I d'Este, like Odoardo Farnese, was avid for military glory, and had always longed for an occasion to display the military skills that were – in his mind – considerable. Prince Mattias of Tuscany, freshly returned from a decade of campaigning in Germany, looked forward to the war.

The effort of the Pontificals was similarly notable. Urban VIII used the crisis to collect silver from the élites, and to impose a substantial head tax.[147] Bercé holds that nearly all of the experienced soldiery hired by Rome was French, particularly the Provençaux recruited from the Papal enclave at Avignon, and transported to Civitavecchia by the galleys of Malta. Many officers were certainly non-Italians, especially French and Swiss, but the local military nobility and others in the clientèles of the cardinals provided experienced cadres. Senior officers like Federico Savelli, formerly of Habsburg service, placed their swords at the Pope's disposal. To the garrisons in Emilia were added a field force numbering 8,000 to 12,000 infantry and 3,000 horse, together with about a dozen cannon. Savelli assembled another army in Umbria to block any invasion coming from Tuscany.

The coalition forces selected competent commanders too: Marco Giustiniano for Venice, with the French chevalier de la Valette as field commander; in Parma the field commander was the French marquis de Sauveboeuf; and Modena enjoyed the services of Raimondo Montecùccoli, released from captivity in Stettin on the initiative of Duke Francesco. The grand duke hoped for the concourse of Ottavio Piccolòmini, who was at the height of his career. He returned to Spanish service, but consented to review the Tuscan army, drilled and fitted out in the latest German fashion.[148] Prince Mattias de'Medici was the titular commander, seconded by Alessandro del Borro, both of whom were very experienced military commanders.

The plan concocted by the diplomats called for an invasion of Emilia from Modena simultaneously with Modenese, Parman and Venetian forces, while the Tuscans attacked in Umbria as a diversion. In practice, each of the allied forces operated independently in a flurry of border skirmishes, with no decisive effect. The Parmans under Odoardo Farnese were not to be distracted from an easy seizure of the town of Bondeno, from which their small army never ventured. Montecùccoli trained a cavalry corps in Modena, but the duchy's other troops were notoriously given to disbanding in search of plunder. On 19 July 1643, Montecùccoli met in battle the Pontifical field army at Nonantola. It was a disjointed, discontinuous mêlée of separate contingents that ended in a Papal rout.[149] Urban VIII berated his nephew Taddeo for his lack of resolve, and sacked commanders for cowardice. A combined siege of Forte Urbano by the coalition

---

[147] *Ibid.*, p. 216.

[148] Barker, "Ottavio Piccolomini (1599–1659)", in *Army, aristocracy, monarchy*, p. 99.

[149] Sandonnini, *Il generale Raimondo Montecuccoli e la sua famiglia*, pt 1, p. 46: and pt 2, pp. 13 and 125.

armies during the summer might have delivered Emilia to the League. Papal troops were wisely dispersed in little garrisons of peasant militia, behind earthen ramparts hastily erected by scores of engineers using Dutch and French techniques.[150]

Elsewhere, the Papal troops displayed more initiative. A force of some 6,000 crossed the Po north of Ferrara and established a bridgehead in the Venetian Polesine, and fortified the south bank at Pontelagoscuro. These troops mishandled the poor Venetian levies and militia there, and caused great damage before retiring. A Venetian army of 9,000 then invested Pontelagoscuro, while a fleet landed a raiding party at Cesenatico and burned the town. This time the Papal forces held their ground and after some very stubborn fighting repelled several assaults on the fort in September 1643. The combat there took on a ferocious character not matched elsewhere.

Grand Duke Ferdinando II began to recruit in earnest in the summer of 1642, but it took time to assemble soldiers, and willing veterans were a rare commodity in neutral states during the Thirty Years War. Soldiers were enrolled in Tyrol and in Germany, but it is difficult to know just how many men were bought this way. Most of the Tuscan soldiers were drawn from the peasant militia, the *bande*. Late in 1642, about 11,000 men assembled for inspection below the walls of Cortona, while more than 2,000 others had been dispatched north to Modena. About 10,000 troops encamped in Sienese territory, poised for an invasion of Umbria.[151] Prince Mattias and his brother the grand duke were preparing a secret invasion too, in the form of an attack on the Papal States by a large bandit force from the kingdom of Naples. Tuscan envoys were in liaison with Cesare Squilletta of Catanzaro, known as fra Paolo. His band was to scour the area from the Abruzzi to Rome, while another bandit leader, Pagani, was to surprise (and presumably sack) either Rieti or Spoleto with a thousand outlaws. The Tuscans were finally ready to march in June 1643, in cadence with their allies. The commanders left the court at Florence with a host of gentlemen adventurers, to join the assembled army near Montepulciano. There were eight Tuscan regiments composed of garrison troops, militia and veteran mercenaries, in all amounting to 7,000 infantry, plus a German infantry regiment. In addition there were 2,000 horse, of which a quarter was German, a regiment of dragoons or mounted arquebusiers, and 400 additional cavalry composed of deserters from armies operating in northern Italy. The artillery train was composed of 18 cannon. For Tuscany, this was a very large force. To it, one must add the troops scattered in the fortifications of the grand duchy, along the coast, in the major citadels, and in garrisons strung along the border.

---

[150] On the important place of such fortifications in the war, and the gradual supplanting of Italians by French specialists, see the article by Renzo Chiovelli, "Ingegneri ed opere militari nella prima guerra di Castro", *La dimensione europea dei Farnese: Bulletin de l'Institut Historique Belge de Rome*, **63**, 1993, pp. 155–92.

[151] Giorgetti, *Le arme toscane*, p. 433ff.

The pontifical army in Umbria numbered 10,000 infantry organized in five *tercios*, but only part of it consisted of mercenaries, with the bulk comprising local militia. There was in addition a body of 3,000 cavalry of various provenance. Supreme command was held by another Papal nephew, Cardinal Antonio Barberini, with effective field operations directed by the Roman, Duke Federico Savelli. The duke had seen extensive service in the Imperial army in Germany, but repeatedly wrecked armies entrusted to him; but it seems that the Barberini were willing to give him the chance to redeem his reputation. Savelli lethargically watched Prince Mattias' army lay siege to, and capture, the well-stocked fortress of Castiglione on Lake Trasimene.[152] Next the Tuscans captured Città della Pieve in a brief but spirited siege. Having secured the border towns, the Tuscan army proceeded to march on Perugia by way of the shore of Lake Trasimene. As they progressed, their field army contracted, so the grand duke called up more militia. Del Borro and Mattias caught most of the Papal army under the Neapolitan general, Della Morra, in the field at Mongiovino in the rolling hills south of Perugia on 4 September 1643, and routed it in a brief battle. They captured 1,000 men along with the commander and all his senior officers. Again, Savelli was never far off with a large force of Papal troops, but he always moved too cautiously to accomplish anything. The Tuscans might have taken Perugia soon after, where much of the nobility was sympathetic to the grand duke, but they lacked a secure route for supplies, and entrenched their forces instead.

Direction of the Papal war effort passed increasingly to the more competent and energetic Cardinal Antonio Barberini, and to the comte de Valençay. Faced with crumbling armies routed in direct confrontations with the allied armies, the Pontifical commanders opted instead for a series of diversions and raids, the aim of which was to disorganize and divide the invaders. Valençay, leaving Bologna in October with 4,000 infantry and 1,000 horse, crossed the Apennines in the hope of surprising the Tuscan city of Pistoia. Forewarned, the peasants and townsmen buttressed the gates with masses of earth, and manned the ramparts. The Pontificals made a halfhearted attempt to scale the walls, before ravaging the villages around the city, almost within sight of Florence. Then they retreated northwards, losing part of their rearguard to Montecùccoli at Sambuca. Valençay's raid succeeded in forcing Prince Mattias to shift troops from his army before Perugia to garrison the Apennine fortresses and passes. Another column of Pontifical troops under the Genoese, Federico Imperiale, seized the border village of Monterchi in the upper Tiber valley, from which it was possible to harass the Tuscan army's supply line. There was much desultory raiding back and forth in the valley, with small forces of mercenaries aided by the rural militias. Finally, a small army of Pontificals invaded Tuscany from the south, hoping to capture the isolated town of Pitigliano. A Tuscan force routed that army near Sorano, and captured its artillery and baggage. This did not stop the raiding against the villages

---

[152] See the encyclopedia entry for Fulvio della Corgna, in Valori, *Condottieri e generali del Seicento*, p. 96.

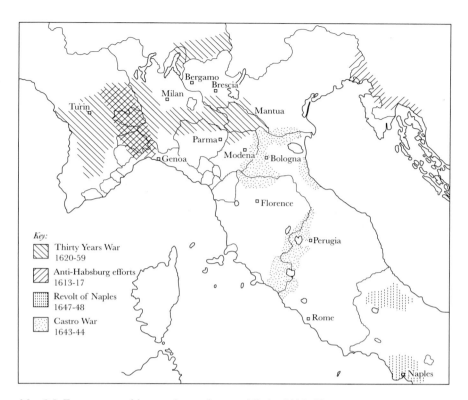

Map 3.3 Zones ravaged by war in north-central Italy, 1613–59

perched on the frontier, where soldiers hoped to capture livestock and booty. Behind the border, Savelli prepared Orvieto and Viterbo to withstand sieges, levied more militias and directed fortification works. As the border fighting continued it was clear that Papal armies were not near imminent collapse. Urban VIII was recruiting his biggest army ever, to replace troops who deserted or fell sick to malaria and typhus. The effective diversionary attacks, coupled with the failing health of the intransigent pope gradually convinced the belligerents that a negotiated settlement was preferable to a new campaign. The cardinals opened peace talks in January and by March 1644, a general peace was concluded that restored Castro to Duke Odoardo, but that otherwise reverted to the *status quo ante*. Urban VIII died several months later, to the general satisfaction of everyone save the Papal nephews.

The affair was revived in 1649, when Pope Innocent X sent a new bishop to Castro without securing the approval of the duke, Ranuccio II. Assassins dispatched the bishop in the countryside by order of the Parman first minister, the Provençal Jacques Gaufrido. The Pope immediately declared war on the duchy and collected armies in Latium and Emilia. On 18 August 1649, a Parman army of only 2,500 men met a Pontifical force of comparable size not far from Bologna. Legend has it that both armies fled simultaneously after the first volley, but that the Pontificals rallied first. Demaria affirms instead that at least a third of the Parmans lay dead and wounded in the skirmish, and the rest ran demoralized back into Modenese territory.[153] Gaufrido was executed for cowardice shortly after. The same month, a column of 2,000 Papal soldiers invested Castro, weakly defended by two or three hundred soldiers. As punishment for the bishop's murder, the Pope transferred the seat of the diocese to Aquapendente, expelled the inhabitants of the town, and ordered it to be demolished to its foundations. Hardly a trace of it remains today.

The Castro War illustrates some difficulties which states had in mobilizing for war without permanent cadres in place. No doubt some of these difficulties stemmed from the competition with great powers for a limited pool of mercenaries and the nobles who could command them. Nevertheless, none of the armies dissolved from complete lack of efficiency, and by the end of 1643 the improvised armies consisting substantially of peasant militias were beginning to function more efficiently.[154] Like the Thirty Years War, the Castro War should be seen as one of the last illustrations of the state's military capacities before the establishment of standing armies with permanent regiments. In both cases the heavy taxes imposed to pay for soldiers, in the Spanish dominions, in the Papal states and in the various principalities, were suppressed as soon as the crisis passed. The legacy of the Thirty Years War in Italy was principally that of widespread destruction in the Po valley, from which it quickly recovered, and economic and demographic collapse that had long-term effects. North of the Alps, where the damage inflicted and the loss of life was much greater, princes sought ways to retain as many of their colonels and soldiers as their finances would allow. For them, the mid-seventeenth century was a turning point of considerable import.

---

[153] G. Solari, *The House of Farnese*, p. 247. See also Giacinto Demaria, "La guerra di Castro", *Miscellanea di Storia Italiana*, 3 ser., vol. IV, 1898, p. 254.

[154] Charles Carlton charts the progressive improvement of English militias under the direction of Thirty Years' War veterans during the British civil wars, which were unfolding simultaneously. He points out that the mercenaries helped professionalize and render effective militia armies, in a process which took about two and a half years. We see something comparable happening in Italy too. See C. Carlton, *Going to the wars: the experience of the British civil wars, 1638–1651* (London: 1992), p. 19ff.

Chapter 4
The Venetian epic, 1600–1718

The military potential of the aristocratic republic

The inherent weakness in the defence of the Venetian empire was that both of its extended flanks had to be protected, each from a different threat. The Spanish Habsburgs to the west, the Austrian Habsburgs to the north and east, and the Papal States to the south were all potentially hostile powers surrounding the republic in Italy. Venice once lost control of the Terraferma briefly after the crushing defeat of Agnadello in 1510, but soon reconquered it. Beyond the Adriatic, risk of war with the Ottoman Empire, the source of much of its lucrative trade, was a permanent risk. Venice retained the allegiance of the Slovenes of Istria, the Croats of the Dalmatian coast and archipelago, and the Greeks in Corfù and Crete. In Dalmatia the local élites spoke Italian and the Catholic population traditionally served in the Venetian army and fleet.

The republic of San Marco enjoyed power and prestige drawn from its wealth; but, in addition, Europeans widely admired the Serenissima's collegiate government for its stability, and this too was jealously guarded by the patrician families who constituted the state. The government was perpetually wary of its own citizens' loyalties and ambitions. Venetian nobles could not bear arms for another state or prince, on pain of their family's expulsion from the ruling councils. Also, the Senate mistrusted any Venetian acquiring too much power. A long-established custom gave overall command of the army to foreigners, like the Genoese Giustiniani, the French Protestant Rohan, the Swede Königsmark or the Saxon Schulemburg, who were closely watched by administrators entrusted with matters of supply and payment. On the other hand, only Venetian patricians could command galleys. The fleet was usually large enough to provide virtually any patrician who wanted it a regular commission.

In 1560, of approximately 150,000 inhabitants, roughly 2,500 adult patricians – those whose houses were inscribed in the Golden Book – were eligible to govern the state. As a body this élite was diverse enough. Available to them were about 800 posts of varying importance and income. Most patricians moved from one office to another over their career, not accumulating power or creating too great a clientèle in any branch of government. The richer families were often quite large

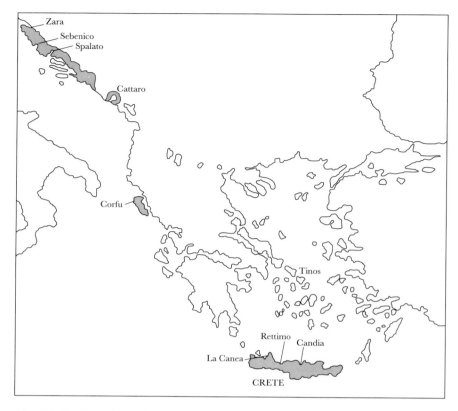

Map 4.1 The Venetian seaborne empire, *circa* 1620

and divided into multiple branches, as elsewhere in Italy. There were 80 males in the house of Morosini in 1591, for example. Many houses had ties to the aristocracies of the subject towns or the overseas empire. While each family pursued its own strategies of dynastic integrity and career specialization, the majority was still active in commerce, even after the loss of Cyprus in 1570.[1]

Collegial bodies like the Council of Ten, answerable in all major decisions to the Senate, conducted foreign policy and war.[2] In wartime, the Ten met daily in

---

[1] On Venetian government and the aristocracy, see the rapid overview by Yves Durand, *Les républiques au temps des monarchies* (Paris: 1973), pp. 80–149. Concerning specifically the activities of the patriciate, see the book by Alexander F. Cowan, *The urban patriciate: Lubeck and Venice, 1580–1700* (Cologne: 1986); and by James C. Davis, *The decline of the Venetian nobility as a ruling class* (Baltimore: 1962).

[2] The political direction of the Venetian military administration is explained in great detail by J. R. Hale, in M. E. Mallett & J. R. Hale, *The military organization of a Renaissance state* (Cambridge: 1984), pt 2 (1509–1617).

Venice and read dispatches sent from the field or the fleet, called experts to advise them, and held their war council below a great wall-map painted in the antechamber. This way, civilians retained a general view of the war and decided upon the basic strategy. The Senate also took measures to raise and supply the army and the fleet, and construct fortresses. The crucial military administrators were the proveditors, who functioned as paymasters, controlled supplies and administered fortresses, and generally oversaw logistical details. There was no clear hierarchy: some had jurisdiction over a single town or castle, while others surveyed whole districts or operational theatres. Not until 1617 did the Senate rank the commander-in-chief of the army above the proveditors in the councils of war. These administrators were most frequently Venetian patricians, who by virtue of their monopoly over the command of galleys had some military experience and training.[3] There was not, in Venice, the rigid distinction between a military nobility seeking an outlet for their ambitions in war, and a courtly or urbane city aristocracy satisfying its martial thrills vicariously. As time progressed, this changed only slowly, owing to the gradual demographic implosion that was characteristic of Italian patriciates almost everywhere. For several reasons, syphilis, perhaps, the Counter-Reformation appeal of the church, and most important, through the restriction of marriage, families were not replacing their numbers in succeeding generations. By 1610 there were 2,100 adult male patricians, and only 1,660 after the plague of 1630–31. The smaller élite was required to govern and defend the same territory as before.

Lepanto and its aftermath confirmed the republic's status as a major power in the Mediterranean. From a peacetime force of 9,000 men spread across the empire in garrisons, the *Serenissima* in 1570 raised an army of 36,000 men, hired partly on the international manpower market. In 1573 Venice had put 130 galleys to sea, with 23,000 infantry on board.[4] It maintained a fleet half the size of the Ottoman one and garrisoned the Empire, the Terraferma and the lagoon too, all with the most modern *matériel*. Like other states before the advent of the standing army, Venice considered it sufficient to maintain an infrastructure capable of raising a field army at short notice. With the approach of peace, it laid off soldiers and stored most of the galleys until the next emergency. It was artificial to make strong distinctions between land and sea forces, since the soldiers embarked and disembarked as the occasion required. In 1600 the peacetime strength of

---

[3] Mallett & Hale, *The military organization of a Renaissance state*, p. 264ff. Many sought combat experience to demonstrate their competence. The septuagenarian Niccolò Contarini, proveditor of the field army in the Gradisca war, swam the Isonzo river with his troops in 1616 in the assault on the city. See the encyclopedia entry in Valori, *Condottieri e generali nel seicento*, p. 95.

[4] J. R. Hale, "From peacetime establishment to fighting machine: the Venetian army and the war of Cyprus and Lepanto", in *Il Mediterraneo nella seconda metà del '500*, G. Benzoni (ed.) (Florence: 1974), pp. 163–84.

the army oscillated around 9,500 men, which was considerable for a smaller state.[5]

The Terraferma was too prosperous for soldiering to be attractive to the population or to the nobility. Apart from the poorer and more isolated province of Friuli, recruiting agents seldom plied the Terraferma looking for bodies. Of the military entrepreneurs employed by Venice in 1615, at the onset of the Gradisca war, only about half were Venetian subjects, while most of the others hailed from north-central Italy and Corsica.[6] Recruits for its infantry companies could be had from Croatia and Greece, under their own captains and colonels. Venice also relied extensively on the services of 'foreign' Italians recruited from the Adriatic watershed, like the Romagna behind Faenza and Forlì or the Marches and the Umbrian hills beyond.[7] Until 1582, when the duke passed into the Spanish clientèle, the duchy of Urbino was an important source of mercenaries, where Venetian diplomats counted the total population and available militiamen almost as if they ruled them.[8] Since the patriciate of the capital city was not jealous of its military monopoly, service for Venice allowed considerable social mobility for talented nobles and *roturiers*. Corsicans were a good example of this, for they served in large numbers, and their captains were kept under contract in Venetian pay. Giacinto Peri began as a simple soldier, and upon his release from service integrated into the Veronese nobility. There were true dynasties of such officers, like the Pozzo di Borgo.[9] Venice also employed Protestant infantry like the Swiss Grisons, for the patricians were not squeamish over such trifles.

Venice hired light cavalry from its overseas empire for skirmishing and scouting. There were Greek *stradioti*, who were practically brigands, liable to plunder indiscriminately if they were not closely watched. Corsicans were sometimes used on horseback to track bandits in the Alpine frontier, along with the Albanian and Bosnian light cavalry, who were frequently Moslems, complete with accoutrements of turbans and scimitars. Venice also recruited cavalry from much of Italy, especially from Friuli, the Veneto, Lombardy and Umbria. They were designated as light cavalry, but only to distinguish them from the ponderous gens d'armes encased in plate armour. About a thousand of them served during the Mantuan and Valtellina wars with the Habsburgs.[10] The merchant republic still employed

---

[5] Mallett & Hale, *The military organization of a Renaissance state*, p. 213. By way of comparison, the French army in the decade after 1600 numbered only 12,000 men.

[6] *Ibid.*, p. 345.

[7] *Ibid.*, p. 320ff.

[8] J. Dennistoun, *Memoirs of the dukes of Urbino, 1440–1631* (London: 1902), vol. 3.

[9] Hale, "From peacetime establishment to fighting machine", in *Il Mediterraneo nella seconda metà del '500*, p. 167. See also F. Paleologo Oriundi, *I Corsi nella fanteria italiana della Serenissima repubblica di Venezia* (Venice: 1912), p. 8. On Giacinto Peri, see Valori, *Condottieri e generali del seicento*, p. 283.

[10] Mallett & Hale, *The military organization of a Renaissance state*, p. 374ff. See also the very useful little book on the organization of the Venetian army by Ennio Concina, *Le trionfanti et invittissime armate venete: le milizie della serenissima dal 16° al 18° secolo* (Venice: 1971), p. 62ff.

some companies of finely mounted gens d'armes after 1600, drawn from the great families of Venice and the subject cities.[11] In 1590 the alumni of noble riding academies and other nobles, or those *civilmente nato* filled fourteen squadrons of heavy cavalry, reduced to seven companies totalling 400 men in the first decades of the seventeenth century. They were trained to charge in serried order in a set-piece battle, but this occasion never arose. Their role was more generally ceremonial.

Finally, the Venetian army enjoyed the dubious support of a peasant militia, similar to that established in other European realms, from England to Spain, Tuscany and Naples. In the Terraferma alone, officials considered there were about 200,000 men fit for military service, although they armed only a small fraction of that number. On paper, these companies presented a formidable force. Militia or *ordinanza* units were set up early in the sixteenth century, to confront the emergency of the Italian wars. They were extended to Dalmatia during the great Turkish war of 1570, to face the dire threat there. Giacomo Foscarini created a similar force in Crete as part of his military reforms of 1574.[12] Despite the huge number of eligible men, only 20,000 mustered in the Terraferma, and a similar number served in the colonies after 1600. If these numbers appear modest, it was because their limitations were their most remarkable feature. Although militia-men kept their weapons at home (a motley assortment of blade weapons, mostly), their training was limited to a few musters on holidays. Commanders sometimes employed them to augment garrisons, or to pace the ramparts alongside the municipal militias.[13] In the Gradisca war against Austria, Venice occasionally trooped hundreds of them to bolster the mercenaries in the field. Many deserted, and they could not stand against professional soldiers. By the seventeenth century, these bands became ever less reliable, and only the most oppressed peasants consented to be conscripted.

Because of its limited manpower, Venice depended on its fortresses. Verona was perhaps the first city anywhere rebuilt on the Italian trace model, and other pioneering projects were traced out in western Lombardy border towns, like Orzinuovi and Brescia. In all of the Terraferma fortresses, there were perhaps only 2,000 men in 1590, and 3,000 in 1620. The commanders were hardly ambitious and efficient soldiers, as they were generally at the end of their careers. The soldiers were rather like security guards whose task was to open and close the gates.[14] One exception was Palmanova, built in Friuli after 1594, the most impos-ing project of the age. More than 7,500 pioneers laboured to clear the terrain for this great octagonal fortress. It watched the border with Austria, though the

---

[11] J. R. Hale, "Military academies on the Venetian Terraferma in the early seventeenth century", *Studi Veneziani*, 1973, pp. 273–96.

[12] W. Miller, *Essays on the Latin Orient* (Cambridge: 1921), p. 187.

[13] Concina, *Le trionfanti et invittissime armate venete*, p. 44ff. See also Mallett & Hale, *The military organization of a Renaissance state*, p. 354ff.

[14] Mallett & Hale, *The military organization of a Renaissance state*, p. 381ff.

pretext for its erection was to prevent an Ottoman invasion from Bosnia. Despite the huge investment in this particular fortress (or perhaps because of it), Palmanova was never besieged in the history of the republic. At the end of the sixteenth century, Venice began other imposing projects in the island colonies of Cyprus, Crete and Corfù, and then along the Dalmatian coast, at Zara, Sebenico, Trau, and Spalato, supported by the wooden walls of the fleet reserve of 30 galleys. The garrisons most frequently comprised 'foreigners,' with Venetians serving when no-one else was available. In 1590 only about 20 per cent of the captains, and 15 per cent of the troops, were Venetian or hailed from the Terraferma.[15]

Both the wooden walls and the stone walls required abundant artillery. The quality of Venetian guns, especially the bronze cannon cast at the Arsenal in Venice itself, was quite good until the seventeenth century. Iron guns and most of the other military hardware came from Brescia, an international centre of arms and armour production. To train proper gunners to serve them, the larger towns organized artillerymen in bombardier confraternities. Mathematics and the physics of ballistics were taught there for their benefit, but good gunners used empirical methods and improved with practice. In 1600, there were an estimated 600 bombardiers available to the state, but this was an insufficient number for the fleet and the fortresses combined.[16]

Like Italian princes, the republic kept military specialists on call or sought them actively elsewhere, and signed contracts with them to raise experienced troops rapidly. There was no special attempt to recruit Venetian subjects, although the patricians of the subject cities were frequent volunteers. The government accepted all offers from volunteers who paid their own way, as long as they brought less than 30 people with them. The Senate was unwilling to abandon its right to choose captains of companies in the way that had become typical of Spanish and Imperial armies. In peacetime the republic spent about 350,000 ducats annually on the maintenance of its military potential, or about a quarter of its revenue. In wartime it could disburse eight to ten times that amount, as during the Gradisca war against Austria in Friuli. As the international climate worsened in the seventeenth century, Venice's peacetime military expenditure increased to 30 per cent of revenues in 1620, and to 42 per cent in 1641, before the onset of the Castro crisis. From a peacetime strength of 9,000 men, Venice raised its forces to 23,500 in the Terraferma alone during the operations against Austria between 1615 and 1617, and the number remained high during the Valtellina emergency.[17] After the

---

[15] *Ibid.*, p. 351.

[16] Mallett & Hale, *The military organization of a Renaissance state*, p. 398. See also Concina, *Le trionfanti et invittissime armate venete*, p. 101.

[17] For these figures, comparing the proportion of 'defence' expenditures of Venice with those of Piedmont and the Papal States, see Luciano Pezzolo, "Esercito e stato nella prima età moderna: alcune considerazioni preliminari per una ricerca sulla repubblica di

debacle of the Mantuan war in 1629, Venice did not turn her back entirely on Italian politics. Instead the Senate hired the French Protestant general, the duc de Rohan, who recruited 6,000 more infantry and officers in a few short months, and inspected all the fortresses preparing for a renewal of hostilities. He recruited as many Huguenots as he could, with Swiss troops and other foreign mercenaries who formed the nucleus of the army. Rohan tried to push the republic into active war against Spain, and occupy the Valtellina, but the Senate refused to be rushed.[18] The performance of the Venetian army also proved indifferent in the Castro War of 1643. After that, Venetian policy never wavered from an attitude of non-intervention in the great-power struggles that engulfed its neighbours. Its indifference may only have been the outcome of three generations of pressure by the Ottoman Turks on the Mediterranean empire.

The Candia War, 1645–70

The Venetian empire in the Adriatic and the Aegean never numbered more than 400,000 inhabitants, or barely a fifth of the total population of the republic. The coastal strip of Dalmatia provided way-stations and bases for galleys and merchant ships, while depriving potential enemies of bases there. Guarding the narrow entrance to the Adriatic, Corfù was a strategic base of the utmost importance, while Crete provided some important resources in grain, rice and sugar for the metropolis. Although Crete was mountainous, it was tolerably fertile, and supported a population of more than 200,000 people. The Cretans often resisted Venetian rule, with its petty harassment of the Orthodox religion of most Greeks. During the Cyprus war, Turkish raids spurred the islanders to revolt. Part of Crete's tribulations lay rooted in the republic's inability to end the feuds that wracked the island.[19] Venice initially established its control by breaking up the island into almost 500 fiefs, of which 80 per cent belonged to resident Venetian nobles. These were supposed to form the backbone of the defence force and maintain internal order, but most of the fiefs were so small that few seigneurs could afford to maintain war horses. These feudatories' martial skills had largely fallen into abeyance by 1574. Giacomo Foscarini then set up a peasant militia on the Venetian model, paid from the island's treasury.[20] In the seventeenth century, the revolts against the *Serenissima* ceased, making it easier for the Senate to provide for the island's defence against external enemies. Crete absorbed most of the garrisons in the Levant, and required about a third of Venetian military expendi-

---

Venezia", in *Guerre, stati e città: Mantova e l'Italia padana dal secolo XIII al XIX* (Milan: 1988), pp. 13–30.

[18] J. A. Clarke, *Huguenot warrior: the life and times of Henri de Rohan, 1579–1638*, p. 183ff.

[19] Miller, *Essays on the Latin Orient*, p. 187. See also the evocative historical travel guide by Jan Morris, *The Venetian empire: a sea voyage* (London: 1980), p. 74ff.

[20] Miller, *Essays on the Latin Orient*, p. 187.

tures in peacetime.[21] Corvées imposed on the peasantry around the towns obliged them to work on fortification in times of tension with the Ottoman Porte. After 1638, three Dutch military engineers in Candia, skilled in displacing earth, built inexpensive fortifications and gradually projected outworks around the city. The lesser fortified towns had flaws so serious that desultory improvement could not rectify them.[22]

Venice cherished peace with Turkey, for trade with the Ottoman Empire was a cornerstone of the republic's prosperity, even after the Thirty Years War had crippled its foreign outlets. There was always a war party in Constantinople promoting the conquest of Venice's Aegean and Adriatic empire. After Lepanto, and again in the debacle of 1630, Venice seemed an easy target, especially in Crete where Greek loyalty was doubtful. Crete sat astride the great trading artery of the Ottoman Empire, between the Dardanelles and Egypt; it was as peripheral to the other Venetian colonies as it was central to the Ottoman-held Greek archipelago. Relations between the Porte and Venice were nevertheless good until 1638, when the republic seized some contested villages near Zara and Sebenico in Dalmatia. Barbary corsairs that year plundered the Italian coast from Calabria to the Marches, seizing some Venetian cargoes in the process. The admiral, Cappello, retaliated by penetrating the Albanian harbour of Valona with the Venetian fleet, and carried off or destroyed the whole pirate flotilla of 16 Algerine galiots while under the fire of the Turkish guns.[23] This single incident almost touched off a general war. After all, the 28 Venetian ships had bombarded the port for good measure, and partially destroyed a mosque; but since the sultan was engaged in war with Persia, the incident gradually receded from view. A new *casus belli* was provided in September 1644 when six Maltese galleys lurking off Crete pounced on the Ottoman Alexandria convoy, and captured part of it after a bloody battle. Among the prisoners figured a concubine and an infant son of the Sultan himself, whom the knights turned over to Franciscan monks as a convert. The Maltese galleys then sheltered off the south coast of Crete to repair their damage before leaving the Aegean.[24] This tacit support given by a neutral state to warlike actions in the heart of the empire finally moved the grand vizir to break with the republic.

---

[21] L. Pezzolo, "Aspetti della struttura militare veneziana in Levante fra cinque e seicento", in *Venezia e la difesa del Levante, da Lepanto a Candia, 1570–1670* (Venice: 1986), pp. 86–96.

[22] P. Morachiello, "Candia: i baluardi del regno", in *Venezia e la difesa del Levante, da Lepanto a Candia, 1570–1670*, pp. 133–43.

[23] K. Setton, *Venice, Austria and the Turks in the seventeenth century* (Philadelphia: 1991), p. 107ff.; see also R. C. Anderson, *Naval wars in the Levant*, p. 117.

[24] Setton, *Venice, Austria and the Turks in the seventeenth century*, p. 121. See also the dense contribution by the eminent French specialist in the seventeenth-century Ottoman Empire, Robert Mantran, "L'Impero ottomano, Venezia e la guerra (1570–1670)", in *Venezia e la difesa del Levante, da Lepanto a Candia*, pp. 227–32. See also by Mantran, "Venezia e i Turchi, 1650–1797", in *Venezia e i Turchi: scontri e confronti di due civiltà* (Milan: 1985), pp. 250–67.

Venice saw the storm coming, as the Ottomans began collecting troops and ships at Constantinople, although Malta and Sicily also saw themselves likely targets. As on past occasions, the republic began its military expansion to meet the threat. Crete was put into a state of defence by the two commanders of the land forces, the German baron von Degenfeld and the Mantuan prince Don Camillo Gonzaga. The Venetian proveditor Cornaro began to muster the Candian militia, and raised the wages of those who were conspicuously loyal. In February 1645, the *Serenissima* sent 2,500 regular infantry to bolster Crete's garrisons, and recruited 1,000 irregulars in the Peloponnesis and elsewhere in Greece. Two galeasses, thirty galleys and six large warships moored in the capacious Suda Bay, in the north-west corner of the island. Venice beefed up its garrisons in Friuli, Dalmatia, Corfù and on the lagoon itself. To finance these preparations, the Senate resolved, after much debate, to adopt a drastic measure long practised in other states. It sold nobility and citizenship rights for the huge sum of 100,000 ducats per family, with the proceeds going to purchase more galleys, galeasses and other vessels.[25] With the object of the invasion still in doubt, and with so many points to protect, none of the fortresses was really strongly held. Of the eight forts along the north coast of Crete, only Candia had a sizeable garrison of regulars. There were only 10,000 soldiers on Crete in 1645, not including the unenthusiastic local militia. Closer to home, the defences were stouter. In Dalmatia, the Venetians held the coastal towns while a forbidding wall of karst mountains blocked access from the Bosnian interior. The major bases at Cattaro, Spalato, Sebenico and Zara were all well fortified. Venice could also count on the support of the Montenegrins, supplied over the mountain-top from Cattaro.

To feed troops and supplies to all these zones, the republic counted on its ability to fill its ships with men and weapons at short notice. To meet the requirements for crews, Venice rescinded laws requiring oarsmen to be Venetian subjects, and entered the market for galley slaves.[26] Minor shipyards and foundries in Candia, La Canea and especially Corfù, seconded the feverish activity in the Arsenal. They had to produce enough equipment to maintain the fleet of 100 galleys and 12 galeasses that the Senate felt was its necessary reserve. This required a constant supply of wood from the Alps, iron from Germany and Friuli, and hemp from the Terraferma to make rope. In 1650 there was material enough to arm 65 galleys and some galeasses, in addition to the 12,000 muskets stored in the entrepôt. Between 1,200 and 2,000 workers and artisans toiled unceasingly in the Arsenal from 1641 to 1670, making it one of the great workshops of Europe.[27]

---

[25] J. C. Davis, *The decline of the Venetian nobility as a ruling class* (Baltimore: 1962), p. 78ff. Davis notes that 80 families purchased noble status during the Candia War.

[26] A. Wiel, *The navy of Venice* (London: 1910), p. 302.

[27] E. Concina, "'Sostener in vigore le cose del mare'; arsenali, vascelli, cannoni", in *Venezia e la difesa del Levante*, pp. 47–58. See also the description of the Arsenal by an important French spy, son of the minister Colbert, *L'Italie en 1671: relation d'un voyage du marquis de Seignelay*, Pierre Clément (ed.) (Paris: 1867), pp. 232–46.

When the Turkish invasion force left Constantinople on 30 April 1645, ostensibly bound for Malta, it consisted of 80 galleys, two mahones or Turkish galeasses, 20 sailing ships and 200 transports. The Turkish army that disembarked at La Canea in Crete on 24 June is said to have numbered 50,000 soldiers and 30,000 pioneers to work in the trenches, although estimates of Ottoman strength were habitually inflated.[28] The garrison at La Canea numbered only 800 soldiers, with a peasant and urban militia of about a thousand more. Of the city militia, only the Basilean monks proved steadfast. The eight-week siege revealed more the shortcomings of Turkish siegecraft than the determination of the garrison, despite their use of noxious "fumes". Unable to repair the defence works as the Turkish guns battered them, the garrison decided to capitulate after repulsing a few assaults. The disappointing performance of the Cretan militia would be repeated in the following years, for several reasons. First, the 12,000 available militiamen lacked firearms. Men had enrolled, not to fight, but to be exempt from fortification corvées or to serve as oarsmen on the galleys. For the first year, these bands did almost no fighting, apart from killing stragglers. Humane treatment by the Turks, who proved to be much better behaved than contemporary European armies towards civilians, won over most of the population into a passive neutrality.[29]

The Thirty Years War made it more difficult for Venice to find help in Europe. Only the Pope and the Order of Malta gave unstinting support. Innocent X Pamphili sent 1,500 troops raised around Rome to Malta, and another 1,500 to Dalmatia. Six Papal galleys under Prince Ludovisi joined the Venetian fleet. Grand Duke Ferdinando II of Tuscany readied five galleys and 600 troops and sent them as well. The allied fleet also counted six Maltese and five Neapolitan galleys. The united Catholic force gathered under the guns of Suda consisted of 62 galleys, six galeasses, 40 other large vessels and 20 smaller ships, with 3,000 cannon, 15,000 soldiers, 10,000 seamen and 12,000 oarsmen. Venetian ships had not gathered on such a scale since Lepanto. Most of the contingent commanders were impatient to engage the Turkish fleet at La Canea and force a decision, but Admiral Cappello lacked the nerve to gamble everything in a single action. After weeks of wrangling and frustration, the fleet disbanded for winter.

In 1646 the Venetian fleet again assembled in Crete with its allies, minus the Spanish and Tuscan contingents, and again Cappello hesitated to engage. Undisturbed, the Turks simply blockaded Candia with 12,000 men, although less than half of that force consisted of soldiers, the rest being labourers and sutlers.[30] Their

---

[28] Morachiello, "Candia, i baluardi del regno", in *Venezia e la difesa del Levante*, p. 139.

[29] Pezzolo, "Aspetti della struttura militare veneziana in Levante fra cinque e seicento", in *Venezia e la difesa del Levante*, p. 88.

[30] Andreina Zitelli, "Candia soccorsa nella penuria estrema di biade", in *Venezia e la difesa del Levante*, pp. 127–32.

target that year was Rethimnon (Rettimo), reputedly a very strong fortress. It fell in only a few days because of dissension between the Venetian and the foreign troops, primarily French and Flemish. When the Turks seized the town, they slaughtered 88 of the officers and more than 1,500 soldiers, perhaps to strike terror in the garrison of Candia itself.[31]

While most of the Ottoman effort was directed at Crete, a diversionary Turkish force issued forth from Bosnia to occupy Dalmatia. After a short siege in 1646, Novigrad fell. The other towns could be supplied and reinforced easily by sea, however, and the Croats participated wholeheartedly in their own defence. Venice employed Croatian notables as officers and even occasionally as proveditors. By the spring of 1648 a counter-offensive of strong raiding columns from the coast had captured 40 towns and villages in Bosnia.[32] The fierce Croat, Serb and Albanian villagers needed few pretexts to engage in a war of skirmishing and rapine against the 'Turks', and every source underlines the ferocious nature of the endless Bosnian war.[33] These Uskoks or 'Morlacchi' formed bands of guerrillas led by their own captains. Their feuding culture accustomed men to carry firearms everywhere, for their own protection from domestic and foreign enemies.[34] Beyond Dalmatia, the Ionian islanders in Corfù, Zante and Cefalonia manned ships and served in garrisons. One strategy employed by Venice was to stir the Christian populations of the Balkan peninsula to revolt. The revolt in the Epirus of the 'Morlacchi' is said to have diverted about 20,000 Turkish troops to the area.[35] This was a ferocious little war of irregulars ambushing, raiding, and seizing villages from the adversary, all tasks for which the Croatian light cavalry was suited. These troops also accompanied units of the regular army mounting expeditions to seize fortified towns in Turkish Bosnia, like Clissa and Knin. Venice required all males in Dalmatia between the ages of 18 and 50 to serve in the militia, for local defence. The targets they selected were rarely farther than a few days' march. The warriors preferred surprise attacks and ambushes to pitched battles against Ottoman forces, which resembled their own. The republic levied a

---

[31] Wiel, *The navy of Venice*, p. 287.

[32] F. Sassi, "La campagna di Dalmazia durante la guerra di Candia", *Archivio Veneto*, 1937.

[33] F. Babudieri, "Gli Uscocchi: loro formazione e loro attivita a terra ed in mare", in *Le genti del mare Mediterraneo*, Rosalba Ragosta (ed.) (Naples: 1981), vol. 1, pp. 445–98.

[34] See Concina, *Le trionfanti et invittissime armate venete*, p. 33; also C. W. Bracewell, "Uskoks in Venetian Dalmatia before the Venetian–Ottoman War of 1714–1718", in *East-central European society and war in the pre-revolutionary eighteenth century*, G. Rothenberg, B. Kiràly, P. Sugar (eds) (Boulder, Colorado: 1982), pp. 431–47, at pp. 432–5. A number of encyclopedia citations reflect the brutal nature of the Balkan wars. See in Valori, *Condottieri e generali del seicento*, the citations on Vencino Mandusich, p. 216; Francesco Possidaria, p. 303; Ilia Smiglianich, p. 377; Pietro Smiglianich, p. 378; and Stefano Sorich, p. 380.

[35] C. Terlinden, *Le Pape Clément IX et la guerre de Candie, 1667–1669, d'après les archives sécrètes du Saint-Siège* (Louvain: 1904), p. 13ff.

10 per cent tax on the booty the Dalmatians acquired from the Moslems and Christians on the other side of the border.[36]

Venice frantically scoured Europe looking for other resources. Italian states contributed their share. Concina speaks of recruiting colonels, 'merchants of human flesh' who persuaded princes in Parma and Modena to sell their subjects to Venice to balance their budgets.[37] This might be a harsh judgement, for even Farnese and Este princes served in these contingents. Two of Duke Ranuccio II's brothers served the Venetians, Alessandro Farnese as a simple captain of cavalry, and Orazio who accompanied the fleet to the Dardanelles in 1656 as an adventurer. At the outset these Emilian auxiliaries showed little fighting spirit, but like the other infantry they gradually gave a good account of themselves. By 1652 the duke of Parma sent both money and men; Modena and the Papal States joined the effort the following year. After the signature of the Peace of the Pyrenees, in 1659, Piedmont sent entire regiments under the Ferrarese general Villa. The Popes were all ardent supporters of war against Islam. One of the first measures of the newly elected Alexander VII Chigi in 1655 was to recruit Papal troops for service in Dalmatia. Rome also subsidized 4,000 French troops in 1659–60, under the command of Prince Almerigo d'Este.[38] They were wasted in a sortie, and many others, including the prince, died of disease.

The number of troops raised by Venice and her allies in the years following the invasion of Crete was never enough to break the Turkish hold on the island. The Senate then sought to starve the besiegers by interfering with their naval lifeline. In 1647 Admiral Mocenigo decided to block the Dardanelles with a fleet of roundships supported by galleys.[39] This shifted the emphasis of the war from one of siege operations on Crete itself, to a naval war ranging throughout the Aegean sea. The Venetian fleet forced a Turkish one to battle off Chios, where Venice's 13 ships and 16 galleys opposed 27 ships, four mahones and 30 galleys. Despite the disparity in numbers in favour of the Ottomans, the result was indecisive. In March 1648 a winter storm struck the Venetians a severe blow as the fleet sheltered off the island of Psara. Eighteen out of twenty galleys, and nine ships sank in the tempest and the admiral, Grimani, perished with 2,000 men. The survivors turned back to Crete. The following year, however, Admiral Riva possessed a fleet of 19 ships and attending galleys operating in the Aegean from bases in Crete. Most of the ships were by now Dutch and English, with officers

---

[36] Bracewell, "Uskoks in Venetian Dalmatia before the Venetian–Ottoman War of 1714–1718", in *East-central European society and war in the pre-revolutionary eighteenth century*, G. Rothenberg, B. Kiràly, P. Sugar (eds) (Boulder, Colorado: 1982), pp. 431–47, at p. 432.

[37] Concina, *Le trionfanti et invittissime armate venete*, p. 14.

[38] For details on the Papal contribution, see the work by A. Guglielmotti, *Storia della marina pontificia: vol. VIII, A Candia ed alla Morea; storia dal 1644 al 1699* (Rome: 1892), p. 11ff. On the French contingent of 1660, see Setton, *Venice, Austria and the Turks in the seventeenth century*, p. 190.

[39] Anderson, *Naval wars in the Levant*, p. 127.

and crew having hired themselves out to the Venetians. Riva promised compensation for any material damage that might be incurred, and these naval mercenaries once they were insured against property damage, acquitted themselves well, together with the Venetian soldiers on board.[40] They forced their way into Turkish anchorages at Fochies (near Chios) and Smyrna, and ran the gauntlet of shore batteries to destroy most of the Ottoman fleet. The sultan's fleet too, consisted largely of Dutch, English and French merchant ships, with the gunners and crew still in western dress.

These diversions helped. The momentum of the Turkish conquest slowed in 1647, and Candia had time to prepare for an extended siege. Officers divided the city into ten sectors, and allotted civilians a section of the walls. Commanders expelled the useless mouths, set up hospitals in the convents and found men and women to work there. New cemeteries were opened and gravediggers hired to fill them. Lights were placed in the streets to prevent nocturnal gatherings. Frantic activity created earthen outworks beyond the ramparts, such as a hornwork, some half-moons and ravelins, executed under the direction of Camillo Gonzaga and the Dutch engineer Van Wert. The clergy egged on the defenders in the city, some 5,000 soldiers and 10,000 civilians, of whom about a thousand could fight. Their strategy was strictly defensive, for it would have required some 20,000 troops to break the siege and sweep away the Turks.[41] Once the Turks began their sap in May 1648, the war of mines began. Venetian 'moles' sensitive to noises underground burrowed countermines out from the fortress. The engineers participated in the digging and the skirmishing underground in person. After the defenders had worn down the attacking force to a mere 6,000 men, the Turks gave up and waited for the next season. In August 1649, the Turks began to sap the same objectives, the Betelem bastion and the ravelins of Panigrà and Mocenigo, all on the landward side. Several times they captured the outworks, but sudden Venetian counter-attacks drove them off. The chief engineers Bellonet and Vernède, both Frenchmen, kept discovering the mine shafts and, by collapsing them, prevented the Turks from burrowing under the moat. By October the besiegers had worn down their strength. The defenders then moved earth and stone to repair the damage. The Turks achieved little more for the next 18 years.

Because Venice enjoyed superiority at sea, Candia could not be blockaded, but this prolonged the city's agony. Even during the quiescent 1650s the defence of the city was tremendously expensive, costing about 700,000 ducats annually, or a third of the republic's pre-war revenue.[42] As new units arrived continually to replace depleted ones, the make-up of the garrison evolved. In peacetime, they had been mostly Italian, from Emilia-Romagna, the Marches and the Abruzzi,

---

[40] *Ibid.*, p. 137.

[41] Morachiello, "Candia: i baluardi del regno", in *Venezia e la difesa del Levante*, pp. 139–43.

[42] Pezzolo, "Aspetti della struttura militare veneziana in Levante", in *Venezia e la difesa del Levante*, pp. 86–96.

the Adriatic Italy that traditionally looked to Venice. The Croat, Albanian and Greek light cavalry present was often judged negatively for its indiscipline and for its violence against civilians. By 1647 the Venetian Senate was hiring German, Swiss and French regiments wholesale, along with any Italians available for service. The end of the Thiry Years War made hiring easier. The *Serenissima* tried to employ whole regiments of Swedish soldiers by negotiating directly with King Karl X. When baron Martin von Degenfeld retired finally from Venetian service in 1651, he went home to recruit 2,000 soldiers for Candia, where his sons commanded regiments. In a muster of 1651, of 4,440 regular infantry soldiers serving in Candia, the Swedes, Germans, French and Swiss constituted 36 per cent; the Greeks formed almost a quarter (22 per cent), the Corsicans 18 per cent and other Italians 15 per cent; the *oltremarini* (Croats, probably) comprised the remaining 8 per cent. With a troop of cavalry of unspecified origin, and the local militia, the overall strength was about 6,000 infantry and 450 horse, of which 5,347 were fit for battle.[43] The Turks blockading them numbered about 12,000 to 15,000, and there were other Turkish garrisons scattered throughout the island.

Given the stalemate on land, the Venetians escalated their efforts to achieve strategic successes at sea, with their fleets of sailing vessels, galeasses, galleys and transports based in Candia and Corfù. The Ottomans made great efforts to increase their number of sailing ships, buying some outright from English and Dutch merchants, and building a few in the Barbary states where renegades from northern Europe were skilled in such arts. Fontenay estimates the number of galleys available to the Turks at between eighty and a hundred, augmented by a few 'mahones' in imitation of the Venetian galeasses.[44] The greater part of this Turkish fleet left the Dardanelles in June 1651 with orders to engage and destroy its Venetian counterpart. Their 55 ships, 53 galleys and six mahones met the Venetians under Alvise Mocenigo off Santorini (Thera) with a fleet half their size, of 28 ships, 24 galleys and six galeasses. The Venetians got the better of the ensuing mêlée, taking a mahone and ten ships, and destroying five others, netting about a thousand prisoners. Consequently, the Turks dodged the Venetian fleet in 1652 and 1653, and instead supplied Crete by small flotillas sprinting from the Greek archipelago and Anatolia. In return, the Venetian admiral, Foscolo, collected tribute in the Aegean, ravaging islands like Samos that attempted to resist.[45] This was the seaborne version of the 'contributions' employed so successfully by Wallenstein.

Success emboldened the Venetians to send their fleet into the Dardanelles

---

[43] *Ibid.*, p. 87.

[44] M. Fontenay, "Chiourmes turques au XVIIe siècle", in *Le genti del mare mediterraneo*, vol. 2, pp. 877–903, at p. 884.

[45] Anderson, *Naval wars in the Levant*, p. 150.

proper in 1654, provoking panic in Constantinople.[46] The resulting battle in the straits was technically a Turkish victory, since the Venetians lost a few ships and then withdrew, but the attempt to end the war with a spectacular show of force nearly succeeded. It ignited revolts of spahis and janissaries in the capital to demand their pay, and protest the poor prosecution of the war, which should have been more one-sided. In 1655 the Venetians appeared in the Dardanelles again with a fleet of 26 ships, six galleys and four galeasses. On 21 June they bested the Turkish fleet in the passage, burning nine galleys and wrecking more for the modest cost of 300 killed and wounded. Then in 1656 they returned and inflicted a stunning blow to the Ottoman navy in the narrows. The Turkish fleet numbering 79 vessels and galleys was all but destroyed, with only a quarter escaping.[47] The Venetians lost only three ships, and with their allies lost about 800 casualties, for the most part Maltese, although the admiral, Lorenzo Marcello, was killed in the fray.[48] For good measure, the Venetian fleet then captured and fortified the islands at the mouth of the Dardanelles, Tenedos, Lemnos and Samothrace, turning them into bases astride the main artery of the Ottoman Empire.

Flush with success, the Catholic fleet returned in 1657. It was a combination of Venetian, Papal and Maltese ships and galleys under the theoretical command of the Pontifical commander, Giovanni Bichi, a relative of the pope, Alexander VII Chigi.[49] This time the operations proceeded less smoothly. Plague had broken out at Civitavecchia, and there were long quarantine delays at Messina before the Pontificals and Maltese could join the Venetians waiting off Chios. The fleet appeared in the Dardanelles at the end of June, but soon lost hundreds of men who had disembarked for an *acquata* and were ambushed ashore. Constantinople's great fleet was waiting for them in the straits. The battle joined on 3 July was another Venetian victory, with a half-dozen Turkish ships taken or burned, and some galleys beached. On the following day, the impetuous Venetian admiral Alvise Mocenigo sought to complete the victory by torching the abandoned

---

[46] *Ibid.*, p. 151. See also R. Mantran, "L'Impero ottomano, Venezia e la guerra", in *Venezia e la difesa del Levante*, p. 230.

[47] The Venetians destroyed 22 ships, four mahones and 34 galleys, and captured four, five and 13 respectively, taking about 8,000 prisoners in the process; Anderson, *Naval wars in the Levant*, p. 151ff. See also Setton, *Venice, Austria and the Turks in the seventeenth century*, p. 173ff. The prisoners taken were augmented by the liberation of galley slaves, many of whom were Italians. This was the fate of Venetian troops captured by the Turks. See Fontenay, "Chiourmes turques au XVIIe siècle", *Le genti del mare mediterraneo*, vol. 2, p. 893.

[48] E. Rossi, *Storia della marina dell'ordine di S. Giovanni di Gerusalemme, di Rodi e di Malta* (Rome–Milan: 1926), p. 72.

[49] An eyewitness account of this, containing sketches of the fleet in harbour and in array, can be found in G. Cugnoni, "Relazione del viaggio delle galere pontificie in Levante l'anno 1657", *Bullettino Senese di Storia Patria*, 1897, pp. 345–89.

galleys, and directed his great flagship galley over to the shore, oblivious to the batteries there. A cannonball must have hit its powder magazine, for the galley exploded and then sank, killing the admiral immediately and hundreds of men besides. The fleet withdrew from the straits soon after. In another engagement off the Spalmadori islands, the allied fleet destroyed a few more Turkish ships, but at a cost of almost 500 killed and wounded.

These naval campaigns ultimately ended in stalemate too. The Turks began to construct stronger fortresses at the entrance to the straits and increased the garrisons there, preventing the Catholic fleets from taking on water. That put the Ottoman capital out of reach of even the most daring offensive. Venetian fleets were still smaller than their Turkish counterparts, but the allied contingents were increasingly large. In 1658 the Pope sent five galleys and ten vessels, these last carrying thirty or forty cannon each.[50] Malta sent six galleys and a dozen support vessels. There were no easy objectives for them to conquer, however, and the Turks succeeded in recapturing the islands off the entrance of the Dardanelles. Fleet actions were supplemented by a myriad of corsair raids that rendered the Aegean very dangerous.[51] In 1654 a flotilla of Maltese privateers intercepted a Turkish squadron off Rhodes and sank four ships, one of which carried 54 guns.[52]

Despite the stalemate, Venetian attempts against the Dardanelles almost succeeded in disorientating Ottoman policy. Lack of military success and irregular payment soured relations between the sultan and his janissaries. In March 1648 they overthrew Sultan Achmed, and appointed the infant Mehmed IV to replace him.[53] From 1654 to 1657 factional infighting in the harem around the sultan spilled out into the Empire. To pay for the Cretan war, there were extraordinary tax levies and confiscations. The striking of debased coinage inflated the currency and played havoc with the economy. In October 1656, Mehmed Pasha Koprulu was named grand vizir, entrusted with restoring efficiency in the state and the army, and with finding money to prosecute the war more vigorously. At first his efforts sparked tax revolts in Kurdistan, Syria and Egypt, and the apparent weakness of the empire encouraged the Transylvanians to cease paying tribute. It took years for the Porte to restore obedience in the empire.[54]

---

[50] Guglielmotti, *Storia della marina pontificia, vol. VIII*, p. 162ff.

[51] Fontenay, "L'Empire ottoman et le risque corsair au 17e siècle", *Revue d'Histoire Moderne et Contemporaine*, 1985, pp. 185–208. Vacalopoulos, *The Greek nation, 1453–1669* (New Brunswick, New Jersey: 1976), pp. 85–90. The contributions and the losses of the knights of Malta are chronicled in Ettore Rossi, *Storia della marina dell' ordine di S. Giovanni*, pp. 72–6. There are hundreds of pages devoted to the Candian operations in the monumental chronicle by Fra Bartolomeo dal Pozzo, *Historia della sacra religione militare di S. Giovanni Gerosolimitano, detto di Malta* (Verona: 1703), vol. 2.

[52] Anderson, *Naval wars in the Levant*, p. 151.

[53] Setton, *Venice, Austria and the Turks in the seventeenth century*, p. 149.

[54] See the substantial work under the direction of Robert Mantran, *Histoire de l'empire ottoman* (Paris: 1989), at pp. 237–42.

Meanwhile, Venice tried to muster enough troops to break the siege around Candia. The arrival of foreign contingents at the end of the war between France and Spain facilitated this. Almost 4,000 French and German troops appeared under the Papal flag. A thousand regular Piedmontese troops joined the operation too, under the Marchese Villa. An open market was gradually developing by which princes would rent parts of their army to other states, as a way to fill tax coffers while keeping precious troops and officers occupied and experienced. Most of these princes were German, although the dukes of Piedmont and Modena also participated in a modest way.[55] Venice rented, for example, three regiments from Duke Johann-Friedrich of Lunenburg. The elector of Bavaria leased about a thousand men to the *Serenissima* too, as did the duke of Lorraine. These princes considered war against the Turks, even for the sake of Venice, as a just cause, and not merely a business venture. Redlich shows how these petty princes pretended to be an 'ally' of the power at war, and called the fee for their services a subsidy. They all allowed Venice to draw upon experienced veterans and spared the republic the incidental costs of providing its own recruiting infrastructure.

The overall commander after 1660 was the Venetian patrician Francesco Morosini. His first attempt to land an army of 8,000 men at La Canea failed because of bad weather. Then he tried a major sortie from Candia that swept the Turks from their entrenchments and back to their camp. When Christian troops broke ranks in the camp to plunder, the Turkish counter-attack repulsed them with heavy loss. After that, the Turkish offensive against Austria in Hungary (1663–4) gave the Venetians some respite. Morosini's more daring approach was a threat to the Turks, for he ferried troops around to maximum advantage. Early in 1666 he once more landed an army of 10,000 men at La Canea to deprive the Turks of their one major base in Crete. Again, bad weather foiled the surprise, permitting the Turks to reinforce it in time.

Late in 1666, the grand vizir, Fasil Ahmed Pasha, arrived in Crete himself with 8,000 fresh soldiers to review the siege of Candia. For the new commander, the city's conquest had become an affair of Turkish and Islamic honour and a symbol of Ottoman tenacity. Christian sources evaluated the Turkish effective strength on the island in the late 1660s at 95,000 men, but this is much too high. Lufti Barkan has shown how little the peripheral provinces of the empire paid into the central treasury. Regular soldiers paid from Constantinople where not that numerous, perhaps only 88,000 for the entire empire at the end of the Candia War, with the part of the janissaries continually increased at the expense of the territorial cavalry.[56] Whatever their true number, it was considerably more than Venice's forces. The republic and its constant allies Malta and the Papal States could field

---

[55] The development of this practice in the second half of the seventeenth century is analyzed by Fritz Redlich, *The German military enterpriser and his work force*, vol. 2, pp. 5–17. On some of these regiments in Venetian service, see p. 49, and pp. 93–6.

[56] Barkan, "L'empire ottoman face au monde chrétien au lendemain de Lépante", in *Il Mediterraneo nella seconda metà del '500*, pp. 95–108.

only 35,000 men, the majority tied up in garrisons from the Terraferma, Istria, Dalmatia, Corfù, the forts holding out along the north coast of Crete, and finally Candia itself.

The Turks resumed the siege of Candia in May 1667, by opening the saps from the Martinengo bastion to the sea. The meticulous Nani chronicle states that between May and November 1667, the Turks launched 32 attacks and exploded 618 mines. Morosini launched 17 sorties to slow their progress, at a cost of 400 officers and 3,200 soldiers killed. The Turks were soon dug in opposite the bastions and placed 44 great guns opposite the curtain wall.[57] Help came to the Venetians in the form of a new crusade urged by the recently elected Pope Clement IX Rospigliosi. By July 1667 he had raised 1,400 men for service in Crete, and sent another 1,500 in October, all paid from Papal funds, while authorizing the Venetians to recruit their own men from Papal territory.[58] Simultaneously, Papal emissaries toured European courts to extract promises of aid. The duke of Modena saw the occasion as an opportunity to rid the duchy of beggars and bandits, and forcibly recruited many of them for service in Crete.[59] The grand duke of Tuscany agreed to send a battalion, along with the knights of Santo Stefano. Genoa promised a similar number, as did the elector of Cologne and the bishop of Strasbourg. Emperor Leopold promised to send 3,000 men. The duke of Lorraine committed 4,000. The duke of Brunswick, in his enthusiasm for the cause, converted to Catholicism, and sent a contingent, along with the prince-palatine of Sulzbach who contributed a regiment of 2,000 men from his tiny state. With these reinforcements came 600 noble volunteers from France, with their retainers and servants. The knights of Malta maintained over 60 of their number on the island, with a stout and effective battalion, in addition to forces patrolling the Aegean. Feeble Spain sent some troops from Milan, and even tiny Lucca sent some men and money. Nevertheless, despite this enthusiastic response of Catholic princes to the Papal alarm, there were never more than 9,000 men in garrison simultaneously, as the siege wore down both armies daily. In September 1667 Morosini and Villa launched a powerful sortie of 2,000 men to destroy the advance works and to capture the guns, but they were unable to hold in the face of counter-assaults.[60]

In 1668 the garrison made some disquieting discoveries. The engineer captain Andrea Barozzi, born in Crete of Venetian parents, went over to the Turks with his expertise. Renegades were essential conduits of western technical advances to the more conservative and Islamic Turkish empire. Most of the grand vizirs were Balkan converts to Islam, and some of the most important officials in the mid-

---

[57] Morachiello, "Candia, I baluardi del regno", in *Venezia e la difesa del Levante*, pp. 133–43; see also Terlinden, *Le Pape Clément IX et la guerre de Candie*, p. 38ff.

[58] Terlinden, *Le Pape Clément IX et la guerre de Candie*, p. 38.

[59] Amorth, *Modena capitale*, p. 127.

[60] On the wearing down of the defenders in constant action, see Terlinden, *Le Pape Clément IX et la guerre de Candie*, p. 118ff.

seventeenth century were Italians, who taught the Ottomans navigational and metallurgical skills.[61] Barozzi taught them how to use the more advanced Venetian artillery, and gave them plans of the city. Most importantly he introduced the new French technique of parallel siege trenches. He persuaded the vizir to divert the axis of attack from the landward bastions of Panigrà and Betelem, and concentrate instead on the Sabbionera and Sant'Andrea guarding the port.[62] From that point on, the Turks made continuous progress.

By 1668, the garrison began to drop below 7,000 men, the minimum necessary to withstand the Turkish progress, despite the continual arrival of small contingents like the company of Roman gentlemen adventurers, and a battalion from Malta. The garrison lacked trained bombardiers in particular, whose skills could not be improvised. In 1668, only 163 bombardiers served 500 cannon in the fortress. In November, a French expeditionary force of 600 gentlemen arrived under La Feuillade, followed by troops from Lorraine and 1,600 more Venetians. La Feuillade insisted on launching a sortie with only 1,000 men, led by four Capuchin monks and two Oratorian priests brandishing crucifixes. They easily carried the first line of trenches, but this was a ruse well known to the Venetians. A counter-attack from several sides resulted in the slaughter of 270 French aristocrats. The Turks then resumed their progress, making breaches on the face and flanks of the wall, and pounded the ramparts and the city with their mortars. Defenders gradually lacked houses and slept in their ruined quarters and on the ground, as the city crumbled. The year 1668 cost the defenders almost 7,000 killed, plus 2,400 oarsmen and 400 civilians. While the Venetians won a sea battle off Candia, it cost them another 1,200 men killed and wounded.

The Venetians depended upon their technological advantage to offset the disparity in forces. One such was the invention of an excavating machine, to dig mines and countermines, and shift earth to repair breaches in the ramparts.[63] Hard-pressed, the Venetians had long resorted to more occult measures, like trying to assassinate Turkish leaders and renegades. They commonly poisoned water supplies, devising a system for poisoning wells slowly through a perforated vase. The garrison received 1,000 lb (420 kg) of arsenic in 1646 for such ends. Early in the war they had invented a type of nail intended to cripple horses and men, coated in a poison made of excrement, saliva, the fat of vipers, and similar ingredients. They sprayed toxins on the pastures where Turkish horses grazed. A

---

[61] G. Benzoni, "Il 'farsi turco', ossia l'ombra del rinnegato", in *Venezia e i Turchi; scontri e confronti di due civiltà* (Milan: 1985), pp. 91–133. Benzoni claims that between 1453 and 1623, of 48 Grand Viziers, at least 33 were renegades, although he provides little to substantiate it, nor does he distinguish between adult converts, and children and adolescents seized from their parents as part of the *devshirme*.

[62] G. Gullino, "Tradimento e ragion di stato nella caduta di Candia", in *Venezia e la difesa del Levante*, p. 146.

[63] See the short encyclopedia citation on Florio Pistori, in Valori, *Condottieri e generali del seicento*, p. 296.

Map 4.2 Plan of Candia, 1669 *(based on Dapper)*

Jewish physician from Zara, Angelo Salamone, tried to distil an 'essence of plague' derived from excrement, buboes and carbuncles of plague victims. He daubed it on hats and clothes, and then had them captured by Turks and carried into their army. But these experiments in bacteriological warfare were all failures.[64] An English engineer who abandoned Venice for Turkish service purportedly devised poisonous fumes to torment the garrison in turn.[65]

---

[64] Paolo Preto, "La guerra segreta: spionaggio, sabotaggi, attentati", in *Venezia e la difesa del Levante*, pp. 79–85.

[65] See the encyclopedia citation on the lieutenant-colonel Cavalli, in Valori, *Condottieri e generali del seicento*, p. 81.

It looked as if the siege might be broken in 1669 when another French contingent of 6,500 men under the duc de Beaufort disembarked along with a contingent of Maltese and Pontificals 2,000 strong. Louis XIV made limited contributions to Christian nations fighting the Turks during the 1660s as a way of asserting his pre-eminence among European princes, although he would soon revert to the old Turkish alliance.[66] Emperor Leopold dispatched 3,000 troops, Bavaria 1,000, Portugal 1,500. Genoa, Tuscany and Modena sent smaller contingents. The Papal force under the duke of Mirandola was reputedly one of the most effective.[67] The Babel of languages and customs created new problems for the defenders, since protocol occasionally paralyzed the army, and the French in particular often acted unilaterally. They led a great sortie of 5,000 troops on 25 June 1669, but this too was undone. Again, the troops swept the first trenches and surged forward after the retreating Turks. When a barrel of gunpowder exploded, they thought that the Turks were exploding mines underneath them, and the troops began to scatter. A counter-attack resulted in the slaughter of 800 French troops, including the commander, Beaufort, and the sortie ended in disaster. In the following weeks, the survivors were gradually worn down by the heat, the skirmishes and the sapping. As the troops became ever more uncontrollable and insubordinate, the French wished to pull out. Before leaving, their fleet vainly bombarded the Turkish camp, but one of their ships caught fire and exploded during the barrage, killing hundreds. In August, the French were gone, and this sent the message to other contingents that the defence was hopeless. In August more Italian and Venetian troops arrived, but there were only 3,700 men in garrison, many of them sick, alongside 4,000 civilians.[68]

For Venice, the effort had been tremendous, involving never-ending labour, expenditure and sacrifice. It became increasingly difficult to repel the assaults along the wall. The Turks were receiving reinforcements of their own, delivered in Dutch and English ships. Faced with a hopeless situation, Morosini resolved to surrender. In the two years since 1667, the Ottomans had launched 69 assaults and exploded 1,364 mines, and the Venetians calculated that 108,000 Turks must have died. The Venetians and their allies, more reliably, made 96 sorties, and lost 29,028 dead, expending 53,000 tonnes of gunpowder and firing 276,000 cannonballs.[69] Giovanni Sagredo claimed that 280 Venetian nobles perished during the siege, a number equivalent to a quarter of all adult male patricians.[70] No doubt relieved by the end of the siege, the Turks allowed the survivors and the remaining civilians to depart. Constantinople permitted Venice to retain several tiny forts along the north coast of the island, at Grabusa, Suda and Spinalunga. Skirmishing

---

[66] J. Meuvret, "Louis XIV et l'Italie", in *XVIIe siècle*, **47**, 1960, pp. 84–102. See also J. Nouzille, "La guerre de Candie", *Revue Internationale d'Histoire Militaire*, 1987, pp. 115–52.
[67] Terlinden, *Le Pape Clément IX et la guerre de Candie*, p. 206.
[68] *Ibid.*, p. 285.
[69] Morris, *The Venetian empire: a sea voyage*, p. 89.
[70] This is curiously downplayed by Davis, in his *Decline of the Venetian nobility*.

continued in Dalmatia and Bosnia for a few months longer, but peace was finally signed in October, 1671. The war marked the onset of Venetian commercial decline, since the city had been still the chief European trader with Constantinople in 1639. In 1670 it had much ground to recover.[71]

The Morea War, 1684–99

The *Serenissima* did not immediately disarm after the signature of peace with the Porte, despite its desire to return to normal trade relations and recover the primacy lost to its English, Dutch and French competitors.[72] Surprisingly, it paid off most of its debts and restored its finances within a few years. Venetian military expenditure remained considerable. Barbary pirates taking shelter at Castelnuovo and Dulcigno and the nearby Albanian ports under Turkish suzerainty repeatedly visited the Dalmatian coast. The Levant garrisons remained hefty to avoid being overwhelmed by surprise. That of Corfù, with more than 2,000 men, was the largest in the empire. There were also significant forces in nearby Cefalonia and Zante. Besides these stout detachments, the republic decided to follow the lead of other maritime nations like France, England and Holland, and construct a fleet of modern warships, more efficient and better armed than hired merchantmen. It built two of them at the end of the Candia War in 1668. It launched five more from Venetian shipyards before 1680, and another five followed in 1684. Venice bought two more from Savoy, built in the Villefranche shipyards near Nice. The Venetian fleet on paper in 1684 stood at 24 ships (of which 14 were ships of the line), six galeasses and 28 galleys, which was significant by European standards. The quality of the ships and the crews were markedly superior to those of the Ottomans.[73] Venetians continued to experiment with their armaments on board too: one notable essay was to place mortars on deck for shore bombardment, but the recoil proved too powerful.

The Ottoman failure at Vienna in 1683 convinced the cautious senators that the hour of retaliation for the loss of Crete was at hand. They signed an alliance with Austria and Poland on 5 March 1684, committing themselves to an amphibious war in Greece that would draw Turkish forces away from Hungary and Moldavia. Other Italian states immediately promised financial and military assistance for the project. The Tuscans sent four galleys and several hundred soldiers officered by the knights of Santo Stefano. Rome sent its entire squadron of five galleys to the theatre with 400 infantry on board. Malta made an even greater

---

[71] R. Mantran, "La navigation vénitienne et ses concurrentes en Mediterranée orientale aux XVIIe et XVIIIe siècles", in *Mediterraneo e Oceano indiano* (Florence: 1970), pp. 375–91, at p. 377.

[72] *Ibid.*, pp. 375–91.

[73] Anderson, *Naval wars in the Levant*, p. 194.

effort, with seven galleys and 1,000 infantry.[74] These were small contingents, but amphibious warfare was ruinously expensive, and the troops had to take all of their provisions along in transport vessels.

It is not easy to know how heavily Venice drew upon its own population to wage this war. Venetian patricians commanded the galleys, which was their monopoly. They were also officers and proveditors for the garrisons, from the Terraferma to Dalmatia and the islands. Venetian and Croat soldiers constituted almost half of the army of 8,400 setting sail in July 1684 to besiege the island fortress of Santa Maura, off the north-west coast of Greece. Behind the Corfù garrison were 2,000 Ionian auxiliaries serving in the Venetian forces along with 150 monks and priests urging them on.[75] About a third of the army consisted of Brunswickers and Hanoverians, purchased for 200 florins a head. A similar army embarked in 1685, with an assortment of Brunswickers, Saxons and Württembergers enlisting under their own flags, and practising their own religion on campaign. They were paid three months in advance along with all the incidental expenditures. The *Serenissima* confided the shore troops to the Friulian Strassoldo, and vested the ships and supreme command in Francesco Morosini.[76] The proximity of the target to Corfù, which served as winter quarters for a large part of the army and fleet, facilitated operations. Morosini's army picked off the major seaports in the Morea, like Nauplia and Koron in sharp sieges from land and sea, for which the galleys were still well suited. Turkish fortresses were not of modern design and were weakly held. Disease (especially typhus and dysentery) weakened the attackers much more than losses in battle.[77]

As the campaigns progressed, Morosini sketched out plans to modernize the army entrusted to him, along the lines of other standing armies set up in the second half of the seventeenth century.[78] Some changes were cosmetic, such as the introduction of uniforms for the different regiments. More fundamental, he allotted the 9,000 permanent infantry into regiments based on national origin. The largest group was the Italian infantry, though we know little about its area of recruitment. There were also units of *oltremarini* and *oltremontani*, in different uniforms and beating their own marches, all exclusive of hired regiments from other powers. Venice also hired Italian mercenary battalions, from Parma in particular.[79] Moreover, in a Spanish army reform, two regiments serving in Milan

---

[74] For the Maltese contribution, see Rossi, *Storia della marina dell' ordine di S. Giovanni'* p. 77ff. The Tuscan flotilla is studied by Camillo Manfroni, *La marina militare del granducato mediceo*, 2, p. 120ff; as well as by Niccolo Giorgetti, *Le armi toscane*, vol. 1, p. 544ff. The Papal expeditionary force is described by Guglielmotti, *Storia della marina pontificia, vol. VIII*, p. 316ff.

[75] Miller, *Essays on the Latin Orient*, p. 222.

[76] Setton, *Venice, Austria and the Turks in the seventeenth century*, p. 291.

[77] Miller, *Essays on the Latin Orient*, p. 403ff.

[78] Concina, *Le trionfanti et invittissime armate venete*, pp. 11–12.

[79] *Ibid.*, p. 14. See also James Paton, *The Venetians in Athens, 1687–1688, from the "Istoria" of Cristoforo Ivanovich* (Cambridge, Mass.: 1940). Paton notes that Duke Ranuccio II of Parma

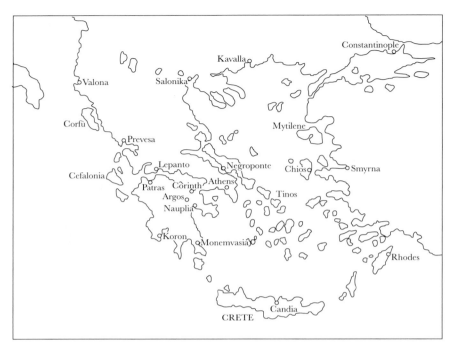

Map 4.3 The Aegean military theatre, 1645–1718

were transferred to Venetian pay. Other Italian troops were less savoury. The Venetians collected auxiliaries haphazardly in the theatre, like the gang of Abruzzi bandits serving in exchange for pardon. They threw a loose unit of bandits and deserters under the Neapolitan outlaw leader, Luca della Rocca, created from the Morea in 1691, into the assault at Monemvasia.[80] A corps of *benemeriti*, deserving soldiers above 60 years of age, performed guard duties. The Italian contingents proved less intractable than the Germans, who answered only to their own officers as far as discipline was concerned. Morosini's harsh, tactless and arbitrary manner breached protocol and the usages that were vital to a seventeenth-century army, especially one consisting of different contingents.[81] As a result, he prized his Venetian troops most, and above all the Croats.

Morosini regimented the *oltremarini*, or Dalmatian infantry and cavalry, in 1687

---

supplied a battalion of infantry for Venice, because he was embroiled in a boundary dispute in the Apennines with Duke Cosimo III of Tuscany, and the two had settled on the Venetian Senate to arbitrate it. Since Tuscany was supplying a contingent each year to the Venetian forces, Parma could not afford not to do likewise: see p. 86.

[80] Concina, *Le trionfanti et invittissime armate venete*, p. 54.
[81] Setton, *Venice, Austria and the Turks in the seventeenth century*, p. 316.

too. They were an admixture of the various ethnic populations of the Adriatic shore and the mountains around them: Cimariots, Morlacchi, Kaiduks and Montenegrins, "*les Iroquois de ces-païs là*".[82] The Cimariots, later known as Capelletti, hailed from the mountains south of Valona in Albania. These were rugged and enterprising, and excellent marksmen. The Venetians used them as assault troops and skirmishers. Balkan Christians were pitiless fighters, especially against the Turks, whom they never took prisoner. They were not very disciplined, and as a result they tended to ravage large districts, capturing slaves, carrying off livestock, and poisoning wells. Around 1690 there were about a thousand of them in Venetian service, and probably more later, comprising four regiments in 1694. There was not much use for heavy cavalry in the Venetian army. In 1692 there were two regiments of dragoons, that is mounted infantry, operating with the army. One was an Italian unit of some 500 men, in the service of the king of Spain, transferred to Venetian pay in 1686. Two hundred more served under the Venetian patrician Grimaldi di Courbon in the Morea after 1687.[83]

The *oltremontani* troops were for the most part Swiss and German infantry, with some French for variety, sometimes serving under Venetian officers. Venice often hired these troops for the campaign under German officers and princes, who lacked a more rewarding war closer to home. In 1687 some 4,000 served under the princes of Brandenburg and Hesse, and 2,500 more under the duke of Hanover. The prince regent of Württemberg, Friedrich Karl, made a fortune recruiting soldiers in the state under his management. In 1687 he contracted to raise three and a half regiments, or 4,500 men, for service in the Aegean.[84] The German contingents were perhaps the conduit by which Venice kept abreast of modern drill and tactics. Papal and Venetian infantry repulsed Ottoman cavalry at the battle of Argos in 1686 using the square formation, which was a recent innovation.

In 1686 this 'Venetian' army oscillating around 10,000 men spent long spells on land in the Greek Peloponnesis under the command of the Swedish general Königsmark, with general strategic direction still entrusted to Francesco Morosini. A victorious set-piece battle of 11,000 troops against a Turkish army at Argos gave the Christians control over most of the region. They then levied contributions on Greek communities to keep the army operative. After the Venetians captured Patras and Corinth in 1687, only the strongly-garrisoned port of Monemvasia held out. Morosini then advanced to occupy Attica and besiege Athens. Its Greek population was welcoming enough, but several thousand Moslem inhabitants withdrew to the Acropolis. They surrendered after a 'lucky' mortar bomb fired by the Venetians blew up the powder magazine stored in the

---

[82] Concina, *Le trionfanti et invittissime armate venete*, p. 31.

[83] *Ibid.*, p. 68ff.

[84] E. A. Vann, *The making of a state: Württemberg, 1593–1793* (Ithaca, New York: 1984), p. 153.

famous temple, until that moment largely intact.[85] The army then wintered in the city, bothered only by the raiding of the Turkish cavalry. When the remnants of the Hanoverian troops withdrew, Morosini decided to evacuate the city, which was too difficult to defend since it was not a port, and evacuated the population with it in March 1688. He traced the new Venetian lines at Corinth and constructed fortifications across the isthmus. The movement of armies only partially reflects the operations in Greece, though. Venetian light cavalry and thousands of Greek irregulars and auxiliaries raided Turkish garrisons and encampments in Attica and Thebes, pinning down 15,000 Turks.[86] Skirmishing was a normal feature of this warfare.

Meanwhile, a second Venetian army waged an amphibious war in Dalmatia after 1686. Diversionary raids launched further north around Sinj in Bosnia drew off Ottoman troops. The Venetian fleet under Admiral Cornaro, augmented by Maltese, Papal, Tuscan and Genoese contingents, besieged Castelnuovo and took it after a brisk siege. When a contagious sickness broke out in Morosini's army in Greece, it was deemed wiser to channel reinforcements to this secondary theatre instead. By March 1687 there were about 10,000 troops there, of whom about 6,000 were Swiss, Bayreuters and Brunswickers. Restive local inhabitants under Turkish rule lent inestimable help to these operations. Their respective clergies incited the Morlacchi and Albanian Christians to revolt. Two thousand Montenegrin auxiliaries operated with Venetian support under the bishop of Cetinje, and the revolt spread from there in 1684 to all of northern Albania. The result of these operations was a continuous and unbroken string of Venetian successes along the coast, from Valona in Albania to Lepanto and Prevesa in the Greek Epirus.[87]

Morosini next began to contemplate the seizure of the great Turkish fortresses north of the Peloponnesis and in 1688 inaugurated the siege of Negroponte (modern Euboea), the conquest of which would deliver the eastern coast of the Greek mainland. The army disembarked there was of unprecedented size for Venice; 16,600 men, of which about 10,000 were Germans and Swiss, and 4,000 Italian infantry, and 1,100 cavalry and dragoons, with combined Papal, Parman, Maltese and Tuscan contingents numbering about 2,000 more men. The local Greek population promised 7,000 irregulars.[88] Unfortunately for the Venetians, it proved exceedingly difficult to blockade the city on the island, and the Turkish fort of Kara Baba on the mainland, simultaneously. This last was the creation of another Italian deserter renegade, Girolamo Galoppo of Guastalla, a dragoon

---

[85] Paton, *The Venetians in Athens*, p. 52.

[86] Setton, *Venice, Austria and the Turks*, p. 316.

[87] Wayne S. Vucinich gives an account of this guerrilla war aided by the Venetians in the Balkans. See his article, "Prince–Bishop Danilo and his place in Montenegro's history", in *East-central European society and war in the pre-revolutionary eighteenth century*, G. Rothenberg, B. Kiràly, P. Sugar (eds) (Boulder, Colorado: 1982), pp. 271–99.

[88] Setton, *Venice, Austria and the Turks*, p. 353.

with some training in fortifications. Galoppo's fort enabled the Turks to prevent a complete blockade, since it fed reinforcements to Negroponte's garrison. The great guns in the fortress smashed the galleys manoeuvring to form batteries. A steady flow of aid from the mainland allowed the Turks in the fortress to make powerful sorties into the Christian trenches. Then the plague broke out in the Venetian camp, killing the commander of the ground troops, Königsmark. Plague was a hazard of war in the Ottoman empire, and was often more lethal than the Turkish army. It appeared early in the campaign, and not all the contingents were familiar with the quarantine regulations, by now second nature to the Venetians themselves. Neglect of precautions was common especially among the German units. By May there were thirty deaths a day from the epidemic, and sixty to seventy new cases daily. By the middle of the month, 600 men in the army had died of it, and thousands more were ill. Worse still, it threatened to break out on the ships and galleys too, where men were packed in great density.[89] After four assaults on Negroponte had been repulsed, Morosini decided to withdraw to Corinth at the end of 1688.

One can draw a sense of the difficulties of these campaigns through the closer examination of the Tuscan contribution. Cosimo III decided to help the Venetians, partly to avoid insistent Austrian demands for contributions to the war under some theoretical Imperial rights. He increased the contingent once it was evident that the Catholic cause was progressing. In 1684 ten Tuscan soldiers were killed and twenty wounded in the siege of Santa Maura, about ten per cent of the battalion. The next year, almost 400 Tuscans, including 43 knights of Santo Stefano, fought at the siege of Koron, and took part in the grand assault on the breach. Cosimo found the resources to send four galleys, four galiots, two other vessels, 70 knights and 800 soldiers to serve at the siege of Modon in 1686. While they shared the glory in the final assault, the Tuscans lost 300 men killed and captured, and 240 more wounded, or two-thirds of the contingent. In 1687 they came again with four galleys, a French ship, an English ship, a corps of 60 knights of Santo Stefano, and another contingent of 800 soldiers. Many of the latter were German mercenaries under the command of the Lorrainer chevalier de Hazard. While they helped capture Castelnuovo in Dalmatia, they suffered losses equivalent to about a third of their force. In 1688, finally, a similar contingent joined Morosini's army before Negroponte. For the Tuscans, this campaign was disastrous. On one day they lost 70 soldiers and five knights of Santo Stefano from a sortie in their sector. On 19 September 1688, nine more knights and 200 soldiers died when another Turkish sortie overwhelmed their trenches. This finally determined the commander, Camillo Guidi, to return to Livorno after two months of fighting, and the Tuscans would not return for subsequent campaigns.[90]

---

[89] Paton, *The Venetians in Athens*, p. 44.

[90] The Tuscan contingents are studied by Giorgetti, *Le armi toscane*, vol. 1, pp. 543–54. See also Camillo Manfroni, *La marina militare del granducato mediceo*, pt 2, p. 119ff. More recent is

The Maltese were more constant, sending at least a battalion of troops every year, and participating in the ground fighting too. The knights paid a toll, however. When the Maltese led the assault on Modon in July 1686, it cost them more than two hundred men, of whom 19 were knights. Ten more knights perished at the siege of Castelnuovo in 1687.[91] The glamour of an unbroken series of conquests brought them back for more, as it attracted other young noblemen cutting their teeth in the military profession. In 1688 the French prince de Turenne arrived in Morosini's camp, with 40 gentlemen in his retinue. Although he was barely twenty, Morosini gave him important responsibilities, and he succeeded in getting himself honourably wounded in the fighting at Negroponte. As other contingents returned to Italy and Germany, he remained behind with the army and was promoted to lieutenant-general.[92]

In 1689 the war entered a new phase. Morosini was elected Doge of Venice, which was unusual for the republic, which traditionally kept successful generals at arms' length, but his successes made him a hero of Venetian and Italian arms. His elevation removed him from the theatre, however. That same year, French devastation of the Rhine Palatinate forced the emperor to shift most of his troops to western Europe. This gave the Turks some respite in the Balkans, and they began to rebuild their strength in Greece and Anatolia. The Venetians were unable to advance beyond the narrow isthmus of Corinth, but the bulk of their army, about 8,000 infantry, finally forced Monemvasia to capitulate. Venice found it harder to pay for military operations, and mutinies broke out for lack of pay. In 1692 the admiral, Corner, attempted half-heartedly to surprise the Turkish garrisons on Crete, but the island was too well-guarded. Although the *Serenissima* retained superiority at sea, its army was too small to undertake anything grand. For want of anything better, the Venetians harassed the Turks with their fleet. In 1687 Admiral Venier repulsed a Turkish fleet off Mitylene, clearly establishing Venetian naval superiority. In 1690, Admiral Dolfin, with only 12 vessels, attacked a Turkish fleet of 36, dispersing them at little loss. The Dardanelles were too well-defended by fortresses to force, so the Venetians limited themselves to levying 'contributions' from the islands. Corsairs flying the Maltese and Tuscan banners infested the Aegean, striking at Greek coastal communities even on the largest islands like Crete, Cyprus, Rhodes, Chios and Mytilene.[93]

Doge though he was, the Senate restored Francesco Morosini to command of the army in the Morea, to break the deadlock. He intended to build very strong fixed defences at Corinth, and then lure the Turkish army into a set-piece batttle where he could defeat it.[94] Moreover, he needed experienced officers and engi-

---

the account by Gino Guarnieri, *I cavalieri di Santo Stefano, nella storia della marina italiana (1562–1859)*, p. 229ff.

[91] Rossi, *Storia della marina dell' ordine di S. Giovanni*, p. 78ff.

[92] Paton, *The Venetians in Athens*, p. 31.

[93] Vacalopoulos, *The Greek nation*, p. 90.

[94] P. Argenti, *The occupation of Chios by the Venetians (1694)* (London: 1935), p. x.

neers, and enough troops to defend the ships from a Turkish naval attack. Morosini, well into his seventies, died in Greece on 6 January 1694, before being able to put his plan into execution. His hand-picked successor was Antonio Zeno, another Venetian patrician who had given a good account of himself. The considerable army under his command at Corinth counted 13,000 foot, 3,000 horse, and some 4,000 Greek auxiliaries. Attrition from disease was about 20 per cent annually, but fresh contingents from Venice maintained that level.[95] Venetian garrisons clung to fortresses from Friuli to Dalmatia, the Ionian islands and the newly conquered Morea. Troops were also required on the galleys and warships of the fleet.

The war council under Zeno believed there were enough troops to attempt new conquests elsewhere, despite Morosini's warnings against dividing Venetian forces while the Turks could still undertake their own initiatives. It devised a plan to land 10,000 men on Chios, while Corner held Corinth with 3,000 troops and the Greek militia. Chios was a tempting target, raided repeatedly by corsairs and knights over the preceding century. The island contained a dense population of 80,000 people, and the city itself boasted 26,000, making it one of the most substantial cities of the Aegean, and far larger than any town yet occupied by the Venetians. Most of this population was Greek Orthodox, but a sizeable Latin Catholic minority could be expected to collaborate. The Moslems would be expelled, and transported to the nearby Anatolian mainland.[96]

The army landed on 7 September 1694, and soon defeated the island garrison. The city, without modern fortifications but containing more than 200 cannon, fell on the 15th. Zeno hoped that the enemy fleet would sally from Smyrna to fight the 21 vessels, six galeasses and 34 galleys that accompanied the 50 fleet transports, but the Turks would not oblige them. The Ottomans had about twenty large vessels of their own, with between 50 and 80 bronze cannon apiece, captained by English, Dutch and French naval officers and renegades. The entire Ottoman galley fleet comprised only about 30 vessels.[97] They were waiting to fight on their own terms. In Chios the Venetian troops under the Saxon general Steinau behaved very badly, plundering Greeks, Turks and Jews indiscriminately. Open favouritism displayed towards Latin Greeks only made the majority Orthodox more sullen and resentful. Zeno had too few engineers available to refortify the city. He then realized that he did not have enough troops to defend both Chios, and the Corinth lines barring entry to the Peloponnesis. When he sent 2,000 infantry and ten galleys back to the Morea, he relinquished all initiative. Moreover, the precious Maltese and Papal galleys had to withdraw every winter, and would not return until the summer of 1695. To defend the island he required 6,000 infantry and 2,000 cavalry, and needed at least 3,200 soldiers more on the

---

[95] *Ibid.*, p. xxii.

[96] *Ibid.*, p. xxxvi.

[97] Fontenay, "Chiourmes turques au XVIIe siècle", in *Le genti del mare mediterraneo*, vol. 2, pp. 877–903.

fleet in case of a sea battle. He had but 10,000 men. As the Turks built up their fleet in Smyrna and an army on the coast nearby, all of Morosini's predictions came true.

Around 1690 a renegade from Livorno convinced the Porte that Venetian superiority at sea lay not with galleys, but with ships of the line, and that Turkey should similarly acquire some. By 1693 the Ottomans possessed a fleet of their own vessels.[98] These were built like a Western ship and manned with the best Levantine troops the Turks could find, while the gunners were often Europeans who did not bother to don a turban for the occasion.[99] On 9 February 1695, the Turkish fleet of 20 ships and 24 galleys engaged the Venetian flotilla of similar numbers. In the battle that followed, the Venetians had the advantage, until three of their ships exploded. The losses for the Venetians that day were about 2,500 killed and wounded, including many patricians. Since neither side forced a decision, another fleet battle occurred ten days later. The rough sea prevented the galleys from capturing crippled warships, so the action consisted of hours of isolated encounters that left hundreds more killed and wounded on each side. Strategically, the Venetians were overextended, outnumbered, and far from their bases and their supplies. On 21 February, Zeno evacuated Chios, but experienced the further misfortune of losing several hundred dragoons when one of his ships ran aground before clearing the island. The considerable loss of life and equipment much diminished the reputation of the republic's navy. Turkish potential at sea was now a challenge.

Until the peace of Karlowitz in 1699, both armies remained immobile on each side of the Corinthian isthmus. The Ottomans gradually suppressed the Greek and Balkan rebellions. Only the occasional fleet action marked the continuation of the war. In 1697 a major sea battle joined off Mytilene, between 26 Turkish and 25 Venetian vessels, was an indecisive mêlée inflicting more than a thousand casualties among the latter. Another battle was fought off the Macedonian coast later that year, after the Venetians bombarded the city of Kavalla, but it too was a bloody draw.[100] The republic had good reason to be satisfied by the treaty, which recognized its conquests made between 1684 and 1687. The Morea became a Venetian colony, along with all the Ionian islands and a few towns in Dalmatia and Bosnia.

The end of empire

For the two subsequent decades, the Venetians applied themselves to developing their new Morean colony, which added about 300,000 Greek subjects to the republic. They prepared to stay permanently by constructing large fortresses at

---

[98] *Ibid.*, vol. 2, p. 880.
[99] Argenti, *The occupation of Chios by the Venetians*, p. lviii.
[100] Anderson, *Naval wars in the Levant*, p. 219ff.

Corinth and the port of Nauplia. From the point of view of the Greeks, the Venetians were no worse than their previous masters, but their taxation system was more efficient, and they resented this in particular. Elsewhere in the Levant, the Venetians held a few forts off the coast of Crete, and the curious island colony of Tinos, a Latin enclave in an Orthodox archipelago. A mere 14 soldiers watched over Tinos, so solid was the traditional loyalty of the islanders. In the Morea about 10,000 Venetian troops, or about a third of the forces of the republic, kept order. Such substantial force underlines the fact that Venice did not disarm with the peace of Karlowitz, but rather maintained a standing army consisting of about one per cent of the population. This put the republic of San Marco on a par, relatively speaking, with France, Piedmont and many German states. During the War of the Spanish Succession (1701–14) the Senate adhered to a costly policy of armed neutrality. Venice refused to heed French siren calls to join the Bourbon alliance, since there was little to be gained by making war on the House of Austria. Imperial armies marched unopposed through Venetian territory to reach the battlefields in Lombardy and Emilia, and the French and Spanish allies (known as Gallispans) foraged around Verona in 1703–4. During that conflict, 5,000 soldiers, mostly veterans, guarded the lagoon and the Terraferma, and another seven or eight thousand sweltered in fortresses in Dalmatia and the Ionian islands. From this position of strength, Venice hoped to accelerate the internal disintegration of the Ottoman Empire.

War between Turkey and Russia in 1710–11 made the Venetians newly hopeful for a further expansion of their holdings in Greece and along the Balkan coast from where Barbary pirates still lunged at Christian shipping with Ottoman complicity. The *Serenissima* wished to exploit Turkish vulnerability to restore the 'most favoured nation' trading status it had once enjoyed, to compete with French, English and Dutch merchants, and regain the rank that the wars had cost them.[101] The republic proffered support to a new Montenegrin revolt, from the naval base at Cattaro. Banditry and warfare were traditional occupations of the tribes of shepherds living in Montenegro and Hercegovina, and were seen as honourable occupations when directed against Turks and other enemies. After the treaty of Karlowitz, the Montenegrins refused to pay tribute to the Turks, so the latter retaliated by burning villages and taking hostages. Danilo of Cetinje, the prince–bishop, organized these bands and co-ordinated their raids, and led a vicious war of religion against those Montenegrins who had converted to Islam, although they raided Venetian territory too on occasion. Turkish forays in 1712 and 1714 did not quell the revolt entirely, but they did sweep the guerrillas and their families into Venetian territory around Cattaro. Bishop Danilo was not a grateful refugee. He sought to undermine the republic's authority in Dalmatia, and contested the Catholic church there.[102] By exploiting the revolt, however, the

---

[101] Mantran, "La navigation vénitienne et ses concurrentes", in *Mediterraneo e Oceano indiano*, p. 379.
[102] Vucinich, "Prince–Bishop Danilo", in *East-central European society and war*, pp. 271–99.

republic had been incautious. The Turks unexpectedly won their war against Russia in 1713. Venice also knew that the Turks would not tolerate a hostile power holding bases so close to the vital shipping routes of their Empire. Their conquest had been possible only because the Ottomans were engaged in a much grander struggle against the Austrians in the Hungarian plain. Excision of the Venetian mole was now a priority for the Porte.

·In 1714 the grand vizir, Damad Ali Pasha, began collecting ships for a great expedition against the *Serenissima*. A year later, the fleet consisted of 58 vessels and 30 galleys, compared to the 19 ships and 15 galleys the Venetians could oppose to it. Between May and September 1715, this fleet and an army said to number 100,000 men invaded the Morea by land and sea. In reality, the army was much smaller, the larger part of it taking the land route via Salonika as a precaution against possible Austrian intervention from the north. Another army transported by sea occupied the various islands in Venetian control, and blockaded the Morean ports.[103] Tinos and Egina, small island colonies, were quickly overwhelmed. If the republic of San Marco still had more than 8,000 troops in the Morea in 1714, its fleet support in the theatre consisted of only eight warships and eleven galleys. Constantinople's rapid conquest of the new Venetian fortresses in a scant three months was nevertheless a great surprise. Ottoman troops pressed Corinth after 20 June, and its 600 defenders resisted but a few days for lack of water. Nauplia was more stoutly garrisoned, with 2,500 men, but the surrounding Greek population refused to help. The violence and impetuosity of the Turkish approach prompted many desertions, until an assault overwhelmed the survivors.[104] At Nauplia, the besiegers captured 126 cannon, 20 mortars and a great quantity of provisions. Modon fell after a short siege, and Monemvasia surrendered without firing a shot. Turkish forces then completed the campaign by reconquering the Ionian islands of Cythera and Santa Maura.

Corfù was the Ottoman target in the 1716 campaign, besieged once before in 1538 but never captured. Its garrison under the command of the Saxon general Schulemburg was a motley collection of 8,000 Germans, Italians, Slavs and Greeks, many having retreated there from more advanced posts. A Turkish army of 30,000 crossed the narrow channel separating it from the mainland, and tried to blockade the island with their fleet. Alarmed at the quick collapse of Venetian forces in Greece, Mediterranean states quickly pledged their assistance, and again the pope, Clement XI, helped cement an alliance of Catholic states.[105] Spain, Portugal, the Papacy, Malta and Tuscany all sent galleys to join the Venetian fleet, which consisted now of 27 ships, opposed to 50 Turkish vessels. As the operations stretched into weeks, the Catholic·forces swelled. The Papal expeditionary force numbered seven galleys, four galiots and seven other vessels, the

[103] A. Bernardy, *L'ultima guerra turco–veneziana (1714–1718)* (Florence: 1902), p. 31.

[104] *Ibid.*, p. 32.

[105] Von Pastor, *The history of the popes from the close of the Middle Ages, vol. xxxiii* (London: 1957), pp. 113–39.

flagship having some 60 cannon. Tuscany made an ineffectual contribution of three ships and a contingent of knights of Santo Stefano. The allied fleet convoyed two contingents of 1,500 troops through the blockade to reinforce the city. Corfù's powerful fortifications compensated for the lacklustre abilities of Venetian generals, and Schulemburg's vigorous defence made Turkish progress very slow and costly.[106] Since the Venetian Senate was reluctant to risk the fleet, there was no climactic battle. The Turkish army finally withdrew after seven weeks, when Austria decided to join the war. With the pressure off Venice, Corfù was saved.

Venice retaliated by fomenting rebellion in Montenegro and Hercegovina, triggered by raids mounted from Dalmatia. The process of regimentation of the Croats and the incorporation of guerrilla units into the regular army reduced the attractiveness of military operations for the participants, however.[107] The Venetian army and fleet were able to bolster the defence of Dulcigno and Castelnuovo against Turkish sieges. Nevertheless, Schulemburg found it impossible to maintain enough troops in the theatre; he needed 30,000 men just to fight a defensive war. Confidence gradually returned to the Venetian army and fleet. In 1717 the admiral, Flangini, decided to blockade the Dardanelles with a fleet of 26 ships, and fought a Turkish force of 38 units. The two navies fought a two-day battle there, in which the Venetians alone lost 1,400 killed and wounded, the admiral being killed by an arrow. His successor, Diedo, was then joined by ten more Catholic warships, and twenty additional galleys, including five Maltese and two Tuscan. In June and July 1718 the Catholic fleet fought a series of battles off Cape Matapan, incurring about 2,400 casualties, for no decisive result.[108] Venice was just beginning to make progress in the Balkans when in 1718 Austria decided to make peace. In the treaty of Passarowitz, Venice retained the Ionian islands and a few large villages on the mainland opposite Corfù, and the *status quo* in Dalmatia, but relinquished the Peloponnesis and the Aegean islands. The *Serenissima* remained at peace with the Porte until the end of the republic itself in 1797.

Schulemburg was lionized as the saviour of the republic, and inherited Morosini's mantel as the father of the army. After the siege of Corfù, the Senate entrusted him with the task of transforming the Venetian army into a professional force similar to armies in Germany, completing the reforms begun by Morosini. By 1724 the Venetian standing army had acquired the structure it would keep for the rest of the century. The number of foot was set at 17,000, in 18 Italian and 11 *oltremarini* regiments of battalion size. While it was a volunteer army, various and sometimes illegal methods of recruitment were tolerated to keep the numbers stable. Recruits signed up for nine years, receiving 20 ducats at the outset, a sum

---

[106] Bernardy, *L'ultima guerra turco–veneziana*, p. 45.

[107] Bracewell, "Uskoks in Venetian Dalmatia", in *East-central European society and war*, pp. 431–47.

[108] Anderson, *Naval wars in the Levant*, pp. 249–69.

so considerable that it virtually held the volunteer hostage. Although there were some recruits from beyond the Alps, the Senate practically ceased to hire large bodies of them in peacetime. *Oltremarini* battalions were mostly Croats. Except the turban, which they lacked, their uniforms resembled Turkish dress.[109] Because of the modest population of Dalmatia, even many of these were Italians, including a thousand Corsicans.

· The various arms gradually became specialized in the course of the eighteenth century, as in modern forces elsewhere. The versatility of Venetian troops on land and sea had been one of their strengths, but it was difficult to provide enough artillery specialists or engineers. After 1757 the Senate formed an artillery regiment on the Prussian model, and then after 1770 created an engineer unit under the direction of some Scottish officers. As the arms became more technical, officials felt it necessary to create special colleges for officer training. Seventeenth-century wars were frequent enough that Venetian patricians or volunteers in the employ of the republic could learn their science in the field. In the more peaceful eighteenth century, a military college was established at Verona in 1764, and a second at Zara in Dalmatia.[110] As a second line of defence, the Venetian militia continued to subsist on paper. The 24,000 men available in the Terraferma were universally considered a sad lot. They were still mustered with their antique armament every two months on the village green, but were incapable of military action. In 1787 the Senate began the practice of drafting militia recruits into the line regiments, as was done elsewhere.[111]

One problem in Venice, as almost everywhere in Italy, was the decline in numbers of the patrician class, due partly to their mediocre economic prospects, and partly to the requirements of status and conspicuous consumption that encouraged families to limit the number of marriages, dowries and heirs. Moreover, even the Venetian patriciate, so secular in many ways, paid its tribute to the Counter-Reformation. Between 1620 and 1760, the number of patricians entering the Church (and by that excluding themselves from public office) doubled. It became necessary to constrain patricians to take up posts in government. Syphilis among patricians may also have influenced natality adversely, without conscious restriction of births. James Davis never specifically says that war could have been a major factor in the decline of the number of adult male patricians in the *Maggior Consiglio*. Davis' own figures of active adult male nobles per decade shows that after the plague of 1630, numbers began to recover. What depressed numbers after that was the brutal Candia War. Numbers then crept upwards until the Corfù war, and then declined again.[112] If there were 2,500 adult male nobles at the time of Lepanto, only 1,710 remained in 1718; 1,300 in 1775 and barely a

---

[109] Concina, *Le trionfanti et invittissimi armate venete*, p. 14.

[110] C. Randaccio, *Storia delle marine militari italiane, dal 1750 al 1860, e della marina militare italiana dal 1860 al 1870*, vol. 1, p. 134ff.

[111] Concina, *Le trionfanti et invittissimi armate venete*, p. 44 and p. 49.

[112] Davis, *The decline of the Venetian nobility*, p. 343.

thousand in 1797, despite the entry of 120 new families between 1645 and 1718 through the purchase of admission. This last was a fiscal measure designed to defray military expenses, not a means of maintaining the number of citizens, so it was discontinued with peace. The family discipline required by the purchase of nobility meant that these new houses were not marrying freely either, and they disappeared more quickly than the old ones.

The combined effect of prolonged peace, and the abandonment of military careers by patricians, who could not fight for a foreign power, meant that Venetian society was quite unbellicose and culturally unprepared for the kind of sacrifices it commemorated for Candia. It is difficult to know who would have become a Venetian officer in the eighteenth century, although senior positions in the fleet were still reserved for patricians. Paleologo Oriundi, working from muster rolls, identifies 64 different colonels in the eighteenth century, the great majority bearing Italian names. I doubt that there were many Venetian patricians among them, although there was one Michiel.[113] Military style became a dress fashion, an affectation and not a career. This laxity gradually spread to the troops themselves. Duties in peacetime were not very taxing. The troops either guarded the fortresses, or patrolled the borders against smugglers and bandits. Every two weeks officers subjected them to some drill, but probably this was not strictly adhered to. Soldiers worked at various odd jobs to supplement their salaries, or served as lackeys to the officers.[114] The pages of Casanova's memoirs depict the somnolence of these Dalmatian and Ionian outposts, the boredom of garrison life, and the non-martial inclinations of the officers condemned to serve there.[115]

San Marco may not have been a spent force. One Italian in six, or about three million people, was a subject of the *Serenissima* at the end of the eighteenth century. The economic resources of the Venetian state were respectable enough too, probably on par with France in per capita wealth, which placed it in the ranks of the more developed areas of southern Europe.[116] Corfù continued to be a military base of regional importance, a considerable fortress with 500 cannon. The fleet resumed military demonstrations in the last years of the republic. The decline of the fleet was not comparable to that of the army, nor did the patriciate abandon it to the same extent. The Senate, which controlled naval matters, tried to maintain standards and equipment. It continued to entice seamen into it, especially from Dalmatia. Such was the lack of volunteers, though, that in 1774, to mount an expedition against Barbary pirates, the *Serenissima* stooped to pressing fishermen's sons. All of the senior posts still went by tradition to Venetian patricians, who were supposed to undergo a four-year apprenticeship on the vessels of

---

[113] Paleologo Oriundi, *I Corsi nella fanteria italiana della Serenissima repubblica di Venezia*, p. 12ff.

[114] Concina, *Le trionfanti et invittissimi armate venete*, p. 21ff.

[115] Giacomo Casanova, *Memoires*, vol. 1 (Paris: 1958), pp. 293–400.

[116] On the vigorous Venetian economy in the eighteenth century, see the thesis of Jean Georgelin, *Venise au siècle des lumières* (Paris: 1978).

the republic. In 1774, a naval academy was established to standardize this training.

Over the 130 years after 1667 Venice's Arsenal built 92 ships of the line and 24 frigates. In a normal year there were about 20 ships of the line, of 64 or 70 cannon (a few in sorry condition), ten frigates, twenty galleys, and about a hundred smaller craft.[117] The fleet gradually grew mouldy for want of use. Sometimes it united with the squadrons of Genoa, Naples and Malta to provide the necessary numbers. Admiral Angelo Emo tried to revive the navy, using as a pretext the eternal struggle against privateers and corsairs. His first task was to impose greater discipline, especially on the officers. He succeeded in restoring some vigour to the fleet in the century's final years. Eight major ships fought some Russian privateers operating out of Trieste in 1787. The Senate launched more determined action against Tunisian corsairs. Twice Emo bombarded the Tunisian shore to deter the Barbary pirates from preying on Venetian merchant vessels. In 1790 he took much of the Venetian navy, six heavy ships, four frigates and various transports and light ships, to bombard Tunis into accepting a truce, although the practical effect of this was negligible.[118] The Venetian republic held so fast to its policy of non-intervention in European conflicts, that it ceased to consider war as a viable policy option in the eighteenth century. Holding this course even in the face of French invasions that paid no heed to established governments, in 1796 it surrendered to Bonaparte without a struggle.

---

[117] In this navy, there were ten generals, 20 ship's captains, 20 frigate captains, 80 lieutenants, and 160 petty officers. While their pay was not good, they all transported cargo on the side on their own account, or even commanded merchant vessels. Randaccio, *Storia delle marine militari italiane*, p. 139ff.

[118] Anderson, *Naval wars in the Levant*, p. 311.

Chapter 5

The Spanish crisis and the rise of Austria, 1660–1710

Spanish exhaustion after 1660

The architect of French pre-eminence after the peace of the Pyrenees was surely Cardinal Mazarin, who conceived and built the imposing edifice of grandeur that Louis XIV would inhabit and enlarge. His patronage of German border states after 1648 made the kingdom a 'German' power to be reckoned with. His influence over the king of Sweden forced the latter to come to terms with his enemies in northern Europe in 1661. French covert military aid to Portugal kept that insurgent kingdom in the field against Spain until it concluded a favourable peace in 1668. Mazarin's shelter and support for the English Stuart dynasty made Charles II a francophile after his restoration in 1661, dependent upon his cousin Louis' financial largesse for most of his reign. England became a satellite kingdom in foreign policy despite its anti-Catholic leanings. Mazarin was especially careful to enhance French power in Italy, expanding the hold over Piedmont (guaranteed by the fortress of Pinerolo) to include other states. Marriages were one traditional tool of such diplomacy, such as that of Victor Amadeus I with Louis' aunt Marie-Christine. In 1655 the heir to the duchy of Modena, Alfonso d'Este, married Mazarin's own niece, Laura Martinozzi, who became regent in 1663. Diplomats made a similar match between Prince Cosimo of Tuscany and Marguerite-Louise d'Orléans, cousin of the Sun King. Each wedding brought scores of French courtiers and their suites to Italian capitals. Simultaneously, the great wigs and brightly-coloured apparel of the French aristocracy displaced the more solemn 'Spanish' demeanour of those courts.

The pre-eminence of French protocol was accompanied by the insistence on formal precedence everywhere for the representatives of the French king. Commanders of French naval flotillas had firm orders to insist that all other fleets salute them first, on pain of hostile riposte. The French on occasion attacked Spanish vessels in peacetime on no other pretext.[1] Louis also picked a quarrel with Pope

---

[1] J. Alcala-Zamora y Queipo de Llano, "Razon de estado y geoestrategia en la politica italiana de Carlos II", *Boletín de la Real Academia de la Historia*, 1976, pp. 297–358, at p. 343.

Alexander VII in 1663 after some French sentries scuffled with Corsican guards outside the French embassy in Rome. The monarch transformed the affair into a major row requiring formal Papal apologies and capitulations. Unlike the king of Spain, Louis held little store by the military potential of Italian states as auxiliaries to the French army. Their neutrality was preferable in French policy to their active alliance. Louis disdained to invite Piedmont, reduced to satellite status after 1659, and with hardly more than a garrison force at its disposal, to join the French war against Spain in 1667–8, nor even the more bitterly fought Dutch War between 1672 and 1678, despite the desire of the dukes to seize territory in Lombardy. Louis never solicited the support of Modena either, even when it was firmly in the French clientèle.[2] Instead, the French king and his ministers raised the odd regiment in the peninsula, like the *Royal italien*, an infantry unit made up of Venice's Candian veterans in 1670. Louvois and his agents recruited about 4,000 Italians in the army build-up for the Dutch War, primarily in Corsica, Parma, Modena and Tuscany.[3] By 1690, when the French army mustered over 400,000 troops, Italians provided seven of the 32 foreign regiments in the Sun King's array, consisting of about 465 officers and 7,100 ranks of infantry, and perhaps one regiment of cavalry. Of these, however, five were rented outright from the duke of Savoy, and should be counted as Piedmontese, rather than French recruits.[4] Of the foreign troops admitted to the Hôtel des Invalides in Paris after 1670, Italians only constituted five per cent, half as numerous as the Irish, and little more than one tenth the number of Germans.[5]

Standing armies were in their infancy in the mid-seventeenth century, and few states maintained forces beyond the skeleton garrisons performing guard duties. Bercé argues that, until 1650, Italian states were still able and occasionally in-clined to make war on each other, and their military institutions and infrastruc-ture allowed this.[6] Nevertheless, those occasions were rare, and Italians eager to pursue a military career generally chose one of the major powers employing them in some numbers: that is, Spain, Austria and Venice, with several of lesser importance, like Piedmont and France. However, at the end of the Thirty Years War in Germany, and then a decade later in Italy and the Low Countries, European armies were pared back to peacetime levels, and respective states paid off their debts. The traditional employers of Italian military nobles were no longer capable of absorbing the high numbers which had been actively engaged in their

---

[2] L. Simeoni, *L'assorbimento austriaco del ducato estense e la politica dei duchi Rinaldo e Francesco III* (Modena: 1986, first publ. 1919), p. 1.

[3] A. Corvisier, *Louvois* (Paris: 1983), p. 252.

[4] *Ibid.*, pp. 517–19.

[5] R. Chaboche, "Les soldats français de la guerre de Trente Ans: une tentative d'approche", *Revue d'histoire moderne et contemporaine*, **20**, 1973, pp. 10–24.

[6] Y.-M. Bercé, "Rome et l'Italie au XVIIe siècle: les dernières chances de l'état ecclésiastique, 1641–1649", *Etudes réunies en l'honneur du doyen G. Livet* (Strasbourg: 1986), pp. 229–37.

service as recently as the 1640s. Spanish service was no longer as attractive after the catastrophe of Rocroi (1643), since its armies were most often defeated. Rocroi may not have been the unique turning point, but it is certain that after the early 1650s Spain entered a prolonged period of decline and defeat that continued unchecked until the War of the Spanish Succession in 1701.

The abandonment of the Spanish army by the Castilian high nobility was apparent from before the time of Olivares, as its interest moved increasingly from military to administrative functions under Philip III. Although violence was still a way of life for most nobles, the Spanish established aristocracy was disinclined to shed its blood on foreign battlefields, apart from aspiring hidalgos in search of status.[7] The demilitarization of the Spanish nobility meant that aspiring captains and colonels no longer raised troops from their own resources, or advanced money to the crown to keep their companies operational. Those traditional perquisites granted to hidalgos, the prestigious habits of the knightly orders, were increasingly given to courtiers and financiers. After 1660 there seemed no link between the bestowal of the habit and a record of service and merit.[8] The evaporation of incentives for nobles to serve the crown led to a gradual deterioration of the bureaucratic machinery that lay behind the army. During the 1630s, virtually the entire organization of war, the fleet, the armaments manufactures, the supply of garrisons and the recruiting apparatus, was placed in private hands. Madrid gradually lost its control over its administration and even local government. The hundred or so grandee families, whose power reached its summit under Charles II (1665–1700), filled the political void.[9] This administrative breakdown was accentuated by the prolonged economic crisis in Iberia beginning with the famines and epidemics of the 1590s, and accelerated after 1609 by the expulsion of the Moriscos to North Africa. Plagues in the 1650s and 1670s added to the negative conjuncture, and the cumulative catastrophes reduced the population of Spain by perhaps as much as a third between 1590 and 1660, leaving the economy in a shambles. Only after 1680 did Spain commence a slow recovery.

Italian nobilities, too, shared this disaffection for the Catholic king's service, and this is visible from the analysis of the thousand aristocrats who were recipients of the Spanish military habits. The Catholic king never restricted these to his direct subjects, bestowing them on 'friends' of the crown wherever they resided.

---

[7] H. Kamen, *Spain in the later seventeenth century, 1665–1700* (London: 1980), p. 247.

[8] L. P. Wright, "The military orders in sixteenth- and seventeenth-century Spanish society: the institutional embodiment of a historical tradition", *Past and Present*, **43**, 1969, pp. 34–70, at p. 50ff; on this point, see also the article by Antonio Dominguez Ortiz, "La crise intérieure de la monarchie des Habsbourgs espagnols sous Charles II", in *The peace of Nijmegen, 1676–1678/79: la paix de Nimègue* (Amsterdam: 1980), pp. 157–68, which places it in the context of a general crisis of regime.

[9] Dominguez Ortiz, "La crise intérieure de la monarchie des Habsbourgs espagnols", in *The peace of Nijmegen*, p. 160ff.

Prestigious houses like the Malvezzi of Bologna, and the Muti of Rome, received several of these prizes over successive generations. A point worth stressing is that recipients resided primarily in the major political capitals. Naples figures far in front, but alongside Milan figure – in approximately equal strength – Rome and Genoa. The surge of awards began after 1610, and continued to 1660, with the provincial aristocracy of the kingdom of Naples and Sicily, and even of Sardinia, being tapped for the first time, as Philip IV and Olivares desperately sought to shore up the monarchy's failing strength. Until mid-century, the place of Rome, Florence, Bologna and even Turin was substantial, with Venetian territories alone spurning the Spanish king's friendship. In terms of relative numbers, the Neapolitan nobility remained far in front, with 185 awards, with Palermo a distant second with 55, and Genoa a close third with 50, ahead of Milan, with 41 bestowals. After 1660, however, a rapid drop in the number of awards makes clear that these aristocracies took their leave of Madrid. Sicilians were disproportionately numerous, but the number of Neapolitans fell by over half, and the Genoese by four-fifths. The aristocracies of Piedmont, Parma, Modena, Mantua, Tuscany and the Papal States disappear almost completely, as the support for the monarchy withdrew into Lombardy and the southern kingdoms.[10]

The prolonged economic crisis of the Mediterranean may have accelerated this withdrawal. Straitened economic horizons for manufactures after 1620 were worsened by the great plagues of 1629–33 in northern Italy, and the disastrous plague of 1656–9 in Genoa and the Mezzogiorno, which depressed the demand for agricultural products. Repeated state bankruptcies by Spain, and the perilous finances of the Papacy and other states at war, meant that interests paid on state bonds were aleatory. Even the well-connected Genoese bankers in Madrid, Andalusia and Naples were not safe.[11] Towards the end of the 1650s, royal coffers were bare. Most towns defaulted on their back-payments and their tax bill, unable to pay the interests on their loans. The crown anticipated dubious revenues, and alienated its tax machinery to foreign financiers, still largely Genoese. It paid out only 40 per cent or 50 per cent of the interest on state bonds, and this struck the aristocracy of the capitals primarily, since they had been the major lenders.[12] New

---

[10] See V. Vignau & F. de Chagon, *Indice de pruebas de los caballeros que han vestido el habito de Santiago desde el año 1501 hasta la fecha* (Madrid: 1901); and Vignau & Chagon, *Indice de pruebas de los caballeros que han vestido el habito de Calatrava, Alcantara y Montesa, desde el siglo XVI hasta la fecha* (Madrid: 1903).

[11] For the financial dangers, see Devèze, *L'Espagne de Philippe IV* (Paris: 1970), vol. 2, pp. 521–32. For the economic crisis in Italy, see R. Romano, "Italy in the crisis of the seventeenth century", in *Essays in European economic history*, (Oxford: 1974), pp. 185–98; and D. Sella, *Crisis and continuity: the economy of Spanish Lombardy in the seventeenth century* (Cambridge: 1979); and C. Cipolla, "Crise à Florence, 1629–1630", in *Mélanges en l'honneur de Fernand Braudel, I: histoire économique du monde méditerranéen, 1450–1650*, (Toulouse: 1973).

[12] On the place of the aristocracy of the capital cities as stakeholders in government finance, see the important theses by J.-C. Waquet, *Le grand-duché de Toscane sous les derniers*

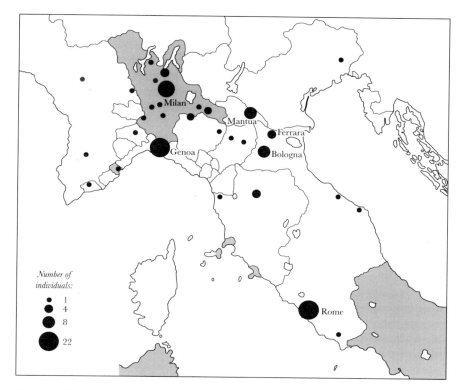

Map 5.1 'Friends' of the king of Spain in central and northern Italy, 1560–1610 (Knights of Santiago, Alcantara, Calatrava and Montesa) *(based on Vignau & Chagon)*

loans were contracted only at usurious rates of interest from the lenders and *asientistas* who were still solvent. Manipulation of the coinage caused rampant inflation and worsened the balance of payments.[13] The gradual wearing down of the royal treasury undermined the combat readiness of the army, just as much as it deprived it of resources. Even the prospect of a major victory, such as the marquis of Caracena's capture of Casale in the fall of 1652, could unlock hidden riches and have aristocrats vying to sell their jewels to raise troops and share in the glory.[14] As an imminently successful conclusion to the war receded, the money

---

Médicis (Rome: 1990); and J. Delumeau, *Vie économique et sociale de Rome dans la seconde moitié du XVIe siècle*, 2 vols (Paris: 1957–9), t. 2, p. 777ff.

[13] For Spain, the groundbreaking work is that of Antonio Dominguez Ortiz, summarized in the article, "La crise intérieure de la monarchie des Habsbourgs espagnols", in *The peace of Nijmegen*, pp. 157–68.

[14] Gianvittorio Signorotti, "Il marchese di Caracena al governo di Milano (1648–1656)", *Cheiron IX: L'Italia degli Austrias*, **17–18**, 1993, pp. 135–81, at p. 155.

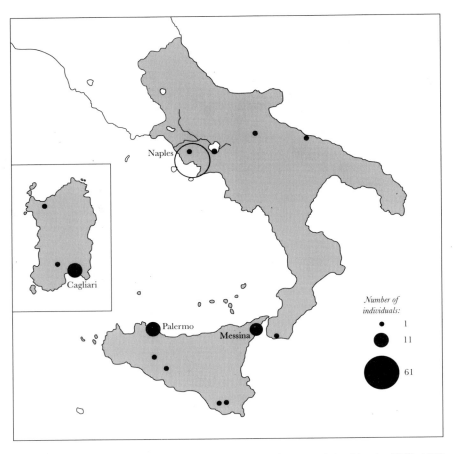

Map 5.2 'Friends' of the king of Spain in the Mezzogiorno and the islands, 1560–1610 (Knights of Santiago, Alcantara, Calatrava and Montesa) *(based on Vignau & Chagon)*

and the goodwill behind it became scarce again. Complete paralysis began in 1662 when Philip IV suspended payments, and after his death his officials decreed a general bankruptcy in 1666.

Such military units that were still in being were skeletal, or else were brought up to strength with hasty levies of vagabonds, criminals or unwilling peasants who deserted at the first opportunity.[15] As an example, one could point to the plight of the Army of Flanders after the peace with France in 1659. The government would not officially demobilize the remaining troops because arrears of pay would have to be made good. It preferred to keep the units on the roster but not pay the

---

[15] A. Dominguez Ortiz, "España ante la Paz de los Pireneos", in *Crisis y decadencia de la España de los Austrias* (Barcelona: 1969, first publ. 1959), pp. 157–93, p. 178ff.

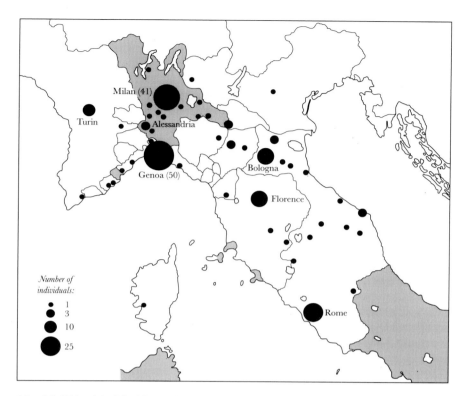

Map 5.3 'Friends' of the king of Spain in central and northern Italy, 1610–60 (Knights of Santiago, Alcantara, Calatrava and Montesa) *(based on Vignau & Chagon)*

soldiers. Desertion reduced the numbers nicely without the crown paying back wages. Thus there were 42,000 soldiers in the Low Countries in 1660, but only 16,000 in 1662 and 11,000 in 1664.[16] After 1664 Philip IV still had 77,000 soldiers under arms. Ten thousand guarded the Low Countries, 16,000 were in Italy, 4,000 in Catalonia, and 11,000 distributed throughout Castile, with most of the remainder along the Portuguese border in Galicia and Estremadura. The old monarch refused to make peace with the Portuguese rebels, so he channelled whatever resources were still available into new campaigns in Estremadura. Spain mounted several invasions of Portugal between 1656 and 1665, but the Portuguese bested them repeatedly, aided by French and English expeditionary forces and military technicians, and by some Italian military engineers of whose exact geographical origin I am unaware.[17] Spanish armies were increasingly motley

---

[16] G. Parker, *The army of Flanders and the Spanish road* (Cambridge: 1972), p. 213ff.

[17] On the Italian engineers in Portuguese service, see Maggiorotti, *L'opera del genio italiano all' estero*, 3 vols (Rome: 1933–9).

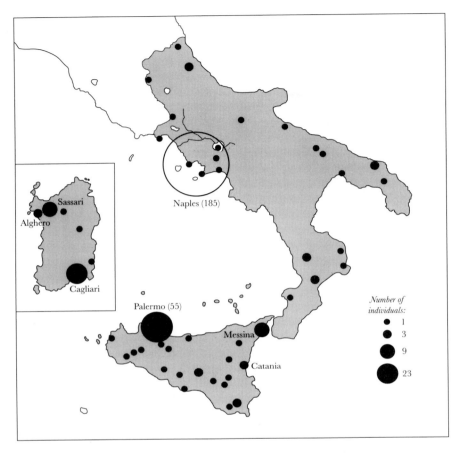

Map 5.4 'Friends' of the king of Spain in the Mezzogiorno and the islands, 1610–60 (Knights of Santiago, Alcantara, Calatrava and Montesa) *(based on Vignau & Chagon)*

collections of Italian and German mercenary regiments and levies of peasant militias that were militarily worthless.[18] On the Estremadura frontier in May 1666, there were only 600 officers and 6,248 cavaliers, not all of whom were mounted. For the infantry there were no fewer than 21 *tercios*: of those, seven were Spanish, five Italian, four German, two Walloon, one French and one Irish. These contained no fewer than 2,000 officers and only 6,920 ranks. In addition there were 3,500 troops in garrisons, including a Swiss regiment.[19] This amazingly high proportion of officers was certainly a sign of disintegration, perhaps the result of nobles raising new undermanned units from their own resources, with the crown

---

[18] Devèze, *L'Espagne de Philippe IV*, vol. 2, pp. 493–500.
[19] Kamen, *Spain in the later seventeenth century*, p. 351.

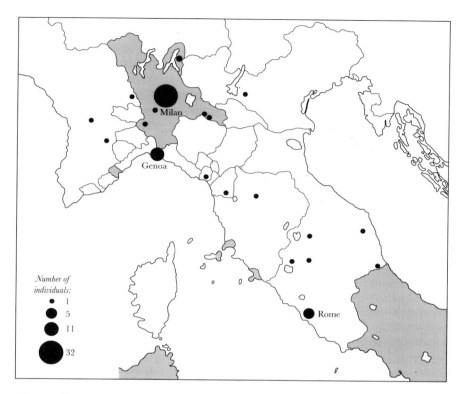

Map 5.5 'Friends' of the king of Spain in central and northern Italy, 1660–1710 (Knights of Santiago, Alcantara, Calatrava and Montesa) *(based on Vignau & Chagon)*

failing to maintain them thereafter. Many in the empire called for a much-needed army reform. There were ever larger numbers of *tercios* in being, but with fewer men in each. Even in the 1650s, the marquis of Caracena in Milan called for a drastic reduction in the number of *tercios* and companies, and the suppression of the practice whereby officers pocketed the pay of the dead and the deserters. This project was not popular, however, in the very patrician class that produced the officers Spain needed.[20]

---

[20] This is noted by Astarita, studying the garrisons in the kingdom of Naples. In 1702, the eight *tercios* in Naples contained only 5,200 men, only a fraction of whom were fit for service. These figures come from the unpublished *tesi di laurea* for the Università degli studi di Napoli, 1982–83 by Tommaso Astarita, "Aspetti dell' organizzazione del regno di Napoli alla fine del Viceregno spagnolo", p. 56. I wish to thank the author for generously allowing me to read his work, which is one of the very rare studies of an Italian army of the period. For the project of army reform in Lombardy, see Signorotti, "Il marchese di Caracena", *Cheiron* ix (1993), p. 148.

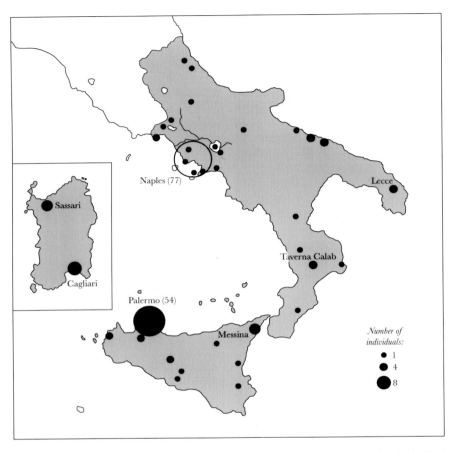

Map 5.6 'Friends' of the king of Spain in the Mezzogiorno and the islands, 1660–1710 (Knights of Santiago, Alcantara, Calatrava and Montesa) *(based on Vignau & Chagon)*

After 1665 Philip IV resigned himself to peace, but it was not signed until after his death in 1668. The weakness of the Spanish Empire excited the appetites of France and England. Louis XIV, whose dowry established in 1659 was never paid, laid claim to the Low Countries in exchange. Without having to expand his army of about a hundred thousand men, Louis expected to swallow up the territory in a military promenade known as the War of Devolution. At the outset of the war in 1667 there were only 2,000 Spanish troops there, and 1,000 Italians, although with local levies and German mercenaries the defenders numbered some 30,000 spread between a field army and many garrisons.[21] They were so

---

[21] Stradling, *Europe and the decline of Spain*, p. 149ff.

outclassed that Holland and England ended their own war and forged an alliance to protect the rump of the Low Countries and preclude their complete conquest by France. In order not to widen the war, and certain of finishing the conquest later, Louis XIV made an advantageous peace.[22] The forces available to continue the war in Estremadura were even more pitiful. In November 1667, a report for the energetic Don Juan, bastard son of the late king, showed the full military establishment in Spain to comprise almost 4,000 officers but only 19,566 infantry rank and file; and 1,300 officers and 7,000 mounted cavalry, with another 2,000 dismounted. The fleet carried an additional 3,300 troops. On the Catalan frontier with France there were 167 officers and 2,567 cavalry, and 780 officers and 2,967 infantry. Garrisons there were all seriously undermanned, and were saved from complete undoing only by French inactivity in the theatre.[23] The spectre of complete collapse in Flanders forced the regency to treat with Portugal.

Spain's imperial force in Europe had just about vanished, since it was as much as the monarchy could do just to protect the loyal provinces of the empire in the face of French aggression. None of the realms of the Spanish House of Austria provided enough revenue to defend another part of the Empire. Madrid's sole departure from a strictly defensive posture was to assist Venice in the crucial stage of the siege of Candia in September 1668. Nine Sicilian and Neapolitan galleys and only 500 troops participated, but none received permission to disembark.[24] Sicily provided about a million ducats of revenue, but the functionaries on the island and, purportedly, the troops in garrison absorbed it all.[25] Theoretically, Sicilian revenues paid for about 8,000 infantry and 1,000 cavalry, and could support a feudal militia of 2,000 and a flotilla of six galleys, from its population of one million people. In reality however, the forces on hand were always much inferior and Sicily provided nothing for the defence of the empire. Its inhabitants felt threatened by a resurgent Ottoman Empire after the fall of Candia in 1669. In Messina, the chief commercial and naval port on the island, the ramparts were readied and artillery provided for the city, and the royal fortresses overlooking the town and guarding the harbour were all improved and their garrisons beefed up. The Spanish crown felt the population to be disloyal or dissatisfied, and one author maintains that the Ottoman grand vizir attracted many disgruntled Neapolitan and Sicilian renegades into Turkish service.[26]

---

[22] Prof. Jean Bérenger, in a private conversation, draws attention to a secret partition of the Spanish Habsburg territories between Louis XIV and Emperor Leopold I precisely in this juncture. Since the sickly infant king of Spain could die at any moment, Louis preferred to soon gain by inheritance what would cost much treasure to conquer. Charles II was not to die until 1700, however.

[23] Kamen, *Spain in the later seventeenth century*, p. 351ff.

[24] K. Setton, *Venice, Austria and the Turks in the seventeenth century* (Philadelphia: 1991), p. 201.

[25] Emile Laloy, *La révolte de Messine, l'expédition de Sicile et la politique française en Italie (1674–1678)* (Paris: 1929), vol. 1, p. 32.

[26] Terlinden, *Le Pape Clement IX et la guerre de Candie*, p. 295.

Naples was still an important resource, albeit one that contributed but a fraction of the money to imperial arms that it had before the revolt of 1647. Since the realm was not directly in danger of attack, Madrid begrudged expenditure on its defence even more than elsewhere.[27] During the 1620s and 1630s, Naples contributed as much as eight million ducats annually to the war effort, while being defended by only 2,400 garrison troops in 1636. Revenues from the kingdom fell from 8 million ducats in 1646, to 5 million in 1648, to about 2.3 million in 1665.[28] The weakening of the state since the 1620s made it almost impossible for viceroys to uproot the habitual corruption, and abuse of power and privilege, now second nature to the nobles and clergy.[29] By the late seventeenth century, annual military expenditures in wartime were closer to one or 1.5 million ducats. The viceroy allocated about half the available troops for the kingdom of Naples to the malaria-infested coastal region of Tuscany and the adjoining island of Elba.[30] Mazarin's naval expedition of 1646, and his support for the uprising the next year, underscored how important the Tuscan presidial state was to the defence of the entire Mezzogiorno. The rest of the kingdom's soldiers were scattered across 22 other fortresses in the Mezzogiorno. After the great revolt, the Spanish crown built cavernous barracks in Naples and nearby Pozzuoli, and a great arsenal in the waterfront citadel. They could house and equip more than 4,000 soldiers, but there was never more than a small fraction of that number available.[31]

Louis XIV's unprovoked invasion of the Netherlands in 1672, and the extension of hostilities to include the Spanish territories in 1673, confirmed the congenital Habsburg weakness. It is difficult to evaluate this in quantitative terms, for as Kamen notes, Spanish historians have neglected a period assumed to be one of unchecked decadence.[32] Besides, the military administration of the Empire was not centralized in Madrid, but was articulated regionally, in Barcelona, Milan, Naples, Palermo, Brussels and in other cities besides, rendering archival research difficult. The crown in Castile continued to pay grandees to recruit and equip soldiers, and there was still no central secretariat governing the army as in France. As a result, the crown had little control over the quality and the discipline of the

---

[27] T. Astarita, "Istituzioni e tradizioni militari", *Storia del Mezzogiorno*, vol. 9, G. Galasso & R. Romeo (eds) (Naples: 1993), pp. 121–56.

[28] F. Caracciolo, *Sud, debiti e gabelle: gravami, potere e società nel Mezzogiorno in età moderna*, (Naples: 1983), p. 286.

[29] *Ibid.*, p. 355.

[30] Tommaso Astarita, "Aspetti dell' organizzazione militare del regno di Napoli alla fine del Viceregno spagnolo", unpublished Tesi di Laurea, Università degli Studi di Napoli, 1982–83, pp. 31–2.

[31] On these constructions, see the report by the French spy, Colbert de Seignelay, *L'Italie en 1671: Rélation d'un voyage du marquis de Seignelay*, Pierre Clément (ed.) (Paris: 1867), pp. 180–90.

[32] H. Kamen, "España en la Europa de Luis XIV", in *Historia de España Menendez-Pidal; t. 28: La transición del siglo XVII al XVIII*, P. Molas Ribalta (ed.) (Madrid: 1993), p. 257.

troops. It bullied or cajoled the Spanish aristocracy into taking up commissions, usually a prerequisite for the court appointments they craved. Ministers felt that the paucity of Castilian officers undermined the war effort, and compelled the monarchy to look for support elsewhere. Spain forged a series of defensive alliances with its former enemies to stem the French tide. Between July 1673 and the end of 1675, Spain subscribed to 12 different defensive treaties with European powers.[33] The war underlined the continuing demilitarization of the Iberian peninsula that could not be offset by Italian recruitment. In 1673 the Spanish army joining the Dutch in the Low Countries numbered only 8,000 men and its morale was very low. A similar crumbling of the army occurred elsewhere. A mere 2,000 men guarded the loyal Burgundian province of Franche-Comté against the threat of French invasion. There was some fiscal improvement through an increase in silver sent from America, and through the continued co-operation of Genoese bankers, but the basic problem was one of military disengagement of Spanish and Italian society.[34] Stradling unconvincingly asserts that the reserves of cannon-fodder in Castile and Naples were rare because of demographic decline. When the troops were Spanish, Andalusian and Galician in particular, they were ever harder to come by.[35]

In reality, the Spanish and Italian populations were on the rebound after the devastating plagues of 1656–9, and these losses were, for Spain, more than compensated by a constant flow of immigration from southern France.[36] Germany, too, suffered frightful losses due to the Thirty Years War, but German soldiers were ubiquitous in Europe for generations after. Rather than 'depletion', one should stress how military service for feeble Spain was not attractive. Even foreign mercenaries preferred to fight for other countries, like France or Venice, despite the higher wages Spain promised. Kamen has measured the plight of Spanish arms from the troops available in Catalonia. Early in the war, in the autumn of 1673 there were in all of the province only 4,300 infantry ranks under 893 officers, and 2,627 cavalry troopers under 173 officers. The garrison of

[33] Alcala-Zamora, "Razon de estado y geoestrategia en la politica italiana de Carlos II", *Boletin de la Real Academia de la Historia*, 1976, pp. 297–358, at p. 315.
[34] Kamen, "España en la Europa de Luis XIV", in *Historia de España Menendez-Pidal, t. 28*, p. 262, notes that the Royal Council in 1672 discussed the troubling lack of interest in Spanish élites for army careers, "la peu d'application des sujets nobles à servir à la guerre".
[35] *Ibid.*, p. 263. Despite these assurances, we are lacking the kind of focus on the rank and file for Spain that André Corvisier has devoted to the French army. For the single exception I know, see Astarita, "Aspetti dell' organizzazione militare del regno di Napoli", p. 194ff, who stresses Andalusian origins of the troops, alongside others from eastern Castile and Aragon.
[36] Kamen, *Spain in the later seventeenth century*, pp. 184–9. Kamen emphasizes that the problem of recruitment was essentially one of low morale, because when the bastard prince Don Juan decided to take power in a *coup d'état* in 1677, he found a willing army of 15,000 men very quickly. See Kamen, "España en la Europa de Luis XIV", in *Historia de España Menendez-Pidal, t. 28*, p. 264.

Barcelona numbered 400 infantry, backed by an untrustworthy militia. By March 1676 the viceroy had but 2,500 infantry in the province, while the garrison of Barcelona numbered only 200 regular soldiers.[37] These figures increased somewhat by the onset of the next campaign, but they remained paltry, for even a small fortified town required a garrison of at least 1,000 men to hold out for any time in a siege. Neapolitan levies sent to Catalonia were not enough to stop French progress.[38] The French made border conquests with only minimal forces and effort. Franche-Comté was quickly overrun by another French army in 1674. Spain was incapable of defending its European possessions elsewhere, as French armies continued to advance in the Low Countries and in Catalonia. Milan was unthreatened only because of Piedmontese neutrality.

In this context of dramatic weakness Messina, one of the most dynamic commercial centres in the Spanish Empire, rose in revolt against Madrid. The situation of the city was special: it was virtually a city–republic whose magistrates held considerable power and autonomy. The source of its wealth, the export of silk, rested on special privilege and monopoly. The city was intensely jealous of its privileges, and sought to expand them by attempting to make the city into the capital of the island kingdom, to the detriment of Palermo. Antagonism between the two Sicilian cities was profound. During the Palermo revolt of 1647, Messina remained loyal, hoping for political dividends. Messina was also the base from which the crown reconquered Naples in 1648. With the renewal of Madrid's efforts to assert its authority over the empire after 1659, the political élites in Castile and those in Messina parted ways. Anticipating trouble, Spain began to fortify the nearby port of Milazzo in 1661. The crown's representative in the city (with the status of viceroy), the *stratico*, gradually increased Spain's authority at local expense. The Walloon prince de Ligne, incurred much hostility in the pursuit of this policy, but his garrison of 1,500 troops kept the city in check. At the slightest incident the troops paraded through the city with their wicks lit and their matchlocks loaded. He armed a faction of the city magistrates favourable to the crown, the 'blackbirds' (a synonym for fools), as auxiliaries. Every incident seemed to deepen the chasm between the crown's servants and the local population. Participation of Spanish troops in local celebrations was felt to be an attempt at intimidation. A famine during the winter and spring of 1671–2, exacerbated the resentment, as the viceroy dispatched ships loaded with grain from Messina to relieve hunger elsewhere. Dissatisfaction on the island was so widespread that in 1672 there were troubles in nearby Catania, and in Tràpani, on the westernmost tip of the kingdom. Some 600 troops were dispatched to the latter city, and about twenty ringleaders of the revolt were publicly executed, in a square packed with Spanish soldiers.[39]

---

[37] Kamen, *Spain in the later seventeenth century*, p. 351ff.

[38] Laloy, *La révolte de Messine*, vol. 3, p. 614ff.

[39] While several books have been devoted to the revolt of Messina, the thesis of Emile Laloy, comprising close to 2,000 dense pages, is still the best. See *La révolte de Messine*,

Repeated Spanish violation of Messina's privileges, the arming of a pro-Spanish minority faction in municipal politics, and the overbearing behaviour of a 600-man garrison under Don Luis de Haro finally culminated in spontaneous rebellion on 7 July 1674. Within 24 hour hours the city's Senate was organizing its own militia to patrol the ramparts. It opened the city gates to admit a peasant host, and distributed arms to most citizens. The Spanish troops fled to the governor's palace, to some outlying redoubts, and to the fort of Salvador, overlooking the harbour entrance. Over the next several weeks the strongpoints on the landward side surrendered to the rebels one by one, much to the relief of the soldiers and their wives. In the citadel, the troops tried unsuccessfully to capitulate for days, because none of the rebels understood wartime usages signalling surrender. Only Fort Salvador, on the mole, held out, since it could receive help by sea. There were soon some 40,000 Messinese citizens and peasants of outlying villages in arms. The rebels found a commander in *cavaliere* Don Giacomo d'Averna, who raised 500 infantry at his own expense in his nearby fief of Mandanice, and his relatives gathered 400 more. He tried to storm the fort at Salvador and repulse the Spanish troops elsewhere with the crowds at his disposal, but there was no order or discipline in his armed bands, and probably precious few old soldiers, owing to Sicily's notorious lack of military proclivities.[40]

Spain's response to the crisis is an excellent illustration of its inability to deal with an emergency at this lowest point in its decline. Within a few days of the initial revolt, the viceroy sailed to Milazzo and established his headquarters there. He collected the galleys and started raising the militia and summoned troops from garrisons across the island. With new taxes he hoped to raise 7,000 soldiers, and 1,000 Spanish regulars to place in garrison. At the outset, though, he had a paltry force of 500 Spaniards, 400 Burgundian cavalry, and 1,000 doubtful militiamen from the island. The *stratico*, Bayona, set about raising 5,000 militia in Calabria, and another 4,000 in Sicily. The 7,700 militia from Puglia and Basilicata, men of the *battaglione*, were also raised and concentrated at Reggio Calabria, where they had to be trained by their general, the Neapolitan MarcAntonio Gennaro. About 1,000 Spanish troops were collected out of various garrisons in southern Italy, to stiffen all of the above. The governor of Milan levied a new regiment of 600 Italians in Lombardy in August, destined for service in Sicily. By summer's end, these forces were ready to blockade the city by land and sea. One problem was that, after garrisoning the myriad towns and villages of the region, only a handful was available in any one place. The various militia forces arriving at Milazzo had no experienced officers, and listened to no-one. Commanders like Gennaro feared for their reputations by having to lead this rabble into battle. In Reggio there was a further contingent of 4,000 men of the *battaglione* available, and a feudal unit sent by the prince of Roccella, but they were useless too, and their demeanour shocked

---

l'expédition de Sicile, et la politique française en Italie (1674–1678) (Paris: 1929). On the rebellion in Tràpani, see vol. 1, p. 188ff.

[40] *Ibid.*, vol. 1, p. 317.

the knights of Malta who saw them.[41] As measures of last resort, the viceroy called up the *saqueta*, or the medieval feudal cavalry militia of Sicily, so expensive to maintain. Negotiations were underway with bandit gangs in the Abruzzi and with Palerman assassins, for at least they were experts with weapons, and better than peasant militias for daring feats. Only 300 Neapolitan and 850 Sardinian regular soldiers could be added to the reinforcements, before Fabio Visconti's *tercio* arrived from Lombardy.

The dilemma for Spain was that there were few alternatives to such mobs. The Spanish crown requested help from its Italian allies as it had done since the beginning of the century. Only Genoa complied, by putting its few galleys and its ports at Spanish disposal in August 1674. The knights of Malta consented to ferry troops to the island, but otherwise declined to take part in the fighting. Grand Duke Cosimo III of Tuscany played a different game. He stressed that the anti-French grouping to which he belonged would suffer if France was to seize the Tuscan presidial territories so weakly garrisoned by Spain. Florence gradually pressed Madrid for their transfer to Tuscan control, as a sign of the 'goodwill' that the king of Spain bore towards his Italian allies.[42]

Louis XIV and his ministers thought of the revolt as a useful diversion of Spanish resources, and sent six warships to show the flag. Their symbolic gesture sufficiently demoralized the defenders in Fort Salvador that they surrendered. Louis then decided to dispatch a larger fleet with a few battalions of infantry under the duc de Vivonne to bolster the city's defence. The numbers were too small to incite the whole of southern Italy to revolt against Spain, but it would have been enough to occupy Reggio Calabria and impede enemy communications from that side. Vivonne could have taken his fleet into the port of Naples itself to cripple the remnants of the Spanish squadron there, but he rejected that too, from the excessive caution that was his hallmark as a commander.[43]

In October 1674, Spain received promises of help from an unusual quarter: the Dutch fleet under the famous admiral de Ruyter. There were still only 2,000 regular soldiers in the Spanish army quartered around the city of Messina. The militia of 8,000 men was largely useless for the skirmishing war that was developing. Seapower remained Spain's trump card. Combined Dutch and Spanish fleets had a good chance of overcoming the recently-formed French navy. There were 22 ships and 25 galleys in the Spanish force in Naples, capable of transporting reinforcements. Shortly after, the new viceroy Villafranca arrived in Milazzo with orders to raise 15,000 regular infantry and 1,500 cavalry, to be recruited from Catalonia, Lombardy and distant Germany. It turned out to be impossible to raise such a large force, for lack of money. A year later, in February 1676, there were

---

[41] *Ibid.*, vol. 1, pp. 324–54.

[42] Alcalà-Zamora, "Razon de estado y geoestrategia en la politica italiana de Carlos II", *Boletín de la Real Academia de la Historia*, 1976, pp. 297–358, at pp. 328–34.

[43] Laloy, *La révolte de Messine*, vol. 1, p. 562. Laloy suggests that Vivonne owed his post to his sister's role as Louis' mistress.

only 9,000 soldiers available, of whom a third were Spanish, another third Germans, and a little over 1,000 militiamen from Naples and Sicily. This number of Spanish troops remained stable after that, as reinforcements trickled in from Lombardy to replace the dead and the deserters. Most of the senior commanders were either Spanish or Italian.

Villafranca proved to be an ineffective viceroy, lodged in Milazzo where a French raid by land and sea almost captured him one morning. His successor was a Guzman, and a soldier too, the marques de Castel-Rodrigo. He renewed the mobilization of the baronial cavalry, as a psychological measure more than anything. The 1,000 horsemen so levied served for only three months. The militia tended to desert, or not to respond to mobilization calls at all. Moreover, Castel-Rodrigo felt that Sicilians were intrinsically no good for war, in any capacity, and that it was pointless to have them around. Spain could not recruit even a single regiment of Sicilians in almost four years of campaigning in the theatre.[44] The main advantage enjoyed by the Spaniards was the lacklustre ability of Vivonne, who maintained a strategic defensive. He neglected to raise any of the Messinese or other Sicilians to augment his forces, save for a single regiment under d'Averna, and this despite the determination of the population to maintain a stout defence. After the defeat inflicted on the Dutch fleet in 1675, Louvois sent 3,000 good French infantry to Sicily, now the foremost theatre for Spain in the war. Vivonne's lack of initiative allowed Spain to strip bare its garrisons elsewhere, to provide troops for the blockade of Messina. The viceroy of Naples, Astorga, needed 1,400 troops in the Tuscan presidial lands, and garrisons scattered throughout the kingdom of Naples. Only at Reggio was there an important force of 2,000 infantry and 675 horse, and a floating population of several hundred militia from feudal levies. Elsewhere, Astorga reduced the garrisons to skeleton forces, like the 250 men in the important coastal fortress of Gaeta, many of whom were married and resided outside the citadel.[45] In Naples there were only 1,500 Spaniards in garrison, mostly recent levies with no experience. On the Adriatic coast, the garrisons were derisory: 100 men at Manfredonia, 40 at Sant'Angelo, 25 at Barletta and only 15 at Trani, all fortresses of modern design. The lack of troops was so dire that the viceroy could not stop the progress of 1,000 bandits in the Abruzzi, and others who plundered Calabria at will, and marauded to the very gates of Naples.

Louis XIV might have tried to rally Italians to him, but this he did not do. Despite offers of service from nobles in the peninsula, he deliberately avoided employing Italians, and refused to send the few Italian troops in the French army to the Sicilian theatre.[46] Instead, he and Louvois saw it as a diversion of Spanish forces, fixing them to ports like Milazzo, Taormina, Syracuse, Palermo and elsewhere. They were pinned down everywhere because French naval power was

---

[44] *Ibid.*, vol. 2, p. 817.

[45] *Ibid.*, vol. 2, p. 146.

[46] *Ibid.*, vol. 2, p. 291.

at its peak. Those ships made continual raids along the coast, but they resembled corsair landings rather than invasion attempts. At the end of 1675, a galley expedition, rowing to the beach under the very walls, seized the fortified port of Augusta defended by only 150 Spanish soldiers and the local militia, and the town was plundered, not held. A landing on the more strongly fortified port of Syracuse was attempted too, but the garrison was larger and refused to yield. Spanish warships also fell victim to French patrols. In January 1676 a naval battle off Stromboli between the French and Dutch fleets was indecisive. The Admiral de Ruyter hesitated to engage because of the weakness of the Dutch fleet and the indolence of his Spanish allies. In April another indecisive engagement took place between the two fleets at Augusta, but this time de Ruyter was killed. Then in June, the French fleet attacked the combined Spanish and Dutch force at Palermo, destroyed several ships belonging to each, and won the initiative at sea. After receiving 3,000 French troops from Toulon, Vivonne had 8,000 troops in total and enjoyed complete freedom in strategic initiative. It would have been possible to capture Naples itself, but lacking vision, the French commander stormed the Sicilian town of Taormina instead. Early in 1677, 1,700 more French troops were sent to Sicily, but they were confined to Messina, extracting contributions from the villages in the district.

The stalemate gradually shifted in favour of Spain, as the Sicilians came to resent the French presence. The kingdom of Naples continued to provide funds for most military operations: its treasury paid out almost three million ducatons over the years, and sent about 17,000 men in total. An important turning point was the coup in Madrid, which saw the late king's bastard son Don Juan, impose himself as the *valido*, or director of government. He emphasized the importance of Sicily in the Spanish imperial system and increased the troop strength there, despite a French invasion of Spain itself. In March 1677 there were over 12,000 regular soldiers, of whom 5,000 were Spanish infantry, 2,300 Italians, 2,200 Germans and Burgundians, and about 800 Sicilian militia, supported by 1,700 cavalry. By February 1678, there were five Spanish regiments, one Sardinian, one Majorcan, one Burgundian, four Milanese, two Neapolitan, three German, one Corsican, one Albanian and four Sicilian militia units. It was thought preferable to reduce the militia from 10,000 men to 2,000, by keeping only the best. Under aggressive officers, like the Roman Piero Paolini, they could perform valuable service, but most of them were good only for eating up supplies.[47] The assembly of such a polyglot force was not without its drawbacks. Spanish officers resented the pretensions of equality of their Italian colleagues, some of whom they considered traitors. Precedence and protocol usages in Castilian favour undermined the cohesion. Italians, but also Sardinians and Majorcans, bridled at this attitude, and serious incidents broke out in garrisons. Rumours held that these tensions between Spaniards and Italians contributed to the loss of Taormina.[48] Of all these

---

[47] *Ibid.*, vol. 3, p. 388.
[48] *Ibid.*, vol. 3, p. 59 and p. 249.

troops, the Germans were considered the best, and the least liable to desertion, but they were also the most expensive.

In 1677, Louis XIV had 11,000 French infantry in Sicily, some cavalry, and the Messinese auxiliaries. This diversion began to draw on French resources as much as Spanish ones, while the Sicilian population was ever less likely to rise against Spain. The great king then began to plot the opening of a second Italian front, by invading Lombardy with Piedmontese help. Normally, that province needed a force of 16,000 infantry and 6,000 horse, of which 7,000 infantry were required to garrison the fortified towns of the duchy. By 1677, however, there were perhaps only 4,000 regular soldiers in the entire province, along with some dispirited militia cavalry. Milan had transferred thousands of troops to Sicily, with many deserting on the way.[49] Some regional nobles began to promise aid to Louis XIV should he decide to invade the region, like the Piedmontese marchese di Parella. Another, Jacomo Celsi, a former lieutenant-colonel of the Venetian army, promised Albanian and Macedonian troops for covert operations. Louix XIV and Louvois listened politely but promised nothing, perhaps in order not to whet the appetite of his Piedmontese satellite.[50]

In April 1678, the new French commander, La Feuillade, received orders from Louis XIV to abandon Messina and to bring the 8,000 troops still there back to France. Over the years, another 6,300 had either died or deserted. Messina was forced to capitulate, paid a colossal fine, lost its trading privileges and was forced to accept a large garrison in a new, strong citadel. Its days as the great commercial centre in southern Italy were over. The campaign ended as a failure for France, at least in the shorter term. In the longer term, the revolt was a serious blow to the integrity of the Spanish empire, and underscored how weak the House of Austria had become. The alliance system – from which Spain had drawn much of its resilience – had withered away, and needed to be cultivated afresh. Continuing support of the Spanish monarchy was no longer in the best interests of the north Italian states, once Spanish military ascendancy was gone, except in the sense that a weak Spanish presence in the peninsula was preferable to a strong French one. Spain maintained the appearance of an alliance with these states throughout the second half of the seventeenth century, and after the Dutch war sought to revive them.

Ferdinando II of Tuscany remained clear of the struggle between Spain and France until his death in 1670. From the 1640s, the grand duchy ceased to lend money to the Spanish crown, which it had supplied before; from 1625 to 1642, Spain extracted 1.8 million *scudi* from the Medici, causing a bankruptcy of Florentine credit institutions when it defaulted on its payments.[51] Tuscan galleys ceased to ferry Spanish troops across the western Mediterranean or along the coast from Naples. Military expenditures – for the weak garrisons around the state

---

[49] *Ibid.*, vol. 3, p. 523.

[50] *Ibid.*, vol. 3, p. 523.

[51] Waquet, *Le granduché de Toscane sous les derniers Medicis*, (Rome: 1989), p. 120.

and the galleys – required about 300,000 *scudi* in 1670, or a quarter of the tax receipts.[52] Florence made much of its alliance with Spain in 1677 when it suggested that Madrid should transfer the sovereignty of the presidial state to Tuscany, to keep it out of Bourbon hands. Having reminded Madrid of the existence of the union of Italian states with Spain, Cosimo III of Tuscany was requested in 1682 to provide troops to garrison Milan, as Spain lurched towards a new war with France. Fearing French retaliation, the grand duke refused.[53] Cosimo III was later emboldened to demand precedence from Spanish galleys in Tuscan waters, and Spain was too weak to resist.

Genoa's contribution to Spain was more crucial. The republic's council sometimes sought to distance itself from Madrid, but there were too many links between the city's richest families and the Habsburg monarchy. For Genoa, Spain was first of all the guarantor of its independence against Piedmontese or French expansion. Significantly, the doge who was elected in 1673, shortly after the Piedmontese invasion, Prince Antonio di Saluzzo, was ordinarily a resident of Naples where he held a fief and business interests.[54] Although they no longer had a stranglehold over the monarchy's finances in Madrid, and despite their gradual naval decline, the Genoese were still redoubtable *asientistas* in Naples and Sicily, and continued to lease galleys to Spain, while making its harbours available to the Catholic king's warships.[55] Connected with that was the privileged access of these families – the Spìnola, De Mari, Doria, Grimaldi, Picchenotti, Centurioni and others – in the transport of huge quantities of specie from Cadiz, as interest on *juros* contracted in Spain, Naples, Palermo and Milan, and transport of treasure between the different Spanish dominions.[56] Genoese galleys and vessels also transported silk from Messina for its manufactures. Genoese investments in the New World, in Spain and in the commercial and agricultural economy of southern Italy were still substantial. For having aided Spain by ferrying troops during the Dutch war, and for building warships for Madrid, Louis XIV decided after 1679 to "mortify" these "Hollandais d'Italie."[57]

---

[52] *Ibid.*, p. 475.

[53] N. Giorgetti, *Le armi toscane e le occupazioni straniere in Toscana*, vol. 1, p. 543.

[54] Argegni, *Condottieri, capitani, tribuni*, vol. 3, p. 77.

[55] Colbert de Seignelay, *L'Italie en 1671: relation d'un voyage du marquis de Seignelay*, p. 283. Another Genoese patrician, Ippolito Centurione, leased a flotilla of eight galleys to Spain in 1665, with which he also transported merchandise and bullion. See, for the naval decline, Gian Carlo Calcagno, "La navigazione convogliata a Genova nella seconda metà del seicento", in *Guerra e commercio nell' evoluzione della marina genovese*, pp. 265–392, at p. 279.

[56] Carlo Bitossi identifies some of these *asientistas* in his article, "Il piccolo sempre succombe al grande: la repubblica di Genova tra Francia e Spagna, 1684–1685", in *Il bombardamento di Genova nel 1684* (Genoa: 1988), pp. 39–69, at p. 55.

[57] Colbert de Seignelay, *L'Italie en 1671*, p. 38. See also the article by Carlo Bitossi, "Il piccolo sempre succombe al grande: la repubblica di Genova tra Francia e Spagna,' 1684–1685", in *Il bombardamento di Genova nel 1684*, at p. 41.

Louis XIV and his ministers, Colbert de Seignelay (in charge of the navy) and Louvois (the war minister), knew that by punishing Genoa they were waging war against Spain, without attracting additional enemies that a campaign in Flanders would entail.[58] With this in mind they weighed their options and calculated the strength of the city. An invasion along the coast culminating with a siege and occupation of the city would have been 'uneconomical', even though the republic disposed of only 3,500 German, Swiss, Italian and Corsican soldiers, of whom no more than half were stationed in the capital.[59] To knock Genoa out of the Spanish alliance, it sufficed to make a 'demonstration' with the French fleet, which had had the upper hand in the Mediterranean since the Dutch War. Genoa had but six galleys and two ships of the line in its navy, and not all of them were fitted out. Louvois and Seignelay chose to treat the republic in the same way they had dealt with Algiers in 1683, by means of a bombardment with a new weapon: the ship-borne mortar or bomb-ketch, which hurled a 90 kg (200 lb) bomb over a kilometre (1,100 yd).[60] Louvois calculated that *un si rude châtiment apprendra aux Genois à devenir sages, et donnera une grande terreur à tous les princes qui ont des villes considérables au bord de la mer.*[61] Six bomb-ketches, escorted by the Mediterranean fleet commanded by Colbert de Seignelay in person, fired about 2,000 bombs over the course of two weeks in May 1684, while the fleet cannon fired about 13,000 stone balls at the city. The Genoese estimate of 3,000 houses destroyed is probably an exaggeration, but the devastation was immense. Seignelay landed about 3,500 infantry in the suburbs to wreak destruction there too, but they left as the militias converged on the city. The governor of Milan, Melgar, sent a thousand Spanish troops into the city during the bombardment, to keep order and to shoot looters. Genoese patricians responded in the short term with gestures of defiance. The republic sided openly with Spain during the summer naval campaign in 1684, sending the fleet to Catalonia where it was decimated by disease.[62] In the immediate years following, Genoa built more warships for Spain. Nevertheless, Louvois' calculations proved correct. The republic stayed out of the League of Augsburg against France, and the great European war of that name in 1689. Genoese military aid gradually ended in the 1690s, as the patriciate's attitude shifted

---

[58] M. G. Bottaro Palumbo, " 'Genua emendata' ": la politica del Re Sole nei confronti della repubblica", in *Il bombardamento di Genova nel 1684*, pp. 21–37, at p. 27.

[59] G. Galliani, "Il 'bombardamento' come atto militare: alcuni interrogativi e considerazioni", in *Il bombardamento di Genova nel 1684*, pp. 95–107, at p. 102ff. The Swiss and Germans garrisoned the city by virtue of a treaty with their home cantons in 1573, and which remained in effect until 1779; p. 96.

[60] Galliani, "Il 'bombardamento' come atto militare: alcuni iterrogativi e considerazioni", in *Il bombardamento di Genova nel 1684*, pp. 95–107, at p. 102.

[61] Colbert de Seignelay, *L'Italie en 1671*, p. 43.

[62] Bitossi, "Il piccolo sempre succombe al grande", in *Il bombardamento di Genova nel 1684*, p. 68.

from pro-Spanish to one of benevolent neutrality towards France.[63] Henceforth, in the words of Giovanbattista Spìnola, the republic would always be compliant to all great princes, and remain simple spectators of the events around them.[64]

The House of Gonzaga remained in the Spanish and Austrian clientèles after the end of hostilities in 1659. In 1662 Carlo II sent home the small Venetian garrison protecting Mantua, without intending to create a force of his own to defend his state.[65] The regent duchess, Isabella Clara, maintained close links with Spain, obtaining a subsidy from Madrid for the upkeep of a garrison in Casale. The duchess also submitted a border dispute with Modena along the Po to the arbitration of the governor of Milan, when both duchies were on verge of war in 1666.[66] Duke Ferdinand Carlo Gonzaga played a more devious game. He belonged to the first generation of unwarlike Italian princes, more apt to savour the distractions of Venice than to seek glory on the battlefield. In 1687 he went to witness the military campaigns in Hungary, but more like a tourist, watching the battle of Mohacs from a safe distance. He returned the year after with a splendid retinue to visit the siege of Belgrade.[67] The duke was already firmly in the French camp, however, having concluded a secret treaty with Louis XIV in 1678, and then selling the fortress of Casale outright to France in 1681. In 1688 he seized the town of Guastalla belonging to a dependent branch of his house, and turned it into a fortress with French help. During the initial phase of the War of the League of Augsburg in 1689, Spanish troops arrived to dismantle the fortress, and then in 1693 Don Vincenzo Gonzaga of Guastalla refortified the place as a Spanish ally. Duke Ferdinando Carlo recovered the Monferrato from France by the treaty of 1697, in a clause meant to deliver the fortress of Casale into the hands of a peaceful power. Ferdinando Carlo remained in the French camp, however, offering Mantua and Casale as a forward base for Bourbon troops in the War of the Spanish Succession from 1701 to 1707. The other duchies also withdrew from the Spanish system in Italy following the Dutch War. Modena no longer renewed its defensive treaty with Spain after 1680. Parma remained formally part of it until 1691, when Louis XIV established an anti-Habsburg league that included the Farnese together with the Este and the Gonzaga, reacting against the forced Austrian contributions of the previous year.[68]

Spanish weakness continued to the end of the century. A genealogical study of numerous Italian aristocratic houses would probably give us an idea just how

---

[63] *Ibid.*, p. 58.
[64] *Ibid.* p. 69.
[65] Coniglio, *I Gonzaga*, p. 451.
[66] *Ibid.*, p. 454.
[67] *Ibid.*, p. 464.
[68] G. Tocci, *Il ducato di Parma e Piacenza* (Turin: 1987), p. 70.

much young nobles spurned military service.[69] Spain relied increasingly on foreign adventurers, and career officers who were neither Spanish, nor even – mostly – noble. It was difficult to regularize their ranks and duration of service, to find a military system that would work in the longer term, in the absence of willing recruits. The shift of power within the Habsburg dynasty from Madrid to Vienna was quite striking, as the Austrian branch built up and maintained a large standing army. The Spanish held Flanders (where there were still 30,000 men) only with Dutch support. Charles II appointed Elector Max Emmanuel of Bavaria as governor-general of the Low Countries, because he brought his own regiments to Spanish service. Spain itself could send neither money nor troops to the region during the War of the League of Augsburg (1689–97). At the battle of Seneffe, the largest of the war, there were only 1,200 Spanish foot in the field, and that contingent decreased thereafter.[70]

The crisis in Catalonia is another illustration of Spanish feebleness. In 1690, the official tally of troops in the theatre was 10,356 infantry and 4,000 cavalry; but the organization of Spanish forces had remained unchanged since the time of Olivares.[71] The soldiers lacked food and basic necessities. The forces were the usual mixture of Castilians, Catalans, Germans, Walloons and Neapolitans, although the best regiments were German units hired entire from their princes, and subject to their own regulations. Urban militias were the backbone of the defence during sieges, and this time the Spanish cause was aided by the indiscipline of the French soldiery. In 1696, by dint of great effort, there were 23,000 troops in the Spanish army around Barcelona. The following year, however, a French army not much larger invested the city by land and sea, and captured it in ten weeks. Spain was then ready to come to terms.

The 10,000 Spanish-paid troops in Lombardy held only through Piedmontese and Austrian assistance. Only Sicily was guarded more tightly than before with 4,000 soldiers and nine ships. Sardinia was 'held' by only 350 soldiers at the end of the century, of which the largest concentration was 200 men in Cagliari.[72]

---

[69] Few such genealogical studies exist, to my knowledge. Authors fixing upon single families sometimes give impressionistic accounts of such service: see T. Astarita, *The continuity of feudal power: the Caracciolo di Brienza in Spanish Naples* (Cambridge: 1991); also, Michèle Benaiteau, "Una nobiltà di lunga durata: strategie e comportamenti dei Tocco di Montemiletto", in *Signori, patrizi, cavalieri in Italia centro-meridionale nell' età moderna*, M. A. Visceglia (ed.) (Bari: 1992), pp. 193–213; Benedetto Croce, "I Caracciolo d'Avellino", in *Uomini e cose della vecchia Italia* (Bari: 1927), p. 138 ff.; see also Angel Antonio Spagnoletti, *L'incostanza delle umane cose: il patriziato di Terra di Bari tra egemonia e crisi, XVI–XVIII secolo* (Bari: 1981), p. 27ff.

[70] Lonchay, *La rivalité de la France et de l'Espagne aux Pays-Bas (1635–1700)* (Brussels: 1896), p. 344ff.

[71] Kamen, *Spain in the later seventeenth century, 1665–1700*, p. 379ff.

[72] A. Mattone, B. Anatra, R. Turtas, *Storia dei Sardi e della Sardegna, vol. 3. L'età moderna: dagli Aragonesi alla fine del dominio spagnolo* (Milan: 1989), p. 101.

Kamen estimates the Spanish fleet in the period (1688) at 26 ships, with 9,000 men and 1,424 guns, and a similar number of galleys, of which a third were rented from Genoa. This was less than a quarter of the French fleet, and was comparable to Venice in number, and probably inferior to it in quality, despite the huge maritime empire it patrolled. The ocean-going vessels were used primarily to escort the Mexican silver that kept the military machine in being.[73] To maintain these minimal forces it was necessary to draw on Naples, the defences of which were pared to the bone. In 1696, of almost 4,000 infantry stationed in the kingdom and the Tuscan garrisons, barely 1,000 were considered fit for service.[74] Cavalry squadrons were insufficiently mounted, and were unsure of their old horses. The viceroy gave gentlemen commissions to raise new units, but none of them ever reached their complement. We find in Naples the same high proportion of officers to ranks that had existed since at least the 1660s in Spain. Astarita estimates that half of the expenditure on the army went towards the salaries of the officers, most of whom were useless for want of soldiers to lead.[75] The difficulties of recruitment meant that anybody who wished could become a soldier of the king of Spain, in contravention of all of the rules governing their levy. Although all the companies analyzed by Astarita were theoretically 'Spanish', about a quarter of the ranks, and fully half of the officers were in fact Italians, in great majority Neapolitans.[76] Few originated outside the lands of the Catholic King. In the face of such weakness, public order broke down in the Mezzogiorno. In the brief periods of peace, the viceroy of Naples, the marchese del Carpio and Stefano Carillo Salsedo tried to stem the tide of banditry, destroying whole villages to punish the inhabitants for supporting bandits, putting prices on the heads of bandit leaders, and giving impunity to those who surrendered.[77] Southern Italy remained tranquil during the War of the Spanish Succession (1701–14), however, as Spanish garrisons were gradually withdrawn to fight elsewhere. In 1707 when the Austrians conquering the kingdom of Naples reached Calabria, there were only 3,000 troops in all the Sicilian garrisons. Spanish decline was relentless.

Austrian horizons expanding

The invasion of Lombardy by Imperial troops, culminating in the siege and sack of Mantua in 1629–30, was no turning point announcing the return of the Holy Roman Empire to Italy. Emperor Ferdinand II's reaffirmation of his right of

---

[73] Kamen, "España en la Europa de Luis XIV", *Historia de España Menendez-Pidal, t. 28*, p. 261.
[74] Astarita, "Aspetti dell' organizzazione militare del regno di Napoli", p. 56.
[75] Astarita, "Istituzioni e tradizioni militari", *Storia del Mezzogiorno*, **9**, pp. 121–56.
[76] Astarita, "Aspetti dell' organizzazione militare del Regno di Napoli", p. 196.
[77] Laloy, *La révolte de Messine*, vol. 2, p. 635.

investiture, during a lull in the Thirty Years War, was a costly gesture. Gustavus Adolphus' invasion abruptly ended the Imperial presence, and Spain remained vigorous for a generation after 1630. Only Spain's exhaustion during the 1650s provided the first pretexts for Vienna to intervene in the Italian theatre with its own resources. In 1656, Emperor Ferdinand III dispatched 4,500 troops to Milan to defend the duchy against France, on the grounds that it was an Imperial fief. Simultaneously, he threatened Francesco I, duke of Modena, with confiscation of his duchy for rebellion, although his quarrel was with Spain. Vienna dispatched a commissioner to the Imperial fiefs throughout northern Italy to levy money from them. Usually, General Enkefort was politely refused entry to the castles, and was occasionally greeted by armed mobs who cared nought that he represented the Imperial dignity.[78] Grand Duke Ferdinando II of Tuscany recognized Spanish suzerainty over Siena, but claimed that Florence had been freed of Imperial allegiance since the Middle Ages. Lucca and Genoa recognized Imperial suzerainty, but claimed exemption from any kind of tribute or taxation. Only Piedmont–Savoy freely admitted to the Imperial tie, and the dukes bore the title of Prince of the Empire – but their policies were the most anti-Habsburg of any state in Italy.[79] Based on the amount of contributions they paid, Italian assistance during the campaigns of 1663–4 in Hungary was negligible. With Tuscany, Emperor Leopold I quietly dispatched a Count Piccolomini to Florence to persuade Grand Duke Ferdinando II to contribute to Imperial coffers, or pay contributions to the Imperial troops sent to Milan. The grand duke insisted upon his independence, and would pay nothing. In 1683, Grand Duke Cosimo III was approached to help finance the campaign in Hungary, and to relieve Vienna. Again, Tuscany refused, but decided to join the alliance against Turkey and help the Venetians in the Aegean instead[80].

Emperor Leopold I tolerated the general refusal of Italians to recognize his jurisdiction over them, without intending to relinquish any of his theoretical rights.[81] His plan was to restore the Empire to its early grandeur by recovering the cities of Dalmatia and the Terraferma from Venice; by punishing the insolence of German and Italian princes, resubmitting them to his authority; and by reuniting the Austrian branch of the Habsburg dynasty with Spain, or at least recovering Lombardy and Naples for Vienna.[82] While princes and subjects rejected Austrian claims of authority over them, they nevertheless conceded that the Emperor had some moral claim to assistance, given freely. Italian participation in the defence of the Empire after 1618 illustrates this ambivalence. From a merely mercenary perspective, there were lucrative posts to be had in the Imperial army. In Florence in particular, there were close dynastic links between the House of Austria and the

[78] Pugliese, *Le prime strette dell' Austria in Italia*, p. 146.
[79] Colbert de Seignelay, *L'Italie en 1671*, p. 269ff.
[80] Giorgetti, *Le armi toscane*, vol. 1, p. 543.
[81] J. Meuvret, "Louis XIV et l'Italie", *XVIIe siècle*, **47**, 1960, pp. 84–102, at p. 85.
[82] Pugliese, *Le prime strette dell' Austria in Italia*, p. 163.

Medici, and the same is true of the Gonzaga of Mantua. Given the multifarious links, it is difficult to detect whether Italian nobles still thought of the emperor as their legitimate sovereign, or the object of special veneration.

The emperors in turn appreciated Italians in a wide range of capacities, artistic, ecclesiastical, military and political, and the contribution of Italians to the Empire was in no way on the decline after the Thirty Years War. Their place was significant on the Imperial Privy Council, the War Council (*Hofkriegsrat*) and the Imperial Conference. Over the entire seventeenth century, Italy provided nine of the 128 members of the Privy Council (seven per cent), most of whom originated outside the hereditary lands of the House of Austria. There were times, however, when their significance was out of all proportion to their numbers, and their influence on the Emperor quite decisive, since numbers and influence do not always coincide. In 1628, of 14 members of the Council, only one was Italian, the Mantuan Rambaldo Collalto, but his star was in the ascendancy.[83] Under Leopold I (1657–1706), the most Italophile and Francophobe of the monarchs, they were more influential. The emperor disdained the German language, preferring Latin and especially Italian, which was the language most often spoken at court and used in official correspondence. His chief minister at the outset of his reign was the peace-loving Venetian-born Count Portia.[84] As if to compensate for the pacific proclivities, and even weaknesses, of his minister, the two most influential members of the council were Italian soldiers, Annibale Gonzaga and Raimondo Montecùccoli, from Mantua and Modena respectively. Leopold came by the services of these men in various ways. Gonzaga, president of the War Council, was a relative of Leopold's stepmother, Eleonora, who had wed Ferdinand III in 1650, and to whom he was very close. The empress and empress dowager played only episodic roles in the formulation of government policy, but they did solicit occasional favours, and were considered friendly to the Italians in Vienna. Montecùccoli was the technocrat, a military organizer and commander of great ability, generally considered the foremost military theorist of the seventeenth century. Leopold's Italian advisers and close collaborators also included priests, like the Capuchin Marco d'Aviano, previously in the employ of Pope Innocent XI Odescalchi, who wanted to unite European nations in a crusade against the Turks, or the Padre Menegatti who conducted secret negotiations for him with France.[85] Around 1670 the place of these Italians was striking, but their numbers waned towards the end of the century.

Montecùccoli was the most important of them all. Certainly he was one of the most cultivated: in 1656 he had helped the Austrian archduke found an Italian

---

[83] H. F. Schwarz, *The Imperial privy council in the seventeenth century*, (Cambridge, Mass.: 1943), p. 114.

[84] J. P. Spielman, *Leopold I of Austria*, (London: 1977), p. 36.

[85] On the personnel of the Imperial government, see the important thesis by Jean Bérenger, *Finances et absolutisme autrichien dans la séconde moitié du XVIIe siècle* (Paris: 1975), pp. 43–90.

literary academy in the capital, and had the reputation of being an intellectual. After the Thirty Years War he was torn between his native Modena and Vienna, until 1658 when the death of Field Marshal Hatzfeld vaulted him to the summit of the Imperial military hierarchy. As *generalissimo* of the field army, he drove the Swedes from northern Germany in the war of the Polish Succession, clinching his reputation for victory. After the death of General Luigi Gonzaga, Leopold appointed him military governor of Györ and commander of the Hungarian theatre, just as the Ottoman Porte decided to renew the offensive in 1663. Fortunately for Austria, the Venetians diverted Turkish resources in the Aegean, and they mustered only 30,000 or 40,000 good troops in Hungary and Transylvania. The Turks captured some towns in Croatia, where one of Montecùccoli's principal subordinates, the Florentine general Alfonso Strozzi, died in a sortie. The sultan's army then tried to force the River Raab and penetrate Austria proper at St Gotthard in 1664. Montecùccoli's field army, composed of an assortment of Austrian troops, Imperial contingents and French auxiliaries, repulsed the Janissaries' assaults with their superior firepower. The event marked the first decisive victory by a Christian army over the Ottomans in the open field. This single success deprived the Turks of the flower of their army, and led to a stalemate peace.

After the battle, Leopold raised Raimondo Montecùccoli to still greater heights, naming him Lieutenant-General of the Empire, a rank just below the emperor in person. The Modenese general then set out to remodel and standardize the Austrian army. He adopted common insignia, if not true uniforms, for the rank and file, following similar reforms in France. He substituted smaller battalions for the traditional *tercios*, and transformed tactics by multiplying the basic formations. Like contemporary armies imitating Swedish usage, he diminished the proportion of pikes in favour of muskets with plug bayonets, and adopted the light regimental cannon. Experience in Hungary, against the Turks, led him to increase the Hungarian and Croat light cavalry, and integrate the Croat light infantry into the main field army. President of the War Council on the death of Annibale Gonzaga in 1668, he continued to work at army reform, even conducting dangerous experiments in person. He remained President of the War Council throughout the 1670s, despite the machinations of a German court faction, envious of his stature, to undo him. His last campaign in 1675 pitted him against the great French Field Marshal Turenne in the upper Rhineland. Gouty and aged, Montecùccoli yet went on to lead Imperial armies into Alsace and Lorraine after the battlefield death of his adversary. His ultimate goal, to be named Prince of the Empire, was achieved shortly before his death in 1680.[86]

---

[86] There are two biographies available: Tommaso Sandonnini, *Il generale Raimondo Montecuccoli e la sua famiglia* (Modena: 1913), focuses on his Modenese ancestry and connections. Thomas M. Barker, *The military intellectual and battle: Raimondo Montecuccoli*, emphasizes the Thirty Years War, and the general's writings. The articles by John Mears, "Raimondo Montecuccoli, servant of a dynasty", *The Historian*, 1970, pp. 392–409; "The Thirty Years

Ironically, Montecùccoli laid the groundwork for the later Germanization of the Imperial army. While the high command was cosmopolitan, he preferred to employ an indigenous common soldiery, and spoke German himself in the heat of battle.[87] Barker affirms that Montecùccoli felt this ethnic uniformity made training and command control easier, and it was not based on the belief that one nationality was more suited for war than another.[88] There were not many officers in an Austrian regiment: four in an infantry company, or in a cavalry squadron, and only about 50 for an entire regiment. Of about 3,000 posts in the Imperial army in 1685, the Italians could have filled at best about 15 per cent, or 450 positions of all ranks.[89] In the Imperial army in 1695, about 25 per cent of the infantry officers, and fully 40 per cent of the cavalry officers were not German. Of 54 colonels in 1684, six belonged to reigning houses in the Empire, nine were princes and counts, and some fifteen enjoyed the right of 'immediacy', that is, belonging to houses theoretically on an equal plane with the House of Austria. With so many princes seeking commands, it might explain why the emperors preferred to promote foreigners and modest nobility from outside the hereditary lands, like most of the Italians alluded to. The cosmopolitan nature of the Imperial officer corps continued to favour Italians, in search of honour and fortune. Elmar Henrich, working from regimental histories, identifies 88 Italians holding the rank of colonel or lieutenant-colonel in the half-century after 1660, which is a decline from the 136 individuals who held that rank during the previous half-century.[90] A considerable number achieved the status of field marshal, the equivalent of general in other armies, which is surprising given that, in absolute numbers, Italians comprised less than ten per cent of the officer corps in 1695. Jean Nouzille finds they comprised but 7.3 per cent of infantry officers of all ranks, and 8 per cent of cavalry officers, totalling little more than two hundred individuals.[91] There must

---

War and the origins of a standing army", *Central European History*, 1988, pp. 122–41; and "The influence of the Turkish wars in Hungary on the military theories of Count Raimondo Montecuccoli", in *Asia and the West: essays in honor of Donald F. Lach* (Notre Dame, Indiana: 1986), pp. 129–45, are all derivative.

[87] Archivio di Stato di Siena, Archivi particolari, Piccolomini Consorteria vol. 25, "Lettere del C. Enea Silvio Piccolomini, tenente maresciallo". See the letter dated from the army, 4 August 1675, where Piccolomini describes the battle at Wilstadt on 29 July, against the French, and Montecuccoli's exertions to spur the soldiers on.

[88]. Barker, *The military intellectual and battle*, p. 68.

[89] Bérenger, *Finances et absolutisme autrichien*, vol. 2, p. 364–6.

[90] The calculations come from the annex of Elmar Jurgen Henrich's MA thesis (Dalhousie University, Halifax, Canada: 1995); "Italian Military Élites in the Service of the Spanish and Austrian Habsburgs, 1560–1700". The source was Alphons Wrede, *Geschichte der K.U.K. Wehrmach: die regimenter, corps, branchen und anstalten von 1618 bis ende des XIX jahrhunders, vol. 1–5: Supplement zu den mittheilungen des K.U.K. Kriegs-Archivs*, (Starnberg: 1985, first publ. Vienna, 1898–1905).

[91] J. Nouzille, *Le Prince Eugène de Savoie et les problèmes des confins militaires autrichiens, 1699– 1739*, Unpublished thesis (Université de Strasbourg: 1979). This substantial work of 1,400

have been a few additional positions, such as governors of fortresses, or militia commanders, like Count Ferdinand Obizzi in Vienna, who took charge of military supply and arms production during the great siege in 1683.[92]

Montecùccoli purveyed military offices to Italian relatives, like the Caprara of Bologna, also related to Ottavio Piccolòmini. All four sons of Niccolò Caprara served in Habsburg armies. Alberto Caprara was Montecùccoli's aide-de-camp before rising to become general. In 1682 he was the Imperial envoy negotiating peace with the sultan in Constantinople. His low opinion of the Turkish soldiery, so inferior to the "genti d'Allemagna" was not entirely borne out by events.[93] Enea Silvio Caprara (whose given name derived from the Piccolòmini family), a senior commander from 1658 to 1697, left a greater legacy.[94] The emperor appointed him commander-in-chief of the Austrian army in Italy in 1692–3, until his trouncing by the French at Marsaglia in 1693. Other Italian generals included the Neapolitan general, Antonio Carafa, who commanded the Italian theatre in 1691, after achieving notoriety in Hungary and Slovakia. Not all enjoyed the longevity required to reach the summit. Two rising stars in the Hungarian campaigns were the Sienese, Enea Silvio Piccolòmini, and Federico Veterani, of Urbino. The first died of plague after leading an army deep into Serbia and Macedonia in 1689. Veterani, described by Spielman as the best and most experienced commander of the theatre, was overwhelmed at Lugos with his whole force in 1695 by the Ottomans, after some maladroit manoeuvring by the theatre commander, Duke Augustus of Saxony.[95] Raimondo's son, Leopoldo Montecùccoli, was on the path of promotion to general when he died in 1698 at the age of 36, and his cousin Ercole Montecùccoli was made cavalry general in 1706, after inheriting Enea Silvio Caprara's regiment in 1701.[96] These were but a few of the most notable Italians whose place was still very significant in Vienna.

John Stoye's recent book devoted to the Bolognese military patrician, Luigi Ferdinando Marsigli, one of the more eclectic minds of his day, charts a pattern borne out in other cases.[97] He went to Constantinople with an Imperial mission in 1679, when he was barely twenty and learned a bit of Turkish out of curiosity. His real gift was for mathematics, which he applied to various fortification projects in Spanish Lombardy before leaving for Vienna in 1683 as an understudy to his co-citizen Enea Silvio Caprara. Captain of a German infantry company, Marsigli was entrusted with scouting, sketching the terrain features and designing field

---

pages deals with the Hungarian theatre primarily, but plumbs the administrative depths of the Habsburg army.

[92] J. Stoye, *The siege of Vienna* (London: 1964), p. 103.

[93] Stoye, *The siege of Vienna*, p. 52.

[94] Mariani & Varanini, *Condottieri italiani in Germania*, p. 241.

[95] Spielman, *Leopold I of Austria*, p. 160.

[96] Sandonnini, *Il generale Raimondo Montecuccoli e la sua famiglia*, p. 169 and p. 194.

[97] J. Stoye, *Marsigli's Europe, 1680–1730: the life and times of Luigi-Ferdinando Marsigli, soldier and virtuoso* (New Haven, Connecticut: 1994).

fortifications along the Raab river frontier. While at this task at the head of some Piedmontese dragoons, the Turks captured him. He 'served' at the siege of Vienna as a slave in the Ottoman camp. After escaping in 1684, his career resumed in the guise of a siege expert and military engineer. The emperor appointed him inspector of the 27 engineer officers in 1687. Marsigli's patrons were not always fellow Italians. His co-citizen Enea Silvio Caprara was always cool to him, but Antonio Carafa helped, as did Count Rodolfo Rabatta. He was on better terms with Ludwig of Baden, Chancellor Stratmann and the duke of Lorraine. Beginning in 1687, the emperor entrusted him with diplomatic tasks; negotiating the Imperial takeover of Transylvania, and being the Emperor's personal 'orator' in Rome, exhorting the Pope to send more money. Marsigli also actively served on campaign, as an artillery expert at the successful siege of Buda in 1686, and again at the siege of Belgrade in 1689. While part of the Italian-led spearhead into Serbia and Macedonia, he charted the topography of the district, and surveyed a military road through the Danube narrows known as the Iron Gate, leading into Bulgaria. His career then stalled for a few years as an Ottoman counter-offensive took back the lands south of the Danube. After curiously serving as 'secretary' to an English embassy in Constantinople, Marsigli finally reached the rank of colonel, promoted with two other Italians, Count Scipio Bagni and Count Giovanni Andrea Corbelli, which supposedly caused a great stir in Vienna. There was indeed an active pro-German lobby led by Marshal Rudiger von Stahremberg, hero of the siege of Vienna, who disliked non-Germans in general, and Italians in particular.[98]

The colonelcy was the first of the lucrative ranks in the Imperial army. While not the outright owner of the regiment, the colonel was the crucial administrative functionary, with virtually absolute authority over officers and men. The duties were primarily administrative and clerical: dealing with the smooth flow of supplies and recruits to the unit, competing with other colonels for resources in Vienna, supervising company accounts, selecting and promoting subordinates, and disciplining the thousand or so officers and ranks in the field. Colonels sold commissions in their unit, or charged fees for advancement when officers were promoted. They were still partly military entrepreneurs, making extra money from recruitment, pocketing the wages of the dead or deserters, and keeping back part of the money due to the troops for equipment. Around 1685, an Austrian colonel made an annual 10,000 to 12,000 florins, compared to the 500 florins received by the average knight of Santo Stefano.

Marsigli seems to have been a passably competent administrator, who supplied his troops adequately and kept them in hand. On the operational front he enjoyed mixed success. Caprara blamed him for leading the army into a swampy morass which permitted the Ottomans to overwhelm the isolated Veterani at Lugos. Notwithstanding that quarrel, the Emperor promoted him to the rank of

---

[98] *Ibid.*, p. 39.

lieutenant-general at the beginning of the Spanish succession conflict in 1702, and assigned him second-in-command of the Austrian fortress of Breisach on the Rhine. When that fortress, weakly held and poorly provisioned, surrendered to the French after a three-week siege in 1703, Marsigli and his superior, Arcos, were made scapegoats. The latter was executed by a court martial. The tribunal discharged Marsigli from the Imperial army with dishonour.

Despite the important role played by Italians and other 'Latin' officers, the rank and file were overwhelmingly Germans. The cheapness of the Austrian troops made them attractive to Spain, over other German mercenaries. Leopold I felt bound by dynastic loyalty to proffer to his beleaguered cousins in Madrid any resources he could spare. In 1663 he sent 6,000 Imperial troops, including the Carafa regiment, to Milan. For Vienna, sending valuable regiments to Spain was a way of ceasing to pay for soldiers without disbanding them, and then recruiting them all over again. In 1664, 7,000 more troops went to Italy and the Low Countries, allowing Spain to transfer its precious few veterans to fight the Portuguese. Service in the Spanish army was still possible for Imperial officers, and promises of pay were attractive, but few seem to have made the switch. After the 1660s, it was rare for Austria to transfer regiments to Spain, save in the framework of a formal alliance against the common enemy France, and even then, only under the command of an Imperial general.[99]

Even after Montecùccoli's great reforms, the Imperial government hired and retired the military establishment as needed. In 1660, after the war with Sweden, only about 20,000 men remained under arms, mostly in over 50 little garrisons along the vast border with the Ottoman Empire, from Croatia to Slovakia.[100] Their numbers were doubled to meet the threat from Turkey, but Leopold subjected the army to massive layoffs in 1668, much to the chagrin of Annibale Gonzaga, who wanted to stabilize effective numbers. The army began to expand again with the onset of the Dutch war in 1672, but the sovereign reduced it with the peace in 1678. When the Turks invaded Hungary again in 1682, there were only 36,000 men under arms, widely scattered in garrisons. In response to this new crisis, which put Vienna itself at risk, Leopold and his ministers formed 18 new regiments, half of them infantry and half cavalry. Austria's army continued to expand after that, and various states in the Holy Roman Empire sent additional contingents under overall Imperial command. By 1700, the emperor could field an army of 116,000 men, and no less than 133,000 in 1710, the year of greatest effort. After 1689 war broke out with France too, so that Austrian troops were required everywhere. In 1710 the bulk of the army was still in Hungary, suppressing a rebellion there. There were also 16,000 men in the Netherlands and northern France, 31,000 in northern Italy, 7,500 in the newly conquered kingdom of Naples, 5,000 in Bohemia and Silesia and 12,000 more in Catalonia. These

---

[99] Bérenger, *Finances et absolutisme autrichien*, vol. 1, p. 121.
[100] *Ibid.*, vol. 2, p. 337.

numbers do not include between 10,000 and 20,000 Serbian and Croatian irregulars settled on the Danubian frontier with the Ottoman Empire.[101]

The Achilles heel of such a huge organization was supply and finance, which was famously archaic and resisted rationalization. Willing reformers, such as Count Rabatta and the archbishop of Vienna, Buonvisi, suggested improvements, but Emperor Leopold disliked changing set procedures. Successive popes helped finance the expansion of effective forces, following its traditional policy of assisting the emperor in his wars against Turkey. In the late sixteenth century, Clement VIII spent about a million and a half *scudi* over several campaigns. During the Thirty Years War, Rome sent an additional three million *gulden* to help the Catholic cause. Alexander VII resumed this financial aid in 1663, by taxing the Italian clergy and the Order of Malta. He sent about 200,000 *scudi* and paid for some additional supplies. During the great war after 1682, this Papal assistance changed in scale. By imposing an extraordinary tax of one per cent on church capital, and by selling church ornaments, the Pope sent 600,000 florins to the emperor in 1683, and 200,000 more to Poland. The Pope also prompted other states to respond. The clergy of Spain sent 200,000 florins, and Tuscany and Genoa sent money and gunpowder at the Pope's command.[102] In 1685 the money for the war came almost entirely from the Church, as Innocent XI ordered the Austrian clergy to sell all the property they had acquired in the previous sixty years, and to give the proceeds to the crown. On Buonvisi's express orders, this money went directly to the field commanders to pay the troops and buy supplies. Bérenger speaks of a tradition by which the Pope sent five million florins to aid the Austrian war effort between 1683 and 1689. Austrian clergy also collaborated by subjecting their income to a five per cent tax. All told, Papal subsidies entailed the transfer of 19.6 million *scudi* between 1542 and 1716.[103]

In the search for money to proceed with this expansion, credit played only a minor role, as the emperor borrowed only 22 million florins in fifteen years, mainly from Italian banking dynasties. For most of the expenditures, however, the emperor's subjects let themselves be taxed. In 1668, a year of major cutbacks, the Imperial budget allocated 1.7 million florins to military expenditure, and 1.4 million on civilian expenditures. After 1672, these sums escalated relentlessly. After 1685 the expenditures reached about 12 million florins, then 16 million in 1693, and finally almost 23 million in 1695, all in a period of deflation. After the peace of 1698, the peacetime military budget was 'only' 14 million florins. What sweetened the pill of enormous tax increases (of 1,000 per cent) was the real prosperity in the Empire occasioned by territorial expansion and, not least, the permanent lifting of the scourge of raiding by Valachs, Tatars and other assorted

---

[101] D. McKay, *Prince Eugene of Savoy* (London: 1977), p. 103ff.

[102] On Papal financial support for Catholic military enterprises, see Wolfgang Reinhard, "Finanza pontificia e stato della Chiesa nel 16 e 17 secolo", in *Finanze e ragion di stato in Italia e in Germania nella prima età moderna*, (Bologna: 1984), pp. 353–87.

[103] Bérenger, *Finances et absolutisme autrichien*, vol. 1, p. 168.

Ottoman light cavalry. Left undisturbed by war for a century, Bohemia and most of Austria gradually recovered from the damage of the Thirty Years War. The taxes that were the fruit of economic recovery were paid primarily by the social élites – the Church, the wealthy nobles and entrepreneurs, who all profited from the expansion of the state. The buoyancy of the economy masked for a while the inefficiencies in the system, the resistance of the provincial estates and assemblies, and the modest tax pressure on the peasantry (who paid substantial feudal rents and services, however). In order to cover military expenditures, Imperial ministers pared back all other categories, and sacrificed civil expenditures with a light heart.[104]

With such a massive effort in the direction of raising money for the war, and since soldiers' pay, arms and horses were so cheap, one might think that Imperial armies were adequately funded. In reality, the opposite was true. As during the Thirty Years War, the military establishment was much larger than the state could pay for. As a result, the Imperial army was prone to operate unpaid, and soldiers and officers together asserted a right to plunder. Italian generals like Carafa and Caprara were not the worst offenders, but their memorable rapacity in Hungary, Transylvania and northern Italy was often counter-productive to the Imperial policy they were sent to apply. Hungary was especially restive. Barker speaks of Vienna's project to 'Bohemianize' the kingdom in the 1670s, referring no doubt to the quadruple process of imposing Catholicism as the sole religion; submitting the Magyar nobility to central Austrian rule; subjecting it to heavy taxes; and finally rewarding faithful German and Italian servants of the emperor with the lands of Magyar rebels.[105] This policy collided repeatedly with the sense of privilege and autonomy of the Magyar nobles, who drew strength and encouragement from the proximity of the Ottoman Empire and from the emissaries of Louis XIV. Only periodic uprisings in Hungary moderated Vienna's ambitions. While Hungarians resented the German presence, they could not expect better from the emperor's Italian servants, beginning with Giorgio Basta in 1605. Montecùccoli developed an intense dislike of Hungarians during his campaigns in the Danubian region after 1661. He felt they were by nature unstable and rebellious, and had to be governed with an iron fist. Austrian rule he thought justified, by the Habsburg claim on the kingdom after 1528; by virtue of its crusading mission against Islam; and by simple right of conquest.[106] As partisans of vigorous Counter-Reformation methods against the Calvinist-leaning Hungarians, Italians could be relied upon to be firm with rebels. Luigi Ferdinando Marsigli, once an understudy to Carafa in Transylvania, subscribed to this same ideal, that when dealing with Hungarian

---

[104] Bérenger, *Finances et absolutisme autrichien*, vol. 2, p. 575ff.

[105] R. J. W. Evans, *The making of the Habsburg monarchy, 1550–1700*, pp. 237–65. See also John A. Mears, "The influence of the Turkish wars in Hungary on the military theories of Count Raimondo Montecuccoli", in *Asia and the West*, pp. 129–45.

[106] Mears, "The influence of the Turkish wars in Hungary on the military theories of Count Raimondo Montecuccoli", in *Asia and the West*, pp. 129–45, at pp. 136–7.

subjects, "repression was nine-tenths of government".[107] Military commanders requisitioned supplies and money there more vigorously than they did in western Europe. Caprara had a bad reputation, but so did German commanders like Heister.

The soldier with the most sinister reputation in the brutal application of Imperial rule was no doubt Antonio Carafa. This Neapolitan fled to Vienna from his native city as an adolescent, *per iuvanilem ferociam*, having assassinated an enemy during a religious procession, in the presence of the viceroy! Entering Imperial service in 1665, he advanced gradually in the ranks of the army, becoming a cavalry colonel in 1672, then general in 1680, and field marshal in 1685, adorned the following year with the title of Count of the Holy Roman Empire. As a general he was cautious and unenterprising, but this was not the career for which he is best remembered. Leopold dispatched him to Slovakia in 1684 to restore his authority there after the siege of Vienna. Wherever Carafa took Austrian soldiers, repression, extortion and looting followed. Having reportedly uncovered an extensive plot at Eperjes (Presov in Slovakia) in 1687, he set about to uproot every trace of it by terrorist methods. His military tribunal tortured witnesses, and executed notables without fair trial or appeal, despite the emperor's instructions to use caution. His biographer, the philosopher Vico reports that he beheaded ten notables, and hanged many commoners after an expeditious court martial, to instil fear.[108] After this success, Leopold sent him to bring Transylvania under Austrian control in a similar fashion. Carafa intended to eliminate the privileges of the Estates there, and impose sweeping absolutism.[109] In 1689, he was appointed military commissioner-general of Hungary, with the task of finding food, money and supplies to keep the Habsburg army in the field. It was the opportunity to make a considerable fortune, since the army immediately enforced his decrees.[110] His excesses there led to a new promotion and a similar task in Italy.

Austria was never able to concentrate all its strength either in the east against Turkey, or in the west against France. The Imperial Council was split between the 'Easterners' calling for the priority of the crusade against Islam, and the 'Westerners' appealing to the emperor to resist the French policy of nibbling away at the borders of the Empire. Italians tended to belong to the former group, encouraging the crusade in Hungary, and they were aided by the emperor's Catholic outlook. While Leopold feared Louis XIV, he long felt that the French menace could wait. Rhenish electors of the Empire at first placed themselves among the clients of the

---

[107] Stoye, *Marsigli's Europe, 1680–1730*, p. 169.
[108] Vico's Latin biography is summarized by another Neapolitan philosopher, Benedetto Croce, in his "Giambattista Vico: scrittore di storie dei suoi tempi", in *Uomini e cose della vecchia Italia* (Bari: 1927), p. 248ff.
[109] Spielman, *Leopold I of Austria*, p. 129.
[110] Stoye, *Marsigli's Europe, 1680–1730*, p. 129.

French king, but the Sun King's policy of 'reunions' pushed most German states into an alliance looking to Vienna for leadership.[111]

The Turkish menace was more immediate, however, and spectacularly underscored by the siege of Vienna in 1683. Leopold's traditional advisers who considered the Turkish threat as an urgent crusade were often ecclesiastics, like the Hungarian Eymeric Sinelli, Cardinal Buonvisi and above all the Capuchin friar, Marco d'Aviano. Not content to be a spiritual adviser to Leopold, d'Aviano travelled with the army on campaign, and became a sort of talisman for it, rousing the troops before battle with impassioned sermons and harangues in Italian.[112] As the victory at Kahlenberg and the conquest of towns in Hungary succeeded each other, Magyars were bound to the Empire more effectively than before. By the 1690s, Hungary began to contribute effectively to the alliance. Enea Silvio Caprara began to turn the kingdom's militia into a more effective force, capable of an adjunct role to the field army.[113] In 1689, flush with victories in Hungary, and unwilling to make peace with the sultan, Leopold was forced into war with France. The 24,000 men left in the east maintained a defensive posture in southern Hungary, while the rest of the Imperial army shifted to the Rhine, to the Low Countries and to northern Italy. The emperor made Caprara supreme commander of Imperial forces in 1689 but for several campaigns he accomplished nothing. After his defeat by the French in Piedmont in 1693 he was transferred to Hungary, before being graciously dismissed in 1696.

The commitment of important Imperial forces to northern Italy in the 1690s marks the beginning of a new 'Austrian' era in Italian history that would continue to the conclusion of unification of the peninsula in 1866. In Vienna's favour was the frustration of Italian élites with the French king's threat to stability in the peninsula, and his objectively pro-Turkish policies in Europe. The seizure of Casale and Strasbourg, on the same day in 1681, demonstrated the offensive strategy of Louis and his advisers. Genoa's bombardment created unease in Italian courts. Louis' pressure on the Pope to concede church revenue to him, by occupying Avignon in 1688, alienated Rome. The growing English and Dutch economic presence was followed by their higher diplomatic profile in Turin, Florence and Genoa, and they encouraged resistance to Louis. The brutal French invasion of the Rhine Palatinate, provoking a general war in Germany just as Vienna was rolling back the Turks in the Balkans, made the Sun King look like a bad Catholic, and a bad Christian.[114]

All these developments undermined the political advantages that Mazarin had acquired for France in Italy by 1660. Louis XIV was abandoned by his

---

[111] Bérenger, *Finances et absolutisme autrichien*, p. 101ff.

[112] Spielman, *Leopold I of Austria*, p. 118.

[113] *Ibid.*, p. 119.

[114] Meuvret, "Louis XIV et l'Italie", *XVIIe siècle*, 1960, pp. 84–102. For the European context of the 1680s, see also C. Boutant, *L'Europe au grand tournant des années 1680: la succession palatine* (Paris: 1985).

Piedmontese satellite, Victor Amadeus II, who preferred to take his chances with the League of Augsburg formed in 1686 to stop French aggression. The sole French strongpoints in the theatre were the Alpine fortress of Pinerolo in Piedmont, and Casale Monferrato isolated in Mantuan territory. The emperor used the presence of his army in the theatre to reassert his theoretical Caesarean rights and his suzerainty over the north Italian states. The Imperial military commissioner he entrusted to coerce Italian states to pay 'contributions' was Count Antonio Carafa, whose notoriety for his high-handedness in Hungary preceded him. In 1691, the emperor had an irresistible argument in his favour; the presence of a large and turbulent army that needed winter quarters and regular provisioning. Italian states now paid 'contributions' as far as they were in the path of the troops. The maintenance of large standing armies made the seizure of neutral territories for supply purposes a strategic imperative, particularly since the enemy could be expected to act similarly.[115] Mantua, practically a French ally, paid the huge sum of 500,000 *scudi*; Parma paid 260,000 *scudi*, plus free passage and feeding of the troops. Genova contributed 180,000 *scudi*, and Lucca, with its small population, paid 103,000 *scudi*. Thereafter, Vienna referred to these states – Parma, Modena, Mantua, Tuscany, Lucca and Genoa – as its 'vassals'. Instead of a series of military alliances, where the king of Spain courted and feted Italian princes, and gave them command over Spanish armies, the north Italian states were now summoned to give money and provisions, and they had no influence over military decisions. These contributions were paid only to the extent that Austrian military presence could not be resisted. Tuscany therefore paid about 115,000 *scudi* in 1692 and 1693, but only 50,000 in 1695, and 123,000 in 1696; its payments then ceased.

Count Carafa left a profound impression on the princes and diplomats with whom he was to 'negotiate'. For one thing, his instructions pointedly emphasized matters of protocol. In every situation, in army camps, on battlefields and anywhere else, he was to have precedence over Spain, treating Milan, where Carafa had his headquarters, as a simple Imperial fief. If the governor of Milan would not accede to this situation, he was to keep camp apart from them, even on campaign. It was preferable to lose a battle, than to concede precedence to vassals. Carafa was to insist absolutely that the place of honour be reserved for him, over the governor of Milan, the duke of Savoy, the grand duke of Tuscany, or any other prince. Critics pointed out that this precedence went to his head, since he was *huomo superbissimo*, treating the duke of Savoy with haughtiness even in Turin.[116] Carafa was thought to have only two principles of conduct: that always, and everywhere, he was to be the emperor's faithful watchdog; and second, to consider it unforgivable not to carry out the emperor's instructions to the letter no matter what the nature of the task. He reportedly had a more appealing 'Neapolitan' side where he could descend to the level of his interlocutors with fulsome pleasant-

---

[115] F. Szabo, *Kaunitz and enlightened absolutism, 1753–1780* (Cambridge: 1994), p. 275.
[116] Pugliese, *Le prime strette dell' Austria in Italia*, p. 165.

ries, courtesy and compliments, but this was to lull them into further concessions.[117]

The Tuscan plenipotentiary in Milan, Angeli, recorded the tenor of some of these discussions. The Imperial commander told him how the emperor had entrusted him with troops to lead into Italy, furnished them with uniforms, horses and arms, and sent him on his way, saying *Buon viaggio, Carafa!*. This meant that it was the field marshal's responsibility for their maintenance, and since he was not ready to pay it from his pocket, the Italian princes would have to find the money themselves. In the full regalia of the knights of Malta, topped by an enormous wig, Louis quatorze-style, the general then invited the Tuscan to put himself in his shoes, before resorting to the dire threat, *Necessità non ha legge!*.[118] Faced with this attitude, and masses of hungry soldiers, most princes paid. When the duke of Parma refused, an army of 4,000 horse descended upon the duchy and extracted much more than Carafa had demanded. Genoa escaped with less, but only because it mobilized its army in the border passes and threatened to fight.[119] Excessive intransigence led to Carafa's recall, and he was replaced by Caprara, who was not much more flexible. Italian states continued to pay as long as they were in harm's way. During the War of the Spanish Succession, the grand duchy paid nothing for as long as the Bourbons were in the ascendancy. After the Austro-Piedmontese victory of 1706 at Turin, however, the Medici paid a colossal 465,000 *scudi* in 1707, and between 100,000 and 200,000 *scudi* in each of the four subsequent years.[120] In this way, the Italian states paid over two million *scudi* between 1707 and 1713. Whenever the emperor sent contingents of troops into the peninsula, as in 1718 for example, he forced the Italian principalities to contribute significant sums for their maintenance on the pretext of Imperial rights.[121] Only Piedmont refused utterly to comply, since it disposed of significant military resources of its own.[122]

Imperial agents like Caprara and Carafa were replaced after 1693 by the more urbane Prince Eugene of Savoy, a young French-speaking aristocrat whose parents were Italians at the court of France. His elder brother, Louis-Jules, commanded a regiment of Piedmontese dragoons in Imperial service in Hungary, where he was killed in a skirmish with some Tatars in 1683. Louis XIV and Louvois rebuffed Eugene when he tried to buy a regiment in the French army, so he went to Vienna instead as a volunteer. Leopold considered him an Italian, and Eugene quickly attached himself to the Italian lobby, headed by the Spanish

---

[117] F. Niccolini, "Cosimo III de'Medici e Antonio Carafa", *Archivio Storico Italiano*, 1938, pp. 69–91 and pp. 180–215.

[118] F. Niccolini, "Cosimo III de'Medici e Antonio Carafa", *Archivio Storico Italiano*, 1938, pp. 180–215.

[119] *Ibid.*, pp. 69–91 and pp. 180–215.

[120] Waquet, *Le grand-duché de Toscane sous les derniers Médicis*, p. 89ff.

[121] *Ibid.*, p. 89ff.

[122] Pugliese, *Le prime strette dell' Austria in Italia*, p. 169.

ambassador Carlo Emanuele d'Este, marchese di Borgomanero.[123] By December 1683 he was a colonel of dragoons. He also accepted the revenue of two Piedmontese abbeys offered by his uncle, Duke Victor Amadeus II, to help him maintain his princely rank in the army. His career blossomed during the campaigns of Hungary against the Ottomans. Despite his sumptuous train he invested great sums in the mounting and equipment of his regiment and acquired the reputation of a strict disciplinarian and a good organizer. Leopold made him commander-in-chief of Imperial troops in Piedmont in 1693, and promoted him to the rank of field marshal, but relegated Italy to the back burner for the duration of the war. He was given command of the Italian theatre again in 1701 with an important field army. Having invaded Mantua and levied important contributions on it, Eugene was then blocked by a French general with talents equal to his own, the duc de Vendôme. Even with the defection of Piedmont to the Austrian alliance in 1703, Eugene made no progress.[124]

In 1706, Eugene received reinforcements and returned to Italy to prevent the fall of Turin and the elimination of Austria's Piedmontese ally. His victory, with Victor Amadeus II, over the French army under the walls of the city was the crucial event in Italian history during the eighteenth century. The Spanish regime in Lombardy collapsed when the French troops disappeared over the Alps. Simultaneously, Eugene liberated from Bourbon occupation those principalities that had tied their destinies to Vienna, and bound them more firmly to the House of Austria. Modena, for example, moved gradually from the French sphere of influence to the Austrian one: from 1673 when Maria Beatrice, daughter of the duke, married James, future king of England and solid French client, to 1695 when the duke married a close relative of the empress.[125] The threat to deprive the Este dynasty of its duchy produced a rapid reorientation in Vienna's favour. Modena's duke, Rinaldo I, wed a daughter of the duke of Brunswick in 1695, placing himself thereby in the Imperial camp. His sister-in-law Amalia d'Este wed the future Emperor Joseph in 1699, further tightening these bonds. When war broke out in the Po valley in 1701, the duke transferred his fortress of Brescello to an Imperial garrison, and withdrew his court to the Papal States to await developments. Modena was occupied by a high-living, spendthrift, but friendly and disciplined French garrison until after the battle of Turin. Duke Rinaldo then

---

[123] On the role of Carlo d'Este, see Thomas M. Barker, *Double eagle and crescent: Vienna's second Turkish siege and its historical setting* (Albany, New York: 1967), pp. 5, 79, 207. See also Henrich, "Italian Military Élites in the Service of the Spanish and Austrian Habsburgs, 1560–1700" (MA thesis, Dathousie University, Carada: 1995), pp. 212–13.

[124] For a biography of Prince Eugene, see Derek McKay, *Prince Eugene of Savoy* (London: 1977).

[125] Amorth, *Modena capitale*, p. 163. See also Riccardo Pacciani, "Temi e strutture narrative dei festeggiamenti nuziali estensi a Modena nel Seicento", in *Barocco romano e barocco italiano: il teatro, l'effimero, l'allegoria*, M. Fagiolo & M.-L. Madonna (eds) (Rome: 1985), pp. 204–216, at p. 214.

returned in the baggage of the comparatively ill-behaved German troops.[126] In 1707, an Austrian army invaded the Papal states and went on to conquer the kingdom of Naples.

Imperial ambassadors in Rome had already made known their intentions to recover their master's 'prerogatives', and to confine the Pope to the ecclesiastical sphere, in the 1690s.[127] In 1706 the new emperor, Joseph I, declared unilaterally that Parma, Ferrara and Comacchio were Imperial, rather than Papal, fiefs and proceeded to quarter troops on them.[128] Austrian troops had been quartered on Ferrarese territory since the beginning of hostilities, ignoring Pope Clement XI's protests that heretic Danes and Brandenburgers were plundering shrines and making demands upon monasteries. In 1704, he threatened both French and Austrian generals with excommunication, with no effect. Angered by Prince Eugene's levies, Clement excommunicated him in August 1707. In response, the prince, encouraged by the dukes of Savoy and of Modena, mounted a formal military occupation of Comacchio and its district in May 1708, and proceeded to detach it from the Papal States. Only then did the Pope order his fortresses to be put into a state of defence, and recruit soldiers for a field army, to be raised from nothing. The papal commander, Luigi Ferdinando Marsigli, laboured to build a paper army of great strength. In September, when Marshal Daun invaded the Papal states and marched through Emilia and Romagna, Marsigli's raw levies wisely kept out of the way. The Imperial army continued its leisurely promenade towards central Italy until the Pope capitulated in January 1709. Austria continued to levy 'contributions'.[129]

After 1711, the new emperor, Charles VI, unsuccessful candidate to the Spanish throne, reigned over an Empire in which about a third of his subjects were ethnic Italians. Vienna acquired Lombardy, Mantua, Naples and Sardinia by the treaty of Utrecht. Charles' closest advisers were Spaniards and Italians who followed him from Barcelona and Madrid, and he kept a Spanish council in Vienna peopled largely by these exiles. In the army, Prince Eugene was the most decisive voice. Italians had an opportunity they could seize in the Holy Roman Empire. Paradoxically, however, we see the rather abrupt decline of positions open to aristocrats from Italy in the Spanish service, and the gradual marginalization of them in the Imperial service too. This partly reflects a demilitarization of Italy itself. What also transpired simultaneously, was a militarization of Germany under the influence of victories in Hungary, and the repeated aggression of Louis XIV. Both events served to maintain large numbers of troops in

---

[126] Amorth, *Modena capitale*, p. 163. See also by Luigi Simeoni, *L'assorbimento austriaco del ducato estense*, p. 5ff.

[127] Von Pastor, *The history of the popes from the close of the Middle Ages, vol. XXXII* (London: 1957), pp. 662–9.

[128] Von Pastor, *The history of the popes, vol. XXXIII*, p. 21.

[129] Von Pastor, *The history of the popes, vol. XXXIII*, pp. 55–64. See also Stoye, *Marsigli's Europe, 1680–1730*, pp. 271–5.

being. It is striking to note the difference in the degree of militarization of the two countries towards the end of the seventeenth century. Germans were fighting not only in the armies of the emperor, where they constituted the great majority of the rank and file, but also for Spain, for Holland, and for Venice in the Aegean. German soldiers comprised a large segment of the enormous French army, and similarly of the little garrison armies of the Italian states.[130] They fought as well for the kings of Denmark and Sweden, who had possessions in northern Germany, and as well in Poland and Russia.

Troops in the Empire had been financed through the system of regional 'circles' (the fiscal subdivisions of the Empire, with larger states alongside smaller ones) since the late sixteenth century, where the regional states and the circle directors used the tax levy powers accorded by the emperors to treat the smaller unarmed states as they pleased. Thus there was an incentive for the smaller states to see to their own defence and create their own military forces and deprive outsiders of their pretext for imposing contributions. They could then 'rent' these troops to other states to help defray their cost. A case of a small state following this path would be the county of Lippe in Westphalia. The decisive moment came in 1698 when the count sought to increase the levies in peacetime to maintain a standing force. The count, Friedrich Adolf, succeeded in maintaining about a battalion of soldiers, which was then integrated into the federal military system at the disposal of the emperor in Vienna.[131] Other German regional states evolved in a similar fashion. If they did not have their own army, Imperial commanders tended to treat them in cavalier fashion, wintering their troops on them, and exacting contributions from them arbitrarily. Larger states preferred to provide their own troops, and force the small statelets around them to contribute to their upkeep. This development did not occur overnight, nor did it take place everywhere, but rather depended upon the desire of particular princes to enhance their 'glory' with the army as an instrument of prestige and of power.

In Bavaria the permanent mercenary army dates from 1657, but it remained very small until Elector Max Emmanuel (1679–1726) raised 8,000 men to aid the emperor against the Turks in 1683. Bavarian noblemen were disinclined to serve in this army, the senior posts in which were often conferred on Frenchmen and Italians.[132] In Catholic Bavaria, as in the Austrian Empire, the Church was a more attractive source of employment for the upper class. In Protestant Germany, the degree of militarization of the aristocracy seems to have been much higher. The Turkish war was also decisive in Saxony, for which Elector Johann Georg raised 20,000 men. The sums the Saxon Estates accorded for military expenditures sextupled between 1661 and 1681 since the delegates saw military offices as

---

[130] See for example the Tuscan guards, in F. Duffo, *Florence au XVIIe siècle, sous les Médicis (1673)* (Paris: 1934), p. 41.

[131] G. Benecke, *Society and politics in Germany, 1500–1750* (Toronto: 1974), p. 326–31.

[132] F. Carsten, *Princes and parliaments in Germany, from the fifteenth to the eighteenth century* (Oxford: 1959), pp. 399–421.

suitable employment for young nobles. Saxony maintained an army of 30,000 men for many years, because the Turkish War was followed immediately by the War of the League of Augsburg, and the Great Northern War, which lasted until 1720.[133] Württemberg's regent, Friedrich Karl, set himself up during the Dutch war as a military enterpriser in the service of the emperor, persuading the circle of Swabia to help maintain what were his personal regiments. This ended with the peace with France after 1677. Some of these forces were henceforth maintained as a standing army of the duchy, and the others rented to Venice. The regent rented 4,500 troops to the republic, but he could recall them. In 1688, when Württemberg was drawn into war against France, it still had no army. There were however thousands of Württembergers fighting for Venice, several thousand recruited for Holland, and more in the contingent of the circle of Swabia in Hungary. The regent mobilized more soldiers when France invaded the duchy in 1691. Then in May 1691, Karl Friedrich announced the conversion of the territorial militia into a standing army, under his own command, and instituted compulsory conscription.[134] The critical moment for Württemberg, as for Lippe, came in 1698 when the war ended with France and Turkey.

The duke decided that although a permanent army of 3,000 troops (about one per cent of the population) would be but little defence against France, an army was a necessary component of his *gloire*. Duke Eberhard Ludwig, no Francophile, imitated Louis XIV's monarchy. Power focused on the person of the prince in his palace, supported by a permanent army. An army of his own made it possible for the duke to dispense with the Estates, hold his rank with the chief vassals of the emperor, and free the duchy from being a quartering ground for Imperial soldiers. The Württemberg army was relatively important, given the limited population of the state, and comparable to Modena in Italy: 6,000 troops after the war of the Spanish Succession; 12,000 in 1735, and 10,000 in 1763. These German states, therefore, had troops to rent and to serve the emperor. Their standing armies responded to complex issues in the emergence of states in central Europe and in the Imperial system. Italy, on the other hand, was peripheral to the system, and for the most part was a reluctant partner in the process. This would have dramatic consequences in the eighteenth century.

---

[133] *Ibid.* pp. 239–47.
[134] Vann, *The making of a state: Württemberg, 1593–1793*, p. 156.

Chapter 6
Profiles and careers

Lessons from the encyclopedias

My narrative until now has dwelt primarily upon the colonels and generals, the most visible stars in the constellation of Italian officers. Before going further, it is time to go beyond the biographical information and make some generalizations about the social group in our narrative. Who were they? Where did they come from? Where did they choose to fight, and when? The answers to these questions should reveal some fundamental traits of Italian and European politics of the era. Three Fascist biographical encyclopedias help elucidate those problems. The works were probably designed to be complementary in a rough sort of way. Not only did their compilers format the entries identically but, among more than 4,100 entries, they duplicate no more than a few score. They make the same basic assumptions as to the identity of 'Italians' in the seventeenth century: the entries include a few Savoyards who moved in court circles in Turin and some Croatian notables living in the Italian-speaking cities along the eastern Adriatic; they integrate the Venetian families established in Crete for generations; and they count Corsicans as Italians without hesitation. The compilers also tend to see 1700 as their cut-off point, although many Maggiorotti engineers belong to the eighteenth century, and a handful of Argegni's cases extend into the period after the Spanish succession.

Some shortcomings of the source affect its reliability. Both compilers and typesetters working from manuscripts introduced many mistakes. The multitude of these – mistaking Spanish for Imperial service, for example, or inverting a date – makes me doubt that the compilers were professional historians. Compensating for the many lacunae posed another challenge, particularly regarding dates of activity and place of origin. Both can often be found in the comprehensive lists of the knights of Santo Stefano and of Malta, published since the seventeenth century. Besides people of uncertain attribution, several hundred individuals remain without identified place of origin. Not by chance they served primarily in Venetian service. I doubt whether most of them were nobles. Deriving a sense of the military proclivities for each region requires a clear idea of the geographical distribution of nobles. I know of no study that quantifies nobles by residence, over the entire Italian area. Surely such distribution would have been unequal. In the kingdom of Naples, some writers suggest that most of the aristocracy, and all of the best families, resided in Naples itself after the late sixteenth century.[1] Considerable differences in the distribution of noble warriors may simply reflect distribution of nobles *per se*. It is instructive to compare the lists of noble families in northern and central Italian mid-sized cities where hundreds of houses existed, to Puglian communities of similar dimensions studied by AngelAntonio Spagnoletti, where there were at best a few dozen.[2] Nevertheless, the data from the enlistment rolls of the knights of Malta, and of the awards of entry into the Spanish military orders corroborates the overwhelming weight of Naples in the total number of candidates from the kingdom.

In short, most military officers mentioned in the encyclopedias appear to have been urban nobles of medieval pedigree (but not necessarily ancient urban residence), whose families were prominent in local government. It is not always easy to determine residency. While aristocrats generally possessed a conspicuous *palazzo* in a good neighborhood in the city that served as the symbolic seat of their house, living expenses were much lower on rural estates and in country towns, where they may have spent much or most of their time. It is impossible to make firm distinctions here since, even in the same family, urban and rural residency might differ for each individual, or for the same individual over the course of their lifetime. Italian nobles were anchored to their cities, nevertheless, in a multitude of symbolic, economic and political ways, and people thought of urban history through the actions of the noble dynasties that resided there.

The military nobles hailed, for the most part, from Italy of the medieval communes. This term designates a broad swath of towns autonomous since the twelfth century, from eastern Piedmont, to the Veneto, stretching into Tuscany, Umbria and the Marches and then becoming rarer as one progressed further south. Of the 3,462 individuals for which we have certain or probable place of origin, the great majority – 84 per cent – came from the north and centre of the country. Of the remainder, 10 per cent came from the kingdom of Naples, 2.7 per cent from Sicily, and a mere 0.3 per cent from Sardinia. Even in southern Italy, there is enormous disparity from one region to another, and a clear domi-

---

[1] Franco Valsecchi, *L'Italia nel seicento e nel settecento: società e costume* (Turin: 1967), p. 196, fixes the number of noble families living in Naples in the year 1600 at 800. On the noble way of life in Naples, see the article by Gerard Labrot, "Le comportement collectif de l'aristocratie de Naples à l'époque moderne", *Revue Historique*, 1977, pp. 45–71.

[2] Examples of cities rich in noble families are Piacenza and Siena. For the first, see E. Nasalli Rocca, "Il patriziato piacentino nell' età del principato", in *Studi di paleografia, diplomatica, storia e araldica in onore di Cesare Manaresi* (Milan: 1953), pp. 225–57. For Siena, see G. Baker, "Nobiltà in declino: il caso di Siena sotto i Medici e gli Asburgo-Lorena", *Rivista Storica Italiana*, 1972, pp. 584–616. In contrast, see the appendix to the book by Angel Antonio Spagnoletti, *L'incostanza delle umane cose: il patriziato di Terra di Bari tra egemonia e crisi, XVI–XVIII secolo* (Bari: 1981), pp. 117–25.

nance of the urbanized regions over the rural hinterland. About 90 per cent of those from the kingdom of Naples came from the capital city, and a handful of small towns in Campania province, like Amalfi, Salerno, Nola and Capua. Officers from the Abruzzi and Puglia account for only half of one per cent each of the total Italian sample; Calabria barely provides one tenth of one per cent, and Basilicata half that, with only two identified individuals. The Sicilian warriors similarly were urban in origin, from the two rival 'capitals' of the island kingdom, Palermo and Messina, sharing three-quarters of the island's contingent between them.

The contrast is markedly north/south even in central Italy too. Although the Papal states provide 14.4 per cent of the sample, the southernmost districts contribute the fewest examples. Like Naples in the Mezzogiorno, Rome, the great capital, attracted aristocrats like a magnet. Rome and Latium together provide 4.7 per cent of the total, but Latium without Rome contributes only 0.9 per cent. Umbria musters less than 2 per cent of the total Italian sample, from all of its medieval communes. Across the Apennines, however, the Marches contributed 3.4 per cent, and the Romagna with the district around Bologna belonging to the Papal States furnished 4.3 per cent. The duchy of Urbino was held to be a reservoir of soldiers for Venice, and then Spain at the end of the sixteenth century. Its presence seems to wane after the extinction of its ruling dynasty and its devolution to the Papal States in 1631; Urbino, Pèsaro and Gubbio have only a modest place, perhaps understated in the sample.[3]

The Italy of the warrior nobility deployed north from Siena in Tuscany, to Emilia, southern Lombardy and into the Veneto. The grand duchy of Tuscany, with only half the population of the Papal States, furnished a roughly equal number of military nobles, 13.3 per cent of the whole. They were concentrated in the two capital cities, Florence of the *Stato Vecchio* with 217 identified officers, and the much smaller city of Siena, with 100. Judging from the encyclopedias alone, Siena figures among the most 'militarized' cities in the country, quite out of proportion to the other cities of the duchy like Pistoia, Arezzo and Pisa. Siena's hinterland contributed a clutch of warriors too, from small towns like Montalcino and Castel del Piano. The mercantile republic of Lucca provided only 0.4 per cent of the whole, in contrast. North of Tuscany, the military contribution of the Po duchies appears quite substantial, where the duchies of Parma, Modena and Mantua account for 8.3 per cent of the whole. Here too, the court cities, Mantua, Piacenza, Parma and Modena account for 90 per cent of those officers. The Ligurian coast and Corsica furnished a respectable 7.3 per cent, given their small populations. Most of the Ligurian candidates were Genoese patricians, so active in galley service for Spain. Corsican officers fought in many armies, and there was always work for them, even if their nobility was not always assured, and they were

---

[3] J. Dennistoun, *Memoirs of the dukes of Urbino*, 3 vols (London: 1902), vol. 3, p. 133. The author cites a local chronicler who indicates 50 volunteers from Gubbio, including 30 officers, present at Lepanto in 1571. None of them figures in the encyclopedias.

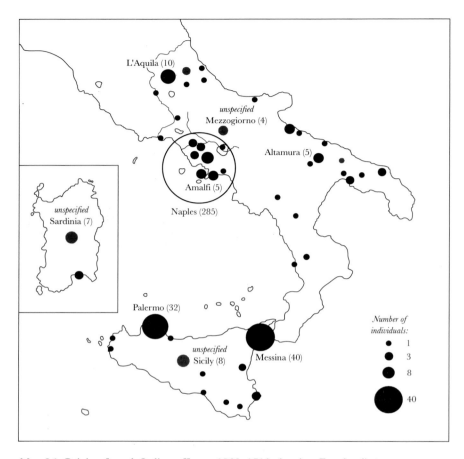

Map 6.1 Origin of south Italian officers, 1560–1710 *(based on Encyclopedias)*

inclined by geography and political isolation to seek their fortune abroad. The Spanish duchy of Milan, and its dependencies in the Monferrato and the Valtellina, also belonged to Italy of the warriors. Milan's patriciate provided only about half the Lombard candidates. A surprisingly high proportion came from Alessandria which, if one allows for its modest population of barely 10,000 inhabitants, must rival Siena as a nursery of military careers. Other cities of the Lombard region, like Pavìa, Novara, Lodi, Tortona, Como and Cremona, contribute only a few careers apiece. The whole territory contributes 9.5 per cent of the total cases.

The most fertile soil for military careers was not Piedmont, but rather Venice, which was the most resolutely commercial state in Italy. Venice was under extraordinary pressure from the Turks after 1645, yet it did not relinquish its empire without an epic fight, and appeared to have the upper hand until the

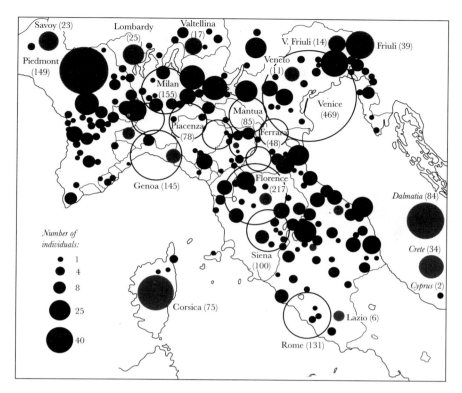

Map 6.2 Origin of north Italian officers, 1560–1710 *(based on Encyclopedias)*

collapse during the summer of 1715. The encyclopedias indicate no fewer than 810 officers originating from Venice and its empire, and over half of those were inhabitants of the capital. The Venetian houses established in Crete provide one per cent of all the encyclopedia entries, and the Dalmatian officers account for 2.4 per cent. The lagoon capital city and its Italian hinterland still account for 20 per cent of all the careers in the encyclopedias. There were significant numbers of them in the largest cities such as Bergamo, Brescia and Verona, and other concentrations in Udine and along the Friulian frontier. In comparison with Venice, the contribution of Piedmont looks surprisingly modest. The Piedmontese distribution is unusual for Italy in that the nobility of the capital does not appear to dominate the numbers at all. Turin was the origin of less than one per cent of all the Italian military careers, and the five largest cities of the duchy – Mondovì, Asti, Chieri, Vercelli and Nice – together account for another one per cent. Instead, the bulk of the careers spring from fiefs and small towns scattered throughout the region. Piedmont constituted a periphery of the Italian world of the cities until the eighteenth century, and the place of the rural-based nobility was still considerable.

Finally, a sprinkling of Italian military nobles originated beyond the confines of 'Italian' states in the territories belonging to the Austrian Habsburgs. Two-thirds of them lived along the Friulian marches with Venice, and a third of them descended from the Tirolean Alps in and around Trento, comprising 2.3 per cent of all careers.

If the great majority of the nobles were urban-based, many feudal dynasties appeared prominent before 1650 – the Saluzzo, Gattinara, and Medici di Melignano in Lombardy and Piedmont, the Malaspina and Pallavicini in the northern Apennines, the Montauto and Bourbon del Monte on the Tuscan and Umbrian confines, and the Sforza di Santa Fiore, Orsini and Colonna in the Roman Campagna. It is doubtful that these lords were primarily country-dwellers.[4] True power was political power, and in the seventeenth century this was exercised from the cities and from the princely courts. As for the fief-holding urban nobility of Naples, it is unclear whether they lived in their urban *palazzo*, even after the progressive urbanization of the aristocracy in the sixteenth century provided virtually every family with a Neapolitan address.

This impression of the dominance of capital and court cities is reinforced if one isolates the twenty cities providing the most careers. Venice, with 469 identified officers, leads the group, since its patricians enjoyed a monopoly over the major political offices of the republic, and theoretically held sway over officers' positions in the navy. Besides functions that were exclusively martial, patricians were appointed proveditors to oversee military operations and supply, which frequently put them into harm's way. The six other cities with a hundred careers or more were all capitals – Naples, Florence, Milan, Genoa, Rome and Siena – although the degree of effective autonomy varied considerably from one to another. In the second cohort of seven cities with at least forty careers each, only one never held administrative sway over a substantial territory: Mantua, Piacenza, Parma, Ferrara and Modena were all seats of important courts at one time or another. Ferrara and Messina retained substantial administrative autonomy, and the latter pretended to be the political capital of Sicily, to spite Palermo. Only Alessandria could never claim such a role. Even in the last cohort of six cities with more than twenty-nine careers apiece, two were authentic capital cities, Palermo and Turin; Bologna retained considerable autonomy in relation to Rome; while Brescia, Bergamo and Udine were district administrative seats of the Venetian republic.

---

[4] For specific cases, see C. Argegni, *Condottieri, capitani, tribuni* (Rome: 1936), vol. 2, p. 35, for Vespasiano Gonzaga; pp. 119–28, for Malaspina di Lunigiana; pp. 133–68, for Malatesta di Romagna; pp. 354–75, for Orsini di Lazio; p. 377, for Ottonelli di Frignano; pp. 439–40, for Pio di Carpi; and vol. 3, pp. 77–108, for Saluzzo di Piemonte. See also Valori, *Condottieri e generali del Seicento*, pp. 211–13, for Malaspina; pp. 181–2, for Guasco di Gavi; and p. 341, for San Giorgio di Monferrato. There are numerous other examples.

While these nobles may have come from families represented in the government of the state, and were familiars of their princes, it does not follow that they served their prince foremost. There seems to have been a process by which local nobles eventually looked to their princes for employment; that is, that the small territorial garrisons and court pageantry satisfied the ambitions of the local nobilities. That development, however, was an aspect of the demilitarization process of smaller states not likely to wage war. Early modern armies were in no way 'national', since they were temporary formations and as such ephemeral. Nobles who made a career of war, or who wished to take part in great events for just a few years, were likely to seek out whatever occasions gave them the most favourable possibility of advancement. This can be inferred from the encyclopedia entries.

The most popular service before 1650 was no doubt for the Catholic king. 'Spanish' armies were polyglot hosts drawing men from across Europe, and outside the Mediterranean theatre the Italians were rarely more than a quarter or a fifth of the whole. It is worth underlining the fact that the king of Spain was the only monarch who attracted southern Italians, Sicilians and Sardinians into military careers, apart from a few Neapolitan noblemen whose horizons were wider. Interestingly, Italian officers before 1610 were more likely than not subjects of other princes; only 47 per cent, of those for whom I can trace the origin, came from Lombardy, Naples or Sicily. Almost a fifth of the Italian officers in the Spanish army came from the Papal States, and another 15 per cent came from the Po valley principalities. Finally, a sprinkling of Tuscan and Venetian subjects from Florence and Siena, Friuli and the eastern Lombard cities like Bergamo and Brescia made up the rest. This proclivity remains valid into the seventeenth century too. While the proportion of subjects of the king of Spain rose to 60 per cent of the Italians, the absolute number of candidates increased too. This left plenty of room for others. Central Italians from Tuscany and the Papal States made up most of the remainder. Even after the collapse of Spanish power during the reign of Charles II (1665–1700), Italians who were not subjects of the king of Spain comprised about a third of the Italian officers in his armies, with the Papal States and Parma proving the most loyal area. There is at least one caveat to this schema, in that subjects of 'foreign' governments held fiefs in Spanish territories in Italy and possibly beyond. The Genoese in particular were prominent feudatories in the Apennine borderlands and in the kingdom of Naples, although they resided in their native city.

Cross-border recruitment would be easiest to understand for the Papal army, for the elected sovereign immediately showered manna, in the form of patronage, on his relatives and friends from his native city. The intricacies of international politics made it rare for a Spanish subject to be elected pontiff. Prelates preferred to elect subjects of 'neutral' Italian princes, without cumbersome ties to Spain, France or the Empire. Thus, there was a heavy preponderance of prelates from Tuscany and the Papal States in the College of Cardinals, and this is reflected in

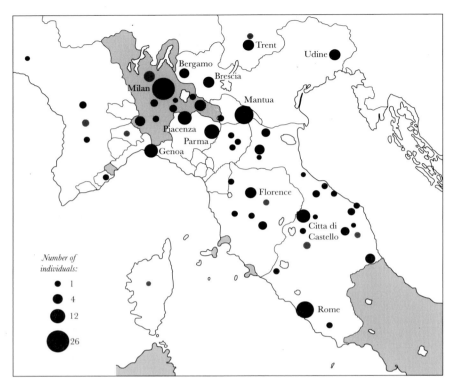

Map 6.3 Origin of Italian officers in Spanish service, 1560–1610 (northern and central Italy) *(based on Encyclopedias)*

the recruitment of military officers too.[5] Before 1610, about 72 per cent of the officers came from the Papal States, including the 'fief' principalities of Urbino and Ferrara, while 13 per cent came from Spanish territories of north and south Italy. After 1592, however, the election of a series of popes from Tuscany, or with deep roots in the grand duchy bolstered their proportion to 13 per cent during the first half of the seventeenth century. After 1650, the election of two Tuscan popes with a famished clientele – the Chigi of Siena and the Rospigliosi of Pistoia – increased the Tuscan proportion to 25 per cent, which, added to the 64 per cent from the Papal States, comprised nine-tenths of the officer corps of Italian origin. The encyclopedia data are corroborated nicely by the list of Italian officers in Papal service in 1667, exploited by Georg Lutz. The unrestrained preference of Alexander VII for his Sienese compatriots meant that almost 15 per cent of Papal officers hailed from that single, relatively minor town. Otherwise, Papal recruit-

---

[5] Renata Ago, *Carriera e clientela nella Roma barocca* (Rome: 1990), pp. 22–5, and in particular the table on p. 24.

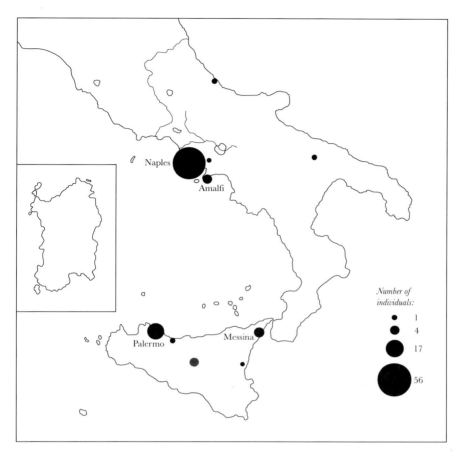

Map 6.4 Origin of Italian officers in Spanish service, 1560–1610 (southern Italy) *(based on Encyclopedias)*

ment across the Papal States, Tuscany and the central Po valley is quite clearly reflected.[6]

In two 'militarized' Italian states, the proportion of the natives increased over the seventeenth century. For Venice before 1610, roughly two-thirds of the officers of Italian origin came from the empire, including Veneto-Cretans and some nobles of Croatian extraction. The *Serenissima* had no qualms about appointing Greek, Croat and Uskok subjects to its officer corps, usually at the head of 'ethnic' irregular units. Most of the rest were drawn from the Papal territories (17

---

[6] G. Lutz, "L'esercito pontificio nel 1677: camera apostolica, bilancio militare dello stato della Chiesa e nepotismo nel primo evo moderno", in *Miscellanea in onore di monsignor Martino Giusti, prefetto dell'Archivio segreto Vaticano* (Vatican City: 1978) II, pp. 33–95.

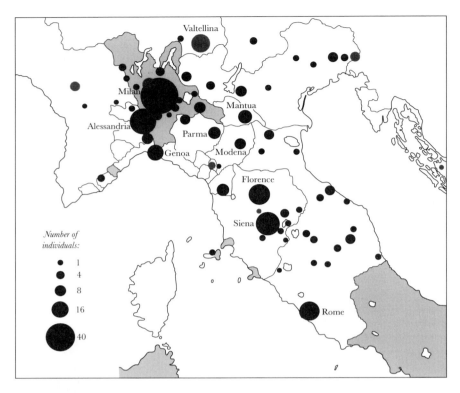

Map 6.5 Origin of Italian officers in Spanish service, 1610–60 (northern and central Italy) *(based on Encyclopedias)*

per cent) and the Po valley duchies (11 per cent), which looked eastward to the Adriatic shore. The gradual mobilization of the republic after 1614, and its involvement in wars both in Italy and in the Aegean placed new emphasis on the martial spirit of the patrician class. Venetian subjects comprised 72 per cent of the officers of Italian origin, with the Pope's subjects and a strong contingent of Corsican captains, constituting 8 per cent each, making up most of the remainder. After 1660, Venetian subjects made up almost four-fifths of the Italian officers, with the remainder coming from across north-central Italy and Corsica. For Corsicans, Venetian service held many rewards, since they commonly attained higher ranks there than they did in the Genoese army, and it was possible to retire into the upper reaches of 'civil society' in the Terraferma.

Similarly, in Piedmont, the gradual mobilization of the state in response to military crisis drew increasingly upon the prince's subjects. Before 1600, when Piedmont was a gadfly in an anti-French coalition, Piedmontese and Savoyards comprised about 37 per cent of the 'Italian' officers in the army, with no regional group dominating the remainder. The duke possessed a solid clientèle in cities like

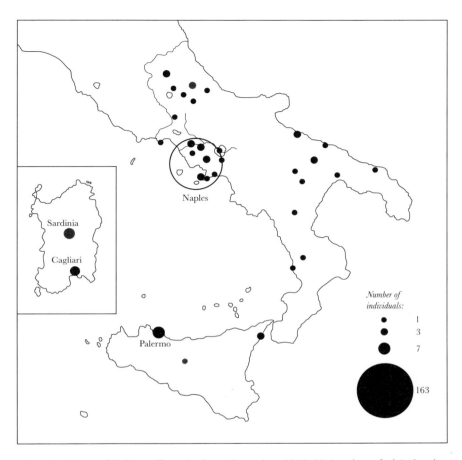

Map 6.6 Origin of Italian officers in Spanish service, 1610–60 (southern Italy) *(based on Encyclopedias)*

Brescia and Bergamo in the Venetian republic. His pro-Spanish and pro-Catholic policy made his patronage attractive for Lombards, Emilians and even Neapolitans. The increase of the army after 1613, and its reckless commitment to the Monferrato war drew on Piedmont foremost, doubling the contingent of local nobles to 69 per cent of the Italians. Successive dukes laid the structures for this expansion from the sixteenth century onwards. Youths were invited to the court to serve as pages, and were given military instruction. Secondly, families aspiring to the nobility were allowed entry into Piedmont's equivalent to the Tuscan and Maltese crusading order, the Order of Santi Maurizio e Lazzaro, which seems to have been restricted to the subjects of the duke.[7] Venetian and Papal subjects

---

[7] Merlin, *Tra guerre e tornei: la corte sabauda nell' età di Carlo Emanuele I*, p. 60.

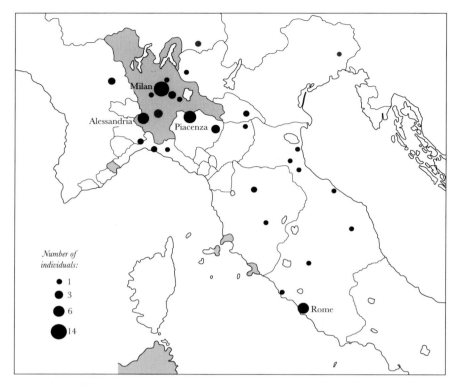

Map 6.7 Origin of Italian officers in Spanish service, 1660–1710 (northern and central Italy) *(based on Encyclopedias)*

provided most of the others, with 10 per cent each. Tuscans showed no interest in Piedmont, and Genoa was an enemy. Finally, in the great wars of the end of the century, Piedmontese subjects comprised no less than 87 per cent of the Italian officers in the army, with a few Lombards and Emilians to help them. Far from constituting the embryo of a 'national' Italian army, the Piedmontese officer corps became purely a regional, north-west Italian force.

Italian officers also served in two armies whose princes held very little territory in the peninsula. After the duke of Savoy had seized Saluzzo in 1588, France held no Italian territory at all. On the other hand, Italians played an active role in the French civil wars of the late sixteenth century, and the great Italian regencies of Caterina de'Medici, Maria de'Medici and Cardinal Mazarin kept a few doors open. Italian service in France paled beside the Swiss and the German, though and, according to our source, gradually declined from 86 careers between 1560 and 1610, to 73 during the age of Richelieu and Mazarin, to just 44 under Louis XIV when the French army was at its largest. For most of this period, central Italians dominated, with the survival of patronage networks in areas where French

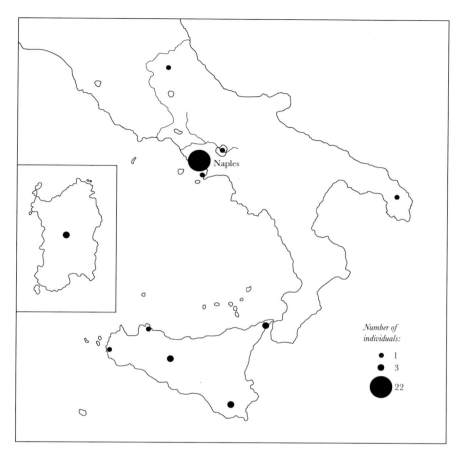

Map 6.8 Origin of Italian officers in Spanish service, 1660–1710 (southern Italy) *(based on Encyclopedias)*

support was strong during the Italian wars of the early sixteenth century. In the first period, a third were Papal subjects and a quarter were Tuscans, with another third scattered through the Po valley duchies and Piedmont. After that, Italians served the French only sporadically, from the same territories. Only after 1660 do we see a new development, the integration of Piedmontese officers into French service. Very, very few Italians in French service were subjects of the king of Spain or the emperor. The encyclopedia indications are not entirely corroborated by the fairly complete list of regiments commissioned by the French monarchy between 1560 and 1710, compiled by General Susane in the nineteenth century. Of the 71 Italian colonels leading a unit, 24 served in the first half-century, including five Neapolitans and a Lombard who seem to have been exiles in the years immediately after 1560. The period of the Thirty Years War saw 29 Italian-led regiments

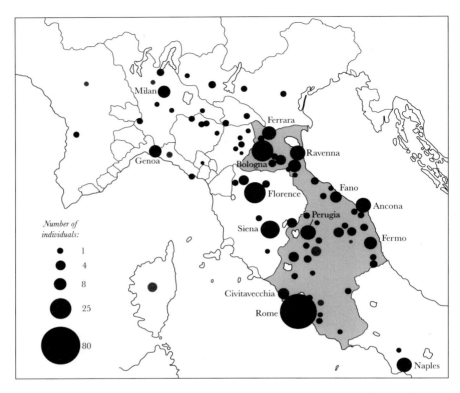

Map 6.9 Origin of Italian officers in Papal service, 1560–1710 *(based on Encyclopedias)*

in French service, although a few of these may have belonged to Parman, Mantuan and Modenese allies during their short dalliance with France. The period of French ascendancy and the great mobilization under Louis XIV saw only 18 commissions, and most of these were to Piedmontese colonels whose units were intermittently incorporated into the Sun King's order of battle. Of the 61 cases in which it was possible to assign a geographical origin, the Piedmontese comprised a third of the total, Corsicans provided eight more: the Po valley duchies and Ferrara together contributed twelve, and the Papal States less Ferrara provided six. Tuscany trailed with five colonels, and the Venetian cities provided three more.[8] This source permits us to see only the identity of the colonels, however.

The emperor held sway on the periphery of the Italian world, in the Tirolese Alps and in eastern Friuli. Nevertheless, service in Imperial armies was an attractive option open to Italians from most of the peninsula, with the exception of areas

---

[8] L. Susane, *Histoire de l'ancienne infanterie française* (Paris: 1853), vol. 8; and by the same author, *Histoire de la cavalerie française*, 3 vols (Paris: 1874).

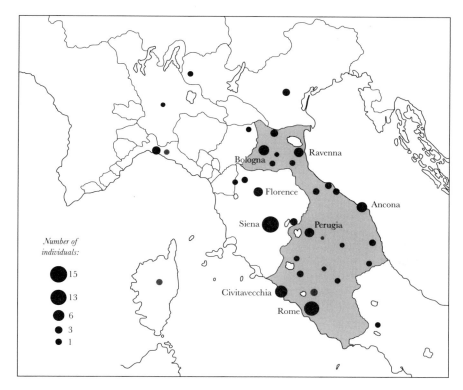

Map 6.10 Origin of Italian officers in Papal service, 1660–1710 *(based on Encyclopedias)*

south of Naples. There was little moral impediment to Italians offering their swords to the German emperor, since the Pope sanctioned his war of 'confessional absolutism' against the Protestants. The emperor's subjects before 1610 comprised but 3 per cent of the total of Italians; the big contingents were subjects of the Pope (30 per cent), the king of Spain (18 per cent) and the Po valley duchies (16 per cent). During the Thirty Years War, Tuscans constituted 31 per cent of the Italian officers, while Venetian, Papal, the Po valley principalities, 'Spanish' subjects and direct subjects of the emperor contributed about 12 per cent each. This wide base of support for the emperor in Italy continued after 1660 in the great wars against the Turks and the French.

The other territories recruited their officers locally, with the exception of the grand duke of Tuscany, about a third whose knights of Santo Stefano hailed from areas outside Tuscany over most of northern and central Italy, principally in Umbria, Romagna and the Marches. While Genoa hired Corsican mercenaries aplenty, their officers tended to be patricians from the *dominante*. The Gonzaga dukes drew principally from the capital city, and 'foreigners' counted more heavily in the total than the dukes' own subjects from the Monferrato. The dukes

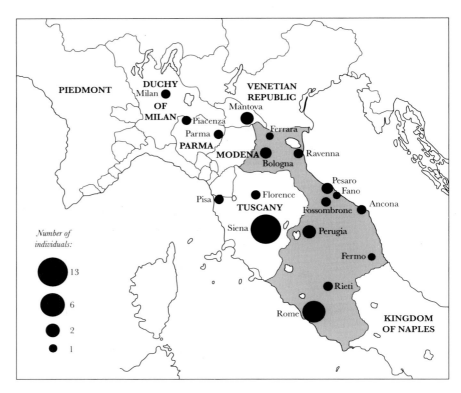

Map 6.11 Origin of Italian officers in Papal service, 1667 *(based on Georg Lutz)*

of Modena on the other hand, retained the fidelity of Ferrarese nobles for half a century after that city reverted to the Papal states in 1598. Finally, in the Farnese duchy, Piacenza's aristocracy was consistently more martial than Parma's, situated as it was close to the battlefields of Lombardy and the great axes of military troop movements along the Po, and between Milan and Genoa.

Whatever the regional distribution of military service, there was a temporal distribution even more telling. That Italian society underwent demilitarization is never disputed. No-one has ever fixed the date of such a process. Historians who fixed upon the end of the Renaissance have often followed Guicciardini, in pinpointing the decline to the outset of the Italian wars. Popular historians like Luigi Barzini, or recent scholars like Richard Goldthwaite, speculate that the early sixteenth century was the decisive moment.[9] AngelAntonio Spagnoletti speculates, more convincingly, that such a process began after the middle of the

---

[9] Luigi Barzini, *The Italians* (New York: 1983, first publ. 1964), pp. 276–98. See Richard Goldthwaite, *Wealth and the demand for art in Italy, 1300–1600* (Baltimore: 1993), pp. 167–70.

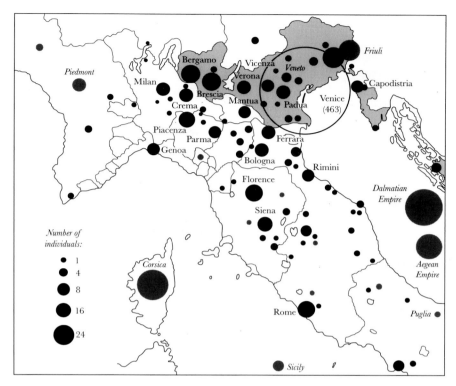

Map 6.12 Origin of Italian officers in Venetian service, 1560–1710 *(based on Encyclopedias)*

seventeenth century. He ascribes demilitarization to a combination of considerations, such as the waning of religious fervour, the decline of the Turkish peril, and the deepening economic crisis. The fascist encyclopedias help us explore his intuition in more depth.

Choosing a single, representative decade of military commitment for each officer is a bit arbitrary in instances where a career in the service of a single prince or republic spanned decades, but such constancy was infrequent. This statistical artifice allows us to chart a chronology of military careers with rough accuracy. Because some individuals served several masters, there are more career 'segments' than there are individuals in the sample. There are 4,505 such 'segments' for the span between 1560 and 1710, which can be broken almost neatly into three equal periods containing a half-century each. The first span includes the great maritime wars against the Ottomans and their Barbary allies at sea, the first phase of the Dutch revolt (ending in 1609), the French wars of religion (pacified in 1596) and the Imperial campaigns against the Turks in Hungary (concluded in 1606). The earlier decades were the most momentous, with the nadir in the 1580s. A second half-century after 1610 corresponds nicely to the prelude and crescendo of the

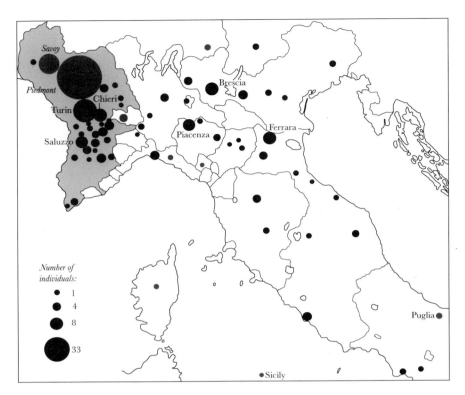

Map 6.13 Origin of Italian officers in Piedmontese service, 1560–1710 *(based on Encyclopedias)*

Thirty Years War in Europe, in all its ramifications, from the revolt of Bohemia to the peace of the Pyrenees between France and Spain in 1659. Even the Cretan war between Venice and the Ottoman Empire experienced a lull in the late 1650s. Finally, in the last period, European wars in which Italians played a part fall into two neat baskets; the campaigns against a resurgent Ottoman Empire, from the 1660s to 1699; and the various European coalitions designed to block French expansion, which mobilized unprecedented numbers of troops until 1714.

From a chronological ordering of the six most important armies in the encyclopedia sample, none contradicts the general trend towards a decline in the late seventeenth century, although in the Piedmontese case I suspect that the source is too incomplete regarding the sudden build-up of the army after 1689. Naturally, the numbers of all six armies rose and fell according to the vagaries of international tension. A first decline followed the end of the great Mediterranean conflict against the Turks. Numbers increased gradually again to their highest levels during the Thirty Years War, with a great peak in the 1640s (almost 800 career

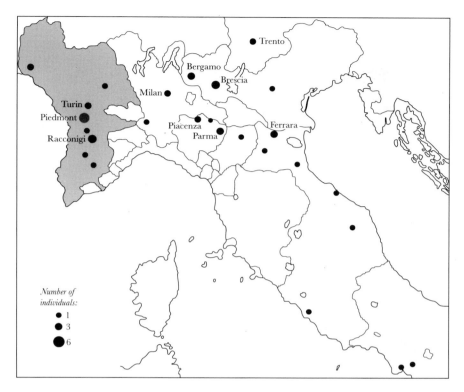

Map 6.14 Origin of Italian officers in Piedmontese service, 1560–1610 *(based on Encyclopedias)*

segments), which saw war break out everywhere. Only Venice's struggle against the Turks kept the numbers substantial for the next two decades. For Spanish service, this decline was especially dramatic, from 563 career segments in the half-century before 1660, to a mere 98 over the next fifty years. Papal army service segments dropped from 219 to 73 over the same period, as Rome eschewed Italian politics in favour of limited operations against the Turks. With Venice, the drop from 615 to 393 may reflect a growing dependency on foreign contingents hired wholesale, especially Germans. Imperial careers fell from 206 to 136; and those with the French from 73 to 44. So even in the most rapidly expanding armies of the late seventeenth century there appeared to be ever less room for Italians, or else markedly fewer ambitious nobles from the peninsula. Only for Venetian and Austrian service was there a brief recovery in the 1680s, before a steep drop there as well. A decline there certainly was, but it was not linear and unbroken.

The more episodic military activity of nobles for the half-dozen minor states

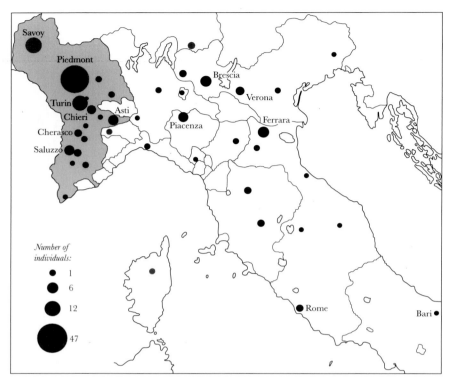

Map 6.15 Origin of Italian officers in Piedmontese service, 1610–60 *(based on Encyclopedias)*

also fits well into this schema. We see a limited Genoese mobilization during the 1570s when Corsica was at risk, and the republic briefly stumbled into civil war. From the 1590s to 1630, Mantua and Genoa were both forced to mobilize against Piedmont in the Monferrato wars and the succession crisis. The Thirty Years War and the Castro War sucked Parma and Modena into brief conflicts against Spain and the Papacy. Thereafter, the number of military careers sustained by these states trailed off to virtually nothing, with the single brief exception of Genoa during the Piedmontese invasion of 1672.

We can refine this first impression by looking at the number of Italian officer casualties – those killed in battle, with those who died on campaign, usually of disease or drowning. The total number of these (including a few Neapolitan, Sicilian and Piedmontese Vaudois rebels) is 687, roughly a sixth of the sample. Wounds were considered by the compilers less 'glorious', or they were originally not noted, so that the number of wounded is much smaller' 303, and a small handful of these were recorded as having been wounded more than once. The first peak, inserted in the 'calm' of the late sixteenth century, occurs in the 1570s,

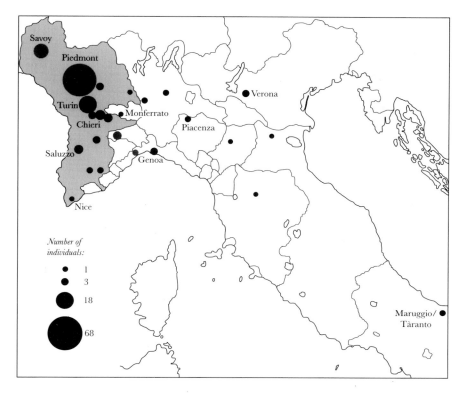

Map 6.16 Origin of Italian officers in Piedmontese service, 1660–1710 *(based on Encyclopedias)*

owing mostly to the war in the Mediterranean, Cyprus and Lepanto, but also in part to the campaign in Flanders. The number of killed and wounded rises after 1600, and remains high throughout the 1630s, 1640s and 1650s, because of the Thirty Years War, the Barberini War and the Venetian campaign in Crete. The level remains high in the 1660s, but this results entirely from the Venetian struggle for Candia during the climactic years 1667–9. After that, the number of casualties drops suddenly, rises slightly in the 1680s because of the war against the Turks in Hungary and the Morea, and then drops again.

Military officers and military 'enterprisers'

Knowing who most of the officers were, where they came from, and the armies in which they served, gives us a few clues about what may have motivated them. Surely, motivation is a complex phenomenon, rarely occurring in a virulent monocausal flash. Giulio Savorgnano, a Venetian general, explained in 1572 that

241

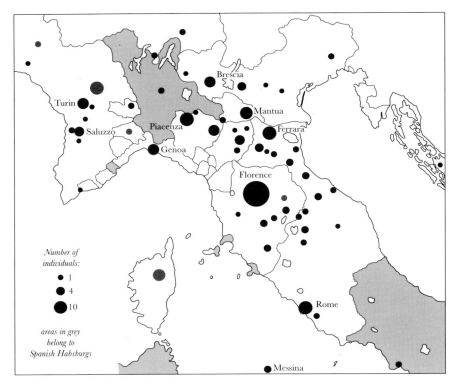

Map 6.17 Origin of Italian officers in French service, 1560–1710 *(based on Encyclopedias)*

men enlisted in armies to escape from being poor artisans, or to avoid arrest or a criminal sentence, or to see new things, to pursue honour (these were few), to follow and serve their masters and hopefully acquire a windfall of plunder.[10] Add to these a moderate desire to defend the Catholic religion, and to live up to the considerable peer pressure in their confined urban communities, and we have a few of the pertinent reasons why young Italian nobles joined armies in the early modern period. All of them had to have an adventurous spirit, for the trade was not for the faint of heart. The role of honour is perhaps understated, but the concept is also difficult to define. Put simply, motives lay somewhere between the stark pursuit of personal self-interest and selfless altruism. Naturally, there was usually some admixture of the two.

The motive we perhaps understand best is the desire for wealth. The develop-

---

[10] M. S. Anderson, *War and society in Europe of the old regime, 1618–1789* (New York: 1988), p. 46.

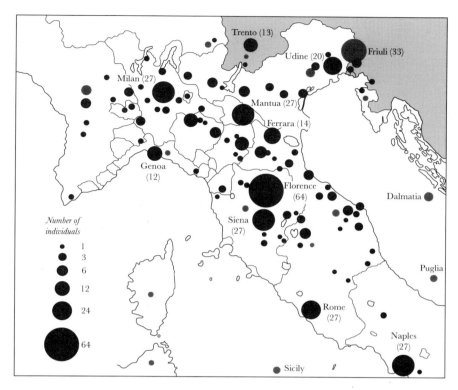

Map 6.18 Origin of Italian officers in Austrian service, 1560–1710 *(based on Encyclopedias)*

ment of modern armies was probably the single most pressing issue to most states of the time, and served as a powerful stimulus to government efficiency. Early modern states had no budgets in the modern sense, and there was not an easy way of knowing how much the crown owed, or how much was owed to it. There was no financial planning, and revenues might vary wildly from one year to the next, making previsions impossible. There was one constant, however: early modern governments almost always spent more money than they took in, and states were chronically short of resources. This is why agreements with private military entrepreneurs (or compliant princes) looked attractive, because it solved several problems at a single stroke. By divesting itself of much of the mechanics of financing armies, the state reduced the problem of the irregularity of its supply, and the misappropriation of funds by officials with powerful friends. As James Dennistoun long ago concluded, "This system suited all parties for the great powers were able to have an ample force in a short time, without waste of treasure. The petty sovereigns eked out of it additional revenues, and gave military employ-ment to those who desired it, and whose restless spirits would have been danger-

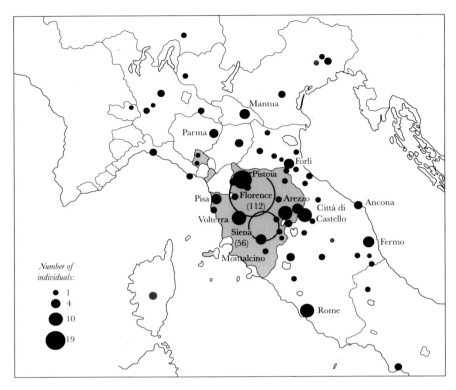

Map 6.19 Origin of Italian officers in Tuscan service, 1560–1710 *(based on Encyclopedias)*

ous at home".[11] War paradoxically contributed to the public peace by removing potential troublemakers.[12]

These military 'enterprisers' (as they are now usually described) descended from the Renaissance *condottieri*, who were large-scale military contractors and simultaneously warriors, functionaries and businessmen.[13] Typically, while they

---

[11] Dennistoun, *Memoirs of the dukes of Urbino*, vol. 3, p. 148.

[12] Stuart Woolf is more explicit: "I would suggest that such employment performed the function of a safety valve, removing financially needy and potentially rebellious nobles from states whose absolutist rulers were still endeavouring to extend and impose their authority". This may be true at the end of the wars of Italy when the homicide rate appears to be very high, but it does not seem to be true for the end of the Thirty Years War, when the rate of violence seems to have been dropping. See S. Woolf, "Intervento", in *Patriziati e aristocrazie nobiliari: ceti dominanti e organizzazione del potere nell' Italia centro-settentrionale dal XVI al XVIII secolo: Seminario di Trento*, C. Mozzarelli & P. Schiera (eds) (Trento: 1978), pp. 81–6.

[13] The term is Fritz Redlich's. See his important work, *The German military enterpriser and his work force: a study in European economic and social history*, 2 vols (Wiesbaden: 1964). For his view of the Italian *condottiere* as the prototype, see p. 29.

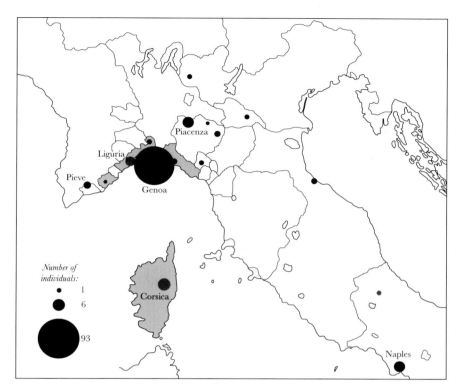

Map 6.20 Origin of Italian officers in Genoese service, 1560–1710 *(based on Encyclopedias)*

advanced their own cash to the warlord – and this might be a sovereign prince, a city–state or a republic – they borrowed more from other princes, noblemen, merchants and their own subordinate officers. The prince or his ministers did not pay the troops directly, for this would have required a more efficient and numerous bureaucracy than these states could afford, and more scrupulous honesty, exact book-keeping and impersonal relationship than was commonly expected. Instead, they handed just enough tax money to the commanders to maintain their credit-worthiness, and to allow them to reimburse money advanced by their subcontractors.

Military entrepreneurship functioned at several levels. The army commander extended credit to the warlord as the latter advanced sums to collect regiments and provisions. Below him were the colonels, who actually contracted for men and materials. Colonels made a profit from several sources: a profit margin in the contract; trading in armour, weapons and provisions for sale to their men; and pocketing soldiers' wages, either by padding the muster-rolls on pay-day, or by appropriating pay due to soldiers who had died or deserted. Colonels were also captains of their own companies, and pocketed that money while giving a pittance

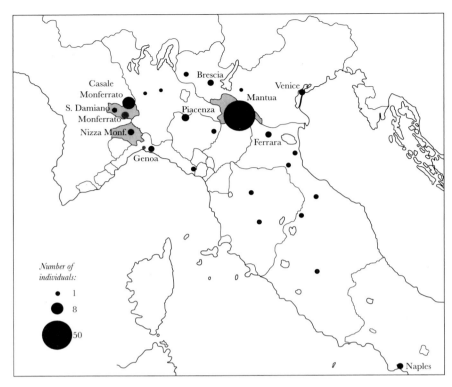

Map 6.21 Origin of Italian officers in Mantuan service, 1560–1710 *(based on Encyclopedias)*

to some lieutenant to direct it. It was standard practice to pad the payrolls for muster purposes, and then contrive to have fewer soldiers for successive pays. The company captain was the final link in the chain. He was often a sub-contractor supplying recruits to keep his company up to strength. Even captains needed to have some assets to thrive, like the ability to pawn jewellery or mortgage an estate, or tap friends and relatives for a sum to keep the unit going while awaiting reimbursement from above. The business conduct of just about everybody was marred by dishonesty, from the sovereign who 'verified' the accounts and contracts passed, to the colonels and captains who padded the musters, to the soldiers who deserted from one company only to enlist in another and pocket the enlistment bonus. However, there were real chances of social advancement even from bankrupt warlords. Princes often rewarded deserving officers with gifts of jewellery, weapons or horses, paid their claims with real estate at a low assessment, or gave them title to estates confiscated from a defeated enemy.[14]

Since the colonel took such an active role in recruiting and equipping his

---

[14] Redlich, *The German military enterpriser and his work force*, p. 50ff.

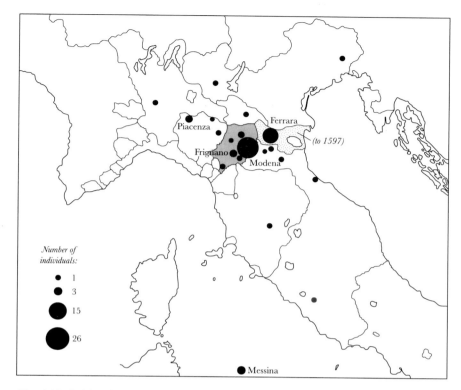

Map 6.22 Origin of Italian officers in Modenese service, 1560–1710 *(based on Encyclopedias)*

regiment, it came to be recognized as his own, virtually a form of property, or at the very least a branch of the state over which he had a right of pre-emption and preferment. A colonel might own several regiments, and lead only one of them himself, entrusting each of the others to a subaltern, a lieutenant-colonel. The emperor soon deprived owners who were not active field commanders, for colonelcy entailed active service in the field with all of its risks and perils. As a form of property, the colonel could will a regiment to his relatives, although the warlord always had the right to intervene, or even disband the unit. To retire a colonel against his will was a risky business, however, as the loyalty of the troops was to him alone, and a regiment was liable to disband after his removal. This is why the princes allowed incompetent or incapacitated commanders to continue.

On the crudest level, one could therefore explain the attraction of a military career by the chance of wealth and power it offered. Most princes counted upon the nobles they retained at their court. In Italy, these were generally not numerous, except when they comprised a bodyguard of nobles. Princes maintained a number of military professionals, usually nobles, whose experience, contacts and 'credit' they utilized in case of need. The best of these men received a salary in

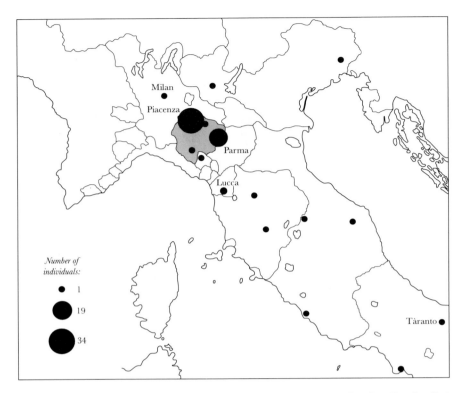

Map 6.23 Origin of Italian officers in Parman service, 1560–1710 *(based on Encyclopedias)*

peacetime, as a kind of retaining fee, called in Germany the *Dienstgeld*. Paid to a few men on a yearly basis, the money pledged their loyalty and readiness to serve whenever the prince required it. Meanwhile, they fulfilled ceremonial roles and served as 'ornaments' for the court. Alfonso II d'Este, duke of Ferrara employed the Neapolitan warrior Giulio Cesare Brancaccio to sing with his *basso* voice in accompaniment to the court ladies, though the old soldier pined for more warlike functions.[15]

Although German military enterprisers have been best studied, it is possible to depict their Italian counterparts from the mid-sixteenth century onwards. They were a significant minority among the hundreds of enterprisers active during the Thirty Years War. Redlich studied 1,500 commanders of all nationalities in Germany during the Thirty Years War, their numbers reaching an apex of 400 active between 1630 and 1635.[16] Most of them were Protestants, or Protestant

---

[15] B. Croce, "Un capitano italiano del cinquecento: Giulio Cesare Brancaccio", *Critica*, 1932, pp. 458–72.
[16] Redlich, *The German military enterpriser and his work force*, vol. 1, p. 171.

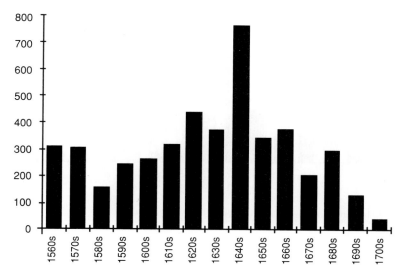

Graph 6.1 Italian military careers, 1560–1710 (in career segments)

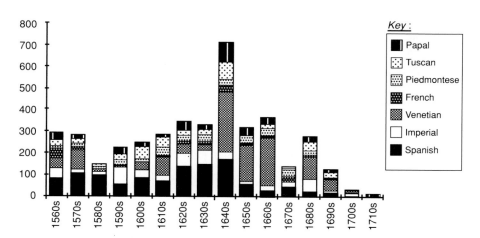

Graph 6.2 Chronology of Italian military career segments, 1560–1720

converts to Rome. About 300 were active there at any moment at the height of the war in the 1630s, and about a fifth of those in Imperial service were non-German, with Italians comprising the most significant part of those. While the great majority held but a single regiment, the seventeenth century saw some increase in the scale of entrepreneurship. Successive and cumulative contracting for several regiments led to multiple ownership, and a greater concentration of military 'capital'. That produced ever more lieutenant-colonels working for salaries and living in

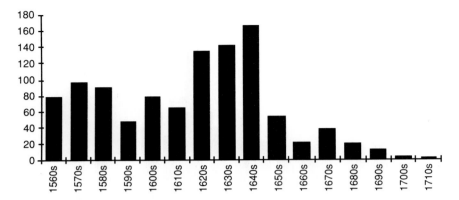

Graph 6.3 Italian nobles in Spanish service, 1560–1720

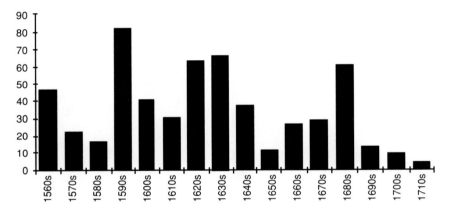

Graph 6.4 Italian nobles in Imperial service, 1560–1720

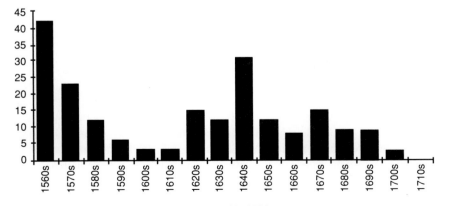

Graph 6.5 Italian nobles in French service, 1560–1720

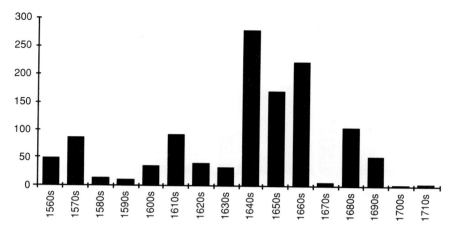

Graph 6.6 Italian nobles in Venetian service, 1560–1720

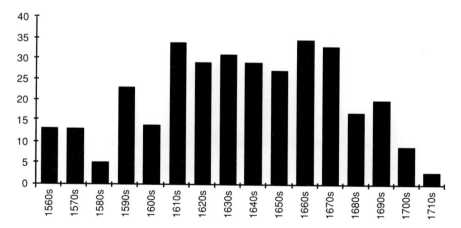

Graph 6.7 Italian nobles in Piedmontese service, 1560–1720

hope of being promoted to a colonelcy with the next vacancy. Ambrogio Spìnola's Spanish *coup* in 1602 constituted the most significant single Italian investment. A large proportion of the multiple owners in Imperial service between 1625 and 1640 was Italian, including Girolamo Colloredo, Annibale Gonzaga, Ernesto Montecùccoli, Ottavio Piccolòmini, Francesco del Carretto and Tommaso Cerboni. Only a few were rich enough and willing to take the risks involved in owning multiple regiments, though there were bankers who were willing to finance them. The most successful ones usually had supportive relatives and were careful to construct their own clientèles as they rose. Both Raimondo Montecùccoli and Ottavio Piccolòmini were of modest nobility with successful

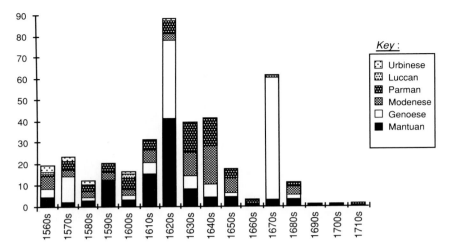

Graph 6.8 Italian military careers in minor states, 1560–1720

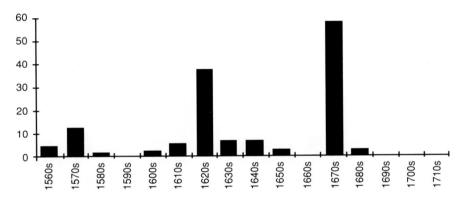

Graph 6.9 Italian nobles in Genoese service, 1560–1720

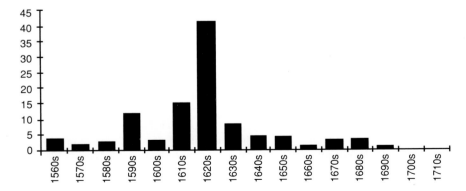

Graph 6.10 Italian nobles in Mantuan service, 1560–1720

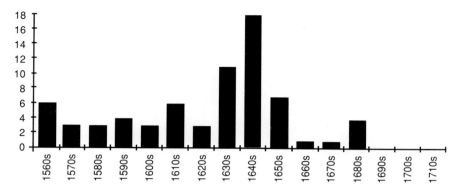

Graph 6.11 Italian nobles in Modenese service, 1560–1720

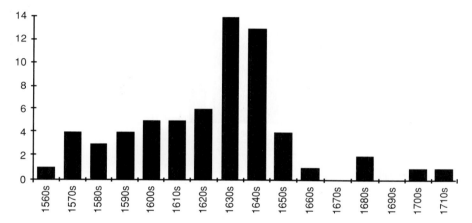

Graph 6.12 Italian nobles in Parman service, 1560–1720

forbears. They in turn aided their own network of relatives: the Caprara of Bologna were related to both families after mid-century. While this eased the way into commissions for their relatives, it did not diminish the danger inherent in army life. Piccolòmini's brother, several nephews, and an illegitimate son were killed in battle. Nevertheless, there were real dynasties of military commanders of whom the Piccolòmini and Montecùccoli are exemplary but not unusual. Redlich asserts that a search through genealogies would reveal that the 1,500 military enterprisers of the Thirty Years War belong in reality to a few hundred extended families and kin networks.[17]

Most Italian military enterprisers came from the peninsula's richest families. Quite a number of them were princes, including several Medici cadets in Tus-

[17] Redlich, vol. 1, p. 296.

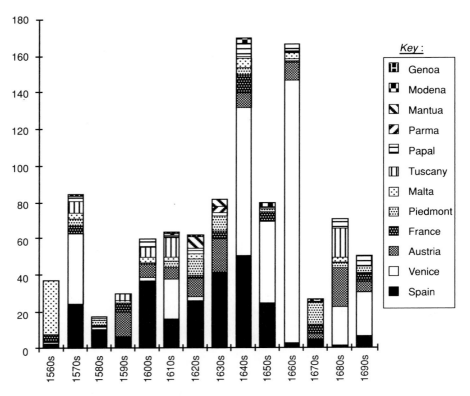

Graph 6.13 Total Italian casualties, 1560–1700

cany, and princes from the Della Rovere, Este, and Gonzaga dynasties in Urbino, Modena and Mantua respectively. Others were high-born urban patricians, like Duke Federico Savelli of Rome, who rose to the top despite his notorious incompetence, or several members of the Sienese house of Piccolòmini. In Spain there was the belief that a man's ancestors were no less (and maybe more) important than his own qualifications for high command.[18] There was a general sense, at least among the noblility, that they had the innate moral qualities to lead and command troops. Kings appointed grandees, princes and great nobles to lead armies because they could recruit soldiers with greater ease, especially from their home districts where they had favours to collect. These lords stood at the head of a network of clientèles and connections. Great nobles with deep pockets also attracted the soldiery to their units, especially if they advanced their own money to pay troops' wages or to keep them fed and warm. Their success at recruiting

---

[18] Thompson, *War and government in Habsburg Spain, 1560–1620*, p. 48ff.

and the subsequent coherence of their regiments depended upon these resources, and on their organizational skills.

Not all of the successful enterprisers were *bona fide* nobles. These officers were expected to lead their troops, and the casualty ratio was often horrendous for them.[19] With time, there were not enough nobles to fill the positions of command and the non-nobles took their opportunities.[20] The Imperial army in particular was open to commoners in the lesser echelons. Only a minority of the junior positions was filled by nobles, since the native Austrian and Bohemian aristocracy was not militarily inclined.[21] While the great aristocracy dominated the higher ranks, this was not an absolute rule, and talented individuals from modest backgrounds could rise to great heights, like the Colloredo brothers from Venetian Friuli, of petty nobility. Some were authentic *roturiers*. Tommaso Cerboni rose from obscure origins in the Tuscan mountain town of Castel del Piano, to own two Imperial regiments in the 1620s. His family was aggregated to the Sienese nobility two years after his death in battle in 1629. Even more spectacular was the rise of Matteo Galasso, whose father was a Neapolitan officer settling in Trento in the late sixteenth century. Their fortune they owed more to raw talent. A competent commander would always be at a premium and enjoy recruiting advantages, and soldiers wanted to fight for a winner because it optimized their own chance of survival and the likelihood of scooping up booty.[22] In Galasso's case, he surged to the top of the relatively small Bavarian army, before transferring to Imperial service under Wallenstein. By 1633 he was second-in-command of the Imperial forces, and esteemed for his abilities.

Great nobles were nevertheless preferred as senior officers, in part because they carried the burden of recruitment. Recruiting was an expensive business, for the soldiery was more mobile, and attached to their pay and to their skins, than the officers. This is what made it so vital to have as leaders men of 'credit' and influence. In Spanish service, the selection of a titled aristocrat as commander of a *tercio* implied that he would disburse significant sums to create the unit. This practice continued to the end of the Habsburg regime in 1700. Some nobles thought that this was a way for Olivares to tax the nobility surreptitiously. Whether they had pertinent military experience was a minor consideration.

---

[19] J. Wood, "The royal army during the early wars of religion, 1559–1576", in *Society and institutions in early modern France*, Mack Holt (ed.) (Athens, Georgia: 1991), p. 16ff.

[20] A. Corvisier, "La noblesse militaire: aspects militaires de la noblesse française du XVe au XVIIIe siècle: état des questions", *Histoire Sociale / Social History*, 1978, pp. 336–55, at p. 346.

[21] J. Nouzille, *Le prince Eugène de Savoie et les problèmes des confins militaires autrichiens, 1699–1739* (unpublished thesis, Université de Strasbourg: 1979), p. 182. The author provides a table of the social origin of infantry officers by rank in the Imperial army in 1695. Seven out of eight marshals were nobles, 12 of 15 colonels and 25 out of 35 lieutenant-colonels, but only 75 of 301 captains were noble, and 25 of 400 lieutenants.

[22] C. Carlton, *Going to the wars: the experience of the British civil wars, 1638–1651* (London: 1992).

Inexperience could be mitigated by appointing military advisers, or 'councillors of war' from the lower-born veterans who directed operations in the field, and to whom the *maestro di campo* was expected to defer.[23]

In Italy the viceroy in Naples or the governor of Milan designated recruiting districts, and appointed a commissioned captain to raise troops there, earmarked for a specific campaign. If a whole *tercio* was being raised, the *maestro di campo* would oversee the operation. As the campaigning continued, the unit would suffer from having too many officers, who would refuse to serve as simple soldiers. To make good the losses, commanders recruited on the fly, from friendly and enemy armies alike. Redlich cites the example of a Bavarian regiment of 1,000 men which was probably ethnically homogeneous at its creation in 1644, but which soon contained soldiers of seventeen nationalities, including over 200 Italians.[24] Since finding enough soldiers was never easy, sovereigns were prepared to accept many irregularities.[25]

One idiosyncracy was the 'gift' of a company; that is, recruiting and equipping a unit at a nobleman's considerable expense, only to place it at the disposal of his sovereign. The prince then had only to pay (or pretend to pay) the soldiery to keep the company in existence, and to provide the donor with an officer's commission and stipend. It was a way for inexperienced nobles to begin a military career at an honourable rank. It was also a way for out-of-favour nobles to redeem themselves for some *faux pas*. The king of Spain accepted increasing numbers of these 'gifts' in the 1580s and 1590s as recruiting began to flag. The recruiting noble paid the expenses of the unit until its embarkation for Flanders or elsewhere. It was not entirely disinterested, of course, since the enterpriser received a proper officer's commission and wage, and probably a right of preferment of junior officers too. Initially, though, the outlay would have been considerable, and fraught with risks.

By 1600, several states were recruiting and supplying units by granting licences and signing contracts with individuals. The Spanish crown, despite its Indies riches, was the first to succumb to this privatization on any scale, as the war of Flanders and Mediterranean defence drained the treasury faster than it could be filled. Despite a stated preference for direct royal control over military expenditure, Philip II embarked on a new policy in the 1590s when the Genoese financier Agostino Spìnola agreed to provide monthly instalments of 200,000 *scudi* to the army of Flanders. In 1592 another Genoese banker, Tommaso Fiesco, became crown factor transferring royal funds to Italy and the Low Countries. The Spanish system relied on a continuous shifting of troops from one theatre to another, and

---

[23] Thompson, *War and government in Habsburg Spain*, p. 146.

[24] Redlich, *The German military enterpriser and his work force*, vol. 1, p. 456.

[25] See also the case of late seventeenth-century Naples, where the 'Spanish' companies in garrison contained large numbers of local recruits, and where even most of the officers were Neapolitans. Astarita, "Aspetti dell' organizzazione militare del regno di Napoli", p. 194.

the money (or letters of exchange) had to travel the same circuits as the soldiery. Gradually, Spanish ministers farmed the pay of different contingents out to different contractors who had ready access to specie, and they skimmed off a profit on this transaction. After 1600 the entire army of Flanders was entrusted to just one of these financiers, Ambrogio Spìnola, who providentially happened to be a gifted strategist. After 1608, these Genoese bankers were paying the garrisons in Spain itself. In 1632, all the Castilian garrisons were paid out of the coffers of a single banker, Octavio Centurion, the Hispanicized scion of a Genoese finance family.[26]

While many decried the system of granting *asientos* to wealthy financiers, it offered short-term advantages. According to Thompson, what made people so uneasy was the social mobility and the fluidity attached to this system. There was a perceptible shift from central to centrifugal government at work in Spain, from public to private administration. Most opinion was in favour of direct royal control. The *asiento* opened all kinds of secondary business avenues, exemptions and monopolies that were very stimulating. Also, many *asientistas* were foreigners, with the Genoese and the Portuguese taking the brunt of hostility. On the other hand, it was one-half or one-third cheaper than the royal administration, and more efficient too.[27] By 1660, a Colbertian programme of centralized control over the army and fleet was out of the question, with Spain moving in a direction opposite that of other western European countries.

There were periods when the enterprisers in the field could make colossal fortunes almost overnight, which was unsettling for the crown as well as the taxpayers. The most outrageously successful belonged to Austrian service. Ottavio Piccolòmini was given a huge part of Wallenstein's estate, some 300,000 florins, after he helped engineer his patron's assassination. When he entered Spanish service the following year (1635) Philip IV endowed him with the duchy of Amalfi in the kingdom of Naples. Then there was the windfall booty accruing to the successful invasion of Picardy and Île de France in 1636, when his cavalry patrols pushed to the outskirts of Paris.[28] Who knows how much he and his officers might have collected in this manner? This palls compared with the providential booty taken by the Imperial commanders when Mantua was stormed in 1630. The plunder from the city was estimated at 18 million *scudi*, much more than the entire Imperial revenue of the time. The two commanders, Aldringhen and Galasso, staked out the ducal palace as their share, netting about eight million *scudi*.

Apart from such accidents, the commanders could make money from a host of means, some judged admissible, others not. They could sell safe-conducts or leaves, for example. In the Imperial army, colonels enjoyed the right to sell commissions for junior officers, and sell other kinds of permissions too. They could levy 'contributions' on villages and towns in their path, and then pocket the

---

[26] Thompson, *War and government in Habsburg Spain*, p. 86ff.
[27] *Ibid.*, p. 257.
[28] Lonchay, *La rivalité de la France et de l'Espagne aux Pays-Bas (1635–1700)*, p. 76.

money themselves, letting the soldiery fend for themselves. Francesco del Carretto di Grana was notorious for this. The practice of officers stealing soldiers' wages was also very widespread. Ernesto Montecùccoli was reputed to be a rapacious extortionist of friend and foe alike, and two generations later, Caprara and Carafa earned similar reputations. Then, when cash was hard to come by, especially after 1650, officers were paid largely in kind, in so many rations. This was not an administrative abstraction, for officers maintained hangers-on, servants and stable-boys taking care of their horses. In the later seventeenth century, the state gradually replaced the colonels in the supply of weapons, clothing and horses, although the colonels continued to be the principal channel of payment. Opportunities for embezzlement for senior officers included retaining recruitment money and soldiers' pay intended to reimburse civilians required to quarter them, keeping campaign stores and funds to purchase equipment and clothing, and selling leaves, promotions and 'surplus' stores. This changed slowly after a new bookkeeping system was introduced in the Imperial army from 1681.[29]

Plunder was an essential feature of war. Redlich chronicles the evolution of the practice from the late middle ages, when it was considered normal, to the eighteenth-century marginalization of it. Medieval lords saw war as an extension of the feud, and it was legitimate to inflict maximum damage on the enemy and his vassals.[30] It was also considered rightful to hold captives taken in war to ransom, a rule that included kings like François I, taken at Pavia in 1525. The incentive of booty was that it kept the soldiery eager for action, while the officers could hope to recoup the cost of their commission or their investment. Looting began to be regulated in articles of war, drafted by sovereigns and states every time the troops were mustered, as part of an attempt to keep them in hand. The articles redrafted by the emperor in 1570 to reimpose discipline on the Imperial troops in Hungary considered it natural that arms and weapons of captives should belong to the captor. The heavier material such as artillery and ammunition belonged to the emperor, as well as flags, standards and kettledrums that were symbols of victory, although these would be given to the army commander by the captors in exchange for some tangible reward. When soldiers lived at their host's expense, the regulations required them to behave decently and modestly, and not to steal or to wreck their lodgings. These rules still held, by and large, throughout the Thirty Years War, in Italy as in Germany, and were observed by all the armies. Prolonged non-payment of troops, however, detracted from battle-worthiness, since the men were continually scrounging for subsistence or plunder. At the first sign of victory, the troops would disband, and even the officers would break ranks to scoop up whatever they could.[31] Only the articles of 1668 prohib-

---

[29] T. Barker, *Double eagle and crescent*, p. 175.

[30] F. Redlich, *De praeda militari: looting and booty, 1500–1815* (Wiesbaden: 1956).

[31] *Ibid.*, p. 42. Luigi Ferdinando Marsigli at Buda in 1686 acted no differently from the soldiery in this respect, save that he was tempted more by manuscripts than gold. See J. Stoye, *Marsigli's Europe, 1680–1730*, p. 45.

ited deliberate destruction of houses, fences, and tried to limit the damage wrought by the army on friend and foe. Prisoners were thereafter consigned to the general of the army, and exchanged with the enemy in an annual trade, with cash values for each rank.

In place of the confused search for plunder, commanders and princes began to organize it, and render it more efficient, taking care to spread it throughout the army. The practice of levying 'contributions' became the touchstone for operations everywhere. Warlords, and particularly the emperor and the king of Spain, could no longer dream of paying the loans they undertook out of their regular income. When the army was ready to disband from lack of payment, discipline ceased to be enforced, and the soldiers took what they wanted. This was usually a desperate measure, to be avoided if possible. 'Contributions' were a tolerated form of wholesale robbery to reimburse the enterpriser. Since this collection was so violent, who could tell what sums commanders really levied? Towards the end of his life, Raimondo Montecùccoli reminded the emperor that he had never been motivated by gain, and defied anyone to prove that he ever took money from a city. The contributions given to him by Hamburg, Lübeck and other cities, he turned over in their entirety to the war chest. But this reminder underscores how such behaviour was not the norm for generals.[32] Really talented and well-organized enterprisers like Alessandro Farnese, or Wallenstein, could supply almost everything through this form of requisitioning. If soldiers exhausted the quartering area, however, the enterpriser might go into debt. Commanders could often die penniless, owed huge sums by their warlord.[33]

Gradually, the captain became central to the maintenance of the regiment. Already at the end of the sixteenth century, many captains took care of the recruiting themselves. For every colonel there were many captains, most of them of modest means. It was all they could do to keep their company up to strength and appropriately armed. One captain in a peacetime army for whom we have some information was the young Giulio Mazzarini (later Cardinal Jules Mazarin), who served in Torquato Conti's Pontifical army sent to the Valtellina to disentangle the French and Spanish in 1626 and 1627. He took his commission as a client of the Colonna family of Rome, for whom his father was estate manager. Mazarin's specific task was to tutor and guide another Colonna who was a captain in the *tercio* raised by Don Francesco Colonna, prince of Palestrina. Although he had already taken minor clerical orders, he lived as an officer in Ancona and Loreto where he was garrisoned with his company. He was always careful to be elegantly dressed (as a layman), to be generous with his hospitality, to keep a good table, and maintain the appearance of noble liberality, to disguise the fact that he was not, in fact, a nobleman. Here he first showed his diplomatic skills as a humble

---

[32] Sandonnini, *Il generale Raimondo Montecùccoli e la sua famiglia*, p. 78.

[33] Redlich, *The German military enterpriser and his work force*, vol. 1, p. 257ff. In one example, the heirs of colonel Aldobrandino Aldobrandini were able to collect the great sum of 60,000 florins, only long after his death.

emissary and messenger between the hostile armies. This diplomatic function was hardly original to Mazarin, since Ottavio Piccolòmini, Antonio Carafa, Raimondo Montecùccoli and a host of others learned the art of negotiation while in the army, and astute negotiators with good connections could advance from the field to the court. Most of his work revolved around disciplinary concerns. His company of 235 men strained the public peace, as they deserted, plundered, and brutalized each other and their hosts. Since Mazarin frequently had to disburse his own money for quartering his troops, he was very diligent in being reimbursed. While these sums were not colossal (once for 229 *lire* and another time for 340 *lire*), they were significant for such a lowly personage who was required to live by his wits.[34]

When war became better controlled from the centre, it ceased to be an avenue of great wealth, save for a few commanders. On the contrary, it could be a source of real impoverishment for parents who required hundreds of *scudi* to set up a cadet with a horse, weapons and pocket-money; or for conscientious junior commanders intent on keeping their units equipped and up to strength; or even for colonels if the prince dissolved their regiment or forced them to retire. Giving command of a fortress to an old or unfit general was an honourable sinecure to stave off poverty. The more provident tried to diversify their income into land, and jewels and plate, but also in bonds and loans on governments. Raimondo Montecùccoli reflected how service to the emperor had caused him more sacrifice than reward, in a letter written around 1643, just before his elevation to colonel. He explained how he had paid the ransom of his first captivity out of his own pocket, and emptied the substance of his house to further Imperial designs. When he left Imperial service to fight for the duke of Modena in Italy, the crown gave his regiment to another officer without reimbursing him for the horses he had bought for his troopers, or paying his arrears. Apart from the 3,000 florins the emperor owed him, he was penniless.[35]

Unemployment, or the dissolution of the regiment before the investment could be recouped, were also risks. For incompetence, the colonel or general was sometimes deprived of command at short notice. The prince sometimes 're-formed' or dissolved the regiment and then gave a recruiting patent to someone else. Peace in 1648 entailed the reduction of the Imperial army and forced the retirement of numerous commanders.[36] Until the final decades of the seventeenth century, armies expanded and contracted with every crisis and every treaty, leaving many officers out in the cold. Imperial regiments in particular could be taken from, or ceded to, Spain, Bavaria, Venice, the Pope, Lorraine, and occa-

---

[34] H. Coville, "Documents sur le capitaine Jules Mazarin", in *Mélanges d'archéologie et d'histoire, de l'école française de Rome*, 1914, pp. 200–34.

[35] Sandonnini, *Il generale Raimondo Montecuccoli e la sua famiglia*, pp. 58–9.

[36] Mears notes, however, that an effort was made to retain experienced officers and military specialists in prevision for the next buildup. See J. A. Mears, "The Thirty Years War and the origins of a standing army", *Central European History*, 1988, pp. 122–41.

sionally even Protestant states, frequently with a change of officers. The officers themselves were ready to seek better fortunes elsewhere, either out of dissatisfaction with the army, or just in search of more money. As the number of military enterprisers diminished, the emperor tried to recompense his senior officers by promoting them to higher commands, with little real responsibility. In 1700, there were twenty field marshals in the Austrian army, although only a few would ever be given autonomous commands.[37] For Italians, however, the alternatives were few. The ability to move back and forth between the Spanish and Imperial branches of the House of Austria, especially before 1660, was considerable. Venice and occasionally France served as outlets too. Where officers went depended upon their connections and their individual outlook.

The risks of this life were therefore considerable. Most glaringly, the work was dangerous. Of the 1,500 entrepreneurs of all nationalities in Redlich's files, 214 died in battle or of wounds.[38] The encyclopedia sample death rate is about 17 per cent, which includes deaths from disease or by accident on campaign. Besides fatal risk, there was the possibility of capture, which would entail having to pay a ransom. The number of enterprisers who survived, and prospered, and ended the war with great gain, like Ottavio Piccolòmini, was very small. Most enterprisers served until nearly the end of their lives, if they did not die on campaign, and withdrew to a feathered nest. Montecùccoli, who had a reputation for honesty, left a fortune of over three million florins in 1680, equivalent to the annual military expenditure of the empire during the 1660s. Beneath the rank of colonel, however, there were only crumbs to be had. The pay for captains dropped by half between 1640 and 1690, denoting a gradual change in the military condition. The mercenary motive cannot by itself explain the attraction of such careers.

Honour and reputation

It is not at all proven that military careers were lucrative for most of those youths who joined armies in the sixteenth and seventeenth centuries. Indeed, one reason the nobilities of the capital cities were so inclined to war, is that their families were richer than provincial nobles, and they could afford the expenditure. They saw war as a calling, a field of competition with their peers in which money was flaunted as lavishly as their valour. If waging war was a form of conspicuous consumption for the rich, however, the contracting economy of the Mediterranean in the seventeenth century put it out of reach for many. Moreover, the patriciates in the capital and court cities were also the heaviest investors in government bonds. The stakeholders in Spanish finances, and even in Tuscany and Rome where government agencies lent this capital to the king of Spain and

---

[37] McKay, *Prince Eugene of Savoy*, p. 35.
[38] Redlich, *The German military enterpriser and his work force*, vol. 1, p. 370ff.

the emperor, were vulnerable to severe losses when the princes defaulted, although only detailed research will reveal how much this handicapped military families.

In Italy, perhaps more than elsewhere, noble families expected their members to put the interests of the 'house' before their personal desires, for the *casa* included not only living kin, but also dead ancestors and unborn children. The real test came during the seventeenth century as the sources of wealth dried up. The aristocracy clung increasingly to its agricultural estates which could not be expanded or split. A tremendous desire for stability and permanence enveloped the aristocracy as a whole, but this immobility could be maintained only with great discipline. Whether this entailed a sociological determinism by which parents earmarked younger sons for military careers far from home is an open question. Chagniot does not find such a situation in France, and Italianists have never studied that question from sound genealogies.[39] Before the seventeenth century, it was often customary for sons to share the estate equally, living together in a single dwelling that served as the ancestral manor. As the economic crisis deepened in the peninsula, it became more common to place the greater part of the state in entail, called the *fedecommesso*, under a single head. This status forbade the heir-designate to diminish the estate either by legacy or by sale, and required instead its transmission intact across several generations. Some larger families with multiple branches established a *consorteria* which specified joint ownership of seigneurial rights and fiefs, but this was out of reach for most.

One result of such restrictions was for junior members of a family to forego marriage. In order to attract the few available grooms, parents increased the dowries for their daughters to dangerous levels.[40] This forced other daughters to enter convents, while half or most of the sons in the family would remain bachelors, in or out of the Catholic church. Many noblemen mated with women outside marriage, like Imperiale Cinuzzi of Siena, who beseeched his brothers to look after the pregnant concubine he had brought back from Flanders, as if she were his wife.[41] Early in the seventeenth century, the Catholic authorities stamped out such cohabitation in Italy, however.[42] Only the eldest son would marry, inherit

---

[39] J. Chagniot, "Ethique et pratique de la 'profession des armes' chez les officiers français au XVIIe siècle", in *Guerre et pouvoir en Europe au XVIIe siècle* (Paris: 1991), pp. 79–93.

[40] O. di Simplicio and S. Cohn, "Alcuni aspetti della politica matrimoniale della nobiltà senese, 1560–1700 circa", *Annali della Facoltà di Scienze Politiche de l'Università degli Studi di Perugia*, **16**, 1979–80, pp. 313–330. Di Simplicio and Cohn link the problem of the demographic decline of the aristocracy, revealed by Baker, to the contracting agricultural economy, and to the growth in dowry levels. See also Baker, "Nobiltà in declino: il caso di Siena sotto i Medici e gli Asburgo-Lorena", *Rivista Storica Italiana*, 1972, pp. 584–616.

[41] Gregory Hanlon, "The demilitarization of an Italian provincial aristocracy: Siena, 1560–1740", *Past and Present*, **155**, 1997, pp. 64–108.

[42] Oscar di Simplicio, *Peccato, penitenza, perdono: Siena 1575–1800* (Milan: 1994), pp. 183–208.

the estate, and dole out an annuity to his siblings. The system was not entirely closed, since mothers could apportion their dowry property for sons and daughters alike, and nobles could earn a decent income through their outside activities in the Church, the court, the bench and in some professions like medicine.[43] Individuals who succeeded – by attaining high rank in the army, or in the diplomatic or administrative service of their prince, by the astute management of their estates, or by climbing the hierarchy of the Church – were then expected to spread the wealth and patronage to their relatives.[44] In the second half of the seventeenth century, nobles sought clerical benefices more eagerly than ever before, giving it some measure of control over tax-exempt church property.[45] In southern Italy, Delille notes how the great aristocracy was able to convince the crown to grant it wider title to the fiefs they held, thereby creating a market in feudal properties that helped them consolidate their fortunes. With Papal dispensations, aristocrats married their closest cousins to avoid alienating land or valuables in the form of dowries. Nobles needed positions at court, special tax privileges and sinecures to make ends meet, and the prince dispensed all of these. As a consequence of these various forms of retrenchment, the number of nobles declined from the late sixteenth century to the mid-eighteenth century. Princes and governments created new nobles everywhere, but the newcomers were progressively enjoined to give up activities that contrasted with the ideology of aristocratic liberality and decorum.[46] In most cities mercantile activities entailed a derogation of noble status. Under great pressure to uphold their rank, new nobles placed such restrictions on their children that such families were more likely than most to become extinct or lose noble status.

Gérard Labrot treats our presumption of noble concern for lucre as *sottement bourgeois*.[47] What military service gratified and enhanced immediately was status. So central was military glory to a working definition of nobility, that even a thin veneer of martial virtue added some lustre to one's name. The eagerness with which rising families steered a son into the knights of Malta or Santo Stefano is one sign of this. His title *cavaliere* dignified them all and served as public

---

[43] For a comparative view of laws governing inheritance, see the long contribution by J. P. Cooper, "Patterns of inheritance and settlement by great landowners from the fifteenth to the eighteenth centuries", *Family and inheritance: rural society in western Europe, 1200–1800* (Cambridge: 1976), pp. 192–312. There are a number of important studies on the contraction of Italian noble families. The most ambitious is by Marzio Barbagli, *Sotto lo stesso tetto: mutamenti della famiglia in Italia dal XV al XX secolo* (Bologna: 1984).

[44] See the article by Renata Ago, "Ecclesiastical careers and the destiny of cadets", *Continuity and Change*, 1992, pp. 271–82.

[45] Di Simplicio, *Peccato, penitenza, perdono*, pp. 84–5.

[46] G. Vismara, "Il patriziato milanese nel cinque-seicento", in *Potere e società negli stati regionali italiani fra '500 e '600*, E. Fasano-Guarini (ed.) (Bologna: 1978), pp. 153–72.

[47] Gérard Labrot, "Le comportement collectif de l'aristocratie de Naples a l'époque moderne", *Revue Historique*, 1977, pp. 45–71, at p. 46.

acknowledgement of the family's noble status. It mattered little if he served his time on the galleys.[48] It is thus difficult to distinguish between those for whom a military career was a rite of passage or a necessary stage on the way to a grander station, and those who awaited the next campaign with eagerness. Moreover, military service washed away the shame of a criminal record, and princes generally turned a blind eye to misdeeds their officers had committed in other jurisdictions. Some of the Montecùccoli clan indulged in sordid vendettas, and many others took their bad habits into the army with them.[49] Noblemen would also rush to participate in some great military campaign, hoping to join the ranks and 'be there' for the great occasion perceived as a turning point in European history. Lepanto and the siege of Malta were two such events, as was the siege of Buda in 1686.

Though they might seem to be antithetical, status and ambition were closely related. In Spain and Italy, noblemen raised troops and led them on campaign as a favour to the monarch. They could also exercise their patronage through such levies, appointing clients to the junior posts in the unit. It was also a way of displaying some *prepotenza*, of levying contributions on vassals, or settling scores. Military service by nobles could help obtain a title, a place at court, or obtain pardon for a crime, or permit the devolution of a fief on a branch of the family.[50] These considerations explain the eagerness with which Italian princes served the emperor and the king of Spain.[51] Mantuan courtiers enhanced their status by joining their duke on campaign in Hungary in 1595. Noblemen in Turin couched their participation in the duke's adventures in terms of feudal obligation, but there was clearly a sense that the duke owed them something in return.[52] If cash rewards were not feasible, then titles, and offices and fiefs with autonomous jurisdiction also served as capital in an economy fuelled by prestige.[53] The late sixteenth century witnessed the transformation of Italian urban notables into legal nobles with a near-monopoly over functions of government. We see a rush to acquire titles and to reinforce lines of social demarcation. Nobility, however, also required a lifestyle predicated upon generosity, bravura, and an anti-economic

---

[48] F. Angiolini, "La nobiltà 'imperfetta'; cavalieri e commende di S. Stefano nella Toscana moderna", *Signori, patrizi, cavalieri nell' età moderna*, M. A. Visceglia (ed.) (Bari: 1992). This is also the thrust of the book by AngelAntonio Spagnoletti, *Stato, aristocrazie e ordine di Malta nell' Italia moderna* (Rome: 1988).

[49] Sandonnini, *Il generale Raimondo Montecuccoli e la sua famiglia*; see the appendices dealing with relatives of the Austrian general.

[50] Thompson, *War and government in Habsburg Spain*, p. 119.

[51] For a specific example, see Michèle Benaiteau, "Una nobiltà di lunga durata: strategie e comportamenti dei Tocco di Montemiletto", in *Signori, patrizi, cavalieri in Italia centro-meridionale nell' età moderna*, M. A. Visceglia (ed.) (Bari: 1992), pp. 193–213, at p. 205, concerning the Tocco di Montemiletto in the kingdom of Naples.

[52] Merlin, *Tra guerre e tornei*, p. 125.

[53] The expression is Labrot's, "Le comportement collectif de l'aristocratie de Naples a l'epoque moderne", *Revue Historique*, 1977, pp. 45–71, at p. 70.

ethos to which only the wealthy could aspire. To prove one's quality it was not enough to brandish an extract from a parish register, but rather conform to this ethos – or better still, display what one social psychologist calls 'superior conformity'.[54]

In the burgeoning literature on the nature and definition of nobility, leadership in war took pride of place. The wave of genealogies published after the late sixteenth century put an emphasis on the glory that military pedigree reflected onto successive generations. These ideas were grounded in feudal concepts of knighthood and chivalry, themselves sustained by a vast literature. Young Raimondo Montecùccoli, setting out on campaign at age 19 described to Duke Francesco of Modena his intention to learn military discipline as "the foundation of every office and every honour".[55] The sentiment of the destiny of the house, or *casa*, and the worth of its traditions, seems stronger in the military and courtier houses than in those from commerce and the bar. In Siena, at least two-thirds of the old noble families could boast a warrior in their ranks in the century and a half after 1560, and among those, the average was more than four warriors each, as opposed to the newer, less prestigious houses where military careers were rare.[56] This pattern is found even in minor cities like Jesi in the Marches, where only the old noble families furnished candidates for the Venetian, Imperial and Papal armies for several generations, until this activity disappeared utterly in the eighteenth century.[57] At the opposite pole on that scale, Charles Emanuel I of Savoy went as far as to decorate part of his palace with the dukes his ancestors bearing arms and armour, to remind himself of his place in the series.[58] The custom of the Venetian patriciate to bring back its war dead for burial in family chapels springs from a similar sentiment.[59]

It is extremely common to find dynasties of military officers, sometimes from father to son, but more often from uncle to nephew. Hale has underlined how many multigenerational families served Venice in the sixteenth century. Fathers were succeeded in a captaincy or a *condotta* by sons, nephews replaced uncles, or one brother another. For these families, promotions were always easy, whether their background was Italian, Croat or Greek. The state aimed to reward the loyalty of the family for its long and faithful service. This prevented them from

[54] For a survey of these outward signs of nobility, see Giovanni Muto, "I segni d'onore: rappresentazioni delle dinamiche nobiliari a Napoli in età moderna", in *Signori, patrizi, cavalieri in Italia centro-meridionale nell' età moderna*, M. A. Visceglia (ed.) (Bari: 1992), pp. 171–92.

[55] Sandonnini, *Il generale Raimondo Montecuccoli e la sua famiglia*, p. 34.

[56] Hanlon, "The demilitarization of a provincial Italian aristocracy: Siena, 1560–1740", *Past and Present*, **155**, 1977, pp. 64–108.

[57] R. Molinelli, *Città e contado nella Marca pontificia in età moderna* (Urbino: 1984), p. 148.

[58] Merlin, *Tra guerre e tornei*, pp. 186–8.

[59] Alexander F. Cowan, *The urban patriciate: Lübeck and Venice, 1580–1700* (Cologne: 1986), p. 103.

leaving to fight elsewhere, for market prices. Venice also established a rudimentary welfare service for the aged and infirm, and confided its less threatened castles and fortresses to over-age officers. The Venetian case is interesting because the officers as a rule were not patricians, nor even subjects of the republic, and presumably had no ideological ties to the regime.[60] An aristocratic example from the kingdom of Naples would be the Tocco di Montemiletto, who provided soldiers for generations from the sixteenth to the eighteenth century. Both the elder and the cadet branches provided four or five officers simultaneously to the king of Spain. GiovanBattista II commanded the garrison at Taranto in the late sixteenth century, having reached the rank of *sergente-maggiore*, or major. Giovanni and Francesco Tocco were at Lepanto, while a third brother Costantino commanded a company of Italian infantry for the duke of Savoy, when this last was a satellite of Madrid. In the next generation, Leonardo Tocco was *maestro di campo* leading a *tercio* to the relief of Turin in 1641. In the eighteenth century, other members of the Tocco di Montemiletto family pursued military careers in the kingdom, though perhaps without ever seeing battle. Michèle Benaiteau notes that even when they held formal commissions from the state, these posts brought with them considerable expenditure. A military career for the Tocco di Montemiletto was not a way to earn money, but to enter the company of that aristocracy that basked in the king's friendship.[61] In Papal Ferrara the situation of the Bentivoglio family was somewhat different. The head of the house, Enzo, tried to maximize family wealth in the 1620s and 1630s so that his sons might find decent careers in foreign armies or in the Church. Enzo's sons Francesco and Ermes followed careers in soldiering, through the family's longstanding alliance with France. But as there was no new wealth, so there was no new space for ambition.[62] It was wealth that was the springboard for lucrative careers in the army, and not the reverse. It helped to fall back on the concept of honour to justify this path, although it may have been honour defined negatively. What nobles rejected was military service merely for money's sake. So despite the unlikelihood of making a fortune at war, many nobles still looked to the army for employment.

Competition among individuals for titles and offices also extended to displays of magnificence and taste, which drew heavily upon family revenues. Goldthwaite is correct to emphasize that display, which is at the heart of feudal culture, applied to war too.[63] Historians are struck by the profusion of plate and horses, carriages and rich apparel among the officers. The cardinal–infanta of Spain sought to reduce the burgeoning ostentation that swelled the baggage trains of the army in

---

[60] Mallett & Hale, *The military organization of a Renaissance state*, p. 317ff.

[61] Benaiteau, "Una nobiltà di lunga durata", in *Signori, patrizi, cavalieri*, pp. 193–213.

[62] On the Bentivoglio of Ferrara and Modena, see Janet Southorn, *Power and display in the seventeenth century: the arts and their patrons in Modena and Ferrara* (New York: 1988), pp. 75–88.

[63] Goldthwaite, *Wealth and the demand for art in Italy*, p. 153.

Flanders.[64] Croce points to the regal train of the Neapolitan Tuttavilla brothers, Francesco and Vincenzo on campaign in Catalonia, and the ill-fated Francesco Toraldo who helped sick or unfortunate subordinates from his own purse by lavishing attention on them. The Sienese Giovanni Bichi turned his cramped galley quarters into a stately chamber suitable for playing the role of *grand seigneur*. Enea Silvio Piccolòmini depended upon remittances from his father in Siena for similar expenses, which he tried to justify in his letters home. Once, he bragged about the tent he had made for him in Cologne, the most magnificent in the Imperial army, which helped him hold his own against more highly placed Italians against whom he measured his progress.[65] While the display of such wealth on campaign increased the risk of losing it, or indicated ransom levels to their captors, it increased their 'visibility' in the crowd of officers and so enhanced their chances of promotion. Money was necessary in part to maintain their rank within the army, to maintain a 'train' that attracted the services and gratitude of clients. Redlich cites Galasso and Piccolòmini as upstarts wishing to be treated as counts and princes, and placing great value on lavish consumption and display, and enjoying wielding patronage to great or notable families, perhaps because their own backgrounds were lower to middling aristocracy.[66] Unlike the magistrate, the military noble lived on representation, maintaining a lifestyle at the limit of, or beyond, his possibilities. At court, they had to spend without wincing, to convince princes, ministers or senior officers of their usefulness.

This visibility was not just for personal satisfaction, for relatives at home lived in tight communities eager for news from the field. The bearing, promotion, success and failure of every town's officers were unfailingly commented on at home, just as their letters were passed around to friends and relatives.[67] Many nobles held a tarnished reputation to be worse than death or mutilation. If the acquisition of honour was expressed in public and visible ways, so was its loss. Cases of such misadventures surge from the encyclopedias. After he gave up a fortress too hurriedly, the governor Cerruti was court-martialled for cowardice in Mantua, and subjected to an expulsion parade through the capital where the

---

[64] Lonchay, *La rivalité de la France et de l'Espagne dans les Pays-Bas*, p. 61.

[65] This propensity for display is noted by M. S. Anderson, *War and society in Europe of the old regime*, p. 58. For particulars, see Croce, "Scene della vita dei soldati spagnuoli a Napoli", in *Uomini e cose della vecchia Italia*, p. 139ff. On Bichi, see Guglielmotti, *Storia della marina pontificia*, vol. VIII, p. 162. On conspicuous consumption in the camp, see in the Archivio di Stato di Siena, Archivi Particolari, Piccolomini Consorteria, vol. 25; lettere del C. Enea Silvio Piccolomini; in particular, the letter dated from Strasbourg, 14 July 1675.

[66] Redlich, *The German military enterpriser and his work force*, vol. 1, p. 449.

[67] Archivio di Stato di Siena, archivi particolari, Consorteria Piccolomini, vol. 25, letter of 20 March 1662; see also John Stoye, *Marsigli's Europe, 1680–1730*, p. 12. Elmar Henrich notes that a third or a half of the broadsheets celebrating the victories of Vienna and Buda were composed in Italian, in his "*Italian military elites in the service of the Spanish and Austrian Habsburgs, 1560–1700*", p. 229 and p. 231.

population pelted him with stones and refuse. Abusive crowds milled around the *palazzo* of Fulvio della Corgna in Perugia, and executed him in effigy after he turned Castiglione del Lago over to the Tuscans. The entire city heaped scorn upon him and his house, which was one of the foremost in Umbria. The nobleman took refuge with the grand duke in Florence, but we can assume that Tuscan nobles held him in similar contempt. Venice cast its unsuccessful generals into prison, and if they refused to return, commemorated their dishonour on a marble plaque affixed to the Doge's palace.[68] Such shame was almost impossible to redeem. Ferdinando Marsigli spent years trying to justify himself at the Viennese court after his disgrace in 1703, and then travelled from one capital to another to plead his case.[69] Shame also fell heavily onto the victim's offspring. Not only was Zaccaria Sagredo's reputation destroyed when the Imperials routed his Venetian army in 1630, but the stain was cleansed only by the battlefield death of his son Bernardo in Crete.[70]

The pursuit of noble causes

The above focuses strictly on what one could term 'selfish' interests motivating these individuals to risk their skins and their fortunes in battle. How sensitive they were to higher causes is difficult to determine. The aristocratic ethos in Spain held that a warrior fought for glory and from a sense of duty to his sovereign.[71] His reward was the gratitude of his ruler, and the property of his enemies. The two 'ideals' to which nobles could refer without blushing, were fidelity to their prince and service to God. Italian nobles seemed to measure up adequately to both, since very few fought their legitimate prince, or against the 'Catholic' cause in the ranks of Protestant or Islamic armies.[72]

Italian nobles in the crusading orders of Malta and Santo Stefano should be

---

[68] There are several examples in the encyclopedias; see Valori, *Condottieri e generali del Seicento*, p. 85, for Cerruti; p. 96, for Fulvio della Corgna; p. 94, for Giovanni Contarini; and pp. 311–12, for Pietro Querini, who died in prison after demonstrating incompetence or irresolute command at Chios.

[69] J. Stoye, *Marsigli's Europe, 1680–1730*, p. 258. Similarly, Carlo Ventimiglia justified himself for the loss of Taormina in 1677, in a letter sent to all the courts of Europe; see Valori, *Condottieri e generali del seicento*, p. 421.

[70] Valori, *Condottieri e generali del seicento*, p. 336–7, for Agostino, Bernardo and Zaccaria Sagredo.

[71] R. Puddu, *Il soldato gentiluomo: autoritratto d'una società guerriera. La Spagna del cinquecento* (Bologna: 1982), p. 8.

[72] Stuart Woolf speculates on the frequency of military service against their own princes. On the basis of the encyclopedias, this appears to be very infrequent. The closer analysis of Siena reveals very few cases. See Woolf, "Intervento", in *Patriziati e aristocrazie nobiliari*, p. 85. See also Hanlon, "The demilitarization of an Italian provincial aristocracy: Siena 1560–1740", *Past and Present*, **155**, 1977, pp. 64–108.

considered apart, because of the tangible benefits of status their members and their families derived from the 'habit'. These Orders resembled religious orders of monks in their constitutions, and assumed the existence of a religious vocation. Sanctity they realized sword in hand in the defence of Truth, against the enemies of the Church. The Order of the Knights of Saint John of Jerusalem, the oldest and the largest of these, recruited young men and adolescents from all over Catholic Europe. After the French, who constituted about half, the second largest component was Italian, who comprised about one knight in three, or three in ten during the early seventeenth century.[73]

AngelAntonio Spagnoletti holds that, as the aristocracies were increasingly employed in the bureaucracies of their state of origin after 1650, there were fewer available to be knights of Malta. The geography of their recruitment is a kind of photographic negative of the integration of élites into the modern state. He looks at 3,448 Italian knights from the seventeenth and eighteenth centuries by situating them in the political context of their city and state, for different periods. The knight's family reaffirmed its traditions and its ambitions by directing a son to the order, and in some cases, parents sent a son into the service deliberately to diversify the family's resources and connections. Gradually, over the course of the seventeenth century, recruitment of Italians flagged. The order remained important primarily in the minor towns, away from the political capitals.

The knights of Santo Stefano, on the other hand, enhanced the authority of the prince, while keeping the Barbary pirates in check. The order differed from that of Malta in that its members could marry, and transmit their 'habit' through inheritance. Property the families assigned to the *commenda* entered ecclesiastical jurisdiction. Spini sees it as just another way of creating a *fedecommesso* of family property, placing it outside the bounds of whatever could be seized for non-payment of debt.[74] Even more than the order of Malta, the order of Santo Stefano was an institution ready to register the progress of new families seeking social recognition. The grand dukes were ready to overlook some defects in the genealogy of the applicant in exchange for a 'topping up' of the capital consecrated to the organization. Of 695 *commende* founded between 1563 and 1737, over a quarter had the capital increased to compensate for an imperfect pedigree. To compensate, and so as not to dilute the noble nature of the institution, Ferdinando II decreed in 1638 and 1665 that knights must marry noblewomen, or at least the daughters of other knights. Angiolini concludes that the Medici dynasty felt it necessary not to alienate the lesser nobility or deprive them of the social recognition they craved. Letting them join the order of Santo Stefano was a way of recognizing their status. Over time, and much earlier than for the knights of Malta, membership in the order became more honorific than martial. The grand duke granted entry to mature men as a personal favour to some nobles so as to

---

[73] A. Spagnoletti, *Stato, aristocrazie e ordine di Malta*, p. 66.

[74] G. Spini, "Introduzione", in *Architettura e politica, da Cosimo I a Ferdinando I* (Florence: 1976), pp. 9–77; at p. 57.

retain the *commenda* in their family. When he reduced the number of galleys after the 1620s, fewer knights could go on patrol and acquire experience. Numbers remained largely stable, but those with military experience were ever rarer by the early eighteenth century. So this military order demilitarized.[75]

'Loyalism' or 'royalism' must certainly count as a motivating force for a good part of the military aristocracy. Guicciardini, when explaining the downfall of Italy to foreign conquerors, contrasted the loyalty of French barons to their king, to the egotistical instincts of Italians.[76] In the Italian principalities, the introduction of Spanish court etiquette and protocol replaced the familiar atmosphere with a stiffer observation of propriety based on rank and function. Consequently, this vaulted the prince far above the station of mere nobles.[77] The growth of such courts in the seventeenth century, with their elaborate ceremonies and entertainments, and ever longer lists of appointments, tied nobles more closely to their princes. Pages in particular were imbued with these values, and then 'placed' in the army or the church as they preferred.[78]

The attraction was perhaps strongest in the Spanish dominions. Very few Neapolitan or Lombard officers fought for anyone but a Habsburg prince. These noble families, however powerful they might be in remote fiefs in their patrimony, vied for the attention of the king of Spain and the viceroys in Naples and Palermo. Their physical transfer to the capital cities during the sixteenth century, to display their willingness to serve the crown, was an important step. This fuelled an intense competition for honours and offices at the court and in the army which was more often cause of indebtedness than of enrichment. The viceregal courts legitimized their social and political hegemony, their privileges and their monopoly over the top positions; there was an effective 'partnership' to govern the kingdoms together.[79]

The Imperial myth that attracted Italians to Vienna is more difficult to explain, but the biographers of Raimondo Montecùccoli and Ottavio Piccolòmini leave no doubt that they 'bought' the cause of the emperor without reserve, and that many other Italians debated its merits seriously, like the commander of the Mantuan fortress who desired to discuss whether an Italian could surrender to the emperor in good conscience.[80] Perhaps the emperor's most attractive feature to Italians was his commitment to the Catholic cause, for it assured them preferment in the

---

[75] F. Angiolini, "La nobiltà 'imperfetta': cavalieri e commende di S. Stefano nella Toscana moderna", in *Signori, patrizi, cavalieri nell' età moderna* (Bari: 1992), pp. 146–66.

[76] Guicciardini, "Storia d'Italia", *Opere*, V. de Caprariis & R. Ricciardi (eds) (Milan: 1961), p. 439.

[77] Dennistoun, *Memoirs of the dukes of Urbino*, vol. 3, p. 187. See also Pierpaolo Merlin, *Tra guerre e tornei*, p. 4ff.

[78] For an example from the court of Modena, see Sandonnini, *Il generale Raimondo Montecuccoli e la sua famiglia*, p. 29.

[79] Aurelio Musi, *La rivolta di Masaniello nella scena politica barocca* (Naples: 1989), p. 89.

[80] Valori, *Condottieri e generali del Seicento*, p. 97, Angelo Corner.

competition with Protestants of equal talent. Piccolòmini entered the plot to assassinate his patron Wallenstein primarily because the former was an ardent supporter of war until total victory for the Imperial cause.[81]

Convergence of the Habsburg Imperial dignity, Madrid's tranquil rule over much of Italy, and their joint promotion of the Catholic cause made it easy for conscientious Italians to choose this camp even in the face of adversity. The very cardinals of the church were sometimes generals, though not usually fighting enemies of the faith.[82] Religious zeal may also have motivated many Italians to join the orders of Malta and Santo Stefano, even if the typical knight fell far short of Guarnieri's depiction of their upright character. There may have been a 'Catholicization' of war from the mid-sixteenth century onwards, as the Pope spent treasure to help Spain and Austria achieve victory. The theme of the Christian knight became a common one in Italian literature.[83] Friars exhorted young men from the pulpit to participate in war. Colleges staged depictions of victorious war against a heathen adversary, usually the Turk.[84] Each victory over an enemy of religion was celebrated in a flurry of renderings of the *Te Deum* in every Italian city; and each death of an Italian noble on campaign was marked in his native city with a procession and cortège celebrating his piety and heroism. Sandonnini attributes Montecuccoli's choice of Imperial service, and his rapid advance, to the rigorous religious upbringing he received from his pious mother.[85] He did not fail to make offerings to the shrine of Loreto after the victory of St Gotthard, acknowledging the aid of the Virgin Mary. Other Italians made offerings to shrines in their native cities to publicize the workings of Divine Providence, and to thank the Virgin Mary for delivering them from peril.[86]

From all of the above, it is difficult to sketch the portrait of a 'typical' military

---

[81] Mann, *Wallenstein*, p. 792.

[82] I have identified seven, all in the first half of the seventeenth century; only one, Guido Bentivoglio, fought against the Protestants in Flanders. Three servants of the king of Spain fighting in Lombardy were Giacomo Trivulzio and Agostino Spìnola, son of the famous general, and Giannetino Doria, who led Spanish troops from Sicily to the aid of Genoa in 1625. The papal nephew Antonio Barberini led armies into battle personally during the Castro War. Cardinal Alessandro Bichi fought with the French army under Mazarin after the fall of the Barberini clan in the 1640s, but as a volunteer rather than as a general officer. One more cardinal, the Dominican Maculani, was a fortifications expert.

[83] A. Prosperi, "Il 'miles christianus' nella cultura italiana tra '400 e '500", *Critica Storica*, 1989, pp. 685–704.

[84] G. Hanlon, "Celebrating war in a peaceful city: festive representations of combat in Siena, *ca.* 1570–1740", in *Self and Society in Renaissance Italy*, W. Connell (ed.) (Berkeley, forthcoming, 1998).

[85] Sandonnini, *Il generale Raimondo Montecuccoli e la sua famiglia*, p. 75.

[86] For example the Madonna di Provenzano in Siena, object of vows, sabres and banners from Paolo Amerighi, Antonio Malavolti and Marco Antonio Zondadari. See Valori, *Condottieri e generali del Seicento*, p. 10, for Amerighi, p. 213, for Malavolti, p. 439, for Zondadari.

noble, for the more we learn about them, the more diverse they seem. Jonathan Dewald, writing of the French nobility, emphasizes their individuality and the futility of pointing to a single representative experience. These men had multiple relations to the court, to money, administration, new technology and new situations.[87] Perhaps this is true not just of nobles, for they celebrated their individuality more freely, and we know them better from the documents they have left us. Perhaps success and fortune in the army depended on a particular kind of assertive personality. Redlich describes the 'German' military enterpriser in unflattering terms, as generally being "tough and grasping, even when they were not immune to loftier motives for fighting". They were "insensitive, but shrewd and great organizers. They were big men, mercenary, brutal, inclined to violence, unrestrained, cantankerous, addicted to gambling for large sums, drinking hard and other vices".[88] The Italians may have been more educated than the norm, less inclined to drink, and ready to justify their actions in reference to their Catholic faith, but for the rest, this portrait may be accurate.

Writing of the Germans in particular, Redlich states that their education was summary, except for those who began as pages at princely courts, where they learned to deal with influential people at an early age.[89] Barker, comparing the German military enterprisers with the Italians, hazards that the Italians would have been more cultivated on the whole, owing to the standard education offered by Jesuit colleges and the military academies that flourished in the cities.[90] Some German commanders were notorious for their alcoholism; Italians, like Ottavio Piccolòmini or Luigi Isolano, however, were more addicted to gambling huge sums. The encyclopedia literature frequently gives examples of this pathological propensity which was socially acceptable once placed in a warrior context. Brief allusions to an "exuberant and irreverent" nature (Artale); a "dissolute and soldierly" behaviour (Giovanni de'Medici) tell us something, as does the probably apocryphal anecdote about Giovanni Serbelloni who once lost a battle for having refused to read a dispatch that omitted some of his titles.[91] Eloquent too was the behaviour of those many nobles who punctuated their career by murdering enemies and not infrequently family members too, like Bartolomeo Faneschi of Montalcino, whose career in the Venetian army was launched by some 'youthful crimes' in his home town; or Antonio Folco, alias Il Turco, who brought his Abruzzi outlaw followers into Genoese service.[92]

---

[87] J. Dewald, *Aristocratic experience and the origins of modern culture: France, 1570–1715* (Berkeley, California: 1993), pp. 45–65.

[88] Redlich, *The German military enterpriser and his work force*, vol. 1, p. 64.

[89] *Ibid.*, vol. 1, p. 157ff.

[90] For rapid comparisons, see Barker, *The military intellectual and battle*, p. 9 and p. 52.

[91] Valori, *Condottieri e generali del seicento*, p. 15, for Giuseppe Artale; pp. 114–15, for Giovanni de'Medici; pp. 369–70, for Giovanni Serbelloni.

[92] Valori, *Condottieri e generali del seicento*, p. 143, for Bartolomeo Faneschi; and p. 152, for Antonio Folco.

In such a competitive atmosphere, honour and interest, idealism and personal advantage were closely bound together. Manifestations of overbearing arrogance were not considered scandalous, for they were challenges thrown down by men who prided themselves on daring.[93] Protocol, power and representation were so closely bound together, that disputes over precedence or procedure commonly hampered operations. If anything brought these Italians together, it was their ethnic clannishness in foreign service, and their readiness to advance other Italians, assuming that other 'nations' would do likewise. Their 'interest', like their ideals, was still largely supranational. They could not know, in 1700, that the states to which they offered their swords would soon strengthen around concepts of ethnicity and territoriality, making their service redundant. As their presence waned, it became ever more difficult for their relatives to lobby for them, and to 'work the court' to obtain advancement. This would then discourage newcomers unable to squeeze through the narrow opening.

Italian society demilitarized as aristocrats withdrew from European armies. One might object that war as a calling continued to be part of the Italian aristocrat's world-view. This is partly true, for the oldest families continued to provide modest numbers of soldiers throughout the century, as in Siena for example, where the Piccolòmini continued to provide the Empire with enthusiastic recruits.[94] The decline in numbers may have been due to the process of demographic implosion affecting the nobility as a whole, as one consequence of the economic crisis. Historians studying Venice, Milan, Florence and Siena have been able to chart this steep fall. In Florence, the nobility lost two-thirds of its numbers between 1500 and 1750. Siena passed from 259 houses in 1560 to 107 in 1764, with the period of rapid decline beginning in the late seventeenth century. The military officers themselves were largely bachelors, or married later in life, thereby accelerating this process.[95] But these considerations only underline the waning importance of the military class in Italian society. Moreover, since wealth and advancement were difficult to achieve through this avenue,

---

[93] Jean Chagniot addresses the problem of competing claims of precedence amongst officers in the French army in, "Ethique et pratique de la 'profession des armes' chez les officiers français au XVIIe siècle", *Guerre et pouvoir en Europe au XVIIe siècle*, p. 85.

[94] Hanlon, "The demilitarization of an Italian provincial aristocracy", *Past and Present*, **155**, 1997, pp. 64–108.

[95] The relentless demographic decline of urban patriciates in the eighteenth century is the object of a considerable literature. For a sample, in addition to those studies evoked in previous chapters, see Emilio Nasalli Rocca, "Il patriziato piacentino nell' eta del principato", in *Studi di paleografia, diplomatica, storia e araldica in onore di Cesare Manaresi* (Milan: 1953), pp. 225–57; for Florence, see R. Burr Litchfield, "Demographic characteristics of Florentine patrician families, 16th–19th centuries", *Journal of Economic History*, 1969, pp. 191–205; for Milan, see Dante Zanetti, "The patriziato of Milan from the domination of Spain to the Unification of Italy", *Social History*, 1977, pp. 745–60; for several examples from Puglia in southern Italy, see AngelAntonio Spagnoletti, "*L' inconstanza delle umane cose: il patriziato di Terra di Bari tra egemonia e crisi, XVI–XVIII secolo* (Bari: 1981).

families steered their male progeny and cadets onto alternative roads. Litchfield notes how the Tuscan patriciate invested the duchy's bureaucracy in the second half of the seventeenth century, snapping up an increasing number of permanent positions. Moreover, the age of noble office-holders dropped on average by six or seven years, to include those youths who had previously spent time on galleys or in army camps.[96] Even more than the bureaucracy, the Counter-Reformation church in heady expansion gave new employment for noble youths, in new canonical benefices reserved for social élites, but also for tonsured clerics established in modest benefices by their families.[97] If the Sienese example is at all typical, aristocratic families avoided the risks of an investment in military glory, and preferred those positions that provided their progeny with a steady income.

---

[96] R. B. Litchfield, *The emergence of a bureaucracy: the Florentine patricians (1530–1790)* (Princeton, New Jersey: 1986), p. 134 and p. 185.

[97] O. di Simplicio, *Peccato, penitenza, perdono: la formazione della coscienza moderna: Siena 1575–1800* (Milan: 1994), pp. 83–5.

Chapter 7
The Piedmontese exception

The development of the Piedmontese military state

Piedmont was the only Italian state to evolve along a north European pattern in the early modern period, where the dukes of Savoy enforced their absolutist pretensions with a significant army, in which nobility served. In this unusual evolution, geography certainly played a part. The sixteenth-century duchy was a rather loose and heterogeneous Alpine feudal state without a central focus. Part of it looked toward Lyon on the Rhône, part towards German-speaking Switzerland, and part towards the upper Po valley which was a backward cul-de-sac compared to Lombardy or Venetia. Duke Charles III (1504–53) employed no mercenaries, nor did he have permanent and assured taxes by which to pay any. France occupied Savoy and Piedmont in the 1530s without much resistance, in order to ensure free access to Milan, the prize it sought. The Swiss Protestant league detached parts of Savoy, and Calvinist Geneva broke away, while Spanish troops occupied Vercelli to keep the French army from Milan. The heir to the throne, Emanuel Philibert, used his birthright – being a nephew of Charles V – to cut a figure in the Hispano-Imperial army. He proved to be one of the emperor's ablest generals, winning the decisive battle against France at St Quentin in the Low Countries in 1557. With the peace of Câteau-Cambrésis in 1559, the duke recovered most of his states, save for Geneva, which was permanently lost. Spanish garrisons held eastern Piedmont until, after many Piedmontese demonstrations of good faith and more or less spontaneous contributions to the Habsburg cause, they relinquished them in 1575. Emanuel Philibert would have preferred to expand his duchy by intervening in the ongoing religious struggle in France, but for the moment concentrated on putting his state back in order.

The duchy lacked any kind of permanent tax in 1559, so the establishment of the *taille*, on the French model, was a crucial innovation. Since both clergy and nobility enjoyed fiscal privileges, it fell primarily upon the peasantry, as in France. The taxes financed a programme for modern fortifications, of which the duke was a true enthusiast. He ordered refortification of key towns like Montmelian in Savoy, and Fort Joux near Geneva, and established forges and foundries to equip them with cannon. Emanuel Philibert subjected his nobles to a stricter application of feudal law, awarding investiture only in exchange for military service. Apart from their contributions there was practically no army, just some noble body-guards. In 1566, the duke created the military 'household', comprising a few companies of horse and infantry. These served alongside a company of noble gens d'armes as was the fashion at the time, the members of which were more courtiers than soldiers.[1] Besides his bodyguards, the duke planted garrisons in the major towns. These were old and trusted servants, more like faithful retainers than resolute veterans. In 1566, there were 1,200 men in garrisons, with 250 in the citadel of Turin, 100 each in Mondovì on the Ligurian confines, and Bourg-en-Bresse near the Saône frontier with France, and 163 in the Mediterranean port of Nice.[2] He spread most of the others across a score of places in small numbers. With the establishment of regular taxes, this number increased to about 3,000 men, comparable to Tuscany or the Papal States and in no way original. To complete this array, Emanuel Philibert founded the Order of Santi Maurizio e Lazzaro in 1570, on the model of the Order of Santo Stefano, with about seventy knights belonging to it. He sent three galleys to the Holy League fleet fighting at Lepanto, and not long after that there were seven of them operating out of the Provençal port of Villefranche, near Nice, the duchy's only harbour. This naval force employed several hundred soldiers, although other private galleys and corsairs operated under the Savoyard flag. After the duke's death in 1580 this naval organization rapidly fell into decay, and only three galleys were maintained thereafter.[3]

Political historians remember Emanuel Philibert best for peasant militia he created. This was no innovation, for the *bande* of peasant infantry existed in Tuscany for several decades; there was also the *battaglione* in the kingdom of Naples, the *ordinanze* of Venice and others besides. It was a volunteer militia, a 'home defence' force not meant to stand in the open field, although its effective numbers were quite important considering the limited dimension of the state. There may have been 15,000 militiamen for Piedmont, and 8,000 more in Savoy, of which perhaps 10,000 were willing to follow the duke on campaigns outside their immediate district.[4] These peasants enlisted, as elsewhere, in exchange for

---

[1] Nicola Brancaccio stresses the military attributes of these early institutions. See N. Brancaccio, *L'esercito del vecchio Piemonte: gli ordinamenti, vol. 1, 1560–1814* (Rome: 1923), p. 14. Walter Barberis stresses the ceremonial functions of these 'servants' in the duke's household: W. Barberis, *Le armi del principe: la tradizione militare sabauda* (Turin: 1988), pp. 7–18. Their place at court is examined in an article by Cristina Stango, "La corte di Emanuele Filiberto: organizzazione e gruppi sociali", *Bolletino Storico-Bibliografico Subalpino*, 1987, pp. 445–502, and especially pp. 484–7.
[2] For the garrisons in 1560, see Barberis, *Le armi del principe*, p. 65. Those of 1566 are enumerated in Brancaccio, *L'esercito del vecchio Piemonte*, p. 23ff.
[3] Brancaccio, *L'esercito del vecchio Piemonte*, p. 59.
[4] Barberis, *Le armi del principe*, p. 19ff. On the effective forces, see W. Barberis, "Aristocratie

privileges enhancing their status in their communities. Barberis sees a deliberate plan followed by successive dukes of to diminish the power of the aristocracy by depriving them of their military monopoly. Among the more attractive provisions were privileges of immunity to imprisonment for debts, to avoid personal arrest or to have their assets seized in lawsuits, all common practices in sixteenth-century villages. Only their own officers could judge them. They could bear arms every-where, and liberally availed themselves of this provision with their assortment of swords and knives. They could wear finery and ribbons normally prohibited to people of their status by sumptuary legislation. Cavalry militiamen, who provided their own horses, enjoyed the right to hunt with dogs, like seigneurs. After five years of service they could legally fight duels with nobles to defend their honour. Troopers and their wives could wear silk and hats with gold trim and feathers like any noble.

Militiamen were no mere commoners. To command their companies (for there was no unit larger) the duke appointed trusted noblemen. He could confer on retainers and notables to whom he owed favours of all kinds, the title of captain of militia, which carried little responsibility.[5] The infantry companies remained loosely organized, containing anywhere from 400 to 1,000 men. Cavalry compa-nies were much smaller, and numbered from 25 to 100 troopers each, but every horseman rode with one or two mounted servants similarly armed. There was a feudal militia too, capable of raising a force of 1,500 horse. On paper this organization numbered 24,000 men, but only a third of that was good for crossing the border and fighting elsewhere. Modest numbers of them fought in several theatres. Emanuel Philibert sent a cavalry contingent to aid the emperor in Hungary against the Turks in 1566.[6] The following year an expedition intervened in the French civil war, and again after 1574, alongside professional soldiers hired by the duke.[7] Since they were not especially effective, he preferred to transform many militia obligations into a tax in wartime.

The Piedmontese gradually acquired the reputation of being warlike, even if for everyone, from militiamen to feudal lords, military service was primarily a vehicle for status, privilege and private interest.[8] Certainly, the dukes set out to create a large category of people who served them. As he dismantled their traditional

---

et tradition militaire au Piémont, XVIe–XIXe siècles", *Revue d'Histoire Moderne et Contemporaine*, 1987, pp. 353–403, at p. 360ff.

[5] Barberis, *Le armi del principe*, p. 46.

[6] Brancaccio, *L'esercito del vecchio Piemonte*, p. 23.

[7] See J. Wood, "The royal army during the early wars of religion, 1559–1576", in *Society and institutions in early modern France*, Mack Holt (ed.) (Athens, Georgia: 1991). How many of the Piedmontese troops were militia is not stated. Brancaccio ventures that most of them were militiamen, in *L'esercito del vecchio Piemonte*, p. 23.

[8] See in particular Barberis' article, "L'economia militare e la sua funzione di disciplinamento sociale nel Piemonte sabaudo", *Annali dell' Istituto Italo-Germanico di Trento*, 1991, pp. 25–42.

'private' military potential, the duke gave them a specific function. Barberis' assertion is true also of the militiamen, often village notables with the means to acquire weapons, armour, and sometimes horses, training with them from time to time, on feast days. Barberis goes farther and rejects the idea that the Piedmontese were effectively warlike, but they became good at playing war.[9] The argument is interesting but is marred by the author's disinclination to study the frequency of their employment, and the performance of these troops in battle.

When the dukes wanted to wage war, they relied instead on a different source: the 'servants' who ate at their table. Like other princes, the dukes paid some gentlemen of various provenance who bore the titles of 'colonel' or 'captain', but who had neither soldiers nor non-commissioned officers to command. These soldiers receiving the duke's *dienstgeld* numbered 28 in 1562, and 41 in 1576.[10] This was a group of old 'comrades-in-arms', who were masters of warlike skills. All were experienced recruiters. They could supply him with effective forces at short notice, as classic military enterprisers: Alfonso d'Este from Ferrara could furnish 600 horsemen and 2,000–3,000 Italian infantry; Ferrante Vitelli from the Tuscan borderlands could raise 1,000 soldiers, and was an expert in fortifications. Emanuel Philibert also recruited German and Swiss soldiers, preferably Catholic, under Giovanni Federico Madruzzo, of the Trentino ruling family. In addition, the native nobility saw military service as its birthright, especially in the cavalry. Some took leave of the duke to seek adventure elsewhere. In wartime they could themselves raise troops or lend money to their prince, in the hopes of appointment to a court office, or a fief.

A prestigious position in the army led naturally to a place at the court. These retainers gave the small court in Turin its austere, martial air.[11] Both Piedmontese and 'foreign' gentlemen used military service as a stepping stone into power circles. Don Andrea Matteo Acquaviva, prince of Caserta, offered his services as a 'general of cavalry' by arriving from Naples with a retinue of 100 horsemen recruited at his own expense. This was his way of buying a generalcy, with the appropriate salary and perks, but this was likely to cost him as much as he was paid, if not more. It was rewarding on an ideological level, since it permitted him to advance within his own caste and cultivate appearances of glory.[12] Status entailed, moreover, appearing in the various plays, cavalcades, ballets and other festivities at court, which also permitted one to get ahead in the battle for precedence. Artillery officers directed fireworks displays. Whenever war gave way to peace, these men fell back on their court function as decorative soldiers.[13]

Charles Emanuel I, who succeeded his father in 1580, was especially avid for battlefield glory and proved to be one of the most incautious rulers of the age. He

[9] Barberis, *Le armi del principe*, p. xviii.
[10] *Ibid.*, pp. 65–71.
[11] Merlin, *Tra guerre e tornei*, p. 1.
[12] Barberis, *Le armi del principe*, p. 114.
[13] *Ibid.*, p. 120.

schemed to expand the state however possible. In July 1582 he attempted to seize Geneva, with the (plausible) justification that it was the capital of heresy in Europe. Not having the resources to prevail in a quick attack, the gamble degenerated into a series of skirmishes that required huge expenditures in fortification and garrisons. Profiting from the endless civil war in France, in 1588 he escaladed the walls of Saluzzo, the French possession south of Turin and annexed it outright, claiming (implausibly) that it was a menace to Catholicism in Italy.[14] In 1589, with Spanish support, he almost reconquered the Vaud (French-speaking Switzerland), but again lacked the means by which to lay siege to the large and stout fortress city of Geneva. He intervened in the later stages of the French civil wars, on the side of the Catholic League, hoping to conquer Provence and Dauphiné with Spanish backing. Such was the assistance of Spanish troops (10,000 in 1592) and Spanish subsidies that this was war between France and Spain with Piedmont as the proxy.[15] Charles Emanuel reached Marseilles at one point, but the fortunes of war shifted as the Huguenot commander Lesdiguières brought ruin to Savoy. The duke's expansion policy westward failed spectacularly after 1598, when Henri IV conquered all the Piedmontese territory held north of the Rhône, the districts of Bresse, Bugey and Gex. France kept it in exchange for Saluzzo by the treaty of Lyon in 1601. This incidentally reinforced the Italian character of the duchy. In December 1602, Charles Emanuel tried to compensate for this loss by storming Geneva by surprise, and almost succeeded, but this was not something that could be repeated.[16]

The only available targets now were the Monferrato, the republic of Genoa, and Spanish Milan, besides some daydreaming about liberating the Balkans from the Turks at the head of an insurrection financed by Spain.[17] The duke tried each of these. He entered Henri IV's league of primarily Protestant states on the point of going to war with Spain in 1610, and suffered no little humiliation when the French king's assassination forced a rapid demobilization.[18] Invading the Monferrato in 1614 and 1617, Spain's muscular intervention blocked Charles Emanuel each time, and he retained his initiative only with ongoing French and Venetian financial backing. Piedmontese troops never won an important battle against the Spanish coalition, but they were never shattered either. The Spanish siege of Vercelli in the spring of 1617 lasted six long weeks. Its fall forced Charles Emanuel to treat with Madrid, but its stubborn and frightfully bloody resistance became a symbol of Italian resistance against Spain. After fruitlessly joining the German Protestant League in Germany in 1618, hoping to be proclaimed king of

---

[14] R. Quazza, *Storia politica d'Italia: preponderanza spagnola*, p. 389.

[15] *Ibid.*, p. 389ff. See also the book by Roger Devos & Bernard Grosperrin, *La Savoie de la Réforme à la Revolution* (Rennes: 1985), p. 90ff.

[16] Devos & Grosperrin, *La Savoie de la Réforme à la Revolution*, p. 96ff.

[17] A. Tamborra, *Gli stati italiani: l'Europa e il problema turco dopo Lepanto* (Florence: 1961), pp. 21–40.

[18] Quazza, *Storia politica d'Italia: La preponderanza spagnola*, p. 409.

Bohemia, the duke played the French card next in 1619 by marrying his son to Louis XIII's sister, Christine de France. In 1625, having knit a fragile alliance with Holland, England, France and Venice against Spain, Charles Emanuel's army tried to seize Genoa and the Ligurian coast, on the coat-tails of Lesdiguières' French army. Vigorous Spanish intervention foiled this too. During the war of the Mantuan succession he switched sides twice, first by joining Spain to seize a portion of the Monferrato, then rallying to France when Louis' army invaded Piedmont, and finally joining Spìnola. At the duke's death shortly after, in 1630, Piedmont had lost more territory than it had gained.

The duke fought in person at the head of his army, and his sons Victor Amadeus and Tommaso joined him there. His ducal bodyguard sometimes swelled to thousands of men. Charles Emanuel, more urbane than his predecessor, continued to organize his court on military lines. Many courtiers fought in the ranks of the army, or else accompanied the duke in the rigours of a campaign.[19] The several score gentlemen of the chamber were primarily military advisers. Pages at the court were officers-in-waiting. Even the gentlemen serving at the ducal table had posts in the army. His chief officials, the major-domos, were practically all military experts. The most important of them served as counsellors of ducal policy, like the Brescian general, Count Francesco Martinengo.[20] As under Emanuel Philibert, most of them came from other Italian states, like the Ligurians Doria, Pallavicino and Spìnola; the Milanese Arconati; the Rangoni, Forni and Villa, subjects of the duke of Ferrara and Modena; the Parmans Cavalcà and Scotti; the Malaspina of the Lunigiana and the Muti from Rome. After the marriage of Victor Amadeus with Marie-Christine in 1619, many Frenchmen made their appearance and rendered similar services.[21] To hope for advancement, they were expected to draw upon their own resources to help the duke win his wars, and were subject to forced loans even when they were serving on campaign.[22] Such loyalty the duke rewarded with an inflation of titles, awards of fiefs, and *commende* in the order of Santi Maurizio e Lazzaro. Those who did not co-operate, or who adhered too closely to the wishes of foreign princes, he neglected or crushed.[23]

Such noble docility, and the interested goodwill of his allies made it possible for the duke to have large forces in being at short notice. This adventurist policy rested on troops raised on the fly, from wherever they could be found. In 1615, as an example, Charles Emanuel raised a regiment of Swiss, then another of Valais infantry, and then intermittently other regiments from Piedmont and Savoy. By the mid-1620s, the duke's army reached important dimensions. If in 1614 there were only 3,600 infantry and 1,250 cavalry, by 1625 there were 25,381 infantry

---

[19] Merlin, *Tra guerre e tornei*, p. 60ff.
[20] On Martinengo, see Merlin, *Tra guerre e tornei*, pp. 102–8.
[21] *Ibid.*, p. 22ff.
[22] *Ibid.*, p. 125ff.
[23] *Ibid.*, p. 129.

and 1,213 horse, not including militia. Among these mercenaries, there were from five to seven regiments of Piedmontese infantry, seven or eight thousand peasant militiamen, and another 2,000 men in garrison. The feudal militia was mustered in 1623, and then again in the campaign against Genoa but it was of dubious value. In 1625, the greater part of the ducal troops were ethnically French, the best of them being Lorrainers, with nine regiments in 1625, and seven in 1626. Italian troops, that is, Lombards, Neapolitans, Romans, and sometimes Corsicans too, enlisted whenever the duke was a Spanish ally. Of the Italians there were four regiments in 1600, two in 1624, two in 1626 and six in 1627–8. None of these formations was permanent. When the duke planned to side with Spain, he had to divest himself of the quarter of his army (or more) recruited in France, and find others to replace them.[24] In the sixteenth century, many troops came from the Papal States. Thereafter, such mercenaries were more often Swiss, conveniently close by, or German Protestants, like those under Ernst von Mansfeld who was the duke's agent negotiating with the Bohemian rebels in 1618.[25] In an emergency, it was possible to have tens of thousands of men arriving in Piedmont, of all nationalities, ready to fight. With the end of war in sight the duke, like his adversaries, laid off as many soldiers as he dared. Effective forces expanded and contracted like a bellows.

Even after Charles Emanuel's death, the size of this 'Piedmontese' army continued to oscillate wildly. From 7,350 professional troops in 1630, there were 12,250 in 1635 at the onset of the Thirty Years War; then 15,710 in 1637, and 18,000 in 1649. French troops continued to be used in entire regiments during these years, and the Savoy regiment in particular commonly employed subjects of the king of France. Then in 1660, after the peace, effective strength fell to 5,400 men. When in 1672 Duke Charles Emanuel II invaded the republic of Genoa unprovoked, he brusquely increased his army to 26,178 men, including over 2,000 troops rented from the elector of Bavaria. There were also three regiments of 'Italians' in this invasion force. With the ensuing peace, however, effective numbers dropped to about 6,000 men.[26]

At the outset of his reign in 1630, Victor Amadeus I sought to obtain peace from France and Spain with the best terms possible, losing only Pinerolo, which was an open door to the French army. Cardinal Richelieu soon lured him into an alliance with France with the prospect of territorial aggrandizement in Lombardy, and the conferral of the much-desired royal title of the king of Cyprus. This latter would enhance his status in relation to the other princes of Italy and the Empire. By the treaty of Rivoli in 1635, Piedmont joined the French coalition against Spain, along with Parma and Mantua. The duke's decision had disastrous conse-

---

[24] Brancaccio provides tables permitting one to follow these levies. See, *L'esercito del vecchio Piemonte: gli ordinamenti*, p. 81ff.
[25] Kleinman, "Charles-Emmanuel I of Savoy and the Bohemian revolt of 1619", *European Studies Review*, 1975, pp. 3–29; at p. 9.
[26] Brancaccio, *L'esercito del vecchio Piemonte*, p. 130.

quences, for the French did not commit the troops to the theatre that they promised, and Spain pressed them harder than they anticipated. By December 1636, both of Victor Amadeus' brothers had changed sides, with Prince Tommaso of Savoy commanding Spanish armies in the Low Countries. This may have been with the complicity of the duke himself. The offensive war rapidly turned defensive as Parma and Mantua pulled out of the alliance, and Turin was feverishly fortified.[27] Victor Amadeus, in command of French troops, carried the day at the battle of Tornavento, which ended the threat of immediate invasion. He died in suspicious circumstances soon after, in the prime of youth, while his infant son of five years died the next year, leaving only a baby and the unpopular duchess Christine as regent.

When Prince Tommaso returned to Piedmont and enlisted the support of his brother, Maurizio, Piedmont slid into civil war, with the brothers seizing several key fortresses. Behind the parties contending for control of the duchy, Richelieu and Olivares guided the movements of each side, with only Pope Urban VIII trying to negotiate a quick conclusion. The critical event was the siege of Turin, which lasted for over a year, from July 1639 to September 1640, in which Tommaso besieged the citadel, while a French army besieged him in turn outside the city. Piedmontese forces dissolved into competing factions owing obedience primarily to their officers. Once Tommaso reached a compromise with the duchess regent, Richelieu appointed him commander of the French forces in the field until his death. French troops garrisoned Turin itself until 1645, and then the citadel until 1657, close to the end of the war. French troops then gradually withdrew from Vercelli, retaining only Pinerolo.[28] A quarter-century of war wrought considerable destruction on Piedmont, due to the scavenging of the soldiers, the diseases they transmitted from place to place (like the plague of 1630), and the quartering of troops during winter on rear areas which had been spared the trauma of campaigning. Villages were required to supply the bread, the straw and oats for the horses, bedding for the soldiers, beasts of burden and carts, and sometimes to advance money for the payment of troops. The state rarely reimbursed these obligations. To provide food and shelter for unruly troops on the move was mostly the obligation of the parish. The work this provided and the provision of armaments for the army did not offset the cost.[29]

For more than a generation after the end of the civil war, Piedmont was a docile satellite of King Louis XIV. Duke Charles Emanuel II sought ways to maintain the nucleus of a trained army, which gave him legitimacy and freedom of policy, while remaining solidly within the French alliance, which afforded him protection. The duke used his army to fight a guerrilla war in the Alps against the

---

[27] On the fortification of Turin during the crisis, see Martha Pollak, *Turin, 1564–1680: urban design, military culture and the creation of the absolutist capital* (Chicago: 1991), pp. 88–118.
[28] Pollak, *Turin, 1564–1680*, p. 145.
[29] Devos & Grosperrin, *La Savoie de la Réforme à la Revolution*, p. 128ff.

French-speaking Vaudois Calvinists, or Valdesi. His generals ravaged their villages and displaced their populations with only limited success. The most vigorous campaign against them, using Irish mercenaries and Apennine bandits, took place while the war with Spain continued, in 1655.[30] Not much progress was made after that, despite new attempts to repress them undertaken in 1663 and 1664.[31] It was not a way to train troops to fight a modern war. Another undertaking was to dispatch an expeditionary force to Candia to aid the Venetians, under the Ferrarese general, Villa. A force of 1,000 embarked in 1659, to keep the siege going, and two entire regiments followed them in 1660.[32] Here the duke himself acted in the capacity of a military enterpriser, one of those princes who kept an army in being in peacetime by renting it to a friendly power. Losses were considerable, however. What made this sacrifice worthwhile for Charles Emanuel II was that in exchange for this aid, Venice recognized his claim to royal title, and the republic's diplomats acted accordingly.[33]

During the 1660s, Charles Emanuel II followed the French example and created a Piedmontese standing army of six permanent regiments, of a single battalion each, with two more raised between 1667 and 1673. In 1669 he reformed the territorial militia as well.[34] He awaited the moment to undertake something grand, but his powerful relative, Louis XIV, who was loathe to allow Savoyard expansion into the most populated parts of Italy, held him in check. The occasion presented itself in the summer of 1672 when Louis XIV provoked the Dutch War, and avoided opening an Italian theatre of operations. Duke Charles Emanuel desired to annex some coastal fiefs in western Liguria controlled by Genoa. He also wished to take advantage of an impending *coup* within the Genoese state, planned by the exiled patrician Rafaelle della Torre. When the Genoese government discovered the plot, the duke ordered a two-pronged invasion against Albenga and Savona after a fatal moment of hesitation that allowed the republic to mobilize.[35] After a few weeks of intense fighting (where Genoa's Corsican levies were especially effective ambushing columns in the Apennine passes), the Piedmontese were forced to retire. The Corsicans and Genoese almost entirely killed or captured one large contingent at Castelvecchio. The only Piedmontese prize was the feeble fort of Ovada, while the Genoese troops captured the coastal town of Oneglia, and threatened to seize Nice too. The unprovoked invasion of Genoa proved to be a complete débâcle.

Rather than disband his army, as previous dukes had done, Charles Emanuel II consolidated it. Following a practice common in Germany, where small states

---

[30] Valori, *Condottieri e generali del seicento*, p. 8, Giacomo d'Allinges.

[31] Brancaccio, *L'esercito del vecchio Piemonte*, p. 120.

[32] *Ibid.*, p. 123.

[33] Quazza, *Storia politica d'Italia: La preponderanza spagnola*, p. 532.

[34] Pollak, *Turin, 1564–1680*, p. 174ff.

[35] Quazza, *Storia politica d'Italia: la preponderanza spagnola*, p. 543.

wished to maintain the cadres of a large army, he leased regiments to his patron, Louis XIV. This was a legitimate way of keeping regiments intact but not on the payroll. In 1673 he rented four regiments to France for operations in the Low Countries, followed by a cavalry regiment, baptized 'Royal Piémont', which was quickly incorporated into the French army.[36] The only condition placed on their use was that they were not to be used directly against Imperial forces, since the duke was a Prince of the Empire. The duke then rotated Piedmontese officers rapidly through the units so that more of them might obtain combat experience, and be ready to train and lead a larger Piedmontese army when the next war came along.[37] In 1676–7, Louis made overtures to the duke for a joint invasion of Lombardy, held by only 6,000 'Spanish' infantry and 2,500 cavalry. Spain was so deeply involved repressing the Messina rebellion, that its forces elsewhere were skeletal. The plan came to naught, though, for Louis XIV would not permit significant expansion of Piedmont, and simply intended the negotiations to induce Spain to make peace. A further setback to any dreams of expansion towards Lombardy followed in 1681 when France bought Casale Monferrato from the duke of Mantua, and turned it into an advance base in northern Italy. The duchy was now squeezed tightly between that fortress and Pinerolo.

Smothered by the protection of Louis XIV, there was only one other avenue of military activity left to the duchy, and that was to prepare for a defensive war, by improving the network of fortresses. This commenced as soon as the last French garrisons left in 1659. The great showpiece of military engineering was the citadel of Turin, which was the key to the duchy. It held out in 1640 even after the newly completed fortifications of the city were delivered by a ruse to Prince Tommaso. Administrative growth and reconstruction after the war made Turin one of the few Italian cities to experience any expansion in the seventeenth century. Its population in 1571 was about 14,000 inhabitants, which was comparable to Mondovì. With the expansion of the court under Charles Emanuel I, and a more resolute centralization of government, the city began to expand. In 1604 there were 20,000 inhabitants, and 24,000 in 1614.[38] A new enlargement of the city was planned and then executed in the 1670s, allowing the population *intra muros* to grow to about 40,000. The fortress city grew such that only a major army could blockade it completely and still have troops left to push siege operations. Earthwork fortifications were relatively cheap to build, and were effective against cannonshot, but they were then clad with stone or brick to give the illusion of strength, and to reduce maintenance costs of constantly shifting and eroding earth.[39] With his capital enlarged and fortified, and with the basis of a permanent and well-trained army, Charles Emanuel II could hope for an opening to resume the policy of expansion so often frustrated.

[36] Brancaccio, *L'esercito del vecchio Piemonte*, p. 133.
[37] Laloy, *La révolte de Messine*, vol. 3, p. 76.
[38] Pollak, *Turin, 1564–1680*, p. 85. See also Merlin, *Tra guerre e tornei*, p. 37.
[39] Pollak, *Turin, 1564–1680*, p. 217.

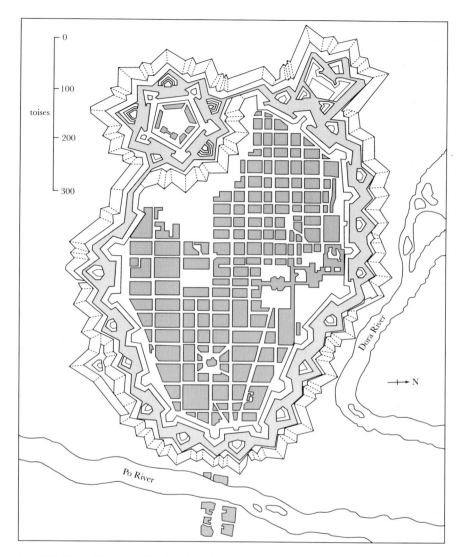

Map 7.1 Plan of Turin, 1695 *(based on Ancelin)*

The great wars and Piedmontese survival, 1690–1748

Victor Amadeus II was only nine years old when his father died in 1675. Like his predecessors his childhood passion was for soldiers and all things military, and he dreamed of great accomplishments while his mother, a French princess, ruled as regent in close contact with the court of Louis XIV. Bourbon tutelage paradoxically proved beneficial to the assertiveness of the ducal regime, for it gave the regent the means to impose absolutist policies *à la française*. A tax uprising at Mondovì against the salt gabelle in August 1680, which enjoyed timid support from the local élites, threatened to spread to other districts. The next year a small ducal army of 3,000 men fought a bitter guerrilla war in the hills around the village of Montaldo. Each truce was broken the moment officials tried to levy the new taxes. Louis offered French troops to suppress the rebellion, which helped the young Victor Amadeus II impose new imposts on Mondovì, Ceva and other districts along the Ligurian border that had long harboured salt smugglers.[40] The suppression of armed rebellion allowed the duke to increase his taxes considerably in subsequent years.

The French king's policies were not always in Piedmont's interest. After Victor Amadeus tugged effective control away from his mother, Louis XIV and the Pope pressured him to complete the Revocation of the Edict of Nantes by uprooting or exterminating the Vaudois Protestants in their Alpine valleys. A Vaudois guerrilla campaign in 1686 made it impossible for the Piedmontese army to impose itself on the remaining 15,000 heretics. A French contingent under Marshal Catinat then overwhelmed the mountain fighters and ejected them into Switzerland. This war of religious unity cost about 2,000 dead, about 5,000 Valdesi converted, and about 3,000 were deported to the duchy's fortresses and from thence to the malarial rice-bowl along the Po to work as landed labourers.[41] Only a few thousand more escaped northwards. Although this persecution had widespread popular appeal in Piedmont itself, Victor Amadeus felt humiliated by this loss of autonomy with respect to a powerful neighbour who had no hesitations about extending French policies to satellites.[42]

The duke's only recourse was to increase the number of his troops as high as he could afford, from around 6,000 men in 1676 to about 8,000 in the following decade. The infantry consisted of ten 'national' regiments, but three of those were rented to France in 1686 and were deployed in the Low Countries. Victor Amadeus' decisive moment to assert his independence came in 1690 when William III, king of England and *stathouder* of the Netherlands, invited him to join the League of Augsburg to stem French aggression. English and Dutch commercial progress in the Mediterranean after 1660 made them political forces to be reckoned with. The maritime powers considered Piedmont a useful base for an

---

[40] See the article by Geoffrey Symcox, "Two forms of popular resistance in the Savoyard state of the 1680s: the rebels of Mondovì and the Vaudois", *in La guerra del sale (1689–1699): rivolte e frontiere del Piemonte barocco* (Milan: 1986), pp. 275–90. See also Quazza, *Storia politica d'Italia: preponderanza spagnola*, p. 47.

[41] G. Levi, *Centro e periferia di uno stato assoluto: tre saggi su Piemonte e Liguria in età moderna* (Turin: 1985), p. 15.

[42] Symcox, "Two forms of popular resistance", in *La guerra del sale*; see also Quazza, *Storia politica d'Italia, preponderanza spagnola*, p. 571.

invasion of France. With their huge subsidies, the duke could expand his army to new levels. Subsidies were vital, for when Victor Amadeus declared war, Louis XIV simply confiscated the regiments rented to France, and imprisoned the officers. The duke planned to conscript six per cent of all eligible males, trained more effectively, for service beside the regular troops. In the interim, six Dutch regiments sent from Holland blunted the progress of a French attack.

A French army under Catinat conquered Savoy without much resistance. Louis XIV then desired to punish Piedmont for its defection. Catinat's troops devastated much of the region, although not as systematically as the brutal and counter-productive dismantling of the German Palatinate two years earlier. Louis and Louvois advocated scorched-earth measures for two reasons: first, to teach the duke a lesson about power, and secondly, to force the Piedmontese army and its Spanish and Austrian allies to stand and accept battle. They achieved only the latter of these objectives: Catinat soundly defeated the allied armies at Staffarda near Saluzzo on 18 August 1690, largely because of Piedmontese overconfidence.[43] Militia bands, however, opposed French depredations, especially around Asti and Alba. Victor Amadeus had allowed the Protestant Vaudois to return to their valleys before the beginning of the war, and in exchange for toleration they willingly served as sharpshooters in the Alps. By 1692, the allies had seized the initiative and invaded Dauphiné, treating occupied districts with the same rigour as the French treated Piedmont. In the following campaign, however, Catinat trounced the Piedmontese army again at Marsaglia on 4 October 1693 and inflicted tremendous losses on it. Since the theatre was but a sideshow compared to the huge armies operating in the Low Countries, the French lacked the troops to undertake important sieges. Allied subsidies made good the losses and the Piedmontese troops increased to 23,000 men in 1695. The duke hired regiments wholesale from Germany or Switzerland, rented and then laid off from one campaign to the next.[44] Two Swiss regiments hired in 1691 he consigned to garrison duty. In 1693 the duke employed a Bavarian regiment, another from Brandenburg and a third from Westphalia. In 1694 four Bavarian battalions fought in Piedmontese service. After 1694, Victor Amadeus abandoned his allies in exchange for the recovery of Pinerolo, and the demolition of Casale. Diplomatically, this represented a significant success, although his allies charged him with duplicity. By 1697 he mobilized new troops to join France to speed a general conclusion of peace.

The period after 1690, then, is not so much important for the creation of a standing army, which already existed, but with its change in scale and effectiveness. With the conclusion of hostilities, Victor Amadeus II launched important tax reforms to sustain a large peacetime force. Public debt payments stood at approxi-

---

[43] Quazza, *Storia politica d'Italia: preponderanza spagnola*, p. 576. For details on these campaigns, see E. de Broglie, *Catinat: l'homme et la vie (1637–1712)* (Paris: 1902), pp. 52–105.
[44] Brancaccio, *L'esercito del vecchio Piemonte*, p. 188.

mately 20 per cent of revenue, which was not dire in comparison with France.[45] His network of French-style intendants increased the efficiency and authority of central directives in the provinces.[46] When resentment against new taxes sparked new unrest around Mondovì in 1699, he suppressed the revolt brutally. Increased revenues also allowed the duke to strengthen existing fortifications. Turin became in the process the most heavily fortified city in all of Italy. Other considerable fortresses ringed it, like the cities of Vercelli, Asti, Susa, Cuneo and Alba, and smaller, purely military hilltop strongholds like Verrua on the Po, and Bard at the entrance to the Val d'Aosta. Nice and Villefranche were important places, as was Montmelian in Savoy. To co-ordinate the raising and maintenance of troops, the direction of fortifications and the provision of *matériel*, the duke established an embryonic war ministry in 1692. Until then, officials entrusted with different aspects of military administration consulted him personally.[47]

The duke suddenly lost his room for manoeuvre in 1700 when the death of King Charles II of Spain opened the problem of his succession. Castile acclaimed Louis XIV's grandson Philip and the Bourbon administration quietly took control of Milan and Naples. The House of Savoy was now penned in by the Bourbon dynasty and could expect no assistance if it were attacked. When Emperor Leopold I declared war to contest the succession in favour of his own Habsburg dynasty, Victor Amadeus II was in the French alliance with nothing to gain from it. A contingent of five or six thousand Piedmontese operated lethargically with the Franco-Spanish forces (or Gallispans, as they were known) against the Imperials in Lombardy, but Victor Amadeus secretly negotiated with Austria and the maritime powers of Holland and England. Piedmontese commanders contrived never to aid the French materially in their campaign. Finally, in 1703, with the duke's double-dealing an open secret, the French army surrounded and disarmed Piedmont's best regiments, some 4,500 troops, and summoned the cities to open their gates to Bourbon garrisons. Savoy was almost immediately conquered and the Gallispans launched raids on Piedmont. Pushed into a desperate situation by his pursuit of expansion, the duke declared war on Louis XIV.

At this critical juncture, military expenditures quadrupled between peacetime in 1700 and 1704, until they represented 58 per cent of the regular revenues of the state. Subsidies from Holland and England provided a comparable amount, equal to 40 per cent of state revenues, channelled entirely into the war effort. Recruitment reached levels unknown until then, as the regular army increased rapidly to about 35,000 men in 1705, exclusive of militia and irregulars.[48] Piedmont armed

[45] E. Stumpo, "'Vel domi vel belli'; arte della pace e strategie di guerra fra cinque e seicento: casi del Piemonte sabaudo, e della Toscana medicea", in *Guerre, stati e città: Mantova e l'Italia padana dal secolo XIII al XIX* (Mantua: 1988), pp. 53–68, p. 60.

[46] On the administrative reforms of Victor Amadeus II, see Geoffrey Symcox, *Victor Amadeus II: absolutism in the Savoyard state, 1675–1730* (Berkeley, California: 1983), p. 119ff.

[47] Anderson, *War and society in Europe of the old regime*, p. 102.

[48] Symcox, *Victor-Amadeus II*, p. 138ff.

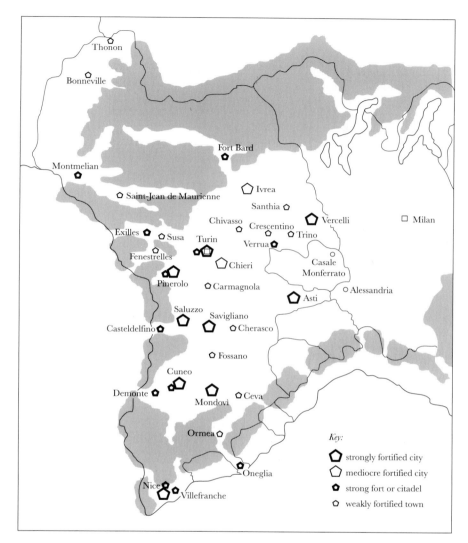

Map 7.2 Piedmontese fortresses, *circa* 1700

eight new infantry regiments in 1704, and eight more the next year, along with cavalry and dragoons. This permitted the army to maintain its effective strength despite the loss of several fortresses and the capture of their garrisons. In addition, the militia played an increased role. After calling up 10,000 militiamen in 1704, the duke concentrated the best of them (about 4,200 men) in large units, called 'provincial regiments', alongside local levies performing transport, fortification and guard duties.[49] Still other irregular bands, including the Vaudois, continued their attacks on the French in the mountains. Finally, Victor Amadeus II raised mercenary troops on the international market, more expensive than local recruits, but more dependable. In the dire situation of 1703, he threw together a regiment composed of Germans, Swiss, English, Dutch and French Huguenots under the Frenchman Desportes. Then in 1704 he hired three German regiments, six regiments of Swiss, (laid off in 1705), and then two full regiments of French Huguenots, also laid off when the crisis passed in 1708.[50] By such measures, Piedmontese forces remained at significant levels.

Such desperate measures offset the scarcity of Imperial troops, diverted to operations in Germany and Hungary. The adroit French commander Vendôme blocked the river crossings into Lombardy with one army, and ate away at Piedmontese territory by siege with another. Victor Amadeus kept the field with his troops, but due to the necessity of placing garrisons everywhere, his field forces were meagre. In the summer of 1706, Vendôme's successors inaugurated the siege of Turin itself. Operations advanced so slowly that Eugene of Savoy was able to lead his field army in a rapid march over hundreds of kilometres along the Po valley to join Victor Amadeus on the heights above Turin. On 7 September 1706, a combined assault on the Gallispan trenchworks from the west broke the Bourbon army. Its scattered remnants retreated towards Milan or across the Alps, opening the way for the Austrian conquest of all the Spanish territories in Italy. In the autumn and winter of 1706–7, Piedmontese troops even joined an Austrian invasion of Provence, and the siege of Toulon, although it was unsuccessful.

As Italian operations wound down after 1710, Victor Amadeus kept his forces at about 22,500 regulars, a number he maintained after the peace of 1713. As a reward for his participation in the anti-Bourbon alliance, the Emperor transferred parts of western and south-western Lombardy, including the city of Alessandria, together with the Mantuan Monferrato, to Piedmontese sovereignty. This first expansion of the state included some of the most densely populated countryside in Italy. Furthermore, the allies awarded him distant Sicily, with its much-coveted royal title, as part of the spoils. He immediately set out to remodel Sicily on Piedmontese lines, to the sullen resentment of the population there. He launched a small navy of four galleys and four warships for coastal defence, and garrisoned 10,000 Piedmontese troops on the island, less to defend it against attack than to intimidate his subjects.[51] On 1 July 1718, under the pretence of sending help to Venice in the Adriatic, a Spanish fleet transported an army to Sicily in defiance of the treaty of Utrecht, and quickly reconquered it, to the applause of the Sicilians. The allies quickly expelled the Spanish in turn, but Piedmont lost Sicily in the peace that followed. Victor Amadeus II received the much more sparsely popu-

---

[49] Brancaccio, *L'esercito del vecchio Piemonte*, p. 206ff.
[50] *Ibid.*, p. 212.
[51] Symcox, *Victor Amadeus II*, p. 171.

lated and primitive island of Sardinia instead, which also had a royal title. The territory had few ports or towns to defend, and precious little revenue to tax. The duke then continued to increase the efficiency and revenues of the Piedmontese heartland undistracted.

Victory in 1706 restored Piedmont's hopes for gradual expansion, now that rival powers sat on each side. When Victor Amadeus II relinquished government to his son in 1730, there was little change in policy. Charles Emanuel III had been trained in war from youth by his father. He joined the Bourbon coalition against Austria in 1733 in the war over the Polish Succession. This conflict was in part spurred by the Spanish desire for revenge against the Habsburgs, and the recovery of its former Italian territories. In exchange for his support for the Spanish recovery of Naples, Charles Emanuel thought it possible to annex the duchy of Milan. Piedmont was for the Bourbons an ally worth courting, for after mobilization the state deployed 1,000 officers and almost 40,000 soldiers. About a third of the wartime army consisted of foreign mercenaries, of whom most were Germans. Together with French troops in Piedmontese service, they comprised the crack units in the army.[52] The state increased its militia levies, and enrolled (sometimes forcibly) volunteers from Piedmont and Savoy, who served for six to eight years. Spanish and French troops in the theatre left the Piedmontese little leeway, and the Gallispans did most of the fighting in the three campaigns from 1733 to 1735. French intervention prevented all of the Milanese passing to Piedmont, but the king of Sardinia (as the duke was now called) netted the Langhe fiefs in the Apennines, Tortona, Arona at the foot of the Alps, and the important town of Novara, not far from Milan, from the peace of 1738.

These new conquests permitted a peacetime standing army of 30,000 regulars, or over one per cent of the total population, for the most part Piedmontese. They helped achieve victory in the War of the Polish Succession without fighting a significant battle. This could only encourage Charles Emanuel's intention to intervene in the next international crisis, the War of the Austrian Succession after 1740, by turning to the side offering the best hope of expansion. Gradual build-up brought the army close to 55,000 effective soldiers (including the provincial militia regiments) in 1747. This level of two per cent of the total population, while lower than that of Prussia or Sweden, was far ahead of France, Austria and most other European states, and certainly had no rival in Italy.[53] The territory was ringed with significant fortresses: Valenza, Alessandria, Casale, Ceva, Verrua, Chivasso and Asti in the lowlands, besides Turin; in the Alps, Bard, Exilles, Susa, Fenestrelle, Perosa, Demonte, Saorgio, with Ivrea and Cuneo in the rear; Nice, Montealbano and Villefranche in Provence; and Montmelian in Savoy.

One prerequisite allowing this exceptional build-up must have been Piedmont's

---

[52] S. Loriga, *Soldats: un laboratoire disciplinaire; l'armée piémontaise au XVIIIe siècle* (Paris: 1991), p. 33.
[53] See the table in A. Corvisier, *L'armée et société en Europe de 1494 à 1789* (Paris: 1976), p. 126.

policy of increasing the number of noble families, most of which served the state in some capacity. Here too the kingdom was singularly out of step with the evolution in Italy, where the number of noble families declined markedly after the middle of the seventeenth century. Stuart Woolf has attempted to measure this. In the age of Emanuel Philibert, there were 1,800 vassals or fiefholders in Piedmont: by the 1780s there were 5,800 of them. For the early eighteenth century, there were about 3,000 noble families, since there were more fiefholders than there were noble families. This number increased too, since the royal domain sold 819 titles of nobility between 1722 and 1796.[54] This élite lacked a strong distinction between robe and sword, since army service led quite naturally to court positions, and even the civil officials had close links with their landed estates.[55] Most new nobles came from mercantile or bureaucratic backgrounds, but the Savoy dynasty successfully militarized them. Both rich and poor nobles served in the army. There were periods, notably in the late seventeenth century, when military service for foreign princes was popular, especially the emperor in Hungary, and then in descending order, France, Spain, the German states and Mantua. Giovanni Levi hazards that, like the duke, Piedmontese nobles were careful not to commit themselves to a single patron. The Tana family, prominent in Chieri, did not all return to Piedmontese service when the duke broke with France in 1690. One of them remained a colonel in French service. Although the duke confiscated his lands in 1694, his relatives' pleas restored his fortune after the war ended.[56] Levi sees duplicitous behaviour as part of a wider preoccupation with stability and security, that was as typical of the Piedmontese nobility as it was of the peasantry. How loyal the Francophone Savoyard nobility was to the person of the duke is more difficult to assess. Bourbon armies occupied Savoy repeatedly. In 1690, many nobles in that region pledged their loyalty to the French king. Savoy was occupied during the War of the Spanish Succession too. Spanish Bourbon troops occupied it in 1742 almost without resistance. Savoy increasingly represented a pawn for a state that became increasingly Italian in composition. The Savoyards duly noted this and were not hostile to the Gallispans as a result.[57]

The loyalty of the population and the effectiveness of the army were most severely tested in the War of the Austrian Succession after 1742. For two years, Charles Emanuel III listened to offers from the Habsburgs and of the French and Spanish Bourbons. This time, he decided to side with the Empress Maria Theresa. In exchange, Austria relinquished from the outset its hold over some of the most lush districts of Lombardy, abandoning Vigevano and all of the territory west of the river Ticino, and all lands south of the Po. Additional territories were to be seized forcibly from neutral Genoa. The Piedmontese advantage now was

[54] Loriga, *Soldats; un laboratoire disciplinaire*, p. 77.
[55] S. J. Woolf, *Studi sulla nobiltà piemontese nell' epoca dell' assolutismo* (Turin: 1963), p. 136 and pp. 156–160.
[56] G. Levi, *Inheriting power* (Chicago: 1986), p. 132–4.
[57] Devos & Grosperrin, *La Savoie de la Réforme à la Revolution*, p. 441.

that the Alps were a serious barrier to a French invasion. No route through the Alps was less than 200 km (125 ml) long. Troops moving through it had to pass as a thin thread along a single track, and commanders could assemble them for either attack or defence, at a single point, only with great delay.[58] Furthermore, no roads were passable by wheeled vehicles. This restricted armies with pack-horse trains with artillery and baggage to just a few passes: Tenda, Mont Cenis, Montgenèvre, and the Great and Little Saint Bernard passes into the Val d'Aosta, in addition to the rugged coastal road through Genoese territory.

Urged on by Queen Elisabeth Farnese, who wanted Italian thrones for her sons, the Spanish made great efforts to rebuild their navy and their army. They joined the league against Austria and Piedmont to acquire at least the duchy of Parma, the queen's birthplace, where the Farnese dynasty had been extinguished in 1731. To this effect Spain marched two autonomous armies into the theatre, one from Naples, and the other through France, which wanted to remain neutral with Piedmont while not impeding the ambitions of its Spanish cousins. In 1742 a Spanish army with French auxiliaries, and guided by the French strategist Bourcet, marched through Dauphiné to occupy Savoy. Charles Emanuel tried to defend the duchy with 10,000 men, but was unable to winter them there. When he tried to take them back across the Alps into Piedmont in the dead of winter, many died or were disabled by exposure. Charles Emanuel sent other troops to help Austria capture the duchy of Modena, a Bourbon ally, and to confront the Spanish army in Romagna. The first campaign thus ended in something of a draw.

Successive campaigns illustrated the geographical advantages enjoyed by a state subject to invasion through a rugged mountain chain. In 1743 Madrid ordered the Spanish army to advance into Piedmont to compensate for the setback they suffered at Camposanto, near Bologna. Charles Emanuel had 40,000 troops facing the Spanish in the Alps, and kept them at bay by winning a big skirmish. The following year, the king of Sardinia looked forward to the campaign with confidence, for he disposed of an army of 50,000 troops. He knew that serious military operations could last only from July to September, and that the republic of Genoa was still neutral.[59] A Franco-Spanish field army numbering 46,000 men concentrated near Nice, but a third of that had to be deducted as screens and garrisons as it advanced. This force occupied Nice and Villefranche without too much difficulty, despite the presence of the British fleet supplying the defenders. Against this invasion, the Piedmontese field army comprised about 26,000 men, subtracting the garrisons, with only 11,000 men at the strongest point. This regular army was supplemented by militia resembling a *levée en masse* in the area of operations. Armed peasants usually dispersed in the presence of large enemy corps, though, and were more useful for harassment. Constant attacks by these bands against supply convoys hampered French progress.

---

[58] Spenser Wilkinson, *The defence of Piedmont, 1742–1748* (Oxford: 1927), p. 3.
[59] *Ibid.*, p. 107.

In their advance, nevertheless, the French pushed the Piedmontese out of the Varaita valley and captured the small place of Demonte. To help stem the tide, the Piedmontese minister, the marchese d'Ormea, personally raised 10,000 peasants around Mondovì, and marched them to Cuneo. The French ferocity against these guerrillas only fuelled their desire for vendetta. Once the Gallispans broke into the plain, they settled into a siege at Cuneo, which the Piedmontese general, Leutrum, defended with 3,200 regulars and a large body of militia.[60] To break the siege, Charles Emanuel collected about 25,000 men and mounted an attack on an equal number of Gallispans north of the city, at Madonna dell'Olmo. Losses were heavy in the course of the day at 4,000 men per side, but the Piedmontese withdrew in good order. The lingering of the unbroken Piedmontese army in the vicinity hindered the progress of the siege. By October it was snowing in the Alps and Cuneo was still holding out. Behind the siege line, in a tenuous thread leading back into France, no less than 23 French and Spanish battalions, or almost 18,000 men, guarded the supply lines through the Val di Stura. Having overextended their stay, the Gallispans then withdrew entirely.[61]

The campaign of 1745 was much more threatening because when the Genoese learned that Piedmont intended to occupy their port of Finale, they threw themselves into the Bourbon alliance, and opened the mountainous southern border of Piedmont to invasion.[62] Charles Emanuel based the principal Piedmontese force of 12,000 regulars and 6,000 militia around Ormea, although other militia patrolled the valleys leading to the Ligurian coast. One band, a couple of thousand strong, burned the Bourbon supply depot at Ventimiglia. More regulars and the Vaudois militia screened the Alpine frontier to prevent a French advance from Dauphiné on Turin. The main Gallispan army centred on Genoa numbered some 70,000 men, of which 10,000 were Genoese and 6,000 Neapolitans, these last two of doubtful quality. It advanced rapidly north from Genoa and into the Po valley, capturing Tortona in August. Spanish forces then separated from the French to occupy the former Farnese duchy, taking Piacenza by escalade, and then Parma. This split the defenders in two, with the Austrians retreating into Lombardy, and the Piedmontese nervously screening their eastern border. Turin's troops camped behind entrenchments along the River Tanaro, with Alessandria on their flank. In a daring assault, however, columns of French, Spanish and Neapolitan troops overwhelmed that line and routed the Piedmontese entirely. This allowed the invaders to invest Alessandria in early October, and overrun much of south-eastern Piedmont. By November, the French occupied the Monferrato. The Spanish for their part advanced trium-

---

[60] Piedmontese generals were very frequently foreigners, like the German Leutrum. See Barberis, *Le armi del principe*, p. 151ff.

[61] Wilkinson, *The defence of Piedmont*, pp. 133–74.

[62] The involvement of Genoa in this war has been studied with great detail by Gaston Broche, *La republique de Gênes et la France pendant la guerre de la succession d'Autriche (1740–1748)*, 3 vols (Paris: 1936).

phantly into Lombardy, capturing Pavia and then Milan. In this triumph, there were three troubling aspects. First, as Bourbon forces advanced and captured important fortresses, they had to place large garrisons in them to maintain supply links to Genoa. Their field army diminished with every success. Secondly, Alessandria and Asti still held out, and had to be besieged or blockaded. Finally, the French advanced westwards into Piedmont. Spanish troops advanced eastward into Lombardy. The separation of the Bourbon armies created an unhoped-for occasion for the Austrian army, which received reinforcements daily.[63]

Elisabeth Farnese in Madrid insisted that Spanish troops hold Parma and Piacenza, however distantly it placed them in relation to their French allies. Not wanting to separate the armies, the French marshal, Maillebois, joined his ally at Piacenza, abandoning the invasion of Piedmont. At the beginning of 1746, the Austrian and Piedmontese forces then enveloped the whole Gallispan army north of the Po, cutting it off from its supplies. Maillebois succeeded in breaking out of the noose and regaining contact with his base, with the Spanish troops in tow, but Bourbon troubles were just beginning. Philip V of Spain died in the interval and his son Ferdinand VI decided to cease offensive operations, but kept the decision secret from his French allies. Ferdinand systematically blocked any French attempt to regain the initiative. Maillebois retreated along the Ligurian coast, abandoning Genoa to its fate. The Austrians and Piedmontese in turn invaded the eastern fringe of Provence, aided by the British fleet, and Charles Emanuel occupied as much of the Ligurian coast as he could. But a revolt in Genoa against its Austrian captors hampered the advance of the Austro-Piedmontese. Genoese levies resisted an Austro-Piedmontese blockade for several months, and small packets of French troops then slipped through the British naval blockade to keep the siege going.

Austria's and Piedmont's siege of Genoa, or more exactly, of the mountain redoubts overlooking the city, dominated the last campaign in 1747. The city might have fallen, but the French decided to save it by invading Piedmont from the Alps. The army of the Chevalier de Belle-Isle advanced from Dauphiné across the Alps to Fenestrelle, the shortest route to Turin. Quickly, Charles Emanuel shifted troops back, where they dug in atop a mountain ridge. French forces attacked in a frontal assault, in a closed space, against an entrenched army overlooking them. Even their scaling ladders were too short. The battle was a massacre, with Belle-Isle among its victims. While such a rash and ill-conceived assault was a setback, the diversion did save Genoa, which France steadily reinforced by sea. King Ferdinand changed his mind about the outcome of the war, and decided to commit Spanish troops again to combat roles. The Gallispans began to advance once more in Liguria, although peace intervened soon after.

The result of this war for Piedmont (the last one in Italy before the French Revolution) was a significant success from the point of view of the king, and

---

[63] *Ibid.*, vol. 2, p. 70ff.; see also Wilkinson, *The defence of Piedmont*, pp. 224–56.

perhaps one for his army too. Walter Barberis has emphasized how the army was technically backward, as the campaigns after 1742 revealed. If it is true that after the siege of Cuneo in 1744 the commander of artillery condemned all the guns in the fortress, one wonders how it held out for so long. Barberis also notes that in December 1746 it was necessary to borrow cannon from the English fleet offshore to advance the siege of Savona.[64] The criticisms may or may not be justified. Nevertheless, there were three set-piece battles with the French army, one of the most successful armies of that war. Those contests resulted in a draw (Madonna dell'Olmo); a rout (the Tanaro line) and an easy victory (Fenestrelle). My purpose here is not to echo Italian patriots on the efficiency and extraordinary combat fitness of the Piemontese army. It suffices simply to point out how it stood up to the test of combat in a long war.

France's alliance with Austria in 1756 deprived the Savoy dynasty once again of an opportunity to expand. Austrian Lombardy after 1748 was just a wedge between the Ticino and the Oglio rivers, but remained the economic hub of the Po valley and was jealously guarded by Maria Theresa. Nevertheless, the Piedmontese army continued to expand, continued to articulate its component units and enhance its combat potential, in anticipation of the next war. One innovation was the creation of a small flotilla, to help protect Sardinia from incursions of Barbary corsairs. In 1760 Charles Emanuel III bought two frigates in England, officered them with Englishmen, and scoured the Ligurian coast for seamen. Villefranche was an adequate base, small, but strongly fortified and well stocked with material.[65] Army reforms in 1775 and 1786 created new élite corps, two regiments (dubbed legions, from Roman usage) of light infantry or skirmishers, and some local artillery. On the eve of the Napoleonic invasion in 1796, the army counted 71,738 men, of which 5,000 were cavalry. It was not immune to the kind of politicking and relaxation of discipline underway in France, but Bonaparte still took it very seriously.[66]

Concluding the narrative, it is worthwhile citing the thesis of Enrico Stumpo, who has attempted to measure the economic impact of war, and the cost of the army. Piedmont was not just 'involved' in wars; the Savoy dynasty, one prince after another, provoked them or welcomed them. Between 1600 and 1713, there were 38 years of effective war, and 19 years of skirmishing. Stumpo estimates that the plague of 1630 killed eight times as many people in the region as all these conflicts combined. War damage was confined to agriculture, and left the fixed infrastructure intact. The population increased, while agricultural production rose and diversified in the same period. Unlike most of Italy, where there was a long agricultural depression, in Piedmont the value of land increased about 60 per

---

[64] Barberis, *Le armi del principe*, p. 192.

[65] On the Piedmontese flotilla, see C. Randaccio, *Storia delle marine militari italiane, dal 1750 al 1860, e della marina militare italiana dal 1860 al 1870*, vol. 1 (Rome: 1886), p. 12ff.

[66] Brancaccio, *L'esercito del vecchio Piemonte*, p. 299.

cent in the turbulent period between 1680 and 1717.[67] There were many examples of productive investments, both by the state and by local communities, both in manufactures serving the war effort, and in products for consumption and export, even in war years. The Savoy dynasty used war to take over land, people and economic resources. For this effort it organized and stimulated production.

Wars also increased the power and presence of the state in every district. Heavy wartime taxation, more or less rationally distributed, kept the duke's obligations to his richest subjects modest. Duplicitous diplomacy aimed to achieve the maximum result for minimal efforts. Consequently, allies paid much of the cost. Over 35 per cent of the cost of the Monferrato war, for example, was paid from Venetian and French treasuries. The war of the League of Augsburg was made possible by foreign subsidies and even more so the War of the Spanish Succession, when 50 per cent of the cost of troops and provisions was borne by the allies, primarily England and Holland. Piedmont's army made exactions by the emperor out of the question, although Piedmont was the only Italian state to explicitly recognize Imperial suzerainty. Much of this acquired, or saved, revenue was spent in the local economy. Piedmontese lenders carried most of the public debt, unlike the Spanish or Neapolitan regimes. By the middle of the eighteenth century, half the local communities were free of debts. It seemed, perversely, that economic growth occurred in periods of strong surges in government expenditure.[68] To leap from there to the conclusion that war was the principal cause of economic and institutional progress is too bold, at least as a rule, for we have seen that the Thirty Years War, even without prolonged fighting in the region, wrought long-term damage to the development of southern Italy and weakened both the state and the economy. In Piedmont, though, war and economic development went hand in hand.

Inside the Piedmontese army

We have several good studies of the standing army of Piedmont, mostly for the eighteenth century, and it is possible to see how it fared with respect to other European forces of the time. The dukes followed a conscious policy of marginalizing the nobility in the key offices of the bureaucracy, like the Intendancies. On the other hand, the officer corps enjoyed great prestige. In the regular army, at the head of militia companies, in the garrisoning of castles and

---

[67] The argument is articulated in two pieces: E. Stumpo, "Guerra ed economia: spese e guadagni militari nel Piemonte del seicento", *Studi Storici*, 1986, pp. 371–95; and "'Vel domi vel belli'; arte della pace e strategie di guerra fra cinque e seicento", in *Guerre, stati e città*, pp. 53–68.

[68] Stumpo, "Guerra ed economia: spese e guadagni militari nel Piemonte", *Studi Storici*, 1986, pp. 371–95. He sees this growth in Tuscany too, in the years of heavy contributions to Austria. Peaceful Tuscany slowly declined economically, however.

fortresses, military functions were placed above civilian ones in both protocol and pay-scale. Salaries for the senior ranks were higher than those in the civilian bureaucracy, and held a corresponding precedence.[69] As in other armies, there were possibilities for colonels and captains to enhance their incomes by furnishing equipment to their units, with corresponding subsidies from the crown. It is doubtful that this income was adequate for the noble lifestyle that officers were supposed to display at all times. Especially in the lower levels, up to that of captain, their salaries were barely adequate to maintain them, and many officers lived in relative squalor. Army commissions were not bought and sold, as they were in France. Holding one was not a sign of wealth and influence, and it required both money and connections to advance quickly.[70]

Barberis insists on how deep-seated aristocratic prejudices were in this institution, how ideologically partial the officer corps was to traditional notions of chivalry, and how they resisted innovation. He sees the Piedmontese nobility becoming obsessed with its feudal roots, and with the myth of the mounted knight. They neither studied war, nor showed much interest in artillery or fortifications, which artisans and bourgeois served.[71] The school to form military engineers was opened only in 1739, and the War of the Austrian Succession revealed some of these shortcomings. Whatever the case, the army in the eighteenth century was one of the most important career outlets for the nobility. Loriga, examining 868 nobles from four Piedmontese provinces in 1734, found that 62 per cent of the males above the age of fourteen followed some kind of career. The most important of these was the Church, which occupied about 30 per cent of all adult male nobles. The army was the choice of about 16 per cent, and a rough third (31.2 per cent) of Piedmontese noble families had at least one member in the army in 1734. Nor were nobles always desirous to be cavalry officers, if they could climb the hierarchy more quickly in the infantry. Many officers were not noble, though; 34 per cent were *roturiers* in 1767, concentrated especially in the lower ranks, and in the infantry and artillery.[72] Often, *roturier* officers began their careers as simple soldiers, but very few of them could reach lieutenant-colonel status. Many of those who were technically noble had bought their titles. Old noble families sometimes intermarried with these newcomers, or with wealthy *roturiers*. Military function and old nobility were therefore not synonymous. If older nobles clung to military vocations to set themselves apart, it only made the army look more attractive to newcomers in search of social legitimacy.

Promotion and career success, studied with some acuity by Sabina Loriga, was a complex issue. Advancement was often through protection and selection by the colonel, who had his own clientèle and his own criteria. The principle of selection operating there was not especially based on class or privilege, but in large part on

---

[69] Barberis, *Le armi del principe*, p. 171.

[70] Loriga, *Soldats*, p. 91.

[71] Barberis, *Le armi del principe*, p. 105 and p. 192.

[72] Loriga, *Soldats*, p. 73.

charisma. Colonels placed great emphasis on what we would consider attitudinal aptitude for command, or leadership quality. The officers, especially at lower levels, were keenly aware that they were being judged not only by their hierarchical superiors and their peers, but also by their soldiers who were usually ready to 'test' them, and worst of all, cause them to lose face.[73] Promotion also depended upon being known at court in Turin. Court life required continual entertainment, and was a more effective barrier to promotion for those who had only their army stipend to live on. The king allocated most court functions to junior officers who had given at least several years' service to the army. The Piedmontese officer corps was thus a complex creation, both an institution justifying the existence and the traditions of the nobility, and a reservoir of talents drawn from a broad section of the social élite.[74]

The rank and file present another case. They too were heterogeneous. Piedmontese and Savoyard infantry, foreign mercenaries, and local militias each had their own characteristics. Mercenaries were the most expensive and required more care. The dukes were not above using subterfuges to attract prime candidates. They would plant recruiting agents as soldiers in other armies, entrusted with picking out good men and inciting them to desert and re-enlist in the Piedmontese army. Another method was to rent entire regiments in Germany. They tended to leave for more highly paid armies when they had the chance, however. Commanders often settled for less. Sabina Loriga has examined the recruitment dossiers for much of Piedmont. The towns supplied 30 per cent of the volunteers to the regular army, which was somewhat higher than their place in the total population (20 per cent), and the middling towns of 5,000 to 8,000 inhabitants in particular furnished a disproportionate number. The army recruited best in those areas with many agricultural migrants. Despite this tendency, eighteenth-century Piedmontese soldiers were not the scum of the earth, as popular imagination improbably depicts them. Some 18 per cent were sons of artisans, and 13 per cent had prosperous parents, like merchants, notaries or landlords. They were overwhelmingly in their late teens and early twenties when they enlisted. Rather than describe them as poor, it would be more accurate to call them marginal, or rootless, many joining the army to escape from different kinds of problems. Recruiters knew how to frequent rural fairs, and then make their presence obvious towards the end, when drunkenness and the ensuing brawls created situations from which young men would be inclined to walk away.[75]

Once in the army, their life was not especially hard or dangerous, outside wartime. Soldiers were fed and given some pocket money. They mounted ten guards a month, at six hours a stint, and except for that they could wear civilian clothing and go wherever they wanted, not having a fixed hour to return at night. It was not uncommon for them to work part-time for urban artisans to increase

---

[73] *Ibid.*, p. 117.
[74] *Ibid.*, p. 85ff.
[75] Loriga, p. 153.

their earnings, particularly in peacetime. Soldiers were everywhere with civilians, in the churches, the cafés, the *veillées* or evening gatherings in winter in private houses, in the marketplace and in the workshops. The soldiers led a life close to that of civilians in the garrison towns, and there were usually all manners of persons coming in and out of the barracks during the day. Women and children, vagabonds and prostitutes always encumbered military buildings. This was because the army recruited married men as well as singles; most of the women were considered regimental prostitutes even when they were married. Peacetime garrison life was only risky in the sense that garrison mortality was triple that of adult civilians, because of the ease with which fevers spread through the cramped barracks.[76]

For the most part they seem to have been content even if, like soldiers elsewhere, they did not earn much money. Although they enlisted for six years, most of them served for only two or three. Like soldiers elsewhere they adopted *noms de guerre* or nicknames. The army for them was an identity, and a framework. Since men were continually moving in and out of the unit, it did not have a strong *esprit de corps*. Moreover, like the officers, most soldiers took liberties with their uniforms, decorating or adapting them to their individual taste. If the Prussian disciplinary model was upheld as the most effective one in the eighteenth century, there was a widespread feeling that the Italian character was refractory to such harsh discipline and that it was perhaps more suitable to Germans, or to men without honour.[77]

The Piedmontese militia suffered a period of relative decline in the seventeenth century, when it was rarely used for any but auxiliary purposes. Unwilling candidates could always find and pay replacements. Victor Amadeus II recast the whole system in 1713, by creating the 'provincial regiments', whose members lived a normal life outside wartime. An older type of militia comprising all able-bodied men between the ages of 18 and 50 survived too, but it had no fixed structure, and was meant to be mobilized only in exceptional circumstances. The 'provincial militia' was subject to two annual training periods, meant to teach the art of war to civilians. Every war wrenched them away from civilian life. Local society preferred to have the poorest youths, with no connections, drafted by the military authorities. Since they were only part volunteers, they were not as reliable as regular troops, and even less useful than the bands of mountaineers who skirmished for booty. Whole regiments of militia, moreover, were prone to homesickness or nostalgia that sapped their combativity and afflicted entire battalions at a time, given that the camaraderie of these soldiers was especially strong. Military authorities were constantly seeking ways to keep the troops amused and their spirits up. One way to gratify them was to give them privileges and exempt them from some taxes, and give them honorific privileges at home, like a place of

---

[76] *Ibid.*, p. 57.
[77] *Ibid.*, p. 206.

honour in religious ceremonies, or the right to wear swords in public, like the aristocracy.[78]

Tensions that existed, in what was probably a typical army, were a constant source of worry to the officers. Troop inspections were mostly an occasion to find out what the grievances were, and defuse them. Soldiers were not always passive, and let their grievances against certain officers become known, through placards. Men sometimes beat up their officers, too; officers are mentioned in 38 per cent of the brawls concerning soldiers. But in a more general fashion, desertion was a more effective way of discrediting officers. They knew that their officers were afraid of losing them, and everyone knew that a spate of desertions represented bad hierarchical relations in the unit. The civilian population tolerated deserters and gave them at least a minimum of complicity. Frequently, though, deserters soon rejoined the ranks, sometimes in another unit under a false name, and sometimes signed up in a different army. Most were content to rejoin the Piedmontese army, officially, and with a pardon from the minister of war. The continual need for soldiers persuaded the king to be indulgent with the soldiers, and few officers thought it wise to be harsh. They were disinclined to punish infractions harshly, even when the war ministry demanded it. Soldiers knew that they were precious to the state, and the foundation of its policy of expansion.[79] By the eighteenth century, Piedmont was the lone Italian territory with such ambitions.

---

[78] *Ibid.*, p. 157ff.
[79] *Ibid.*, p. 172.

Chapter 8
The Great Powers and Italian demilitarization, 1700–1814

The Italian military low-pressure zone

During the War of the Spanish Succession in Italy (1701–13), Italian states passively watched the combats from the sidelines, with the notable exception of Piedmont. There was much at stake for all of them. Italian fief-holders and princes alike had to choose between a large Bourbon army in the Po valley, and their Imperial Habsburg suzerain who could deprive them of their title for rebellion. Most fief-holders had to declare themselves before it was clear which side would prevail. Some noble families solved the dilemma by having members fight for each side, so that whichever side won the war, their family's fortune would be safe.[1] Others were tied by sentiment and by interest to one of the competing powers. Houses with ancient ties to Spain, like the Doria and Spìnola of Genoa, declared for Philip V and lost. Duke Ferdinando Carlo of Mantua chose the French alliance in 1681 when he sold Casale Monferrato to Louis XIV, and appreciated the 'subsidies' from Paris thereafter. By a secret treaty of February 1701, the duke let Bourbon troops enter his capital on the fiction of *force majeure*, and with French subsidies provided a few thousand soldiers for the common cause. Mantuan troops saw much action, but were never considered reliable. After 1704 they fell under the control of the French commander Vendôme, with the duke a simple spectator.[2] For his loyalty, the duke's possessions became the battleground between Bourbon and Habsburg forces until Prince Eugene's victory at Turin in 1706.[3] Ferdinando Carlo chose the wrong side and the emperor deprived the Gonzaga dynasty of the state it had ruled since the Middle Ages.

Mantua's misadventure demonstrated how much the emperor's pretensions over Italy had escalated. From the 1660s onwards, Leopold I increased his

---

[1] S. Pugliese, *Le prime strette dell' Austria in Italia*, p. 201.
[2] F. Fantini d'Onofrio, "Le fonti e la storia: la guerra di successione spagnola a Mantova attraverso la corrispondenza ai Gonzaga da Mantova e Paesi (1701–1708)", in *Guerre, stati e città: Mantova e l'Italia padana dal secolo XIII al XIX* (Mantua: 1988), pp. 427–66.
[3] *Ibid.*

demands upon the north Italian states for subsidies, under the pretext that they still belonged to the Empire. After the victory of Turin, the Austrian claim to suzerainty became bolder, since it was the legal underpinning for the right to levy huge contributions. The tone of relations between the emperor and the Italian princes changed too, with Vienna considering the latter to be vassals, and punished them for non-compliance with military lodgings. Vienna pretended not to understand the difference between a small fief and a principality, and so treated them all as subject territories. No longer did the emperor send an important dignitary as an emissary with a request for Italian princes to send aid, but instead addressed the same letter to each. He notified them that he intended to winter his troops on them, and invited them to send an official to Milan to work out the details with the military governor.[4] Joseph I took a leaf out of Louis XIV's book by employing jurists to uncover the legal justification for the extension of Imperial jurisdiction over areas hitherto considered outside it. In 1708 Vienna declared Parma and Piacenza part of the Empire, notwithstanding a consensus in Europe that they were Papal fiefs. Pope Clement XI Albani resisted this bitterly, by excommunicating Prince Eugene and his generals, and dispatching a few hundred troops to help garrison Parma. The Farnese duke still could not prevent Austrian columns from launching devastating foraging raids.

Vienna escalated its pretensions by proclaiming Ferrara and Comacchio, both part of the Papal States proper, to belong to the Empire too. Imperial forces crossed Papal territory at will, first in 1707 when an army of 10,000 marched south to conquer the kingdom of Naples, and again from 1708 to 1710. This policy was only the Austrian version of the French 'reunions', and every local success encouraged the emperor to widen his demands. After 1708, he proclaimed his suzerainty over Sicily, and intensified the pressure on Modena, Tuscany, Genoa, Lucca and Parma to accept the principle of his sovereignty. In 1713, Austrian troops occupied Parma militarily, against the wishes of the Farnese duke, to collect the dues that it had unilaterally imposed. Grand Duke Cosimo III of Tuscany was more successful in wriggling out of these demands, like the huge sum of 300,000 doubloons, and winter quarters for the Imperial armies, announced after the battle of Turin.[5] Cosimo's non-compliance planted the seed for Austria's intention to take over the duchy if the Medici dynasty were extinguished, however. After the war, the emperor's apologists repudiated Papal temporal power almost everywhere, and advanced Imperial pretensions to Venice and the Terraferma too.[6] In Italy, only Duke Rinaldo II d'Este (1697–1737) of Modena, unswerving partisan of the Emperor, encouraged these claims, since he hoped to lead an Austrian army into the Romagna and recover Ferrara for his house.[7] A

---

[4] Pugliese, *Le prime strette dell' Austria in Italia*, p. 214.
[5] Giorgetti, *Le armi toscane*, vol. 1, p. 556.
[6] Pugliese, *Le prime strette dell' Austria in Italia*, p. 237.
[7] Von Pastor, *History of the popes since the end of the Middle Ages*, vol. 33, p. 48.

French occupation of his state from 1702 to 1707 only attached him more firmly to Vienna. In 1708 the duke commanded an Imperial–Modenese army of 12,000 men stationed in Parma and in the Papal states, while Austrian forces under another command held his own fortress of Mirandola.

Naples and Sicily contributed to the Bourbon effort for as long as they belonged to Spain, but Austria took control in 1707 and squeezed them too. Naples sent galleys and troops to help the Imperial effort in Catalonia, under General Sormani. By war's end, military expenditure in Naples equalled about 70 per cent of effective revenue.[8] It does not appear, however, that many Neapolitans rallied to Vienna, nor did the emperor, Joseph I, or Charles VI (after 1711) seek to extract resources other than money from the kingdom. Following the peace of Utrecht, which awarded Austria the duchy of Milan and the kingdom of Naples, the duchy of Mantua and Sardinia (exchanged for Sicily in 1720), Imperial strength seemed enormous. In 1715 the Austrian army alone totalled 144,000 men, second in Europe after France. From it, Vienna earmarked 20,000 men for Lombardy and 14,000 for Naples.[9] They were never that numerous, but they overwhelmed the military potential of every state but Piedmont and Venice. Just as important to Austrian hegemony in Italy as the number of troops stationed there, was the French strategic withdrawal from the peninsula in the eighteenth century. Apart from backing the ambitions of the Madrid Bourbons, Paris had no coherent Italian policy. Italian princes faced with Austrian pretensions duly noted this when they conceived their own projects.[10]

Austria's conquest of Naples occasioned little celebration in the Mezzogiorno. All of the troops stationed there were Germans, and their equipment was Austrian. The army was still largely that created by Montecùccoli and enlarged by Eugene of Savoy. The Imperial council with jurisdiction over Italy completely dismantled and suppressed the old and moribund militia institutions.[11] A dozen Italian regiments raised by Spain were merged into only two, in 1720.[12] While Neapolitans paid for 20,000 soldiers, only 7,000 guarded the fortresses, and a few thousand more held the presidial state along the Tuscan coast administered from Naples. Vienna hoped that the nobility would rally around the emperor and Austria as they had around the king of Spain, but few were so inclined. Conse-

---

[8] A. di Vittorio, "Un caso di correlazione tra guerre, spese militari e cambiamenti economici: le guerre asburgiche della prima metà del XVIII° secolo e le loro ripercussioni sulla finanza e l'economia dell' Impero", *Nuova Rivista Storica*, 1982, pp. 59–81; at p. 63.

[9] J. Nouzille, *Le prince Eugène de Savoie et les problèmes des confins militaires autrichiens, 1699–1739*, p. 631.

[10] Luigi Simeoni, *L'assorbimento austriaco del ducato estense e la politica dei duchi Rinaldo e Francesco III* (Modena, 1986; first publ. 1919), p. 1.

[11] Michelangelo Schipa, *Il regno di Napoli al tempo di Carlo Borbone* (Naples: 1923), p. 21ff.

[12] Lawrence Sondhaus, *In the service of the Emperor: Italians in the Austrian armed forces, 1814–1918* (Boulder, Colorado and New York: 1990), p. 3.

quently, the demilitarization of the aristocracy that had begun half a century before, continued apace.[13]

After Utrecht, the Austrian empire was far-flung, and extremely diverse, extending from the southern Low Countries, to Naples, Sicily and Milan, and across the bulk of Danubian Europe as far afield as Transylvania. Victories in the War of the Spanish Succession and the Turkish wars made the emperor direct sovereign over 16 million inhabitants around 1730, second only to France in Europe. Of these 16 million, six million or 37 per cent were ethnic Italians.[14] In 1725 the emperor's subjects paid taxes worth 36 million florins. The military expenditures alone oscillated between 23 million and 32 million florins, and commonly constituted 70 per cent of government expenditure in wartime. Charles VI (1711–39) tried to force the peripheral regions to contribute more to the centre. Heavy military taxation actually benefited the economies of the hereditary lands, to the detriment of Brussels, Milan and Naples.[15] Military expenditures (and also no doubt misappropriated tax money too, for the Austrian fiscal system was notoriously inefficient) benefited manufacturing in Austria and Bohemia. New mercantilist companies, the free ports of Trieste and Fiume, and various other tax shelters were powerful stimuli to the economy around the capital. Profits from government loans also returned to Vienna to be spent there. This redistribution of financial contributions fuelled the aristocratic and ecclesiastical building boom in Vienna and Prague after 1683. Wealth was generated precisely among those groups most directly involved in war finance.

Austria's peacetime army oscillated between 80,000 and 130,000 men, well below the benchmark of one per cent of the total population found in some other states. The king of Prussia maintained 80,000 soldiers from a population of two million inhabitants, but this was an extreme.[16] Precious few Imperial troops were Italian. Guido Quazza provides a list of standing Imperial units in 1734: of 46 line infantry regiments, only one was Italian. Only one of twenty cavalry regiments was Italian, and none of the sixteen regiments of dragoons or hussars. Of the new levies for the War of the Polish Succession (1733–5), only two of ten infantry regiments, and none of the five cavalry regiments was Italian. Contingents rented from various German states then augmented the emperor's forces. The total number of troops in 1734 was 259,000 men, of whom probably less than 10,000

---

[13] T. Colapietra, "Prestigio sociale e potere reale nell' Aquila d'antico regime (1525–1800)", *Critica Storica*, 1979, pp. 370–87. Colapietra finds virtually no trace of soldiers amongst the 143 members of the city council of Aquila in the Abruzzi in 1717, even though all of them were nobles. He notes (p. 386) that during the seventeenth century, the officials outnumbered the soldiers aggregated to the nobility, until the closure of the group to newcomers in 1668. Military nobles were never numerous on the city council.

[14] G. Quazza, *Il problema italiano e l'equilibrio europeo, 1720–1738* (Turin: 1965), p. 28ff.

[15] Di Vittorio, "Un caso di correlazione tra guerre, spese militari e cambiamenti economici", *Nuova Rivista Storica*, 1982, pp. 59–81.

[16] Corvisier, *Armées et sociétés en Europe moderne, 1494–1789*, p. 126.

were Italian, and most of those were new levies.[17] After 1735 there remained only two Italian regiments in the army, both based in Milan, and they took on an increasingly Lombard character.[18] Beyond these, however, one must remember that Austria called upon its 'satellites' in Italy, as in Germany, to provide troops for its wars. These were few, however, compared to Germany. A Tuscan regiment saw active service in the Seven Years War after 1760. Modena continued to rent troops to the emperor, although I am not certain the troops were Italian. These numbered about 1,500 in 1737; and three infantry and a cavalry regiment in 1757, in Lombard garrisons, making the Milanese available for service elsewhere.

Despite the size of the Imperial army, it was a fragile colossus. Army efficiency had made little progress since the time of Montecùccoli. In 1740, of 144 persons working for the Council of War (*Hofkriegsrat*) in Vienna, effectively only four people dealt with military matters. Most of the money for the upkeep of the troops in the Italian theatre was still in the hands of Milanese financiers.[19] Moreover, the number of troops assigned to a theatre by the administration was purely theoretical. Of the 13,000 men posted to Milan in 1718 and paid from its treasury, thousands were missing from the rolls. Officers still frequently defrauded the troops of their pay and provisions and incited them to desert. Only after 1748 was it possible to make the province of Milan pay for the upkeep of 28,000 troops assigned to defend it. The person in charge of reform after the disappointing War of the Austrian Succession was the general, Marchese Luca Giovanni Pallavicini, who tried to raise a Lombard army in the region. He failed too, for numbers were always inferior to expectations. In a year of peace (1751) it was necessary to replace at least ten per cent of the recruits, due to sickness, death and desertion.[20] Despite his attempts, it seems that few recruiters actively sought to employ Italians in the army. There were few Italian soldiers in the ranks already in the time of Montecùccoli, despite their prominence among the officers. Eugene of Savoy explicitly discouraged recruiting Italian troops. If the emperor, Charles VI, was an

---

[17] G. Quazza, *Il problema italiano e l'equilibrio europeo, 1720–1738*, p. 415ff; "Etat général des troupes de l'Empereur et de leur déstination pour la campagne de 1734".

[18] Sondheim, *In the service of the Emperor*, pp. 2–5. Sondheim notes that the Austrian recruiting regulations of 1715 and 1722 stipulated that non-Germans, or *Welschen* should be barred from the regiments, but the Habsburgs inherited a few Italian regiments from its conquest of Italy, which were merged. Karl Roider also notes that army recruiting regulations frowned upon particular nationalities – namely, French, Italians, Swiss (!), Poles, Hungarians and Croats – "because they do not adjust easily to our type of comradeship and are the greatest cowards and braggarts, who go from one army to another and even lead astray and debauch good men". Roider emphasizes that these regulations of 1722 set forth ideals, and were not always practised. See Karl A. Roider, *The reluctant ally: Austria's policy in the Austro-Turkish War, 1737–1739* (Baton Rouge, Louisiana: 1972), p. 20.

[19] C. Donati, "Esercito e società civile nella Lombardia del secolo XVIII", *Società e Storia*, 1982, pp. 527–54, at p. 530.

[20] *Ibid.* On Pallavicini's efforts, see p. 550.

Italophile, the old marshal advocated the army's 'Germanization'.[21] He wanted the bulk of the army to be ethnically German and homogeneous, although he tolerated other nationalities. Yet he preferred German troops to all others, and kept newly conquered provinces in German hands. Later emperors, like Francis I and Joseph II, did not have a high opinion of Italian soldiery, although the two Lombard regiments fought adequately against the Turks in Hungary in 1788–90. It is true that when French revolutionary armies advanced in Italy in 1795, both virtually disintegrated, and only an insignificant number of Italians fought for Austria after the French takeover of the region.

In stark contrast to the feeble affinity of ordinary Italians for the Imperial army, they were still numerous among the senior officers early in the eighteenth century. Christopher Duffy considers that these officers still enjoyed a high reputation for their manners and their skills.[22] Austria's officer corps was still among the most cosmopolitan in Europe, and the most 'democratic' in the lower echelons where non-nobles held most of the commissions.[23] Italian commanders were still prominent in the War of the Austrian Succession, like the Genoese Antonio Botta Adorno, but after that their numbers and importance waned. By the Seven Years War, if not long before, there was no longer an Italian 'lobby' in Vienna enjoying the emperor's preferment. Reciprocally, Italian aristocrats may have spurned an army in which such a high proportion of officers consisted of non-nobles, and where senior ministers and generals sought to discount social status when considering promotions.[24] Lawrence Sondhaus counts 24 Italian generals between 1740 and 1790, about half of whom came from Lombardy.[25] Milan's patriciate was rather overshadowed by generals from elsewhere. In 1747, of 271 senior officers in the Imperial army, only seven were Milanese, and only one of 28 field marshals. Milanese patricians thereafter deserted the Austrian army. In 1797, of 422 generals and senior officers, only one remained, a lieutenant field-marshal named Belgioioso. Their percentages fell from 2.5 during the War of the Austrian Succession, to a mere 0.2. I have no specific earlier figures for Milanese, but we should recall here that Italians comprised 15 to 25 per cent of senior officers in Wallenstein's army, and still about 8 per cent in 1700. The decline appears relentless in the one European army where Italians were welcome. Claudio Donati analyzes this further by systematically studying genealogies. From the early seventeenth to the early eighteenth centuries, among the 23 foremost Milanese families, at least 33 individuals followed a military career. Twenty-four more served between 1700 and 1763, but only six in the remainder of the century.

---

[21] McKay, *Prince Eugene of Savoy*, p. 214.
[22] C. Duffy, *The army of Maria Theresa: the armed forces of Imperial Austria, 1740–1780* (New York: 1977), p. 25.
[23] Nouzille, *Le prince Eugène de Savoie et les problèmes des confins militaires autrichiens, 1699–1739*, p. 182.
[24] F. Szabo, *Kaunitz and enlightened absolutism, 1753–1780* (Cambridge: 1994), p. 275.
[25] Sondhaus, *In the service of the emperor*, p. 7.

Donati suggests that most of the nobles wanted to serve in the Milanese civil administration instead.[26]

If the Austrian army 'Germanized', the renascent Spanish army shed its Italian component in the eighteenth century too. It was recast in the crucible of the civil war, following its gradual breakdown under the last Habsburg king, Charles II (1665–1700). The unreformed institution still relied heavily on the *asiento* system, on the regular rotation of *tercios* to different parts of the empire, and on antiquated tactics that the French likened to duels.[27] Philip V officially reconstituted the army in 1704, along the French model, and placed it in the hands of French officials in his retinue. An overhaul in Spanish financial and administrative practices, also directed from Paris, facilitated its resurgence.[28] In 1703 the kingdom's revenues amounted to only 12 million escudos. Abolishing the privileges or *fueros* of Valencia and Aragon helped centralize the administration, and new gabelles and the reincorporation of alienated rights further strengthened the crown. Most of the financiers, now Spanish, accepted reimbursement in the debased coinage of Castile, reducing the export of specie. Revenues soared to 26 million escudos in 1713, of which 18 million were assigned to military expenditures.[29] By 1711 (after the Netherlands and Italy had been lost), Madrid financed 116 infantry battalions, of which twenty or twenty-five were foreign (mostly French, Flemish, Walloon, Irish or German), for a total of about 70,000 men, in addition to 20,000 horse. The quality was still unsatisfactory because the force was so new, and because it took time to reconstitute a proper officer corps. Madrid's aim was to advance lesser nobles to the fore based on their experience, and to persuade the grandees to begin their careers at a subalternate level to learn the trade.[30]

During the War of the Spanish Succession, many Italians held prominent positions, perhaps because they were aristocrats, unlike most of the Spanish officers. Fleeting accounts of the campaigns mention the same families in Spanish military service for generations – the Caràcciolo, Caetano and Cantelmo of Naples, Guasco of Alessandria, and Pio of Milan, for example. Henry Kamen notes moreover the gradual replacement of French advisers and officers by Italian

---

[26] Donati, "Esercito e società civile", *Società e Storia*, 1982, pp. 527–54. Donati is the only historian I have encountered who has used the Fascist encyclopedias in an attempt to gauge the participation of Milanese nobles in military service.

[27] H. Kamen, *The war of succession in Spain, 1700–1715* (London: 1969), p. 59.

[28] *Ibid.*, p. 43.

[29] H. Kamen, "España en la Europa de Luis XIV", *Historia de España Menendez-Pidal; t. 28: La transiciòn del siglo XVII al XVIII*, p. 286ff.

[30] G. Quazza, *Il problema italiano e l'equilibrio europeo*, p. 394ff. Quazza reproduces in an appendix the fascinating report by the Piedmontese diplomat, the marchese di Triviè, judging the worth of this new army in 1711. On the substitution of the 'patrimonial' concept of military office, with that of a 'career' beginning in the lower echelons, see Francisco Andujar Castillo, *Los militares en la España del siglo XVIII: un estudio social* (Granada: 1991), p. 102.

ones, as anti-French sentiment deepened in Spain. By 1711 grandees lamented that Italians and Flemings ran the country. The foremost general of the Spanish Bourbon king was the duke of Pòpoli, a Cantelmo. At war's end in 1714, this Italian presence increased through the king's marriage to the ambitious and domineering Elisabeth Farnese, who brought the low-born Parman Cardinal Alberoni to Madrid as her adviser. New Italian faces with old names took command of key posts: a Spìnola became governor of Valencia, a Grimaldi was governor of Cadiz, and Italians took ministerial positions too.[31]

When Alberoni supplemented the new army with a fleet, Spain returned in force onto the international scene. The cardinal hatched the scheme to invade Sicily with a seaborne army in 1718, and expel the Piedmontese in a quick campaign, before the Imperials engaged in Hungary could react. The project backfired by triggering intervention from all the European powers. Nevertheless, the Spanish fleet and army were now capable of significant operations, and were looking for an opening in Italy. The looming Tuscan succession in 1731 called for its transfer to Prince Charles, backed by a force of 6,000 Spanish soldiers. Then with the outbreak of war in 1734 (over the succession in Poland), Philip V transported over 20,000 troops to Tuscany with the aim of reconquering the kingdom of Naples. A crowd of nobles and adventurers, including many Italians, latched onto the expedition, as the Spanish military promenade bottled up the principal Austrian garrisons. Most of the Neapolitan nobility, deaf to Austrian appeals, turned out to applaud the 16-year-old King Charles. Naples' citadels capitulated after a *pro forma* siege of several days. The only battle in the campaign took place outside Bari, at Bitonto, where a Spanish army of 13,000 stormed an entrenched Austrian force of equal size and took most of it prisoner. After that, the conquest proceeded at a leisurely pace with the sieges of Pescara, Capua and Gaeta, all significant fortresses defended by German units and the debris of a Neapolitan regiment.[32] Then, in August, the Spanish fleet transported another 13,000 men to conquer Sicily. The Austrian viceroy held out in Syracuse with only a handful of troops, while the Spanish occupied Palermo and Messina without firing a shot.

This new-model Spanish army and its officer corps has been studied recently by Francisco Andujar Castillo, who sifted through 4,800 individual officers' files. The major reforms of 1702–4 transformed the old structure of *tercios* into regiments, battalions and companies, completely eliminating recourse to *asientos*. Only the king had the right to assign officers to a unit. Alongside the new regular battalions, the French advisers created a new militia, with some attempt made at a system of conscription. By 1734 it comprised 33 regiments. Paris and Madrid attempted to remilitarize the Spanish aristocracy as well, with some success. In the second half of the seventeenth century, only about half the officers were noble, and many of

---

[31] Kamen, *The war of succession in Spain*, p. 55 and p. 117.
[32] See the account of the campaign in M. Schipa, *Il regno di Napoli al tempo di Carlo Borbone* (Naples: 1923), p. 101ff.

those originated outside Spain. Senior Castilian officers saw military preferment as part of their family patrimony, and the crown actively encouraged this, expecting the grandees to raise troops themselves. In the eighteenth century, Madrid established the army cadet corps on the French model. Candidates had to be noble and have the financial resources to maintain their rank. Nobles were also promoted more quickly, and they held a virtual monopoly of the senior ranks. As a result, the proportion of noble officers passed from 60 per cent between 1700 and 1725, to almost 90 per cent after 1776.[33]

The Spanish army employed foreign battalions (mostly German) and foreign officers in the eighteenth century, and these last were most frequent at senior levels before 1750. For the entire officer corps over the whole century, these foreign officers were 1 per cent Sicilian, 0.5 per cent Neapolitan, 0.5 per cent Milanese, 1 per cent other Italian; barely 2 per cent hailed from the Low Countries, and the remainder came from over much of Europe. Foreigners from lands under Spanish dominion constituted 11 per cent in 1715–35; 4 per cent in 1736–55; 2 per cent in 1756–75, and 0.5 per cent in 1776–1800. The 'Italianization' of the upper echelons at the end of the War of the Spanish Succession was apparently a fleeting moment. Andujar Castillo's figures are not more precise as to geographical provenance, but it is easy to conclude that there was little room for Italians. That space was rapidly shrinking as more Spaniards returned to the profession of arms.[34]

France continued to maintain the largest European establishment, with 200,000 peacetime effective soldiers, and more than double that at full mobilization. For the eighteenth century, it has been the object of a groundbreaking study by André Corvisier who focused not on the officers, but instead on the rank and file. Extrapolating from the *contrôles de troupes*, he calculates that foreigners in the wartime year of 1711 comprised about 50,000 men, or about 15 per cent of the army, and 20,000 in the peaceful period between 1716 and 1733.[35] Foreigners were attractive, for they saved a king's subject and deprived the enemy of a mercenary. On the other hand, they were more expensive, and they deserted more easily. In the French army, there were many thousands of Germans, Swiss and Irish. The number of Italians was lower than virtually any other group. The *Royal Italien* infantry battalion numbered about 600 men, most of whom were Piedmontese. In 1739 the crown established the *Royal Corse*, for a second battalion.[36] The ethnic composition of the various units was not rigorous, though. For the whole army in 1716, there were only about 1,500 Italians. Piedmontese comprised a large quarter of them; a small quarter came from the grand duchy of

---

[33] F. Andujar Castillo, *Los militares en la España del siglo XVIII: un estudio social* (Granada: 1991), p. 159.

[34] *Ibid.*, p. 315.

[35] A. Corvisier, *L'armée française de la fin du XVIIe siècle au ministère de Choiseul: le soldat*, 2 vols (Paris: 1964), vol. 1, p. 259.

[36] *Ibid.*, vol. 1, p. 548.

Tuscany and the republic of Lucca; 10 per cent were Lombards, and the remainder came from the rest of the peninsula. Recruiting in Italy was feasible only when Piedmont was a French ally.[37] In the eighteenth century, then, Italian troops virtually disappeared from fighting armies across Europe, and in their stead a handful of officers served the three Catholic monarchs.

We should examine, before leaving this aspect of demilitarization, the role that Italian nobles played in the crusading orders. Only the knights of Malta continued to play any role after the siege of Corfù. Malta was first and foremost a fortress of incredible dimensions by 1700. Redoubts and batteries overlooked not only Valletta and its suburbs, but every bay and shelter. In 1716 it had a permanent garrison of 3,000 men, in addition to about 600 knights and 7,000 militia.[38] The order regained new vigour at the turn of the century, and complemented its galley fleet with a flotilla of sailing ships of fifty or sixty guns apiece. Besides raiding Barbary commerce, it went to the aid of the Spanish-held port of Oran in 1707. It was their last land engagement. At the time of Venice's Corfù war, its galleys and its five warships made the Maltese fleet larger than those of Naples and Sicily, the Papal fleet, and the Tuscan navy. But these ships were not well built and Malta could not afford to raise troops in addition to its ships, as it had done in the seventeenth century. After 1710, the income of the order was unable to cover the expenditure on the fleet.

International pressure put more and more Moslem territory out of bounds to this fleet. Even Malta's police role was insignificant next to the French patrols, though sometimes the galleys and the vessels of the order would tag along, to be useful. France and Venice forbade attacks on the Greek islands or the Turkish coast. In the second half of the eighteenth century, the Adriatic was placed off limits too.[39] Though forbidden to sail anywhere north of the line Sicily–Gibraltar, they often ignored those rules. From 1700 to 1765, the knights captured or sank only 56 vessels. While there were twenty or thirty corsair vessels flying the Maltese flag in the seventeenth century, there were only about eight in the 1720s, and then four or five after that.[40] With such little scope for offensive action, few knights acquired much military experience. It became more difficult to convince them that the 'caravans' were worthwhile, and in 1723 the Grand Master had to order many knights to report to Malta. Caravans were increasingly limited to excursions and cruises between Italian ports, and the knights spent their time carousing or going to the theatre. Protocol visits, with long interludes in port, and their train of

---

[37] A. Corvisier, vol. 1, p. 273.

[38] The scale of the fortifications, and the many stages of their elaboration is followed in the book by Quentin Hughes, *Fortress: architecture and military history in Malta* (London: 1969).

[39] R. Cavaliero, *The last of the crusaders: the Knights of St. John and Malta in the eighteenth century* (London: 1960), p. 82.

[40] This decline was matched by that of Algiers, which had only eight sailing ships and nine galiots active in 1737. See Peter Earle, *Corsairs of Malta and Barbary* (London: 1970), p. 45.

compliments and festivities, took their place. The cannon served mostly to fire salutes.[41]

This 'demotivation' then spread to recruitment. The number of Italians gradually diminished to about a quarter or less of the knights. Spagnoletti maintains that as the Italian states expanded their bureaucracies, fewer nobles were available to serve as knights of Malta. From 1719 to 1789 there were but nine Italian entries annually, on average. Southerners, and 'provincials' originating in small towns, made up an increasing proportion of them.[42] When Bonaparte arrived in Malta in 1798, there were only a few dozen Italians there. Of the 362 knights left, 260 were French, and few of those gave much thought to resisting. The Corsican general drew from Valletta 1,200 cannon, 40,000 muskets and 1.5 million tonnes of powder for his Egyptian campaign, which gives an idea of Malta's potential.

The knights of Santo Stefano had virtually lost their seafaring ways too, and only a few went on patrol each year: this despite a recruitment of almost two thousand men into the order between 1660 and 1737.[43] The last significant Barbary prize was taken in 1719. There were only three galleys left and a few unserviceable ships afloat at the turn of the century. In 1716 the Tuscan contribution to the Venetian defence of Corfù made a very bad impression on everyone.[44] In conclusion, it seems that the eighteenth century witnessed an extremely low level of militarization in the Italian peninsula, and few Italian nobles sought these careers elsewhere. The armies that had hired them in some numbers no longer needed their services, and there were no credible alternatives left among Italian princes, apart from the duke of Savoy.

Minor states rearm

Italian princes were quite conscious of their military limitations, and some of them wished to build up what complacency and neglect had worn down. The first half of the eighteenth century, which made Italy a battlefield on three occasions, witnessed some interesting attempts to recast armies much in the same way that Spain had done. They failed. But their attempts illustrate many of the difficulties princes encountered. Italian states still set aside a significant part of their revenues for defence, but this entailed mostly the upkeep of fortresses constructed in the

---

[41] C. Petiet, *Ces messieurs de la religion: l'Ordre de Malte au dix-huitième siècle ou le crépuscule d'une épopée* (Paris: 1992), pp. 136–41.

[42] A. Spagnoletti, *Stato, aristocrazie e Ordine di Malta nell' Italia moderna* (Rome: 1988); p. 63ff.

[43] F. Angiolini, "La nobiltà 'imperfetta'; cavalieri e commende di S. Stefano nella Toscana moderna", in *Signori, patrizi, cavalieri in Italia centro-meridionale nell' età moderna*, M. A. Visceglia (ed.) (Bari: 1992), pp. 146–66, at p. 152ff.

[44] C. Manfroni, *La marina militare del granducato mediceo*, pt 2, p. 120.

preceding one and a half centuries. Their paltry garrisons were unfit for service in the field. In the Papal States, after servicing the debt, military expenditures were the largest single item, accounting for about 20 per cent of all revenue in the early eighteenth century. Successive popes after the late seventeenth century sought to enhance military professionalization by delivering soldiers from the evils of nepotism.[45] The Papal States' military establishment of 5,000 men, scattered from Avignon to Ferrara, Ancona and Rome, was utterly incapable of military initiative. Small garrisons counted together did not comprise an army.[46] Similarly, Tuscany and Genoa disposed of only about 2,500 garrison troops each, and their respective militias were useless. Tuscany, in 1718 posted 1,700 troops in Livorno, and 700 more in Portoferraio on the island of Elba. Other garrisons were insignificant, like the 50 soldiers in the citadel of Siena, or the 150 men guarding the sizeable fortress of Grosseto in the coastal plain. The fortresses themselves were often splendid works, well stocked with cannon. The Fortezza da Basso, largest of the Florentine citadels, had 165 cannon, but only 100 men in garrison. Radicòfani, at the south-eastern entrance to the grand duchy, also probably had fewer men in garrison than there were artillery pieces on the ramparts. Most forts only had a custodian and an artillery inspector. Compounding the small number of troops was their pitiful condition. Many regular soldiers were aged, often blind or lame.[47] There were only a few cavalry companies, and the grand duke's personal guard numbered only 80 men, all Germans. There was not even a thought of resisting any great power solution to the problem of the dynasty's extinction.

Parma

One prince who sought to reverse the demilitarization process was Duke Francesco Farnese, who acceded to the throne of Parma in 1694. With the wintering of Austrian troops still fresh in his mind, he resolved to prevent the duchy from being a feedbag for the great powers. When the War of the Spanish

---

[45] See the detailed study of the Papal army for 1667 (and not 1677, despite the article's title), by Georg Lutz, "L'esercito pontificio nel 1677: camera apostolica, bilancio militare dello stato della Chiesa e nepotismo nel primo evo moderno", *Miscellanea in onore di Monsignor Martino Giusti, prefetto dell' Archivio Segreto Vaticano* (Vatican City: 1978) vol. 2, pp. 33–95. From Lutz's identification of Papal officers at the end of the mandate of Alexander VII Chigi, it appears that at least 15 per cent of them were natives of Siena, like the Pope. See also my article, "The demilitarization of an Italian provincial aristocracy: Siena 1575–1740", *Past and Present*, **155**, 1997, pp. 64–108.

[46] Hans Gross, *Rome in the age of enlightenment: the post-Tridentine syndrome and the ancien régime* (Cambridge: 1990), p. 140.

[47] A review of these little garrisons in the statelets of northern Italy is contained in the work by Guido Quazza, *Il problema italiano e l'equilibrio europeo, 1720–1738*, p. 64ff; for Tuscany in particular, see Harold Acton, *The last Medici* (London: 1980, first publ. 1934), p. 272.

Succession broke out in Italy at the start of 1701, the duke raised 28 companies of professional troops, to deny foreign armies access to the duchy. Realistically, he apportioned them equally between Parma and Piacenza, the duchy's fortress capitals, for garrison duty.[48] Within a short time, Duke Francesco had raised his garrison army to 3,500 infantry, and completed it by reviving the training musters of the huge militia force of 38,000 men. By appointing military commanders over the soldiers and militiamen alike, the duke exercised not a little patronage power. Senior officers were almost all members of the duchy's oldest families, like the Anguissola and the Scotti, fixtures at the court since the beginning of the seventeenth century. Nevertheless, in this sizeable army, a single company of Irish Guards, or about a hundred men, was the only unit that we would call 'combat-ready'. The captain of the Irish Guards enjoyed the highest salary of any officer in the duchy.[49] Parma's army was too tiny to deny access to the duchy by French and Austrian troops, who contested it as a battleground until 1707. These troops could keep the Bourbons and the Habsburgs out of the cities, however, unlike neighbouring Mantua and Modena. Following Prince Eugene's victory at Turin, Austrian troops occupied the duchy regularly in winter quarters until 1713. Consequently, the Parman army appeared quite superfluous.

Once, the duke threw his army into a war against an adversary his own size. Tensions arose between Parma and Modena in 1701 after Parmans had helped demolish the Modenese fortress of Brescello under French supervision, and Duke Rinaldo d'Este swore vendetta. A pretext arose in 1711, when both states claimed a tiny piece of riverbank land along the border stream of the Enza. The Parmans delimited the little territory with a row of poplar trees, and planted a customs house on it to show the flag. On 21 May, hundreds of Modenese soldiers and militiamen stormed the little hut, cut down the poplars, and then built a redoubt on the spot. Duke Francesco flew into a rage when he heard about the provocation, and ordered his army to avenge the affront to his sovereignty. On 25 May, about 6,000 Parman regulars and militiamen, ostensibly commanded by General Anguissola, but deployed by the Irish captain, Harvey, stormed the Modenese trenches. About half a dozen men died in the attack, where the vastly outnumbered Modenese 'army' took to its heels. On 1 June, the victorious Parman forces returned to the capital in a victory parade, with crowds hollering "Viva! Viva!" to the accompaniment of trumpets and drums. Outside the belligerent states, however, the public greeted this lilliputian 'war of the poplars' with derision. The Austrian military governor of Milan and Grand Duke Cosimo III of Tuscany defused the whole affair, as they had similar conflicts a century before.[50]

Duke Francesco Farnese also committed troops to help Venice in its struggle with Turkey over Corfù and Dalmatia, from 1715 to 1719. This was a continua-

---

[48] M. Zannoni & M. Fiorentino, *L'esercito farnesiano dal 1694 al 1731* (Parma: 1981), p. 14.
[49] *Ibid.*, p. 20.
[50] *Ibid.*, pp. 42–5.

tion of a seventeenth-century policy under which Parma raised the troops, and Venice paid for them in the theatre of deployment. One battalion went to Greece during the Morea war, where it remained until 1699. Francesco contributed another battalion, called the 'Parma,' and dispatched it to Corfù in 1715 just in time for the siege. Most of its 600 men died of typhus and similar diseases. Then in 1717 he sent a second battalion, raised under his personal supervision and in his quality of grand master of the Constantinian knights of Saint George. Duke Francesco saw this unit as a tool to bolster his claim to the 'throne' of Macedonia, so he invested in it all his prestige and much of his revenue. He required its officers to be nobles of the finest pedigree. Deployed first in garrison in Spalato, in 1718 it formed part of the Venetian army besieging Dulcigno in Montenegro. About a third of its effective numbers became casualties, but very few from combat.[51] Raising troops for these two battalions proved difficult. The duke coerced some of his feudatories to contribute men to it, and sent out orders to empty the jails. One energetic seizure of 30 householders in their own homes one night frightened scores of individuals into seeking refuge in churches and the *palazzi* of prominent individuals.

With the death of Duke Francesco in 1727, his successor pared the army of Parma back again to a few companies of garrison troops, ornamented by some ceremonial horse guards, totalling about 1,600 men. The busiest contingents were probably the cavalry companies, assigned to maintain public order in the remote countryside, and patrol the borders against smugglers.[52] Many soldiers, together with the officers, were Italians from other regions, or Catholic foreigners. When the last Farnese duke, Antonio, died in 1731, the emperor, Charles VI, occupied the state of Parma immediately with 5,000 men under the command of the Lombard general, Carlo Stampa. This rendered vain any Papal claims for the duchy's devolution to Rome. It was then the object of fierce fighting in 1745–6, for Elisabeth Farnese desired that Spanish troops should occupy and hold it at all costs. With the establishment of a Spanish Bourbon branch there in 1748, the duchy ceased to have a significant army.

Genoa

More defenceless still was the republic of Genoa, with about 2,000 soldiers for a population of over 400,000, strung out along the coast from Provence to Tuscany. Genoa itself boasted considerable fortifications, built after the Franco-Piedmontese invasion of 1625. Owing to the Piedmontese menace, so did some places on the northern edge of the Apennines, like Gavi, Ovada and Novi Liguria. From the moment of the first great rising of 1729, however, Corsica was the republic's Achilles heel. The quick loss of control over the island underscored how

---

[51] M. Zannoni, p. 51ff.
[52] *Ibid.*, p. 102.

militarily supine the republic was. In 1731 Genoa requested military intervention by Imperial troops available in Lombardy, which was virtually a recognition of its vassal status. A corps of 4,000 infantry under the prince of Württemberg landed in August. The guerrillas tried to draw the Austrians inland into the mountains, where they could harass them more effectively. By 1732 about 10,000 troops, perhaps all Germans, hunted the active rebels. The guerrilla bands signed a treaty with an amnesty in 1732, but the Genoese soon broke it, and a new revolt broke out. Imperial troops quelled it again in 1733, but the next year there were new skirmishes when Austrian troops withdrew to defend Lombardy from a Bourbon invasion.[53] Behind the instability was the lack of political co-ordination among the Corsicans themselves, whose clan structures made it almost impossible for inhabitants of one village to follow a leader from another. Corsica was an archetypal feuding society. The Genoese had tried to ban firearms from the island in 1715, without success. To demonstrate the ungovernability of the island, the Genoese published the figure that in the 32 years preceding, there had been 28,715 homicides, or an average of 900 annually, for a population of barely 100,000. Corsican patriots did not contradict this figure, but simply attributed it to Genoese *malgoverno*.[54]

The rebels felt that only an outsider could unify them against the little Genoese garrisons clinging to the rugged coastline. A strange individual, an adventurer and swindler from Westphalia, Theodore de Neuhoff fell into the leadership role, after he stole a ship full of arms in 1736 with the intention of selling the weapons to the insurgents. Since he pretended to be a Spanish grandee, the Corsicans elected him king. Theodore's 'reign' lasted but a few months, and he fled in fear of vendetta after exercising the most rudimentary discipline. His troops numbered at most several hundred, and were prone to fighting each other. Nevertheless, these bands were fairly successful against their opponents. Genoese troops (Germans in large part) were demoralized and withdrew to their garrisons. Around Bastia, the capital, there were at most 169 rebels sniping at the 500 men blockaded inside. Whenever the Genoese took the offensive, it was in small units of three or four hundred men. To collect these, it was necessary for the republic to reduce to almost nothing the garrisons along the Riviera.[55]

After Austria's defeat in the War of the Polish Succession, Genoa requested help from France. In 1738 the French marshal, Maillebois, landed thousands of French troops in Bastia, mostly mobile light infantry. To quell the rebellion outright, Maillebois launched columns well into the interior, to occupy the

---

[53] On the background to the revolt, see the long polemic by the *abate* Costa, *Giustificazione della rivoluzione di Corsica* (Oletta, Corsica: 1758). The course of the early revolt is narrated in the book by André le Glay, *Theodore de Neuhoff, roi de Corse* (Paris: 1907), p. 8ff.; and in the thesis by Gaston Broche, *La république de Gênes et la France pendant la guerre de la succession d'Autriche, 1740–1748*, 3 vols (Paris: 1936), vol. 1, p. 29ff.

[54] Costa, *Giustificazioni della rivoluzione di Corsica*, p. 28ff.

[55] Neuhoff, *Theodore de Neuhoff, roi de Corse*, p. 110.

Balagre and the Goro valleys. About a thousand Corsicans made a stand around Zicavo, but in September 1739, Maillebois crushed it with a rush of four battalions. A few survivors lived as bandits in the mountains after that. With the outbreak of the War of the Austrian Succession after 1745, when Genoa decided to participate in the Bourbon alliance, the Corsicans rebelled again, this time with the support of the English fleet. Bastia capitulated to a Corsican army of 1,400 men who descended from the mountains, but this was their only cohesive action. They then broke up into competing bands, and the guerrilla war continued until the republic of Genoa finally sold the island to France in 1768.

The irony in this situation was that Corsica contained the most militarized population in Italy, and its soldiers had long been the pillars of the Genoese state. While these troops were always numerous, their leaders were confined to subaltern-level positions, and were only promoted when the republic was in danger. Genoa retired many Corsicans promoted to the rank of colonel, on the half-pay of reformed officers. France, Venice, Tuscany and the Papal States had all appointed Corsicans as army commanders, governors of fortresses, governors of provinces, and even as field marshals. Neuhoff established a list of Corsicans serving as soldiers in various armies around 1743, and the numbers he lists are corroborated by other sources. There were 750 in Papal service; almost 900 enrolled in the Venetian army; another 900 in the Bourbon armies of Spain and Naples; 400 in French service where they constituted a regular battalion; a few score each in the armies of Piedmont and Tuscany; and finally almost 1,500 in Genoese service. The 4,600 Corsicans in active military service, constituted about 4 per cent of the entire population. This figure was comparable to the most militarized zones of Europe.[56]

The creation of a proper Genoese army was the sudden outcome of a threat against the *dominante* itself. Patricians fought only defensive wars, and had a long tradition of depending upon allies to save themselves from Piedmontese or French invasions. The republic depended upon foreigners to repress the revolt in Corsica, but after 1740 and the outbreak of war everywhere, it was bereft of regiments for hire. Genoa hoped to remain neutral in the conflict raging all around it, even when Lombardy became a battlefield. It also hoped that the various belligerents would respect its neutrality and not violate its territory. In January 1742, however, the Spanish landed a large expeditionary force at La Spezia, expecting right of passage into the interior. This was not illegal under international law, and was a frequent practice despite the protests of interested states. Later that year, the Corsicans rose in rebellion again, this time with the material aid of Piedmont (which desired the outright conquest of the republic and of the island), and of Britain, which needed a naval base of operations in the western Mediterranean. Genoa's neutrality was mocked still further in early 1743 when Piedmont signed the treaty of Worms with Austria for an all-out war against France and

---

[56] Neuhoff, p. 303.

Spain, which recognized its intention to occupy and annex part of the Genoese state.[57]

The republic only tardily consented to protect itself, by boosting its garrisons in Finale and La Spezia in Liguria, by floating a loan for a million *scudi*, and by calling France and Spain to its assistance. By the end of 1744, French and Spanish troops occupied parts of the Riviera, and pushed the republic into a formal alliance. The senate finally resolved to raise an army of 10,000 men, with Genoese patricians becoming officers in the new regiments. France's ambassador did not have a high opinion of the discipline of the troops, nor of the spirit of subordination of the officers, for Genoese nobles had not served in armies in any numbers for many decades.[58] Troops comprised mainly the local peasantry. The French considered these forces useful for guard duty, and for screening less critical areas. They did show a great deal of enthusiasm in the campaign of 1745, although the officers knew nothing about warfare. Bands of Ligurian peasants armed and led by Genoese patricians guarded passes over the Apennines. They resembled the more experienced and enterprising Piedmontese armed mountain companies, and like them they were basically civilians, not covered by the laws of war. From Genoa a huge Bourbon army tramped northwards into Lombardy, with several thousand Genoese regulars tagging along. With the shift of military fortunes back in Austrian favour, the republic sensed the danger. Immediately it ordered 9,000 more recruits into the regiments.[59]

When the French and Spanish withdrew into Provence and Languedoc in 1746, they abandoned Genoa to its fate. Its garrison of 10,000 troops might have resisted, but morale collapsed and the city admitted an occupation force led by a disgruntled Genoese patrician in Imperial service, Antonio Botta Adorno. Maria Theresa wished to punish the republic for having opposed her, and she imposed on it a huge 'contribution' of almost four million *scudi*, the equivalent of two years of revenue for the state. In addition, the city had to pay the subsistence cost of an Austrian garrison of 7,000 men. The magnitude of the Austrian exactions, and the hostility of the empress towards the republic finally pushed the population into open revolt, led at first by the urban workers, in December 1746. When the crowd overwhelmed the garrison, Botta Adorno withdrew into the mountains to blockade the passes leading into the city. His forces were harassed there by the peasant bands. The bulk of the Austrian army was hundreds of kilometres distant, having launched an invasion of Provence. Inside Genoa, a new militia of 6,000 men was formed on the structure of the artisans' corporations and guilds, to bolster 3,000 regulars. A few French artillerymen broke through the British naval blockade to stiffen the force. This militia rabble was considered adequate whenever an operation required *élan*, but very mediocre whenever obstinacy, discipline, or even

---

[57] Broche, *La république de Gênes et la France*, vol. 1, pp. 82–108.

[58] *Ibid.*, vol. 2, p. 55.

[59] *Ibid.*, vol. 2, p. 95.

steady work was required. They were also prone to sudden panics. Gradually reinforced by small packets of Gallispan regulars, the Genoese contested the Apennine redoubts with the Imperial army with some success. By late 1747 there were 7,000 French and 3,500 Spaniards actively helping the defence, so that the city was safe. The siege ended when the French mounted a diversionary invasion of Piedmont, forcing Charles Emanuel III to withdraw his army to confront it. With the end of the war the Genoese army dissolved again.

Modena

The only state besides Piedmont intent upon maintaining a strong army over a longer period was the duchy of Modena, whose forces probably always consisted of more than one per cent of the civilian population. Like their counterparts of the House of Savoy, the Este dukes were capable of switching alliances to defend their interests or support claims upon their neighbours. In the War of the Spanish Succession, Duke Rinaldo II threw in his lot with the Habsburgs, to the detriment of the population. He hoped by that to receive the fief of Mirandola as a reward, and possibly recover Comacchio from the Pope if the war extended there. He allowed Prince Eugene to hold his principal fortress of Brescello along the Po, which effectively ended his pretence of neutrality. When Eugene was repulsed, the Bourbon troops entered the duchy and occupied it. The duke returned to his capital only in November 1706, in the baggage of the Imperial army.[60] He was never able to shake off the status of an Austrian puppet, held tightly in the grip of Imperial troops. Because of Spain's (or rather, Elisabeth Farnese's) aggressive policies in Italy, Duke Rinaldo preferred the proximity of Austrian protection. During the War of the Polish Succession in 1734, he advanced money to the Austrian commander, and then supplied auxiliary troops for the Imperial army. Fearing Bourbon retaliation again, he left his capital for Bologna until the end of the war, in 1736.[61]

The advent of Francesco III in 1737 brought no immediate policy shift. As the duke desired to acquire military glory in a manner no longer typical in Italy, he fought against the Turks in the Hungarian campaign of 1737, in the capacity of Imperial general of artillery.[62] In 1739 Modena alone of Italian states sent troops – 1,500 men raised in Germany – to increase the emperor's armies in Hungary.[63] At the end of the war, the duke was loathe to dissolve these battalions. Likening his potential to that of Piedmont, he built a road over the Apennines to Massa, opening his line of communication to the sea. Energetic recruiting and purchase of weapons in Austria raised his army to a level well above that of his

---

[60] Amorth, *Modena capitale*, p. 163.
[61] Simeoni, *L'assorbimento austriaco del ducato estense*, p. 14.
[62] Amorth, *Modena capitale*, p. 180.
[63] Pugliese, *Le prime strette dell' Austria in Italia*, p. 273.

neighbours.[64] Duke Francesco III d'Este was one of those ambitious princes who could not resist competing for a piece of the Austrian empire after Frederick II of Prussia invaded Silesia in 1740. Now favourable to the Bourbons, the Este prince soon obtained a Spanish subsidy, to increase his army from 3,000 men to 8,000. He planned to join the Spanish campaign in Lombardy as supreme commander, the echo of a common seventeenth-century practice. Unfortunately for him, though, the Austrians and Piedmontese reacted quickly to the threat, and promptly invaded the duchy in 1742. They captured the city of Modena after a month-long siege, and then besieged the citadel. The Spanish did not move quickly enough to effect the planned junction with the Modenese. The duke had to flee his duchy, and thereafter trailed behind the Bourbon troops, disappointed that he was not treated as a fully-fledged ally.[65] He learned nothing from the experience, even despite losing his lands in Hungary as punishment. After 1748 he immediately began to prepare the next war, rearming his state with French subsidies. Francesco intended to play a major role in the Lombard campaign, to expand his state and to acquire military glory for his house. The Bourbon–Habsburg alliance of 1756 precluded any such war in Italy, much to the duke's disappointment.[66] After his death in 1763, an archduke of the House of Austria ruled in Modena.

Tuscany

In Tuscany, the new Habsburg regime attempted to recreate a military force after the extinction of the Medici dynasty in 1737. The Lorrainers dispatched to Florence by the sovereign, Francis of Lorraine, husband of Maria Teresa, decided to create a small but efficient army of six battalions, totalling about 4,000 infantry, and to disband the traditional peasant militia. Most of the garrison troops were to be Tuscans, but the officers were to be preferably Germans or Lorrainers, and their task would be to discipline the soldiers along lines common to northern Europe.[67] The results were so disappointing that Vienna declared Tuscan neutrality during the War of the Austrian Succession, and Spanish troops crossed it unopposed.[68] At the end of 1747, there were about 3,000 regular troops, plus some badly trained militia, still in service. A new plan provided for increasing the Tuscan army to 5,000 troops, and integrating them into the standing forces of the Austrian empire. The largest of the three regiments was to be composed of Germans. Small numbers of Germans had served as soldiers in the duchy since the Castro War, if not before. Their peacetime function was to guard the ports,

[64] Amorth, *Modena capitale*, p. 180.
[65] Simeoni, *L'assorbimento austriaco del ducato estense*, p. 20ff.
[66] *Ibid.*, p. 36.
[67] Giorgetti, *Le armi toscane*, vol. 2, p. 16.
[68] *Ibid.*, vol. 2, p. 16ff.

enforce quarantines, and track smugglers. A considerable amount of money, over two million lire in 1753, was spent on the force. Then in 1756, the outbreak of the Seven Years War provoked a panic among the young men of the grand duchy. Vienna ordered 3,000 troops to prepare to leave for Germany. The foreign officers complied immediately, but many Tuscan soldiers did not want to leave the grand duchy. The force left for Silesia only at the end of 1758. This first contingent was followed by 1,500 reinforcements in 1759, and others thereafter to replace the losses from battle and disease. Although Italy was not a theatre of operations, the population feared the imposition of conscription. About 4,000 young Tuscans slipped out of the duchy into the Papal States so as not to be conscripted, which was a significant drain on a total population of about 800,000.[69] The aspirations of Tuscans to be left out of great-power politics were quite clear.

The Neapolitan military experiment

The Neapolitan example of an attempt to remilitarize is no doubt the best, because it was the most sustained, and consciously took as its model the rebirth of the Spanish army. The adolescent King Charles received 14 battalions of infantry and 2,000 cavalry from the Spanish army, with an abundant artillery, as an outright gift from his father, Philip V in 1734. This was to be the nucleus and the fighting core of a Neapolitan army. With his ministers, Charles then drew up plans for a standing army of 32,000 men, in 19 infantry regiments of two battalions each, and five cavalry regiments. Charles called upon the Neapolitan aristocracy to help provide men, and recruiting parties sought to enrol veterans all over central and northern Italy, and in Switzerland. Many Austrian prisoners also enlisted.[70] Subsequent experience was that the results fell far short of expectations. By 1737 there were only 18,000 infantry and 2,500 horse available, including three regiments of Swiss and a Greco-Albanian regiment. Most of the other soldiers were Spanish, or other foreigners, although there were Neapolitan officers aplenty, drawing generous pay.[71] Nothing had been done to alleviate the dependence upon a foreign military infrastructure, as under the Austrian Habsburgs. The equipment came overwhelmingly from abroad, particularly from France.

Charles was given this army in the expectation that he would use it to further Bourbon objectives in Italy. In 1741, a Spanish seaborne invasion force landed at La Spezia and Orbetello in Tuscany to eject the Austrians from Parma and Lombardy. Together the Spanish armies in Italy numbered 40,000 men, not including the Neapolitans. Charles' mother summoned him to send 12,000 men northwards to join it. Under the duke of Castropignano, these Neapolitan troops

---

[69] Simeoni, vol. 2, p. 58ff.
[70] Schipa, *Il regno di Napoli al tempo di Carlo Borbone*, pp. 328–30.
[71] *Ibid.*, p. 330.

accompanied the Spanish general, Mortemar, to Emilia. Their plan was to rein-force Modena, whose duke had declared for the Bourbons, and then advance together on Milan. This army wintered in the Marches, before moving north in April 1742 to join the Modenese. Too late to prevent Modena from being overrun, the troops then retreated into Umbria, ignoring Papal remonstrances, to protect Naples from the north. The campaign was not successful, and the 'Nea-politans' returned much diminished, in September 1742.

At the end of the year, a British fleet appeared off Naples and summoned Charles to withdraw from the war immediately, under threat of bombardment of his capital. Charles had no navy, and few shore defences, so he acceded to the ultimatum. The experience spurred him to repair the fortifications of the king-dom, to build some warships, and to raise new units. He created ten new 'national regiments', on the Piedmontese pattern, by scouring the land for recruits in 1743, and assembled some 32,000 men, although it was impossible to sustain such a host for long. Although they were purportedly trained and drilled on the Prussian model, the Piedmontese ambassador who saw them was not impressed. Mean-while, the Spanish army took the offensive again into Emilia. It fought an Austrian army to a draw at Camposanto, near Bologna, before retreating into central Italy again.

In 1744 the Austrians took the offensive in Italy, intending to reconquer the kingdom of Naples. When the Spanish army under de Gages retreated through the Marches and the Abruzzi, Charles decided to rejoin the war and mobilize all his army at Capua to stop the invasion. Of the 18 regiments in the army in 1744, five of them were provincial ones in desperate condition, and one regiment mutinied so as not to have to go on campaign, and had to be forcibly disarmed. Of the remaining regiments, at least seven were foreign: Walloon, Swiss or Spanish. The Austrians sent a battalion of infantry into the Abruzzi to raise it against the Bourbon dynasty. Since there were no garrisons, Vienna rallied much of the province, and some influential nobles defected to it. As the Austrian invasion materialized, many barons expressed conspicuous discontent with Bour-bon regime. In July, King Charles marched with 3,000 men to retake the region, and quickly suppressed the revolt. The Spanish and Neapolitan armies then joined and stood off against an Austrian army of comparable size but of superior quality at Velletri, in the Papal States just south of Rome. Despite the uneven quality of his army, Charles gambled his kingdom on a single battle. On 11 August 1744, after a standoff of several weeks, the Austrian General Lobkowitz stormed the Bourbon lines, and his grenadiers almost captured de Gages, the duke of Modena and King Charles sleeping in the town. When the Austrian soldiers stopped to plunder the houses, they lost their momentum. The Hispano-Neapolitan army recovered and repulsed them. Even some provincial regiments gave a good account of themselves that day.[72]

After the battle, the Austrians withdrew to Lombardy and the Spanish and

---

[72] Wilkinson, *The defence of Piedmont, 1742–1748* (Oxford: 1927), p. 182ff.

6,000 Neapolitans followed them, under General Vieuville. The Neapolitans aided the offensive northwards from Genoa, and as second-rate troops they often guarded fortresses in captured territory. Victories in the summer and fall of 1745 came too easily. When the counter-attack came at the end of the year, the Bourbon forces were in an exposed position around Piacenza, with their lines of communication to Genoa cut. A first attempt to break out failed with heavy losses. Then the Gallispans, with the Neapolitans trailing, succeeded in poking a hole through the Austrian line and rushed south to regroup. The Austro-Piedmontese subsequently captured a large part of the Neapolitan force (mostly foreign regiments) deployed in isolated garrisons. When Ferdinand VI of Spain pulled out of the war in secret soon after, hostilities ended for the Neapolitans too.

In creating the twelve national regiments in 1743, Charles wanted to create an instrument of 'national cohesion'. He clearly needed to attract nobles into the army, to draw them away from the capital, and to tie them to the regime through the concepts of honour, duty and obedience.[73] The Abruzzi revolt, and the murmuring in Naples just strengthened his determination. Many officers posted in provincial garrisons were foreigners who had helped him conquer the kingdom a decade earlier. They were Spaniards and Walloons, Flemings and Parmans who began their careers as cadets in the Spanish army. They had chosen a military career out of family tradition, and because they considered it a source of honour, virtue, prestige, all according to the ideology of aristocracy. Enticing the Neapolitan nobility into the institution meant entering a process of reciprocal faith and collaboration. It was an imperfect union. Great nobles expected to have access to regimental commands for their sons, but without effective service on their part, like the courtly officers of Parma or Rome. Senior command was an appropriate appendage to their rank, and was not understood as a trade or profession to be mastered. On the other hand the army became a means by which lesser nobles could reinforce their status, especially holders of minor fiefs or those living in provincial towns. Over time, they reduced the place of the great nobility of the capital in the officer corps.[74] But the military efficiency of the institution gained nothing in the exchange. An inspection of Sicilian defences in 1760 revealed that the state of the regiments on the island was disastrous, the ships were only warships on paper, and that powder and munitions were lacking everywhere. The institution was quite hollow.[75]

---

[73] A. M. Rao, "Antiche storie e autentiche scritture: prove di nobiltà a Napoli nel settecento", *Signori, patrizi, cavalieri in Italia centro-meridionali nell' età moderna*, M. A. Visceglia (ed.) (Bari: 1992), pp. 279–308, at p. 280. See also Maria Grazia Maiorini, "Nobiltà napoletana e cariche amministrative: i presidi provinciali nel Settecento", in the same collection, pp. 309–25, at p. 312.

[74] Maiorini, "Nobiltà napoletana e cariche amministrative", pp. 309–25. See also Rao, "Antiche storie e autentiche scritture", pp. 279–308, at p. 286.

[75] G. Giarrizzo & V. d'Alessandro, *La Sicilia dal Vespro all' unita d'Italia* (Turin: 1989), p. 449.

Under King Ferdinand in 1765, a reform of the army boosted its effective strength to 35,000 men, or about 0.7 per cent of the population. There were plans to create a Swiss and Italian élite unit of 2,600 men, 23 regiments of line infantry comprising 26,000 men, and eight regiments of cavalry, with an artillery corps and some light troops. The greatest stumbling block to the realization of this ambitious project was the training of officers and non-commissioned cadres. After 1770 the crown proposed creating a noble cadet corps of several hundred members, but the Neapolitan nobility was still reluctant to commit itself to effective service in isolated garrisons. The English Jacobite court favourite, John Acton, designed another reform in 1788, by which the numbers were to be increased to 58,000 soldiers in peacetime, and 61,500 in wartime. This included 15,000 men in a provincial militia, equipped in the Austrian style. The artillery component was to be tripled and patterned after the latest French innovations, and the cavalry modelled on the Prussians. Despite the energy of its creator, the plan failed. In 1791 there were only 18,000 troops available, and only three regiments were up to strength. Acton filled other units by attracting deserters from Venetian service. French officers, who were very important before the Revolution as drillmasters, left with the outbreak of events in France, and were replaced by Germans. The rank and file resented the harsh Prussian discipline and deserted. In a frantic attempt to improve the army, Acton sent officers to Bologna to study mathematics, and to France and Austria to study engineering and army administration. He buttressed the fortifications of the kingdom, and built a weapons factory near the capital, at Torre Annunziata.[76]

Acton also took into hand the creation of a navy, for he had been a naval officer in French and Tuscan service, and had combat experience against the Algerine fleet. At the time of the Bourbon conquest in 1734, the navy was almost nonexistent: it was helpless when the English fleet appeared in 1742. Charles built a few frigates and some galleys in Naples and Palermo, and commissioned them to Spanish officers, but they were still incapable of undertaking anything significant. Acton had been recruited in Florence specifically as a naval expert, in 1778. He proposed building a real navy, and transformed the shipyards at Castellammare into the largest naval yard in Italy. He launched a ship of the line every year, besides smaller warships. By the time of the French Revolution, the Neapolitan navy consisted of 12 ships of the line, 12 frigates and 100 minor vessels, sailed by over 8,000 seamen. Naples also bought two large warships from the knights of Malta, and a large frigate from the East India Company. Of the larger vessels, he sent five in 1783 to bombard Algiers, along with some smaller vessels. To staff this creation, he called upon his Tuscan connections to provide naval officers, and created a naval academy to attract young aristocrats. The best cadets went to train

---

[76] On Acton and his projects, see the work by Harold Acton, *The Bourbons of Naples (1734–1825)* (London: 1956), p. 222ff. See also Anna Maria Rao, "Esercito e società a Napoli nelle riforme del secondo settecento", *Studi Storici*, 1987, pp. 623–77.

aboard foreign naval vessels, and most of them served on French and British warships.[77]

In 1793 Naples joined the anti-French coalition. The forceful queen, Maria Carolina, sister to Marie Antoinette, was viscerally hostile to the events unfolding in France, which were starting to have echoes in the capital. The Neapolitan army joined the British and Spanish at Toulon in 1793, but this resulted in defeat. In 1795, four cavalry regiments joined the Austrians in Lombardy against the French revolutionary army. The queen, pressed by Austria and England, decided to resume hostilities against France in 1798, to the almost universal disapproval of her war minister and the senior officers. When the French revolutionary army invaded the kingdom, the army of Naples, although numerically superior, dissolved on contact. Most of its 50,000 men were green recruits, wretchedly officered and incompetently led by the Austrian general, Mack.[78] They were capable only of skirmishing, and after a few days of fighting, Naples was occupied.

Bonaparte and the new Italian army

In 1800, Napoleon established the republican regime in northern Italy upon the bayonets of his troops. Élites there had long since abandoned military careers, which had become the object of scorn. National Guards set up to legitimize the regime numbered only 9,000 Italians, extremely undisciplined and unwarlike, under a plethora of 'political' officers, frequently Italian Jacobins in the baggage train of the French army. President Melzi d'Eril in Milan set out to create a new 'Italian' army, but it got off to a slow start, with only 4,000 volunteers in 1802, although a law provided for a military reserve of 60,000 men. The inability of Italians to wage war was a commonplace, even among administrators, who blamed the long peace for having extinguished the military spirit. Plans for conscription, and especially of requisitioning (the old 'contribution' under a new name) were extremely unpopular. Of the first 18,000 men drafted, only 3,000 complied. Napoleon was fully conscious of the difficulties of creating an army in a country where military traditions had disappeared, and was less concerned about the number of recruits as of the quality of the junior officers and sergeants.[79]

Bonapartist mythology credits him with 'democratizing' the officer corps. That may be overstated. He too decided to create two élite corps whose members would be drawn from the upper classes, as a way of rallying nobles around his regime. Their numbers were slow to increase, but they did perform enthusiastically on the battlefield.[80] The army finally attained its recruiting goals between 1810 and 1812, reaching a good technical and disciplinary level, comparable to

[77] C. Randaccio, *Storia delle marine militari italiane, dal 1750 al 1860*, vol. 1, p. 73ff.
[78] Acton, *The Bourbons of Naples (1734–1825)*, p. 238ff.
[79] F. della Peruta, *Esercito e società nell' Italia napoleonica* (Milan: 1988); p. 45 and p. 135.
[80] *Ibid.*, p. 143.

French units of the Napoleonic army. Between 1800 and 1814, the kingdom of Italy with its six million inhabitants supplied about 200,000 soldiers, of whom over half died abroad. Losses were heaviest in Russia, and in Spain where Bonaparte employed them extensively. They provided important contingents in Napoleon's last campaigns in Germany in 1813. Since then, the formation of this Italian army has been held to be decisive for the formation of an Italian national conscience, and the creation of a modern state.

The restoration, however, just confirmed the Austrian hegemony that Vienna had consistently claimed since 1690. Throughout the eighteenth century, the Viennese Habsburgs extended their permanent control over key territories in the peninsula, from Lombardy and Mantua in 1707, to Tuscany in 1737, Modena in 1767 and arguably even Naples under Queen Maria Carolina. Austrian pretensions over the Papal fortress of Ferrara, and then over the Venetian Terraferma and Dalmatia, resulted in unchallenged control by the age of Metternich. Austrian control was unencumbered by alliances with Italian princes, and was not dependent upon the service, the wealth or the idealism of the peninsula's élites.

Chapter 9
The military imagination

Applied Ariosto

Military values, whether virtues or vices, do not exist in a cultural vacuum. Since society recognized war as the social purpose of the nobility and the resort of kings, war had been idealized in story, song and image. Even in the centuries before realist canons in art became the norm, the image of war was a vehicle for concrete ideas about politics, society and social relations that enshrined the superiority of the old nobility. Not all was imaginary, far from it. Princes expected their military servants to accomplish bold deeds at the risk of their lives, and to display a disregard for their persons which they would recompense appropriately.[1] Princes sometimes held military accomplishments to be the prerequisite for the attribution of political or ceremonial functions at the court, a practice explicitly followed by Charles Emanuel I in Turin.[2] The desired impression was to adorn the sovereign with a garland of fearless, distinguished and selfless servants of high birth whose sense of adventure was second only to their fidelity. The most elaborate literary expression of this world was the chivalry romance, an extraordinarily popular art form enjoying an unbroken vogue from the fifteenth until the early decades of the seventeenth century. Earlier romances blended historical figures and fictitious knights from Antiquity and the Middle Ages. The High Renaissance reworked prose romances into rhyme, for easier recitation and greater elegance, and elaborated stories inside stories. The reading and listening audience of these works was quite wide, for both sexes. Counter-Reformation preachers deemed most of this escapist and exotic literature inoffensive. The most celebrated single voice was Ludovico Ariosto, a poet at the Este court of Ferrara in the 1520s, whose *Orlando*

---

[1] J. B. Wood, "The royal army during the early wars of religion", in *Society and institutions in early modern France*, Mack Holt (ed.) (Athens, Georgia: 1991); pp. 6–33. Filippo Strozzi's army before La Rochelle in 1573 reportedly lost 266 officers killed and wounded, which constituted a casualty level for them of about 50 per cent. Other authors note high rates of mortality of officers in the Imperial army at White Mountain (1620) and Alte Veste (1632). See G. Mann, *Wallenstein: his life narrated* (New York: 1976), p. 590.

[2] Merlin, *Tra guerre e tornei*, p. 149.

furioso saw as many as 183 printings in Italy from 1516 to 1600 and spawned countless imitations.[3] It wove intricate adventures of kings, princes, knights and their female counterparts in an enchanted world, roughly articulated around the emperor Charlemagne and his epic war against the Moors. That particular work was the literary 'best-seller' of late-sixteenth century Italy.[4] Emerging from this we also see a revival of the concept of the 'Christian' knight who upheld orthodoxy and good religion, risking martyrdom in the good fight.[5]

This chivalric image held such appeal in western Europe during the Renaissance that the most important rulers of the age referred to it as a maxim of government. Charles V had the greatest claim to the patent, since he descended directly from Charlemagne, and his title and jurisdiction surpassed all of his rivals, especially in Italy. "Medieval Italian imperialism looked towards the North for the return of the Emperor, expecting to see him coming at the head of an army of shining knights to bring back the golden age of peace and justice, a pathetic, but deep-seated illusion. . . ."[6] Charles cultivated and extended to Italy the Burgundian honour of the Golden Fleece, which placed him at the centre of a select group of great nobles who pledged to further the cause of Catholicism and Empire. Bestowing the Golden Fleece on *los potentados* was but one of his rewards. Charles and his successors married them to his Spanish viceroys, and to his illegitimate children, obtained cardinals' hats and dukedoms for their progeny, and appointed them generals to his armies.[7] Frances Yates attributes Charles' success to a desire for order and stability that only a charismatic figure with great resources could satisfy.[8] In Naples (and in Sicily equally), the Spanish viceroys understood the importance of prestige, rank and honourable employment for the nobility. Beginning with Pedro de Toledo in the 1530s, these great lords depended upon the *effetto Corte* to draw the nobility from the countryside, and to integrate those residing in the capital into the ceremonial life of the palace.[9]

Charles' prestige spawned imitations of imperial protocol at all of the regional Italian courts. After the partition of the Habsburg domains in 1555, the naked power of the emperor in Italy was slight. Imperial fief-holders gravitated towards the local princely courts that exerted their own attractions and conferred even

---

[3] Paul Grendler, "Chivalric romances in the Italian Renaissance", *Studies in Medieval and Renaissance History*, 1988, pp. 57–102.

[4] C. Bec, *Les livres des Florentins (1413–1608)* (Florence: 1984), p. 72. See also Grendler, "Chivalric romances in the Italian Renaissance", *Studies in Medieval and Renaissance History*, 1988, p. 80.

[5] A. Prosperi, "Il 'miles christianus' nella cultura italiana tra '400 e '500", *Critica Storica*, 1989, pp. 685–704.

[6] F. Yates, *Astraea: the imperial theme in the sixteenth century* (London: 1975); p. 5.

[7] M. Rivero Rodriguez, "Felipe II y los 'Potentados de Italia'", *La dimensione europea dei Farnese; Bulletin de l'Institut historique belge de Rome*, **63**, 1993, pp. 337–70.

[8] Yates, *Astraea*, pp. 22–5.

[9] Musi, *La rivolta di Masaniello nella scena politica barocca*, pp. 70–71.

greater rewards. Genoa forced the fief-holders along the Riviera to confide their castles to the republic, and to build residences in the capital. In Tuscany, feudatories pledged 'friendship' to the grand duke, before accepting honours and charges that transformed them into courtiers residing in Florence.[10] Similarly the Orsini, Colonna and Sforza of Santa Fiora deserted their castles for palaces and offices in Papal Rome.[11]

Most of the early courts, like those of Emanuel Philibert of Piedmont in Turin and Pier Luigi Farnese at Parma and Piacenza, retained a military climate, and a simplicity (or brutality) of manners.[12] The generation after Lepanto displayed more interest in culture and display. There was no dichotomy between soldiers and art patrons in late sixteenth-century Italy, just as flamboyant costume and decoration was not held to detract from martial spirit.[13] The most eager warriors were simultaneously the princes most concerned with the urbanity of their entourage. The dukes Alfonso II d'Este in Ferrara, Charles Emanuel I in Turin, Francesco Maria della Rovere in Urbino, Vincenzo I in Mantua, Ferdinando I in Florence, and in later times Francesco I d'Este in Modena were as avid to leave artistic monuments to their glory as they were to cultivate warrior virtues. They basked in the glow reflected by the real or mythical warriors they kept at their courts. At the court of Modena in 1629, of the 130 members of the household receiving a stipend, there were eighteen *cavalieri*.[14] These were the individuals who followed princes on campaign, like Vincenzo of Mantua, Odoardo of Parma, Mattias of Tuscany or Francesco of Modena, not to mention the followers of the Piedmontese dukes.

Members of various companies of gens d'armes or *corazze* that added martial pageantry to ceremonies under the pretext of protecting the prince were more doubtful warriors. They slipped into personages drawn from the pages of romances, and adopted emblems and mottos. Emblems, mottoes and devices were launched in Italy with the French occupation of Milan in 1499. French captains adorned themselves with such elegant insignia on their breast and back, that Italian captains soon sported them on their clothes and banners too. The device was nothing more than a symbolical representation of a purpose, a wish, or a line of conduct, expressed by means of a motto and a picture that reciprocally ex-

---

[10] Pugliese, *Le prime strette dell' Austria in Italia*, p. 85ff.

[11] Jean Delumeau, *Vie economique et sociale de Rome dans la seconde moitié du XVIe siècle*, 2 vols (Rome: 1957–9), vol. 1, p. 434.

[12] For Piedmont, see Pierpaolo Merlin, *Tra guerre e tornei*, p. 1; and Cristina Stango, "La corte di Emanuele Filiberto: organizzazione e gruppi sociali", *Bolletino Storico-Bibliografico Subalpino*, 1987, pp. 445–502. For Parma and Piacenza, Marzio Achille Romani, "Finanza pubblica e potere politico: il caso dei Farnese (1545–1593)", in *Le corti farnesiane di Parma e Piacenza (1545–1622)*, 2 vols, Marzio Achille Romani (ed.) (Rome: 1978), pp. 3–85, at p. 27.

[13] Anderson, *Army and society in Europe of the old regime*, p. 58.

[14] Southorn, *Power and display in the seventeenth century*, p. 58.

plained each other. Early themes were largely military or chivalric in inspiration, although the humanists gradually developed others during the sixteenth century. Their vogue became fixed after 1531 when Alciati published a catalogue of such signs. The work knew more than 150 editions, mostly in the first half of the seventeenth century.[15]

Princes enhanced the pageantry of their entourages by creating companies of gens d'armes in the second half of the sixteenth century. Duke Alfonso II of Ferrara may have set the precedent with his 60 *gentiluomini d'onore*, augmented by a ceremonial guard of 100 halberdiers and 100 horse guards.[16] In Mantua, Mozzarelli notes how a significant segment of the urban élite affected a noble lifestyle and pledged itself to serve the Gonzaga princes. The stern and miserly Duke Guglielmo conceded privileges to them, particularly in the realm of representation, and the right to carry weapons. He placed the Mantuan company of gens d'armes, fixed at 75 nobles, on the payroll in 1580.[17] The profligate Duke Vincenzo then multiplied privileges and distinctions like titles. In Mantua they staged a magnificent cavalcade on the occasion of Duke Vincenzo's coronation in 1587. These noble guards wore scarves embroidered with mottos on themes of love, with jewelled chains, hats with plumes, shirts with lace and pistols adorned with gems. Italian and German bodyguards, true soldiers attached to the duke, were luxuriously fitted out too.[18] The Gonzaga Order of the Redeemer, a crusading order of only 15 knights founded in 1608 without galleys or ports, fulfilled the same pageant function. Similarly, in the Farnese duchy the *corazze* consisted of two companies of nobles, one in each capital, who escorted the duke on special occasions. Fathers transmitted the office by inheritance to their sons, and in the eighteenth century its members still sported the archaic armour of over a century previously.[19]

The Medici were not far behind. Their first company of gens d'armes was a *bona fide* military unit reserved for gentlemen, formed in 1562 by Cosimo I. He assigned about 400 of them to the chief cities of the state, in Pisa, Pistoia, Arezzo and Siena, and drew upon the local nobility for membership. Part of the year the members served at the court in Florence.[20] Before long, the military attributes of

---

[15] On these devices generally, see Mario Praz, *Studies in seventeenth-century imagery* (Rome: 1964), 2nd edn, p. 55ff.

[16] Quazza, *Storia politica d'Italia: preponderanza spagnola, 1559–1700*, p. 114. See by the same author the article on Duke Alfonso II d'Este in the *Dizionario biografico degli Italiani*, vol. 2, pp. 337–41.

[17] Mozzarelli, *Mantova e i Gonzaga dal 1382 al 1707*, p. 75ff, p. 98, p. 104.

[18] M. Bellonci, *A prince of Mantua: the life and times of Vincenzo Gonzaga* (New York: 1956), p. 114.

[19] Zannoni & Fiorentino, *L'esercito farnesiano dal 1694 al 1731*, (Parma: 1981), p. 101.

[20] Angiolini, "Politica, società e organizzazione militare nel principato mediceo", *Società e Storia*, 1986, pp. 1–52, at p. 23.

the group vanished. In the late sixteenth century, Grand Duke Ferdinand I reformed it again, retaining only 100 gentlemen from Florence and Siena each, all from the noblest houses.[21] Other noble gens d'armes served in the militia cavalry, by special privilege of the grand duke after 1632. This way the prince ingratiated himself with the principal houses of the state, and provided a sinecure and a theatre for members of a potentially turbulent group.[22]

Such companies were also part of the court life of Spanish dominions. Garcia of Toledo sponsored an Academy of Knights in Palermo incorporating *cient nobles en los quales se incluye casi todo el Reyno*. None could be commanded in war by any other person but the king.[23] But the military reference was entirely symbolic. In Naples, this guard, called *I Continui*, similarly comprised 100 noblemen, one half Spanish and the other Italian, for the viceroy's personal service and escort.[24] In Messina, the aristocracy expressed itself in the creation of the Order of the Star, a company of 100 knights. Each was to practise equestrian arts and the handling of weapons, and have four squires apiece ready to serve in war. This too was a ceremonial organization, recruited among the city's most aristocratic families. Only they could ride horses before the senators in civic festivals.[25] After the mid-seventeenth century, however, court protocol preferred the bewigged civilian courtiers with no military references at all, on the model of Paris.

Aristocrats who crowded around the thrones of Italy in the manner of feudal knights also valued titles and fiefs more than ever before, and pressed their respective lords to create new jurisdictions. The prince obliged them, having several good reasons to do so. First, the new fiefs – or the redistribution of old ones when the line extinguished – added money to the treasury. Emanuel Philibert, who created new titles in Piedmont, saw them as a means of disciplining and controlling his nobility. Charles Emanuel used them consistently after 1600 in order to domesticate the nobility at his court and tie them to his person.[26] Even in the more peaceful Tuscany, the grand duke required new fief-holders created after 1590 to serve at court for a month out of every year. By the mid-seventeenth century, the defeated urban patriciates of Florence and Siena were effectively

[21] G. Hanlon, "Celebrating war in a peaceful city: festive representations of war in Medicean Siena", in *Self and Society in Renaissance Italy*, W. Connell (ed.) (Berkeley, forthcoming, 1998).
[22] Arnaldo d'Addario, "I 'capitoli della militia' e la formazione di un ceto di privilegiati alla periferia del principato mediceo fra XVI e XVII secolo", in *Studi in onore di Leopoldo Sandri* (Rome: 1983), vol. 2, pp. 347–80, esp. pp. 376–8.
[23] F. Benigno, "Aristocrazia e stato in Sicilia nell' epoca di Filippo III", in *Signori, patrizi, cavalieri in Italia centro-meridionale nell' età moderna*, M. A. Visceglia (ed.) (Bari: 1992), pp. 76–93, at p. 81.
[24] A. von Reumont, *The Carafas of Maddaloni: Naples under Spanish dominion* (London: 1854), p. 46.
[25] E. Laloy, *La révolte de Messine*, vol. 1, p. 51.
[26] Merlin, *Tra guerre e tornei*, p. 131.

transformed into docile courtiers, though at some cost to the jurisdictional integrity of the state.[27] Sovereigns often justified fief-granting with economic arguments, expecting the grantee to colonize his jurisdiction, and develop its industry and commerce in his own self-interest, particularly in isolated zones that yielded little revenue to the state, and which required more intensive policing.[28] The kings of Spain gave the example. In Lombardy they conferred the titles of count and marchese without diminishing the strength of royal jurisdiction. Acquiring a noble title was an important step for a family's ascent into the Milanese patriciate, and the crown could exact a stiff fee for the honour.[29] In the Mezzogiorno, on the other hand, Galasso and Villari argue that Spain's need for cash to finance its wars led to the extension and reinforcement of feudal jurisdictions at the crown's expense. This would lead to the clientelism that plagues the region to this day.[30] With the inflation of honours, and the proliferation of titles, Italian nobles competed to enhance the trappings of their status. One manifestation among the highest aristocracy was the fictitious genealogy, with its basis in a mythical ancestor.[31] Interest in heraldry exploded in the sixteenth century, at first without any regulation. The state only gradually imposed ordered hierarchies in which families displayed on their blazons their subordination to the Church, the prince, and the emperor.[32]

All these traits stem from the urbanization of the aristocracy, and the intense rivalry and competition among noble houses for prestige, consideration and employment. Conspicuous consumption was one weapon in the struggle for pre-eminence. The early seventeenth century in Sicily saw a rise of street festivities, of splendid cavalcades, fireworks and bull-baiting among aristocrats. Nobles celebrated their virtues with tournaments, jousts, carousels, fencing schools and parades of knights, all in an urban setting. These made a great impression on

---

[27] I. Polverini Fosi, "Un programma di politica economica: le infeudazioni nel senese durante il principato mediceo", *Critica Storica*, 1976, pp. 660–72, at pp. 666–8. This question is developed also by Claudio Donati in his *L'idea di nobiltà in Italia* (Rome: 1988), p. 215.

[28] Luigi Amorth discusses the creation of new ducal fiefs, in the Apennine hinterland of Modena, in *Modena capitale*, p. 108ff.

[29] G. Vismara, "Il patriziato milanese del cinque-seicento", in *Potere e società negli stati regionali italiani fra '500 e '600*, E. Fasano-Guarini (ed.) (Bologna: 1978), pp. 153–72, at p. 169.

[30] G. Galasso, "La feudalità napoletana nel secolo XVI", in *Potere e società negli stati regionali italiani fra '500 e '600*, E. Fasano-Guarini (ed.) (Bologna: 1978), pp. 241–57, at p. 254; see also R. Villari, *La rivolta antispagnuola a Napoli: le origini, 1585–1647*, pp. 235–9.

[31] Donati, *L'idea di nobiltà in Italia*, p. 219.

[32] R. Goldthwaite, *Wealth and the demand for art in Italy, 1300–1600* (Baltimore: 1993), p. 167. The author's assertion that nobles did not emphasize their servitude to princes in their heraldry no longer seems true in the seventeenth and eighteenth centuries, judging from the profusion of such symbols as imperial eagles, helmets and cardinal's hats placed on top of them.

contemporaries.[33] Benigno calls this a new aristocratic 'urbanity' that was part of the attraction of a capital city where the viceroy held court. Parading itself around the palace courtyard or the city streets, the nobility displayed its cultural aspirations: "select and renowned everywhere, liberal and magnanimous, affable and physically attractive, enemy of merchant greed, expert in military art and in fighting, music-loving and prompt to cultivate letters". This model of the perfect noble, published in Naples in 1580, enjoyed an extraordinary literary fortune and echo.[34]

Print and paint also amplified the military reputation of the house by evoking its history. Scribes combed the archives of their cities for documents highlighting the deeds of the ancestors of contemporary patricians, often subsidized by the latter. Such histories resolutely focused on nobles in the past, and were complemented by *compendia* of the deeds of noble families arranged alphabetically by house, or by field of achievement.[35] Soldiers and their relatives lost no opportunities to proclaim their military successes by decorating their *palazzo* interiors with frescos or paintings of battles in which they distinguished themselves, and battle painting was a widespread *genre* in the seventeenth century.[36] Mattias de'Medici desired to make it clear in his *palazzo* that visitors were in the house of a soldier. Raimondo Montecùccoli and his ancestors also commissioned paintings of the battle of St Gotthard, and the capture of Kanizsa to hang in their houses in Bologna, in Modena and in the castle of Montecùccoli, the feudal seat.[37] More prosaically, they embellished their *palazzi* with portraits of ancestors in armour and panoply, along with seascapes and scenes of Malta or Livorno. Another form of street theatre exalting the house's military virtues was the funeral. Funeral cortèges of most nobles were elaborate parades. Families expended considerable treasure to celebrate a soldier's passing, such as the burial of the Sienese Carlo Piccolòmini in 1627, complete with all the trappings of warfare.[38] Chapels not

---

[33] F. Benigno, "Aristocrazia e stato in Sicilia", in *Signori, patrizi, cavalieri*, p. 78 and p. 88. See also Silvia Carandini on outdoor festivities featuring nobles, *Teatro e spettacolo nel seicento* (Bari: 1990), p. 16ff.

[34] G. Muto, "'I segni d'onore'; rappresentazioni delle dinamiche nobiliari a Napoli in età moderna", in *Signori, patrizi, cavalieri*, pp. 171–92, at p. 179.

[35] In Siena there were at least four of these *compendia* before 1700. See G. Hanlon, "The demilitarization of a provincial Italian aristocracy", *Past and Present*, **155**, 1997, pp. 64–108.

[36] See the example of Prince Mattias de'Medici in the article by Stella Rudolph, "A Medici general, Prince Mattias, and his battle-painter, il Borgognone", *Studi Secenteschi*, 1972, pp. 183–91.

[37] Sandonnini, *Il generale Raimondo Montecùccoli e la sua famiglia*, p. 77.

[38] Valori, *Condottieri e generali del seicento*, p. 288, Carlo Piccolomini. Enea Silvio Piccolomini's passing in Serbia was also commemorated in pomp in 1689; see Hanlon, "Celebrating war in a peaceful city", in *Self and Society in Renaissance Italy*, W. Connell (ed.) (Berkeley, forthcoming, 1998). For the Genoese and Venetians, see also the Valori citation on Ambrogio Doria, p. 129; and A. Cowan, *The urban patriciate; Lübeck and Venice, 1580–1700* (Cologne: 1986), p. 103, for Venetian practice of bringing back war dead.

infrequently displayed military trophies publicizing the great events in which members of the family participated. They all held significance for the family's history, proclaimed its pretensions and gained ground in the competition for honour.[39]

The spirit of competition also underlay the intense display of urban spectacles, in which the aristocracy promoted and participated in the various forms of street theatre. The participants often articulated this around military themes, whether or not they possessed such credentials themselves. In Modena such spectacles, which included jousts, mock battles and knightly cavalcades, immediately followed the transfer of the Este dukes to the city from Ferrara in 1598.[40] One military spectacle was the Modenese army filing through the gates of the city, setting out on campaign against Lucca in 1613. Gleaming armour and multicoloured pennants and feathers were intended to show that the Modenese meant business.[41] The dukes of Modena retained the joust in their panoply of dynastic festivals, in its most archaic forms, perhaps longest of any Italian dynasty. One of the last references to actual tilting of knights I find, took place in Modena in 1652, where the warlike Francesco I personally led a team into the lists. Raimondo Montecùccoli accidentally killed a relative there with his lance.[42]

The joust was only one form in the repertoire of battle-theatre. Another, more elaborate spectacle, the *naumachia* flooded the *cortile* in five feet (1.5 m) of water and recreated battles against Turkish galleys.[43] Common too, was the assault of a mock-fortress in a city square or, in one very elaborate Neapolitan case in 1672, on an island. Organizers amplified these with elaborate fireworks displays enhancing the pathos and the dramatic atmosphere.[44] It would not be too far-fetched to

---

[39] One example of the abundance of military mementoes in a peaceful cleric's possession is contained in the post-mortem inventory of the *abate* Galgano Bichi, whose palace was so ornamented because of the eight knights of Malta the family had produced in the preceding century: Archivi di Stato di Siena; Notarili Post-Cosimiano Originali 1430, Filippo Donati a Siena, 12 August 1727 to 9 November 1728. That inventory has been transcribed and astutely analyzed in an honours thesis by Kate Wilson, for Dalhousie University, Canada, 1994.

[40] Amorth, *Modena capitale*, p. 17.

[41] *Ibid.*, p. 40ff.

[42] Sandonnini, *Il generale Raimondo Montecùccoli e la sua famiglia*, p. 63. Amorth also cites a great tournament in Modena on the occasion of the duke's marriage with Lucrezia Barberini in 1654, with an aside that such events took place even outside great dynastic events. See his *Modena capitale*, p. 108.

[43] Roy Strong, *Art and power: Renaissance festivals, 1450–1650* (Woodbridge, Suffolk: 1984), p. 127ff.

[44] For examples of such festivals, often commemorating actions against the Turks, see the article by Elvira Garbero & Susanna Cantore, "Le entrate trionfali", in *Teatro a Reggio Emilia*, S. Romagnoli & E. Garbero (eds) (Florence: 1980), pp. 20–52, at p. 20, for Reggio Emilia; for the Neapolitan case, see Hanlon, "Celebrating war in a peaceful city", in *Self and Society in Renaissance Italy*, W. Connell (ed.) (Berkeley, forthcoming, 1998).

emphasize the martial evocation of the galley, or an entire squadron, when it delivered illustrious passengers to their destinations, as outdoor theatre. Booming cannon and soldiers' volleys announced the disembarkation of an ambassador, a royal spouse, or even a prince of the Church into a joyous city.

The sixteenth century mixed both medieval and ancient classical references in its glorification of military virtue. The Renaissance exalted heroes, in antique armour, ornamented swords and breastplates with cameos, mounted on majestic horses, adorned with plumes, among thickets of spears and clusters of banners.[45] One may doubt the relation of these representations to war, apart from a merely evocative one. They paled in comparison with the combat sports practised in fifteenth-century Burgundy.[46] In Italy, such jousts seem to have been commonplace in towns where nobles presided, until the middle of the seventeenth century. Aristocrats who sponsored these events preferred tilting in turn at a fixed object, rather than simulating combat. Huizinga considered these an elaborate and expensive form of play that celebrated the martial skills of a warrior class. As play, any utilitarian motive recedes to the background.[47] A popular 'psychological' interpretation of play-fighting makes it the ritualization and neutralization of violent aggressive impulses in both individuals and groups.[48] It is not difficult to find examples of such events in centres that were not active seats of princely rule. In Siena, Reggio Emilia and Bologna, such recurrent festivities celebrated a noble marriage, or the visit of a foreign dignitary.[49] The organizing committee, often composed of academicians, orchestrated the challenge around some amorous argument in flowery and ponderous prose or verse. The aim of the participant was to splinter as many hollow lances as possible, and score additional points for good strokes, before a gallery of lords and ladies. It was pure theatre, and contrary to Strong, I do not think it had much relevance – even as a dramatization – to real wartime prowess.[50] Anglo calls it a kind of anachronistic posturing, the purpose of

---

[45] M. Praz, *Studies in seventeenth-century imagery* (London: 1939), p. 172.

[46] R. Goldthwaite, *Wealth and the demand for art in Italy, 1300–1600*, pp. 157–64. The point is raised by Alan Young too, who notes the taming of these spectacles in England after the fourteenth century, into elaborate pantomimes. See A. Young, *Tudor and Jacobean tournaments* (London: 1987), p. 22ff.

[47] J. Huizinga, *Homo ludens: a study of the play-element in culture* (Boston: 1955, first publ. 1944), p. 89ff.

[48] F. Cardini, "Il torneo nelle feste cerimoniali di corte", *Quaderni di Teatro*, 1984, pp. 9–19.

[49] For Siena, see Hanlon, "Celebrating war in a peaceful city", in *Self and Society in Renaissance Italy*, W. Connell (ed.) (Berkeley, forthcoming, 1998); and Alberto Fiorini, *Metamorfosi di una festa: dalle "pugna" al "palio alla tonda" (1581–1720)*, (Siena: 1986). For Reggio Emilia, see Garbero & Cantore, "Le entrate trionfali", *Teatro a Reggio Emilia*, p. 52; for Bologna, see Lenzi, "Teatri e anfiteatri a Bologna nei secoli XVI e XVII", in *Barocco romano e barocco italiano: il teatro, l'effimero, l'allegoria*, M. Fagiolo & M. L. Madonna (eds) (Rome: 1985), pp. 174–91.

[50] Roy Strong, *Art and power: Renaissance festivals, 1450–1650* (Woodbridge, Suffolk: 1984),

which was to make a fine display, with no desire to risk injury. The event was then relayed by pamphlets and paintings. As a spectacle, this kind of joust had extraordinary longevity, lasting most of the seventeenth century, if not beyond, in most of the 'noble' cities of the peninsula.[51]

These were also occasions for aristocrats to celebrate the prince's glory, and display their skills in his presence.[52] Alfonso II d'Este in Ferrara may have devised the prototype in 1561. His tournament followed a literary libretto, with an appeal to champions, an exchange of printed challenges, and a 'combat' in which knights pretended to fight. Every gesture formed part of a carefully scripted fantasy inspired by chivalry romances.[53] Fulvio Pacciani, secretary and counsellor to dukes Alfonso and Cesare d'Este theorized about the necessity for the prince to sponsor such festivities, arguing that it allowed him and his subjects to get to know one another. From this socializing came a kind of political familiarity that built a consensus among subjects, and between the subjects and the prince. Most often, such tournaments unfolded along a preset theme in episodes, acted out by participants.[54] The presence of this opulent nobility at court was not wasted on spectacles they organized themselves for their own renown. Organizers increasingly managed the spectacle to ensure that the ruler was always the victor. This was easy to arrange because the fighting was phased out after the 1550s. In Florence, the Medici exalted the tournament to the norm of festival art (see Strong) to justify the new order of things; a mixture of classical mythology, *Orlando furioso* and Florentine history, all celebrating the dynasty. The Medici themselves were slow to design a permanent court theatre, but they did build lists in the courtyard of their residence, the Palazzo Pitti, and held events following a loose plot into which contending knights could weave their own allegorical story-line. The knights were occasionally led by the grand duke in person.

The most consistently committed sponsor of such festivals to promote the dynasty and its policies was Charles Emanuel I of Piedmont, as Roy Strong and Pierpaolo Merlin have demonstrated. These pageants were part of his policy to rival both Madrid and Paris in magnificence, and to show off the loyalty of his nobles. After 1600, the use of such spectacles to justify the policies of the House of Savoy became systematic, and the duke himself was the author of many of the

---

p. 12. See also Hanlon, "Celebrating war in a peaceful city", *in Self and Society in Renaissance Italy*, W. Connell (ed.) (Berkeley, forthcoming, 1998).

[51] For Sidney Anglo's comments, see the "Introduction", in *Chivalry in the Renaissance* (Woodbridge, Suffolk: 1990), p. xii. See for Ferrara, J. Southorn, *Power and display in the seventeenth century*, pp. 130ff.

[52] Strong, *Art and power*, p. 12. Alan Young applies this model to England in *Tudor and Jacobean tournaments*, pp. 22–5.

[53] Lenzi, "Teatri e anfiteatri a Bologna", *Barocco romano e barocco italiano*, p. 178.

[54] See the article by Riccardo Pacciani, "Temi e strutture narrative dei festeggiamenti nuziali estensi a Modena nel seicento", in *Barocco romano e barocco italiano*, M. Fagiolo & M. L. Madonna (eds) (Rome: 1985), pp. 204–16.

programmes.[55] Charles Emanuel and his leading courtiers were the principal participants, in a show usually reserved for a palace audience.

After mid-century, non-military festivities gradually came to the fore. Sidney Anglo describes this as the process of transmutation from the knight to the courtier, with tournaments evolving into court masques and horse ballets.[56] Costume was more important than swordplay long before 1600, with the tournament itself more a theatre for fashion than for bravura, and this is reflected in the literature narrating the events. Armour was too ornate for combat, and armourers sometimes constructed shields with hidden mechanisms causing them to fly apart on impact, for the entertainment of the spectators. When chariots and floats multiplied, the great cavalcade became the primary focus.[57] Music and dance were integrated into the action too. The joust celebrated in Bologna in 1639 was almost entirely sung, with continual scenery changes, and culminated in formations of knights on foot and on horseback manoeuvring before the audience.[58] Such spectacles became carousels and horse ballets performed in the prince's presence. Their lavishness increasingly led to their takeover by the court, which emphasized classical decorum and parade-ground order, removing them from the streets and squares, and shifting the events to permanent structures.[59] The joust and the cavalcade or carousel were transformed into pageants and opera, with a drift towards amorous themes. Horse ballet veered towards the masque and the court ballet. Knights descended from their horses and gave themselves to dance. Guided by their dancing masters, they recast their gestures to be more restrained and graceful. Even fencing put the emphasis on posture, and sensitivity to the gestures and movements of others.

The place of such spectacle was no longer the courtyard of the palace, or the lists in the city streets or at the gates, but in a theatre. The first ones were flimsy but lavish structures constructed anew for each occasion. Italy's first permanent court theatre was conceived by Duke Ranuccio Farnese at Parma, and not officially opened until 1628.[60] Across northern Italy, wealthy nobles built their own. In Ferrara, *cavaliere* Enzo Bentivoglio was one of the first to build one, after 1620. Baroque theatres contained an array of machines for special effects that

---

[55] Merlin, *Tra guerre e tornei*, p. 165–76.

[56] Anglo, "Introduction", in *Chivalry in the Renaissance*, p. xiiff.

[57] Richard Barber and Juliet Barker, *Chivalry and pageants in the Middle Ages* (New York: 1983), p. 162. A detailed example of the great cavalcade overshadowing the joust itself, at Palermo in 1680, is related by Giovanni Isgrò, *Feste barocche a Palermo* (Palermo: 1981), p. 111ff.

[58] Lenzi, "Teatri e anfiteatri a Bologna", in *Barocco romano e barocco italiano*, p. 189.

[59] Mark Motley, *Becoming a French aristocrat: the education of the court nobility (1580–1715)* (Princeton, New Jersey: 1990), p. 146. The model is Italian. See Silvia Carandini's overview of all these festivities and their shift towards the permanent theatre, *Teatro e spettacolo nel seicento* (Bari: 1990); in particular, p. 94ff. and p. 174.

[60] Drei, *I Farnese: grandezza e decadenza di una dinastia italiana*, p. 196. See also Southorn, *Power and display in the seventeenth century*, p. 79ff.

enhanced the magical and theatrical atmosphere. Baroque display gradually edged out martial echoes. Ornate coaches, similarly, evinced the horse and the cavalcade in city pageantry. The effect was not the same, for the heavy coaches were boxes filled with nobles of all ages and physique, and of both sexes.[61] The military evocations vanished entirely. The carousel gradually displayed horsemanship more than any other feature, such that the equestrian arts remained an essential part of noble youths' training throughout the eighteenth century. Those festivities still featuring battles tended to fix upon the Turk as the enemy.[62] Finally, in the last decades of the century, even evocative combat gave way to the more abstract depiction of a 'conceit' through a 'machine'. In Reggio Emilia in 1683, organizers erected one such object in the street to celebrate Habsburg victories over the Turks.[63] Another, built in Modena as part of the marriage celebrations of the duke in 1695, eliminated every reference to the world of Ariosto. It was a conceit entitled *Il tempo bruciato*, 'easy to comprehend', constructed of geometrical figures superimposed one over another.[64] The waning of the martial evocation parallels, with some lag, the withdrawal of the Italian aristocracy from active roles in European wars. By the eighteenth century, only vestiges remained.[65]

Other forms of playing at war, enjoyed by nobles and populace alike, endured longer. Popular games in medieval Italy were often ritualized forms of warfare, and the genre called *mazzoscudo* (mace and shield) was widespread in Tuscany and Umbria. They lasted in various forms down to the end of the eighteenth century. The purpose of these games was to exercise young men and to make them fierce and strong, and humanists invoked the examples of Macedonia and Sparta to justify them.[66] They were to the communal militia what the tournament was to the feudal knight, with similar invocations and challenges by the nobility taken from romances. One variant in Pisa, called *ponte*, was 'played' with a clublike shield, and

---

[61] Hanlon, "Celebrating war in a peaceful city", in *Self and Society in Renaissance Italy*, W. Connell (ed.) (Berkeley, forthcoming, 1998).

[62] See the article by Elvira Garbero & Susanna Cantore, "Le entrate trionfali", in *Teatro a Reggio Emilia*, p. 20. See also Hanlon, "Celebrating war in a peaceful city", in *Self and Society in Renaissance Italy*, W. Connell (ed.) (Berkeley, forthcoming, 1998).

[63] Garbero & Cantore, "Le entrate trionfali", in *Teatro a Reggio Emilia*, p. 52.

[64] Pacciani, "Temi e strutture narrative dei festeggiamenti nuziali estensi a Modena nel seicento", in *Barocco romano e barocco italiano*, p. 216.

[65] Claudio Donati, "L'evoluzione della coscienza nobiliare", in *Patriziati e aristocrazie nobiliari: ceti dominanti e organizzazione del potere nell' Italia centro-settentrionale dal XVI al XVIII secolo: Seminario di Trento, 1977*, C. Mozzarelli & P. Schiera (eds) (Trento: 1978), pp. 13–36, at p. 34.

[66] Hanlon, "Celebrating war in a peaceful city", in *Self and Society in Renaissance Italy*, W. Connell (ed.) (Berkeley, forthcoming, 1998); see also Fiorini, *Metamorfosi di una festa*, p. 9. The best treatment of the general subject may still be that of William Heywood, *Palio and Ponte: an account of the sports of central Italy from the age of Dante to the XXth century* (London: 1904).

the team's aim was to seize control of the bridge. In 1574, for example, the mêlée between the two teams, each of several hundred participants, lasted for two hours. Civic authorities gradually reduced it to one hour in 1650, and to 45 minutes in 1686, but there was never any lack of willing participants, nor any sign of detachment from the crowd. The winners lit bonfires, waved banners, beat drums, sounded trumpets and sang their valour, while the losers on the other bank brooded. A few days later followed the Triumph, with a cavalcade of men in military costume leading a great float on a martial theme. Heywood assures us that disturbances during these celebrations were rare.[67] Other festival games involved stone-throwing. Perugia banned the most brutal of these in 1425, but forms of it lingered, as in the 1582 granducal wedding celebration in Florence, where numerous participants were left dead and wounded, and military intervention was required to stop it.

Late sixteenth-century Florence played *calcio,* a kind of soccer, probably little more than a fistfight at first, spoken of as a *battaglia.* The object of the players was to drive the ball with feet or fists to the opposing team's end of the field. Players were exclusively nobles, aged 18 to 45, handsome and vigorous, of gallant bearing and good report. Although the game itself lasted less than an hour, a great pageant and procession of youths decked out in gorgeous costumes preceded it. Florence's company of gens d'armes and other noblemen in a great cavalcade filed before the grand duke. On the field, the participants deployed into squadrons as for battle, and advanced into the enemy zone by assault and battery.[68] In Siena, the corresponding game was the *pugna* or the 'fist'. It was said in 1425, and echoed often later, that the onlookers derived most of the amusement from it. Teams drawn from each of the city's three main districts arrayed in the great square, and the participants bandaged their heads and fists to limit the damage. Occasionally organizers threw a ball into the square as well, but the *pugna* could dispense with it. Sometimes in the excitement, the ritual would break down and a battle royal would develop uncontrolled, with the participation of the lower classes and some onlookers. Municipal organizers gradually limited the duration of this game too, which in the eighteenth century began to seem ill-suited for the celebration of religious holidays. In its place they substituted more sedate pageants, cavalcades, and ultimately the Palio, or horse race around the square.[69] These games gradually lost their powerful sponsors after 1750, and the new Habsburg dynasty was not partial to this kind of festival. In 1807 the queen of Etruria, a Bonaparte, describing the *ponte,* called it too trivial for war and too violent for peace, so abolished it.[70]

---

[67] Heywood, *Palio and Ponte,* pp. 95–134.

[68] *Ibid.,* pp. 164–80.

[69] Hanlon, "Celebrating war in a peaceful city", *in Self and Society in Renaissance Italy,* W. Connell (ed.) (Berkeley, forthcoming, 1998).

[70] Heywood, *Palio and Ponte,* p. 134.

Towards a disciplinary society?

American historian Ellery Schalk has recently sketched the evolution of the self-presentation of the French nobility throughout the sixteenth and seventeenth centuries, and how their ideas drifted away from an emphasis on military virtue, towards ideals of breeding and education that high birth required.[71] Claudio Donati's similar work on ideas surrounding nobility in Italy is less strongly chronological. Both are built wholly on literary evidence, but despite that defect there is a certain plausibility in the argument. The point of departure for such an evolution was probably the spread of institutions promoting knightly skills. These were both an initiation to the martial arts, and a forum for the elaboration of a code of ethics. This code was the *scienza cavalleresca*, elaborated gradually by hundreds of authors refining the ideas of honour and virtue. Its basic premise was that true nobility stemmed from, and carried on, a military tradition, celebrated it through ritual that Donati calls a 'lay liturgy', and confirmed it by resolute defence of one's good reputation. Donati sees it as an urban freezing of aristocratic values of honour and challenge over generations.[72]

One feature of this noble culture that emphasized martial posturing was the personal challenge or the duel. After the mid-sixteenth century, Italy was the scene of an extraordinary flowering of the duelling manual, and of a curious code of honour that nourished it. The *Duello* of Muzio, first published in 1550, underwent twelve editions before 1585, not counting the translations into French and Spanish. Between 1541 and 1563 seventeen published works appeared dedicated specifically to the duel. They were but the beginning of the wave, which probably hit its peak in Italy during the last years of the sixteenth century.[73] Theorists held the duel to be a privilege of nobility, but it was rapidly imitated lower down on the social ladder, for possession of weapons was very widespread. Honour was a precious good that nobles, and soldiers of all kinds in particular, were to hold higher than all else. It took little to provoke someone to draw their sword. If the challenger and his opponent conformed to the rules, the outcome was considered, if not legal, at least legitimate. One finds that such vocabulary, attitudes and gestures were as commonplace among peasant militiamen as they were among nobles. Simultaneously a groundswell of writings condemned this lore and ex-

---

[71] E. Schalk, *From valor to pedigree* (Princeton, New Jersey: 1986). See also Claudio Donati, both his *L'idea di nobiltà in Italia* (Rome: 1988); and "L'evoluzione della conscienza nobiliare", in *Patriziati e aristocrazie nobiliari*, M. A. Visceglia (ed.) (Bari: 1992) pp. 13–36.

[72] Donati, "L'evoluzione della coscienza nobiliare", in *Patriziati e aristocrazie nobiliari*, pp. 25–8. See also by Donati, "Scipione Maffei e la scienza chiamata cavalleresca: saggio sull' ideologia nobiliare al principio del settecento", *Rivista Storica Italiana*, 1978, p. 30ff.

[73] Donati, "L'evoluzione della coscienza nobiliare", in *Patriziati e aristocrazie nobiliari*, p. 19ff.

horted nobles to refuse the challenge, but it is difficult to know what impact they had, lacking close studies of the practice.[74]

The duel regulated and disciplined the more savage vendetta. Such concern for discipline and regulation sprang from the same wellspring as the Protestant and Catholic Reformations, which were also preoccupied with order. While the intensity of religious devotion waned after 1650, the concern for social control redoubled. From the outset, moralists sought to inculcate self-control. After 1600 the principles of Roman stoicism, which enjoyed considerable appeal towards the end of the Reformation, seeped into the military sphere. Humanists had been trying since Macchiavelli to bring modern warfare into line with ancient practice, held to be superior. Neostoic philosophy of action, constancy, self-control and obedience appealed to commanders who needed good order and discipline among the soldiery. Piety, and the defence of honour and dignity, held central places too. These principles could be buttressed both by moral education, such as was imparted in the colleges, and by mechanical drill.[75] The most widely read military theoretician of the century, Raimondo Montecùccoli, was deeply imbued with the neostoic philosophy of Justus Lipsius, the history of Tacitus and the political thought of Machiavelli.[76]

Self-discipline eventually collided with the *scienza cavalleresca*. Ideologically, the first effective refutation of duelling came only in the first years of the eighteenth century, when the Veronese noble Scipione Maffei published a scathing critique of that whole culture. Educated in the noble college of Parma at the apex of its influence in 1690, Maffei looked back on this athletic and physical education as ideal training for young men. What disgusted him was the futility of this duelling knowledge outside the scope of a legitimate army career. The whole ethos of the futile challenge, the taste for provocation, the inclination to strut about armed with sword and dagger, had to disappear from a well-policed and a disciplined republic.[77]

Noble academies, which had a didactic function for young men and were separate from the companies of gens d'armes, spread more genteel models through the upper classes. From the outset they appealed to governments as a way

---

[74] On the nature of the literature devoted to the point of honour, see the book by Frederick Robertson Bryson, *The point of honor in sixteenth-century Italy: an aspect of the life of the gentleman* (New York: 1935).

[75] On the relation between neostoicism and the formation of the modern state, see the book by Gerhard Oestreich, *Neostoicism and the early modern state* (Cambridge: 1982, first publ. 1980). Oestrich provides a thumbnail description of these neo-stoic virtues on p. 83. An example of an early Italian military handbook preaching such ideals is Flaminio della Croce, *Theatro militare del capitano Flaminio della Croce, gentil'huomo milanese* (Antwerp: 1617), p. 72 and p. 272.

[76] T. M. Barker, *The military intellectual and battle: Raimondo Montecuccoli and the Thirty Years' War* (Albany, New York: 1975), p. 68ff.

[77] Donati, "Scipione Maffei e la Scienza Chiamata Cavalleresca", *Rivista Storica Italiana*, 1978, p. 30ff.

of taming riotous youth. Venice had the turbulent patriciate of its subject cities in mind. Deprived of serious political power, or access to military commands in the navy, and forbidden to study outside the republic, these young nobles could profit from the academies as finishing schools. Societies of nobles in the subject cities of the Terraferma combined to do honour to the horse, and to teach young nobles how to ride with noble bearing. The governor of Verona established the first of these in 1565, with 65 members. Padua launched one in 1608, with the support of the republic; another followed immediately after at Udine in Friuli; yet another was established at Treviso in 1610. These colleges all employed a riding master, a weapons instructor, a dancing-master and a mathematician, teaching an assortment of motor and intellectual skills. The physical emphasis was foremost, as the masters strove to impart a grace and suppleness, a corporal *sprezzatura* in their pupils. Each youngster had to maintain a good charger, and possess two sets of armour, one for personal combat, and another for riding in the ring. Horsemanship emphasized the jumping and stylish steps not dissimilar to dance.[78] These academies also taught the science of fortifications and military tactics, dispensed by competent instructors. Even Galileo gave public lectures and private tutoring, in the principles of fortification, at Padua. Academies encouraged the nostalgia for a more swashbuckling life that was part of the romance culture. Hale sees them as playing at being northern nobles.[79] The model then spread from Italy to northern Europe, and particularly France, where the curriculum emphasized the trio of physical exercises: riding, fencing and dancing.[80]

Jesuit colleges for nobles relayed these arts too. An initiative of Saint Charles Borromeo created the first at Milan in 1574, and similar foundations followed in Parma, Ferrara, Modena, Mantua, Florence, Brescia, Bologna, Siena and Turin. These colleges were deliberately exclusive, catering mostly to nobles from out of town. For example, of the hundred or so students in the Sienese Collegio Tolomei, only ten were from local families, while most of the others came from cities like Bologna or Parma. Many Germans studied in Italy as part of their *Kavalierstour*, and they transmitted the forms and content of Italian baroque culture to their homeland.[81] Since the youths were outsiders, lodging in the college, they were subject to strict controls. The colleges dispensed the same humanist education as other colleges gave non-nobles, including Latin, mathematics, law, rhetoric, and proper style and speech, but adapted the curriculum especially to their status. The aspect that set these places apart was the emphasis on 'knightly arts'. Duke

---

[78] On the development of the Italian equestrian arts, see Young, *Tudor and Jacobean tournaments*, p. 67.

[79] J. R. Hale, "Military academies on the Venetian Terraferma in the early seventeenth century", *Studi Veneziani*, 1973, pp. 273–96.

[80] Motley, *Becoming a French aristocrat*, p. 124ff.

[81] Gian Paolo Brizzi, *La formazione della classe dirigente nel sei-settecento: i seminaria nobilium nell' Italia centro-settentrionale* (Bologna: 1976), p. 30ff.

Ranuccio Farnese formed his pages in the college he founded at Parma in 1601, alongside about three hundred other youngsters, mostly from elsewhere in Italy. The duke imposed this courtly curriculum on the Jesuits, who were reluctant to teach dancing and martial arts, which they declared at first to be contrary to good morals.[82] On the duke's insistence, the good fathers oversaw student instruction in the use of the broadsword, the sword, the dagger, the sabre, the halberd, the training pike, the military pike, the banner, movement in formation, musketry and horsemanship. The horse was the attribute of the gentleman as the pen was that of the magistrate. This training for war they directed against a generic enemy, implied to be the Turks. College theatre reinforced this by dramatizing European victories against them, especially in the late seventeenth and early eighteenth centuries. These colleges were the primary training ground and school of discipline for officers, especially at the end of the seventeenth century when enrolments were at their peak. They compensated for the lack of military academies *per se*.[83]

Most youths entered the college at about the age of 12, and remained for six years on average.[84] Here the noble cadets found the intellectual baggage they would need to make their way in the world, and the social connections that would open positions in the Church, the army and the administration. All gentlemen were held to be conversant in the basic knightly arts: fencing, equestrian arts and dancing. Yet the colleges offered many more skills: these included geography, fortification, French, and practice on a number of musical instruments. In Bologna, the range of these lessons reached 58 specific courses in the eighteenth century, including protocol, personal carriage and bearing. The students who took lessons of fortification (until about 1750) and geography underwent a very broad instruction of military and civilian architecture, perspective, arithmetic, mathematics, algebra and geometry. An academy opening with ducal patronage in Turin in 1678, specified that the noble youths were to *acquérir la politesse, et se produire dans le monde . . . par des tournois, les Ballets, les Carrouzels, et quantité d'autres Festes galantes*, to learn how to *monter à cheval, à courre la Bague, les Testes, et le Facquin, à danser, à faire des Armes, à voltiger, le maniment des Armes, les Evolutions militaires . . . et les Mathematiques et le Dessin.*[85]

Military education was only tardily confided to proper military colleges, geared

---

[82] The book by Brizzi examines a number of these colleges over the seventeenth and eighteenth centuries. See *La formazione della classe dirigente nel sei-settecento*. On the Parman college and the conflict between the prince and the Jesuits, see Giovanni Drei, *I Farnese*, p. 196ff.

[83] Brizzi, *La formazione della classe dirigente*, p. 167. Brizzi estimates the proportion of students at Bologna who later followed army careers at 12 per cent.

[84] *Ibid.*, p. 13.

[85] W. Barberis, *Le armi del principe*, p. 177.

to giving professional and technical skills to future officers in the standing army. The model was French, and the Bourbon king, Charles, established the first Italian institution (for the navy) in Naples almost immediately after his conquest of the kingdom in 1734. An artillery school followed in 1744, and an engineering academy ten years later. These were bare-bones operations, amalgamated into the *Reale Accademia Militare* in 1769. Along with ballistics and tactics, they taught experimental physics and chemistry to graduating classes of young officers. In order for all cadets to attend classes in Naples, garrison units rotated through the capital every four years. Despite its technical thrust, the intended audience was the aristocracy of birth, and adolescent sons of army officers, to inculcate good intellectual and political habits into them.[86] Comparable institutions were created in Modena, Livorno and Vicenza in the second half of the eighteenth century.

The technical orientation of the new colleges recognized that warfare had become more scientific, requiring an ability to calculate mathematical forces. Martha Pollak, who is interested in the hugely important subject of the visual culture and aesthetic preferences of engineers, has studied the broader cultural ramifications of this. She sees it expressed in the architectural aesthetic of the new Turin, as it expanded under the guidance of the dukes. Intellectual foundations for this current were drawn from antiquity and given new impetus during the Renaissance. Pollak dates the renewal of interest in the military treatise in Rome to 1534 when Pope Paul III consulted a panel of specialists to advise him on the fortification of Rome.[87] Italian military treatises multiplied, while humanists, courtiers, and soldiers alike collected them. Duke Emanuel Philibert of Savoy was one enthusiast. He spent much time with his military architect Francesco Paciotto, designing fortresses and war engines. When in the seventeenth century, Victor Amadeus I refortified the expanding capital Turin, he laid out the new streets on a grid pattern.

Architects who conceived these buildings and laid them out on uniform lines were usually engineers, themselves products of military culture. Civil architects too, practised as military engineers until the middle of the eighteenth century. Continual exchanges between military and civic design, especially in the aesthetic of regularity, uniformity and austerity, influenced city planning. Advances in surveying, cartography and topographical draftsmanship, mathematics and geometry all enhanced military engineering. The sense of regularity and order was only partly utilitarian; it was a preference, perhaps the ancestor of our functionalist, or minimalist aesthetic.[88] Turin was not the only example of it. Livorno's regularity, and even more the utility and 'good order' of the naval arsenals there

---

[86] Giuseppe Ferrarelli, *Memorie militari del Mezzogiorno d'Italia* (Bari: 1911), p. 12ff.

[87] M. Pollak, *Turin, 1564–1680: urban design, military culture and the creation of the absolutist capital* (Chicago: 1991), p. 19.

[88] *Ibid.*, p. 217ff; on the aesthetic preferences of engineers for order, regularity and uniformity, p. 5.

and in Venice, seduced the young Colbert de Seignelay.[89] The encyclopedias suggest that Italy of the engineers was almost entirely confined to the centre and north. The cities producing the largest numbers of them were Florence, Venice and Milan, with a curious concentration in the Marches, from towns like Urbino, Ascoli and Fossombrone, from whence Renaissance engineers first appeared in the fifteenth century.

Writing of French aristocrats, Jonathan Dewald notes how the military life inculcated in them a special sensitivity for precision, empirical knowledge and appreciation of technical progress, as geometry and ballistics transformed their way of fighting.[90] Too much has been made of the 'bourgeois' nature of the technical arms.[91] Besides the *roturier* military engineers proper, officers appeared who had few notions of geometry, but who understood the principles of fortification, material technology, manipulation of earth and stone, shovelling and hoeing to build traces and profiles, moats, bastions and courtines. They knew how to calculate ground, time and costs, just as they knew how to form soldiers into lines and columns and move them around in formation.[92] The sixteenth century was overwhelmingly dominated by Italian engineers, but this was no longer true by the time of the Thirty Years War, when French experts in particular brought innovations to Italy, a full generation before Vauban. The Castro War, for example, witnessed the proliferation of new fortifications projects throughout Central Italy, built cheaply and rapidly out of earth.[93] Fortification by then was no longer the preserve of soldiers, engineers and military architects, but also attracted mathematicians, writers, and even ecclesiastics who considered it to be a practical application of geometrical principles.[94]

One can overstate the impact of the army as a disciplinary instrument on western culture and society. Sabina Loriga underscores how far the Piedmontese army fell short of the neostoic archetypes of professional officers, servants of the crown. She and others have noted how much soldiers, and their officers, were a

---

[89] Colbert de Seignelay, *L'Italie en 1671: relation d'un voyage du marquis de Seignelay* (Paris: 1867), p. 122.

[90] Jonathan Dewald, *Aristocratic experience and the origins of modern culture: France, 1570–1715* (Berkeley, California: 1993), p. 53ff.

[91] W. Barberis, *Le armi del principe*, p. 192, maintains this position, but provides little evidence to support it. He is not followed by Loriga.

[92] P. Morachiello, "Candia: i baluardi del regno", in *Venezia e la difesa del Levante, da Lepanto a Candia, 1570–1670* (Venice: 1986), pp. 133–43.

[93] R. Chiovelli: "Ingegneri ed opere militari nella prima guerra di Castro", *La dimensione europea dei Farnese: Bulletin de l'Institut historique belge de Rome*, **63**, 1993, pp. 155–92. On the growing influence of French engineers by late century, see A. Blanchard, "Ingénieurs de sa majesté très chrétienne à l'étranger, ou l'école française de fortifications," *Revue d'histoire moderne et contemporaine*, **20**, 1973, pp. 25–36, at p. 34.

[94] Chiovelli, "Ingegneri ed opere militari", p. 177. Cardinal Vincenzo Maculani, a Dominican from the duchy of Parma was perhaps the foremost military engineer of the peninsula; p. 168.

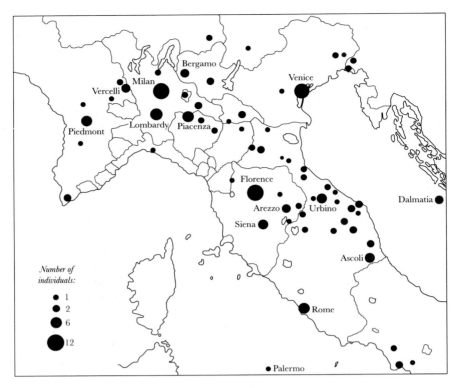

Map 9.1 Origin of Italian engineers, 1560–1710 *(based on Encyclopedias)*

point of contamination for illicit books and ideas. The officers in garrison were the principal reading public for the more daring tracts of the *philosophes*. They could easily contaminate the rest of society, because of their close contact with the civilian population. Many foreign soldiers were Protestants, like the Swiss who celebrated their religious services without much hindrance. There were many marriages between Lutheran soldiers and Catholic girls. Even in the ferociously Counter-Reformation state that was Piedmont, soldiers were uncertain Christians, and much of the Piedmontese soldiery did not bother with confession and communion, that was considered obligatory for the rest of the population.[95] The state placed military efficiency above ideological commitments, and it was no different in France or Austria, or even Spain.

What really weighed on the sense of professionalism of the officers, to cite Loriga, was not how tightly they maintained their noble caste, or how well they understood the technical aspects of their trade, or how smart their soldiers looked on the parade ground. The art of the officer was that of instilling confidence in his

---

[95] Loriga, *Soldats*, p. 60.

soldiers. The attitude of the troops could weigh heavily on his professional self-image. He had to be wary of reacting rashly without proper control, and thus be diminished in the eyes of his men and other officers. Armies were institutions where a young nobleman learned the art of commanding, together with the sense of duty and obedience. By 1750, many noble families saw it as a place where young men underwent an apprenticeship. For many, it was a temporary career. About a fifth of the officers in the Vercelli regiment served for less than ten years. Both aristocratic and *roturier* families expected the army to educate and transform their sons, especially if the family status was uncertain. The colonel was a person for the family to cultivate, as someone who could adopt the role of a guidance counsellor. The youth endured the institution for a few years, and acquired verbal measure, emotive distance, and the way of dealing with others, especially those with greater power. The army taught him how to move about in the institutional world. From that position, he could then be active in the wider civilian society around him. In the militia regiments, and in peacetime, the officer's life was more civilian than martial.[96]

Finally, the army was most useful as a stepping stone to a career at court. Loriga is probably right in seeing the court as the ultimate disciplinary institution, where everything was charged with ritual and protocol. Individuals there were defined by their function, and the place they occupied in the whole. Their bodies had to be continually contained and dominated. At the court, the education of feelings began with the control of language. It was necessary to express oneself with order, clarity and precision, and to weigh each word with discretion. A good officer had some of this courtly background. He was capable of motivating and persuading his soldiers without having to have recourse to physical punishment: knew how to be respectful towards their superiors, affable with his comrades, and not harsh with his own men.[97]

The 'disciplinary society' sprang from several military wellsprings working in tandem. A few observers were sensitive to the 'good order' emanating from the great peasant militias, maintained by every Italian state in the seventeenth century. Their numbers around 1600 may have been as high as a quarter of a million individuals, though they were not uniformly warlike.[98] One French traveller repeated the commonplace that they, rather than the skeletal troop of guards in the fortresses, kept Tuscany free from disorder. Watching the muster of 2,000 militiamen at Prato in 1673, he praised their appearance, and their stern faces or *bonne mine*.[99] This discipline is not at first glance a logical outcome, for the militia was still recruited by appealing to peasants vanity, and their aversion to servile tasks.

---

[96] *Ibid.*, p. 120ff. On the army as an institution providing social legitimacy for both officers and soldiers alike, see p. 220.
[97] *Ibid.*, p. 208.
[98] M. Rizzo, "Istituzioni militari e strutture socio-economiche in un città di antico regime: la milizia urbana di Pavìa nell' età spagnola", *Cheiron*, 1995, pp. 157–85.
[99] F. Duffo, *Florence au XVIIe siècle, sous les Médicis (1673)* (Paris: 1934), p. 41ff.

Cavalry militiamen were village notables whose wealth allowed a certain flamboyance that militia service put on display. Poor peasants, asked to state their rank to the magistrate, responded proudly, *sono soldato onorato*, before adding that hoeing and shovelling constituted their livelihood.[100] They exchanged periodic service to their prince for some fiscal advantages and for exemptions from demeaning corvées. Militia membership reinforced social hierarchy to be sure – in Parma there were frequent complaints that officers abused their ranks by forcing them to perform work details for their private advantage – but militiamen were not at the bottom of rural society.[101] The prince trusted them to keep muskets and swords in their homes, and confided to them the task of keeping order in the countryside, under the close watch of their officers. These last constituted a dense network of notables and retired officers whose families governed the towns and villages of Italy.[102] The institution often fell far short of the desired effect. Smugglers on the border near Bologna enrolled *en masse* in the Papal horse militia, with its ample privileges, for it allowed them to roam the district at will with their firearms. For local magistrates, militiamen were often the primary troublemakers, and in the Papal States judges often wilfully ignored their privileges.[103]

Technological developments rendered the militiamen of dubious military utility. Only professionals trained to fight in large bodies could prevail in the field. In 1600 it took two minutes for an experienced arquebusier to reload and fire,

---

[100] A. d'Addario, "I 'capitoli della militia' e la formazione di un ceto di privilegiati", *Studi in onore di Leopoldo Sandri*, vol. 2, pp. 347–80.

[101] Luciano Pezzolo emphasizes how militia systems help create popular consensus for the political order, since it entrusts and enhances the maintenance of order while according them a myriad of social and fiscal privileges. See Luciano Pezzolo, "Esercito e stato nella prima età moderna: alcune considerazioni preliminari per una ricerca sulla repubblica di Venezia", in *Guerre, stati e città: Mantova e l'Italia padana dal secolo XIII al XIX*, pp. 13–30. On the coercion of militiamen by their officers, see Mario Zannoni & Massimo Fiorentino, *L'esercito farnesiano dal 1694 al 1731* (Parma: 1981), p. 109.

[102] We lack firm information on the military backgrounds of militia officers, who are just now starting to attract attention. See Zannoni & Fiorentino, *L'esercito farnesiano dal 1694 al 1731*, p. 20; Georg Lutz identifies a few of them in his survey of the Papal army in 1667, "L'esercito pontificio nel 1677", in *Miscellanea in onore di Monsignor Martino Giusti*, vol. 2, pp. 33–95, at p. 70. Surely most of the approximately 14 per cent of civic nobles holding office in the towns of the Marches and classified as 'military' nobles, must have been militia commanders. See B. G. Zenobi, *Ceti e potere nella Marca pontificia: formazione e organizzazione della piccola nobiltà fra '500 e '700* (Bologna: 1976), p. 255. Giovanna Benadusi likewise indiscriminately conflates militia commanders in Tuscany with soldiers, and equates their tenure with military 'careers'. See G. Benadusi, "Career strategies in early modern Tuscany: the emergence of a regional élite", *Sixteenth Century Journal*, 1994, pp. 85–99.

[103] G. Brunelli, "Poteri e privilegi: l'istituzione degli ordinamenti delle milizie nello stato pontificio tra cinque e seicento", *Cheiron*, 1995, pp. 105–29.

requiring dense masses of steady pikemen to protect them.[104] More effective firearms required more linear infantry formations, and enough officers and non-commissioned cadres to drill recruits and keep them steady in the field.[105] The complementary nature of cavalry, artillery, pikemen and musketeers required a body of knowledge and a corpus of practices that took on a more abstract and mechanical form. The tactics of the eighteenth century imposed a rigid discipline on the soldiers, enabling them to advance simultaneously in straight lines, to fire in volleys, and to switch formation from line to column under fire with a minimum of trouble. Soldiers became cogs in a giant machine with multiple intricate parts, each having a specific function and intended to produce a specific result. Order was everything. The ordering technique of the army was drill. Michel Foucault describes it as an eighteenth-century science of bodily subjection. The soldier was something constructed along a specific textbook model. Theory held that it took three weeks to fashion the body of the recruit to obey. Maurice of Orange and Gustavus Adolphus introduced the first of these innovations shortly after 1600. Drillmasters conducted manoeuvres with watch in hand, submitting and transforming the body by a process of continuous coercion.[106] Military discipline increased or enhanced the power of the body, while diminishing its resistance to authority. This training often required a closed space where it could be imposed, like the college, the hospital and the barracks, all institutions that multiplied after 1650. A disciplined soldier could obey promptly and blindly any command. It became possible to recognize the best subjects not by their physical strength, which was now less important, but by their demeanour, their *bonne mine*. Duke Francesco of Parma was not alone in demanding that recruiters find men who had the air of soldiers; men who were muscular, of good appearance and who showed by their face and their bearing that they were not merely peasants in uniform.[107]

One visual pillar of this change was the uniform. It was of recent origin, virtually unknown before the Thirty Years War, when soldiers affected a certain fancy in their apparel, like bandits. Its introduction into the French army dates from the great reorganization begun by war ministers Le Tellier and Louvois in 1662, and was complete only at the end of the century. The uniform suppressed the soldier's individuality and panache.[108] The transition was neither smooth nor sudden. In the Piedmontese army, the duke first distributed uniforms to the troops

---

[104] Geoffrey Parker, *The military revolution: military innovation and the rise of the West, 1500–1800* (Cambridge: 1988), p. 17.

[105] Piero Pieri, *Guerra e politica negli scrittori italiani* (Milan: 1975, first publ. 1955), p. 65; see also Loriga, *Soldats*, p. 220.

[106] M. Foucault, *Surveiller et punir: naissance de la prison* (Paris: 1975), p. 137ff.

[107] Zannoni & Fiorentino, *L'esercito farnesiano dal 1694 al 1731*, p. 82.

[108] Daniel Roche, *La culture des apparences: une histoire du vêtement (XVIIe–XVIIIe siècles)* (Paris: 1989), p. 211ff; see also Loriga, *Soldats*, p. 106.

in 1671. Usage in the field often tattered them, so the soldiers and officers replaced these articles with others of their own choosing. Resistance to the uniform often came from the captains, who resented the egalitarian idea behind it. In the French army, the decisive stage came in 1710–20 when all the different ribbons, feathers and other distinguishing finery were withdrawn from the soldiery. There may have been such regulations in Piedmont, but both officers and soldiers took liberties with their uniforms, adding badges and other personal identification marks. Officers decorated their shirts with lace, or wore large cravats, placed flowers or feathers in their hats, inflated the tail of their hair, and otherwise adapted or modified their uniforms with other pieces of different colours, continually transforming their military paraphernalia.[109]

Despite all of this twisting of the logic of the uniform, Daniel Roche holds that it ultimately affected the character of its wearer by transforming individuals into a purposeful group with an *esprit de corps*.[110] The uniform was widely worn in the eighteenth century, especially in Piedmont with its peasant militias. It was part of the way in which the army modified the gestures and the behaviour of men, making them desirous of more order themselves. Army authorities then intensified the process after the 1750s, by embracing the officers as well as the troops, for even they wore the uniform, which differed only in the quality of the cloth and the distinctive symbols of rank. Soldiers increasingly resembled their officers in their grooming and appearance. This discipline was then transmitted to habits of hygiene. The soldier had to cook, sew, wash his clothes and keep them presentable. Uniforms were also attractive. By symbolizing power and majesty, they played a significant role in recruitment.[111]

Already by the end of the eighteenth century, some European armies had reached levels of uniformity and efficiency that caused contemporaries to marvel. One Piacenzan chronicler described the army of Prince Eugene on its march to relieve Torino in 1706 as marching in such good order, and with such silence that it resembled a huge procession of Capuchin monks![112] Hyperbole aside, Sienese chroniclers in the eighteenth century were similarly impressed by the discipline of the Spanish and Austrian armies, and noted the frequent use of the firing squad to maintain it.[113] In order for such discipline to work, as Foucault justly notes, there had to be a penal mechanism. The system coerced those who fell short of the rules. The Parman army applied such discipline to its new regular forces and its militia troops indiscriminately, much to the resentment of the latter. Those who contravened an order were forced by their officers to run a gauntlet of musket butts, or were placed on a device – of French invention – that stretched

---

[109] Loriga, *Soldats*, p. 106.

[110] Roche, *La culture des apparences*, p. 218.

[111] *Ibid.*, p. 221ff.

[112] Zannoni & Fiorentino, *L'esercito farnesiano dal 1694 al 1731*, p. 40.

[113] Hanlon, "The demilitarization of a provincial Italian aristocracy", *Past and Present*, **155**, 1997, pp. 64–108.

their arms and legs.[114] Italian armies, however, were 'Latin' forces, akin to the French army of the young Napoleon. Like the French and Spaniards, they were more amenable when motivated by honour, than when they were bullied into obedience.[115]

The effect of militia service and military drill on the efficiency of the state was probably weak compared to the tremendous effects of military taxation. Behind the growth of armies in the late seventeenth century was the growth in the portion of tax revenue appropriated by central government. In Germany, Carsten has demonstrated the means by which princes browbeat their towns and assemblies into granting heavy, permanent increases in taxation, entirely destined for the standing army. Mercantilist schemes to increase the volume of commerce and enrich the towns had this as their *raison d'être* too. The Austrian empire similarly worked to bypass its assemblies, and to integrate the peripheral regions to the centre, primarily by forcing them to pay higher taxes. Italian generals like Montecùccoli, Caprara and Carafa all advocated this policy in Hungary, under which that kingdom would lose its privileges, its exemptions, and its very constitution, to increase the size and efficiency of the army.[116]

Most of Italy escaped such pressure. Jean-Claude Waquet estimates that Tuscans carried the same tax burden in 1560, 1660 and still in 1726, before the reforms of the Habsburgs. This explains the extraordinary stability in the early modern duchy.[117] In Tuscany, as in many other parts of Italy, the nobility was not legally exempt from most taxes, as in France. They enjoyed, however, the right to fix their own tax assessment, which they systematically underestimated. The court nobility, and the nobles in the capital also held bonds on the state debt, which bore reasonable rates of interest. Lacking a sizeable corps of tax inspectors, the grand dukes were obliged to administer new taxes and loans in such a way that the stake of the patriciate in the tax machinery was not threatened. Finally, nobles had access to the grand duke and his ministers, whose personal sympathy and intervention could 'adjust' their bill in case of difficulty. Nor should we forget the legal situation of the Church, which was exempt from state taxes. The clergy did not have to declare its revenues, and churchmen frequently took control over the property of family members precisely to remove it from state taxation. If social discipline there was, it was probably tied to the massive entry of Italian aristocrats into key positions in the Church at the time of the application of the Tridentine reforms.[118] Tuscany experienced significant increases in taxation only

---

[114] Zannoni & Fiorentino, *L'esercito farnesiano dal 1694 al 1731*, p. 20.

[115] Loriga, *Soldats*, p. 212. For the nature of Spanish soldiery, see Guido Quazza, *Il problema italiano e l'equilibrio europeo*, p. 394ff.

[116] For a number of German states, see F. L. Carsten, *Princes and parliaments in Germany from the fifteenth to the eighteenth century* (Oxford: 1959).

[117] J.-C. Waquet, *Le grand-duché de Toscane sous les derniers Médicis*, p. 576.

[118] The working of the Tuscan fiscal machinery, and the place of the patricians in it is the subject of Waquet's big thesis, *Le grand-duché de Toscane sous les derniers Médicis*. On the

in 1756, when the Habsburg administration needed money to fight the Seven Years War. The administration of the Duke Francis of Lorraine (1737–65), well staffed with French-speaking Lorrainers and Germans, deliberately sought to uproot the lax standards and special privileges that they identified with Italian *malgoverno*.[119] Most other regions of Italy were similarly spared. When Duke Francesco of Parma raised his companies of regular troops in 1701, he financed them with loans and luxury taxes on wigs and bonnets, rather than resolutely milk the population. Within a few years, he had to curtail the effective numbers drastically.[120]

In seventeenth-century Italy, only Piedmont underwent such dramatic change. The first permanent taxes date from Emanuel Philibert. Charles Emanuel I doubled taxes in Savoy after the onset of the Monferrato wars, from 740,000 *livres* in 1610, to 1,500,000 in 1625.[121] The tax pressure was increased again early in the reign of Victor Amadeus II, with the suppression of salt smuggling around Mondovì. Local officials argued about their ancient privileges and their fiscal autonomy. Soon, however, the prince's larger army could nip in the bud any incipient refusal to pay the assigned taxes.[122] In the early eighteenth century, new emphasis on better appraising wealth, and levying taxes more efficiently, resulted in massive new cadasters from which to fix assessments. Even if such estimations were inaccurate, and not able to incorporate the myriad ways in which the population drew its income from the soil, it enhanced the state's fiscal potential immeasurably.[123] By the late eighteenth century, however, only three Italian regions had been so transformed: Piedmont, Austrian Lombardy and Tuscany, each of which was required to maintain large military establishments.

The ideal outcome of this evolution was exemplified by the Prussian military state, with its drillbooks and its examinations, and its very harsh punishments and summary judgment of offenders. Foucault's analysis goes further than

---

number of ecclesiastics in Tuscany, see E. Stumpo, "'Vel domi vel belli': arte della pace e strategie di guerra fra cinque e seicento: casi del Piemonte sabaudo e della Toscana medicea", in *Guerre, stati e città: Mantova e l'Italia padana dal secolo XIII al XIX*, pp. 53–68.

[119] J.-C. Waquet, *De la corruption: argent et pouvoir à Florence* (Paris: 1987), pp. 218–20.

[120] Zannoni & Fiorentino, *L'esercito farnesiano dal 1694 al 1731*, p. 20.

[121] Merlin, *Tra guerre e tornei*, p. 92.

[122] G. Symcox, "Two forms of popular resistance in the Savoyard state of the 1680s: the rebels of Mondovì and the Vaudois", in *La guerra del sale (1689–1699): rivolte e frontiere del Piemonte barocco* (Milan: 1986), pp. 275–90.

[123] Geoffrey Symcox emphasizes the importance of the land tax, the *perequazione* in the fiscal arsenal of the Piedmontese state. See his *Victor Amadeus II: absolutism in the Savoyard state, 1675–1730* (Berkeley, California: 1983), p. 192ff. For the actual process of elaborating the cadaster (an official land ownership register compiled for tax purposes), see Giovanni Levi, *Le pouvoir au village: histoire d'un exorciste dans le Piémont du XVIIe siècle* (Paris: 1989, first publ. 1985), p. 220.

that advanced by drillmasters. As a machine, and an effective one, the army represented an approach and a grand design that could project its image on the whole social body. Erving Goffman and Michel Foucault launched the debate in the social sciences around the notions of discipline and coercion, and their centrality in western culture. The debate fed a certain historical literature that was only interested in negative aspects of discipline, censure and reprobation, repression and exclusion, and utilized interpretative ideas of social opposition that were too simplistic. In Sabina Loriga's view, Foucault underestimated the extent of social interaction among individuals placed in the institutions he wrote about.[124] Order certainly had its limits, and historians have been justified in showing the persistence of old mental habits of disorder, of laxness, of confusion, and a general resistance to rationalization. Loriga looks at the institution not as a place where the individual was set apart from society, or subjected to it, but also a place where individuals benefited from a certain protection, and even a legitimate status to which they clung. The army was one of these 'normative' institutions inhabited by individuals who had different social and cultural experiences, but who were dependent upon each other. It was part of a set of institutions, from the court to the charitable organizations, each with its particular function, which tried to form obedient subjects, and to integrate them into a wider social project.[125]

The 'German' model exemplified by Prussia, and copied more or less successfully by other states, was not just a military reference, but a model for society with conscious reference to ancient Sparta. The extension of this model to a project for society produced what one might call militarism. Militarism more generally can be defined as a social structure whereby political power and social esteem were distributed in favour of the military class. The crown realized it by centralizing power over its soldiers.[126] The absolutist state was an excellent vehicle for it. It rationalized and regimented political life, broke the power of independent nobles, and created a hierarchy of officers and officials. To return to our situation, it is doubtful that this archetype could be applied to any of the Italian states, but certainly Piedmont came closer to it than any other. The king and his leading officials, from Victor Amadeus II onward, would not have seen this project with a jaundiced eye, and in fact were consciously working to this end.

Northern Italy's Austrian overlord embraced this model at the end of the eighteenth century, with results that are difficult to determine. Emperor Francis I, Maria Theresa and especially Joseph II, all strove to render the bureaucracy impersonal, to bind it by norms and regulations, and to place it beyond favouritism. The purpose of this bureaucracy was to make the state as homogeneous as

---

[124] Loriga, *Soldats*, pp. 11–23.

[125] *Ibid.*, p. 23.

[126] Hans Speier, *Social order and the risks of war* (Cambridge, Mass.: 1969, first publ. 1952), pp. 230–52.

possible, and to maintain a large military establishment to defend and increase it. The Prussian army state seduced Joseph II in particular, who consciously modelled Austrian policies on it. As a philosopher–prince, Joseph looked beyond the immediate issue of more soldiers for the army, and saw instead a utopian resuscitation of ancient Sparta that could transform the state into a super-efficient entity.[127] From mid-century, the army was the object of reforms designed to render it uniform and efficient. The adoption of the drill-manual-cum-officer's handbook, the Field Service Book of 1750 was one such measure. After 1766, Joseph undertook to conscript peasants into the army on a part-time basis, the canton-system that worked so well to provide Prussia with a citizen-army. He applied it first to the heartland of the Empire, and then with mixed success in the Trentino in the last decades of the eighteenth century. The Spartan army-state model, like the French nation-in-arms, further augmented the disparity in militarization between northern Europe and Italy.

The nobility in state service gradually assimilated these political ideals: the standing army 'professionalized' the aristocracy.[128] In Piedmont, the only really relevant Italian case, the army extended the prince's authority. In this way, it became the leading institution of the state, and its 'functionaries' inculcated the ideal of service in the public interest. The defence of the state and loyalty towards the sovereign became the keystone of a whole social system. The army reflected the image of the rationality of the state, to use Barberis' terms.[129] Few served the order of Malta in the eighteenth century, and even fewer left their native land to fight in more exotic foreign wars, like the Marchese Victor Amadeus Solare di Govone, who abandoned his Piedmontese officer's commission to fight the Turks in Moldavia.[130] Élites were now incorporated in overarching state institutions building a Hegelian future.

Conclusion: a project for research

Few specific events announced the decline of the Italian military tradition, which makes it difficult to set out a precise chronological framework. Between Lepanto and Bonaparte's invasion, nevertheless, demilitarization there was. The review of the literature underscores how active Italian nobles were in the great European wars of their time, and how the underlying structures of military readiness were still in evidence during the first half of the seventeenth century, even in the

---

[127] Szabo, *Kaunitz and enlightened absolutism, 1753–1780* (Cambridge: 1994), p. 260 and pp. 283–5.

[128] Corvisier, *Armées et sociétés en Europe de 1494 à 1789*, p. 117.

[129] Barberis, *Le armi del principe*, pp. xviii–xx.

[130] Loriga, *Soldats*, p. 85. On the abandonment of the order of Malta by Piedmontese nobles, and the increasing control over those who remained by the prince, see Spagnoletti, *Stato, aristocrazie e ordine di Malta nell' Italia moderna* (Rome: 1988).

absence of a standing army. To explain the ensuing 'absence', it might be easiest to indicate the last occasions when the different forms of military intervention took place. Italian predominance in fortification had come to an end by 1640 when French experts came to the fore. The last wars waged by Italian states against each other were the Castro War in 1642–4, and the unsuccessful Piedmontese invasion of Genoa in 1672. Italian noble volunteers ceased to flock to armies after the siege of Buda in 1686. Italian contingents played central roles in many great battles of the first half of the seventeenth century. But after 1660, only Argos in 1685 comes to mind, apart from the Piedmontese campaigns. Apart from Piedmont still, the last offensive operations launched by an Italian army on its own were the Morea campaigns of the 1680s, and the failed operation against Chios in 1695.

The last Italian regiments raised for Spanish service – from the purses of great nobles – date from the first years of the eighteenth century. Vienna raised few Italian regiments after the Thirty Years War, notwithstanding the huge sums of money it extracted from northern Italy. In the eighteenth century, apart from the king of Sardinia, Charles Emanuel III, only one Italian prince, Francesco III d'Este of Modena, led an army on campaign. The last great Hispano-Italian fleet launched from Italy was probably in 1641, for the relief of Tarragona. Naples' last successful amphibious expedition against a European power was in 1650, when it recovered Porto Longone from the French. The last naval battles against the Turks were those fought in 1718 in the Aegean. The decline of the activity of the crusading orders follows the same chronology, from large-scale operations until the Candia War, a resurgence of activity during the Morea War, and then a long decline after 1720, in both recruitment and combat experience. One could perhaps multiply similar observations, pointing to the way Italian states increasingly lagged behind their neighbours after 1650.

A proper demonstration of Italian demilitarization over more than two centuries is clearly beyond the capacity of one researcher or two, which is why I consider this book to be a *pré-enquête*. Part of the difficulty owes to the dispersion of the archives. Each state contains archives concerning the raising of troops, the attribution of commands and the search for cadres. The secret of Italian demilitarization is partly to be found in the internal evolution of the Spanish monarchy, and requires some work at Madrid and Simancas. The archives of the Austrian monarchy in Vienna will similarly reveal the number and identities of Italian noblemen serving in the Imperial army. There are no doubt documents in Brussels, Munich, Paris and Malta that would elucidate our subject. Each Italian political capital – Turin, Milan, Venice, Parma, Modena, Florence, Rome and Naples – contains administrative documents, such as recruiting patents, that will one day reveal some clues to the paradox of demilitarization.

A proper study must go even farther, however, and try to find some types of documents in widespread use everywhere that could reveal the varying presence and proportion of military nobles over time. Ideally, such a study would employ a team of historians spread evenly over the country, using similar sources and methods from the outset – say, ten researchers each with three or four cities to investigate. I have attempted such a method elsewhere using the testament as an instrument used by much of society and identical in form and content across every region.[131] Such a study should reveal the incidence of military aristocrats and their family context, and we should be able to see the frequency of their appearance. Surveying several hundred wills for each city, choosing aristocratic wills primarily (although not exclusively) would allow us an insight into the special morphology of each patriciate and the place of military nobles in the whole. By comparing wills of different periods, it would be possible to isolate and evaluate the presence not only of individuals in military careers, but also of military dynasties, and as they receded, to chart which areas of activity became a surrogate.

More literary sources, widely available in Italian archives, would be the various *compendia* and catalogues celebrating the achievements of local families, in the diverse spheres of noble activity: service in the army, but also the Church, the state, the bar and the arts. Finally, some systematic use of genealogies could chart for each region the incidence of service. Valuable lessons could be gleaned from that monument of genealogical scholarship, the *Famiglie illustre* by Pompeo Litta, and other works of its kind. Within a few years it should be possible to have a better understanding of the process of demilitarization, its specific chronology, its regional variation, together with the alternative activities of the nobility, and ultimately to isolate the economic and social background of the process.

---

[131] G. Hanlon, "The demilitarization of an Italian provincial aristocracy", *Past and Present*, **155**, 1997, pp. 64–108.

Index